3RD EDITION

The IMC
HANDBOOK

Readings & Cases in Integrated Marketing Communications

EDITORS

J. STEVEN KELLY
DePaul University

SUSAN K. JONES
Ferris State University
Susan K. Jones & Associates

RICHARD A. HAGLE
RACOM Communications

© 2015 by Racom Communications

Published by
Racom Communications
150 N. Michigan Ave.
Suite 2800
Chicago, IL 60601
800-247-6553
www.racombooks.com

Editor: Richard Hagle

Catalog-in-Publication information available from the Library of Congress.
Printed in the United States of America
ISBN: 978-1-933199-06-1

This book is dedicated to:

Kathleen, Alison, Jerry, Joseph and Clara
—Steve Kelly

Bill, Shannon, Katie, Sheridan, Scott and Tonia
—Susan Jones

Ruth, Matt, Mio, Mara, Scott, Jesse, Tara
Tristan, Ian, and Heather
—Richard Hagle

CONTENTS

Acknowledgments   ix

About the Case Writers' Workshop and the Development of This Book   x

I. READINGS

1. Solving Marketing Problems with an Integrated Process   1
   Don E. Schultz, Northwestern University and Agora, Inc.

2. What Is a Brand (And Why Does It Matter?)   13
   Derek Moore, Founder, Kick-Start Collective

3. Customer Relationship Management   24
   Robert Galka, DePaul University

4. Creative Strategy in Integrated Marketing Communications   38
   Susan K. Jones, Professor of Marketing, Ferris State University
   Principle, Susan K. Jones & Associates

5. An Introduction to Database Marketing   51
   Arthur Middleton Hughes, Director, Subscriber Acquisition Strategy,
   E-Dialog.com and Vice President, The Database Marketing
   Institute, Ltd.

6. Media Planning: The Business End of Advertising   59
   Marian Azzaro, Roosevelt University

7. The Economics of Database Marketing   69
   Robert Weinberg, RW Consulting

8. Search Engine Optimization (SEO) and Paid Search   85
   James Moore, DePaul University

9. Business-to-Business Marketing   103
   Victor L. Hunter, Sheila T. Zelenski and Jeff J. Kreutzer
   Hunter Business Group, LLC

10. Business-to-Business Lead Generation   121
    Ruth P. Stevens, eMarketing Strategy

11. Consumer Privacy: Knowing Your Customers Without
    Really "Knowing" Them   132
    Jennifer Barrett Glasgow, CIPP, Global Privacy Officer,
    Acxiom Corporation

12. Multichannel Marketing   142
    Debra Ellis, Wilson & Ellis Consulting

13. History Matters: International Direct Marketing From 1981 On   150
    Charles Prescott, The Prescott Report

14. Multicultural Marketing in the U.S.   160
    Jaime Noriega, Ph.D., DePaul University

15. Contact and Call Centers   177
    Mitchell A. Lieber, Lieber & Associates

16. Social Media Marketing: Building, Nurturing and
    Sustaining Relationships   202
    Stephen K. Koernig, DePaul University
    Neil Granitz, Professor of Marketing, California State University,
    Fullerton

17. Mobile Marketing and the Mobile Decade to Come   218
    Mickey Alam Kahn, Editor-in-Chief, www.mobilemarketer.com

18. DRTV and Integrated Marketing   225
    Timothy Hawthorne, Founder, Chairman and
    Executive Creative Director Hawthorne Direct

II. CASES

1. Allstate Insurance: Building Relationships through
   Email Campaigns   243
   Blodwen Tarter, Golden Gate University
   Mary Caravella, University of Connecticut
   Debra Zahay, Northern Illinois University

2. American Cancer Society, Chicago Chapter
   May Walk and Roll Event Marketing Campaign   254
   J. Steven Kelly, DePaul University
   Frank K. Bryant, Cal Poly Pomona
   RayeCarol Cavender, Virginia Tech
   Kate Stevenson, DePaul University
   Regine Vanheems, Université of Paris I—Sorbonne

3. Amtrak: A Communications Planning Challenge   262
   Marian Azzaro, Roosevelt University

4. Busch Gardens®: Planning for a Wild Direct & Interactive
   Marketing Ride   269
   Lisa D. Spiller, Christopher Newport University

5. Domino's Pizza: Growing Sales With Technology   292
    Matthew H. Sauber, Eastern Michigan University
    David W. Marold, Eastern Michigan University
    Alicia Anderson, Eastern Michigan University

6. ECB.com: Customer Profiling and Segmentation   310
    Debra Zahay-Blatz, Aurora University
    Blodwen Tarter, Golden Gate University

7. GreenolaStyle: Brand on a Mission   316
    Drai Hassert, Loyola University Chicago
    Stacy Neier, Loyola University Chicago

8. Häagen-Dazs® Loves Honey Bees   332
    Blodwen Tarter, Golden Gate University
    Jack Saunders, Golden Gate University

9. Hi-Ho Silver: Using Metrics to Drive Integrated Marketing
    Communication Decisions   343
    Lisa D. Spiller, Christopher Newport University

10. Kiln Creek Golf Club & Resort: On Par for an Integrated Marketing
    Communications Campaign to Acquire New Members   367
    Lisa D. Spiller, Christopher Newport University
    Carol Scovotti, University of Wisconsin-Whitewater

11. McDonald Garden Center   379
    Lisa D. Spiller, Christopher Newport University
    Carol Scovotti, University of Wisconsin-Whitewater

12. NueMedia, LLC: Redefining Business Media for Customer-Centric
    Marketing   395
    Carol Scovotti, University of Wisconsin-Whitewater

13. Peninsula SPCA   408
    Lisa D. Spiller, Christopher Newport University
    Carol Scovotti, University of Wisconsin-Whitewater

14. Primetime Developmental Playthings, Inc.   422
    Harlan Spotts, Western New England College
    Greg Baleja, Alma College

15. The San Francisco Symphony Turns One Hundred: Marketing a
    Cultural Centennial   440
    Blodwen Tarter, Golden Gate University

16. Star Island: The Paradox of Management   446
    Jan P. Owens, Carthage College

17. TurboTax® Tries Direct Response Television . . . Again   450
    Blodwen Tarter, Golden Gate University

18. VIPER: SmartStart—From Curiosity to Conversion: How VIPER
    SmartStart Leverages Mobile Technology to Generate New Customers 465
    David W. Marold, Eastern Michigan University
    Lisa D. Spiller, Christopher Newport University

19. Zappos: Ensuring a Good Fit—Fortifying Customer Service and
    the User Experience at Zappos   480
    Deborah Cowles, Virginia Commonwealth University
    Jan P. Owens, Carthage College
    Kristen L. Walker, California State University Northridge

ACKNOWLEDGMENTS

The editors would like to acknowledge the exceptional contributions of the authors of this book's cases and readings. Their names and affiliations are listed at the beginning of each piece. Their willingness to share their research, experience and knowledge with professors and students is very impressive, and much appreciated. Their generosity is exceptional as well: all contributors to this book have agreed that 100% of royalties will go to DePaul University's Interactive Marketing Institute.

The editors would also like to thank the past and present trustees and staff members of the Chicago Association of Direct Marketing Educational Foundation for conceiving and guiding the creation of the DePaul Case Writers' Workshop, and for continued strong support of the Workshop.

Thanks are due as well to the Direct Marketing Educational Foundation's trustees and staff for several years of generous financial support and guidance to the Workshop.

We would like to acknowledge that great effort and support was given to this and many other projects by the Chicago Association of Direct Marketing Educational Foundation.

THE DePAUL UNIVERSITY CASE WRITERS' WORKSHOP AND THE DEVELOPMENT OF THIS BOOK

Since its origins in the mid-1990s, the DePaul University Case Writers'Workshop has nurtured the development of more than 40 original cases in Integrated Marketing Communications. The authors of these cases include professors, adjunct instructors and professional writers from all over the world. Case subjects include companies and agencies focused on financial services, product marketing, services marketing, online marketing, the non-profit world, and much more.

Dr. J. Steven Kelly is the Director of DePaul's Interactive Marketing Institute and an Associate Professor of Marketing at DePaul. He spearheaded the development of the DePaul University Case Writers'Workshop with funding and direction from the Chicago Association of Direct Marketing Educational Foundation (CADMEF) and the Direct Marketing Educational Foundation (DMEF). These foundations have supported the Workshop because of the strong and demonstrated need among professors and students for timely, authoritative and meaty cases focused on direct marketing, interactive marketing, advertising, sales promotion and public relations. As a former educator/trustee of the DMEF, former chair of CADMEF and current CADMEF trustee, Marketing Professor Susan K. Jones of Ferris State University joined forces with Dr. Kelly in 2002 to help nurture case creation and prepare the cases for publication. With the help of RACOM Communications publisher Richard Hagle, Dr. Kelly and Professor Jones commissioned the development of the authoritative readings that accompany the cases in this book.

READING

1

Solving Marketing Problems with an Integrated Process

DON E. SCHULTZ

Northwestern University and Agora, Inc.

A s long as there have been buyers, makers, and sellers, there have been exchange challenges and opportunities. Historically, exchange problems were solved on an individual level. The seller had immediate and personal contact with the buyer in the market, in the bazaar, or through shops and other locations. Thus, the seller could learn what the buyer wanted and the buyer could express his or her wishes and desires. While the system was personal, it wasn't very efficient.

As the marketplace evolved, it became more complex. Industrialization created factories and mass production. More formal distribution systems emerged. Thus, the distance between the buyer and the maker increased, even though the seller's channels and distribution systems helped make the market more efficient. The major problem, of course, was because of the increased distance and layers of distribution, the maker didn't really know the buyer's need. Likewise, the buyer often didn't know where to find the maker's products.

As the market became even more diffused over time, both in terms of products and through geographical expansion, the makers and sellers invented what we now call "marketing" to solve the lack of maker-buyer closeness. In its simplest form, marketing is or has been nothing more than a number of activities that makers/sellers use in an attempt to close the gap between themselves and the buyers. For example, the maker/seller now uses tools such as customer research, logistics and distribution, marketing communication, and the like to try to better understand current users and prospective buyers.

U.S. Marketing Development

During the 1930s and 1940s, when the U.S. market was "massifying," the marketing function was formalized inside many consumer product organizations. That is, the marketing group developed internal approaches they believed would help them, as the maker, close the distance gap initially with the distributor/seller and ultimately with the end-user or buyer. As might be expected, most of those approaches dealt primarily with what the maker could or was able to do, that is, to move the products that

1

had been made from the factory through the various sellers on the way to the end-user. The maker also developed communication tools to advise buyers of what products were available and where sellers were located. Unfortunately, few of the steps or activities the seller developed had much do with what the consumer wanted or needed. The activities were primarily focused on what the seller had or could make available and what the firm wanted to accomplish. In other words, an "inside-out" approach was the first stage of most marketing.

These initial "marketing efforts" were formalized in the 1950s into what is now known as the 4Ps approach to marketing. The 4Ps, of course, are product, price, place (distribution), and promotion. All were tools, activities, and elements the sellers controlled and could manage in their various attempts to encourage sellers and end users to purchase what they made or wanted to sell. Thus, most marketing concepts, and indeed the entire field of marketing as we know it today, were developed as a series of internal activities and efforts that sellers could use to assist them in better dealing with an increasingly complex, distant, external distributor and end user customer.

Clearly, since the 1950s, when the 4Ps concept was developed, many marketplace changes have occurred among makers, sellers, and, mostly, among end-users or buyers. Yet, the 4Ps are still the general, rule-of-thumb, starting place that most marketers use to try to get buyers to accept their products. They are activities the marketer controls or has available. This 4Ps approach is clearly apparent in the framework still used for most marketing instruction and almost all marketing textbooks. It assumes the marketing system is something the seller uses to influence or persuade end-users and even channels to buy, use, or consider.

As the marketplace developed through the decades of the 1970s, 1980s, and up to the 1990s, it became clear to many observers that the power in the marketplace was shifting from the maker/seller to the customer/buyer. Much of that power shift came as a result of the development and diffusion of information technology through the Internet. For example, the commercialization of the Internet, the World Wide Web, and the development of various forms of electronic communication, social media, and mobile telephony all gave buyers more information about and access to makers and sellers and the products and services available to them around the world. The traditional buyer constraints of time, geography, distance, and lack of information rapidly melted away. This diffusion of information through various technologies is what is driving most of the change and changes in marketing and marketing communication today.

The overproduction and oversupply of many products and services that came as a result of the makers and sellers use of technology contributed to that shift as well. In short, in the last 15 years or so, buyers have come to dominate the makers and sellers. Buyers know what they want and have a variety of ways to access products, services, and, of course, the makers and sellers. Makers and sellers know primarily what they have to offer, and, often know little about their customers or prospects. Customers know what they want, what their problems are, and are looking for solutions, not just products. Thus a gap continues to exist, and likely is widening between the maker/seller and the buyer even though the new technologies will hopefully close some of that gap. So, while buyers were developing ways of meeting their changing needs and requirements, makers and sellers seemingly have remained mired in the internally-focused 4Ps concepts of a supply-chain approach. That is, make the product, push it out into the marketplace and then try to find buyers for what has been made.

The problem today is that the 4Ps approach, developed over 50 years ago, was created for a marketing organization, a marketplace, and groups of customers, channels, and consumers that are dramatically different now than they were then. The 4Ps approach also is primarily managed for and by people inside the various "making and selling" organizations. Thus, because of their focus, they often have little knowledge, understanding, or regard for customer wants, needs, or requirements. They often perceive their job to be to manage the activities they control and to persuade and "sell" the products they have available. So, while buyers have gotten closer to sellers, the sellers, and particularly the makers, have not gotten very much closer to their buyers.

Enter Integration

In the late 1980s, a movement called Integrated Marketing Communications, or IMC, began in the United States. Initially, IMC was focused primarily on how to align and coordinate the firm's marketing communication activities. That is, the goal was to "integrate" all the communication efforts the firm was sending out to prospective buyers so that the consumer received a clear, concise view of the product or service being promoted. The premise was, as it had been in the 4Ps approach over the years, that if the maker or seller could develop effective selling messages, the buyer would respond. Thus, the concept of IMC originally developed as a way in which the maker or seller could get closer to the buyer by aligning and integrating internally the various marketing and communication tools the selling company used. Clearly, there were also some cost-efficiencies inherent in such a system, but, those were returned primarily to the seller, not the buyer.

Using this view, the first IMC efforts were focused on creating "one sight, one sound" for the maker or seller. The basic premise was that these "integrated communication activities" would provide a more effective and efficient selling tool for the marketer or seller. It was hoped this integration of communication might also offer some customer or buyer value as well, but that was expected to come as a by-product of the effort, not as the primary goal.

As information, transportation, logistics, and distribution techniques improved in the 1980s and 1990s, the concept of integration began to expand. It became clear to most maker and seller managers that integration was needed to organize all the firm's efforts to focus on serving customers, rather than just focusing on what had been made. Thus, integration provided the conceptual base for what has now become supply-chain, CRM and other management approaches and activities. The supply-chain is, of course, simply an extension of the 4Ps idea. That is, sellers, by managing various activities they control, should, would, or could be able to create marketplace value by enhancing the activities involved in creating, producing, and distributing products and services and making them available to buyers. For example, by reducing time to market, creating just-in-time distribution systems, enlarging economies-of-scale that enable lower end-user pricing and the like, sellers believed they could create more value for the buyer and, of course, more profit for the marketing organization.

And, that, essentially, is how the marketing systems developed during the decade

EXHIBIT R1.1

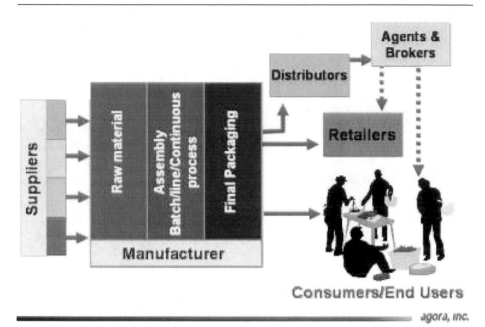

agora, inc.

of the 1990s. A supply-chain approach in which the maker and seller attempted to integrate and align ways and methods of creating what they believed would be actual or perceived value for the buyer. That concept is illustrated in Exhibit R1.1.

The supply-chain approach is a great idea, at least from the seller's point of view. It is practical and possible, and it adds value that the maker and seller input to the products being made which can then be accessed by the buyer. This "inventorying of value" is truly the heart of the 4Ps marketing and supply-chain system. In too many cases, however, this "inside-out" system is out of sync with what customers want or need. The reason? It is still based on the 4Ps, that is, what the maker and seller want to sell and can do with the products and services, what value they input into the products they make that can be acquired by consumer through their purchases. Thus, much of the marketing focus today continues to be on managing the elements and activities the marketer controls, not on what customers want and need. That simply means that the maker and seller are still focused on the development of the supply-side elements (i.e., products or services), the pricing of those products or services to provide a return to the marketing organization, distribution in ways that are most effective and efficient for the seller, and an outbound promotional communication system that is focused on efficient delivery of the marketing organization's messages and incentives. So, while we use new terms, such as supply-chains, the approach is still based on the basic elements of the 4Ps of marketing.

EXHIBIT R1.2

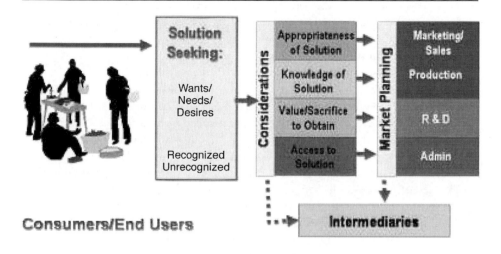

agora, inc.

An Alternative View of Integration

In the early 1990s, an expanded and alternative view of integration began to develop in the Integrated Marketing Communications department at Northwestern University. That view was a composite approach, suggesting that rather than developing integrated approaches from the view of the marketing organization or the seller, better marketing results could or would come from developing an integrated approach around the views and needs of the customer or buyer. Using a variety of existing tools and approaches in new and different ways—data and databases, interactive communication systems, financial models of customer income flows, and the development of processes rather than more corporate functions—a new demand-based marketing system began to emerge. That's illustrated in Exhibit R1.2.

The IMC approach, as it has been developed at Northwestern, is just the reverse of the traditional 4Ps marketing approach. Rather than looking at how the seller can create value for the buyer, it starts with identification of the problem solutions or benefits customers want, need, and desire. Rather than identifying how the organization wants to sell, it starts with how customers want to buy. Rather than looking at how the organization wants to price the product or service, it starts with the level of value the customer is seeking and how much sacrifice (i.e., money, time, effort, etc.) they are willing to make to obtain that value. And, rather than looking at what the marketing organization wants to tell the customer, the IMC approach starts with what the customer wants or needs to know about the solution to their problem, question, or concern, and how they, the buyer, would like to obtain the information that would enable them to make informed and relevant purchasing or acquisition decisions.

Moving from Functions to Processes

The primary difference in the IMC approach to developing marketing solutions and the traditional methods based on the 4Ps that have been used for the last 50 years, is the introduction of a marketing communications process. Process is a methodology that can be used to solve problems in a rational, information-based, consistent way starting with the customer needs and moving all the way through the process to resolution. Best of all, the IMC process is quantitatively based, that is, it's organized around and on a financially measurable, accountable approach, an area in which marketing and marketing communication practice has been notoriously weak.

For the most part, organizations lack processes in dealing with customers. Many have no specific group dedicated to customers or customer understanding. This responsibility is commonly shared among a number of internal groups ranging from market research to customer service. Thus, there is no locus of knowledge representing the customer, the customer's views or the customer's needs.

Much of the problem comes about because most firms, both large and small, are organized around some type of functional structure. In this system, managers report upward, vertically to other, higher level functional managers. Unfortunately, there is little or no cross-functional activity between the multiple functional groups. Further, marketing generally is only one of the functions found in an organization that makes and attempts to sell something. Those marketers are often disconnected from the other value-producing or developing elements inside the organization. The typical structure of many modern-day companies is illustrated in Exhibit R1.3.

As can be seen, in organizations of this type, marketing is simply one of the organizational functions, along with finance, human relations, operations, and the like, on

---

EXHIBIT R1.3

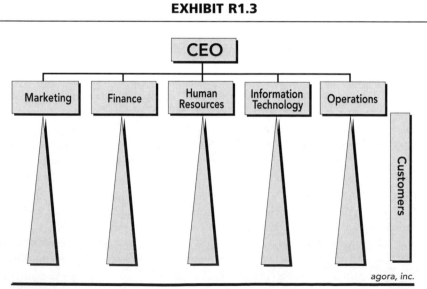

agora, inc.

Source: Adrian Payne

which the firm is structured. All these functional groups report upward in some type of command-and-control system. Managers of the functions are dedicated to maximizing the facilities and resources they control or for which they are responsible. (That's really what the 4Ps is all about, managing the internal resources of the firm.) Customers, as shown, are off to the side, in essence, an afterthought. The assumption is that if each of the functions does its job, optimizes its resources, and meets management's goals, customers and buyers will magically appear. They will buy the firm's output, and come back for more, hopefully, on a continuing basis. Clearly, this is a supply-chain approach that suggests that, somehow, the organization can create value within the functions and find some way to deliver those values to the customer or buyer without knowing much, if anything, about the needs or goals of the customers they are trying to serve. It's a 4Ps approach, applied to the entire organization.

While the structure shown above might have been relevant in the 1940s and 1950s, when the 4Ps and current-day marketing management theory and practice were developed, it is less relevant today. What is needed in the 21st century is an integrated process or system that focuses on customers and brings all the functional elements of the organization together to meet customer needs and solve customer problems.

One approach is illustrated in Exhibit R1.4. As shown, there are five "process steps" required to bring the firm closer to the customer and to align and integrate the organization from the customer's perspective.

The introduction of these new processes can, if not properly introduced and aligned within the organization, create problems for the functionally organized maker or seller. It requires that the various functional groups work together and relate to customer needs, not management mandates. It requires an external view of the marketplace, i.e., what customers want and need, not what the organization can or is capable of producing. It challenges the seller to think "demand-chain," not "supply-

EXHIBIT R1.4

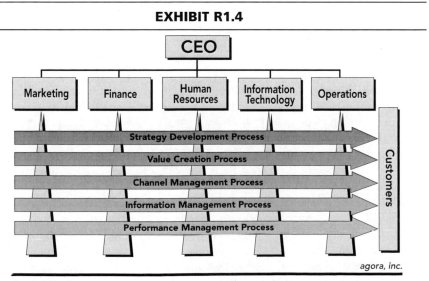

agora, inc.

Source: Adrian Payne

chain," a radical departure from what most managers are accustomed and trained to do. In short, it requires a different type of maker or seller organization than the one that was in place when the 4Ps were first developed in the 1950s.

While the change in the seller's focus is dramatic, results can be, and often are, dramatically greater for the organization that is able to take on and master this type of realignment. Examples of organizations that have either mastered this approach or are well on their way to doing so include Apple, FedEx, Starbucks, Cisco, and General Electric.

Quite honestly, this change from "supply-chain" to "demand-chain" is one of the biggest challenges facing most "selling" organizations today, that is, moving from a production to a customer orientation. Or, better said, moving to a buyer view from a maker or seller view.

Providing Students with Relevant Tools to Make the Change

The question, of course, is what do all these changes mean for the marketing or marketing communications student? This is a marketing and marketing communications case book. It's filled with examples and illustrations of marketing organizations that have goals and objectives. It challenges the student to find solutions to the marketing problems that managers have identified and described in some detail. The situations inside the organization are given. The marketing organization is in place. The student, attempting to solve or provide alternative methods of finding relevant answers to the questions raised, can't change the management . . . can't change what the organization does or makes . . . can't totally re-do the marketing system. All the student can do is take the information given and try to offer pertinent answers or meaningful solutions to the problem. The beauty, of course, is that as a student, you are working within the confines of the classroom. Thus, you are free to experiment, to question, to challenge conventional wisdom. You are free to explore, and, most of all, it is hoped that you will challenge existing thinking. That becomes increasingly important in an interactive marketplace where customers and buyers often have as much or more information about the marketplace and certainly their need than do the sellers or suppliers.

So, what we believe the student needs to accomplish the tasks requested and required in this text is a new problem-solving process. A method of gathering the right information. A process of thinking through to find the relevant alternatives. A road map to follow in evaluating those alternatives and selecting the most appropriate solution. And, that's what the IMC process is designed to do. Provide a system that starts with the customer and then leads through a logical and relevant process that enables the student or manager to generate rational, or at least reasonable and practical, solutions.

The IMC process described below is not some academic concept that sounds good in the classroom, but is totally unusable in the "real world." This approach has been accepted and implemented by a large number of companies all over the world and is in the process of being implemented by hundreds more. It works for organizations as diverse as IBM, Hyatt Hotels, and 3M. It is in place in geographies as widespread as

Finland, Australia, and China. In short, it is a new, more effective way to analyze, think about and solve marketing and communication challenges in the 21st century.

The IMC Process

The IMC process consists of five continuous and repeatable steps. It starts with the customer (it can be either the seller or the end user) and moves through how the marketing organization understands what solution the customer is seeking or the alternative ways in which the buyer's needs or wants can be filled. To do that, the maker or seller must first identify the customer or prospect and their needs or wants. Next, the marketing organization, because it has limited resources, must define which customers its products and services are best suited for and how much time and effort the firm can invest in these identified customers or customer groups. That requires some type of customer valuation.

Next, the marketing organization must find some way to communicate with the buyer or customer, and then measure the results of those communication plans. Once that is done, the marketing organization must measure and evaluate the results and then recycle the process.

With this continuous process approach, IMC moves away from the "campaign" or short-term thinking that is used in most marketing and communication planning and implementation systems. Campaigns have finite and limited time frames. IMC assumes the customer is a dynamic individual or firm that changes over time. Thus, the IMC process is continuous and ever-adapting and is designed to change as the customers or buyers the organization is attempting to serve change and evolve.

Following is brief description of the IMC process. Since the description of the process is limited, the student will have to rely on the instructor to provide additional detail. Or, the student may wish to consult one of the available IMC texts.

The process, as shown in Exhibit R1.5, is built on a logical, step-by-step approach; therefore, it is not difficult to follow. The only caveat: The basic assumption of the IMC process is that the maker or seller within the marketing organization has some type of behavioral data on the customers or buyers it wants to serve and that is stored in some type of a database. The cases that appear in this text are clearly of that type. Thus, customer information is accessible and usable in developing solutions to the cases and work problems assigned. Given that qualification, here's the IMC process in brief.

The Process Chart

An overview of the IMC process is shown in Exhibit R1.5.

As noted, the IMC process is a series of five interlocking steps, providing a closed-loop investment and return system. That simply means that once the IMC planner has completed the fifth step in the process, that is, budgeting, implementation and evaluation, the process is repeated. That is why the IMC process is a continuous learning system that focuses on taking the results of the current marketing and communication programs, evaluates the results, and then suggests changes or adaptations that should be made in the next series of communication efforts.

The best way to learn the IMC process is a walk through the methodology.

EXHIBIT R1.5: THE 5-STEP INTEGRATED MARKETING COMMUNICATION PROCESS

1. Customer Identification
   From Behavioral Data

5. Budgeting,
   Allocation,
   Evaluation &
   Recycling

2. Valuation of
   Customers/
   Prospects

4. Estimating Return-
   on-Customer- Investment

3. Creating & Delivering
   Messages & Incentives

agora, inc.

Step One: Customer Identification from Behavioral Data

The key to understanding buyers or customers is to be able to look at them as people, not as demographic groups, psychographic cohorts or slices of a firm's sales pie. People buy products and services, not demographic groups and not psychographic units. And, to effectively develop marketing communication messages and incentives that will be of value to the customers and prospects the marketing firm wants to serve and to solve the problems they have, the marketing communications manager needs to identify customers who might have those needs or wants. There are any number of ways to identify customers, but the most common is through some type of analysis of the information commonly held in a database. That provides the clues and direction in finding a relevant solution to the customer's actual or perceived problems.

Step Two: Valuation of Customers and Prospects

To develop effective, efficient plans and programs, marketers must invest in various forms of marketing communication in an attempt to influence buyer behaviors. That means the planner must find some way to determine how many units customers buy or might possibly buy and convert that into dollars. The firm invests dollars in marketing communication, and, therefore, some estimate of how many dollars should be invested in customers and prospects in terms of marketing communication funds and what type of returns the firm might achieve or are required. This generally is determined through an estimate of what the present or future income flows from those customers might be.

Step Three: Creating and Delivering Messages and Incentives

To develop and deliver effective marketing communications messages and incentives is the key to any successful marketing communications program. Those messages and incentives should have some behavioral impact on customers and prospects. And, by delivering those messages and incentives effectively and efficiently, the marketer should be able to see some behavioral reinforcement or behavioral change in those customers and prospects.

Step Four: Estimating Return on Customer Investment

If the marketer is able to develop and deliver effective messages and incentives to the identified customers and prospects, there should be some behavioral change or reinforcement among those selected groups. And, if enough is known about those customers or prospects, the planner should be able to forecast what those results and returns might be. Thus, the planner must focus on both the expenditures to be made and the returns which might be achieved.

Step Five: Budgeting, Allocation Evaluation, and Recycling

If the planner has some idea about the returns that can or will be achieved, a realistic marketing communication investment plan can be developed. Budgeting or expenditures, therefore, are at the end of the process rather than at the beginning. The logic is simple: unless and until the planner knows enough about the customers and prospects to estimate their present and future value to the firm, it is quite difficult to estimate what level of marketing communication investment to make in them. Thus, unless and until an estimate what level of return might be achieved, it is almost impossible to determine how much could, would or should be invested. So, the final step in the IMC process is to invest the firm's resources in marketing communication programs directed to the selected customers, measure the returns, and use that as the base for the next level of investment.

With the completion of the five-step process, an Integrated Marketing Communications process or plan has been developed. We know the customers or prospects we want to reach. We know enough about them to make reasoned and reasonable investments in them through various marketing communication activities. We know we are attempting to influence the behaviors of those customers or prospects and if we are successful, we have some idea of the returns we will receive. As a result, we have closed the loop on our IMC process. That "closed loop" approach is illustrated in Exhibit R1-6. As shown, by knowing the current value of the customer or prospect, we can make a managerial estimate of what we might invest. We can then measure the hopefully increased value of the customer and thus close the loop on the process.

While there is still much work to be done to implement the marketing communication program described, the success of those programs should be much easier given the insights that have been developed using the 5 Step process.

EXHIBIT R1.6:

Closed Loop IMC Process

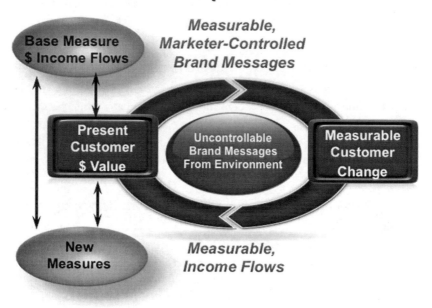

On to the Cases

With this view of an Integrated Marketing Communications approach, you should be able to master most any of the cases you will find in this text. Granted, each will and should challenge your thinking, your logic, and your creativity, but, hopefully, this discussion of IMC will help you meet those challenges both in the classroom and in the "real world."

Don E. Schultz is Emeritus Professor (In Service) of Integrated Marketing Communications at the Medill School at Northwestern University and a partner in Agora, Inc., also of Evanston.

READING
2

What Is a Brand?
(And Why Does It Matter?)

DEREK MOORE, FOUNDER
Kick-Start Collective, Brand & Marketing Consultancy

Of all the millions of adjectives that have been applied to the topic of branding over the years, the very first one was "painful." At least, that is, if you were the cow.

In fact, branding of products was born when the product being branded was meat on the hoof. Back in the days when Chicago held the title of Hog Butcher to the World, the top cattle ranches gained a reputation for producing cattle that proved more tasty and desirable. In time, finer restaurants recognized the cows, which provided consistently good product, wore certain brands and they proved willing to pay more for these future juicy entrees—and less for others. Naturally, what started as a way for the cattlemen who raised those prize cattle on the open range to distinguish their cows from others and to thwart rustlers—namely burning their brand into the flanks of their animals to eliminate all question of ownership—these "brand owners" realized their brands came to stand for a promise of better beef. And they made every effort to maintain that promised quality because it drove their profits.

Although the concept of branding has since spread into countless other categories of goods and services, the concept behind it has remained remarkably unchanged. A brand's purpose is still to assure buyers that they are justified in paying more for a product that is, to all outward appearances, the same. If buyers are willing to do so, the brand is doing its job. If not, then it's not.

At the top of this essay, we mentioned the millions of words already devoted to this subject. In my judgment, many if not most of those words over the years have been more theoretical than usable. As a practicing creative professional in the brand agency world for 30-plus years, this author will try to offer a theoretical framework of branding only insofar as it can help the reader in practical applications—the only kind, after all, that will ever cause those applying them to be hired, promoted or fired.

Every Brand is a Promise

A brand is a persona that envelops the product. It makes a promise to the buyer that the product will carry the traits the brand is known for. When the product is bought

13

and used, the product—and with it, the brand—either succeeds or fails in keeping that promise.

The dustbin of history is filled with once-great brands that lived by their promise, then died when they lost touch with the consumer and ceased to fulfill it. Examples are countless, but here are just a few:

- BlackBerry once dominated the smartphone industry (insofar as the phones at one time were likened to being as addictive as drugs and called "crack-berries"), but is now on the brink of fading into extinction because in 2007 Apple, a new entrant into the smartphone arena, began delivering an arguably better user experience with its iPhone.

- Kodak dominated the camera and film industry for more than 100 years and at its zenith in 1996 was ranked as the fourth most valuable global brand. But Kodak's star lost its luster when it failed to capitalize on the transition from film-based media to digital media. It is a sad irony that Kodak actually invented the first digital camera but failed to adapt to the changing market, as it did not stop investing in film and film-related technologies until 2003, by which time it was too late. Kodak was ejected from the Dow index in 2004 and filed for bankruptcy protection in 2012. It has sold thousands of its valuable digital-imaging patents at fire-sale prices to a consortium led by Apple, Google, and Microsoft. And it has emerged from bankruptcy a shadow of its former self, which many are saying is sure to fade away like an old photo left in the sun.

- Another brand that has disappeared altogether was the proverbial "canary in the coal mine" for what happens when a brand fails to live up to its promise: the Oldsmobile brand that was part of General Motors, a wounded giant whose crash to earth is still creating financial ripples to this day. Named for Mr. Ransom E. Olds, the brand long embodied the innovative spirit of its founder. Contrary to modern belief, the dynamic Mr. Olds geared up an assembly line long before Henry Ford did. He started two car companies, the other bearing his initials REO (producer of the real-life REO Speed Wagon). Olds cars were the first to offer curved dashboards, and later, as part of General Motors, the first brand with automatic transmissions and air conditioning. In the 1970s, the brand claimed the number-three selling car in America: the Cutlass Supreme.

  The engine of Oldsmobile's destruction was, in part, literally an engine: the Chevy V8 mislabeled as the justly famous Olds "Rocket V8." This clumsy sleight-of-hand was made necessary by GM's overly enthusiastic parts consolidation across all its divisions. GM and Oldsmobile ultimately lost a highly publicized consumer class action lawsuit over the engines, not because they didn't run well, but because they weren't the genuine Olds engines the brand and its advertising promised. A few years later, Olds made the first of several futile stabs at image repair with the ad campaign "This is not your father's Oldsmobile," which failed because the product again didn't keep the promise: In most respects, it *was* your father's Oldsmobile. The brand emerged so mortally crippled that even a genuine freshening of its products a decade later barely slowed its final descent into oblivion. The failure of the Oldsmobile brand was merely an early warning symptom of the disease that would later bring GM to its knees when the financial markets imploded and the brand that was once the top selling automotive brand in the world declared bankruptcy and had to shed its Pontiac, Saturn, Saab, and Hummer brands in order to survive and recover.

Now we are watching once highly valued brands like Yahoo, Dell, Sony, Motorola, Sears, JC Penney, Volvo, and Mitsubishi Motors struggle to remain viable and valued in the minds of consumers. Only time will tell if the efforts to renew, refresh or reposition these brands will be successful and they can regain their once vaunted value.

Measuring the Value of a Brand

A brand is a measurable business asset. One such measure is the Interbrand/Business Week list of Best Global Brands, which ranks brands according to each brand's estimated asset value to its owner. For 2013, the number-one brand on this list was Apple, with a brand valuation at $98,316,000,000, followed by number two Google at $93,291,000,000 and number three, Coca-Cola, with a brand valuation of $79,213,000,000[1]

At the first writing of this essay in 2009, Coca-Cola was the number one global brand, so because it is an easy product for us to wrap our heads around, let's look at how this brand value thing works. The value that a brand can add to its raw materials is intuitively obvious when one considers that each serving of Coca-Cola sold at fountain outlets consists of a few cents worth of syrup mixed with a cupful of carbonated water, yet easily commands a price upwards of $3.00, depending on the venue. Why do consumers pay this price rather than drink generically sugared sparkling water? Because the Coke brand promises them more than a carbonated, sweetened liquid. It promises a familiar experience, emotional as well as sensory, made richer by the memories of Cokes past and the emotional qualities ("real thing" genuineness, wholesomely effervescent fun, community with other brand adherents) that have been invested in the product by its long-term advertising and marketing communications.

Similarly, although Apple makes a considerable upfront investment to develop each new generation of its core operating systems, software, and hardware products, it then amortizes that investment over millions of copies. Let's take look at the top-of-the-line iPhone 5s with 64GB of flash memory for example. It has a bill of materials and manufacturing cost estimated $218.30 dollars, yet the phones command the premium price of $849 for an implied profit margin of 74%.[2] Each iPhone fetches hundreds of dollars for Apple, simply because the Apple brand promises the end user uniquely dependable ease of use, security and interoperability with their other Apple

---

[1] Source: Interbrand's Best Global Brands 2013. Survey of major consumer brands, owned by publicly held companies, sold under the same brand name internationally. Proprietary method of valuation combine three factors: a financial analysis of revenues specifically attributable to the brand, a measure of how the brand influences customer demand at the point of purchase, and a numerical benchmark of the brand's ability to secure ongoing customer demand.

[2] Source: IHS Press Release; *Groundbreaking iPhone 5s Carries $199 BOM and Manufacturing Cost, IHS Teardown Reveals,* September 25, 2013

and non-Apple devices and a level of design and craftsmanship rivals often imitate but arguably few can match. And while some would argue quite successfully that there are more capable smartphones available and at a lower price point, Apple generally delivers on this promise, and it's a benefit most consumers and businesses consider important enough to pay for even though there are perfectly serviceable alternatives available.This is also proved by the fierce loyalty the Apple iPhone brand also engenders. According to research from Consumer Intelligence Research Partners, 81% of existing iPhone users purchased another iPhone during the year over which the research was conducted, compared to only 68% of existing Android smartphone users who bought another Android device. More dramatic is the fact that nearly three times as many Android users jumped to the iPhone as iPhone users who switched to an Android device.[3] Why? Because the iPhone delivers on the promise the Apple brand makes.

Who Is Your Brand Identity?

Customers relate to the most effective brands in terms of personality traits they care about and understand from experience. That's why brands that connect with consumers are the ones that *act and behave like human beings.*

It logically follows that smart marketers try to determine what kind of person the consumer wants as their product friend. What kind of clothes would they like their preferred brand to wear? How would s/he talk? Every brand has a set of attributes, whether its stewards realize it or not: its guiding principles, identity, personality, and set of behaviors, including what the brand does for "work" and how it differs from others in the same field of work, that the consumer observes and judges it by. Each of these attributes, in turn, corresponds to an observable human trait: the values the brand has that guides what it does; the benefit having a relationship with that brand will bring, and the way that brand engages with the world around it, how it acts, talks and looks. Figure R2.1 illustrates a simple process the author uses in helping discover and codify those attributes and how to distill from the attributes the promise the brand will make to those willing to engage with it.

These traits apply not only to what the brand's identity actually is today, but also what its owners and their agencies *want* it to be. Thus it is an equally valid tool for the maintenance of successful brands, the rehabilitation of existing brands or the creation of entirely new ones. Carrying the Figure R2.1 example forward, Figure R2.2 illustrates the brand values, benefit and personality that the author recently developed for Bernie's Book Bank, a nonprofit in the Chicago area that distributes new and gently used children's books to children who own no books of their own.

Once identified, these traits shape the single, whole personality that the marketing communications should logically assign to the brand. The sum total of which should deliver on the brand promise, which is the distillation of all of the brands characteristics and reason for being.

Just as brands and their advertisers can usefully think of human traits in forming a brand, consumers inevitably do the reverse as well: taking a set of traits and anthro-

---

[3]Source: All Thing Digital, *iPhone Leads Android in Smartphone Loyalty,* August 23, 2013.

EXHIBIT R2.1: THINK HUMAN™

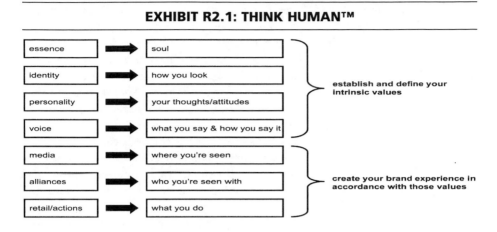

Think Human is a trademark of The Marketing Store® 2011

pomorphizing it into an imagined personality. A Coke drinker spoke of the beverage in an interview as an energetic pick-me-up roommate. Similarly, while Windows computer users spoke of their PCs as objects or tools, Macintosh users spoke of their Macs as people, some even giving them names. And once consumers make a brand their friend, their loyalty to it can be fierce. Hence the legendary brand rivalries of Coke vs. Pepsi, Ford Man vs. Chevy Man, Microsoft vs. Apple. What makes these arguments so passionate is that they're personal.

Such a strong identity is, of course, the envy of every marketer. The only way to get it is through unshakable consistency of voice. Every touchpoint between the brand

EXHIBIT R2.2: THINK HUMAN, APPLIED TO A SPECIFIC BRAND

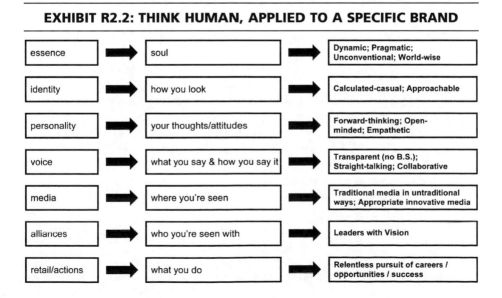

and its audience and adherents–everything: brand advertising, but direct marketing, social media posts, annual reports, press releases, promotions and public statements by company executives—should reinforce, never undermine, that identity and promise. As an example, if a Microsoft spokesman confided that a new edition of its operation system software was basically a bug fix, he might well be commended for his candor, whereas if Tim Cook said the same thing about a new Apple release, it would probably cause a firestorm of outrage from the faithful. Different brands generate different expectations.

From 2006 to 2009, Apple and their agency TBWA\Media Arts Lab wisely capitalized on this anthropomorphism of brands in it's famous, Get a Mac, advertising campaign where the cool, hip and warmly accessible Mac played by Justin Long would often open the commercial with, "Hi, I'm a Mac." And the more staid, business-like and awkward PC played by comedian John Hodgman, would intone, "And, I'm a PC." This campaign perfectly illustrates brand personification and how universal a properly positioned brand identity can be. Incidentally the launch of this campaign coincided with changes in signage and employee apparel at Apple retail stores, which underscores the power of a completely integrated approach to marketing communications. A campaign so successful that *AdWeek* named it, "campaign of the decade" in its best of the 2000s roundup in 2009[4].

A Brand Is More than Its Communications

The Microsoft/Apple example above illustrates a universal truth: A brand, like a person, must always be true to its own personality if it expects to be trusted. But this truth extends beyond even a company's various public pronouncements, all the way to its actions and its products. Those manifestations, in turn, will not be consistent unless the *company itself* is built around the brand's promise. In this way, too, the brand is like a person, because it ultimately won't be trusted if it pretends to be something it's not. It is likewise important to remember that brands, like humans, can ill afford to get *too* set in their ways; change, flexibility and growth are all part of a healthy existence be it a person or brand. Brands can and do evolve without losing their core promise, essence, or values.

The four-quadrant construct is a typical way of evaluating brand consistency (Figure R2.3). The four areas shouldn't really be viewed as polar opposites, but rather as four areas that should all be in harmony with each other if the company is to work cohesively toward its branding goal.

One company whose success has flowed from a high level of brand consistency is BMW. Its customer-facing brand skin of "The Ultimate Driving Machine" is well served by a company whose internal culture is dedicated to the very similar goal of "Engineering excellence for driving experience," a goal that's understood and accepted by the vast majority of BMW employees. By contrast, Ford has tried on identities like so many hats: innovation ("Ford has a better idea"), solidity ("Quality is Job One") and emotion ("Bold Moves") and continual improvement ("Go Further") to

---

[4] Ostrow, A. (2009, December 14) Get a Mac named ad campaign of the decade. Mashable.

EXHIBIT R2.3: ANATOMY OF A SUCCESSFUL BRANDING COMPANY

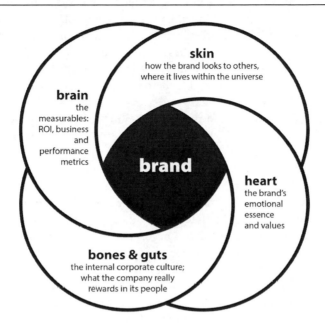

name a few. But in a company dominated in reality by its finance executives, each of these skins was betrayed as false by a lack of gut-level support. Expressed as a generalized equation:

$$\text{Brand Expectation} \pm \text{Brand Experience} - \text{Brand Perception}$$

Or to put it another way:

$$\text{Brand Promise} \pm \text{Brand Reality} = \text{Brand Perception}$$

Brand-forward companies like BMW and Apple enforce their consistency by structural means. Everything about their business must pass through the screen of meeting the brand strategy. This business approach requires strong discipline from the top, but that is not to say that such companies must deny genuine empowerment to employees or avoid decentralization in operations. Rather than trying to act as Soviet-style micromanagers of ideological purity, it means top management must achieve something far more productive and difficult: getting all employees to buy into the *underlying principles* and to internalize them.

One essential way to rally employees to your brand is to develop brand values that are clearly crystallized and easy to understand. Apple's products and software design are driven by only one value: simplicity. No thick owner's manuals, no confusing commands, and no expectation that the consumer should have to "figure it out." The machine should be an extension of your wishes. Plug it in, get to work. This philosophy has informed product functionality, styling, advertising, and the identification of new markets to conquer.

There are other ways to rally employees around your brand personality. Research showed that United Airlines was delivering some of the worst customer service in its industry. In a seeming paradox, United and its agency wholeheartedly launched the major image campaign "Fly the Friendly Skies." This direction was not chosen in denial of the problem, but in fact to address it. Management gambled—successfully— that United's own rogue employees would hear the company's loudly stated new persona and be accordingly shamed into better service performance. Interestingly, United's current agency, McGarryBowen, has recently returned to this iconic campaign (originally created by Leo Burnett in 1965 and shepherded by them until 1996) as it tries to reestablish United's brand positioning as the world's leading customer focused airline.

Listening is a trait that all successful branding companies share, but not all do it the same way. Procter & Gamble, one of the most successful brand builders ever, is quite literal-minded in its listening. It probes consumers for immediate needs the consumer can clearly articulate (whiter whites, dandruff relief) and creates products to meet them. By contrast, Apple looks beyond what customers *say* they need and tries to read between the lines to provide what doesn't yet exist, but that they would crave. This approach requires a leap of faith by the company's top management, with all the attendant risk. At its best, this approach results in paradigm-changing successes like the iPod, iPhone and iPad. At its worst, it yields products that lead to head-scratching over their failure to live up to the hype and expectations, such as the much-mocked Apple Maps application which was designed to replace Google Maps on iPhones.

The Customer Owns the Brand—Literally

The more trusted the brand, the higher the expectations of the faithful will be. Porsche enjoys a fanatical following of millions who see the brand as the world's specialist in rear-engine sports cars that require enormous skill to drive. When Porsche introduced the 928 and 944 models, the cars were beautifully styled to most eyes, brilliant performers by any objective measure, and priced with the same exclusivity as before. But they committed the unpardonable sin of carrying their engines in the front, giving them different handling characteristics than previous Porsches. Porschophiles bitterly denounced the new models, collectively dismissed them as "not true Porsches," and ultimately hounded the models from the marketplace. More recently, Porsche endured the same criticism again after risking brand dilution to raise much-needed cash with the four-door, front-engine, mass-market SUV, Cayenne, and sedan, Panamera.

The lesson is that once a brand has achieved great success, its fans become more than mere followers or cash contributors. In a very real business sense, they become the brand's co-owners, and as such they cannot be dismissed casually. With the rise of social networks, online forums, blogs, and consumer-generated creative content, consumers have taken unprecedented power to interact with the brand on *their* terms, not those of the marketer. It may have smacked of gimmickry when *Time* and *Advertising Age* magazines both named the Everyman consumer as their Person of the

Year and Ad Agency of the Year, respectively, in 2006 but that doesn't mean they were wrong.

A painful lesson in this new reality was provided to Dell Computer by a single consumer named Jeff Jarvis. You may recall him as the lone blogger who ranted about Dell's poor after-sale service when Dell responded poorly to the defects in his new laptop. Armed with little more than the Google-friendly phrase "Dell Hell," he saw his complaint gain momentum in the blogosphere until his noncommercial site became one of the principal Google hits for anyone who wanted to know about Dell customer service. Even though its customer service was in truth no worse than most, Dell saw its service reputation—and ultimately its stock price—suffer severe and lasting damage. Another tragic "beginning of the end" story that is being played out before our eyes with Dell's desperate attempt at saving itself by going private.

A branding company's perceived intent seems to be key in determining consumers' reactions when the brand makes a misstep. An illustration of this rule, but one quite different from Dell's, is the aforementioned Apple Maps application. While Apple Maps itself generated much negative press and could be judged a failure in consumer acceptance, Apple didn't appear overall to have lost a lot of customers over it. Insofar as the intent of the app to be a simpler, faster, and cleaner mapping application than Google Maps is defensible as consistent with the brand's mission, the brand's adherents seem to have taken Tim Cook's apology for Apple Maps at face value and are basically willing to forgive it.

The Role of Tactical Media: Great Brand Marketers Resist Petty Temptations

Applying the notion of brand consistency to advertising and marketing, anyone can see that "brand" advertisements such as the 30-second TV spot or the full-page magazine ad should reflect the brand's values. The greater managerial challenge comes with response-oriented tactical media, such as social marketing, web advertising, and direct marketing. In these media, numerous tactics have proven themselves as effective *short-term* attention-getters and response stimulants. Many have descended into cliché, such as the obnoxiously vibrating banner ad or the mail envelope that appears to contain a check from the government. Nonetheless, if measured only by immediate metrics, they still work. This quantifiable performance boost, in turn, has given these tactics a fierce body of adherents who hawk them to branding companies as more "scientific" marketing methods.

For any marketer with aspirations of building or sustaining a viable brand in the longer term, this crystal-meth potency is exactly what makes these "made you look" gimmicks so dangerous. If a local VW dealer steps before the camera in a monkey suit, his sales boost comes directly at the expense of the millions VW has spent to meticulously build the brand's contemporary, understated image. In a franchise industry such as cars or restaurants, it's not always possible for a brand's marketing managers to rein in the independent business owners with whom they're linked. But to the extent that the brand's stewards do have control of the image the brand presents to the public, it's very much in their own larger self-interest that they use it.

This is not to belittle the importance of tactical media by any means. Instead, it's to remind that a brand's tactical communications should draw on a brand's equity and reinforce it in a positive cycle of brand-building, rather than recklessly spend it down. Target is an excellent example of a brand that successfully meets intense sales pressure with marketing that maintains a consistent face. The leader in cheap chic always presents a clean, uncluttered look dominated by red and white, the signature bullseye logo, and an aura of fashion in both its brand and retail advertising. From the most lavish prime-time spot to the lowliest Sunday morning FSI, the Target message of "Expect more.Pay less" is consistently maintained. Just as important, the retail experience in Target *stores* is consistent with this promise as well.

Some rules of tactical marketing are absolutely valid and workable for any brand. For example, any direct response solicitation in any medium should always make it clear what is being offered and present the consumer with a clear and easy way to order it. Others are far from universal gospel. In the author's personal experience, a high-powered direct response consultant earnestly told a direct marketing agency that green outer envelopes depress response and should *never* be used. At the time, the agency was developing the first comprehensive direct mail campaign for John Deere, the venerable farm-based brand legendarily linked to the color green. Naturally, green envelopes in this case increased the response rate immediately because it was more important to invoke the promise of a well-known and beloved brand than to avoid a color that sometimes proves less successful in generic situations.

The Marketer's Role in Branding

As elaborated above, the ideal marketing mix is one where *all* media both invoke the brand successfully and build upon it further. As a marketer, whether at a company or its agency, you have a promise to keep on behalf of the brand. To keep that promise, you have to know exactly what the promise *is*.

This requires a thorough understanding of the brand at all levels. If the brand's own stewards can't give you a clear picture of the brand persona, you can outline your own findings or impressions of the brand and then ask them, "Is this your brand?" Useful insights can also come from the outside. Those who are not stakeholders in the brand—the press and public—can provide some of the most objective viewpoints on it.

The press generally must maintain a delicate balance between satisfying its readers and viewers with legitimately useful information on the one hand, while avoiding offense to advertisers on the other. As a result, any errors it makes in assessing a brand are likely to be in the direction of excessive charity. In the case of larger consumer brands, spontaneous consumer feedback on the Internet can provide the opposite slant. While some might dismiss consumer forums and blog posts out of hand as unrepresentative, irresponsible or worse, these venues do reflect the views of those consumers who have the most passionate feelings about the brand. And whether those emotions are generally positive or negative, the strong motivation of the posters, combined with the power of search engines, guarantees that they *will* be influential. Just ask Dell.

Armed with this information, it is possible to discern what the brand really is—

whether its nominal owners recognize it or not—and what its disciples want it to be. Properly used, it is the knowledge that leads to more successful branding decisions by companies and agencies alike. When a brand's messaging is consistent in presenting a personality the consumer wants to know better, and the brand experience then fulfills that promise, the consumer is happy to pay more. This is the value of a great brand—and the value of great brand marketing.

DEREK MOORE is the founder of a brand and marketing communications consultancy called Kick-Start Collective.He has earned hundreds of awards while revitalizing numerous major brands. Derek led the integrated marketing creative group at Leo Burnett, then ran Foote Cone &Belding/Chicago's direct and interactive agency FCBi as Managing Director before taking the creative helm at the multimedia agency The Marketing Store. He then joined the non-profit film company EthnoGraphic Media as their Chief Marketing Officer. Derek also has been an occasional guest lecturer at Northwestern University's Medill School of Journalism and columnist for DM News magazine.

READING
3

Customer Relationship Management

ROBERT GALKA

DePaul University

This article will provide the reader with an understanding of Customer Relationship Management (CRM), and its application in marketing and sales. It will demonstrate how CRM aligns business processes with customer strategies in an effort to build customer loyalty and increase profits. It will further illustrate how:

- Relationship marketing—with its emphasis on building connections as opposed to merely creating transactions—has created a new marketing paradigm. Thus, one-to-one marketing and a customer-centric focus become as important (and perhaps more relevant) in today's environment than mass marketing and the traditional Four Ps of Marketing (product, price, place, and promotion).
- Organization culture and structure are critical to a CRM strategy.
- Data management, data platforms, and customer data development are key CRM technology enablers.
- Organizations are leveraging tools and strategies in their efforts to sustain and grow business-to-business relationships.
- Organizations are incorporating CRM into their overall marketing strategies, or in some cases making CRM the foundation of their marketing strategies.
- Organizations are evaluating their CRM efforts.
- Companies are analyzing how to manage the huge amount of data generated via social media channels and determine the relativity to their respective CRM strategy.
- Privacy and ethical issues have created challenges, but also opportunities, for organizations as they attempt to implement and maintain a CRM strategy.

Organizations have created many acronyms and phrases to describe their efforts in sustaining and growing relationships with their customers—all focused on increasing profitability while satisfying the customer. One-to-one Marketing, Relationship Marketing, Relationship Management, Customer Relationship Management, Customer Relationship Marketing, and Customer Experience are some of the ways that organizations have described these efforts. In fact, some organizations feel that *technology* is CRM. The following discussion will define these terms and leave the reader with a firm understanding of the magnitude of CRM.

The Principles of CRM

CRM can be defined as a process that maximizes customer value through ongoing marketing activity; founded on intimate customer knowledge established through collection, management and leverage of customer information and contact history.

As the acronym indicates, the focus of CRM is the customer. Existing customers as opposed to new ones are the primary focus. However, acquiring new customers and bringing them into the "pipeline" or "funnel" are necessary for any business to thrive over the long term. The knowledge base on existing customers contained in a CRM system will, in fact, aid in the acquisition of new ones. As companies gather information about their current customers, view their purchase history and interactions with the organization, compute customer lifetime value and word-of-mouth effect, and understand what motivates them to increase their purchases or "trade-up" to higher-priced items, the company cultivates a knowledge base that will enable it to attract other customers like the ones it has.

Likewise, as companies gather information about current customers who don't buy frequently, buy products or services only when they are on sale, frequently return merchandise and complain often, the company fosters a knowledge base that will enable it to avoid attracting more of these types of customers. It is anathema for some marketers to consider avoiding certain types of customers; after all, once in the company fold, wouldn't it be possible to market some products and services to them at a profit? Perhaps not! A long-distance telephone company currently has 20 million subscribers who never have used their long-distance services. This extremely large customer base costs the company millions of dollars each year simply because it has to mail out statements indicating that they have a zero-dollar balance.

Many current non-users are also long-time customers. Consequently, the purpose of a CRM methodology is not to retain or keep customers that would otherwise switch to a competitor. Nor is the purpose of CRM simply to please customers—any company can do this by giving the product or service away for free. The purpose of CRM is to *identify, retain and please the right kind of customer and to foster their repeat usage.*

While weeding out least-profitable customers is an important function of CRM, companies such as L.L. Bean, Lands' End, Amazon.com, high-end resorts, and top-tier retailers use CRM to make their customers feel that they are important assets to the company. These companies use CRM to establish relationships with their customer base that cultivate loyalty and trust, and enable the company to offer products and services that are price-inelastic. As companies shift from mass marketing to one-to-one marketing, they shift from broadcast (sending the same message to many different people) to dialogue (real-time communication with their customers).

Thus, the goal of CRM is not merely to establish and maintain a relationship with customers, but rather to increase the strength of the relationship from acquaintance-ship to friendship to partnership. One must not overlook the fact that there must be some mechanism in place to feed potential customers into the system; i.e., to convert strangers to acquaintances. Some feel that mass marketing efforts will therefore always have a role since they focus on bringing strangers into the "funnel" so that some can be turned into acquaintances and then friends and then partners. In marriage, having a partner is very useful in fighting off other suitors; likewise in business. A partner, by definition, implies one's customer is impervious to competitor's offerings.

A straightforward answer to "why adopt CRM?" is that adopters can enhance productivity across the entire range of key marketing functions:

1. Identifying prospects
2. Acquiring customers
3. Developing customers
4. Cross-selling
5. Up-selling
6. Managing migration
7. Servicing
8. Retaining
9. Increasing loyalty
10. Winning back defectors

History and Development of CRM

One would think that it would be relatively easy to pinpoint the origins of a field coming to the forefront of business in the mid-to-late 1990s. Not so. There are many different views as to what led to CRM as we know it today. The roots of CRM are varied: philosophical, technological, functional, and organizational. A better and more thorough understanding of CRM can be achieved if one understands its history and development.

Relationship Marketing focuses on building relationships as opposed to generating one-time transactions. What's more, its underlying tenet is that customer retention is one of the primary determinants of company profitability. These were two of the underlying concepts leading to CRM. *Relationship Building* inherent in business-to-business and industrial marketing was emulated by CRM in the business-to-consumer environment. *Services Marketing*, with its focus on improving service quality, and *Marketing Research*, with its measures of customer satisfaction regarding service quality, both contributed to CRM.

Companies in a variety of industries began to adopt direct-response marketers' use of *One-to-One Marketing* with great success. Relational databases allowing for customer data integration, and the proliferation of personal computers to analyze the data, meant that those closest to the customer could act on their own findings. Material *Requirements Planning* (MRP) and *Enterprise Resource Planning* (ERP) were forces leading to CRM because of their focus on and use of databases. Rising costs of promotional campaign development and media buys led to campaign management tools—an important segment of CRM. *Sales Force Automation Tools* were developed to improve sales force productivity and documentation but are increasingly used to strengthen relationships and improve satisfaction.

Telemarketing centers gave way to *Customer Contact Centers* (CCCs) and when

CCCs took on customer service and support application functions, we had what many call the first CRM initiatives. *Direct Marketing* (DM) focuses on one-to-one relationships with customers and prospects. DM relies upon databases, files, secondary data and other techniques to support this one-to-one relationship-building effort. DM uses campaign management techniques that are based on customer lists containing variables that companies could target for smaller, more focused promotional campaigns. Companies could plan, target, schedule, and measure responses to each campaign and modify future campaigns based on the results.

Some feel that CRM had its origins in marketing research's *Customer Satisfaction Studies* of the late 1970s (actually, marketing researchers were studying customer attrition and customer satisfaction at least a decade earlier than this), and its relationship with *Total Quality Management* (TQM) in the late 1980s. CRM is dependent upon information technology in the form of a database that enables marketers to capture customer information, access it in a timely fashion, and communicate with customers in a one-to-one fashion. With consumers today using a variety of touch points in their relationships with companies, it becomes important for companies to collect and manage this information and use it as a resource in strengthening bonds with their customers.

The majority of CRM strategies started out as point solutions satisfying the needs of a single department or function. Departments and functions used local databases, and none were linked. The data warehouse, a centralized cross-functional database, was introduced to provide a single vision of the customer across all functions and departments. The customer data comes from all business areas: billing, customer contact, marketing, and so on, providing what is referred to as a 360-degree view of the customer. CRM suites were developed to integrate all of the point solutions, but these must be consistently upgraded as well. For example, with the growth of multichannel users, the focus of CRM expanded to include the Internet and e-commerce.

Relationship Marketing and CRM

With CRM's dependence on data, hardware, and the software to run it, it is easy to lose sight of the reasons why companies have CRM in the first place. CRM and its goal of helping companies attain high levels of trust and commitment from its customers gets to the very heart of a company and its marketing efforts. CRM is built on the philosophical base of relationship marketing. Relationship marketing, with its focus on customers as opposed to prospects; relationships rather than one-time transactions; individuals as opposed to masses; and the attempt to improve the company's offerings to each individual by learning more and more about each individual's needs; has reshaped the entire field of marketing.

Marketers began focusing on customers as a result of technological advances, the success of direct marketing efforts, the realization that customer retention was the key to corporate profits, and the application of relationship building techniques from industrial and business-to-business markets. In addition, CRM is a win-win situation for companies and their customers. With CRM, companies can lower acquisition costs, increase profits through cross-selling and up-selling, increase positive word of mouth, and differentiate offerings based on customer value. What's more, CRM provides customers with greater decision-making efficiency, reduced risk, savings, ease of shopping, and recognition. All of this leads to greater employee satisfaction and better service.

Organization and CRM

Organization dynamics—including the organization's value chain—directly impact any CRM strategy. Technology is rarely the cause of CRM failures. Most CRM initiatives fail due to organizational issues such as:

- Internal communications
- Political dynamics
- Organizational structures
- Reward systems
- Lack of leadership and executive involvement
- Misinterpretation that technology is the solution
- Lack of knowledge and training
- Process planning
- Inadequate or no change management methodologies
- Weak flow-through after technology implementation

Analytics and customer relationships must be at the top of everyone's mind. Appropriate CRM skill sets must be identified and necessary training made available. CRM efforts must be quantified and measured. Marketing and technology must be interlinked from a strategic position.

Surveys performed by multiple analysts that follow the CRM industry have consistently shown that over 75% of CRM initiatives are inhibited by ineffective *Change Management*. One CRM key success factor is human resources. Employees must have both an emotional and a knowledge "buy-in" to the organization's CRM efforts and methodology.

Organization structures must have a certain level of bureaucracy in order to operate successfully. Typically, the existing organization structure is not optimal for a CRM initiative. Functional or silo-based structures are usually the most challenging to work within for any CRM effort. There will be separate managing departments or areas of activity for different business disciplines. Typically, each area will prioritize its activity based upon maximizing its own performance. There is usually no reason to reset its priorities in an effort to assist another function beyond its defined and agreed-upon responsibilities to that respective function. This is a key inhibitor for CRM.

From an organizational perspective, there are two major challenges related to technology. The first is the purchase, integration, continuous improvement and scalability of equipment and software. The second is that of perception. Many organizational decision makers believe that CRM is technology, and that once the technology is implemented you are practicing CRM. Technology is simply a CRM *enabler* that organizations leverage when implementing their CRM strategy. It may be a key component of the strategy but it is not CRM.

Organizations do not compete with each other. Rather, *value chains*, of which an organization is a member, compete with each other. A CRM methodology must incorporate all members of the value chain, from manufacturer to end user. Failure to include all members relative to their value almost assuredly weakens the organization's CRM efforts.

CRM and Data Management

Creating a single accurate view of a customer is a key to CRM success. It is probably the most difficult CRM-related task a company must undertake, but if not done optimally, it can inhibit the best CRM strategy. It is extremely time consuming, very complex and very detailed work. It takes a certain discipline to create an optimal, data-integrated environment. The steps (listed in order but often managed dynamically based upon the respective solution) necessary to perform this methodology are:

1. **Touchpoint identification:** This is the process of identifying every location within the organization as well as within the value chain that a customer can interact with the respective organization or its value chain partners. B2C examples would be P.O.S. (point-of-sale), phone, web, customer service, survey, promotion response, distribution. B2B examples may include procurement, sales, and technical support. These sample lists are of course not all inclusive of the various interaction touch-points.
2. **Define how data is collected:** I.e., human, technology, self-reported or generated versus two-way exchange.
3. **Establish data collection rules:** This is the process of setting priorities for data variable collection from each touchpoint.
4. **Define the data collection process:** Specific process steps, timing, and security.
5. **Place data in similar formats (optional):** Some software that will work with the collected data requires it to be in the same of similar formats.
6. **Split data into two areas—linkage and non-linkage:** Linkage data is any set of variables that can be used to identify the customer. Non-linkage data is everything else. Name and address or customer loyalty card numbers are examples of linkage variables. Products purchased would be non-linkage data. Non-linkage data can contain an extremely large number of variables. A unique number can be assigned to both so that both parts of the customer data, linkage and non-linkage, can be connected together later. Splitting data is not always necessary, but in many instances it improves the efficiency of the processing of linkage data—through those steps necessary to enhance customer matching across multiple interactions and transactions.
7. **Standardize and correct linkage data:** Commercial software is used to correct errors in any addressable variable (e.g., street name, ZIP code, email address).
8. **Postal processing:** Ensures that the most current customer address will be used as well as improve mailing efficiency. There are multiple processes in this step and the USPS website (www.usps.com) is a good source for information on what is involved with this process. This varies by country and best practices in countries are usually used along with local partners in the respective country.
9. **Linkage identification:** This step is sometimes referred to as de-duplication

or merge/purge. It identifies each appearance of a customer's multiple set of interactions or transactions and links them together. This is a critical step as it helps build a centric view of the customer, a critical success factor for CRM.

10. **Data enhancement:** Secondary sources of information are added to the customer information to enhance the view of the customer. (e.g., demographic variables, secondary sources).

11. **Data suppression:** Use data captured about customers to suppress from a variety of activity such as: reduced or eliminated marketing efforts to nonprofitable customers; adherence to customer request for non-interaction; and legal and ethical conformance (children, prisons, deceased, military, and fraud detection).

12. **Consolidate data:** Link data together.

13. **Prepare data for respective database update process.**

These steps have been listed as a serial process. They can be executed in real time, in part, or in whole, depending upon the requirements and resources, both technical and financial. The data integration process is a key success factor as it creates a single —and hopefully accurate—view of the customer at a point in time.

Technology and Data Platforms

Discussions of technology can be overwhelming and, to many business students, intimidating. The following discussion and diagrams have been developed in such a way as to link the CRM strategy with technology at a functional level.

Exhibit R3.1 illustrates a typical data warehouse environment. The Operational Data Store (ODS) is a database designed to hold limited information that is relative to a current customer interaction and can be accessed quickly. The Data Warehouse (DW) contains all relative marketing information. It is designed for efficient storage and security. It is not designed for quick access. A Data Mart (DM on this model) is a subset of the DW and contains information extracted from the DW for a specific purpose. This consumer finds that the Web and the phone are the two easiest ways to interact with the organization. A noninclusive list of other interaction sources appears in the left side of the exhibit. Data Preparation appears twice. The elongated cylinder represents a batch or semi-batch environment of data preparation steps. The Data Prep that appears within a database icon in the middle of the figure depicts the same data preparation functions occurring in real time. The functions are integrated into the customer interaction. For example, a person using the Web to make a purchase may have the information they entered processed through the data preparation steps instantly while they are at the web site.

This is how a web site completes a form once the customer enters limited information about themselves. That is, the limited information is matched against their complete information resident in the ODS. While one ODS icon appears, it should be pointed out that many ODSs can be created and used by companies. In fact, some companies create the ODS first and the DW later, using the ODS for both functions. In a way, this is a less risky approach as the marketer learns more about what information is available before designing the DW.

EXHIBIT R3.1: THE CRM PROCESS

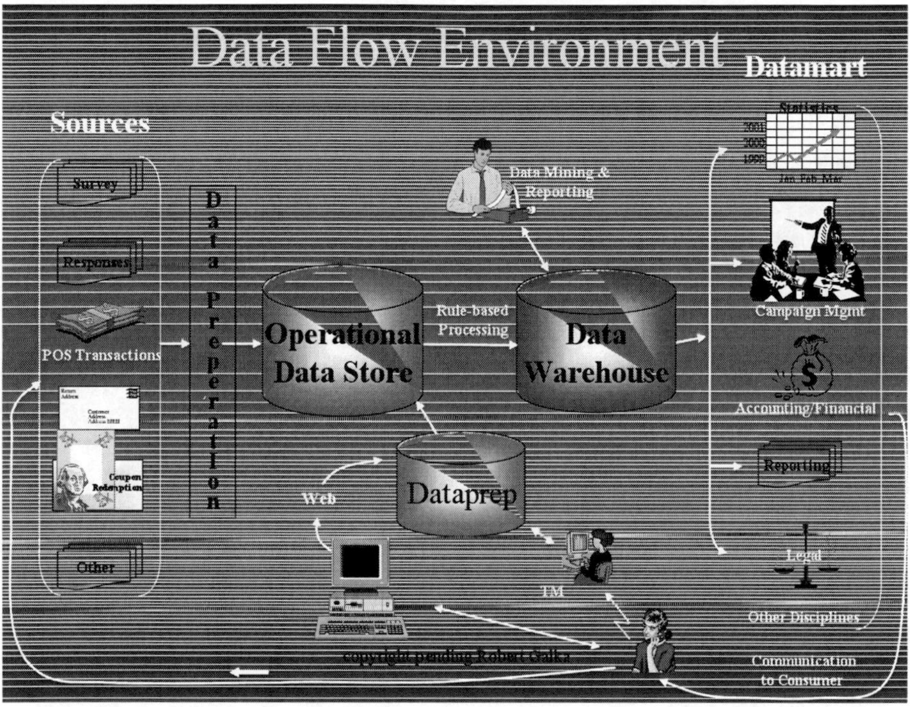

Some companies for financial or strategic reasons never build a DW and stay with the ODS or build a DW years later. The DW is updated by software with information that comes from one or more ODSs. The arrow depicts this update in the middle of the figure. It should be pointed out that the man accessing the DW via double arrow at the top of the figure is reading only, and not writing to the DW. The double arrow indicates a query and subsequent response from the query. This can be a time-consuming method of accessing information, but sometimes it is necessary to query the DW. The most efficient and common means of accessing information is via a Data Mart. DM examples appear on the right side of the figure. They are created as separate databases.

Different business requirements necessitate different DMs as the software used to access the DM is usually designed to support a particular business application. A marketer may use campaign management or decision support tools to access relative information. Statisticians may require certain samples to run models. Finance may be looking at revenue and cost information. Legal may be interested in liability. Each of these functions probably has an optimal software product that is used to access the DM. The arrows from the DMs back to the consumer indicate that some action is taken with the consumer after information on the consumer has been processed via some DM activity.

EXHIBIT R3.2: THE CRM PROCESS

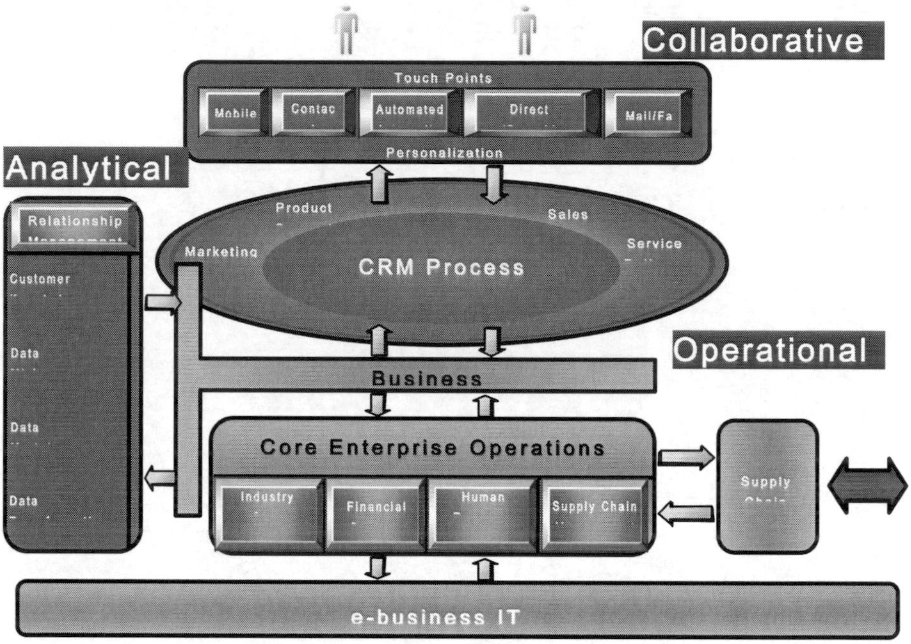

Source: IBM Integrated Customer Information

This is a generic description that compensates for different technology approaches and naming conventions. Oracle, for example, provides the same functions but their technical solution is different. They use a hub approach where all information is centrally located and other entities and access points are on a perimeter ring. This approach may not fill all of the company needs, and therefore more data base entities may still need to be developed by the company.

Exhibit R3.2 illustrates CRM and technology on a much wider scale than the prior exhibit. Here it is shown that the CRM effort is highly dependent on other activity. One can conceptualize three main areas of activity: Collaborative, Analytical, and Operational. The arrows connecting these areas have been referred to by some as bolts, in that software and hardware must be bolted together from one area to the next to ensure optimal flow of information critical to the CRM effort. Middleware is the name used to describe the hardware and software required to bolt these areas together. *Computer Telephony* (CT) and telephone interaction are key CRM enablers. There are many resources devoted to the art of CT and telemarketing.

Radio Frequency Identification (RFID) is becoming a key CRM enabler. It is being adopted currently as a cost-cutting strategy in many business areas. However, forward- looking companies are starting to look at this technology as the new differentiator related to building customer relationships. Eventually, a company will have to adopt these emerging technologies to just meet (not exceed) a customer's expectation.

Knowledge Discovery

CRM initiatives have resulted in the accumulation of what some may say is too much data. Data by itself is not actionable and must be turned into knowledge. There are many approaches used to turn data into knowledge. Organizations find themselves using some or all of these techniques, as each respective situation will dictate an optimal approach. Statistical analysis tests for statistical correctness of models create a hypothesis to test for significant relationships and tends to rely on sampling. *Online Analytical Processing* (OLAP) delivers facts based on historical data. Data mining is more interested in finding data patterns by the exploration of large amounts of data and attempts to predict what may happen next. Organizations that utilize predictive analysis can double their ROI. Organizations use these techniques to perform segmentation, gain a better understanding of their customers, increase profitable customer retention and/or acquisition, eliminate efforts to sustain relationships with unprofitable customers, create up-sell and cross-sell strategies, perform risk assessment, generate response models, and improve the processes that serve the customer, reduce fraud, and identify risk.

Sales Strategy and Technology

Sales forces are experiencing significant new internal and external challenges in managing customer relationships. The internal challenges include integrating the use of new *Sales Force Automation* (SFA) tools and the use of CRM systems into their sales process. The external challenge for sales forces is to manage customer relationships better in a more competitive environment. In order to accomplish that task they incorporate technology to make important customer information available to provide the right offer to customers at the right time. The single greatest impediment to effective CRM operation within the sales function is the lack of sales force participation.

Today, sales forces must provide solutions to complex customer problems. The demands on sales forces go far beyond typical prospecting, qualification, networking, and presentation strategies. Today, due to industry consolidation, the answer to how to solve a customer problem usually involves sales force decision making.

The following strategies are now utilizing new data resources and better analytics to improve company performance with retailers:

1. Category Management (CM)
2. Account Specific Marketing (ASM)
3. Continuity and Frequent Shopper Programs (FSP)

CRM's value to salespeople translates into the following areas:

- CRM must save the salesperson time.
- CRM must save the salesperson effort.
- CRM must make the salesperson more productive.
- CRM must streamline the decision-making process for a sales organization.

Marketing Strategy and CRM

The types of companies that benefit most from CRM are:

- **Those with a steep skew**: i.e., when customers' value to the company varies widely. Companies with a shallow-skew customer base, where profits generated by each customer are more or less the same, won't benefit as much.
- **Those with multi-channel customers**: The high-value customer is a multi-channel user and companies must integrate field sales, store, telephone, and Internet sales and service approaches and identify customer interactions with each touchpoint.
- **Those in "lost for good" markets**: In such markets, customers face high switching costs, concentrate their business with one vendor, and change vendors very reluctantly. Companies in such markets can increase profits through customer development strategies linking customers even closer to them through ordering, delivery and inventory systems.

Significant profitability can result in the short term through the use of "tactical CRM." For tactical CRM to result in quick-wins for an organization, it must first determine which stage of the customer-business life cycle it wants to focus on: acquisition, development, cross-selling, up-selling, retention, servicing, loyalty or win back. After these determinations are made, then tactical actions can be taken. Companies selling contract services (telecommunications, magazines, health club memberships) traditionally focus on customer acquisition, retention and win-back. Companies that have created high exit costs for their customers (retail banks, for example) focus on customer development. Fashion retailers focus on cross-selling and up-selling to their elite market segments. Automobile manufacturers focus on up-selling. Some organizations, such as supermarkets, with their loyalty programs, and university alumni associations, with their affinity group programs, do far less than they are capable of in the area of strategic CRM and tactical CRM.

There are a variety of CRM strategies based upon the customer business cycle stages of acquisition, retention, and win-back. Retention strategies include a wide array of possibilities. Bonding can be both programmatic (rewards programs) and humanistic (preferential treatment). The use of the idiosyncratic fit can make each strategy more effective. Personalization and customization are also effective retention strategies, whether implemented over the Web or during a general service encounter. Cross-selling and up-selling have direct profit implications; and the often overlooked strategy of managing migration may be four times as effective as general retention strategies. Use of "profit-driving" as a segmentation variable focuses a company's attention on profitable market segments. CRM may also be used as a brand-building tool and a method to more effectively manage brands.

CRM Program Measurement and Tools

Where marketers once focused on measuring aggregate market share, they now focus on measuring their share of wallet, share of stomach, share of trips, etc., for distinct buying units such as individuals, couples, families, businesses and other organizations. While aggregate measures of marketing success are still important, they have been supplemented by an increasingly large number of measures useful to those involved in an organization's CRM efforts. For example: effectiveness in acquisition, bonding development, behavior changes, retention, prevention of downward migration, win back, company efficiency, employee behavior, computation of Customer Lifetime Value (CLV) and customer equity, critical incident analysis, acquisition/defection matrices, RFM, event history models for predicting customer response rates,

Privacy and Ethics

CRM requires a quid-pro-quo between the organization and the customer. This information and benefit exchange supports CRM. It also allows the organization to confirm a customer's expectations on privacy, which if executed properly can support its legal and ethical compliance effort.

The propensity to share customer information within the organization in support of a CRM effort or the organization's willingness to sell that information is a rising consumer concern. Another major consumer concern is the tracking of online activity and the threat of identity theft. The organization has to balance its need for information with its adherence to the customer's privacy expectation.

Many larger organizations have assigned executive ownership with the creation of a Chief Privacy Officer (CPO) position. A good practice is for organizations to monitor the FTC privacy website (www.ftc.gov/privacy) for current information on U.S. legislation, trends, best practices, and current cases.

Non-U.S. privacy strategies can be more complex. Organizations should hope for more rather than less documented legislation. It is easier to manage a privacy strategy when rules are defined. The worst situation exists when privacy guidelines are vague and open to interpretation. This creates the most risk for companies. The European Union has been aggressive in its approach to consumer information usage and consumer privacy. Latin America and Canada are almost as aggressive as the European Union. Japan has incorporated recent legislation as well.

The Future of CRM

The following discussion deals with projections of what is likely to occur, as opposed to fact.

The majority of U.S. companies are still floundering with CRM. There are mixed messages concerning CRM performance. This is particularly confounding when everyone agrees, conceptually, with the need for CRM and its strategic applications.

Challenging economic conditions have created an environment where CRM is a critical component of an organization's strategy as it attempts to reduce costs and increase revenue, both of which are key benefits gained by adopting CRM methodologies.

Organizations are "drowning" in information precipitated by increased Internet activity. CRM strategies enable organizations to filter out "noise" and focus on that information which directly impacts their efforts to sustain and grow customer profitability.

Major shifts in technology capability have precipitated changes in customer behavior and have created new market dynamics which impact CRM strategies. Brick and Mortar retailers are becoming showcases used for experiencing the good. Customer loyalty can be compromised via competitor phone messaging while in the company location. Geofencing is a new way to effectively communicate in real time. Mobile phones are becoming the major communication vehicle and also act as a digital wallet. Proliferation and enhanced capability of mobile phones have resulted in an overwhelming amount of data which must be transformed into information and knowledge to be leveraged in sustain and building relationships.

Monitoring social media conversations supports the effort of capturing the voice of the customer. This captured information can then be used to measure potential success of new products and services, suggest modifications to features and functions, and possibly offer new uses and applications. Facebook and Twitter are increasingly becoming valuable channel intermediaries.

Social trust can emanate from brand communities and social media channels. Structural ties with the customer can be made easier using these new channels of interaction. Crowdsourcing strategies are inexpensive methods of including the customer in the organization's marketing effort.

Neurometric and Biometric technologies are being used by "neuromarketers" to analyze brain wave response to organization messaging.

While dramatic increases in use of consumer mobile devices and social media channels have created new CRM opportunities, there are also new challenges. In addition to maintaining hardware and software compatibility while managing consumer expectations, organizations must adapt to new consumer interaction behavior patterns at multiple generation levels.

Longitudinal research efforts may be utilized more effectively due to the fact that it is much easier to collect information and in real-time.

The future of CRM technology promises significant improvement in CRM functionality to expedite the managerial and diagnostic system application processes. The future result will be CRM systems that are better able to provide insight into customer behavior and relationship development.

Technical improvements in CRM will be matched by improvements in Enterprise Resource Planning (ERP) systems. In theory, the future of CRM technology will be the seamless integration of customer demand with production, delivery, and billing. The direction of manufacturing, logistics, and accounting operations will be far more efficient. Companies will realize bigger gains in productivity as system integration provides for significant improvements in productivity.

In order to predict the future of CRM technology, it seems reasonable to consider where the corporate leaders in the field are investing their dollars, before drawing any conclusions. In recent years, there has been a significant CRM industry consolidation. Microsoft has begun to turn its attention to the CRM space, but acquisitions have established Oracle, salesforce.com, IBM, SAP, and SAS as the current titans. Google is a rising force as it has both the technology as well as the customer information necessary to sustain relationships with consumers.

Note: Material adapted from *CRM: The Foundation of Contemporary Marketing Strategy*, Routledge Taylor & Francis Group, 2013, by Roger Baran and Robert Galka

ROBERT J. GALKA (MBA Kellogg Graduate School of Management Northwestern University) is an Executive in Residence at DePaul University, where he teaches Marketing Principles, Marketing Strategy, CRM principles and strategy, data analysis, campaign management, data mining, and measurement graduate classes. He has 25 years of experience in business development, strategic planning, relationship marketing strategy, general management, information systems and direct marketing. His last position was a General Manager for a strategic business unit providing strategic marketing solutions including CRM. He frequently teaches professional programs in CRM, lectures on multiple marketing topics internationally, advises on CRM in the U.S. and abroad, has several published works, is heavily involved in Online Learning methods and class development including CRM, and is active in the Predictive Analytics Master Degree Program at DePaul University.

READING

4

Creative Strategy in Integrated Marketing Communications

SUSAN K. JONES

Professor of Marketing, Ferris State University

Principal, Susan K. Jones & Associates

The concept of *Integrated Marketing Communications* (IMC) makes absolute sense—so much so that novices in the field may wonder what all the commotion is about. IMC suggests that marketers look at the customer first—his or her preferences, buying patterns, media exposure, and other factors—and then expose that customer to products and services that fit the customer's needs via a mix of communication methods he or she finds attractive and credible. As Don E. Schultz, the late Stanley I. Tannenbaum, and Robert F. Lauterborn asserted in their classic book, *The New Marketing Paradigm: Integrated Marketing Communications*, IMC challenges marketers to "start with the customer and work back to the brand."

Why was this revolutionary? Not because it was a new or controversial concept, but because a whole culture of agencies, in-house departments, and consultants had grown up around the notion of separation for advertising, direct marketing, sales promotion, and public relations efforts, rather than the harmonious, customer-centered planning process that IMC requires.

At its worst, this old-style culture leads to arguments among professionals as to how a media budget will be split: how much for general advertising, how much for direct marketing, how much for digital advertising, and so on. More recently, arguments have erupted as to where social media fits into the picture. Should it be considered part of direct marketing? Public relations? Advertising? Sales promotion?

Such "turf wars" have very little to do with what the *customer* wants or needs. They rely on chauvinistic notions that "my method is better"—that direct marketing is inherently superior to sales promotion, for example, or that general advertising is more refined, and therefore more appropriate, than "pushier" direct marketing techniques.

Because of the paradigm shift required in order to implement IMC, advertising professionals and their counterparts in direct marketing, sales promotion and public relations continue to work to come to grips with this concept. As with other deep cultural changes, intellectual acceptance may long precede the ability to embrace the gains and losses inherent in this new way of doing things. While the evolution continues, this conceptual framework may help creative people to understand IMC and use its tenets to their advantage.

The Four Elements of IMC

Integrated Marketing Communications encompasses *general advertising, direct marketing, sales promotion* and *public relations.* Some IMC campaigns feature aspects of all four elements, while others may eliminate one or more elements for strategic reasons. The American Association of Advertising Agencies defined IMC as follows:

> Integrated Marketing Communications is a concept of marketing communications planning that recognizes the added value in a program that integrates a variety of strategic disciplines, e.g., general advertising, direct response, sales promotion and public relations and combines these disciplines to provide clarity, consistency and maximum communications impact.

In an integrated campaign, *general advertising* shines at strengthening brands and brand equity while *direct marketing* builds relationships and dialogue and provides the means to close sales. *Sales promotion* provides short-term buying incentives for both consumers and the trade. *Public relations*—mainly publicity in this case—offers third-party endorsements and extra reinforcement for the paid advertising messages. None of the four elements is inherently superior or inferior; they all have important functions in an integrated campaign. The campaign should focus on a "big idea" and a graphic look that threads through all four elements. This maximizes the chances that consumers will get the message and then have the message reinforced and layered in their memories without the "cognitive dissonance" that arises from mixed messages or incongruous graphic elements.

The Creative Process in Integrated Marketing Communications

The best integrated marketing campaigns begin with the disciplined application of creativity theory. We all are gifted with the ability to exercise the creative process. However, optimizing our results requires us to understand and apply that process patiently, and step-by-step.

The Italian sociologist Vilfredo Pareto said that an idea is merely a new combination of old elements. Take a kaleidoscope, for example. It contains myriad bits of color, forming into many different patterns as the kaleidoscope turns. The pattern is never the same twice, yet it combines all the same ingredients. The Bible says that "there is no new thing under the sun"—only unique ways of relating old elements. Creating a marketing idea, then, is the result of a step-by-step process designed to identify relevant elements and arrange them in new and effective patterns.

Creativity Formulas

There are as many written creativity formulas as there are technique checklists for copy and art. Some of these step-by-step processes come from advertising "creatives," while others are advanced by academicians through their study of the history of ideas. Following are abbreviated versions of two such helpful creativity formulas.

1. James Webb Young's *A Technique for Producing Ideas*:
   * Gather raw materials
   * Mental digestion
   * Incubation
   * Eureka!
   * Testing

2. The late Eugene B. Colin's *How to Create New Ideas*:
   * Pick a problem
   * Get knowledge
   * Organize knowledge
   * Refine knowledge
   * Digest
   * Produce ideas
   * Rework ideas
   * Put ideas to work
   * Repeat the process until it becomes a natural habit

A quick read through these idea-generating formulas shows that the basic process follows a predictable pattern: outlining the problem, gathering information, evaluating information, walking away from the problem to let the mind do its work, enjoying one moment when ideas strike, weighing the pros and cons of various ideas, and then implementing the best idea.

Brainstorming

One of the most effective resources for idea generation is brainstorming. While it's possible to "brainstorm with yourself," most creative experts agree it's not preferable. Working with others lets you benefit from different perspectives, experiences, and thought processes, and also builds excitement and enjoyment. Here is a brief, step-by-step plan for effective brainstorming.

1. Identify a specific question that brainstorming will attempt to answer.
2. Select a neutral and nonjudgmental facilitator.
3. Gain agreement that all participants are to be considered equals during brainstorming, no matter what their usual status in your organization.
4. Shake things up with a new location, new space configuration, music, lighting or other elements designed to change perspectives.
5. State your question beginning with the phrase "In what ways can we…" and begin brainstorming, with people calling out their ideas one by one.
6. Encourage participants to build on the ideas of others.
7. Use the resulting "laundry list" of ideas for a later refinement process based on budget, logistics, timing, uniqueness, target market and other factors.

Creative Strategy and Positioning

In a good marketing plan, creative objectives and strategies are clearly articulated. And before the first word is written or a single line drawn, the copywriter and art director should accept and understand the *creative strategy statement* for the job they've undertaken. While many agencies and companies employ more comprehensive creative strategy formats, an informal creative strategy can be used as a minimum entry point. Such a "simplified creative strategy" must include descriptions of:

- **The target market**—demographics, psychographics, segmentation strategies and characteristics. Smart marketers often discuss both the general target market and one specific prospect—described by name and in so much detail that the copywriter is able to write "one on one" to that person.
- **The competitive benefit**—What your product or service delivers uniquely and meaningfully to individuals in the target market. Ideally this section will also include support for the benefit—sometimes called "permission to believe."
- **The objective**—In general advertising, objectives focus mainly on informing, persuading or reminding people about the product or service. In direct marketing, it usually focuses more specifically on attracting leads and/or selling products. Sales promotion objectives concentrate on maximizing short-term incentives, while public relations objectives—when they are part of an IMC plan—generally have to do with generating non-paid publicity.

Discipline yourself to agree with your creative partners, clients, and/or account people on at least these three concepts, and you'll stand an excellent chance of delivering creative work that all agree is "on strategy" the first time around.

In addition, a well-written *positioning statement* helps creative people to focus on the members of their target market with strong and specific messages that answer the prospective buyer's question, "What's in it for me?" You can create a simple positioning statement by filling in these blanks:

To the (TARGET CONSUMER), (NAME OF BRAND) is the brand of (COMPETITIVE FRAME) that (BENEFIT).

Here is an example of a positioning statement using this format:

To (FAMILY FOOD SHOPPERS WHO ARE CONCERNED ABOUT DIET), (MAZOLA) is the brand of (MARGARINE) that (TASTES BETTER THAN ALL OTHER LEADING HEART-HEALTHY SPREADS).

Creative Concepts in IMC

While some creative strategies and tactics are unique to certain elements of IMC, there are other concepts that apply across the board. These include print ad how-tos such headline writing, layouts and illustrations and tips for readability.

Headline Writing

Observe people flipping through newspaper and magazines, or browsing on the Web, and one thing becomes readily apparent: each article or ad has only a split second in which to engage the prospect's attention—just as do the articles themselves.

The headline is considered the most important element of a print advertisement. This is equally true online. Thus, a smart copywriter will invest all the time and care necessary to make each headline irresistible. A good headline flags down qualified prospects and lures them into the body copy. A good headline has no extra words to slow the reader down, and every word in it is working hard to get the message across. A good headline is in active voice.

One of the classic ways to master this skill was to work for a daily newspaper writing news story headlines. Today an equivalent challenge would be to write headlines for stories online. Journalists are taught to answer six questions in each news presentation: Who, what, where, when, why and how? These are the questions people want answered immediately about most any situation or opportunity—and thus they are powerful idea starters for headlines. It may also help the fledgling writer to consider some of these headline methods as idea starters:

- Give news
- Tell how-to
- Inspire curiosity
- Pose a challenge
- Pose a question
- Appeal to the reader's self-interest

Print Layout and Illustration Types

Many of today's print ads—if they are not direct-response oriented—fall in to the category of "poster" or "fashion" layouts. They include little more than a headline, a dominant picture that bleeds off the page, a line or two of copy or even no copy at all, and a logo. This type of ad can be quite effective at building a brand image or at reminding customers and prospects about a dominant, leading product. But if your advertising is aimed at informing or persuading the reader, or at obtaining leads or sales, the layout will have to make room for some copy and possibly one or more response devices. Typical layout types and their characteristics include:

- Standard—Dominate visual at the top of the ad, headline, body copy and logo.
- Editorial—Looks like an article in the publication where it is placed. Copy-heavy; few if any visuals.
- Poster or Fashion—Dominant visual bleeds off the page. Headline and logo; little to no body copy.
- Picture-Caption—Headline at the top; pictures with captions to lead the reader through a story or process; logo at bottom.
- Comic Strip—The ad takes the form of a comic strip with the copy in "balloons" indicating the spoken words of the characters; logo at bottom.
- Picture-Cluster—Like the standard layout except with a montage of photos instead of just one.
- Direct Response Ad—With coupon and/or prominent toll-free number and/or referral to a Web site or landing page. Should have persuasive copy that is long enough to convince the reader to take the next step by asking for more information or purchasing the product.

Typical illustration types used in print ads include:

- Product alone (Example: a hot car).

- Product in use (Example: prepared food product—not just the box it comes in).
- Product with people (Example: person using a smart phone—not just the smart phone itself).
- Results of using product (Example: person with toothy white grin—not the whitening strips that did the job).
- Comparison or contrast (Example: Huge stack of laundry done with one container of concentrated laundry detergent across from much smaller stack done with one container of regular-strength competitor).
- Trade character—(Example: the Geico Gecko).

Readability

To make your copy readable, follow a few basic rules. These include:

- **Serif vs. sans serif type**—Serif typefaces (the ones with the "squiggles" on the letters like Book Antiqua) are easier to read for long blocks of copy. Sans serif typefaces (the plain ones like Arial) have a sleeker and more modern appearance and are best used for headlines and short copy blocks. On the World Wide Web, however, sans serif typefaces are preferred for all copy because the serif "squiggles" can become muddied in an online presentation.
- **Type styles**—Don't use more than two type styles in any one presentation unless you are highly expert at type selection and presentation. Don't use ALL CAPS much as they are the equivalent of shouting and are difficult to read. Watch out for reverse type (light colors reversed out of dark backgrounds). They may be attractive in a design sense, but they are very difficult to read in blocks of copy.
- **Type size**—Body copy smaller than 8 pt. may be difficult for anyone to read—especially older individuals. Readable body copy is usually in the 10-14 pt. range. Anything larger than 14 pt. is called "display type" or "headline type" and should be used for headlines and subheads.
- **Leading**—Leading is the space between lines of type. Adding at least a point of leading between lines increases readability.
- **Writing tips for readability**—Forget what your English teacher told you about long paragraphs with topic sentences. Advertising paragraphs are short—no more than seven lines in most cases. Advertising sentences are short. One and two-word "sentences" are sometimes used for emphasis. Select "juicy" words that pop "word pictures" into your reader's mind—but never use a complex, three-syllable word when a simple one will do. "House," not "habitat" or "love," not "affection" for two quick examples.

Creative Concepts in General Advertising

The Big Idea

Very few people in your target market are going to slow down long enough to "figure out" your ads if they are not simple and clear on first viewing or reading. For this reason, general advertisers find it effective to focus each of their campaigns on one "big idea" that is executed across all media. This "big idea" is sometimes called a tag line. It may appear as the headline of a print ad, or at the bottom of the ad near the logo. It could be the "hook" of a television or radio jingle, or a tag line at the end of such a spot.

The "big idea" should focus on making your product or company's competitive benefit real and actionable to your target market. It shouldn't be in marketing language—it should be in the language of your target consumers. Examples of classic "big ideas" include AT&T's "Reach Out and Touch Someone," General Foods International Coffee's "Celebrate the Moments of Your Life," Nike's "Just Do It," McDonalds' "I'm Lovin' It," Apple's "Think Different," and Dell's "Be Direct." You will notice that the longest of these is nine syllables. That is by design—that's about all a targeted customer can remember without trying.

Television Basics

General advertising television spots seldom run more than 30 seconds these days, and your average viewer isn't paying full attention. Thus you need to focus on one main idea in your ad . . . there's no time for multiple concepts or a progression of ideas. When developing a TV spot, think the whole thing through in video first—not words. TV's main strength is its visual aspect and the ability to demonstrate things, while copy is secondary in this medium. Creating a TV ad today is much like writing and producing a mini-movie or a music video.

Because so many TV ads these days are subject to "zipping" (fast-forwarding past the ads on a Digital Video Recorder), "zapping" (flipping around other channels during the commercial break) or "flushing" (losing the viewer while they visit the bathroom)—it's important to get your viewer's attention right away. This can be done by various methods—lots of motion, total silence, using arresting sounds, voices or images, arousing curiosity, showing celebrities in action, and so on. In addition, it's important that if you are showing words on the screen, your announcer is also saying those words—otherwise viewers may suffer from cognitive dissonance and won't retain either set of words. But if you are demonstrating something on-screen, it's fine to talk about something else—viewers can see what you're showing them and don't need to have that reinforced so literally.

Here are a few of the typical TV formats you might consider:

- Demonstrations such as product-in-use or a torture test
- Before and after or side-by-side comparison
- Slice of life (often blended with problem/solution)
- A set of vignettes showing various product uses or various types of people using the product
- A short movie with the product blended in
- Testimonials or celebrity endorsements

Radio Basics

Whereas television is all about visuals, radio has no visuals—they are left up to the listener's imagination. While television commands the viewer's attention at least some of the time, radio is often used as a companion medium or as background noise while driving, working or relaxing. Radio copy should be conversational and personal—written one-to-one. It's vital go get the listener's attention right off the bat with your ad, too…otherwise it will remain as part of the background noise. This can be done with a unique voice, a call to attention, or selecting out the audience with music or sound effects, among other methods. General-advertising radio spots may be as long as 60 seconds, but as with television, they can only get across one main idea per spot.

A few typical radio formats to consider are:

- Straight announcer (recorded in advance)
- Announcer or on-air personality (done live)
- Dialogue between two people (often blended with problem/solution)
- Jingle—either for the whole spot or blended with an announcer
- Celebrity endorsement (often with announcer lead-in and/or ending)

Retail Advertising Basics

Most effective retail ads in daily or weekly newspapers or on television, radio or via e-mail or web site are comprised of four important elements:

1. Store image—Ads should "look and sound like the store" and have the same "look and feel" as other company promotions.
2. News/timeliness—Retail ads are meant to drive traffic, and thus should feature a certain time-limited sale or offer, new product arrivals, special events or other reasons to visit now.
3. Specifics—Retail customers "shop the ads" and want to know what colors and sizes your turtleneck sweaters come in, what they are made of, the brand name, and so on. Model numbers, series numbers, and other specifics also help customers know what to expect when they get to the store.
4. Price—People in the market for a $100 MP3-CD player likely want neither a stripped-down $29.99 version nor a souped-up $300 job. They want to know the price range of the item your promoting before taking time to visit your store. If you're having a sale or other price promotion, be specific about that as well.

Out-of-Home Basics

Outdoor advertising gurus caution that your general-advertising billboards should contain no more than 7 to 10 words for maximum effect. Sometimes all you need for billboard copy is the "big idea" for your campaign. The most arresting billboards include a dominant, attention-getting visual—but keep in mind that billboards should be in harmony with the "look and feel" of the rest of your ads and promotions. You may be able to sequence your ads so that the first one in a series asks a question, and the next one answers it. Or you may use billboards for a teaser campaign with a bit more added each week or month until the new product, store or event is fully revealed to the viewer. Today's digital billboards open up many possibilities for updating ads on the fly rather than being "stuck" with the same message for 30 days at a time.

Creative Concepts in Direct Marketing

How Direct Marketing is Different

The essential character of direct marketing lies in its *action orientation*. General advertising may inform, persuade or remind prospects about products or services, but it does not sell. To sell, or to invite a step toward a sale, direct marketers include a call to immediate action and an easy-to-use response device. Direct marketers make specific offers: They tell prospects what they're going to get and what they have to do to get it—be it a product in exchange for a price, free information in exchange for a phone call, or some other quid pro quo. In addition to action orientation, direct marketing has several other important characteristics. It is:

- Targeted
- Personal
- Measurable
- Testable
- Flexible

While most any medium can be utilized for direct-response purposes, this section details some how-tos for several of the most prominent direct marketing media: direct mail, catalogs, and broadcast.

Direct Mail

A direct mail package that sells a product or service should take the place of a retail store experience for the customer. For example:

- The outer envelope serves the same function as a store window—to select the audience and entice them inside.
- The letter takes the place of personal sales—using "you-oriented" language to speak directly to the buyer and answer the buyer's objections.
- The brochure takes the place of the product display or demonstration.
- The reply device takes the place of closing the sale.

One of the "pros" of direct mail is that it allows for a variety of formats—everything from postcards to multi-dimensional "bulky packages." In addition to the four "classic package" elements mentioned above, a direct mail package may include such pieces as:

- Business Reply Envelope to make it easy for the prospect to respond
- Premium slip to highlight a free offer
- Publisher's letter to overcome specific objections
- Involvement device such as stickers to indicate selections on the reply form
- Reminder slips
- Article or ad reprints
- Testimonial flyers
- Questions and answers
- Samples
- DVDs or flash drives

Less personal and more promotional than the classic envelope-enclosed direct mail package—but also less expensive in most cases—is the self-mailer. This piece does not come in an envelope—it's folded and/or stapled to encompass all the elements of the letter, brochure and reply device. Postcards are used more and more as mailing costs increase and people's attention spans decrease—they can drive traffic to a Web site or landing page where full information is available, remind subscribers that it's time to renew, or complete other simple and straightforward communications with customers.

Catalogs

When Montgomery Ward and Sears reigned supreme in the world of American catalogs, their thick "wish books" served the purpose of a general store by mail. But as Americans gained mobility and suburbs spilled into what had been remote farmland, many more shoppers were able to visit cities, towns, and outlying malls to make their purchases in person. Thus, catalog merchandisers were forced to find new reasons for being—resulting in today's "niche marketing" landscape.

To succeed in today's competitive catalog realm, each firm must discover and fulfill one or more unmet needs of a target group of consumers. That special niche can be determined through:

- Research to see what catalogs are already in the marketplace and where gaps exist
- Consumer research to determine their unmet needs and wants in terms of merchandise mix
- Exploration of niches based on factors other merchandise such as better selection, finer quality, more affordable price or appealing presentation

Catalogs are merchandise-driven, and it's wise to put your most appealing merchandise, and/or the items with the best margin, in what are called the "hot selling spots." These are, in order of strength:

1. Front cover
2. Back cover
3. Inside front cover spread
4. Center Spread
5. Inside back cover spread
6. Spread near the order form (if your catalog still has one—some firms have tested and found they can get away with online and phone ordering only)
7. On the order form itself (again, if your catalog still has one)

Copywriters often are invigorated by the prospect of a new catalog concept, and the first time through is exciting—what with discovering the merchandise and the target market, setting the tone of the catalog, and so on. But much of catalog copywriting can become a bit dull and repetitive—so writers in this field need to find ways to keep themselves fresh. These methods could include:

- Keeping an eagle eye on the competition.

- Using the catalog's products yourself and observing the reactions of family and friends as well.
- Making friends with the merchandisers to get their perspective on products' unique aspects.
- Thinking like a consumer—what would excite someone about this item?
- Pay attention to results and do your best to increase sales.
- Don't stay in your cubicle—check out customer service, the shipping department and other areas of the company to stay in touch with the overall business.

Broadcast

Direct response TV and radio spots are—by and large—longer and more laden with copy and benefits than their general advertising counterparts. Keep in mind that these spots must overcome inertia to the extent that a prospect picks up the phone, goes to a retail store, or visits a Web site in response to your promotion. Direct response spots often are created on a shoestring, unlike the expensive general-advertising productions that are broadcast for major brands.

Products that perform well in direct response TV spots include those that shine in demonstration, have wide appeal, are not available at retail, and have an acceptable price range—usually not much more than between $9.95 and $39.95. More expensive products can be sold using a two-step approach of lead generation with follow-up by phone or personal sales.

Formats for direct response spots often are similar to those described in the general advertising section, but they must be structured to make a sale. They include considerable repetition, and need plenty of time to get ordering instructions across including the appropriate toll-free number and/or web site.

On the radio, personalities such as Dave Ramsey and Glenn Beck—while expensive to work with—can yield exceptional results when they endorse products on their own talk shows. Radio spots often employ much more humor than direct response television spots—in part because humor offers a palatable way to employ repetition of important points and response information.

Creative Concepts in Sales Promotion

As with public relations, in many cases you will find yourself working with sales promotion specialists to enhance your efforts at spotlighting products or services. In this situation, it is imperative that you ensure the sales promotion program they develop is in keeping with the brand image, "look and feel" and overall campaign theme you have developed for your general advertising and direct marketing efforts.

The most prominent example of sales promotion is the coupon. A typical mistake in developing coupons is to forget to include benefit-oriented material along with the "price deal" or other promotion. Your targeted customers won't care about getting $5 off the regular price of a product unless the product itself intrigues them. Your sales promotion efforts have to help sell the product's attributes and benefits to optimize results.

Sweepstakes and contests are other typical sales promotion efforts. Because of the laws, rules and controversy surrounding sweepstakes and contests, it is wise to engage the services of a company that specializes in running these promotions. Be sure, as always, however, that the theme and prizes they come up with are in keeping with your product's brand image, and appealing to your target market. For example, a grand prize of a Ford Fiesta or F-150 pickup truck might be very exciting to the 18-25-year-old market, while older and more well-heeled empty nesters would be more intrigued by their own version of the "dream car"—a BMW Z-4 or similar.

Creative Concepts in Public Relations

Public relations experts often deem their field more compatible with the management function of business than the marketing function. They consider themselves "the right hand of the CEO," rather than mere "publicity seekers." On the other hand, when we discuss public relations as one of the four main aspects of Integrated Marketing Communications, we are focusing mainly on seeking publicity—which is indeed part of the public relations arsenal.

Public relations efforts can be extremely cost-effective. What's more, having a third party (a magazine, web site, TV show, etc.) say positive things about a product or service is very powerful. The other side of the coin is that since coverage resulting from public relations efforts is not paid for, it is also not controllable. It takes media savvy and careful cultivation to optimize relationships with reporters and minimize chances that a long-sought PR opportunity will turn into a negative story.

While respecting public relations professionals to ply their own craft, IMC creative types will be wise to work with the PR team to ensure that the news releases, special events and media contacts they make are in keeping with the overall brand image and campaign theme being promoted via general advertising, direct marketing and sales promotion.

If you embark on your own publicity program, understand that most news releases will not be acted upon in any meaningful way without follow-up and cultivation of the reporter and/or editor involved. It is important that the same PR professional makes these contacts over time to develop a cordial relationship with each journalist. It is vital that this PR professional take calls and return calls from journalists in a timely manner, too—and not hide from the media if controversy arises.

You should take time to read the publications, Web sites, and blogs, and watch the shows where you would like coverage for your product so that you can make constructive suggestions on where you might fit in—the "Diet and Nutrition" segment on NBC's Today Show, for example…or the weekly executive profile in a regional business publication. And remember that legitimate media outlets are completely separate from their advertising departments and that journalists will not take kindly to suggestions like "We're a big advertiser—we'd like to see you cover this story."

Get to know the publication's schedule and don't call a reporter who is "on deadline." Realize that reporters and editors at legitimate publications and broadcast outlets do not have to give you approval of your expert's quotes or the photos they take—indeed, they make take offense if you ask. Try to come up with information or angles that will intrigue reporters, bloggers and editors as well as their readers and viewers—if you don't get past these gatekeepers, your story will never see the light of day.

Here are some tried-and-true themes to consider for your news releases.

- New Products
- How-to Information
- Controversy
- Celebrity Involvement
- Human Interest
- Timely Information

Putting It All Together

Integrated Marketing Communications efforts can best be orchestrated by a cross-functional team using a comprehensive promotional plan as their "bible." Mutual respect, open communication, and an absolute commitment to focusing on the target consumer—rather than on internal squabbles and turf wars—will help ensure that this team is successful in identifying and executing the ideal mix of general advertising, direct marketing, sales promotion and public relations.

SUSAN K. JONES is a full-time, tenured Professor of Marketing at Ferris State University in Big Rapids, MI, and the principal of Susan K. Jones & Associates, an Integrated Marketing Consultancy. Ms. Jones is the author, co-author or editor of more than 30 books, including this volume (with J. Steven Kelly and Richard A. Hagle). She is a graduate of the Medill School of Journalism at Northwestern University with a master's degree in advertising. She is a member of the Medill Hall of Achievement, a recipient of the Downs Award of the Chicago Association of Direct Marketing, and the Robert B. Clarke Award of Marketing Edge, among other awards and honors. She lives in East Grand Rapids, MI and can be reached at sjones9200@aol.com.

READING

5

An Introduction to Database Marketing

ARTHUR MIDDLETON HUGHES

Director, Subscriber Acquisition Strategy, E-Dialog.com and
Vice President, The Database Marketing Institute, Ltd.

The purpose of database marketing is the same today as it has always been: to create and maintain a bond of loyalty between you and your customers that will last a lifetime. The goal has not changed, but the methods have. We still maintain information about our customers in a database and use it as a basis for our communications with them. In the past we used direct mail and phone calls to communicate. Today we use these plus emails, web sites, cell phone text and web messages and social media. These new developments make communications much less expensive, more frequent, but also much more complex. Most companies have found it useful to hire a service bureau to maintain their databases, and an email service provider (ESP) to send their emails and cell phone messages.

The process begins with a marketing database that keeps all sorts of information about customers: not only what they buy, but their demographics, families, responses and preferences. Information storage has become much more sophisticated—using relational databases—and much less expensive. Moore's Law describes a long-term trend in the history of computing hardware. The number of transistors that can be placed inexpensively on an integrated circuit doubles approximately every two years. The trend has continued for more than half a century and is not expected to stop until 2020 or later. This same trend has affected disk storage and transmission speed and capacity. Result: you can afford to retain and use all the information you can collect about a customer in your marketing programs. The only limitation is the human creative ability and willingness to devise methods for using the data.

The biggest change in database marketing in the last decade has been the arrival of web sites, email and mobile marketing. At first these seemed like a godsend: the main problem with database marketing was the high cost of communications with customers: $600 per thousand messages. You had all this wonderful information in your database that you could use to build relationships, but you were limited, in most cases, to about one letter a month because of the cost. In the last ten years, with web sites including social media, email and the iPhone, you can send messages to your subscribers and customers for less than $6.00 per thousand—a cost so low that the delivery cost is inconsequential.

Email has become the main way to communicate between companies and their customers. Direct mail is still alive and well, but email is gaining on it. There is a third communication means that is also growing: one-third of consumers in both the United States and the United Kingdom are viewing their emails on their iPhone or similar mobile devices. The use of mobile email is most prevalent among younger consumers, with over half of them spending a significant part of every day glued to their phones. Mobile use is exploding in all directions. All of these new communications methods can make use of the information in a customer marketing database.

Here, at last, is a way to use your database to build really close relationships with each customer using the data you have collected. What we had not figured on was that the low cost of email and mobile messages has become a curse.

They have been a curse because marketers have discovered that emails are so inexpensive that you can afford to send messages to your customers every week, or even every day. The more you send, the more revenue you gain. More and more major corporations in the U.S. and elsewhere have been sending emails, and sometimes mobile messages, to all their subscribers all the time. Subscriber inboxes are overflowing. The big problem is that the messages, while they can be, and often are, personalized, are seldom filled with dynamic content based on what we know about each customer. We can have these rich databases, but we do not use the rich data that they hold. To use it requires many creative staff members who dream up the dynamic content. The thought is: "These subscribers over 65 have certain interests, while these other subscribers are college students who have different interests. We will vary our messages based on this knowledge, and also do that for about a dozen other subscriber segments so as to make our relationships richer for them and more profitable for us." Sounds great, doesn't it? That has always been the promise of database marketing. We *could* send dynamic content before when we were sending one message a month. But few marketers today are doing anything like that. They are blasting identical content to every subscriber or customer whose email or address they can get their hands on.

The problem boils down to one simple fact: **The lift we get from dynamic content does not seem to be as great as the lift we get from frequent communications**. You can't afford to do both, so you go with the most profitable.

As database marketers we must deal with the ramifications of this tradeoff between frequency and dynamic content. There are many solutions. Take a good look at this chart:

ROI Comparison	Direct Mail	Email
Pieces Mailed	1,000	1,000
Cost of mailing	$600	$6.00
Conversion Rate	2.67%	0.15%
Sales	26.7	1.50
Revenue per Sale	$100	$100
Revenue	$2,670	$150
Return on Investment	$4.45	$25.00

This chart explains a lot about what has happened to Strategic Database Marketing.

The Old Corner Grocer

In my seven books on database marketing, I described the customer relationships of the Old Corner Grocer and how his loyalty building methods are carried out today by modern database marketing. The analogy is still true.

Back in the days before there were supermarkets, all the groceries in America were sold in small corner grocery stores. In many cases, the proprietor could be seen at the entrance to his store, greeting the customers by name. "Hello Mrs. Hughes. Are your son and his family coming for Thanksgiving again this year?"

These guys built the loyalty of their customers by recognizing them by name, by greeting them, by knowing them, by doing favors for them. They helped by carrying heavy packages out to customers' cars (there were no shopping carts in those days). These veterans no longer exist. The supermarkets put them out of business. Prices came down. Quality went up. The corner grocer had 800 SKUs in his store. Supermarkets today have more than 30,000 SKUs. He had a few hundred customers. Companies today have thousands or millions of customers.

As a result, the familiarity of the Old Corner Grocer that produced loyalty in the old days has become much more difficult to create and sustain — until database marketing came along. Using current techniques, it is now possible for a large corporation with a marketing database to build a relationship with customers that recreates the recognition and loyalty of the old corner grocer. We do this over the phone (using voice, text and emails), through creative use of a web site and emails, and by providing our employees in marketing, sales, customer service or at retail counters and teller windows with the kind of information about their customers that the corner grocers used to keep in their heads. We are returning today to methods that worked wonderfully in the old days. They work today. They build loyalty, repeat sales, cross sales, and profits.

Customers have become dominant. There are, today, in most parts of the US, many different stores selling similar products. Most families and businesses today have PCs and advanced smart cell phones—both equipped with Google—so that they can look up and find any product or service that they want to buy, with comparative prices and customer reviews. You can't fool them anymore. What do they want?

What Customers Want

What has been happening is that the customers are becoming dominant. Companies are discovering what their customers want, and selling them that. It is customer-based marketing. But it is really more than that. What customers want today can be summed up in a few general concepts:

Recognition—That they be recognized as individuals, with individual desires and preferences. They like being called by name.

Service—Thoughtful service provided by knowledgeable people who have access to the database, and therefore know who they are talking to, and what these people are interested in.

Convenience—People are very busy. They don't have time to drive a couple of miles to do business. They want to do business from where they are by cell or landline phone or using the web, with companies that remember their names, addresses, credit card numbers, and purchase history.

Helpfulness—Anything that you can do to make customers' lives simpler is appreciated. Merchants have to think, every day, "How can I be more helpful to my customers?" Only those who come up with good answers will survive.

Information—Customers are more literate today than ever before. They use the Internet. Technical information is as important to many of them as the product itself.

Identification—People like to identify themselves with their products (like their cars) and their suppliers (like their cell phones). Companies can build on that need for identification by providing customers with a warm, friendly, helpful institution to identify with.

Who Do They Listen To?

Increasingly today, customers listen to other customers. They participate in blogs. They read product reviews written by other customers. Young people participate in Facebook and Twitter, exchanging information that suppliers of products and services cannot control.

From 1985 to today, most large modern corporations have built customer marketing databases filled with personal information about their customers. Modern computer technology has been used to create relational databases that store a great deal of information on each household (or company, in the case of a business-to-business product). Retained is not just the name and address, but also:

- Email address, plus the cookies that keep track of their web visits
- Complete purchase history
- Customer service calls, complaints, returns, inquiries
- Outgoing marketing promotions, and responses
- Results of customer surveys
- Household (or business) demographics: income, age, children, home value and type, etc.
- The profitability, Recency/Frequency/Monetary (RFM) code, and lifetime value of every customer in the database.

What changed, however, is the method of using the database to communicate with customers. Before 2000 we had direct mail and telephone. Now, we have the web, email, and mobile devices which have changed everything.

- Every company of any size has a web site filled with information—most with shopping carts.
- Many companies send both catalogs and promotional emails to prospective customers.
- Most companies also send triggered messages to individual customers that make it possible to send each of a million customers a different message, based on the database.

- Most companies send transaction messages ("Your product was shipped today.") which were impossible before (too slow and expensive) and now, not only keep customers informed, but sell them additional products and services.
- Most email and mobile communications today are filled with **links** which mean that every message can be an adventure: a gateway to every product and piece of information that the company has available. Using links you can do research, read reviews, print specifications, compare prices, and buy whatever interests you.

Two Kinds of Databases

There are really two different kinds of databases in any company that is engaged in direct marketing of products and services. One is an operational database and the other is a marketing database.

An *operational database* is used to process transactions and get out the monthly statements:

- For a cataloger, this database is used to process the orders, to charge the credit cards, arrange shipment, and handle returns and credits.
- For a bank, the operational database processes checks and deposits, maintains balances, and creates the monthly statements.
- For a telephone company, the operational database keeps track of the telephone calls made and arranges the billing for them.

A **marketing database** gets its data from the operational database, if there is one. This data consists of a summary of monthly transactions. But the marketing data also includes much more. It gets data from:

- Preferences and profiles provided by the customers.
- Promotion and response history from direct mail and email marketing campaigns.
- Appended data from external sources such as KnowledgeBase Marketing, Donnelly, Claritas, etc.
- Lifetime Value and RFM analysis, leading to creation of customer segments.
- Modeling for churn and next best product.

The marketing database passes data back to the operational database. It may advise the operational database:

- Which segment each customer has been placed in, which may lead to operational decisions. Gold customers, for example, may get different operational treatment.
- Expressed customer preferences leading to different operational treatment: smoking or non-smoking rooms assigned automatically.

The operational database is run by IT. It is run on accounting principles and balances to the penny, since there are legal and tax aspects to its data. It is audited by external auditors. It contains only current data on customers. Old data is archived. There is no data on prospects until they make a purchase.

EXHIBIT R5.1: OPERATIONAL AND MARKETING DATABASE

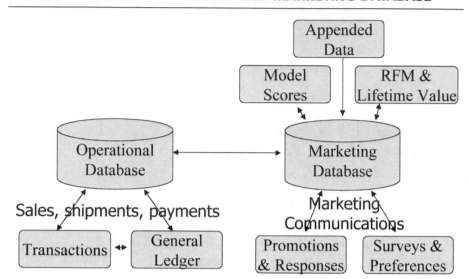

In many companies, there are several marketing databases. For various reasons, the database of catalog customers is often separate from the retail store customer database. The web site and email customer databases may also often be kept separately. From the outside it seems like a simple matter to bring all these databases together so as to get a "360 degree" picture of each customer. But, in fact, this combination is often difficult to achieve. Why should this be so?

The reasons are varied but they often relate to internal company politics. In a typical bank, there are vice presidents for each major product: credit cards, home equity loans, retail (checking and savings accounts), insurance, etc. The credit card manager receives no bonus or special recognition if some of his credit card customers sign up for a checking account. The Retail Vice President gets no special reward if some of his customers apply for a credit card. Yet any analysis of bank customers will show that the more different bank products that the average customer has, the higher will be that customer's loyalty to and profits for the bank. The organization and compensation system does not reflect the theory of customer relationship management.

Sears Canada Shows How It Is Done

This situation was dramatically illustrated by the experience of Sears Canada a few years ago. For historical reasons, Sears Canada had separate operations for the catalog and retail stores. One day they decided to build a combined customer marketing database. Once the database was built, Sears was able to measure the performance of catalog customers vs. retail customers vs. web customers. The data was very revealing. They found that at that time the average catalog customer spent $492 dollars per year. The average retail customer spent $1,102 dollars per year. But customers shopping both channels were spending $1,883 per year with Sears.

This discovery led to a fundamental reorganization of the whole company. A central EVP for marketing was set up who worked across all channels. Bruce Clarkson, General Manager of Relationship Marketing for Sears Canada, didn't stop at integrating catalogs with retail. Using the new database he focused on retention, acquisition and purchase stimulation. He proved that the strongest predictive variable for not shopping the catalog was exposure to bad service: out of stock, or merchandise that was not satisfactory. Sears could prove that money spent on improved service would increase customer retention.

Sears set up an RFM system with 189 cells, tracking recency on a quarter by quarter basis. Clarkson's analysis showed that each quarter between 20,000 and 30,000 new customers acquired a Sears card, bought once, and never bought again. Sears spent a lot of money trying to get the card into people's hands, but was not doing enough to get them to use the card. The new database showed that 14 percent of Sears customers were $2,500 plus buyers who contributed 50 percent of Sears total corporate merchandise revenues. Using their database to see what web site customers did, they found that 97 percent of sales volume was from people who had the paper catalog in front of them.

Sears used and continues to use their database to understand their customers. Then they took that crucial step to change their organization to make use of what they had learned. They became customer focused. It is a tremendous lesson for the rest of us.

Email Marketing Needs to Catch Up

Building a central marketing database is only a first step. In most companies today, email marketing—the most powerful tool available—is not used productively. Direct mail is used carefully because it is expensive. emails are so inexpensive that most marketers send millions of identical messages on a daily basis to subscribers who are overwhelmed and annoyed by their overflowing inboxes. Database marketing is not being used effectively by most email marketers—which means most major corporations today.

This is a message that you will learn from studying about database marketing. You will learn how to determine the lifetime value of your customers and of your email subscribers. You will learn how to use that value to direct and manage your marketing program through all communication channels.

Looked at from the customer's point of view, database marketing through all channels is a way of making customers happy; of providing them recognition, service, friendship, and information for which, in return, they will reward you with loyalty, retention and increased sales. Genuine customer satisfaction is the goal and hallmark of satisfactory database marketing. If you are doing things right, your customers will be glad that you have a database and that you have included them on it. They will want to subscribe to and read your emails. They will come happily to your web site and your retail stores. They will want to receive your catalogs. They will appreciate the things that you do for them. If you can develop and carry out strategies that bring this situation about, you are a master marketer. You will keep your customers for life, and be happy in your work. You will have made the world a better place to live in.

Conclusions

- The purpose of database marketing is to create and maintain a bond of loyalty between you and your customers that will last a lifetime.
- Modern database marketing is trying to recreate for large companies the loyalty enjoyed by the old corner grocers who knew their customers by sight and name.
- Database Marketing has changed significantly due to web sites, email and mobile marketing. These have reduced the cost of communication, but presented a serious problem: There are too many messages.
- Sending dynamically different messages to each customer is the goal, but the lift from customized content is less than the lift from frequent messages: frequency beats customization.
- Electronic links within messages permit customers to do research and discover every product you have for sale and a tremendous amount of previously unobtainable data.
- There are two types of database: an operational and a marketing database. Companies must have both.
- Customers today want recognition, service, friendship, and information. They listen, often, more to other customers than to what you are saying to them.

ARTHUR MIDDLETON HUGHES was Vice President of The Database Marketing Institute. He was the author of *The Complete Database Marketer* (Editions 1 and 2) (McGraw-Hill), *Strategic Database Marketing* (1st, 2nd, 3rd and 4th editions) (McGraw-Hill), *Customer Churn Reduction and Retention for Telecoms* (RACOM 2009) and *Successful E-mail Marketing Strategies* (RACOM 2010).

Media Planning:
The Business End of Advertising

MARIAN AZZARO

Roosevelt University

Media planning is the business end of the advertising business. Media is the marketing communications function responsible for the allocation of millions and millions of client advertising dollars.

There are many jobs in the media business, but this piece will focus on the critical task of planning. It is the job of the media planner to consider an ever-increasing number of media alternatives and recommend placement of an advertiser's message. Media planning professionals can make a big difference in the effective delivery of a client's message. A good media planner can make even bad advertising work for a client. Conversely, a media planner who makes bad or uninformed decisions can bury even the best advertising. In media, it is all about making informed decisions. Media planning decisions are made in the context of the media planning process.

The primary purpose of the media planning process is to identify the one best combination of many media alternatives that will most effectively and efficiently deliver the client's communication to the right target audience. At each major step of the media planning process, critical decisions must be made.

There are three strategic steps to the process: Establishing Objectives, Defining Spending Principles, and Identifying Strategies. Let's consider them one by one.

Establishing Objectives

Every media plan must first express an objective that will establish goals for coverage and delivery of exposures to an appropriate target audience. These goals must be specific and measurable quantitative goals. Note here the use of the word *must*, not *should*. This is very important. While much in media is negotiable, this is not.

In order to gauge effectiveness and efficiency, the media planning process requires a specific and measurable quantitative objective. Other, qualitative objectives can be incorporated, but a proper media plan starts with a quantitative goal.

The details of this quantitative objective statement suggest the focus of a media planner's decision-making. First, it is the identification of "an appropriate target

---

EXHIBIT R6.1: THE MEDIA TARGET FOR PLANNING AND MEASUREMENT

The brand communication strategy for Kraft's Velveeta brand cheese product may state the target audience is "women who cook family meals with cheese." However, the media research and measurement services do not report media measures for "women who cook family meals with cheese." The media planner for the Velveeta business uses syndicated secondary research services like Simmons or MRI[1] to create a customized target definition by combining the profiles of women who buy cheeses commonly used for cooking: cheeses like shredded cheddar or mozzarella, or cheese products like Velveeta or Cheez Whiz. The media planner then designates this newly created profile as the "planning target." Next the media planner studies the demographic characteristics of the customized target (women who buy cooking cheeses) to identify the principle demographic, probably women aged 35 to 64. Finally the planner designates this principle characteristic as the "measurement target."

---

audience." Then, the focus shifts to coverage and delivery of exposures to that target audience.

The Media Target

The media planning process is most often initiated as a subprocess of the advertising or marketing plan, with the target audience for a client's communication already established. If this is the case, then the media planner's role will be to restate the marketing target audience in terms that match up to the typical measures reported by media research services.

Media planners restate the marketing target audience in two different ways, one for planning purposes and one for measurement purposes. The planning target requires a media target definition that allows planners to analyze and evaluate multiple media options relative to the target audience. The measurement target requires a simple, demographic target definition that allows planners to measure and compare the relative effectiveness and performance of alternative media plans. Exhibit R6.1 shows how a media planner might restate a brand positioning target audience for each purpose.

In some cases, media planners may be called upon earlier in the marketing process to help identify the best target audience for all marketing efforts. For example, this might happen when the client assignment is to launch a new product. As described in Exhibit R6.1, media planners can be very creative in finding ways to use the syndicated research services like Simmons and MRI. A media planner can do this by using other products currently in a category, or looking at research on competitive products that will be replaced by the new product.

Media Coverage and Delivery

Once the target audience has been defined, the media planner next considers the question of coverage and delivery of exposures to that target audience. Media plan-

---

[1] To learn more about the major syndicated media research services, visit the Simmons web site at www.smrb.com or the web site for GfK MRI at http://www.gfkmri.com.

EXHIBIT R6.2: THE THIRD TIME IS A CHARM

Advertising works through repeated exposures to a marketer's message. The general rule-of-thumb is that it takes three exposures to ensure effective communication. To understand this rule, consider the fleeting nature of a 30-second television advertisement. Most would agree that it would be lucky if the target audience actually noticed any part of an advertisement on the very first exposure to it. Maybe the consumer saw something that first time that piqued her interest and so she paid attention the next time (the second time) she saw the advertisement. This would be a lucky coincidence. Even so, the consumer, having noticed and paid attention to the ad, still needs to understand and agree with the message before being convinced. Such understanding and agreement *might* be reached on a third exposure to the message, if the message is compelling and clear.

ners use several quantitative measures for this purpose. The most important measures are reach and frequency, impressions, and rating points.

Reach and Frequency. Reach is the number of different people exposed to a message within a specified time period. Reach is usually expressed as a percentage of a total target audience such that reach would never be greater than 100 percent. Frequency is the number of times a person is exposed to a message, usually linked to the same time period as used for the reach goal.

In media planning we use the words reach and frequency to mean coverage and exposures, respectively. These two words together represent a core concept of media planning—trade-offs. Media planners can put together media choices to optimize reach or optimize frequency, or they can work within a budget constraint to balance reach and frequency. The media planner must decide which approach is best for the client's needs.

Media planners make this decision based on the advertising plan, matching the Reach/Frequency goal of the media plan to the corresponding advertising objective overall. If the advertising objective is to increase top-of-mind awareness in order to remind consumers that Brand X is out there, then the corresponding media objective might be to achieve the broadest possible coverage (reach) of the designated target audience. However, if the advertising objective is to convince consumers that Brand X is better than Brand Y, then the corresponding media objective might be more exposure (frequency) oriented. As a rule it takes more exposure to convince a prospect than to simply remind.

Next the media planner considers how much exposure is enough. This is a subject of continuing debate in media planning circles. Some say once is enough; some say three, four, or more. The generally accepted rule-of-thumb is that it takes three exposures to be effective. Exhibit R6.2 shows how it might take three exposures to make sure the advertising works.

Impressions. Impressions are another important and often used quantitative measure of a media plan. Impressions are a summary figure representing the total exposures of an advertising message in a given period of time. The phrase "total ex-

---

EXHIBIT R6.3: CHOOSING BETWEEN MEDIA PLAN OPTIONS

Consider a case of two media plans, A and B. Each plan delivers a total of 1,000 Target Rating Points in one calendar quarter. The media planner must look at the component statistics of the two plans to determine which plan is the best. Plan A delivers 1,000 TRPs with a Reach of 80 percent and an average Frequency of 12.5 times (80 × 12.5 = 1,000). Plan B, on the other hand, delivers 1,000 TRPs with a Reach of 50 percent and an average Frequency of 20 times (50 x 20 = 1,000). If the media plan goal was to optimize Reach, then Plan A would be the better choice.

---

posures" is the key to this measure. With impressions we count each person reached with our message, for every time that person is reached. As such, some people are counted multiple times. In most media plans this is a big number that can be stated either in "gross" terms, meaning a broad measure statistic like TV households, or in "target" terms, meaning a narrow measure statistic like Women 35 to 64.

Rating Points. Rating points are probably the most widely familiar form of media measurement. Most people in the U.S. have heard of the Nielsen[2] ratings for TV shows. The rating of a TV show tells us the percent of a total audience tuned in to that show. We use ratings to compare TV programs across a common audience base and rank programs according to the relative size of the audience tuned in.

Rating points are another measure that can be expressed in either "gross" or "target" terms, such as gross rating points (GRPs), meaning ratings at the household level, or target rating points (TRPs), which means rating points among a specific target audience segment.

Rating points are calculated as a function of percent Reach times average Frequency and knowing this is very important. Exhibit R6.3 shows how a media planner would use this knowledge to choose the better of two similar media plans.

Any one of these measures, reach and frequency, impressions, or rating points, can be used as an effective, quantitative measure of media plan performance. The media planner uses one or all three to compare alternative media plans.

Media Plan Objectives

The best media plan objective defines a specific target audience, a specific percentage of reach, and a certain level of frequency to be accomplished within a specific time frame. Depending on the circumstances, it might be appropriate to use an additional statistic like impressions or rating points together with reach and frequency. Exhibit R6.4 shows several examples of appropriate media plan objectives.

Defining Spending Principles

Budget is always an issue for media planning and many of the planner's decisions are based on working within a budget constraint. A media planner makes trade-offs, like

---

[2] For more information about television ratings, visit the Nielsen Media Research web site at www.nielsenmedia.com.

EXHIBIT R6.4: EXAMPLES OF MEDIA PLAN OBJECTIVES

Each of the following objectives provides a quantitative performance standard. The media planner considers alternative media plans against such a standard to choose the best plan for the client's assignment.

- Reach 80% of women 35–64 an average of 4 times every 4 weeks.
- Reach 50% of men 25–49 an average of 3 times each week before a home football game.
- Reach 70% of the primary target audience 5 times each quarter of the year.

---

reach versus frequency discussed earlier, throughout the plan. Spending principles define priorities that guide the media planner's decisions in making such trade-offs. Spending principles are often determined by the strategic approach to the media plan.

The recommended strategic approach to the media plan can be either defensive or offensive. The defensive approach leads the media planner to identify strategies and allocate the budget in such a way as to defend and support the existing strengths of the client's business. The media planner uses research to prioritize the geographic and seasonal emphasis of the plan based on the client's biggest sales.

In the offensive approach, the media planner sets budget priorities in an aggressive, competitive manner. The client's message delivery is directed offensively and opportunistically toward the areas of greatest business potential, not existing sales. The media planner uses research on the client's product and other factors to prioritize and focus on opportunities for growth of the client's business.

With focus and priorities established, the planner moves on to identify the specific strategies that will ultimately define the media plan.

Identifying Strategies

Strategies represent the means by which we expect to accomplish the objectives of the media plan. We define strategies in specific areas of planning relating to media scheduling, specific geography, and the mix of media by class/type and by specific media vehicle within each class.

Scheduling

Scheduling refers to how advertising is scheduled over the time period of the media plan. Media planners have three choices in this decision: continuous scheduling, flighting, or pulsing.

Continuous scheduling is a pattern that delivers an almost constant level of media support throughout the whole of the media plan period. For example, your favorite local grocery store probably runs a constant level of media support every week. This makes sense because we know that consumers shop for groceries every week.

Flighting and pulsing are patterns of media support delivered in peaks and valleys throughout the time period of the plan. In both cases, the media planner bundles media for heavier delivery in certain periods relative to others. The key distinction

---

EXHIBIT R6.5: REGIONAL COVERAGE OF THE U.S.

Many food products manufacturers started as Midwestern companies located close to raw materials supplies like grain. These businesses grew and distribution expanded effectively to the East but less so to the West. Western expansion was an issue because of the extra time and cost required to move goods through the Rocky Mountains. As a result, new companies started on the west coast to serve western customers. Many Midwestern-based food products companies still suffer weaker sales in the western U.S. Media planners for these national companies often choose to sell off the western region of national media buys.

---

between these two patterns is that a flighted schedule will leave certain periods blank with no media support at all. Media planners will decide to use a flighted or pulsed schedule in cases where a client's business runs in peaks and valleys. For example, if the client is an expensive neighborhood steakhouse, it has likely been observed that business is much better after the 15th of each month. This would be consistent with research indicating the importance of the 15th of each month as a common payday in the U.S. The media planner in this case would schedule advertising messages heavier around the 15th each month to build awareness when potential customers are more likely to have money to go out for dinner.

Specific Geography

In identifying strategies media planners make decisions about the specific geography the media must cover. If the budget is large enough, the media plan might cover all geography where the client's product is sold. However, it isn't always possible or even sensible to cover all geography equally. Sometimes a client's business or business potential is better in a particular geography. The media planner can reflect such differences in the media plan. Exhibit R6.5 presents the general example of major national food products manufacturers.

Mix of Media

The last area of media strategies is to decide media mix by general class/type and specific media vehicles. The term "media class" defines different general types of media including traditional forms like network television, cable television, magazines, radio, and newspapers, as well as other emerging and non-traditional forms like Internet-based and mobile media and a vast selection of out-of-home media forms now available. The term "media vehicle" is used here in reference to specific media choices like television programs by title, cable TV networks, radio station formats, and magazine titles. This is a broad area of media decision-making encompassing thousands of possible combinations and the choices are expanding every day as new media alternatives emerge.

Whether considering traditional or non-traditional media forms, the media planner first narrows the options by media class and then identifies specific choices of media vehicles. Media planners narrow the possibilities by considering each class of media relative to a list of criteria. Some of the more important considerations are the audience/media relationship, the availability of resources (time and money), and the geographic emphasis of the product relative to the media.

Each class of media works in a different way, engaging different senses of its audience and because of this, consumers may feel more or less involved with the media. The media planner is expected to know the facts of the audience/media relationship. A radio listener hears an advertisement, but doesn't see it. A magazine reader sees an advertisement, but doesn't hear it. A typical television viewer might actually hear and see an advertisement, but can't interact with it. If however, that television viewer is watching an advertisement through a cable system Video-on-Demand (VoD) service, then interaction with the product is not only possible, but likely.

This doesn't mean that any one medium is better than another, but one or more media may not be right for a particular client. Consider the example again of Velveeta cheese. If it is important to show a rich, creamy cheese sauce, then radio might not be the best medium to use. Instead, it might be better to use beautiful photography and 4-color reproduction to show that rich, gooey cheese sauce in a magazine advertisement.

Another factor to consider in this area is the active/passive nature of each medium and the corresponding longevity of an advertisement. Print media like magazines, newspapers, and Internet web pages and videos allow viewers a more active involvement with the content. The magazine reader can take an in-depth look at an interesting advertisement at his leisure. As such, a print advertisement has some longevity as long as the consumer keeps the magazine around. Broadcast media including traditional television and radio are more likely to be passive and fleeting in nature; consumers are simply exposed to the advertising message. Newer broadcast media options like VoD make it possible now for consumers to re-watch or refer back to previously viewed broadcast advertisements. If the client's message is complex, then the media planner might recommend a media form where the consumer can take time and refer back to the message.

The availability of resources can be a big factor in media decision-making. Media planners know that advertisements require more or less time and money to produce for the different media. If the client has a message today that she wants to deliver to consumers tomorrow, then the media plan won't use long lead-time media like television or magazines. Instead, the planner might recommend radio, knowing that a live announcer could read from a script, thus getting the message out quickly.

Planners also know that the absolute cost of buying advertising time or space can vary dramatically from one medium to another. At one extreme, the cost of a 30-second television ad to run during the Super Bowl can be more than $2.5 million. In contrast, a national advertisement in the Super Bowl edition of *Sports Illustrated* magazine would cost about one-tenth of that.

In considering geographic emphasis the media planner evaluates each media class for its effective coverage of the product's distribution geography. If a product is only available for sale in the Midwest, then the media planner eliminates media with coverage outside the region. On a more complex level, planners will consider that even the national media delivers its audience differently across the country. For example, the audience for late night television is much better in the Midwest than it is on either coast. Knowing this a planner might recommend the use of late night TV for a national client needing a Midwestern emphasis.

EXHIBIT R6.6: MAGAZINE COVERAGE OF A TARGET AUDIENCE

If your client is marketing a product for young, college-age women 18 to 24 years old, which magazine would you choose: *Cosmopolitan* or *Mademoiselle*? (Note that *Mademoiselle* is now incorporated into *Glamour*, but this theoretical example is still relevant.) Consider the following audience facts[3]:

- The total audience for *Cosmopolitan* at 9 million is more than double the *Mademoiselle* audience of just over 4 million.
- *Cosmopolitan's* coverage of women 18 to 24 is about 2.4 million, while *Mademoiselle's* coverage is about 1.4 million.
- The wasted coverage of people who are NOT the target audience is just over 6.5 million for *Cosmopolitan* (about 72% of the total audience) and only 2.5 million for *Mademoiselle* (about 62% of the total audience).
- While you get a bigger audience with *Cosmopolitan*, you are paying for more wasted coverage, not just for the coverage you want, women 18 to 24.

After narrowing the possible media alternatives by class, planners must evaluate and identify specific media vehicles. Even after eliminating whole classes of media, there are still many alternative media vehicles among which to discriminate. Two of the most important criteria for comparison among specific media vehicles are audience use of the media and audience coverage of the media.

In considering these factors for the more traditional media forms the planner turns once again to syndicated research services such as Simmons and MRI. These services report vast tables of data detailing the demographic, lifestyle, and psychosocial characteristics of the people who use various media. For example, for television alone these services report data on people who watch different program types, cable networks, at different times of day, and even specific TV shows. Media planners use Simmons and MRI reports, cross-tabulating product use (see Exhibit R6.1) and media use, to help them choose the right kind of magazine or the right time of day for an advertiser's message. These services help media planners to know the media use habits of the advertiser's audience. These same services also help planners to see that different media vehicles are more or less focused in their coverage of different audience segments. Exhibit R6.6 presents a discussion of audience coverage among comparable media choices.

When it comes to the emerging and non-traditional media forms, media planners sometimes have to trust their instincts and rely on less traditional, often less proven, research. For example, interactive and Internet-based media forms can offer an amazing amount of detailed information about such things as unique visits to web sites, length of time spent at a web site, number of pages viewed, etc. However, we can't yet have any real confidence in knowing the makeup of the audience behind the Internet terminal. Whatever the research, it is the media planner's job to know the many forms

---

[3] The data for magazine coverage of a target audience was summarized from Simmons NCS Part 1, Spring 1999.

of media and even more importantly, to know whatever she can about the audience for each media form.

The Changing Nature of Media

Throughout all time, the world of media has changed as technological advances have been realized. This was true centuries ago with the invention of moveable type and it is still true today as a result of the invention of the Internet. And, this will be true too in the future as the world moves more towards wireless and cellular mobile communications. With each new technological advance, we see a host of new media forms available for use in delivering marketing messages to consumers. Importantly, even as new media forms emerge, existing media forms remain. The result is the ever-evolving, constantly changing nature of the media business.

The number of media options available today for advertisers and their media planners has virtually exploded. In the preceding sections of this article we spoke briefly about such things as traditional and non-traditional, broadcast and print media forms. In recent years it has become increasingly difficult to characterize media in these same old and familiar ways. Instead we are coming to think of media now in terms of **outbound** and **interactive** forms.

Outbound media are the more traditional media forms, as well as some of the newer forms, where the emphasis is on one-way delivery of a marketing message to a consumer. This would include traditional media like broadcast and cable television, cinema, radio, magazine, newspaper, and most forms of out-of-home from roadside billboards to airport/stadium signage. This definition would also include some of the newer media applications such as sidewalk chalk signage, graffiti/mural messaging, public restroom signage, and all manner of other kinds of signage that we see all around us these days.

Interactive media on the other hand is where we are seeing some of the more exciting new developments of the day. As you would expect, the emphasis in interactive media is on facilitating interactive, two-way communication between the marketer and the consumer. It's not just about delivering the marketer's message, it's about delivering the message in such a way that the consumer can interact with the marketer to ask a question or gather more information about the product. For example, as we discussed earlier in this article, cable system Video-on-Demand services make this kind of two-way communication possible. Television digital video recording (DVR) devices like TiVo offer services like brand "tags" and title search advertising as another way to make television an interactive media form.

The Internet is a largely interactive media form. There are several different ways media planners can use the Internet in an interactive marketing capacity. Some of the more common interactive Internet applications today include web site features like advergames, microsites, and web logs. And, other Internet applications like search engine optimization (SEO) and social networking or virtual reality sites are also ways a media planner can provide an interactive forum for a marketer's message. Consider for example, the Travelocity brand Roaming Gnome character and its Facebook friends' page.

Mobile messaging is another newer class of the interactive media form. Mobile messaging is big business in many parts of the world already and growing quickly in the U.S. Mobile phone users all over the world can use their cell phones today to send and receive emails, text, or multimedia messages, or download games, songs, or videos. In many parts of the world, mobile service providers are making it possible now for marketers to send coupons and other marketing messages to consumer cell phones. In Japan, consumers can use their DoCoMo cell phone camera feature to scan Quick Response codes from product advertisements that allow them to then print coupons for discounts in stores where they shop for that product.

As a whole this is one of the more exciting aspects of the media business, the fact that it never sits still. Technology is an ever-evolving dynamic in the world and media is a technology driven business. As the media and media audiences of the future go increasingly digital and mobile, media planners will be the ones helping the marketing clients of the world to find new ways of reaching and communicating with those audiences.

Conclusion

The media planner is expected to make decisions and recommendations every day. Media is where the client's advertising budget is spent and sometimes the stakes can be high. No matter how large or small the advertising budget, the pressure is always on when you are spending someone else's money.

Media planners have to know a lot, but they don't have to know it all. Minimally, a planner needs to know where to find the facts. Planners use the facts that they learn from media research services to make big decisions and to explain their reasons for each decision. To do this, media planners have to be comfortable reading, interpreting, presenting, and explaining numbers, percentages, and indexes, and what each means for the client.

Good media planners love their work. They get charged up about knowing what kind of audience reads a certain kind of magazine, watches a given TV show, or visits a particular web site. They feel personally motivated to learn everything they can about the existing media and emerging, new media developments. The best media planners are consulted as experts for their knowledge of audiences and specific media usage behavior. Media planners are proud to serve their clients at the business end of the advertising business.

MARIAN AZZARO is a professor of marketing communications at Roosevelt University. Before joining Roosevelt, Azzaro enjoyed a successful 20-year career in business. She spent the first 10 years of her career working in advertising media planning. Then, after earning her MBA, she moved into brand management and marketing communications. Azzaro joined the faculty of Roosevelt University in 1999 where she is now a tenured professor teaching marketing, advertising, and media planning classes. She also serves Roosevelt as the head of its graduate IMC program. Azzaro is the lead author of the media planning textbook, *Strategic Media Decisions*.

READING
7

The Economics of
Database Marketing

ROBERT WEINBERG
RW Consulting

D atabase marketing is regarded as the most quantitative, results-oriented advertising medium. Yet most texts on the subject place little emphasis on the
economic factors needed to succeed or on how to determine profitability
and evaluate performance. Even more surprising is how many database marketers
pay much less attention to understanding their basic economic drivers than they do
to executing superior creative, testing, or media selection. Many traditional direct
marketers and even more dot-commers suffer greatly or even perish due to this
inattention.

Determining Profitability

Three factors determine the level of success database marketers can expect from a
customer relationship.

1. **Sales** net of returns for credit. Database marketing sales are driven by responses
   to the direct media used to promote a product or service.
2. The **contribution** which each sale makes to promotion cost and profit.
   Contribution is simply the amount remaining from a sale after the cost of
   goods or services, order processing and fulfillment, customer service and overhead are deducted from net revenue.
3. **Promotion cost,** or the amount spent to solicit a response from customers or
   prospects.

For a database marketer to succeed, their sales, at a level of response the marketer can
reasonably expect, must generate enough contribution to more than cover promotion costs.

Contribution

The term "contribution to promotion cost and profit" is somewhat unique to database marketing. It quantifies that portion of sales remaining after all the variable costs
of purchasing, handling and shipping a product or delivering a service are paid. This

includes more costs than are encompassed by the term "gross margin" which nets out only the cost of goods sold, but fewer than are encompassed by accounting's standard EBITDA (earnings before interest, taxes, depreciation and amortization). Typical variable costs subtracted to derive contribution include:

- The cost to purchase or manufacture the products being sold or to provide an offered service (e.g. claims costs for insurance, print, delivery and editorial costs for a publication, delivery of wireless, Internet, or similar services for a telecommunications firm).
- Labor costs to enter and process orders plus 800#, Internet and other connect charges.
- Order picking and packing labor and materials plus shipping cost (e.g. UPS, USPS, FedEx).
- Labor needed to receive and process a refund plus any costs incurred to refurbish or dispose of returned items.
- Labor and phone/Internet costs incurred responding to customer service questions (e.g. where is my order) or to handle **non**-revenue calls prompted by promotions.
- Credit card merchant fees.
- Any premium offered for trying or buying a product or service.

Though fixed overhead for such expenses as management salaries, rent, insurance, or corporate allocations is sometimes ignored to determine the contribution figure used to calculate breakeven or the profit/loss from a specific program, to derive true bottom line profitability marketers must know their overhead cost structure.

Exhibit R7.1 shows, in simple terms, the major cost categories subtracted to arrive at contribution as well as its two components—promotion cost and profit. The $24 in costs might include $16 for cost of goods (COGS), $5 in fulfillment expense, and $3 in overhead. Deducting these costs from the average $40 sale leaves a balance of $16 or 40% for contribution. Were promotion costs for this effort to total 25% of sales ($10), then 15% or $6 is left for profit.

At breakeven 100% of **contribution,** $16 in this case, is available to cover promotion costs and nothing ($0) is left for profit. A loss occurs when the promotion cost per order exceeds contribution, or 40% of sales in this example.

The example in Exhibit R7.2 shows a more complete contribution calculation for a typical merchandise sale. This marketer has determined that the average revenue per order is $50. In addition, customers pay an average $6.00 extra for shipping and handling. However, due to a free shipping offer on orders above a stated minimum value, only 75% of customers actually pay this charge. Thus **average** shipping & handling revenue is only the $4.50 shown. Similar weights apply to most other costs as well. For example, since only 35% of orders are placed via an in-bound 800 call, the average $3.25 cost for such orders is assessed only 35% of the time, resulting in an average per order phone cost of $1.26. Similar factors apply to mail and Internet orders.

Applying all these costs and weights results in a net contribution per order of $21.40 or 39.3% of the $54.50 in total average revenue. If $5.50 in corporate and de-

EXHIBIT R7.1: MAJOR PROMOTION COST AND PROFIT CATEGORIES

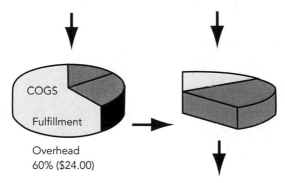

For a Sale = $40.00 (100%)

If Contribution = 40% ($16.00)   *And* Promotion Cost = 25% ($10.00)

COGS

Fulfillment

Overhead
60% ($24.00)

Then Profit = 15% ($6.00)

partmental overhead are added back in, contribution to **overhead**, promotion cost, and profit rises to $26.90 or 49.4% of total average revenue.

Part 1 of the Exhibit R7.2 worksheet contains a comprehensive list of input assumptions though some marketers will require more, fewer, or a slightly different set of items.

Part 2 performs the average order contribution calculation. Columns 1 and 2 [Base Cost and Factor Percent] reflect relevant values from Part 1. In a few cases these require an intermediate calculation that is not shown. Column 3, Weighted Cost per Sale, is equal to the Base Cost times the Factor Percent. Net Cost/Sale is the Weighted Cost factored up to reflect the added amount each **net** sale must absorb for orders returned for credit.

For example, though a marketer incurs order processing, shipping, pick and pack charges on a return, these orders produce no revenue to offset the expense. Thus, they must be borne by those sales that are paid for. In the Exhibit R7.2 example, which assumes a 10% return rate, the Weighted Shipping Cost/Sale of $3.50 is factored up by 1 minus the return rate to derive a Net Cost/Sale of $3.89 [$3.50 ÷ .9 = $3.89].

While the same detailed approach to computing contribution applies to virtually all services, there are typically fewer cost elements for such commonly direct marketed services as insurance, banking, credit cards, subscriptions, telecommunications and fund raising. Cost components for each of these services also vary widely. We will look at these in more detail under *Repeat vs. Individual Transaction Relationships*.

Prepare a detailed contribution calculation like the one in Exhibit R7.2 for any new offer, at least annually for established offers, and whenever a change in product, marketing or fulfillment experience impacts sales or costs. For example, free shipping, discounts, or a shift from telephone to Internet ordering all impact contribution, altering breakeven, profit, and loss levels. When compiling the detailed numbers that go into this computation, work with finance to ensure that assumptions and estimates are as accurate as possible.

EXHIBIT R7.2: DIRECT MARKETING CONTRIBUTION CALCULATION

PART 1—AVERAGE ORDER ASSUMPTIONS

Assumption	
Average Order Value	$50.00
Shipping and Handling	$6.00
Product/Service Cost	$15.00
Cost of Premium	$0.00
Business Reply (BRE) Postage	$0.42
Mail Order Processing/Handling	$2.50
Phone Order Processing/Handling	$3.25
Web Order Processing/Handling	$2.05
Order Picking/Packing	$2.25
Shipping Cost	$3.50
Customer Service Follow-up	$3.00
Return Handling	$2.95
Return Refurbishing	$5.20
Postage Refund on Returns/Exchanges	$3.25

Percent %:	
Returned Goods	10.0%
Exchanges	2.0%
Paying Shipping & Handling	75.0%
Mail Order	10.0%
Phone Order	65.0%
Web Order	25.0%
Postage Refunds	48.0%
Customer Service Follow-up	26.0%
Corporate Overhead	3.0%
Departmental Overhead	8.0%

	Freq. or Rate	Discount or Uncollected
Cash with Order	5.0%	1.00%
Net 30 Days	0.0%	0.00%
Charge to:		
American Express	15.0%	3.00%
Visa	40.0%	2.00%
Master Card	30.0%	2.00%
Discover	10.0%	1.75%
Other Cards	0.0%	0.00%

EXHIBIT R7.2: (Continued)

PART 2—AVERAGE CONTRIBUTION PER ORDER

	Base Cost	Factor Percent	Weighted Cost/Sale	Net Cost/Sale
Average Order Value	$50.00	100.0%	$50.00	$50.00
Shipping and Handling	$6.00	75.0%	$4.50	$4.50
TOTAL AVERAGE REVENUE			$54.50	$54.50
Average Product/Service Cost	$15.00	100.0%	$15.00	$15.00
Mail Order Processing/Handling	$2.92	10.0%	$0.29	$0.32
Phone Order Processing/ Handling	$3.25	65.0%	$2.11	$2.35
Web Order Processing/Handling	$2.05	25.0%	$0.51	$0.57
Order Picking/Packing	$2.25	100.0%	$2.25	$2.50
Shipping Cost	$3.50	100.0%	$3.50	$3.89
Premium Cost	$0.00	0.0%	$0.00	$0.00
Credit Card Discount	$1.16	95.0%	$1.10	$1.10
Bad Debt	$54.50	0.1%	$0.03	$0.03
Return/Exchange Handling	$2.95	12.0%	$0.35	$0.39
Return/Exchange Refurbishing	$5.20	12.0%	$0.62	$0.69
Shipping Cost on Exchanges	$3.50	2.0%	$0.07	$0.08
Postage Refund on Return/ Exchange	$3.25	5.8%	$0.19	$0.21
Customer Service Follow-up	$3.00	26.0%	$0.78	$0.87
SUBTOTAL—FULFILLMENT			$11.81	$13.00
TOTAL DIRECT COSTS			$26.81	$28.00
Overhead—Departmental	$50.00	8.0%	$4.00	$4.00
Overhead—Corporate	$50.00	3.0%	$1.50	$1.50
SUBTOTAL—OVERHEAD			$5.50	$5.50
TOTAL COST			$32.31	$33.50
CONTRIBUTION TO:				
Promotion Cost and Profit		42.0%	$22.19	$21.00
Promotion Cost, OH, and Profit		53.0%	$27.69	$26.50

Promotion or Selling Cost

A second special economic characteristic of database marketing is the importance placed on promotion cost, which should **not** be thought of as the advertising expense common to other distribution channels. Rather, promotion cost is database marketing's true "selling" expense. It is more akin to the cost of running a retail store or supporting a sales force than it is to advertising a retail sale or building brand awareness.

Promotion costs are typically large with 20% to 40% of sales not uncommon. Marketers control and direct this spending by choosing among many media (mail, Internet, TV, etc.) and deciding the content of each (e.g., size of a mail piece or space ad, length of a TV spot). They must therefore be isolated and analyzed carefully.

In most media, determining promotion cost is fairly straightforward. Divide promotion expense, typically from a single provider like a magazine or TV time buyer, by the number of prospects the medium reaches. An ad costing $20,000 in a publication whose circulation is 500,000 costs $.04 per reader or $40 per thousand readers (see *Measuring Success* for more on this) plus a small amount to create and prepare the ad.

In the mail, however, multiple suppliers are generally used for different services, each of which is paid for separately. Services range from printing to lettershop, postage, list rental, and unduplication (merge-purge). To ensure an accurate and **fair** evaluation of promotional success, use these rules to derive an effort's appropriate base promotion cost.

- Charge only for what is spent to print the number of pieces used in a mail drop **if** overages will be used later. If not, charge the full amount to the drop.
- Base list rental and merge/purge costs on the **net** number of names **mailed and paid for,** not gross quantities received.
- In **all** media, account **separately** for such creative and development costs as photography, copywriting, models, layout, and agency fees or commissions.
  —Charge all promotions a creative overhead based on an estimate of the proportion that fixed creative and development costs are of annual variable promotion costs. If fixed annual creative expense is estimated at $100,000 and variable spending is estimated at $1 million, add 10% to the variable cost of **each** effort, whether it is a test or a control.
  —Failure to follow this rule can burden tests with disproportionately high development costs, raising their cost per contact. Control packages or ads, in comparison, incur little if any new fixed creative costs and any amount spent is spread over a larger circulation base, further lowering its impact on the cost per contact. If this bias is not addressed via this suggested approach, winning tests can be discarded owing to an unfair promotion cost comparison.

- To avoid an additional bias in **mail** tests only, calculate profit or loss using **rollout** print and production costs for a piece rather than its actual cost whenever tests are printed in less than control mailing quantities. Allocate the excess costs for these less-than-rollout quantity runs to a testing overhead budget and charge the percentage this amount is of estimated total mail promotion costs proportionately to **all** mail promotions.

EXHIBIT R7.3: RESPONSE CALCULATIONS

	Test Results	
	A	B
Sales	$13,500	$26,000
Orders	270	520
Profit	$900	$1,400
Circulation	15,000	30,000
Profit % of Sales	6.7%	5.4%
Promotion Cost % of Sales	33.3%	34.6%
Sales per 1,000	$900	$867
Orders per 1,000	18.0	17.3
Profit per 1,000	$60	$47

Before leaving this topic we need a word on how to treat Internet promotion costs. Unlike other media, the Internet is unique in that most of its delivery costs are fixed. Except where marketers rent an email list, the cost to actually transmit a message to customers or prospects is negligible. The fixed costs to create and broadcast messages and to maintain sites to which responders are directed to click may, however, be considerable.

The mistake too many users of e-commerce make is to ignore these fixed costs and assume that the low variable cost of contacting prospects means they can send millions of messages with no ill effect as long as even a tiny fraction respond. Even if imprecise, marketers who email existing customers or prospects should attribute **fixed** costs to this medium based on their estimated annual site maintenance expenses divided by a best guess of the number of messages they will send. Though this number is subject to a margin of error, it is preferable to assuming that email promotions are essentially free.

Measuring Success

A final way in which database marketing math differs from traditional approaches to evaluating business outcomes is in its emphasis on relative rather than absolute measures of response, sales and profitability. Example response figures in Exhibit R7.3 show why this is the case.

Were we to evaluate the results of this effort based solely on **absolute** sales, orders and profit, Test B would be judged the better outcome. However, factoring in circulation, contribution and promotion cost we see that, on a **relative** basis, Test A offers a greater financial reward. Though there may be factors that make the Test B outcome acceptable, results cannot be completely or fairly judged until key relative measures are computed.

Because circulation quantities of most database marketing programs vary greatly as do their costs, relative measures provide a simpler, more accurate way than absolutes to evaluate outcomes, set goals, and benchmark results.

Having stated the need for relative measures, which ones are most important and

EXHIBIT R7.4: VALUES AND MEASURES

Absolute Values	Relative Measures
Gross or Net Sales	Sales per 1,000 (Contacts) Sales per Contact
Gross or Net Responders or Orders	Response Percent
Promotion/Marketing Costs	Promotion Cost Percent of Sales Promotion Cost per Piece or Contact Promotion Cost per 1,000
Product/Service and Fulfillment Costs, and Contribution	Percent of Sales Cost per Order
Pre-tax Profit	Profit Percent of Sales Profit per 1,000 Profit per Responder

how are these calculated? Exhibit R7.4 lists the most helpful relative measures corresponding to key absolutes. They range from response percent, widely but mistakenly believed to be the most important, to such less well known measures as sales or profit "per thousand of circulation" (commonly written "/M" or "/K").

Before proceeding, let's look at a simple example to understand how to calculate a per-thousand (/M) measure.

*If a marketer nets $18,000 in sales from a promotion sent to 12,000 households, then sales/M are $18,000 divided by circulation **in thousands**. In this case that is 12 (12,000/1000) and the answer is $1500 ($18,000/12).*

Exhibit R7.5 shows, in detail, how to compute key relative measures.

Breakeven and Profitability

With an understanding of these basic measures and their computation, we can now demonstrate how to establish the breakeven, profit, or loss for any effort, given the price of the product or service, its contribution per sale, and its promotion cost. Profit, using the terms introduced here, is simply contribution minus promotion cost.

Continuing the Exhibit R7.5 example, if each sale is worth $50 of which $16, or 32%, is contribution, and promotion costs are $400/M, then to break even (i.e. to just cover promotion cost) a marketer needs to net [after returns] $400 ÷ $16 or 25 orders **per thousand of circulation.** Sales of 25 orders per/M translate into a 2.5% response rate [25/1000 × 100] and sales/M of $1250 [25 orders/M × $50 per order].

Multiplying orders and sales/M by actual or forecast circulation in thousands gives us total actual or expected orders and sales. In this example, where total circulation is 7000, the number of **net** orders needed to breakeven is 25 × 7 or 175. Breakeven sales are $8750 [breakeven sales/M of $1250 × 7M circulation or 175 orders x $50 per order].

Note the importance here of the sales/M measure. It is the product of the number

EXHIBIT R7.5: CALCULATION OF RELATIVE PERFORMANCE MEASURES

Assumptions

A Selling Price per Order		$50
B Contribution to Promotion Cost and Profit per Order		$16
C Total Circulation		7,000
D Net Orders		250
E Total Promotion Cost		$2,800

Calculate:

F Total Sales	A x D =	$12,500
G Promotion Cost/Piece	E ÷ C =	$.40
H Promotion Cost/M	E ÷ (C/1000) or G x 1000 =	$400
I Response %	(D ÷ C) x 100 =	3.6%
J Sales/M	F ÷ (C/1000) =	$1,786
K Promotion Cost %	(H ÷ J) x 100 = or (E ÷ F) x 100 =	22.4%
L Total Contribution	B x D =	$4,000
M Contribution %	B ÷ A or L ÷ F =	32.0%
N Total Profit	L—E =	$1,200
O Profit/M	N ÷ (C/1000) =	$171
P Profit %	(O ÷ J) x 100 = or (N ÷ F) x 100=	12%

of orders times the average value of each sale or transaction. Except where revenue per sale is constant, sales/M is a better measure than response percent for setting goals and evaluating outcomes. This is because it factors in both response rate **and** average order value.

Before leaving this topic, let's look at a shortcut to computing breakeven sales/M given a promotion cost and contribution. It is: *Promotion Cost ÷ Contribution %*.

Using the Exhibit R7.5 example, breakeven is where promotion cost equals contribution, or 32% of sales. At a promotion cost of $400/M, breakeven = $400 ÷ .32 or the $1250/M shown above.

Were an alternative test package to cost $500/M, breakeven rises to $500 ÷ .32 or $1562.50/M. Dividing by our $50 average order value gives us the net required response rate of 3.125% [31.25 orders/M].

The Math of Repeat or Continuity vs. Individual Transaction Relationships

As mentioned in the section on Contribution just prior to Exhibit R7.2, most database marketing programs fall into one of two categories. In one, a regular stream of promotions is needed to drive additional sales while in the second the buyer, either explicitly or implicitly, agrees to make repeat purchases, limiting greatly the need for routine promotions.

Individual Transaction Relationships

Here marketers hope that, once satisfied with an initial experience, a reasonable number of buyers will eventually repurchase from any one of a typically large number of discreet promotions. Catalogs offering an array of consumer or business products are the most common form of this approach which depends for its success on:

- Keeping the cost of acquiring new customers down (see Acquisition Cost).
- Effectively segmenting the buyer file by such factors as the recency, frequency, amount, or nature of prior purchases.
- Targeting promotions with products and/or offers based on past relationship detail.
- Optimizing the number and timing of promotional contacts.

Despite marketers' best efforts, mail response rates to these promotions are usually in the single to low double digits since buyers have not committed to making an additional purchase. Response may be somewhat higher via outbound telemarketing and lower from emails, but in all cases only a small minority respond to each effort.

For these programs to work, it is critical that the marketer know contribution per order and breakeven. These numbers determine whether a customer will be promoted and in some cases which promotion he or she should receive. Decisions about whom to contact are made for each promotion of which there can be anywhere from a handful to dozens per year.

Repeat or Continuity Transaction Relationships

These relationships are found in a wide array of services. They include such financial services as insurance, banking, credit cards, and brokerage, telecommunications including local and long distance, wireless, cable and DSL, subscriptions for a publication, most fund raising, and such membership programs as auto clubs. They also include a narrow range of products, most commonly book or CD clubs, rental programs like Netflix, food and collectibles.

For credit cards, daily newspaper subscriptions and many other products and services, there is no minimum purchase commitment and the relationship only ends when the customer notifies the marketer—or fails to pay. For some clubs, telecommunications services and others, customers do commit to a minimum number of shipments or payments after which they typically continue to receive the product or service until they ask that it be stopped. In still other cases there is an explicit relationship period with no commitment to renew. However a large minority if not a majority of even first time buyers in fact "renew" with renewal rates almost always climbing thereafter. Insurance, subscription, and fundraising relationships typify this behavior.

Unlike single transaction relationships, promotion costs **subsequent to acquisition** generally play a small role. This is because of buyers' upfront commitment to maintaining a relationship for at least some finite period. It is also common for only a single or closely related product or service to be offered. Segmentation and targeting are also less important though smart marketers will use these tools to boost customer value or to intervene where experience suggests a relationship may be in jeopardy.

The three keys to the success of continuity programs are:

1. Keeping the cost of acquiring new customers down *(see Acquisition Cost)*.
2. Keeping retention rates, especially during early periods, high by reducing the reasons to sever a relationship. Retention factors vary widely based on the nature of the service or product offered. They can include anything from bad debt or canceling a continuity plan, to failure to pay an insurance premium, use a credit card, renew a subscription or make another donation.
3. Increasing the value of the relationship where possible. Examples of this are applying for more insurance, donating more, using a credit card or telecommunication service more often, or renewing a subscription or membership for multiple years.

Contribution remains important though it normally needs to be figured for each payment or relationship period, typically months, quarters, or years. The value for each period subsequent to the first will often change, especially if the marketer can increase the average "sale" for those who remain active.

While the elements going into a contribution calculation vary greatly by product or service, it is always important to understand the long-term value of a relationship. This is so the marketer can set an economically sustainable limit on customer acquisition cost.

Exhibit R7.6 is an example of a long-term model for the sale of an insurance policy. It provides a taste of what marketers should pull together to estimate the value of a repeat transaction or continuity relationship.

The example shows that the discounted 10-year value of a customer is estimated to be $175 ($174,776/1000 initial policy holders). Recognizing that this is only an estimate and a long-term one at that, prudent marketers limit what they are willing to pay to acquire a new buyer of one of these policies to some percentage of the estimated amount. This may be as much 50% or 60%; roughly $87 to $105 in this example.

Alternatively, if history shows the average promotion cost spent to acquire a new policyholder is $100, then the model shows that policies sold must, on average, remain active for just over two years for the company to break even (two year value being $99 per starting policy holder).

For many customers a relationship with a company will extend across years if not decades. These future profit flows must be discounted to reflect the net present value (NPV) of monies that won't be received for some time to come. An NPV function can be found in Excel and on some financial calculators. In the Exhibit R7.6 example which uses a 14.5% discount rate, estimated Year 6 profit is cut almost in half by discounting. Policyholder worth in current dollars is $8,390, not the $16,512 the company nominally expects to earn from them in Year 6.

Once created, these "models" can also be used to perform "what if" analyses. For example, how would long-term value change if Year 1 retention increases to 60%, if the average annual premium grows more quickly, or if claim costs are lowered from 55% to 53% of premiums?

Recognize that the Exhibit R7.6 worksheet represents a lifetime or, more accurately, a long-term value model for repeat relationship businesses. The next section on *Lifetime Value of a Customer* explores this concept further and looks at how a similar estimate might be prepared for individual transaction businesses.

Lifetime Value of a Customer (LTV)

For single transaction businesses, the concept of lifetime or, more appropriately, long-term customer value [LTV] is as important as it is for continuity relationships. In both cases, for a newly acquired customer LTV represents the **net present value** (NPV) of all future **profits** from an **average** customer **exclusive** of the acquisition contact.

It is important to recognize that LTV represents a stream of future **profits**, not sales. Since losing money to acquire a new customer involves an upfront out-of-pocket cost, it is only justified if expected future **profits,** discounted to reflect the time value of money, exceed the loss.

Though a superior marketing database will allow a marketer to calculate a LTV for each buyer, in practice it is normally computed for groups of names. Numerous individual customers have a negative value. For example, those who purchase only once or for a single period typically produce losses, while those remaining active for years generate profits far above the average.

Though LTV can be calculated as an average of all customers, the more media, offers and creative alternatives a marketer employs the more sense it makes to estimate it separately for large, discreet groups. Many marketers find that customers acquired in different media, via substantially different offers or creative approaches, or with different demographic or first purchase characteristics (e.g. first product category or season of purchase) produce widely varying LTVs. Where differences are found, marketers may want to set alternative acquisition cost limits or target promotions to acquire more customers with a higher expected LTV and fewer with lower ones.

Recognize that however it is derived, LTV is a **model** that to a greater or lesser degree predicts future profit streams based on past behavior. Numbers developed for Exhibit R7.6, as in all LTV forecasts, represent an estimate of the future based on what has happened before, perhaps altered to reflect **predictable** changes in response or in business operating or other costs.

Because LTV is only an estimate, and a fairly long-term one at that, most marketers prefer to set conservative limits on the acquisition cost they are willing to incur to acquire a customer. The longer the substantive stream of future profits, the more sense it makes to set investment limits conservatively. Investment limits of 30% to as much as 50% or 60% of LTV or a 12, 18, or 24 month payback period are common.

The approach to LTV seen in Exhibit R7.6 and the one we will look at in Exhibit R7.7 represent expected behavior models. Once developed, they provide a good indication over what period of time a marketer can expect to receive substantive value from a group of new customers.

The bulk of most product marketer profits are returned within one to three years of first purchase. For such services as credit cards, insurance and other financial services, time horizons may be longer, extending to perhaps five to 10 years. Recognize

EXHIBIT R7.6: EXAMPLE CONTINUITY PROFITABILITY MODEL—ANNUAL PREMIUM INSURANCE

	Ratios/ Costs	Year 1	Year 2	Year 3	Year 4	Year 5	Year 6	Year 7	Year 8	Year 9	Year 10
Applications	80.0%	1,250.0									
Renewal Rate	—	55.0%	65.0%	75.0%	80.0%	80.0%	80.0%	80.0%	90.0%	90.0%	90.0%
Policies in Force	—	1,000.0	550.0	357.5	268.1	214.5	171.6	137.3	109.8	98.8	89.0
Average Premium		$250.00	$270.00	$290.00	$300.00	$310.00	$325.00	$350.00	$350.00	$375.00	$375.00
Total Premium		$250,000	$148,500	$103,675	$80,438	$66,495	$55,770	$48,048	$38,438	$37,066	$33,359
Claims Paid	55.0%	$137,500	$81,675	$57,021	$44,241	$36,572	$30,674	$26,426	$21,141	$20,386	$18,347
Issue/Application Charges	$8.00	$10,000									
Annual Billing/Customer Service	$12.00	$12,000	$6,600	$4,290	$3,218	$2,574	$2,059	$1,647	$1,318	$1,186	$1,067
Claims Handling	5.2%	$13,000	$7,722	$5,391	$4,183	$3,458	$2,900	$2,498	$1,999	$1,927	$1,735
Overhead	6.5%	$16,250	$9,653	$6,739	$5,228	$4,322	$3,625	$3,123	$2,498	$2,409	$2,168
Total Expense		$51,250	$23,975	$16,420	$12,629	$10,354	$8,584	$7,269	$5,815	$5,523	$4,970
		20.5%	16.1%	15.8%	15.7%	15.6%	15.4%	15.1%	15.1%	14.9%	14.9%
Operating Income		$61,250	$42,851	$30,234	$23,568	$19,569	$16,512	$14,353	$11,482	$11,157	$10,041
		24.5%	28.9%	29.2%	29.3%	29.4%	29.6%	29.9%	29.9%	30.1%	30.1%
Net Present Value	14.5%	$61,250	$37,424	$23,061	$15,700	$11,385	$8,390	$6,369	$4,450	$3,777	$2,968
Cumulative NPV		$61,250	$98,674	$121,735	$137,436	$148,821	$157,211	$163,581	$168,031	$171,807	$174,776

EXHIBIT R7.7: ESTIMATED LIFETIME VALUE FOR 100 CUSTOMERS ACQUIRED 4 YEARS AGO

Year:	1	2	3	4	5	6
Sales	$2080	$1790	$1025	$590		
Contribution	936	806	461	266		
Promotion Cost	243	193	137	70		
Profit	693	613	324	196	110	60
Disc. Profit (8%)	642	526	257	144	75	38
Cum Disc. Profit	$642	$1168	$1425	$1569	$1644	$1682

that at some point expected future profits are substantially reduced by the compounding effect of NPV thereby limiting any marketer's effective time horizon.

The approach to LTV used in Exhibit R7.7 is more typical of that employed in individual transaction relationships. Unlike the continuity scenario in Exhibit R7.6, marketers who send a steady stream of promotions to past buyers to generate sales incur a substantial, less predictable stream of marketing expenses. These are impacted by how effectively the marketer targets and segments past buyers and on changes in response characteristics. Changes in average order value, seasonality, and competition further complicate this picture, making it even harder to predict sales and profit.

For these reasons, anyone attempting to model their business' profits needs a solid handle on expected overall promotion cost and expected response (average order value **and** response rate) for each customer segment being tracked. The **un**availability of accurate information on customer databases is one of the biggest barriers to marketers developing solid estimates.

The approach shown in Exhibit R.7.7 is a much simplified version of one alternative that individual transaction marketers can use to estimate LTV. It requires a marketer to provide historic sales and marketing costs for a group of like customers acquired at a similar point in the past, typically 3 to 5 years ago. In the absence of Year 5+ detail, this example estimates Years 5 and 6 by fitting a curve to 4 year data.

A business whose estimated LTV is the $16.82 (Cum. Disc. Profit of $1682 divided by the 100 initial customers) estimated above, might be willing to pay $8 or $10 to acquire new customers but surely not as much as $14 or $15, given that changing circumstances leave a healthy margin for error around any estimate.

Though Exhibit R7.7 estimates sales and costs by year, it is preferable to generate data by quarter or half-year. Revenues should include not only direct product sales but also any profits from such ancillary sources as list rental, e-commerce, package inserts, or cross promotions.

This example also assumes that prices and marketing costs have not changed in the last four years. This can be reasonable given recent inflation rates. Marketers impacted by significant price inflation—or deflation in recent years, or by increases in marketing expenses, need to challenge this assumption. Where this is the case, factor historic sales and marketing dollars up or down to better reflect what these numbers look like today.

Before leaving this topic, we should mention how the LTV concept might apply to relationship marketing programs. These efforts include loyalty, reward, and customer communication initiatives. They typically generate no direct revenue, but often incur substantial expenses for marketing, operations and rewards.

Applying LTV to these efforts would require that profits generated by incremental sales from program participants exceed the cost of program operation. While it's almost impossible to get solid estimates of this impact for such large established programs as airline and hotel rewards, for more modest programs, especially start-ups, models and live tests can and should be run to determine whether a planned investment is justified. A live test might see some customers invited to participate while a control group is not given special treatment, at least for an initial trial period.

Acquisition Cost

It was once the case that many database marketers expected to acquire a new customer at no cost or even a small profit. Those days are past for most organizations selling products or seeking a donation. It is even more normal for firms selling services to incur a substantial loss to acquire a new customer relationship.

Database marketing success requires the long-term value of a relationship to exceed its acquisition cost. It is therefore crucial not only to estimate long-term value but to also establish an accurate average acquisition cost per new customer. Fortunately this latter number is much easier to derive than the former. Two measures are commonly used.

1. Acquisition Cost per New Buyer is used and much preferred for Individual Transaction Relationships or whenever there is a substantial **initial** purchase or sale. Its formula is:

$$\text{Acquisition Cost/New Buyer} = \frac{\text{Loss from promotion}}{\text{Number of new buyers acquired}}$$

2. For Repeat Transaction Relationships where initial revenue is modest and/or most names acquired are expected to repeatedly purchase or renew, a more common acquisition cost measure is the Promotion Cost per New Buyer. Its formula is:

$$\text{Promotion Cost/New Buyer} = \frac{\text{Promotion cost}}{\text{Number of new buyers acquired}}$$

Exhibit R7.8 shows how these two measures are computed for a given loss scenario. Note that the difference between the two cost figures equals the per order contribution to promotion cost and profit.

Summary

With this overview, the reader will have gained an understanding of why a solid product or service, direct marketed to the right audience with good creative, can still fail if

EXHIBIT R7.8: DETERMINING A COST/BUYER

	Value	Calculation
Net Average Order	$50	
Contribution to Promotion Cost and Profit	$20	
Promotion Cost	$400/M	
Mail Quantity	100,000	
Orders	1,700	
Sales	$85,000	($50 x 1700)
Orders/M	17	(1700/100)
Sales/M	$850	($85,000/100)
Contribution/M	$340	($850 x 40%)
Profit/M	($60)	($340—$400)
Acquisition Cost per New Buyer	**$3.53**	**($60/17)**
Promotion Cost per New Buyer	**$23.53**	**($400/17)**

the underlying economics do not adequately support the venture. Database marketers must:

- Thoroughly understand the contribution each sale or transaction makes to promotion cost and profit.
- Properly calculate promotion cost.
- Use appropriate relative rather than absolute measures of sales, cost and profits to set goals, gauge success and determine breakeven and other key ratios.
- Make certain the long-term value of newly acquired customers substantially exceeds their acquisition cost.

ROBERT (BOB) WEINBERG leverages 35 years' experience as principal of RW Consulting. His specialties include implementing, improving and analyzing direct and database marketing programs. RW Consulting has completed major assignments for such companies as Coach, Hershey, Hewlett-Packard, Moore Business Solutions Direct, PETsMART Direct, Sara Lee Direct and ServiceMaster. Prior to founding RW Consulting, Bob was President of the Chicago office of Kobs Gregory Passavant. Before joining KGP, Bob was a Senior Manager with Accenture. He is a frequent speaker at industry gatherings worldwide, and a former president of the Chicago Association of Direct Marketing.

Search Engine Optimization (SEO) and Paid Search

JAMES MOORE

DePaul University

In the Douglas Adams book *The Hitchhiker's Guide to the Galaxy*, we encounter "The Guide": an electronic travel guide to life, the universe, and everything. Space is described like so:

> *"Space," it says, "is big. Really big. You just won't believe how vastly hugely mind-bogglingly big it is. I mean, you may think it's a long way down the road to the chemist, but that's just peanuts to space. Listen . . ."*

The Internet feels larger than that. Luckily, we have guides to almost all things on the Internet. Search engines help us find what we're looking for on the Web. Search engine optimization, or SEO, is an Internet marketing process that improves search engine visibility and ranking in a way that attracts qualified traffic to a web site.

Your web site needs traffic the same way your body needs oxygen or water. Without traffic it's as good as dead. You want your web site to be a bustling destination on the Internet highway, a highly sought-after location travelers flock to. You do not want it to be a sleepy little backwater.

The essential concept behind SEO is fairly simple: Craft your web site so that all search engines can read your content. Create content people want to read and link to. Promote your web site. Do all of this better than your competitors.

While the concept of search engine optimization is straightforward, the execution can be difficult. SEO is a rapidly evolving area in which tactics constantly change. Search engines rankings are determined by a series of algorithms. "Black hat" Internet marketers, scammers, and spammers figure out these algorithms in order to fraudulently boost their web sites' rankings. So the computer scientists who build search engines must constantly refine and revise the algorithms in response to these underhanded tactics. For example, the Penguin, Panda, and Hummingbird algorithm updates that Google has employed have sought to circumvent those gaming the system, and allow unique and valuable content to rise to prominence in search engine results.

There is far more to say than can be covered in a single article, but hopefully what follows will provide you with a solid foundation to build upon.

What Is Search?

Broadly speaking, there are two types of search web sites:

1. **Directories.** Analogous to the Yellow Pages, a directory is a categorized listing created and edited by humans. Searchers can browse through categories until they find what they are looking for, or they can enter search terms to locate an entry within the directory. An entry will exist in one place only within a directory.
2. **Search Engines.** A search engine is an index created by computer programs known as robots or spiders that scour the Internet and then report their findings. A series of algorithms define how search results are displayed and ranked. A searcher can enter a keyword query to bring up a Search Engine Results Page (SERP), which lists a series of web site links accompanied by short descriptions or excerpted text from the destination pages.

Historically the two services were separate, but now both services can be found together. For example, Yahoo (http://www.yahoo.com) started life as a directory but now has an integrated search engine (http://search.yahoo.com). Google (http://www.google.com) is primarily known as a search engine but also provided a directory service until 2011. Google has been known to promote the Open Directory Project (http://www.dmoz.org), a directory created and maintained by volunteers.

As ever, there are a couple of exceptions that prove the rule: Mahalo (http://www.mahalo.com), Wikianswers (http://answers.wikia.com), and Yahoo! Answers (http://answers.yahoo.com) are examples of search engines with indexes created by humans.

Google dominates search within the U.S. (and most of the world). Google's competitors have an immense task ahead of them to win back market share. However, rather than competing directly, some companies have tried to distinguish themselves as something more than just a search engine. For example,

—Bing (http://www.bing.com) positions itself as "the decision engine," placing value in helping customers make decisions rather than merely serving up search results. Microsoft has purchased companies like Faircast to improve real-time search, which bolsters the ability to provide relevant results.

—WolframAlpha (http://www.wolframalpha.com) aims for a more exclusive crowd and defines itself as being the "computational knowledge engine." For fun, type in the query "Are you Skynet?" on the WolframAlpha home page.

—Twitter Search (http://search.twitter.com) stresses, "See what's happening — right now." Customers can bypass traditional search, and ask their social networks for answers, or follow rapidly trending topics.

There are overseas territories where local search providers have an edge on Google, such as China's Baidu (http://www.baidu.com) and Russia's Yandex (http://www.yandex.com). However, it is Facebook, with "Graph Search" that is most likely to be a true competitor to Google's dominance. The valuable data within Facebook has the potential to be opaque to Google, and Facebook can offer micro-targeted advertising services that allow for nested filters to identify truly qualified prospects to be converted into customers.

Where to Start with SEO

Search engine optimization can be divided into four areas:

1. **Site design:** How your web site works—its function.
2. **Copy:** The content—words and pictures that communicate effectively to your customer.
3. **Code:** The HTML underlying your web site.
4. **Promotion:** Getting the word out, your "listing, linking and engagement" strategy.

While one person could theoretically handle all four areas, it is a rare individual who excels in all of them. So you may need to direct others to make changes in the areas where your technical skill set is deficient. Remember that SEO is a process—you are never finished.

Determining Your Audience

Start by dividing your target audience into two groups:

1. **External:** Those who come to your web site from search engines
2. **Internal:** Those who are lost on your web site and use search to navigate your web site. They know that your site contains what they are looking for—they just have not found it yet. This group can be further divided into two subgroups:
   a. **External Audience:** Customers, clients, etc.
   b. **Internal Audience:** Employees, stakeholders, etc.

At every stage in the SEO process, determine which particular audience you're serving and keep in mind what their needs and motivation are. Remember that your web site serves a particular purpose—getting your audience to convert on your web site. Do not focus on search engine optimization at the expense of providing relevant services to your audience.

Part 1: Design

The design of your web site should allow for growth and the creation of new pages while providing a clear, understandable structure that facilitates navigation and prevents your customer from getting confused and lost. Ultimately you want a web site in which a customer could land on any page and know almost immediately what the site is for and how to navigate to other pages. Some methods to accomplish this are:

- **Header.** Your header should contain your logo and perhaps a tagline that explains what your web site does. Most customers are used to seeing a search bar in the top right-hand corner of the screen.
- **Breadcrumbs.** Breadcrumbs are an excellent way of presenting exactly where a particular web page is within the hierarchy of a web site. This provides context and an easy way of navigating to similar pages. An example of how breadcrumbs might look is:

DePaul > Continuing Education > Practical Internet Marketing

- **Navigation.** Your navigation scheme should incorporate keywords in the links to areas on your web site. If you have a link to your home page, use the anchor text "[Company Name] Home" (as in "DePaul Home") rather than "Home." By avoiding general terms in favor of specific terms, you provide search engines with more relevant information.
- **Footer.** Provide supplemental navigation in the footer along with contact information (e-mail, telephone, physical address) on every web page. Providing contact information will increase the trustworthiness of your web site (you are now more than a random site on the web—you have a physical presence) and also assist in optimizing your site for location-based search services. You should also provide a link to a contact page. For the anchor text, "Contact [Company Name]" (as in "Contact DePaul University") is preferable to "Contact Us."

The design of your site should incorporate four critical pages:

1. Home page. This page should clearly articulate what you do, or the services you provide, in a few words.
2. About Us. This page should explain in greater detail who you are and what you do. Use specific language and terms that your audience will understand.
3. Contact Us. This page should tell your customer how to get in touch with you. If you expect to create trust you will need at least:
   a. Telephone
   b. E-mail
   c. Physical address
   d. Fax (optional)
   e. Social media. Customers may prefer to interact with you via services such as Facebook or Twitter.
4. Site Map. This page is a directory listing of all areas on your web site (and possibly all web pages).

Responsive Design

The advice above is largely focused on the assumption that your visitors will be interacting with your site on a PC. What is increasingly more likely is that your visitors will be using a mobile device—a smartphone, tablet, or wearable computer (such as Google Glass). Your visitors may swap between these devices, and they will expect a pleasant experience on all platforms. This leads you into the concept of responsive design, sometimes known as RWD (Responsive Web Design). The responsive design philosophy is that the user should not have to worry about which device they use to interact with a web site, or to be unnecessarily forced into zooming in and out (or panning left and right) for basic web site functionality. The site just works.

There are two approaches to take with responsive design:

1. **Mobile friendly, works with everything else.** Here, the site is designed to work well on mobile devices, but also tested and optimized for all other devices in a way that does not break the initial mobile-friendly design.
2. **Platform/device dependent.** Here the site designers anticipate the various platforms (i.e., browsers) and devices (i.e., PC, smartphone, tablet, wearable) that visitor will use and then create versions that work well for each of those platforms and devices. Browser and device detection allow for the appropriate version to be presented automatically. However, the visitor may prefer to be able to override this setting.

Part 2: Copy

A good writer is your most valuable SEO tool. Creating engaging, well-written content can be the best way to optimize your web site. Writing for the Web is not the same as writing for other media. Your best approach is to follow these guidelines:

- Short sentences
- Short paragraphs
- Active language
- Simple language
- Break up the page with headings and subheadings
- Use bullets to simplify concepts

Writers will assist in weaving keywords and key phrases into your web pages. Try not to choose more than one concept to optimize for each web page (which translates to no more than seven words). Follow this process when choosing keywords:

1. Imagine that you are your customer and you are looking for a web page on your site. What words or phrases would you use to search?
2. Now survey others to find out what words they would use. Brainstorm as many words as you can.
3. From that long list of words, reorganize the list into three groups:
   a. **Critical** (no more than seven words)—These are the words that occur most frequently in your surveys or clearly define the concept.
   b. **Supplemental**—Synonyms that might be used in a search.
   c. **Nice to have**—Less essential words that in rare cases might be used in a search.

As your writer creates copy for your web page, she or he will use this list to draft the copy. The critical keywords should appear multiple times on the web page—in the page title, headings, subheadings and opening paragraph. However, this should be done in such a way that the web page does not look like it has been "keyword stuffed." The copy should be pleasant to read and interesting. This is what you pay the writer for. The writer should use the less-critical keywords in the copy, but these can appear farther down the page and with less frequency.

Digging down deeper, you can research which of your keywords are used most frequently in search queries. This may change the order of criticality. Keyword-tracking services you can use are:

- ComScore (http://www.comscore.com).
- Google Adwords: Keyword Planner and Auction Insights (https://adwords.google.com).
- Google Trends (http://www.google.com/trends)
  Use to compare search terms, and to research trending topics and searches.
- Hitwise (Experian Marketing Services) (http://www.experian.com/hitwise).
- Wikipedia article traffic statistics (http://stats.grok.se)
  Beta service, but provides topic popularity results and top 1000 most viewed pages from Wikipedia.
- Wordtracker (http://www.wordtracker.com)
  Wordtracker also provides a SEO Blogger tool and Keyword Questions through their Wordtracker Labs.

For many pages, you should also be guiding your writer with intent. How exactly do you want your readers to act after consuming the content on your page? Make sure that your goals are explicitly explained to your writer. Your web site exists for a reason.

You should also choose to research what your competition is doing. Sites like SimilarSites (http://www.similarsites.com) or HubSpot's Marketing Grader (http://marketing.grader.com) can be very helpful in analyzing what your competitors are up to.

Social Media (perhaps more accurately described as "Emerging Media") has had an impact on web content. People are looking for content to share. With social networks like Facebook or LinkedIn, the image that accompanies a shared link is vital to the popularity of that share—enticing others to engage and hopefully to share further. A boring image may cause prospects to scroll past, but an image that resonates will capture attention. Thus, each page that you want shared should have at least one image that both conveys your message and provides an emotional response. Artistry does not come easily here.

Link-bait (and Top 10 Lists)

Another good use of a writer is creating link-bait. A link-bait web page is one that's so enticing and interesting that other web sites (particularly blogs) provide links to that page. The concentrated number of inbound links (frequently with the same anchor text) is noticed by search engines and raises your results in SERPs. Easy ways to approach creating link-bait are:

- Ten top tips for . . .
- Best and worst . . .
- How to make/save money in five easy steps
- Secret ways to . . .

Perhaps this process has been overused by sites like BuzzFeed (http://www.buzzfeed.com), with "listacles" that promise "15 Things That Look Like Jennifer Lawrence At The Oscars (all of them **adorable**)," but the process of crafting addictive content and copy does provide tangible results. An alternative approach to this is to write something that flies in the face of convention and generates controversy (and plenty of inbound links). Here you want to be careful not to alienate your audience.

Another approach is to create guides, white papers, or instructions that are topical. To capitalize on topicality, you can research what keyword queries are "hot" and see if you are able to write something on that subject. A great resource to see what is "hot" is Google Trends'"Hot Searches":

http://www.google.com/trends/hottrends

Video has an important role to play here. Although the expenditure in creating a video is significantly more than just crafting text, video is a highly sought-after commodity on the Internet. A short video that meets the needs of a prospect may be favored over a text web page by search engines. If you do start to create videos, make sure you create a corresponding transcript. Not only will the transcript help search engine robots properly index your video, the transcript will also assist members of your audience with visual or cognitive disabilities. Given the higher relative cost of video, look for areas where there is less competition.

One final thing to consider with content is citation consistency. Addresses, names, telephone numbers, terminology, and other forms of identification should follow a consistent format. A lack of consistency here can indicate sloppiness to both search engine robots, and actual users of your site.

Part 3: Code

The same list of critical keywords can be used in the underlying code of your web page to optimize your SERP. Here are some strategies that you can follow:

File name

If you are able to define the filenames of your web pages, this can improve your search engine ranking. You want the filename to be meaningful and contain your keywords. Keywords are best separated by hyphens, but underscores are almost as good. For example:

- search-engine-optimization.htm
- search_engine_optimization.htm

Page Title

These should be 40 to 60 characters long. The page title is displayed in the top of the browser window and on the SERP. A meaningful page title is going to make your link enticing on the SERP and gives the search engine more information to work with. My suggestions for structuring this is something like:

- <title>10 best SEO tips for beginners (DePaul University)</title>

but you could choose something like:

- <title>DePaul University: 10 best SEO tips for beginners</title>

The text should be clear and unambiguous.

Description Metatag

Some search engines will display the contents of this metatag on their SERP. Other search engines will not display this information but may use the text as another factor in their ranking algorithms. You have about 250 characters to create an engaging summary of the web page, which should be keyword heavy. For example:

<meta name="Description" content="Search Engine Optimization (SEO) is easier than you think. In this short tutorial we will show you best practices, examples and help get your site optimized." />

Image Alt Text

Alt text is displayed by some browsers as the mouse pointer hovers above an image. The text is particularly helpful to members of your audience who are visually impaired and using screen readers to translate your web page to speech. Every image on your web site should have short (five to six words) alt text that is descriptive and uses your keywords.

Keywords Metatag

The keywords metatag has been abused by unscrupulous search engine optimizers. Most search engines routinely ignore this data. There is little need to use this code, unless you are using this data to improve locally served search results (i.e., you control the parameters of search).

In addition, there are other strategies you can follow to improve the quality of your web site.

Robots

As mentioned earlier, robots.txt can be used to prevent search engines from indexing duplicate content on your web site. Extensive duplicate content will hurt your search engine rankings. You can also use metatags to indicate that certain web pages should not be indexed or links followed:

<meta name="robots" content="noindex, nofollow" />

Favicon

Add these two lines of code to the <HEAD> section of every page on your web site:

<link rel= "shortcut icon" href="favicon.ico">

<link rel="icon" type="image/ico" href="favicon.ico">

Properly Formed HTML and CSS

Avoid the temptation to use Adobe Flash, Adobe PDF and other technologies that search robots have difficulty reading for exclusive content on your web site. If a search engine robot cannot read the content, then how are searchers going to find this information? The bulk of the content on your web site should be in HTML, but you can provide supplementary content in Flash or PDF if necessary. CSS (Cascading Style Sheets) will allow you to separate the semantic meaning from the style of your site. Use proper HTML tags to structure your web pages into a collection of headings, subheadings, paragraphs and bullet points. Always validate your HTML code.

RSS (Really Simple Syndication)

RSS (Really Simple Syndication) is a way you can update readers about new, regularly changing content on your web site. If you are blogging or adding new items to your web site, then you need to publicize this through an RSS feed.

Other Metadata

Increasingly, users and search engine robots are leveraging new forms of metadata to discover content and to rate quality. Hashtags, GPS coordinates, EXIF data, authorship, should be considered.

Finally, be aware that the speed at which your web pages are displayed will contribute to your SERP ranking. Sites that render slowly are less likely to rank highly. Thus, use this information to inform your technology choices. Be aware that if your web pages serve up advertising from a third-party provider, this may slow your site down and hurt your ranking.

Part 4: Publicity

You can automate publicizing articles from your web site by adding tools and buttons that allow your audience to share these pages with a larger audience. Notable examples are:

- Digg (http://digg.com/submit)
- Del.icio.us (http://del.icio.us)
- Facebook (https://developers.facebook.com/docs/plugins/like-button)
- Reddit (http://reddit.com/buttons)
- Twitter (https://about.twitter.com/resources/buttons)

If you are creating video for your site, then consider creating a channel on YouTube. You can then embed your videos on your web site. By doing this, you guarantee that Google is aware of what you have created. More information about this process can be found here:

http://www.google.com/support/webmasters/bin/topic.py?hl=en&topic=10079

Promotion— Directories & The Open Directory Project

Search engines do not have the capability to index all sites on the Internet. To allocate resources appropriately, search engines begin indexing from a set of preferred sites. This set of preferred sites may come from a directory, such as the Open Directory

Project. Thus, it makes extremely good sense to get your web site listed in a directory since this both markets your services in the directory and increases your chance of being indexed by search engines.

Directories include:

- Best of the Web (http://botw.org)
- Business.com (http://www.business.com)
- GoGuides (http://www.goguides.org)
- Jayde (http://www.jayde.com)
- JoeAnt (http://www.joeant.com)

There are two additional advantages to being listed in a directory:

1. **Trust and reliability**. Humans edit directories; this imbues them with a degree of trustworthiness and reliability.
2. **Targeted audience**. Some directories exist within niche areas of expertise or customer focus. Quite often B2B suppliers will be listed in a targeted directory such as B2B Index (http://www.b2bindex.co.uk). If you provide services in these areas, then you need to submit your information to directories.

So what do you need to do to get listed in these directories? Thankfully, the process is extremely straightforward, but it requires some planning and organization. The steps you should follow are:

Step 1—Determine which directories you want to be listed in.

The Open Directory Project (http://www.dmoz.org) is definitely the first directory you want to be listed in, but there are other directories that you should consider as well. One way to begin your search is to look through the Open Directory Project's list of directories, which can be found here:

http://www.dmoz.org/Computers/Internet/Searching/Directories/

Create a list of directories that you have the time and resources to contact. For each directory, read carefully their submission requirements. Some directories will charge for submission. Recognize that your payment does not guarantee placement, merely that someone will review the information you provide.

NOTE: You should only submit a fully constructed web site to directories. Ensure none of your web pages are under construction before contacting a directory. Your web site will be evaluated and may be rejected if considered a work in progress or untrustworthy.

Step 2—Determine where you should be listed within each directory.

Drill down in each directory and choose the most appropriate place for your web site to be listed. Make a note of this location. Check to see that you are not already listed in the directory; if you are listed already, then confirm that your details are accurate.

Step 3 — Write your web site description.

Create a title and description for your web site that closely follows the submission requirements of the directory. Try to ensure that your copy is tightly written but contains appropriate and descriptive keywords, such as:

DePaul University

Largest Catholic university in the United States. Founded in 1898 by the Vincentians. Two Chicago campuses, with four satellite suburban campuses. Courses offered internationally and online.

Most directories will penalize content that looks too much like a sales pitch or advertisement. By ignoring the submission requirements, you run the risk of not being listed.

Step 4—Submit your web site.

Submit your web site to each of the directories. Record the details of each submission and keep this information in an electronic document:

- Name and URL of directory
- Date of submission
- Title
- Description
- Cost (if any)
- Name and e-mail address of person who submitted the listing

Record any subsequent correspondence with the directory.

Step 5—Review and update.

Periodically check to see that your web site is listed correctly. If your site undergoes extensive changes, you may need to update your directory listings. Even though the employees who staff directories are inundated with submission requests, they will appreciate being informed of necessary corrections.

Promotion—Search Engines

Now that we have covered directories, we should talk a little more about search engines and appropriate SEO strategies. There are three stages to the search engine process:

1. **Crawling**

   A search engine robot (also known as a spider) "crawls" the Web following links. As it follows links, the robot attempts to read all Web content it discovers and follow subsequent links it encounters. At the root of each new web site, the robot will look for a file named "robots.txt," which instructs the robot to exclude certain pages from the crawl process. Not all Web content will be read by the robot. Information in images or Adobe Flash may be hidden from the robot. The robot is essentially blind—it reads web page code in a similar way to screen readers for the visually impaired. Websites are crawled periodically. Changes that you make to your web site will not be reflected until your site is crawled again.

2. **Indexing**

Pages that the robot has read are analyzed and information recorded. Information may be cached and metadata (information about information) may be collected.

3. **Presentation of results**

A searcher receives a SERP after entering a keyword query. The results are presented according to relevance, ranking and advertising criteria. In the majority of cases the algorithms that dictate how results are presented are industry secrets, but we can make informed decisions about how these algorithms operate.

So how do you ensure your web site is crawled? Although it is possible to submit your web site and request that it be indexed, the more appropriate course of action is to make sure that sites that are indexed by search engines link to your web site. As search engine robots crawl and re-index these web sites, they will follow links to your site and index you. Thus, you should concentrate on listing your web site in directories and on other web sites (that are crawled by robots).

So which web sites do you want to be listed on? There are sites that will offer to provide inbound links for cold hard cash. There are sites that will provide inbound links only if you provide links back to them. Avoid both of these types of sites. Search engines are not happy with such overt manipulation of the system, as this has a tendency to reduce the relevance of search results. If a search engine employee discovers that your inbound links come from such shady web sites, they will take action to either remove you from their index or reduce your ranking in the SERP.

Your better course of action is to target complementary web sites where a link to your web site is relevant and provides utility. For example, if your site sells books, then you might want to contact authors and ask them to link to your online bookstore. In a similar fashion, you should contact local business bureaus, trade associations, clubs, and relevant organizations and ask them to link to you.

When asking web sites to link to you, the best practice is to provide them with anchor text. Anchor text is the text within a link. Search engines take particular note of anchor text, so you want to avoid inbound links that look like this:

DePaul University has a web site, you can view it **here**.

And move in the direction of links that look like this:

Visit the **DePaul University web site**.

When you contact a web site and ask the administrators to link to your web site, you can provide them with code that ensures you have appropriate anchor text.

Now contacting people and asking them to link to you may sound a little naive and simplistic. You can build a more professional strategy by creating press releases and sending these to the appropriate outlets. Your press releases should also be found on your web site—in a "news", "press" or "media" area. Building upon this, you can create a "link to us" page with example code or incorporate this on your contact page.

Your Next Steps

Getting one page crawled does not guarantee that your web site will have top ranking in SERPs. There are some basic tasks to follow to make sure that your web site is crawled appropriately:

Checking How You Are Listed in Search Engines

Entering the code below (where you substitute your web site URL) will provide you with an understanding of whether your site is listed in the major search engines:

- **Google**
  site:yourdomain.com
- **Yahoo**
  site: yourdomain.com
- **Bing**
  site: yourdomain.com

Using the Lynx Browser

Lynx is a text-only browser that, among other things, approximates how a search engine might "see" your web site. Using Lynx can be an appropriate way of verifying that your site can be crawled by search engine robots. Free browsers can be downloaded from:

- **Windows Version**
  http://invisible-island.net/lynx/
- **Mac OS X Version**
  http://habilis.net/lynxlet/

You can also use online Lynx viewers like:

http://www.delorie.com/web/lynxview.html

If you notice functional problems with your site when viewed through the Lynx browser (such as missing navigation), then you know that search engine robots will have difficulty indexing your site.

Check for Dead Links

Robots are fairly dumb. They will not make informed guesses about the location of your web pages. You need to check your web site for dead links. There are software tools that can assist in this process, such as:

http://validator.w3.org/checklink

Provide a Site Map

After you check for dead links, you need to provide search engines a way to find every page on your web site you'd like them to know about. You can do this by creating an index or site map. A site map is simply a directory listing of pages on your web site.

Create your site map and then provide a link to it on every page of your web site. This helps both robots and humans. If your site has more than one hundred web pages, provide links to just the critical pages and categories (search engines tend to stop indexing links if there are too many on the page).

Spellcheck
Make sure that all content on your web site has been spellchecked.

Create a custom "404: File not found" page
Inbound links may go to pages that do not exist—this generates a "404: File not found" error page. To fix this problem you can create a custom page that indicates that the page that the user is looking for cannot be found but then provides links to other pages on your web site. The structure of this page can be similar to your site map.

Use robots.txt
The robots.txt file can be used to guide search robots through your web site. You can choose to exclude certain pages that you might not want to see on a SERP such as duplicate pages, pages under construction or limited promotions.

Paid Search

Paid Search is one component of Search Engine Marketing (SEM). Like many other practices in Internet marketing, the definition of Paid Search changes over time (and who you are talking to). Paid Search consists of both placing advertisements on Search Engine Results Pages (SERPS), as well as placing advertising on content sites in the form of contextual ads. Vendors who provide this service include Google AdWords, Microsoft AdCenter and Yahoo! Search Marketing.

Example U.S. Paid Search Providers
- 7Search (http://7search.com)
- Ad.net (http://ad.net)
- Advertise.com (http://www.advertise.com)
- adMarketplace (http://www.admarketplace.com)
- Apple iAds (http://advertising.apple.com)
- Ask Sponsored Listings (http://sponsoredlistings.ask.com)
- Bing Ads (http://advertise.bingads.microsoft.com)
- FindIt-Quick (http://www.finditquick.com)
- Google AdWords (http://adwords.google.com)
- Holika.com Online Advertising (http://www.holika.com)
- LookSmart AdCenter (http://adcenter.looksmart.com)
- Marchex (http://www.marchex.com)
- Search123 (http://www.search123.com)
- Yahoo! Advertising (http://advertising.yahoo.com)

Paid Search is one of many channels available to you. For a Paid Search advertisement to be placed in front of a prospect, a set of keywords must be defined for the advertisement. The advertisement will be served dynamically, if the keywords for the advertisement match (to a certain degree) the prospect's search query.

For a contextual advertisement to be placed in front of a prospect, a set of key-words must be defined for the advertisement. The advertisement will be served dynamically, if the keywords for the advertisement match (to a certain degree) keywords in the web page content. Relevance (sometimes referred to as a quality score) and bid cost dictate the ranking and selection of these dynamic advertisements.

When Should Paid Search Be Used?

Paid Search should only be seriously considered when you are able to measure the effectiveness of a campaign. This assumes that you have both Key Performance Indicators/Key Performance Metrics (KPI/KPM) defined and an accurate and timely way of providing analytical data. Otherwise you have no idea if you are actually getting a return on your investment.

Paid Search is of critical importance if you are not achieving the organic search results you need. This may happen when you are in start-up mode (and largely unknown to search engines), or due to listing issues (such as technical or political reasons for not ranking in SERPs).

Your role here is to measure success, and then either adapt or cancel your Paid Search strategies.

Some argue that Paid Search can be used to as a branding tool—pushing competitors out of the picture or reinforcing the brand. Personally, I am not entirely convinced, but this is worth considering. Again, you need to be able to measure effectiveness.

How Can You Improve Paid Search?

Most successful sales professionals know the value of focusing on qualified prospects and ignoring time-wasters. Similarly, you can apply constraints to the display of your Paid Search advertisements, such as:

- Negative keywords
- Geography
- Language
- Seasonality
- Day of week
- Time of day

Let's look at some basic examples of how you might properly constrain your Paid Search advertisements. Imagine you are in the training business, and want to promote your courses through Paid Search. How can we prevent our ads from being displayed to the wrong prospect?

Negative Keywords

There is a world of difference between someone searching for "SEO training" over "free SEO training." Thus, "free" might be an appropriate negative keyword, and you might decide not to advertise to prospects who use that word in their searches.

Geography

If your business only offers training courses in Chicago, then you might want to limit the display of Paid Search advertisements to prospects who are searching in the Midwestern U.S. However, this might prevent Chicago natives from seeing your ad when they are searching while outside of your catchment area.

Language

If your training courses are taught in English only, then you might choose to constrain Paid Search placement to prospects who are searching in the English language (or have localized their browser).

Seasonality

Your (imaginary) training courses may only be offered certain months of the year, or demand for these courses peaks and troughs according to the seasons. If you do not have courses running in the immediate future (or they have just started and you don't accept late registrants), then perhaps there is less need to advertise, and you can hold back on using Paid Search. Conversely, you might want to flatten out demand and advertise more during slow months.

Day of Week

Let's imagine your training courses are tailored for businesses, and you know that prospects only search for courses Tuesday through Friday. You might decide to cut back on advertising over the weekend.

Time of Day

Paid Search involves the allocation of finite resources. You may discover that you get better placement of Paid Search ads if you restrict your bidding until late in the day. Your competitors may have exceeded their budgets by then, leaving you with a less competitive environment.

All things being equal, these constraints will improve your conversion rate. Additionally, a model for success that I suggest is to think about a Proactive/Reactive Split. You want to be proactive in placing your advertisements in front of the right prospects (findability), and then reactive in providing engaging copy that your prospects will favorably respond to (clicking). Context can help—an advertisement on a niche site (versus a portal site) with a similar focus to your web site is more likely to be clicked on (and, therefore, more likely that the prospect will spend longer looking at the advertisement).

Where Paid Search or a contextual ad brings a prospect to a web site, a landing page can be used to increase the chances of conversion. User Testing can optimize both the incentive and your landing page. Your options are:

- **A/B: Two version of one element.**
  Here, 50% of your audiences are assigned your original incentive or web page, and the other 50% see a version with one item changed. The version with better conversion rates is the one you keep.

- **A/B/N: Multiple versions of one element.**
  With this strategy, you randomly assign your audience to multiple versions of your original incentive or web page. In each version, the same element is changed. The version with better conversion rates is the one you keep.
- **Multivariate: Multiple versions of more than one element.**
  This last option is considerably more complex. Here, you randomly assign your audience to multiple versions of your original incentive or web page, where multiple elements are altered. The version with better conversion rates is the one you keep.

As your optimizing process gets more complex, the statistical certainty of your results decreases. You need to have a sufficient volume of prospects for this to be a workable solution. Google provides a free tool within Google Analytics (Content Experiments) that can be used to facilitate the A/B/N testing process on your web pages (for up to five full versions of a page).

Your long-term strategy here is to remove underperforming keywords and advertisements, and simultaneously explore alternative keywords and advertisements. All of the major Paid Search providers have learning resources (and account managers) who can assist you here.

Crafting the right copy is fundamentally important to success. One suggestion on how to design an effective strategy is to use something like Gartner's Magic Quadrant to map where you exist, versus your major competitors. By identifying differences, you can propose a unique value proposition. Beyond that, you need to have a message that speaks directly to your prospect—identify a problem, provide a solution, incentivize your prospects to act immediately.

To conclude, both SEO and Paid Search are long-term processes that involve hard work and continuous oversight. You have to dedicate sufficient resources and steadily focus on incremental improvements to achieve successes. The road may be long and arduous, but the end is rewarding.

Additional Reading

For those interested in digging deeper, here are some books that provide some useful history and commentary. SEO and Paid Search is constantly evolving, so as you approach competency (and hopefully mastery) in these areas please ensure that you engage with various online communities. This is where you will find the most up-to-date advice.

The Search: How Google and Its Rivals Rewrote the Rules of Business and
    Transformed Our Culture
by John Battelle
Portfolio © 2005 (320 pages)
ISBN:1591840880

How to Make Your Advertising Make Money
by John Caples
Simon & Schuster © 1983 (383 pages)
ISBN:0134236084

Search Engine Advertising: Buying Your Way to the Top to Increase Sales
by Kevin Lee and Catherine Seda
New Riders © 2009 (288 pages)
ISBN:0321495993

The Filter Bubble
by Eli Pariser
Penguin Books ©2012 (304 pages)
ISBN: 0143121235

The Long Tail: Why the Future of Business is Selling Less of More
by Chris Anderson
Hyperion ©2006 (256 pages)
ISBN: 1401302378

Everything Is Miscellaneous
by David Weinberger
Times Book ©2007 (256 pages)
ISBN: 0805080430

Too Big to Know: Rethinking Knowledge Now That the Facts Aren't the Facts,
    Experts Are Everywhere, and the Smartest Person in the Room Is the Room
by David Weinberger
Basic Books ©2014 (256 pages)
ISBN: 0465085962

JAMES MOORE is the Director of Online Learning for DePaul University's Driehaus College of Business. He teaches Internet Marketing classes in fully online, blended and face-to-face formats. He attempts to balance his love of technology and gadgets with the knowledge that quick and simple solutions are best. Unfortunately, creating quick and simple solutions often involves a long and complex process.

READING
9

Business-to-Business Marketing

VICTOR L. HUNTER
Hunter Business Group, LLC

SHEILA T. ZELENSKI
Hunter Business Group, LLC

JEFF J. KREUTZER
Hunter Business Group, LLC

Effective marketing to businesses yields an amazing return on investment, if you understand your customer and the potential that each customer represents, optimize your activities, and invest accordingly. While the risk and investment are far greater in marketing to businesses, so are the rewards. This piece will provide you with the basic tools necessary to succeed in business-to-business integrated marketing communications and to effectively combine marketing communications with direct selling efforts.

Business-to-Consumer (B2C) Versus Business-to-Business (B2B) Marketing

To begin it is important to differentiate between marketing to individual consumers and marketing to business buyers. The key differences between consumer and business to business marketing are those of scope, depth and complexity.

Scope

If you miss the mark in demonstrating value to the customer when marketing to consumers, the individual loss is small. However, make this same mistake on the B2B side, and you risk losing many potential opportunities and buyer groups within a single company. Conversely, acquiring, assimilating and growing a single business customer will likely yield high lifetime value and additional revenue through the identification of new buyers and new needs as you penetrate fully into the organization. The lifetime value of a business customer is often many, many times beyond the apparent initial potential. This is due to the opportunities for new relationships, new buyer groups, new product needs and applications. This great potential deserves additional investment in building the B2B relationship, delivering value and action on those things that drive customer loyalty.

103

Moreover, consumer marketers often have a seemingly unlimited universe of prospects to choose from. The opportunity to make mistakes, realign and try again is greater because you usually have millions prospects to approach. In the B2B world, it is typical to have a total universe of fewer than five thousand organizations, making it even more critical to do your research and deliver value from day one.

Depth

Because profitable B2B transactions are a result of strong relationships, the end result of a successful B2B marketing campaign is one where the relationship with your customer is deepened. You deepen your relationship with the business customer by (1) gaining a deeper understanding of your customer—their needs and behaviors, (2) achieving a deeper understanding of the account as a whole—learning about new buyers, influencers, and opportunities, and (3) creating an higher degree of trust by demonstrating value, diagnosing needs and finding solutions.

Of course, this means that B2B marketing focus and processes look quite different from consumer marketing. For example, a critical piece of any business-to-business marketing plan involves proactive calling to identify new buyer groups and decision-makers. Another activity may involve the delivery of value-added communications such as industry articles, to strengthen the bond between you and your customer. The first activity is not relevant to consumer marketing, where few decision-makers are involved in the purchasing decision. The second activity is rarely justified in consumer marketing because both the average order size and lifetime value are too small to justify the investment.

In addition, B2B marketing measurements are different. When marketing to consumers, the desired outcome is a transactional purchase. Therefore, measures are based on the number of responses and subsequent transactions generated by consumer marketing activities. In B2B marketing, the desired outcome is often less tangible. When marketing to businesses, the desired outcomes are building stronger relationships, identifying new buyer-groups, decision-makers and applications and increasing customer loyalty. Therefore, the measures must be set accordingly. So, the right B2B marketing measurements must be broad, deep and complex in order to measure economic value and return as well less concrete outcomes such as customer satisfaction, product penetration, account penetration, referrals, frequency of valued contact, and repurchase rates.

Complexity

The complexity of the buying process is another significant difference between consumer and B2B marketing. Typically, more than one person is involved in a single buying decision, more than one group within an organization may purchase the same type of product, and the decision to purchase may even involve formal processes, committees and preferred provider requirements. It is critical to understand the nature and complexity of this buying process before you embark on marketing strategy. Without knowledge of who within a company makes purchases and how they make those purchases, it is nearly impossible to influence buying patterns.

By understanding these key differences, you can start to develop a B2B marketing strategy that will result in loyal, profitable, and long-standing customers.

The Business-to-Business Marketing Strategy: 8 Business Results

Understanding the critical business results in the B2B space is critical to position your marketing strategy. The eight business results that follow enable your organization to reach organizational goals.

Business Result 1: Customer Acquisition

How can I be sure I'm getting a decent payback for the money we're spending to get new customers?

Getting customers is tough and expensive. It can cost 5 to 15 times more to get a business customer than to keep one and it typically takes more than a year and a half to break even. So, what's the trick? Continuous learning—the kind that results from implementing a measurable process that allows your organization to increasingly understand:

- What organizations and individuals to go after
- Which ones to cultivate and which ones to get rid of
- How to shorten the time it takes to get a prospect to buy
- How to get a higher percentage of prospects to become long-term customers

Critical to Customer Acquisition is the way you manage:

Lead Generation. In simple terms, the objective of lead generation is NOT to simply generate inquiries, based on volume. The objective of lead generation is to generate QUALIFIED leads, defined as prospects that have a need for what is being offered and a higher probability of becoming loyal, long-term customers.

Lead Management. Few processes are more important since, in addition to increasing the chance that the acquisition efforts will produce an acceptable return, a well run lead management process greatly determines whether new customers become long-term, profitable customers.

Prospect Cultivation. Few business-to-business prospects turn into customers instantly. A prospect might want time to be sure that your solution will produce the results they need. Or they may need time to sell internally. It might be that they just have to wait for the next budget cycle. Whatever the reason, if the investments made to generate leads are to be protected, there must be a deliberate process that ensures that the "seeds" planted not only survive but are nurtured into healthy "harvestable crops." Prospect cultivation is generally a dialogue-based process whose purpose is to exchange value in the form of increasing knowledge, understanding, and trust.

Value-Based Contacts. By better understanding the prospects' needs and communications preferences and building them into each contact in the cycle, the effectiveness of acquisition efforts can be greatly enhanced.

New Product Launch. Today's highly competitive and dynamic business climate requires new product approaches that are driven out of a deep, real-time understanding of the anticipated needs of specific segments of customers. Such a level of under-

EXHIBIT R9.1: KEY SALES FUNNEL COMPONETS

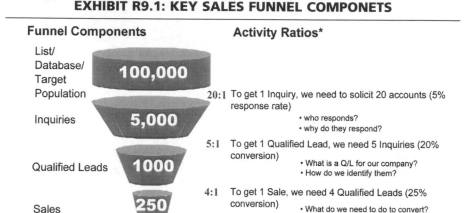

Funnel Components

List/
Database/
Target
Population

100,000

Inquiries

5,000

Qualified Leads

1000

Sales

250

Activity Ratios*

20:1 To get 1 Inquiry, we need to solicit 20 accounts (5% response rate)
- who responds?
- why do they respond?

5:1 To get 1 Qualified Lead, we need 5 Inquiries (20% conversion)
- What is a Q/L for our company?
- How do we identify them?

4:1 To get 1 Sale, we need 4 Qualified Leads (25% conversion)
- What do we need to do to convert?
- How can we increase conversion rates?

If average order size is $100,000 and our revenue goal is $25,000,000, we will need 250 sales ($25m/100K). To get 250 sales, we will need a target population of 100,000 potential buyers (250X4X5X20)
© Hunter Business Group, LLC

standing seldom results from periodic "research events." Rather it develops as an almost natural outcome of day-to-day processes designed to build deeper and more responsive relationships.

Opportunity Management. An effective opportunity management process allows B2B companies to identify and respond to business opportunities quickly and appropriately, and insure the highest conversion rate possible.

The Sales Funnel. Sales Funnel definition and tracking provide visibility into your situation—and provide a tool for managing and guiding the process. The Sales Funnel represents the steps and stages of your standard sales process. A tailored model, each company's Sales Funnel is composed of:

- Source tracking for each lead and opportunity entered into the sales process.
- The stage gates which represent the evidence of progress through the sales process and defining moments within the sales process.
- The key sales activities that are required to progress a lead through each of the stages (Exhibit R9.1).

Business Result 2: Customer Retention

How can we possibly be gaining that many new customers every week and still have stagnant revenue?

Few B-to-B companies make money on the first sale. On average it takes 18 months before a company reaches the breakeven point. This is why customer retention is critical, not only to recover the cost of acquisition, but to fuel overall growth and profitability. Acquisition and retention are often treated as separate and distinct processes but they are really two major phases of the customer lifecycle and are highly interdependent. Keeping customers is greatly determined by which customers are acquired.

And finding good, retainable customers works best when their characteristics are similar to those of the most loyal existing customers.

Critical to Customer Retention is the way you manage:

Assimilation. An old marketing adage says "a customer is not a customer until he or she purchases twice." Today many marketers would say "until he or she has purchased three or four times." Assimilation is the intentional task of getting new customers to purchase two or three times in a relatively short time frame. But the primary purpose of assimilation is not so much the money gained through those additional purchases as it is getting new customers to enjoy multiple positive experiences rooted in the exchange of value.

Reactivation. Reactivation is the process of quickly becoming aware of and appropriately intervening to "rekindle" the relationships and continue to earn a return on your investments.

Customer Loyalty. Loyalty gets more and more customers to experience more and more value over time. Loyalty is earned and profitable growth is realized when the additional transactions are well matched to what specific customers most value. People often talk about an account being loyalty but the only way to achieve total account loyalty is to achieve the loyalty of all the individuals and buyer groups in all of the locations that make up an account. Understanding what customers value and the attributes that define the key drivers of loyalty will increase customer share. The key is that only one customer voice will not give you a clear understanding of what an account values. All the individuals and buyer groups within the account rolled together will help define the drivers that will increase customer growth (Exhibit R9.2).

The Leaky Bucket. If sales are up, life is good! . . . Well, maybe and maybe not. Too often executives can fall into the trap of focusing mainly on top line revenue. In order to make effective business decisions, an analysis of where the revenue is coming from is required. Revenue may be up because the company has gained a lot of new customers, but previously established customers are defecting—in effect, "leaking" out the bottom of our customer pool. If we are successful in replacing the defecting cus-

EXHIBIT R9.2: LOYALTY MEASUREMENT MODEL

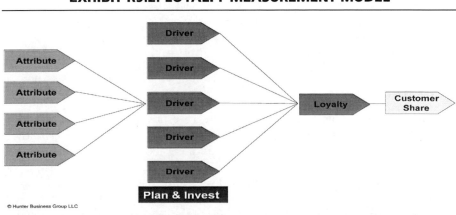

© Hunter Business Group LLC

tomers, the top line growth figures may be attractive—but consider the substantial costs. It is significantly more costly to be acquiring new customers, as opposed to retaining the customers we already have.

Service Profit Chain. How does leadership impact corporate profitability? Good question. That is the very question the Management Interest Group at Harvard Business School set out to answer. The hypothesis was that profitability was a direct result of the strength of an organization's leadership. The results of the study showed that profitability was driven by customer loyalty and supported by effective leadership styles. Additionally, it was learned that there is a direct relationship between employee and customer satisfaction/retention.

Business Result 3: Customer Profitability

How do I know the appropriate amount of money to invest in existing customers?

In the business-to-business arena profitability can be easily leached away if focus on understanding your customers, effectively measuring for customer profitability and using integrated account management is lost. These aspects create a direct line of sight to customer profitability.

Critical to Customer Profitability is the way you manage:

Grading. Not all customers are created equal. Different customers—even those that look alike—can have substantially different potential economic value to a particular organization. When marketers don't recognize this fact, or even when they do recognize it but don't do anything about it, they risk over-investing or under-investing in particular sets of customers. **A grade is not a segment.** Grading is the process of grouping accounts or buyer groups according to their *potential value*.

Segmentation. Defined as a group of accounts, buyer groups or individuals with a common set of attributes.

A segment could be a target; however, segments are often composed of multiple targets:

- Segmentation can be based on firmographics (demographics of companies), demographics, needs, and/or behavioral characteristics
- The best segments are needs and behavioral based
- The best attributes (characteristics of a segment) are "actionable attributes"
- Segments are often based on similar applications

Most companies segment by some form of demographics because it is easy, not because it is effective.

Core and Common Measures. Most all business executives will agree that maximizing customer profitability is critical. The disparity often comes in how to effectively measure customer profitability. Further complicating the issue is that there are two sides of the equation that must be considered, the revenue provided by a customer as one side and the cost of servicing and delivering to that customer as the second component.

Across the B2B environment, a standard set of similar effective measurements and reports have proven to be effective and reliable. The measures used may be less important than using them consistently across the organization. Customer profitability will surely improve when an organization establishes a set of core & common measures, uses them within every department and across all efforts, and takes appropriate actions based on their findings.

Measurement Framework. To maximize the effectiveness of the measurement framework it is critical that we correctly link processes and activities to the results they drive. Our objective is to ensure what we measure is truly predictive of results—avoiding both "black box" syndrome (too few measures, resulting in a lack of foresight on where the business is going) and "white noise" (so many measurements, that we cannot tell the important and indicative from the less relevant). It is critical to complete the measurement framework with the addition of Quality metrics. Quality metrics can often be the most difficult to define and track—but are frequently the most powerful in predicting results.

Integrated Account Management. Functionally, Integrated Account Management leverages and integrates all of the available media options for building this inter-dependent relationship between B2B companies and their customers. Seamlessly integrating email, mail, phone, etc. to support the field and the channel, Integrated Account Management provides a cost-effective model for extending the interactions and coverage we can provide for customers. In addition, it places at our disposal a wider array of tools for communicating with customers in a manner consistent with their preferences and expectations. The net result is a classic win-win situation: greater value and satisfaction for our customers, and greater loyalty and revenue at lower cost for the B2B company.

Business Result 4: Customer Growth
How can I achieve sustainable growth?

Growth can only be achieved by improving value delivery through the overall customer experience—and may be one of the only remaining sustainable differentiation strategies available to the modern firm. If the growth imperative is dependent on business activities in the customer domain, no strategic growth initiative can succeed without leveraging customer insight to improve the value delivered across the entire customer experience. It may sound simple, but listening is the common thread. Listening to the voice of the customer, and then responding appropriately helps uncover what customers want us to know and do—deliver value. To accomplish this we need new tools to hear the voice of the customer and refined methodologies to apply this knowledge.

Critical to Customer Growth is to take on strategic questions through the following concepts:

Customer Loyalty. In some ways, customer growth is long term assimilation. Loyalty gets more and more customers to experience more and more value over time. Loyalty is earned and profitable growth is realized when the additional transactions are well matched to what specific customers most value.

Setting objectives for, and measuring, customer growth requires being pretty specific about defining what a customer is. It helps to think of customers as individuals rather than accounts. Accounts don't buy things—people buy things on behalf of accounts. Emphasizing accounts as customers can actually be a hindrance to customer growth because it tends to permit "laziness" when it comes to really understanding who makes the actual buying decisions, what they value, and how to reach them. It's useful to think about business-to-business customers as networks of individuals clustered into *buyer groups* responsible for sets of specific applications. Larger accounts are typically intertwined networks of multi buyer groups in multiple locations. Using this concept allows customer growth objectives, strategies and tactics to be highly focused.

Account Penetration. Customer Growth through Account Penetration involves identifying and connecting with a growing number of individual buyers within a customer account. In this framework, think of the account as a network of multiple sites, composed of multiple buying groups, composed of individuals with responsibility for specific applications—applications for which your products or services meet the customer needs.

Product Penetration. If Account Penetration is about achieving customer growth by selling your products to more buyers within an account, Product Penetration achieves growth by selling more products to each of those buying groups. Product Penetration is about more than short-term revenue enhancement, though. It is about creating a sustainable, interdependent relationship with your customers which is based upon a broader exchange and delivery of value.

New Product Launch. Most companies measure velocity from the completion of product development to the time the product is introduced to the commercial market. After that date is met, most launches either collapse into chaos or slide into obscurity. Organizations should really focus on the time it takes to fill the sales funnel and realize sales. The speed and methods used to fill the sales funnel will have the greatest impact on your new product's lifecycle—market penetration, product penetration and repurchase—because this is when you build your presence in the marketplace.

Integrated Account Management. Business-to-business marketing and sales executives are urgently searching for new and better ways to find and keep customers. Faced with the triple impact of rising costs, fierce competition, and fickle clients, many organizations are finding a unified solution in integrated account management (IAM)—a form of marketing that takes a proactive and personal approach to managing mutually beneficial customer relationships. IAM allows companies to effectively manage their relationships with customers. It is the customer relationship that drives both growth and profitability. It is why customers buy, what differentiates companies from competitors, and, most importantly, why customers remain loyal. IAM is an integral component of a company's overall relationship marketing strategy

Service Profit Chain. The most direct driver of revenue growth and profitability is customer loyalty. In almost any organization, a small percentage of loyal customers account for the majority of the company's profit and growth. All of which begs the question: how do I increase customer loyalty? The answer is not simple, but the

Service Profit Chain (Service Management Interest Group, Harvard Business School) provides an excellent framework for diagnosing components and building the infrastructure to increase loyalty, revenue growth and profitability.

Loyalty is measured by actual buying behavior. By knowing who your best customers are and what they value, you can target and acquire similar customers with greater potential of becoming loyal and driving business growth.

This understanding must then be translated internally into the skills, behaviors and attitudes of the organization. Employee loyalty is directly linked to customer's perception of value and customer loyalty.

Value-based Contact. It is important to integrate and coordinate communications to provide the maximum value to the customer. Customers today want to be more in control of specifying the content and quality of the communications that are valuable to them. Customers are pleased to provide information on how communications should be delivered, as well as the content, frequency and medium and may indicate that face-to-face contact is not a preferred medium when asked how they want to receive communications. This can come as a shock to Business-to-Business selling forces, or a realization that there are ways to optimize the delivery of value to customers. This realization is the first step to bringing expense to sales ratios down, and to delivering more value to your customers.

Business Result 5: Expense Reduction

How can I reduce expenses in the sales and marketing budget with reduction in growth and retention?

Expense reduction is often seen as doing more with less and that translates to getting less results. In all actuality if expense reduction is done correctly efficiency will be gained and more growth and added customer value can be realized.

The critical concepts to manage for expense reduction are:

Marketing Integration. Customer communications are a key (and effective!) weapon in the arsenal of customer knowledge acquisition and customer relationship building, and customer growth. At the same time, the communications and customer contact can be a hefty portion of our cost to serve. The challenge is to maximize the effectiveness of this tool, while minimizing the costs. New methods of communication, such as e-commerce, are radically changing the cost of communication and customers are rapidly accepting new forms of interaction. These new methods of communicating are fundamentally different and have significantly different costs associated with them. To reduce customer management expenses, organizations should use the lowest cost medium that delivers the highest value to the customer.

Customer Contact Matrix. The Customer Contact Matrix is a planning tool that ensures the investment of sales costs is appropriate for the expected return in sales or revenue. The tool (or plan) aligns sales and marketing investments with the revenue potential of different grades of customer. The objective is to maintain approximately the same level of sales and marketing investment for each grade.

Integrated Account Management. The spiraling cost of keeping field sales reps on the road and collapsing margins from mature products have been a major contributor to entire industries either disappearing altogether or having to radically change how they go about their business. In order to remain competitive, organizations have been forced to better leverage the high cost of face to face visits with lower cost methods of communication with customers. Integrated Account Management is a formularized method for conducting this iterative process. This refining method is done by modifying the media used to manage the customer and the frequency with which those media are used.

Grading. The primary reason to grade customers is to ensure that the investment in those customers matches the expected return.

Lean Six Sigma. Do not be intimidated by the terminology of Lean Six Sigma. The methodology is—simply put—about reducing the complexity in your sales and marketing processes and implementing new, improved processes that function more reliably, effectively, and repeatedly. The methodology includes tools and approaches which allow you to re-engineer your process—simplify; remove the errors; and streamline for greater velocity at lower cost.

Value-Stream Mapping. Value Stream Mapping is a diagnostic tool to understand the current environment and identify areas of waste. Once the current environment is clearly understood, an organization can then prioritize the necessary actions to improve that process. By eliminating the waste, an organization is able to lower its costs while still providing equal or greater value to their customers.

Business Results 6: Sales Acceleration

How can I accelerate my sales to realize growth and profitability sooner?

As the adage goes, "Give me infinite time, money, or quality—and I can accomplish anything". Unfortunately, this is not a luxury with which any are actually confronted. Resources to reach out to customers are not unlimited and must be invested wisely. Fiscal realities of ROI, budgets, and market combined with perishable resources and competitive pressure demand sensitivity to the timing of the sales cycle. A higher velocity sales cycle delivers ROI and economic benefit faster.

Critical to managing sales acceleration are the following key concepts:

Sales Funnel. A key component of the overall sales process is the sales funnel: the steps and stages of our engagement process—defined within the context of our industry and company. We populate the funnel with leads, generated by our outreach and lead generation activities. The funnel itself includes the activities and milestones which mark the progress of that lead towards a sale. Although at a detail level, each customer and sale have their own, unique characteristics—the successful, stable sales process is marked by a standard set of activities and milestones which are part of each sales engagement. Once we understand and designate a standard, repeatable set of steps and stages (milestones and activities) for our company, we can establish targets and measurements for these steps and stages.

Core and Common Measures. We do not need to start from scratch in identifying the key categories for effective measurement. Although the metrics themselves may vary by industry or company, most of the key measurements that indicate health and velocity of the sales cycle are predictable. The focus for measurement is to select the appropriate key measurements, and develop a methodology to collect the data easily and leverage the data into improved decision-making and action.

Value-Stream Analysis. The first step in effectively improving the sales cycle process—as with any process—is to properly diagnose the cause and drivers of the current performance level, whatever that level may be. We must answer the questions, "Which parts of the process are driving the current cycle time and unpredictability?" and "Where can we most effectively make changes to increase velocity and predictability?" Value-Stream Analysis (VSA) provides a diagnostic approach to answering these questions for an organization.

Business Result 7: Sales Coverage
How do I optimize my sales coverage?

Most companies know the basic principle of selling: customers buy from you; so make your customer the focus. Give them what they want or need and they will hopefully keep buying from you. However, in today's world of increased competition and globalization, it takes a bit more to truly design a customer-centric sales model. Effective sales coverage incorporates both a mature understanding of the customer and customer needs, and an economically based design to effectively address those needs.

Critical to sales coverage is gaining an understanding of the following concepts:

Coverage Model Design. Our sales coverage model must encompass a plan to reach the "right" individuals within the account. We know the accounts and the individuals we are trying to reach. We split them up and assign them among our field sales representatives and channel partners, and we have "coverage," right? Wrong. We don't just want coverage; we want a smart, economical coverage model. The most important components are the graded model and integrated account management.

Integrated Account Management. Integrated Account Management extends the reach to our customers, by leveraging each of our field sales contacts with additional phone; email; mail and other lower-cost contacts. By seamlessly integrating across the various media, and employing the media for each message which maps to the customers' preferences. Through integrated account management we are able to increase customers' perception of value; increase loyalty and share of wallet; and simultaneous reduce the cost to serve.

Customer Contact Matrix. Customers are a valuable asset. And like other assets, they require investment. Also like other assets, we can achieve best business results by investing in ways that are commensurate with the expected return of those assets.

We have two primary points of focus: integrating and leveraging the various contact investments to get the maximum impact, and ensuring the total investment is consistent with expected return. The customer contract matrix builds a mix of integrated sales and marketing tactics that leverage lower cost media while delivering effective and valuable contacts.

Marketing Communications. Once you have developed a clear understanding of who your customers are and what they need, this understanding must be DEMONSTRATED via your customer communications, in order to leverage the understanding into more effective relationship-building. Effective leverage of customer knowledge into your communications precludes any kind of "one size fits all approach". Rather, the customer segments and needs that you have worked so hard to identify require tailored communications.

Value-based Content. A key component of building relationships with customers that drive business results is the ability to engage customers with communications content that provides value to the customer. The value in the content delivery transforms the interaction from a "tell—sell" engagement into a delivery of service, that advances the business relationship. Value Based Content requires you understand what the customer needs, media preference for that content and how often they want it.

Business Result 8: Creating a Customer Culture

What do I need to do to ensure that I get the right people in the right roles to impact my B2B marketing?

It is critical to always slow down and define your direction before embarking on a new hiring cycle. This is the ideal time to determine how to improve the caliber of the team and the organization as a whole. We know that when a position opens up, all the forces of nature will converge upon you to fill the position quickly. It is natural to want to grab the last ad or the last set of recruiting material and use it again, just to get things started quickly. However, we cannot stress enough the importance of *hiring slowly*. Get the team together, conduct a *Role Definition Workshop*, and define all the key elements of the position.

Critical to creating a customer culture are the following concepts:

Behavioral Profiling in the Recruiting Process. *"Hire them for what they know. Fire them for who they are."* This statement is an accurate reflection of what happens in most organizations. There are three factors that go into every hiring decision. They are 1) **Talent** or Behaviors, 2) **Experience** and Education and 3) **Chemistry**. Use of this process will allow you to determine **before** you hire a candidate, whether or not they will be successful on the job. While no assessment process is guaranteed, this method has proven the best results. Over 60% of turnover results from people not "fitting" in the culture. And the cost associated with turnover is significant, usually up to three times an individual's annual salary.

Performance and Talent Management. *"You get what you reward, every time."* The Performance Management Process must be developed to drive and reward the right behavior and align with organizational goals and objectives. The Performance Management Process is so much more than an annual appraisal or "completed form." A successful performance and talent management system is based on regular dialog, honest and straightforward feedback using *performance standards,* development planning, incentives and a formal coaching process.

Employee Satisfaction and Loyalty. To quote from the *Service Profit Chain* (Harvard Business School), research has shown that there is a direct link between profitability, customer loyalty, employee satisfaction, loyalty and productivity. The employee loyalty survey that helps the organization understand key drivers and attributes supported by qualitative and quantitative data will help the organization embark on change that has the most impact on employee loyalty. This in turn leads to customer loyalty and productivity.

Change Management. Like a broken link in a chain, if you are missing even one step in your Change Management process, the entire initiative will be weak. While there are many change management models available to businesses today, the core elements are very similar. John Kotter defines a multi-stage process that leadership can use to drive change in a healthy way. The model creates the environment for the change required to move your company forward as you initiate new processes and systems in the B2B marketing space.

B2B Customer Relationship Management

As we have explored, B2B marketing is a process of relationship building. Relationship building requires time and resources; often the same, or similar, type resources tasked with selling your company's products. This is not a constraint, but rather an opportunity to enhance the effectiveness of your company's sales and marketing plans—planning driving measurable execution and performance. Earlier we identified and discussed the eight business results driving Business-to-Business marketing, now we will examine the tactical approaches to growing and managing B2B customer relationships.

The Customer Community Center is the point through which marketing and sales activities are coordinated and implemented. The goal of the center is two-fold: (1) to increase sales productivity, which is measured by comparing sales expenses with sales revenues; and (2) to increase the perceived value, satisfaction, and loyalty of your customers by increasing the frequency of value-based contacts—communications. But, as discussed in the Value-Based Communications and Customer Contact Matrix concepts, the customers' perceived increase in value-based contacts does not come from increasing the size of the field sales team. The most cost effective way to increase the frequency of value-based contacts is implementing an integrated inside/outside sales model. An effective inside/outside sales model leverages cost-effective insides resources to allow more expensive field sales people to focus on strategic face-to-face sales meetings.

An effective customer relationship program should focus on one of the basic sales competencies:

1. Demand or Lead Generation
2. Opportunity or Lead Management
3. Account Management
4. Inside Sales

Each of these competencies presents a focused approach to achieving a defined business result. Demand or Lead Generation is the process of managing customer touches all the way to a purchase order. For commodity products, demand generation may actually include purchasing the product off the web site. For B2B applications, demand generation typically stops at the point where you turn over a qualified inquiry to the sales team.

Examples of the activities of an agent working within this competency include working with the field team to the plan for lead generation activities via mail and email, coordinating issuance of materials and tracking via CRM software, tracking and reporting on response rates by source and time.

Opportunity or Lead Management is the process of rapidly and effectively creating, nurturing, distributing and analyzing leads. The ultimate goal is to increase the likelihood that a lead will convert to a qualified opportunity and then a new, satisfied customer. Examples of the activities of an agent working within this competency include responding to inquiries (e.g., from web, marketing materials, etc.), entering and tracking inquiries in a CRM system, creating and executing contact plans for inquiries, and pre-screening and qualifying leads for field.

Integrated Account Management (IAM) is a system of marketing and selling that is driven out of a proactive, planful, and personal approach to managing mutually beneficial individual customer relationships. In IAM, the account manager uses a variety of contact media to manage customer relationships in an economically prudent manner to drive sustainable, long-term, profitable relationships. Examples of the activities of an agent working within this competency include maintaining and executing the contact plan for leads that will take longer to come to fruition, leverage customer contacts by the field reps with lower cost contact during the sales process, conducting account profiling activities, and serving as the focus on integration between the field sales team and CRM application.

Inside Sales includes IAM, but also includes the actual sales transaction—the production activity that tends to focus on the short-term closing of the opportunity at hand. Examples of the activities of an agent working within this competency are similar to those performed in account management, but also include booking and closing sales.

Standardization

Standardization is one of the many benefits of a process-oriented customer center. Independent of the competency, standardization can be achieved in planning, risk assessment, resource scheduling, program monitoring and control, performance management and reporting templates, and best-practices to name a few. There is a natural progression from standardization, to measurement, to control, and lastly to continuous improvement—competency maturity. Without achieving the first step—standardization—the goal of continuous improvement and excellence may never be achieved. An iterative process to improve competency maturity can be represented by the Deming / Shewart Cycle (Exhibit R9.3).

The four components of the cycle are defined as follow:

EXHIBIT R9.3: DEMING/SHEWART CYCLE

- PLAN—Establish the objectives and processes necessary to deliver results in accordance with the specifications.
- DO—Implement the processes.
- CHECK—Monitor and evaluate the processes and results against objectives and specifications and report the outcome.
- ACT—Apply actions to the outcome for necessary improvement.

Roles

Across Demand/Lead Generation, Opportunity/Lead Management, Account Management, and Inside Sales, six roles exist. Each program type or competency may not contain each role; the scope of the program and client wishes influence the final configuration. The six primary roles are: (1) Inbound Representative; (2) Outbound Account Management Representative; (3) Outbound Lead Generation Representative; (4) Inside Sales Representative; (5) Team Lead; and (6) Program Supervisor. Following is a description of each role and its primary responsibilities.

Fundamentally, the responsibilities of these roles are focused on developing and nurturing client relationships. These roles should perform as an extension of the field sales teams; not a competitor. Successful implementation of an inside / outside model requires appropriate people and process change management. As with any successful organization, its strength is in its people. The concept of Behavioral Profiling, discussed earlier, should be utilized during the recruiting process.

Some of the key traits to seek when staffing for any of the four competencies include:

- Articulate.
- Excellent listening skills.
- Excellent communication skills.
- Familiarity with contact management software.
- Prior B2B experience.
- Prior experience working in a phone-based environment.
- Demonstrated ability to self-manage.
- Demonstrated experience in consultative selling.
- Demonstrated ability to successfully multi-task.

As in many situations, tradeoffs will need to be made. The T.E.C. Model discussed earlier provides a framework for assessing and prioritizing the candidate tradeoffs.

Again, it is imperative to establish and follow a structured recruiting process. The selection of the "right" person from the beginning will contribute to quicker rewards in any of the four sales competencies.

Performance Measurement

An important process associated with any of the four sales competencies is the ability to establish and measure results to plan. Performance management is a systematic process in which a company involves its employees in improving organization effectiveness in the accomplishment of the company's mission and strategic goals. A comprehensive performance management system must include metrics at the employee level and metrics that provide linkage and predictability to organizational mission and goals

The CRM Measurement Framework provides a skeleton for developing and implementing the appropriate measures needed to monitor performance. The framework begins at the top with the results measures. There are a limited number of these measures which generally link to business objectives and goals. The framework then identifies the processes and activities which can reliably and predictably deliver those results. The challenge is to identify the causal relationship (build from the top down). There are two major benefits of the framework:

1. It allows company to focus on measuring the most important things with confidence—desired results.
2. Provides employees with a line of sight as to how their individual activities impact business results.

Key factors to good metric selection include the following:

- Defining results that are closely linked to economic value. Examples include but are not limited to profit, revenue, and market share.
- Clearly understanding and educating people on the processes and activities that will deliver the desired results.
- The correct linkage of activities to results ensures that activity measures are truly predictive of the desired results. Proper linkage also provides employees with a credible and effective line of sight to how their activity performance drives and impacts the business results.
- Identifying quality metrics that cut across all levels of the framework. Proper quality measures ensure activities are performed in the appropriate manner, and with sufficient quality, to deliver the desired results; as opposed to simply "checking the box."

As stated by Harold S. Geneen (1910–1997), " . . . It is an immutable law in business that words are words, explanations are explanations, promises are promises—but only performance is reality."

Reporting

With the implementation of a demand generation, opportunity management, account management, or inside sale program, clear, precise, reporting should precipitate from the program at regular intervals. From a time and cost perspective, good performance reporting should address current program performance to plan and where the program is headed (trends). From a planning perspective, identifying present and future risks associated with the program or market segments being serviced and whether there are any special problems that need to be addressed, and finally, what proactive actions can be taken by management to maintain or improve future program performance.

There are four primary categories of reports (1) Performance reports, (2) Status reports, (3) Projection reports, and (4) Exception reports. Each type of sales competency should publish reports in all of the four categories with a frequency of no more than monthly. Current technology allows many of the performance metrics associated with programs to be reported on a "real-time" basis.

Performance reports indicate the physical progress of the program to date against its goal. Ultimately, success of a program is defined by the sponsor of the program. As such, the desired results, and activities driving those results, will be monitored and reported on. Status reports identify where we are today and report the information from the performance reports in a consolidated, standardized, format. Projection reports calculate and illustrate any forward-looking projections. Finally, exception reports identify exceptions, problems, or situations that exceed the threshold limits on

EXHIBIT R9.4: REPORTS BY GROUP

Group 1	Group 2	Group 3
• Rep Productivity Report (# contacts per day)	• Campaign and Source Report	• Database At-Risk Report
• Variable Compensation Worksheet	• Total # of Opportunities Identlfied, Qualified, Closed	• Field-Generated Opportunities Report
• # of Completed Account Profiles	• Exception Report	• Distributor-Generated Opportunities Report
• New Decision-Maker Contacts Report	• Close the Loop Status Report	
• Campaign Analysis Report		
• Opportunity Status Report		
• Total Inquiries, Opportunities Identified, Sent to Field		
• Through Put Analysis		
• Potential Revenue $ in Funnel / $ Sold Report		
• Call Quality and Monitoring Report		

such items as CRM database quality, program performance to goal, representative performance to plan, along with other such topics.

Standardization across the four sales competencies allows for three primary groups of reports—the Core & Common Reports. The first group (Group 1) of reports is applicable across all four sales competencies. The second group (Group 2) of reports is applicable to demand / lead generation, opportunity / lead management, and account management programs. The third group (Group 3) of primary reports is applicable to account management and inside sales programs.

The table in Exhibit R9.4 identifies the Core & Common reports associated with each group.

Summary

Effective execution of a business-to-business marketing strategy will result in strong, long-term relationships with your customers, regardless of their stage in the customer lifecycle. If this process seems complex and time-consuming, keep in mind that the risk and investment that comes with effective business-to-business marketing is almost always outweighed by the rewards returned to the company.

VICTOR L. HUNTER is founder and president of Hunter Business Group, LLC. He is nationally known for his expertise in business-to-business direct marketing and service to the nation's leading companies. Founded in 1981, Hunter is the first consulting and service company dedicated solely to increasing the productivity of businesses by assisting them to sell products and services to other businesses, institutions, and professionals.

SHEILA T. ZELENSKI and JEFF J. KREUTZER are former associates of Mr. Hunter at Hunter Business Group, LLC, in Milwaukee, Wisconsin.

Business-to-Business Lead Generation

RUTH P. STEVENS
eMarketing Strategy

O ne of marketing's most important contributions to business marketing is generating leads on behalf of salespeople. Lead generation can be defined as identifying prospective customers and qualifying their likelihood to buy in advance of making a sales call.

For salespeople, a qualified lead provided by a marketing department allows the sales rep to spend his or her valuable time in front of a prospect who is likely to buy, instead of squandering the salesperson's skills on cold calling. In short, lead generation programs make a sales force more productive.

If you talk to B-to-B marketers about their goals, they will invariably include lead generation near the top of their to-do lists. A recent study from Marketing Sherpa confirms: The top objective reported by 74% of marketers was "generating high quality leads." The second most important objective, reported by 49% of marketers, was "generating a high volume of leads." A goal named by 40% was "competing in lead generation across multiple media, from podcasts to paid search to webinars to print ads." Lead generation is job one for B-to-B marketers.

A lead consists of the name, contact information and background information on a prospective buyer. A qualified lead is a prospect who is ready to buy. The defining characteristics of "qualified" vary by industry, by company, and by salesperson. Marketers who generate leads must tailor their definitions of lead qualification to the requirements of the sales force they serve.

The process of lead generation is fairly straightforward. It involves a series of steps, beginning with a campaign of outbound and inbound contacts to generate the inquiry and qualify it, to handing the lead to the sales organization, and then tracking the lead through conversion to sales revenue.

The secret to success is in a focus on business rules and process. Lead generation and management is less of the glamorous, creative side of marketing. It is more about developing the rules, refining them, testing, tracking, and making continuous improvements. The company with the best process, executed consistently, is the one with the true competitive advantage.

Campaign Planning: Setting Campaign Objectives

The first step in campaign planning should be to set campaign objectives. Without them, you won't be able to recognize success when you see it. Campaign objectives will typically cover:

- The number of leads expected
- Their degree of qualification
- The time frame during which they will arrive
- The cost per lead
- Lead to sales conversion ratio
- Revenue per lead
- Campaign ROI, or expense-to-revenue ratio

The important point is that the entire process must be planned in advance of making a single marketing campaign investment. Make sure you are able to generate the amount of qualified leads needed by your sales organization, at the right cost. Plan your fulfillment material up front, during the outbound campaign process. Don't leave it until later. And make sure that your interim steps—the processes and people that capture, fulfill, qualify, nurture the inquiries—are in place, with the capacity to handle the flow you intend to create.

Campaign Planning: Calculating Campaign Volume Requirements

To set up campaigns that will provide a predictable, relevant and timely lead flow, here is a simple process to figure out how much campaigning is required to generate a month's worth of leads for a sales team.

1. Estimate the number of qualified leads each salesperson can reasonably be expected to follow up on a month.
2. Multiply that number by the number of reps in a geographic territory.
3. Then divide by the qualification rate you expect for your campaign inquiries.
4. Divide again by the expected response rate on the campaign. This final number will be your campaign volume needed to support that territory for a month. In mail campaigns, you can control the lead flow within the territory by selecting ZIP codes for each volume required. In other media, you may end up with some peaks and valleys that you can smooth out with tactical campaign efforts like telemarketing.
5. Continue the process for each territory, and add up the results. You will have total numbers for your qualified leads, inquiries and campaign volumes for the month.

Campaign Planning: Media Selection

Each communications medium has its strengths, weaknesses and best applications. The campaign must carefully harness the right medium for each job. For generating leads among new prospects, the best choices are search engine keyword bidding, direct mail, and outbound telephone for ongoing campaign work. Exhibiting at trade shows is also effective, as long as the show is well targeted to your audience and attracts a qualified pool of prospects. Also effective are search engine optimization, targeted banner advertising, pay-for-performance content syndication, and referral marketing programs. It's also important to add some downloadable content to your web site, plus a call to action and a dedicated landing page, where you capture visitors' contact information. A technique that's worth exploring is IP address identification, using tools that allow you to find the name of a company that has visited your web site and what keywords they were searching for. Among inquirers and current customers, you may find telephone and email most productive, telephone being more intrusive and email being less expensive than direct mail or print.

Campaign Planning: Offer Development

Like any direct marketing effort, lead generation offers are designed to motivate a response. The offer should provide a reason to act, in order to overcome people's natural inertia. It can be a consumer-like incentive, with personal benefit to the recipient. Or it can be related to solving a business problem.

Offer Checklist

Here are the types of offers frequently used for lead generation. Experiment with as many as you can.

- Free information, aka "content" (research report, newsletter, white paper, case study, video, infographic)
- Premium (a calculator, a book)
- Free trial
- Free sample
- Free self-assessment tool
- Seminar or webinar
- Demonstration
- Discount
- Financing
- Sales call
- Free consultation or audit
- Free estimate

Campaign Results Analysis

Many companies divide their results analysis into two parts: activity-based metrics and results-based metrics. During the long stretch until sales results come in, marketers can still get some interim benefit from analyzing the inquiry and qualification campaign activities themselves.

Activity-based metrics include such indicators as:

- Cost per thousand
- Response rate

- Cost per inquiry
- Campaign turn-around time
- Qualification rate
- Cost per qualified lead

Results-based metrics include:

- Conversion-to-sales rate
- Sales revenue per lead
- Campaign ROI
- Campaign expense-to-revenue ratio

Lead Management

The leverage in lead generation lies not in marketing creativity or in conducting more campaigns. Instead, it lies in converting more inquiries into qualified leads and, then, more qualified leads into sales.

In short, the company with the best inquiry management is the one that will win. Inquiry management is about setting up a solid, methodical process, and then executing it every day.

A Minneapolis-based inquiry management company named Performark conducted a study, wherein they responded to over 1,000 business-to-business advertisements in trade publications. What happened? Performark found that 61% of the inquiries they submitted received absolutely no response, over 60 days. Worse, that result was down from their 1995 experiment, when a mere 43% of the inquiries were ignored.

Remember, these are inquiries resulting from paid advertisements, which carry calls to action, like to a web site or an 800 number. The marketers who bought these ads clearly intended for readers to respond and maybe—one would hope—buy something. But most of these marketers failed to put in place a process to handle the inquiries. To put the best face on this pathetic situation, look at it this way: When things out there are this bad, the company that does handle inquiries well is going to clean up, without investing much at all.

Here are the steps you can take to create a great inquiry management process.

Response Planning

Start response planning early in the campaign development process. Make sure you have a unique code that identifies responses from every outbound communication. This can be a pixel, a priority code, a special 800 number, an operator's name, a unique URL, anything. Offer multiple response media, including phone, web, BRC, and email. And don't be shy about including qualification questions on your reply form or your inbound-phone scripts.

Response Capture

Your response capture process will only work if it's designed by the people who manage the inbound media. Put together a cross-functional team. Then, be sure you consider the best strategy for each medium. For example, make sure your digital inquiries—from email and your web site—are acted on immediately. Log the inquiries into a database and match the name against prior contacts to avoid duplicates.

Inquiry Qualification

Many of your inquiries will require additional qualification before they are ready for hand-off to sales. The secret to qualification is involvement of the sales team in setting qualification criteria. Don't let them tell you they want "everything." But do listen to their views of an ideal qualified prospect. Ask the qualification questions either on the response form or via follow-up communications by email or telephone. Use a scoring system to sort the leads into those that are qualified, meaning ready to be handed off to the sales team, and those that still need marketing attention.

Lead Nurturing

When the prospect isn't ready to see a salesperson (but will be ready eventually), move the inquiry into a "nurturing" process. Nurturing involves a series of ongoing communications, intended to build awareness and trust, and to maintain contact until the prospect is ready to buy. You can use a variety of tactics, from webinar invitations and newsletters, to surveys, white papers and birthday cards. Marketing automation tools vastly assist in managing the complexity of ongoing nurturing communications streams.

Lead Tracking

Let's not forget the process of closing the marketing loop, to attribute a closed sale to a marketing campaign. It isn't easy in B-to-B, but it's worth some effort, if only to justify marketing budgets, not to mention giving you the tools to refine campaign tactics and improve results next time. Supplement your closed-loop tracking system with end-user surveys or data match-back analysis.

Optimize your inquiry management process, and you can triple, even quadruple, your revenues from lead-generation campaigns.

Setting Qualification Criteria

The most important approach to setting qualification criteria is to follow the needs of your sales force. After all, it is they who will be handling the lead and taking it to closure. They know better than anyone the nature of the sales process and what kind of buying characteristics are most likely to be workable for them.

Qualification criteria will vary by company and by industry. In large enterprise marketing, the criteria typically involve the following categories:

- Budget. Is the purchase budgeted, and what size of budget does the prospect have available. You will want to set up categories or ranges, for easier scoring. Some companies request information about the company's credit history here.

- Authority. Does the respondent have the authority to make the purchase decision? If not, you should try to capture additional relevant contact information.
- Need. How important is the product or solution to the company. How deep is their pain. This criterion may be difficult to ask directly, but it can be approached by roundabout methods. "What is the problem to be solved?" "What alternative solutions are you considering?" "How many do you need?" "What product do you currently use?"
- Timeframe. What is their readiness to buy. When is the purchase likely to be. Depending on industry and sales cycle length, this can be broken into days, months, or even years. Also be sure to ask whether they would like to see a salesperson.

Taken together, these key variables are abbreviated as BANT (budget, authority, need and timeframe). Qualification criteria will vary from company to company. Other common criteria include:

- Potential sales volume. How many departments in the company might use this product? How much of, or how often, might they need the product?
- Predisposition to buy from us. Are they past customers of ours? Are they similar to our current customers? Would they recommend us to their colleagues? Are they willing to call us back?
- Account characteristics. Company size, whether number of employees or revenue volume. Industry. Parent company.

Lead Generation Media

Sources of Marketing Contacts

B-to-B marketers have two general sources of marketing contacts: internal and external.

The internal data sources include:

- Sales contacts, whether gathered from the contacts lists of your salespeople or from sales force automation systems
- Billing systems, which provides important information about purchase history, credit worthiness and other transactional data
- Operations and fulfillment systems, which can tell you about a customer's channel preferences and communications needs, as well as purchase frequency data
- Customer service systems
- Inquiry files, i.e., prospects who have indicated interest in more information, whether at trade shows, or at your web site, or having responded to your campaigns

The external data sources include:

- Prospect lists, whether compiled or response files, like catalog buyers and seminar attendees
- Prospecting databases, whether open or closed cooperative databases or proprietary de-duplicated databases
- Email lists, both compiled and response
- Appended information, like SIC code or employee size, purchased from a data compiler

Direct Mail

The work horse medium of direct response communications for lead generation is direct mail, primarily due to the breadth and depth of prospecting data available. Direct mail is very flexible, offering multiple formats, like the #10 business size envelopes or 6 x 9 inch or larger packages, self-mailers, postcards, catalogs and dimensional packages designed to get past the gatekeeper.

Telephone

The telephone has traditionally been a very productive tool for lead generation. The beauty of the telephone is that it is flexible, personal, and cost-effective, and supports both inbound and outbound communications. Outbound, the phone is usually used in lead generation as a substitute for—or a supplement to—direct mail. This function is typically known as "telemarketing," and its power lies in its ability to penetrate small universes effectively. Inbound, the phone is frequently used as a response device, meaning one of several options for prospects to express their interest if they prefer the phone to the web or to a business reply card (BRC).

But there are many other uses of the phone in the world of lead generation. It is effective in response qualification, either inbound or outbound, when the operator poses a series of questions to evaluate the prospect's likelihood to buy. The phone is also productive for lead nurturing, when the prospect is not ready to buy, but the marketer wants to keep in touch, continue the relationship and be there when the time is right to see a salesperson.

Tips on Telephone Scripting for Lead Generation

Business calls shoe treated as a conversation, not a sales pitch.

Because business-to-business contact rates are lower than consumer, your script needs to be developed so it is more persuasive when you do get the prospect on the phone.

Breakthrough creativity is not the key ingredient in successful telemarketing scripts. More important is to follow the established formula, namely, gain attention, establish credibility, qualify the customer and move to the offer and call to action.

Make each script more relevant to the customer's situation than the caller's situation. Position features as benefits. Discuss what's in it for the customer.

Scripts should include an explanation of the reason for the call, such as thanks for visiting our web site, or to learn the prospect's reactions to the materials he reviewed.

Far more important than the script itself is the research and preparation that should precede the call. Encourage your reps to find out in advance everything they can about the prospect and his needs. Visit the prospect's web site, check the financial and trade press for articles about them, and, most obviously, review any information maintained internally on the prospect

Web Sites

The Internet is prized among business marketers for its versatility, reach and flexibility.

The web site can be designed to contribute to the lead generation process in a number of significant ways:

- Registration. Adding a registration area to the home page, with an offer, is an important and low-cost method of generating sales leads
- IP address identification. New tools allow you to identify the company behind the visit to your site, from which you can institute some marketing action, such as telephoning into the company to find out more about their needs
- Fulfillment. Responders can download the content-based offers from your web site, either on the spot or through an email link.
- Landing pages, where inquiry contact data is collected.
- Subscription sign-up. The top right corner of the home page is the best location for making subscription offers to a digital newsletter
- Extranets, or dedicated sites behind the firewall of your best customers, where they can learn about product information, ask to see a salesperson, or even conduct a transaction

Email

Email is a powerful medium for lead qualification and nurturing, not to mention customer relationship management, up-selling and a host of other business marketing applications. Email is not recommended for cold prospecting, however, since it is likely to be seen as spam and deleted.

Here are some tips on the best ways to put email to use in the lead generation process:

- Gather email addresses, and permission to use them, from customers and prospects at every point of contact. Email is generally welcome in business correspondence, so it makes sense to invest in gathering and maintaining as close to 100% email penetration of your customer base as possible.
- Practice good email etiquette. Ask permission to communicate via email. Offer recipients the option to "opt out" of continuing to receive emails, and honor those requests faithfully. Consider creating a contact preference page, where customers can keep you updated on how they want to hear from you.

- Apply the basic rules of direct marketing in your email communications. Test regularly. Use friendly, benefit-oriented copy. Make compelling offers. Ask for the action you desire from the reader frequently within the copy.
- Use email wherever in the sales and marketing process that it applies, like e-newsletters to keep in touch with customers and prospects, and as a personal communications medium from salespeople.

Performance Media

Performance marketing is gaining traction as a prospecting vehicle for B-to-B marketers. In these deals you only pay when your prospect takes the action you're looking for—the click, the download, the purchase, whatever.

The way it works is that the media channel owner conducts a campaign and charges the marketer an agreed price for every respondent according to predetermined criteria. There are scads of ways performance marketing is being applied across the B-to-B go-to-market spectrum, among them:

- **Pay per click.** The granddaddy of performance marketing, the system that sent Google's fortunes into the stratosphere. You only pay when a prospect clicks on your selected keyword(s). The secret to success here is choosing the right keywords and sending the clicker to a brilliantly written landing page, where you have a chance to convert them from a mere clicker to something else, like a prospect with whom you can continue a conversation. Some banner advertising and email rental lists are sold this way, as well.
- **Pay per lead.** This highly popular technique was pioneered by trade publishers looking for ways to extend the value of their customer access. The tech industry world calls this "content syndication," distributing marketers' white papers and research reports, and charging by response. Companies have sprung up offering pay per lead programs via banner ads to a network of publishers, or via email to compiled databases of business buyers.
- **Pay per appointment.** Hiring a telemarketing shop to conduct appointment-setting programs for sales reps is a long-time staple of the B-to-B marketing toolkit, and often priced by the appointment. Myriad call centers offer this kind of pricing.

  But keep in mind the old adage that you get what you pay for. The performance model has an inherent bias against quality. So marketers need to do the math. Avoid this model unless you have good data on conversion rates—conversion to qualified lead, and then conversion to a sale. With that data in hand, you can determine a profitable price and buy leads and appointments as long as you like.

Search Engine Marketing

Search engines can direct interested inquirers to your site at a rapid clip, but they take some time to understand and manage. You need to both submit your site to the top search engines and apply optimizing techniques to achieve higher ranking results. This can absorb the attention of a full-time staffer, or the services of an outside service provider. Another approach is paying for certain key words relevant to your product or company using Google AdWords or other search engine advertising options.

Advertising

Direct response advertising in trade publications, industry vertical publications, and business publications can provide a steady, reliable stream of new prospective sales leads.

The main issue faced by lead generators using advertising is conflicting goals within the company relating to brand awareness versus generating a response. Advertising, whether in print or online, can be very powerful in generating awareness and building brand recognition and positive attitudes. But if your objective is to get leads, the ad must be created for response.

Here follow some tips for successful lead generation using advertising:

- Stress benefits and the offer in every possible element of the ad (the headline, the body copy, the design and the response device).
- Add an offer and a response device to all brand advertising. You'll be surprised, and the sales force will be pleased, with the results.
- Do not permit your lead-generation advertising to conflict with your brand image. All communications must support and enhance your brand. Do nothing to harm it. In fact, you can gain leverage for lead generation from the awareness in the marketplace that the brand advertising has created.
- As print publications migrate to digital media, reach these targeted audiences through banner advertising, retargeting and sponsorship media.

Trade Shows

Exhibiting at trade shows and conferences is a time-honored way to get in front of customers and prospects in a focused, concentrated manner. Attendees are often highly qualified, their minds are on business at the show, and they are seeking solutions to business problems. Regrettably, marketers often squander the opportunity to put trade shows to their best advantage in lead generation. Here follow some suggestions for optimizing trade shows and conferences for generating good quality leads.

- Set your objectives clearly, in advance. If generating qualified leads is job one, then focus all of your show activity toward that goal.
- Design your signage to state clearly what your company does and how it benefits the customer. Passers-by will give you only a few seconds to get your message across.
- Insert one or two qualification questions into your inquiry-gathering process, by attaching a short form to the prospect's business card, or using an electronic swipe tool provided by show organizers.
- Remember that there is a direct inverse correlation between gift-giveaways and inquiry qualification levels. In a highly qualified environment, a show where most attendees are already solid prospects, using an incentive can be an excellent traffic generator. But go slowly when the audience is more broadly based.
- Put in place a process to qualify the leads—or have them contacted by sales—immediately on return from the show.

Referral Marketing

Business buyers are very good sources of referral business for two reasons. First, they are likely to know their counterparts in other companies through their own professional networking. And, second, they are often happy to introduce a solution to a colleague as part of nurturing their web of business relationships. From a marketer's point of view, referrals are an outstanding source of new business. Recommendations from a colleague have great credibility, so not only is the referred prospect likely to be qualified, he is likely to be motivated. The only downside of referral marketing is that the volume of referred business you can ever hope to get is rarely enough to sustain your needs for growth.

Some points to keep in mind when applying referral marketing to the lead generation process:

- Review all your marketing communications, and add a referral request where appropriate.
- Conduct regular referral-request campaigns to your current customer base. You may want to offer an incentive to both the referrer and the referred to increase response.
- Place a pass-along request at the bottom of your emails, especially those that contain valuable information or an offer.

RUTH P. STEVENS consults on customer acquisition and retention, teaches marketing at Columbia Business School, and is a guest blogger at HBR.org and Biznology. Crain's BtoB magazine named Ruth one of the 100 Most Influential People in Business Marketing. She is the author of *Maximizing Lead Generation: The Complete Guide for B2B Marketers*, and *Trade Show and Event Marketing*. Ruth serves as a director of Edmund Optics, Inc., the HIMMS Media Group, and the Business Information Industry Association. She also serves as a mentor to fledgling companies at the ERA business accelerator in New York City. She has held senior marketing positions at Time Warner, Ziff-Davis, and IBM and holds an MBA from Columbia University. Learn more at www.ruthstevens.com.

Consumer Privacy: Knowing Your Customers Without Really "Knowing" Them

JENNIFER BARRETT GLASGOW

CIPP, Global Privacy Officer, Acxiom Corporation

Integrated Marketing Communications involves devoting considerable time and energy to knowing your customers in order to bring them relevant offers at the right moment and to develop long-term relationships. But how much of that energy is involved in understanding your customers' preferences regarding how to handle their personal information, and how and when they would prefer that you contact them? And how much do you know about whether their attitudes regarding use of their personal information could affect their buying decisions, especially online and through other digital media? Surveys show us that today's consumers continue to be extremely concerned about protecting their privacy, which compels us to be respectful in our efforts to develop long-term relationships.

This Is Not a New Phenomenon

Dr. Allan Westin, a Professor of Law at Columbia University and founder of the Privacy and American Business Center for Social and Legal Research, has studied consumer attitudes since 1990. His research breaks the population into three distinct segments—the Fundamentalists, the Pragmatists and the Unconcerned. (1)

- Fundamentalists are individuals who are generally distrustful of companies and favor laws to spell out privacy rights. They generally choose privacy over benefits. This group is the one most concerned about their privacy and the one most likely to hesitate or refuse to provide their personal information.
- Pragmatists are individuals who weigh the benefits of various opportunities and services against the degree of intrusiveness of the personal information sought.

---

1. Privacy Indexes: A Survey of Westin's Studies by Dr. Alan Westin, Professor Emeritus, Columbia University, Teaneck, New Jersey
http://reports-archive.adm.cs.cmu.edu/anon/isri2005/CMU-ISRI-05-138.pdf

They believe that businesses should earn the public trust. They want the opportunity to decide for themselves. Most Pragmatists are willing to provide personal information when asked if it seems reasonable or when some value proposition, such as greater convenience, is offered.

- Unconcerned individuals are generally trustful of businesses about their collection of personal information and are ready to forego privacy rights to secure benefits. For these people, privacy is just not a big issue.

What is interesting about Westin's research is that throughout the 1990s, the Fundamentalists remained around a steady 25 percent of the population. However, between 2000 and 2002, this segment grew to about one-third and held steady for the balance of the decade.

More recently a global study by MasterCard in September 2013, "Around the World in 5 Personas: How Global Consumers Think about Their Data Online"[2], breaks the global population into five personality types:

- Open Sharers (21 percent) are highly digital consumers. They are progressive in their mobile and social media attitudes, exemplifying open behavior in both. These consumers tend to lead a less risk-averse lifestyle in general, including travel and clothing, but especially regarding online activities.
- Simply Interactors (21 percent) are the ultimate social networkers, with nine in 10 accessing Facebook daily. They view social networking as an easy way to stay connected, and feel themselves "missing out" when they are unable to connect with others online.
- Solely Shoppers (21 percent) are characterized by their reliance on the Internet for their shopping needs, both in product research and actual purchase. Indeed it is shopping that drives this persona online, as 73 percent believe online shopping saves a lot of time and hassle.
- Passive Users (20 percent) are not fully convinced of the value of the Internet, and they use the web less than other segments. Broadly speaking, they're risk-averse, not just with the Internet, but with their career, travel, clothing styles, and financial management.
- Proactive Protectors (17 percent) are guarded when it comes to shopping online. They are highly aware of targeted marketing and the ways their data is used to tailor marketing to them, and as a result, are very active in privacy management. Fully 82 percent know marketers can target them based on their search and browsing history, but only 26 percent are willing to be tracked online in exchange for a benefit.

While we might speculate about the reasons people feel the way they do and while there are many interesting observations we can draw from Westin's and MasterCard's research, there is one clear message we must heed: The American public's skepticism

---

2. Around the World in 5 Personas: How Global Consumers Think about Their Data Online by MasterCard. http://newsroom.mastercard.com/documents/around-the-world-in-5-personas-how-global-consumers-think-about-their-data-online/

and even distrust of the business community's responsible collection and use of information is a factor in a large-enough segment of the population that it can't be ignored. The question is: What does that mean to your business, and what are you doing about it?

This trend was first evident in the 1990s with the growing consumer rejection of outbound telemarketing as an acceptable medium for selling products and services. Within a few years, more than 80% of U.S. households had signed up for the Federal Trade Commission's National Do-Not-Call registry, which was launched in the fall of 2003. However, the telemarketing story still has some interesting dynamics from which we can learn some valuable lessons for today.

For instance, a study conducted by the Information Policy Institute in June of 2002[3] found that more than eight in 10 consumers said they had acquired a product or service, given their voting support, or made a donation at least once during the previous year as a result of a call to their household. And seven in 10 of those who have acquired a product or service over the telephone were satisfied with the shopping experience. Yet most consumers wanted to block telemarketing calls to their homes because many were too intrusive and they couldn't make the ones they objected to stop.

In addition to the registry, the FTC revised the Telemarketing Sales Rule [4] in 2002 to limit the number of abandoned calls—calls resulting from making too many advance outbound calls and then not having an available operator to talk to the consumer when the call was answered. Getting a call and having no one on the line when they answered created very real concern for consumers, especially the elderly, who said they feared they were being stalked. This eventually led to regulations about this practice.

More recently, the debate has focused in the online space on evolving data collection and marketing activities, such as behavioral advertising and social marketing. The Federal Trade Commission held a series of behavioral advertising workshops in 2007 and 2008 and published a set of recommended practices in February 2009[5] . This guidance provides insight into how regulators feel about aggressive uses of technology, especially when consumers don't understand how information about them is collected and what their choices are to limit its use.

Also in 2009 the Digital Advertising Alliance (DAA)[6] published the first of their guidelines for third-party collection of data about web site visits, Self-Regulatory Principles for Online Behavioral Advertising. These were followed in 2011 with

---

3. Measuring the True Cost of Privacy: A Rebuttal to "Privacy, Consumers, and Costs" by Michael A. Turner, Ph.D., President and Senior Scholar at PERC (formerly The Information Policy Institute) http://www.perc.net/wp-content/uploads/2013/09/gellmanlong.pdf

4. The FTC National "Do Not Call" Registry Website http://www.ftc.gov/donotcall

5. FTC Staff Report: Self-Regulatory Principles for Online Behavioral Advertising http://www.ftc.gov/os/2009/02/P085400behavadreport.pdf

6. Digital Advertising Alliance Self-Regulatory Principles for Online Behavioral Advertising, Multi-Site Data and the Mobile Environment. http://www.aboutads.info/

Principles for Multi-Site Data and in 2013 with guidance for the mobile environment.

In early 2010, social networks took the spotlight[7] with a focus on the ways in which information posted by users on their public pages is accessed by the commercial sector for a variety of purposes, including marketing. In response, Facebook changed its privacy policy and default settings several times in a short span of time to react to these concerns. Several other social networks reacted similarly.

In 2012, the FTC again published an insightful report, "Protecting Consumer Privacy in an Era of Rapid Change: Recommendations for Businesses and Policymakers." This report sets forth best practices for businesses to protect consumers and give them greater control over the collection and use of their personal data. The FTC also recommends that Congress consider enacting general privacy legislation, data security and breach notification legislation and data broker legislation.

All these examples create two resounding themes: first, the need for transparency about how information is collected and used and, second, the requirement to have an effective and easy-to-use choice to allow consumers to stop overly aggressive marketing practices.

Have We Learned from History?

The drive to legislate marketing activities is not a new phenomenon. We have another clear example of a marketing practice in the mid-1990s that did just that—sweepstakes. The sweepstakes industry was a very profitable one. However, as it became more competitive and consequently more aggressive, dissatisfaction grew with the offers being made and there was much confusion about whether making a purchase would increase the odds of winning. Furthermore, a number of elderly individuals were confused by the wording of the sweepstakes offers, thinking they had won when they, in fact, had received only an entry form.

Repeated complaints to authorities were ignored by sweepstakes marketers. So after several years, Congress held hearings that devastated to the industry. These resulted in the passage of the Deception Mail Prevention and Enforcement Law[8], which spells out what a sweepstakes offer can and cannot say and how it can and cannot say it, even down to the type size and placement of language that explains the chances of winning. The result is that the sweepstakes industry is a fraction of what it was in its heyday of the mid-1990s.

It would seem that we did not apply the lessons we learned from sweepstakes to telemarketing. Have we learned from both sweepstakes and telemarketing and applied those lessons to our practices online, in mobile marketing, and in interactive TV? Only time will tell.

Furthermore, we have a whole set of new and converging issues that have confused

---

7. Privacy Groups Assail Facebook Changes
http://news.cnet.com/8301-13578_3-20006220-38.html
8. Public Law 106-168-Dec. 12, 1999 Deception Mail Prevention and Enforcement Act
http://www.govtrack.us/congress/bill.xpd?bill=s106-335 and the DMA Sweepstakes Do's and Don'ts for Marketers http://www.dmaresponsibility.org/Sweepstakes/

the consumer and turned what was historically only an irritation factor into a legitimate claim about the invasion of one's privacy.

We Must Understand the Consumer's View of Privacy

Direct marketing practitioners would likely say that the sweepstakes, telemarketing, behavioral advertising and social marketing issues should really not be considered privacy issues. Instead, these practitioners would claim that even aggressive marketing tactics are merely irritations to some, not all, consumers resulting in no real "harm." However, consumers don't see this distinction, nor do policy makers and regulators.

The picture is complicated by concerns about identity theft coupled with the rapidly expanding uses of "cookies," geo-location sensing devices, and other passive data collection technologies that monitor and record our every movement. Added to this are larger corporate structures across which more information is being shared and mega-marketing databases are being developed.

We also have continued frustration over spam (unsolicited or undesired bulk electronic messages—either email or SMS), spyware, and phishing (attempts to **fraudulently** acquire sensitive information, such as usernames, **passwords** and **credit card** details, by masquerading as a trustworthy entity in an electronic communication). Studies report that Internet Service Provider filters remove as much as 80 percent of all e-mail as fraudulent. According to Framingham, Mass.-based market-intelligence firm IDC, 2007 was the first year that spam email volumes exceeded person-to-person email volumes sent worldwide. And despite the passage of the CAN SPAM Act [9] in 2003, consumers fear unsubscribing will not make spam stop, so they often ignore the very tool that legislation provided.

If that weren't enough, we are in the age of text marketing to mobile devices based on our location at any given moment, personalized advertising on cable TV based on the shows we watch, RFID tags that can track purchases we have made all the way to our homes, and social marketing based on what kind of friends and fans one has.[10]

While these could be very exciting opportunities for marketers, they also pose the risks of consumer backlash if we don't understand the privacy dynamic. In the consumer's mind, all of these practices to defraud, deceive, track them down wherever they are, and watch everything they do are lumped together and constitute a growing "invasion of my privacy," driving policy makers and regulators to be engaged. And as Abraham Lincoln said, "Public opinion in this country is everything."

---

9. Protecting Consumer Privacy in an Era of Rapid Change: Recommendations for Businesses and Policymakers.
http://www.ftc.gov/opa/2012/03/privacyframework.shtm

10. FTC Compliance Guide for Business for the CAN SPAM Act of 2003 (Controlling the Assault of Non-Solicited Pornography and Marketing Act)
http://www.ftc.gov/bcp/edu/pubs/business/ecommerce/bus61.shtm

Are We Our Own Worst Enemy?

Evidence suggests marketers could easily head down the same path with these new marketing activities that they walked down with telemarketing and sweepstakes. They may be too focused on short-term profits and ultimately sacrifice or severely limit the long-term viability of certain marketing methods.

The movement toward integrated multichannel marketing has reaped great rewards for companies that have successfully deployed the strategy. Peter Drucker wrote that the only reason a business exists is to "get, keep and grow their customers." However, companies can focus too much on the "getting" part and not enough on the "keep and grow" parts. Companies must understand how their customers' attitudes about information use translate into sustaining and expanding a long-term profitable relationship. It goes without saying that in order to be successful today, a company must develop a "trusted" relationship with its customers. And to develop trust, customers have to believe that a company will responsibly use the personal information it keeps about its customers. Furthermore, customers have to be listened to and treated with respect.

Respect is one of the key components of trust. And the good news is that developing an integrated multichannel marketing strategy provides companies with the vehicle for greater customer interaction in order to understand their needs, show respect and learn their preferences. However, it is a cyclical process; in order for customers to be comfortable expressing their preferences, they have to trust a company enough to believe it will honor them. It is hard to understand how sweepstakes offers that misled customers into believing they had won, or telemarketing calls that were overly aggressive, or repeated unwanted emails or text messages where a business refused to honor a consumer's request to stop, can possibly build trust.

Companies Must Discover Their Customers' Preferences!

Everyone engaged in integrated multichannel marketing must learn from these history lessons and begin a dialogue with customers about how personal information is handled while respecting the customers' expressed preferences about how and when to be contacted.

Back as far as the early 1970s, four globally accepted fair information practices were introduced. These were the foundation of the privacy principles commonly recognized today and must become a part of every company's customer relationship strategy:

- **Transparency** in the form of a privacy notice or policy has historically been the vehicle for educating a consumer about information collection practices and providing the foundation for a trusted relationship. It is the means to supply customers with information about (1) who the company is, (2) what information it collects, (3) how the company uses that information, (4) what choices the consumer has about how information is used and shared with others, and (5) how to get in touch with the company.

    One word of caution: Notices should be as short as possible, clear and easy to read. Companies should provide a summary or the highlights of their full privacy notice for the customer if the full, legally compliant version becomes too long and unfriendly.[11] Also, companies should look for more innovative ways to educate consumers about information collection and use practices. The idea of putting an icon on a web site or in an ad that is behaviorally targeted that the consumer can click on to learn more and exercise choice is an example of such an innovative practice. New interactive technologies offer lots of opportunity for creativity that we haven't had available in the offline world.

• **Control** defines what kind of choices a company gives its customers about how their information is used. Control must be both appropriate and effective. It must include offering the customer the ability to opt-out of having information about them shared with unaffiliated third parties for marketing purposes. It should also include a chance for the consumer to express other preferences about how they would like to be contacted by a company.

Thus far, much of the control discussion has centered on whether opt-in or opt-out is the best approach. However, what the consumer wants is a volume control, not just an on/off switch. Keep this in mind when developing an approach to control, for it is a critical means of showing consumers that the company will listen to their feedback and honor their preferences.

It is through dialogue about control that companies can best determine where their customers fall into Westin's three categories or MasterCard's five. This will give a company the needed information to personalize the approach used in marketing and servicing customers in ways that increase the trust factor rather than irritate a customer or even worse, destroy their trust.

• **Access**, the least visible principle, has been a hotly debated topic both in the U.S. and abroad. While only required by a few laws in the U.S., it is a universal requirement in many other countries and one that has become the subject of regulatory debate in the U.S. For now, at the very least it should mean providing a customer with access to information that they have provided and that is critical to a company's decision-making so the consumer can be assured that it is correct. The process of fulfilling a request for access is also a wonderful opportunity to engage in more dialogue with the customer.

Access also implies the ability to correct information that is found to be in error. While this can be complicated and, in some cases, costly for companies, correction must be factored into a company's privacy strategy.

Finally, the issue of authentication comes into play with the access principle. Providing access to personal information to an unauthorized person is a privacy violation, not a confidence-building practice. Careful consideration must be given to authenticating the identity of individuals prior to granting them access, especially to sensitive information.

• **Security** has become a much more important principle over the last few years.

---

11. Ten Steps to Deliver a Multilayered Privacy Notice
http://www.hunton.com/files/tbl_s47Details%5CFileUpload265%5C1405%5CTen_Steps_whitepaper.pdf

This is the one area where there does not need to be any dialogue with the consumer since they expect companies to keep both personal and anonymous information safe. And security is getting harder to provide, with the rapid advancements in technology and more information collected and used by businesses. Finally, security should be viewed not only from an authorized access perspective, but also from an insider theft perspective. A company's own employees may present the greatest risk.

At a minimum, if a company embraces these four principles in its integrated marketing activities, it can begin to move forward with the trust component of the customer relationship. If this is coupled with a marketing approach that shows you respect your customers, you will move even further up the trust ladder.

What Is Required to Gain a Customer's Trust?

While we may not like it, we have to acknowledge that the business community has lost much ground in the trust equation. We have to be on a positive trajectory, and we can.

Marty Abrams, Executive Director and Chief Strategist at the Foundation for Information Accountability and Governance, developed a trust equation some years ago that is still extremely relevant:

(**T = VPS**) **T**rust is the product of "**V**alue" times "**P**rivacy" times "**S**ecurity."

Value can have a scale attached to it ranging from zero to very high. However, **P**rivacy and **S**ecurity are either a one or a zero in the minds of consumers. Thus a problem with either one can totally destroy the **T**rust that has otherwise been developed.

In today's exciting but turbulent times, I believe we need to add one other component to the Abrams trust equation: the variable of Experience (**T=VEPS**). The **E**xperience a customer has in doing business with a company is also a factor in developing or destroying trust and the good news is that **E**xperience, like value, has a scale. Treating a customer with respect greatly contributes to a positive experience even when there are product- or service-related problems.

Some industries, such as financial services and health care, are already regulated and are required to provide notices and offer certain choices. Other industries will become regulated, and we can expect virtually every marketer to be required to follow in some way the four globally accepted fair information practices.

But regulation is never the highway to trust. Regulation, at its best, establishes a foundation on which to build — nothing more. Real trust requires going above and beyond what is required by law. Trust is built on layering three practices together into the relationship a company has with its customers.

The foundation layer is the law. The second layer is industry best practices and the final layer is a company's own policies:

- **The Law:** If all a company has is the foundation based in law, that may keep it out of trouble with the regulators, but it won't achieve a high degree of trust with its customers. Laws are designed to be the baseline, not an example of relationship enhancing best practices.

- **Best Practices:** Following recommended best practices or industry codes of conduct can help move a company's trust rating up. Many industries have developed and continue to evolve their ethical guidelines and recommended best practices that will help build strong long-term relationships. These should be carefully studied and adopted as appropriate.
- **Company Policies:** A high degree of trust, however, will not be achieved without adding onto these first two layers (a) a set of company policies that are appropriate for the company's products and services, (b) a degree of relatability to the kind of personal information a company collects about its customers, and (c) an appropriateness in the various marketing methods used to interact with customers—face-to-face, over the phone, online and via a mobile or other wireless device.

A company that is actively engaged in following the law, adheres to industry best practices, and has developed its own policies and procedures that respond to the concerns and desires of its customers can achieve the highest trust rating possible—and one that contributes to business success. In the book *The Speed of Trust* by Stephen M.R. Covey, the author references a Columbia Business School study by Professor John Whitney who claims that "mistrust doubles the cost of doing business." What more compelling argument do you need to adopt a trust-based business approach to your customers?

Managing the Trust Equation Is Just Good Business!

We can only speculate about what would have happened if we had shown more respect and responded sooner to the concerns consumers expressed about sweepstakes and telemarketing. We might not have a sweepstakes law, and we might not have over 80% of the households on a federally run, national do-not-call registry. That experience shows that if we don't practice responsible use of information about consumers, we will have broad, prescriptive legislation limiting our use of information and potentially even limiting how and when we can use certain media to market and service customers.

You don't really know your customers if you fail to understand where they fall in Westin's or MasterCard's segmentation of the population. And you won't be nearly as successful in keeping and growing your customers if they don't have a high level of trust in you. Find out what each customer's preferences are and use that to make a significant contribution to your bottom line.

JENNIFER BARRETT GLASGOW, CIPP, the first Chief Privacy Officer in the world, manages global information practices for Acxiom Corporation, which helps the world's largest companies transform data into business intelligence. Jennifer is called upon by businesses, policy makers and the media to provide insight on how information enhances business processes while addressing privacy concerns. Jennifer serves on the DMA Safe Harbor

Ethics Committee and was former chair of the Committee on Environment and Social Responsibility, is an Executive Member of the Center for Information Policy Leadership, is an Advisory Board Member for the Political and Economic Research Center, is a board member of the Foundation for Accountable Information Governance and is a member of the University of Texas Chancellor's Council and College of Natural Science's Advisory Council, and the Arkansas Academy of Computing. She can be reached at jennifer.glasgow@acxiom.com.

READING
12

Multichannel Marketing

DEBRA ELLIS
Wilson & Ellis Consulting

M arketing channels are emerging and evolving at the fastest rate in history. The days when marketers could wait months or years to see if a new channel is viable are gone. Waiting can be a death sentence because competition is increasing exponentially. Geographical and logistic limits that historically reduced competitive entrances into regional areas do not exist in the global economy. These changes have permanently altered the way businesses identify and connect with customers.

The definition of a channel as an organizational unit that transfers products and services does not fit the new marketplace. The addition of new customer connection platforms and consolidation of departmental units requires an updated description. A marketing channel is a path that companies use to connect with customers to create relationships and generate revenue. The most prominent paths in today's marketplace are bricks and mortar stores, e-commerce, direct marketing and social media. Mobile marketing is emerging and expected to become a dominate channel. Who knows what the future will bring. (Note: Catalogs, telemarketing, promotional mail, email, and direct response television are considered part of direct marketing for this reading.)

Social media is a game changer, but not in the manner anticipated by early adopters. There is a global conversation. Some of it is about companies, products, and services, but it has not replaced traditional marketing activities. Instead, it provides businesses with unprecedented access to customers and prospects. The promise of one-to-one marketing is realized with social media. Companies can connect with customers and prospects individually, monitor personal conversations, and access friends and family using a variety of platforms. This access comes at a price. Participation is labor intensive and will not generate revenue without a strategic plan that crosses channels. It requires a major organizational shift from silo management to integrated marketing.

Management of the silo model is relatively simple. There are no requirements to integrate or even communicate with other channels. Even if someone tries to integrate, the different systems, processes, and policies limit efforts to cross channel lines. Customers are expected to choose their channel of choice, and if they don't, they are assigned one in an effort to manage the return on marketing dollars.

The silo structure creates a competitive environment within the corporation. Each channel has its own marketing budget. Attempts to bundle offerings meet resistance at every turn because successfully crediting sales to the right division is nearly impossible. Marketing expenses rise dramatically without a matching return. Consistent branding is challenging due to the variances between the channels and their management. And, customers rarely follow their assigned buying patterns. They cross channels expecting to be recognized as a valuable asset wherever they shop.

These challenges started the downfall of the silo channel business model. When economic and customer analytics showed that separate divisions created a redundancy of services and limited growth opportunities, companies began to consider transitioning from multiple channels within separate departments to integrated multichannel management.

Customer expectations are the catalyst expediting the shift to multichannel marketing. Today's consumers are demanding a seamless brand experience. They want the ability to browse through a catalog, order online, and return to the store. Or, they want to order online and pick up at the store. Or, they choose any other combination of service across channels that you can imagine. Providing these options improves the company's overall performance because cross channel shoppers have higher lifetime values than their single channel counterparts and are 25%–50% more profitable.

There are also operational benefits to a multichannel marketing strategy. The consolidation of databases, call centers, and management teams reduces costs. The ease and low expense of listing items online provides a perfect resource for inventory liquidation. email is a cost-effective alternative to snail mail for customer communication. Mobile allows instant access to people while they shop. And, social media expands a company's marketing reach exponentially. The best business strategies use one channel's strength to offset another's weakness.

Multichannel marketing utilizes technological advances to connect with customers in ways unimaginable a few years ago. Detailed information about customers, their buying preferences, and patterns is available. This analysis identifies opportunities and vulnerabilities allowing companies in both business-to-consumer and business-to-business to optimize their return and define new growth strategies.

How do you grow a business? The most common method is to expand existing channels to increase the customer base and sales. If you have stores, open more. If you have a catalog, add mailings. If you have a web site, increase traffic by driving more customers to your existing site or expanding into web communities like eBay and Yahoo!

You can also enter new channels. This approach is more complicated than building on past successes because it requires different processes, tools, and skill sets. Direct marketing companies with analytical backgrounds from catalog, telemarketing, and direct response advertising are best suited for adding Internet, mobile or social media channels. While the media and benchmarks differ, the skill set and tools required to analyze consumers shopping patterns and transactional data are very similar.

Retail stores without a catalog face the biggest challenge as they expand into alternative channels since data warehousing is relatively new to them. Capturing customer information is very challenging when shoppers can enter the store and browse for hours without making a purchase. Cash transactions provide sales data without identifying anything about the customers.

Web sites provide extensive information about customers and their shopping experience. Every click can be monitored to see how consumers browse online. The volume of data available is incredible. Savvy marketing managers are very selective about the data they process. They search for the information that can be used to increase sales, lifetime value, and profitability. This includes customer retention, lifespan, lifetime value, channel flow, and crossover.

Utilizing the data from multiple channels to enhance service and reduce costs is the best growth strategy for retail companies today. It requires a complete understanding of customer preferences and integration of marketing and operational initiatives. Analytics provide the information needed to make quality management decisions.

Customer Analytics

There are seven types of customers:

1. **Newbies**—Customers who have purchased 1 or 2 times. These shoppers have not established loyalty to the company. They may be at a stage where they have limited needs for the product line. Or, they may be testing to see if the quality and service match their standards. Either way, they are not committed to return.

2. **Rising Stars**—Shoppers who have purchased three or more times within twelve months. These customers are trending towards loyalty with increasing sales and responsiveness to marketing. They need encouragement to continue their movement to the next level.

3. **Platinum**—Customers with consistent performance season after season. They respond well to marketing and have reliable buying patterns. This group will typically follow Pareto's law and account for 20% of the customer database while providing up to 80% of the sales. They are the most profitable segment and valuable asset of any company.

4. **Falling Stars**—Platinum customers with reduced performance. They may be nearing the end of their buying lifespan. If this is the situation, attempts to reactivate are futile. In some cases, they become Falling Stars due to a service failure. When this happens, they can be reactivated before they reach the Rest in Peace stage.

5. **Bargain Hunters**—These shoppers only purchase sale items. They respond well to sales and liquidations and rarely transition into the regular customer buying cycle. They are a valuable segment if the marketing is limited to sales promotions. They provide a vehicle for liquidating overstocks and poor buying decisions.

6. **Rests in Peace**—These customers have completed their lifespan with the company. It may be due to a lifestyle change. For example, customers of companies specializing in children's products will leave when their children are grown and return when grandchildren appear. Operational problems can lead to an early termination of the lifespan.

7. **Social**—People who fall into the social type are not customers in the traditional sense. They have not purchased products or services from the company, but they talk about them in social networks. They can add or decrease value depending on the information they share. Monitoring their activity and responding when appropriate is a vital part of an effective marketing strategy.

New shoppers with a full lifespan will typically follow the pattern of Newbie, Rising Star, Platinum, Falling Star, and Rest in Peace. Bargain hunters are easily identified by their product selection. They only buy sale items. Established customers may shift from Platinum to Falling Star back to Platinum as their lives change.

Lifespan is the time that starts with the first purchase and ends with the last. A natural lifespan varies by company and product line. For example, customers for maternity apparel will typically buy for 4–6 months then stop until the next pregnancy. Techies may buy from an electronic store their entire adult life.

The natural lifespan can be altered by the company's performance. Poor service, merchandising, and marketing can shorten the life of a buyer. Inversely, a customer who has cycled into the Falling Star or Rest in Peace segments can be rejuvenated with new product lines, offers, and improved service.

There is a marketing axiom that it costs five to ten times more to acquire a new customer than it does to keep a current one. Customer retention measures the movement of individual buyers to insure that acquisition exceeds attrition. It is possible for a company's customer file to show growth while losing their most valuable buyers. For example, the chart below is an analytics summary for a retail business:

EXHIBIT R12.1: RETAIL ANALYTICS SUMMARY

Customers:	Year 1	Year 2	Year 3
Active	25,756	28,332	31,165
House File Growth Rate		10%	10%
First Purchase	7,727	8,742	9,172
Last Purchase	2,612	4,723	5,247
Acquisition Rate		16.5%	14.9%
Attrition Rate		10.1%	16.7%
House File Mail Count	52,986	61,728	70,900
Avg $/Active Customer	$169.66	$180.46	$208.35
Avg Ord/Active Customer	3.2	3.3	3.5
Lifetime Value	$848.32	$902.30	$1,041.75
Annual Sales	$4,369,763	$5,112,793	$6,493,338
Sales Growth Rate		17%	27%

This company has solid growth in sales and customer base. Their average order and number of orders per customer is increasing. On the surface, it is thriving. Unfortunately, not all is well, because attrition is exceeding acquisition. Newbies are replacing older, more profitable customers. If this fits with the natural lifespan, there is little cause for concern. If not, the source of the problem must be found and eliminated before the enterprise enters a downward spiral.

Lifetime value (LTV) is the present value of customers over their natural lifespan. It is helpful in determining marketing budgets because it provides a tangible indicator of return over acquisition expenses. In other words, it helps marketing teams determine how much money they can spend to acquire a customer and remain profitable. LTV is a relative number since many external factors can alter lifespan, average order, and profitability. The methodology for calculating LTV varies by company due to intrinsic factors.

Channel Analytics

Channel analytics are the metrics specific to the origin. Customer analytics begins with a focus on the complete customer file regardless of channel flow, crossover, or source. The next stage drills down into the data segmenting by origin and movement across channels. For example, customer analytics are created for customers whose first purchase is online. Then, they will be created for customers whose first purchase is by phone or mail. Finally, they are created for in store first purchase customers. Once they are completed, they are compared to determine strengths and weaknesses.

Customers who move across channels are the most valuable segment. These customers are typically more interested in convenience than cost. Service is vital to their shopping experience. It has a long-term effect on customer value and lifespan. Cross-channel shopping allows the buyer to choose their media and provides the company more opportunities to sell. Average orders are higher in dollars and quantity.

Each channel has metrics that are specific to their medium. Store analytics include sales per square foot, comparable store sales, and traffic conversion. Catalog analytics include response rate, income per piece, and fill ratios. web analytics track visitor interaction, conversion patterns, and origin. All channels measure transactional data.

There is also information available about how your customers shop elsewhere. This can be used to identify new product lines or company alliances. There is so much data available that a lifetime could be spent reviewing reports without ever applying the information. It is critical for information managers to avoid data overload and insure data integrity. While some information is interesting, it is hard to leverage it to improve sales or reduce costs. Other analytics may have application and be impossible to validate.

Applicable information is used to create personalized shopping experiences. Studies have shown that the shopping experience is the key factor in customer loyalty and long term profitability. Globalization is eliminating traditional competitive advantages such as unique product lines and pricing since most consumer products are available from multiple sources at a variety of price points. A quick search using a quality search engine will provide a list of competing companies with the same products at a variety of prices.

Multichannel Marketing Management

A positive shopping experience provides the best competitive advantage. Customers return when they have previously enjoyed the convenience and service of a retail operation. A good multichannel model has innovative combinations of channels, systems, processes, and policies designed to match customers' shopping preferences. It creates a unique enterprise that is impossible to duplicate because it has its own personality and corporate culture.

Customers should be encouraged to add channels instead of migrating to another medium. This can be a result of subtle marketing such as adding an 800 number to every web page, a URL to every catalog page, and social media information to every marketing item. Or, it can more aggressive by offering special promotions to customers when they cross channels.

The shopping experience begins when a customer starts the process. It may be an excursion to the store to browse or a mission to find a specific product. Every touchpoint is an opportunity for the company to influence long-term loyalty. A touchpoint is the direct contact between the consumer and the company. It includes direct mail pieces, store interactions, kiosks, package delivery, web sites, call centers, mobile texts, and social media networks. The brand must be consistently promoted at every point to insure a positive shopping experience. For example, a company known for high-quality, personalized service would have superior packaging for every product delivered to a customer's home. Anything less is inconsistent with the image.

Leveraging Resources

One of the major advantages of the new retail multichannel model is the ability to leverage resources between channels. Every unit has unique benefits and limitations. They include:

- Email is an efficient, effective, and economical method for communicating with customers and prospects. As a marketing tool, it provides opportunities to drive web traffic, announce store events, and promote direct mail offerings. Operationally, the proactive communication about service concerns such as inventory shortages and shipping information reduces costs. Disadvantages include a short tail (time between first order and last one for a promotion) and deliverability challenges.
- Stores offer customers the ability to connect with the product and sales team. It is the most personal channel because there is face-to-face contact and the opportunity to touch and test items. How do you adequately describe the feel of silk against your skin? Or, how do you show the detail of a hand embroidered jacket in a photograph. While the store provides the best opportunity for interaction, it is limited in its ability to provide depth of merchandise. Floor space limitations require the merchants to display the very best items and omit others that might become best sellers. Catalogs and web sites can offer multiple combinations of colors and sizes because their inventory housing is less expensive. Strategically placed kiosks offset product display limitations by providing an opportunity for

the customer to place an online or catalog order while shopping in the store. They infinitely expand the sales per square foot potential.

- Catalogs and other direct mail promotions provide shopping convenience. Customers can browse through offerings of items unavailable locally while waiting for the doctor or soccer practice to end. Once they make their decision, purchases may be made via the Internet, call center, or through the mail. Mailing are expensive so total exposure is limited. Space limitations limit the descriptive details.
- Web sites provide the ultimate self-service experience. When they are created with quality usability standards, customers can easily navigate through products and information to find exactly what they need. Orders taken via the web have lower associated costs. Integrating trigger emails with Internet shopping increases sales and profitability.
- Social media provides one-to-one interaction with customers and prospects. It is not a direct sales channel, but it serves well as a funnel for other channels. Customers who interact with company representatives in a social network tend to spend 40%–60% more than their non-social counterparts.

Evolution

Transitioning from multiple channels to an integrated multichannel organization is an evolutionary process. It requires analysis, design, testing, and redesign to find the best operating model for the specific organization. Companies in the same industry, selling the same products will find that their optimal business model is different from their competition.

Creating an optimized cross channel operation is a complex process. There are six stages in the systematic approach. Following these steps provides the process required to incorporate new channels into an existing business as they become viable.

1. **Establish Presence**
   A presence in a channel requires the doors opened, the site launched, promotional pieces mailed, or consistent social media posts. The initial presence doesn't have to be flawless, only functional. Enhancements will come as customer preferences dictate how the channels need to evolve and work with each other.
2. **Align Elements**
   The alignment of product, price, service, and image across channels creates a consistent shopping experience. These items do not have to be the same, but they must support the company's value proposition and match customers' expectations. For example, many retailers offer items unique to each channel to encourage cross channel shopping.
3. **Integrate Channels**
   Channel integration is the most challenging aspect of multichannel management. Established silo operations have a variety of systems, processes, and policies that are often completely incompatible. Their software operates on different platforms; employees have been trained to consider other units as

competitors, and physical locations present barriers. Successful multichannel management requires compatibility and cooperation.

4. **Enhance Performance**

   Technological and analytical advances combined with customer and employee feedback provide new opportunities to improve service and functionality. Capitalizing on these opportunities solidifies the company's market position and encourages long term loyalty.

5. **Leverage Resources**

   Each channel has strengths and weaknesses that differ from others. Using the benefits of one channel to offset the pitfalls of another strengthens the corporation as a whole.

6. **Refine Model**

   Multichannel management is a process, not a project. It requires a climate of cooperation and innovation to be successful. The corporate attitude must be one of continuous improvement. The culture should encourage experimentation as the company navigates through uncharted territory.

DEBRA ELLIS is the principal of Wilson & Ellis Consulting in Asheville, North Carolina. Her firm provides advisory services and customized solutions to direct and interactive multichannel marketing organizations. Wilson & Ellis works closely with clients to fully understand the uniqueness of each organization and find the best strategies for resolving business challenges. Clients have included National Allergy, Hobby Builders Supply, Jacuzzi, Costco, and The Body Shop.

READING
13

History Matters: International Direct Marketing From 1981 On

CHARLES PRESCOTT

The Prescott Report

To look backward for a while is to refresh the eye, to restore it, and to render it more fit for its prime function of looking forward.—Margaret Fairless Barber

Any economic environment is the result of two major factors: demography and technology. Those two elements both describe and dictate an economy. Since 1981, changes in those two foundations have revolutionized the practice of direct marketing and contributed to its international adoption. Direct marketing itself hasn't changed in its principles, wherever it goes: right offer, right person, and right time. As we will show, the best of the best today looks pretty much like yesterday's.

It must be also be noted at the outset that the tools and the prevalence of those tools have changed beyond recognition, and become vastly more common than when Ronald Reagan was President, Margaret Thatcher was Prime Minister of the United Kingdom, or when China and Russia were ruled by Mao and Brezhnev, respectively.

Direct marketing is no longer an exclusive club whose members are predominantly in the United States and in a few European cities. Well over half of all entries and winners of the U.S. Direct Marketing Association's (DMA) annual Echo Awards competition are now from outside the United States. Probably 80% of those submitted to the Cannes competition are likewise.

The spread of direct marketing knowledge and skills has occurred primarily with big brands, which bring their agencies with them. This has been paralleled with the technological revolution, which is now changing direct marketing worldwide and making it an even more exciting discipline.

Agencies Spread the Discipline

Agencies worldwide act as brand advocates. They incidentally become direct marketing advocates. Their influence and impact have gone with — and supported the brands of—many nations, from the United States and the United Kingdom to France, Germany, the Netherlands, Korea and Japan.

A report from GroupM, a WPP company[1] examined the state of use of interactive media in advertising in the 28 countries that were important to the Group. They were able to determine the percentage of media investment spent online, and for what objectives. Importantly, "direct response" as an objective was a common finding within the 10 industries studied. And, yes, the study suggested that "the Internet is direct marketing on steroids," as author Seth Godin noted.

Moreover, as the reference to 28 countries in the GroupM survey shows, agencies and addressable advertising seeking a response are now global.

In a survey conducted by the author, the DMA discovered that direct marketing specialist firms Grey and Proximity had offices in 49 and 48 countries, respectively. And of course Omnicom and WPP, with revenues from brands in excess of $12 and $11 billion respectively, are even more broadly distributed.

It is not just big agencies that spread direct marketing and enhance it. Companies often turn to smaller agencies for local expertise or unique talents. The Interdirect Network of independent database/direct agencies, founded in 1988, has participants in 28 countries. It was formed to help clients execute international or cross-border campaigns. Their client list has recently included British Airways, CompuServe, Glenfiddich, Hapimag, Nilfisk, Shell, Walt Disney, Microsoft, Monroe, G.N.Netcom and Volvo.

Agencies, brands and businesses are now no longer "international", but global, and they have taken direct marketing with them.

How did we get here?

Technology, Infrastructure and Tools

The infrastructure for every aspect of direct marketing has changed, making possibilities that would have been the stuff of dreams 40 years ago. The world has changed beyond recognition, creating opportunities that are beyond even dreams.

Thanks to digitization and the mass production of optical cable, call centers and data processing can be located cost effectively nearly anywhere, making for interesting discoveries of both real and imagined comparative advantages. In 1981, a trans-Atlantic telephone call cost over $5 per minute. With plummeting phone costs, Ireland became the call center capital of Europe and followed this with other technological improvements. As a result, the Irish diaspora came home. India thinks it has discovered a comparative advantage based on the English language and some rudimentary training alone. Results on this score are mixed.

In 1981, according to Freddy Rosales of the Argentine agency di Paola & Asociados, there were no Argentine call centers. These only started in 1989 with two companies and about 150 seats. Now Argentina is internationally competitive as a call center hub.

Digitization makes printing in distant local markets under controlled circumstances possible. Hybrid mail (mail delivered using a combination of electronic and physical delivery) can now work, nearly instantly. The Posts of France, Germany and

---

[1] Interaction: All Change: marketing in addressable media, April 2007, GroupM, London.

Italy all have competing hybrid mail services. The Post from France specializes in competing across the Atlantic to the U.S. market.

The marketing power of the letter has been combined with the distance-dissolving ubiquity of the Web. Until recently, postage costs plummeted and mail volumes increased worldwide. Video, introduced as a marketing tool in the 1980s, was slowly on the way out as merchants moved to DVD and CDs. Now there is resurgence as rich media and video on the Web are used by companies globally.

Digitization makes the Web possible. The Web itself was a toy in the hands of a few scientists in major universities working to build a network of easy communication for scholars. America Online started business as Quantum Service in 1985. Netscape was founded in 1989, and it still took another 10 years for a critical commercial mass to occur. It would not be until the late 1990s that merchants began to understand that the Internet was a real-time interactive shop window.

In the late 1970s there was much experimentation with "video text", which never took off in the United States. In 1978, France Telecom began installing mini-tel machines in French homes, intending for these primarily to be electronic phone number look-up services. They soon evolved into the pre-cursors of online shopping. In fact, their ubiquity actually delayed the take-up of PCs in French homes until the last six years. Since then, that change has dramatically impacted French catalog companies, some of the oldest and largest catalogers in the world.

Computerization has changed the conduct of direct marketing and impacted the world. Most of us can articulate the many benefits of having a 1981-era mainframe computer on our desktop. We can perform database management, analysis, segmentation and regression analysis of startling complexity with relative ease. Art directors have mastered a bewildering array of computer tools to accomplish more cost-effectively the ordinary and mundane and—even more startling—the imaginative. We forget that we could do this already in 1981, just not so easily.

Jon Lambert, president of data processing company Acton, reminds us of the advances in computing since 1981: "The increase in speed and storage and decrease in cost of computers. This is probably more important than the Internet itself because the Internet wouldn't be usable without this functionality occurring. Can you remember as recently as the mid-1980s, having to do massive amounts of backup on those clumsy old reels? An iPod carries a ton more data than a semi-trailer load of those poor old tapes! And you don't have to mail them."

And we could go on and on about digital photography and catalogs, digital printing and new inks. The travel specialist company Thomas Cook demanded that its agencies digitize their artwork and photographs and centrally store them in a searchable database, ultimately saving millions of pounds in photography costs alone.

But there is a context in which all of this occurred that made it all so much more ubiquitous.

Economic, Social, and Political Deregulation; Political Consolidation

The deployment of first copper and then fiber-optic cable created potential, but the potential was not realized until Ma Bell was broken up and the liberalization and privatization wave swept the telecoms world, which has occurred worldwide, from Argentina to Shanghai and Stockholm to Sydney.

This brought down prices and permitted companies to provide customer service globally, 24 hours day, 7 days a week. Customers, be they consumers or businesses, could be touched, assisted, upsold, and mollified at any time for mere pennies a call. Your author can remember being a student in Paris in 1968 and calling home once, by appointment, on Christmas. The cost was prohibitive. Now it is affordable to call home every night from wherever one is.

Deregulation occurred in the air, also. Airlines were freed to compete, first in the United States and then in Europe. Government-controlled pricing came slowly to an end and new entrants appeared to carry people and, importantly, cargo, around the world. Adjusting for inflation and currency valuation changes, it now costs less to ship a 10-pound product by FedEx or even USPS than it did in 1981, and the package arrives in two or three days, not two or three weeks. As shipper or addressee, you can track its progress on the Internet from your desktop computer. (You can also track the flight your daughter is on from Beijing to New York.)

If you are in Japan and you have bought a Dell computer, the computer was probably delivered that way from its factory in China or Malaysia. You call in the order to an international toll-free number on Sunday morning; it's manufactured that afternoon, shipped in the evening, delivered to Japan Monday, matched to a screen and keyboard and delivered to you in Osaka on Tuesday.

Both people and goods travel farther and faster and more cheaply than ever before. This article was written on a computer in an airplane flying non-stop from Shanghai to New York. The round-trip ticket cost $1,308 dollars, about the price of a good Italian men's suit in Milano, or one month's rent in a Boston studio apartment, or six months' salary for a recent university graduate in computer science from a Chinese or Indian university.

That last example hints at another dramatic revolution of a political nature: the opening of China. This is proving to be one of the most phenomenal developments of all, and it is one example of the other great deregulation that began with the Uruguay round of trade negotiations and the creation of the WTO. Like NAFTA and the creation of the European Common Market, the passage of investment funds and goods has been eased incredibly over the last generation, literally dissolving borders. True international business-to-business direct marketing has increasingly made economic sense, especially over the last 15 years, as businesses discover that tariffs are lowered or removed.

The greatest of these deregulations, the creation of one European economic area, is perhaps the most historically significant event of all times. It is producing radical changes in Europe. Brilliant visionary leadership, acting at the conclusion of World War II, understood that for peace to last in Europe, where nations had been at war with each other since pre-history, the borders needed to be weakened and the economies integrated. Their vision brought peace, and an increasing "field of peace" reaching even the Russian border. It also has resulted in one of the world's richest laboratories for "international marketing".

In 1981, there were real borders for people, money, and goods in each European country, each with its own economic policy. In 1992, the borders came down. In short, the monopolies of each country on the regulation of their economies and markets were abolished. And with the introduction of the Euro in 2002, one of the most astounding peaceful revolutions in history has taken yet another major step, one that increasingly makes a marketer's dream of Europe-wide campaigns and business possible.

Signage provider Seton, with businesses throughout Europe, now uses one catalog layout for the region, but local language copy in a common template of product pictures. The Swiss and German websites share an online catalog (with turnable pages) in German. Where it can, it has one price insert in Euros.

Brussels is now so important to direct marketing as a profession that the national DMAs found it critical to establish FEDMA in1992, which has been followed by the Internet Advertising Bureau, an American export.

Finally, one of the greatest, and also peaceful, revolutions of the century occurred in 1989 when the Berlin Wall was smashed, the Cold War ended, Russia began to develop and Eastern Europe began its interrupted journey toward fulfilling its pre-World War II promise as a thriving modern economic area. Of course, with the end of Russia's controlled economy, Finland had to learn a new trade other than being an entrepot trader between Russia and the world, and the Finns have unleashed their technical excellence and given us Nokia and Telia and a myriad of technological forerunners.

Direct marketing is starting to thrive in Eastern Europe and the Baltics, demonstrated by the success of direct response television and catalog company Studio Moderna, and the fact that at least six direct marketing associations have been established in that region in the last few years.

China was a very grim place in 1981. Shenzhen was a farming village with no hotels, just a government rest house. I stayed there. Now, Shenzhen and the surrounding Guangzhou Province originates somewhere in excess of 50% of all merchandise sold in consumer catalogs in the United States and Japan. China now has two fledgling DMAs, competing post offices, at least four nationwide catalog companies, offices from all of the major direct marketing agencies, and a population so mobile phone crazy that some people have as many as four or five.

Also under this heading of "deregulation," two quiet but nevertheless very important demographic changes must be noted. In the developed part of the world, women have entered the workforce in large numbers, transforming the size, make-up and dynamics of family life in Japan, the United States and Europe, as well as shopping habits.

Liberalization has unleashed creative energy and able hands. Currently one-third of the Commissioners of the European Commission are women. As a corollary, families have become smaller, more urban, and wealthier. In fact, in all but a few of these regions, smaller families mean a shrinking population whose average age is rising. What these families buy, and how, has changed.

Women have developed a new image of themselves as independent and self-actualizing members of the wider community. They work in offices and need business attire. More of them raise their children as single parents. Families need prepackaged meals.

Paradoxically, in Japan and the United States, what these families have less and less of is time, which direct marketers help save by providing distance purchasing options through catalogs and the Internet. In Japan, China and France, many catalog orders tend to be "group orders" from informal sets of workmates in an office, who are predominantly women.

Parallel with the evolution of smaller families, we have the graying of the workforce in the industrialized countries. Graying and rich. According to the OECD, some 75% of the assets and two-thirds of the stock market wealth of the 29 wealthiest countries in the world are owned by people over the age of 50. In short, the average age of the consuming public in the best markets for the consumer side of our industry has increased by some 15 years in the last 25 years!

The Spread of the Practice. Who Do You Mail To? Direct Marketing Finds New Niches

If you wanted to do a mailing promoting your products into Asia, Europe or Latin America in 1981, you had a tough time finding lists. Not much existed except the usual magazine suspects. In fact, you probably couldn't even find many of those, and what you did find was on these huge tapes, that were bulky and slow to ship. Technology today reduces costs, eliminates loss, and speeds up the process. No shipping tapes around at great expense. You click "attach" and "send", or simply paste to the SMTP address, and it's done. The data can go to the client or processor on the other side of the world in seconds, for free, not in a week and for a lot of money.

There was a period when such lists were relatively available as publishers and conference businesses generated new names to file at a rapid clip. International English publications were especially responsive lists. Some of these are still used, and they have been joined by new conference and loyalty program lists, but in fact, practitioners complain that the universe is somewhat stunted.

More and more countries have legal systems and ethical standards that have discouraged owners from sharing data. Recent legal changes regarding privacy in Germany, basically requiring permission from an individual to transfer his name and address to another company, have hurt the list industry there. And, of course, some paranoid markets still exist where you have to trust your mailing to a lettershop that literally applies the labels—markets like China and sometimes Brazil. But even in China, lists at last are appearing, and among major companies in Brazil the list practice looks like it does anywhere else.

The Universal Postal Union Has Played a Role

In 1998, the United Nations specialized body known as the Universal Postal Union established a self-funding project known as the Direct Mail Advisory Board (DMAB). It was charged with assisting Posts in developing direct mail programs. Through its program of in-person and online training, research and publication, it has introduced the disciplines of direct marketing and direct mail to many Posts. As a direct consequence of its work, there are robust postal product offerings, infrastructure and even direct marketing membership associations in many countries, including Saudi Arabia, China, South Africa, Brazil, and the Caribbean and in Central Europe.

For example, acting on the information gained from the DMAB, China Post has partnered with Acxiom to establish a large database of consumer data, with about 10 data points. As of this writing it contained about 150 million individuals. This is not much in a country of over a billion, but this is probably the most attractive consumer population. It has also established a China Direct Mail Association to help spread knowledge of the practice.

The Posts of South Africa and Brazil, learning from the DMAB, Royal Mail (UK) and Deutsche Poste, have talented professionals in their Direct Mail Centers who hold direct marketing courses and offer guidance and information about direct mail and direct marketing in general. In addition, South Africa has over the last several years rapidly expanded its address system into rural areas, enabling small communities to participate more fully in the economy. The Brazilian Post partnered with the largest consumer bank in Brazil, Bradesco, to establish branches inside postal facilities throughout the country, giving access to financial services to hundreds of millions who previously were unbanked.

Strong supporters of the DMAB, the New Zealand and Australian Posts, had previously developed vast survey-based databases of consumer responses to lengthy questionnaires. This data is used by mailers and other direct marketers as both prospect lists and for database enhancement. In support of promoting more international mailing, the New Zealand Post has originated a project at the Asian Pacific Postal Union, an intergovernmental organization of 31 postal administrations, to build a similar multi-country database to support the growth of direct mail in these markets.

Credit and debit cards have flooded Europe and Japan and are making huge headway in Brazil, making purchases at a distance more secure for companies and more convenient for consumers. China is just starting down that road.

However, as effective as the practice of using lists to mail offers has become in of all these new markets, in the more mature markets and in some markets with poor postal service (e.g., South Africa) the new data and the new consumers are being found on the Internet or through their mobile phones, not through the Post from subscriptions and other mailings.

The new data is not as frequently being found through offline mailings, but through carefully attracting visitors to Web sites with the new digital tools and tactics of search engine optimization, online behavioral advertising, social media, and mobile marketing. Data is more and more being carefully given by individuals directly to the sites they frequent and trust. Often the registration process elicits very scant identification, a name and e-mail address. This data becomes a challenge to link to other meaningful data, and this is a new challenge.

This pattern, begun in the United States, is being repeated around the world. The world is now a "consumer pull" world, and the challenge of direct marketing is to understand how consumers can be drawn into dialogue at one's Web site, or even through the mail, by the use of the new prospecting tools: search engine optimization, banner advertising, mobile marketing and the affinity marketing practices inherent in the new social media tools.

This does not mean the death of direct mail. In the industrialized countries, mail still receives a significant portion of the direct marketing budget, and in fact the largest part of the United States marketer's direct marketing budget. What it does mean for many Posts is that they now need to refine their parcel delivery offerings for all those online purchases. It also means that e-commerce merchants are the new "catalogs" in terms of "new names to file" and data exchange.

And What of Creativity and Problem-Solving?

All of these changes make for more, better, more effective, more economical, and increasingly more international direct marketing. Skills have been translated, transferred, and adapted. The digital world and online marketers who scoffed at direct marketing as "old-fashioned" have discovered the magic of the algorithm, something understood by the direct marketing world since Bill Fair and Earl Isaac's application of predictive analytics to credit analysis.

The skills are being applied. To demonstrate this, I dipped into the archives of winners of the Echo awards from more than three decades ago for samples to show what was and reached out to agencies around the world for samples that show what is.

At that time, the Echo competition was enlarged to encompass all types of media and changed its name from "The Best of Direct Mail". (Four years later, the Direct Mail Marketing Association would become the DMA.).

Here are a few observations after reviewing some 30 winners from the 1980s and some dozen or so campaigns sent to me in the 2000s.

1. One campaign was for a dead technology, but its attention-capture device might have legs. Lear Siegler won a Gold Echo for its b2b mailing of a stopwatch to CEOs to promote its "mail mobile," a mail delivery machine that follows a painted magnetic path along the floor of a large building. The CEO is invited to start the stopwatch and send it to himself through the interoffice mail from another part of his building. I suppose the idea of "efficiency testing" is still valid, but the mail mobile is, alas, no more...the one at Reader's Digest chirruped out a friendly and cheerful little "beep" when it stopped, and gave a double warning "beep-beep" good-bye when it was about to set off.

2. When you see some of the old winners today, you'd think they were just invented. One medical campaign with an edge might still fly today, at least in Canada. It reflects the Charles E. Frosst & Co., Ltd.'s Canadian nature. The campaign consisted of a series of different sample mailers for a pain-relieving medicine, an aspirin variant. The eight mailers each had a different photograph of a fruit or vegetable being subjected to a particularly painful experience, a split green pepper being sutured, a cucumber in a bear trap, a leaf of lettuce being ironed, a watermelon with a meat clever imbedded in it. Even today, Canadian marketing still has much that is idiosyncratic, even shocking, and quite often very humorous.

3. Some campaigns look very familiar. GE did a series of b2b mailings to potential power generating and distribution companies (engineer buyers of technical products—talk about database challenges!) to promote a PCB substitute called DiElecktrol that was promoted as safe. The mailing started with an empty aquarium and continued with sand, a little underwater castle, seashells, etc. Respondents got a salesman's call complete with fish and water in the last package. Gold then and Gold just a few years ago to a Norwegian firm using at least two of those many steps to promote their group trip to the DMA's Annual Conference in Chicago.

4. Some winners showed technology on the march. Indra AB of Sweden with its "King Meatball" campaign to caterers promoted its new machine-made "contact" fried meatball as a tastier and more economical alternative to handmade fat-fried meatballs. Gold for an increase in sales of 98% over the handmade control meatball.

5. "Free" works. Always has, always will. Jeweler Hans Péclard of Switzerland earned a Gold Echo for a traffic driver to its first-ever trade fair booth in 1978 in Geneva: a genuine certificate of one share of DeBeers Company stock to the first 1,000 visitors to its booth. Cost: SFr 60,000. Revenue: SFr 1.2 million. ROI of 200.

6. Also "free," and *in memoriam,* once-mighty and now-deceased TWA promoted its first cross-country flights on Lockheed's new L-1011 with an American Express statement stuffer of coupons for a drink or free headphones on the new flight. The stuffer looks like a briefcase and opens to show a TWA brochure with coupons inside: involving, to the point, value, targeted. Response of 12.5% on 350,000 mailed.

Today we have a wider variety of media to choose from, but the messages have to be localized to the culture and audiences to be successful, and the themes of solving a problem and engaging the target are constant. Colleagues around the world have sent some wonderful examples.

1. The mail in any market still works well as a testing environment and client generator. In Argentina, Banco Privado is primarily an online bank and has only two branches. It tested four different prize premiums in four different packages offering a credit card account. The winner by a large margin was a miniature of a small bed complete with mattress and sheets which had a real credit card "under the mattress". This played to the thrifty "old-world" Argentines' sense of thrift and distrust of banks.

2. Also a very "culture-dependent" campaign, and a very sophisticated mail piece, was a Guinness loyalty program mailing in Malaysia that would only work in a Chinese environment. The mailing consisted of a sophisticated constructed piece with many paper cut-outs of Chinese New Year iconography. These cut-outs celebrated traditions going back 2,000 years. The totality of the message is that the recipient is part of a special group of men who are "in the know", who are loyal to friends and family, who are competitive and successful but generous. In short, the recipients are Chinese men of substance who are proud of their culture and their accomplishments. Response and result data were spectacular.

3. In yet other media, India TV channel SAB used broadcast and online video to attract new contestants and viewers for its version of "The X-Factor". In the piece, an iconic "holy beggar" has no success finding food in a village he has recently come to. Prompted by a heavenly voice, he displays his "X-Factor", a talent for playing hard rock guitar, and is feted by the whole village.

4. In China, Japan and South Africa, much of direct marketing is mobile marketing and experimentation is proceeding at breakneck speed. Here, the brands are most definitely at work. Johnson & Johnson enjoyed a significant success with a mobile coupon campaign for its launch of ACUVUE Vivid Style contact lenses.

Consumers redeemed the m-coupon for free trials at participating stores and submitted their own photos via MMS to participate in a "most vivacious eyes" mobile picture voting contest. Since most of the entrants were young women, naturally most of the voters and phone numbers acquired were young men.

5. Finally, it is being discovered worldwide that social media can be targeted and made into a response and engagement tool. In Spain in 2009, an unknown author with a small publisher needed to publicize his novel, *The Wounded Copilot*. A combined direct mail and social media campaign created interest by allowing readers to determine the book's ending. Literary critics received a leaflet that released fake blood. Other influential people received a launch invitation that was perforated with a bullet hole. The launch itself took place at the theater which was the site of the book's story. All readers were invited to choose online how to resolve one of the book's incomplete plots. The book's print run increased 40%.

So, the creativity and problem-solving of the campaigns from the 1980s would still work nicely alongside the new entrants that are winning prizes, and satisfying clients, today. The skills and sophistication of direct marketing experience are now widespread. However, many younger practitioners who have cut their teeth on Web site design and campaign management are unaware that they are "doing direct" and are unaware of the history and gems of knowledge that are older than they are. As Mark Twain said, "When I was a boy of fourteen, my father was so ignorant I could hardly stand to have the old man around. But when I got to be 21, I was astonished at how much the old man had learned in seven years."

It now should prove worthwhile for marketing professionals worldwide, whatever their experience level, to look back, and look around. Someone may have the answer to their client's problem. When you need inspiration, an afternoon browsing in one of the industry's archives of winning campaigns, such as the DMA's Echo library, or the UK DMA's awards, would be well-spent.

Pre-Internet promotions and post-Internet campaigns have much in common. It is true that one needs the SEO and the analytics and the social media presences to get people to a Web site, and a reason for them to register or otherwise engage. But, one also needs one or more of these brilliant "old" ideas to continue to get them to respond. Now marketers can deploy their "new" bright ideas faster, more economically, and more broadly than ever before. But they will need to speak Chinese in China, Spanish in Spain . . . and not just the language but the culture of the language.

Since graduating from Harvard Law School in 1974, CHARLES PRESCOTT's career has focused on international corporate, securities, finance, and new country development law and projects. He most recently served as Vice President, Global Development at the Direct Marketing Association (DMA) of the United States and in October 2009 was appointed an Adjunct Director of the Board of Directors of the US DMA. He is the publisher of The Prescott Report, a newsletter of international direct marketing.

READING
14

Multicultural Marketing in the U.S.

JAIME NORIEGA, PH.D.
DePaul University

As a land of immigrants, multicultural marketing has always been a relevant issue in the U.S. With every wave of immigrants that helped populate this country, its new inhabitants brought with them different customs, beliefs, and languages. As a result of this, bilingualism was relatively common in the 19th century, and marketing communications no doubt reflected this diversity of languages. In fact, it wasn't until 1906 that Congress enacted an English language requirement for citizenship. At this point assimilating to the dominant culture and language became a practical and sometimes necessary measure for immigrants in order to secure a bright future.

Nowadays, however, English is no longer regarded as such a sacrosanct, unifying, and defining element for the nation and its citizens. And thanks to the still-growing global economy and the emergence of transnational communities, it is much easier for immigrants and their descendants to retain or reestablish cultural, social, economic, and political ties to their home country. As a result of this, multicultural marketing is once again at the forefront of U.S. marketers' concerns.

What is Multicultural Marketing?

The term *multicultural marketing* refers to a marketer's efforts at communicating with and serving a target market which is somehow different from its general market. These target markets are usually made up of subcultures: a group of people who hold beliefs, values, customs, and other cultural characteristics which differentiate them from other members of the same society. The factors that make these markets different from the general market may include race, ethnicity, nationality, religion, age, and gender. Here we will concentrate on racial and ethnic minorities, which are often the most misunderstood groups marketers have to deal with.

In many cases, these cultural differences will dictate changes in the marketing mix (the 4 Ps of marketing—Product, Price, Place, Promotion). At a minimum however, communicating a selling message to a target market outside of the general market will usually require an adaptation of the "promotion," or how the selling message is conveyed. There are also a number of ethnic minorities for which it may be necessary to change the language and the venue in which the message is delivered.

This reading will summarize the three largest minority groups targeted most often by U.S. marketers: Hispanics, Blacks, and Asians. We will then discuss some of the ways in which these groups have been traditionally targeted both in mainstream advertising and via targeted advertising. In the last section we will discuss some of the new ways in which academic research is beginning to describe and understand multicultural markets.

U.S. Hispanics

Because of its size, continuing growth, multiple language usage, and continually evolving nature, the Hispanic/Latino market in the U.S. has been a very challenging group for marketers to reach effectively. The length and breadth of this section is a testament to the complexity of this often-elusive consumer market.

According to the U.S. Census there are currently approximately 50 million Hispanics in the U.S., a number expected to grow to 133 million by 2050. They are the largest minority in the country and had an estimated purchasing power of $978 billion in 2009, which is projected to reach $1.3 trillion by 2014, as reported by the Selig Center for Economic Growth.

In the recent past, Hispanics have achieved a number of milestones that the popular press has been quick to report. In July of 2002, the U.S. Census Bureau reported that Hispanics had surpassed African Americans as the largest minority group in the U.S. Hispanics currently account for more than 15% of the U.S. population. There are currently more English-language Hispanic themed television shows than ever before along with a multitude of highly successful cross-over Hispanic performers. On television, especially in youth programming, there are numerous Hispanic surnamed characters that have been integrated into Anglo or multi-ethnic casts. With every successive election, the popular press emphasizes the growing importance of the Hispanic vote. And during the past decade, Hispanic purchasing power has been growing at a rate twice that of the overall national rate. These statistics are quite significant because research has shown that as minority groups gain political and economic clout, they are more likely to feel comfortable exercising their cultural identity.

Following are a number of important Hispanic demographics and statistics summarized from the U.S. Census:

- The median age for Hispanics is 27 years of age, 9 years less than the U.S. general population.
- Almost one-third of the U.S. Hispanic population is under 21 years of age.
- Hispanic households are more likely to include children than non-Hispanic households.
- Hispanic households are more likely to consist of extended family members than non-Hispanic households.
- The current U.S. Hispanic population is more than 60% native born.
- Traditionally, the U.S. Hispanic population has been concentrated in seven states: California, Texas, New York, Florida, Illinois, Arizona, and New Jersey.

- However, from 2000 to 2007, the largest increases in the U.S. Hispanic population occurred in states that previously had only a small Hispanic presence.

These are some previously identified characteristics of the Hispanic consumer market: [1]

- Prefer name brands.
- Are fashion conscious.
- Prefer to shop at smaller stores.
- Do grocery shopping several times a week.
- Prefer fresh food items.
- Do not like to use coupons.

It should be pointed out that these consumer behavior characteristics are based on earlier research. As Hispanics continue to acculturate, it is believed their behavior will fall more in line with that of the general population.

Aside from these facts and assumptions, other important factors may help marketers connect more meaningfully with this growing and changing consumer group.

Spanish, English, or Both?

It is estimated that whereas 20% of Hispanics speak only Spanish and an equivalent number speak only English, the remainder—60%—speak both English and Spanish. In general, English monolingualism was thought to be the natural consequence of cultural assimilation for non-English speaking immigrants; however, an emerging body of sociological research suggests that bilingualism is not only a plausible outcome for Hispanics, but also an actual one. Longitudinal research conducted by Rubén Rumbaut in 2002 specifically found that U.S. Hispanics' ability to speak and read Spanish actually improved from their teenage years to their twenties. This new pattern of language shift is different for Spanish speakers when compared to other immigrant groups or to Spanish speakers from earlier waves of immigration.

Another indication that bilingualism is a growing reality among U.S. Hispanics is the significant growth of bilingual publications. As reported by Western Publication research, in 2000 there were approximately 58 bilingual Hispanic newspapers in the U.S. By 2007 that number had grown to 189, a 225% increase. By comparison, Spanish language Hispanic newspapers experienced a 30% growth in the same time period, from 492 to 638 publications nationwide. And of particular interest to adver-

---

1. Donthu N. and Cherian J. (1992) "Hispanic Coupon Usage: The Impact of Strong and Weak Ethnic Identification" *Psychology & Marketing*, 9 (6): 501–510; Mulhren, F.J. and Williams, J. D. (1994) "A Comparative Analysis of Shopping Behavior in Hispanic and Non-Hispanic Market Areas," *Journal of Retailing*, 70 (3): 231-251; Rossman M.L. (1994) Multicultural Marketing : Selling to a Diverse America, New York : AMACOM; *Rafeedie*, C., Godkin, L., Valentine, S., and Swerdlow, R.A. (2006) "The Development of a Model Specifying the Differences in Hispanic and White Adolescents' Consumer Behavior," *International Journal of Management*, 23 (3): 597–605; Chattalas, M. and Harper, H. (2007) "Navigating a hybrid cultural identity: Hispanic teenagers' fashion consumption influences," *Journal of Consumer Marketing*, 24 (6): 351–357

tisers, a 2008 study of Hispanics in San Diego, California conducted by Meneses Research & Associates found that 82% of respondents preferred to receive information from advertisers in <u>both</u> languages.

This emerging language usage pattern has opened the door to some bold new approaches when communicating with this consumer group.

In 2007, a family-owned Honda dealership in Florida decided that the best way to cut through the clutter of television advertising would be to broadcast a Spanish-language TV commercial on a general-market English language network. The ad featured all family members and some employees speaking Spanish with a noticeable Anglo accent but delivering a warm, appealing, and convincing message. Although the dealership did receive some negative feedback as a result—threatening and ugly phone calls and emails from viewers (including some Hispanic viewers)—not only did they receive overwhelming statements of support, this tactic also ultimately increased overall sales.

More recently, in 2009, a leading U.S. car manufacturer took a gamble by placing a Spanish-language TV commercial during a Hispanic-themed English-language entertainment show. The gamble paid off, leading to several requests for additional information; however, surprisingly, some viewers requested the information in Spanish, others in English. Although one cannot determine the precise reason behind viewers' language choice for the additional information, there are a number of assumptions that can be made; some of which are quite surprising and useful in understanding the complex manner in which language plays a part in many Hispanic consumers' lives:

1. It is possible that program viewers favor English over Spanish.
2. This preference might reflect a higher proficiency in English than in Spanish.
3. Even if English is their preference, at least those viewers who responded to the commercial apparently did not mind being "addressed" in Spanish.
4. Regardless of their language proficiency, many viewers understood Spanish well enough to respond to the commercial.
5. Although viewers who requested the information in Spanish may be more comfortable with their native language, they were nevertheless enjoying English language programming.

The success of efforts like these seem to imply that determining which language to use when targeting Hispanics is not a simple choice based on the age or generation of the specific Hispanic target market, as has been suggested before. At least in some cases it appears that although using a Hispanic consumer's native language—even within English language media—may not be necessary, it may nevertheless be helpful, and potentially fruitful. In the last section I will discuss why there may be some instances in which targeting bilingual Hispanics with an English language message may be preferable.

Hispanic, or Latino?

It would not be very surprising to discover that the majority of Americans believe *Latino* is the preferred term with which to refer to this group. After all, it is the term they are most likely to hear being used in the mainstream media. And who can forget Associate Justice of the Supreme Court Sonia Sotomayor's ". . . wise Latina" comment during her confirmation hearings? The term *Latino(a)* is widely used by established business people, politicians, and celebrities. And the point here is that "established" usually also means "older." According to a 2008 study of more than one thousand 14- to 24-year-old Hispanics in eight major U.S. markets, conducted by The Intelligence Group, a New York based research firm, these young individuals preferred the term *Hispanic* to *Latino* by almost a 3 to 1 margin (56% vs. 19%; 11% preferred the term *American* and the rest had no preference). This is not a trivial point given the comparative youth of the Hispanic population; furthermore, the choice to identify oneself as either Hispanic or Latino is often a personal matter which may involve taking a political and/or social stand. As poet/writer Sandra Cisneros explains the distinction between the words *Hispanic* and *Latino*: "It's not a word. It's a way of looking at the world. It's a way of looking at meaning." Given this, it may be helpful for any marketer targeting this group to consider the potential consumer's age before referring to them as "Latinos" or "Hispanics," if such a label is deemed helpful or appropriate as a way of reaching out to this consumer group.

Blacks/African Americans

The politically correct term for this racial group is African American; however, this is an inaccurate term which often causes confusion over the size and composition of this consumer market group. Strictly speaking, the term *Black* describes a race whereas *African American* is more aptly described as an ethnicity. In fact, many textbooks stress the diversity of the "African American" population by pointing out that it includes individuals of Caribbean descent as well as other groups defined by the Census; Black-Hispanic for example. As the term implies, an African-American is a person of African descent, and clearly not all Blacks living in the U.S. fit that description. For the purpose of this chapter however, we will use the more commonly accepted term *African American* with the knowledge that at least some of the numbers may actually refer to the Black race as a whole (especially since the U.S. Census Bureau lists this category as "Black/African American.")

According to the U.S. Census, there are currently about 40 million African Americans in the U.S., a number expected to grow to 57 million by 2050. They are the second-largest minority in the country and had an estimated purchasing power of $910 billion in 2009, which is projected to grow to $1.1 trillion by 2014, according to the Selig Center for Economic Growth.

African Americans have been part of the general population for so long that they share the same language as the general population. Thus for most product categories, many marketers attempt to reach this group through their general-market advertising—often making sure that at least some of the models or spokespeople are also African American. Marketers usually rely on the audience profiles provided by media outlets in order to ensure their message is reaching a substantial number of African American consumers. There are, however, a number of specialized products that still benefit from targeted advertising. Such advertising is usually placed in predominantly African American TV or radio programming and several national and local magazines and newspapers specifically targeted to this population segment.

Following are a number of important African American demographics and statistics summarized from the U.S. Census:

- The median age for African Americans is 30 years; six years less than the general population.
- More than 50% of African American consumers are under the age of 35.
- The top five African American cities are: New York, Chicago, Detroit, Philadelphia, and Houston.

These are some previously identified characteristics of the African American consumer market:[2]

- Prefer popular and leading brands.
- Are brand loyal.
- Are more likely to engage in conspicuous consumption (purchasing items that signal success).
- Spend almost a third more on clothes than the general market consumer.
- Spend 10% more on grocery shopping than the general market consumer.
- Support African American community retailers.
- Trust African American media more than mainstream media.

Asian Americans

According to the U.S. Census, there are currently about 14.5 million Asian Americans in the U.S., a number expected to grow to 34.4 million by 2050. They are the fastest growing minority in the country (percentage wise) and had an estimated purchasing power of $509 billion in 2009, which is projected to reach $697 billion by 2014, as reported by the Selig Center for Economic Growth.

Asian Americans are by far the most diverse minority group in the country and can include South Asians from Bangladesh, Bhutan, India, Maldives, Nepal, Pakistan, and Sri Lanka; East Asians from China, Hong Kong, Japan, Macau, Mongolia, North Korea, South Korea, and Taiwan; and Southeast Asians from Brunei, Burma, Cambodia, East Timor, Indonesia, Laos, Malaysia, Philippines, Singapore, Thailand, and Vietnam. The U.S. Census Bureau and other research entities often also include native Hawaiians and other Pacific Islanders as Asian Americans.

Given the many different nationalities and regions represented by this group, members of the Asian American community speak literally hundreds of different languages and/or dialects. As varied as this group is, according to the U.S. Census Bureau only six different ethnicities make up 90% of this population: Chinese, Filipinos,

---

2. Rossman M.L. (1994) Multicultural Marketing : Selling to a Diverse America, New York : AMACOM; **Fisher,** C. (1996) "Black, hip, and primed (to shop)," *American Demographics*, 18 (9): 52–58; St. John, B. (1998) "African-American trust minority media first," St. Louis Journalism Review, 28 (209):3; Bush, A. J.; Smith, R. and; Martin, C. (1999) "The Influence of Consumer Socialization Variables on Attitude Toward Advertising: A Comparison of African-Americans and Caucasians," *Journal of Advertising*, 28 (3): 13–24; Witt, L. (2004) "Color Code Red," *American Demographics*, 26 (1): 23–25.

Indians, Vietnamese, Korean, and Japanese. It is perhaps because of this diversity of cultures and languages that U.S. marketers do not target this group as a whole with any comprehensive national campaigns. At the local level, however, marketers have at their disposal numerous print publications and local broadcast channels and programs, each targeted to the six major groups of Asian Americans as well as many of the other nationalities within this minority group. Grassroots marketing by way of event sponsorships also gives marketers access to members of the many national groups which are part of this highly sought-after minority group.

Reflecting their status as members of collectivist societies, Asian Americans are very family oriented. They are also very hard-working and place a very high value on education. Their higher than average household income makes them a highly sought after target market.

Following are a number of important Asian American demographics and statistics summarized from the U.S. Census:

- The median age for Asian Americans is 32 years of age, four years less than the general population.
- 52% of Asian Americans have completed at least 4 years of college, more than any other U.S. population group.
- The median household income for Asian Americans is $69,000+; almost 25% higher than the U.S. average.
- Only 36% of Asian Americans are U.S. born; and of these, two thirds are first-generation Americans.
- Almost 50% of all Asian Americans live in Los Angeles, San Francisco, New York, Honolulu, and Sacramento.
- Asian Americans are more computer literate than the general population.
- Asian Americans are more likely to have Internet access at home than other minority populations.

These are some previously identified characteristics of the Asian American consumer market:[3]

- Value quality and prefer upscale brands.
- Are loyal consumers.
- Respond very well to targeted selling/advertising.
- Consumption decisions tend to be male dominated.
- More likely to buy online than the general population.

---

3. Rossman M.L. (1994) Multicultural Marketing : Selling to a Diverse America, New York : AMACOM; Steere, J. (1995) "How Asian-Americans make purchase decisions," Marketing News, 29 (6): 9; "Asian Americans Lead the Way Online," Min's New Media Report, December 31, 2001; Fetto, J. and Gardyn, R. (2002) "Cyber Tigers," American Demographics, 24 (3): 9–10; "Asian American Market Profile," Magazine Publishers of America (2004): Accessed September 2010 at http://www.magazine.org/ASSETS /BF4E8BCE5E9D4847BA537A448EE20EF4/ market_profile_asian.pdf; Martin, B. A. S., Kwai-Choi Lee, C., and Feng Y., (2004) "The Influence of Ad Model Ethnicity and Self-Referencing on Attitudes," Journal of Advertising, 33 (4): 27–37.

EXHIBIT R14.1: MULTI-ETHNIC MODELS AD EXECUTIONS

- Asian Americans from countries where owing money is seen as taboo are reluctant to buy on credit.

Multiculturalism in the Mainstream

Marketers who wish to appeal to different ethnic or cultural markets within their general market advertising instead of, or in addition to, their targeted marketing efforts tend do so in one of two different ways.

We Are the World

Some advertisers feel the best way to appeal to a diverse cross section of the American consumer population is to be all inclusive. These ads, which are hard to miss, usually feature one or more models/spokespersons of every conceivable race or ethnicity, presumably reflecting the actual population in the given marketplace (see Exhibit R14.1). These advertisements are noticeably different from other general market advertisements which will often include almost exclusively Anglo and African American protagonists. In general, this all-inclusive approach may work just fine especially in major cities where people of different cultural backgrounds are more likely to coexist amicably enough. However, the potential danger of using this approach is best illustrated by putting it in an international perspective; this all-inclusive approach would be disastrous in some countries where although many different races and or ethnicities may coexist, they may not only not get along, they may even despise each other.

The lesson is clear: Whether or not all the relevant races and ethnicities are represented in one's advertisements is not as important as how those different individual groups feel about being depicted together. In some parts of the U.S. this may be a risky approach because market research is not likely to uncover these intergroup dynamics. Racial or ethnic intolerance is not a socially desirable trait; therefore, if asked, it is doubtful that too many individuals would express intolerance for other races or ethnicities regardless of their actual feelings.

Who Are You?

A more recent and seemingly safer alternative that many advertisers now use is actually so ubiquitous that it has now been ridiculed on national TV. A recent television advertisement for U by Kotex tampons cleverly parodies other commercials in its product class, calling them "obnoxious". In the commercial, a very attractive model dressed in white in an all-white background divulges the many advertising tactics used by marketers and at one point states: ". . . You can relate to me because I'm racially ambiguous. . . ." Many print and broadcast advertisers now feature models and/or spokespersons whose race or ethnicity is hard to determine (see Exhibit R14.2). Once the accepted standard, it is increasingly rare to see television or print advertisements in which the principal spokesperson is a blue-eyed blonde.

The growing popularity of this approach suggests that it is working well. However, it is important to consider how this execution corresponds with empirical research. Studies have shown that when ethnic minorities receive a selling message, they prefer to see models/actors/ or spokespersons that look like them; presumably, if consumers can relate to the faces they see, they are more likely to be persuaded to buy the adver-

EXHIBIT R14.2: RACIALLY/ETHNICALLY AMBIGUOUS MODEL AD EXECUTIONS

tised offering. It should be pointed out, then, that featuring a racially ambiguous model or spokesperson in one's advertising is not quite the same thing as featuring a model of the same race(s) as one's target market(s). The intent of the former seems to be to *prevent negative feelings* a consumer may feel when receiving a persuasive message from someone outside of their racial/ethnic group. After all, the most accurate way to characterize a racially ambiguous spokesperson is to say they "could pass" for many races/ethnicities, whereas the latter approach attempts to *promote positive feelings* by delivering the same message via someone who is *clearly* a member of the racial/ethnic group being targeted.

Both the "all inclusive" and the "racially ambiguous" approaches assume that neither the product nor the message requires any further adaptation in order to appeal to various racial or ethnic target markets.

Regardless of which of these two approaches marketers use when attempting to reach a diverse consumer marketplace through their general market advertising, television may be a different story. When advertisers decide to deliver their selling message via television, they usually assume a network's audience profile will be a good indication of which different ethnic or racial consumer groups will be watching. However, marketers seldom think twice about how well each targeted consumer group is represented in the shows within which they are placing their advertising. Although few would argue that racial/ethnic diversity is a reality of the marketplace, television programming usually fails to reflect the true diversity of the U.S. population. As reported by *Entertainment Weekly*, Table R14.1 shows a comparison between the number of characters depicted in scripted television series in five major networks (ABC, NBC, CBS, FOX, The CW) during the fall of 2008 and actual U.S. population figures based on analyses of 2007 U.S. Census data.

Considering the amount of news coverage regarding the growth of the Hispanic/Latino market in terms of population as well as political and spending power, it is surprising to see it is by far the most under-represented ethnic group on television. Although they are now the largest minority U.S. population, on television they represent just over 6% of television characters.

If we consider the extent to which so many marketers are relying on product placement rather than traditional TV advertising, these disparities gain a special sig-

TABLE R14.1: DIVERSITY ON TELEVISION

Race/Ethnicity	U.S. Population	TV AVG	ABC	NBC	CBS	FOX	The CW
White/Anglo	66.2%	74.72%	78.2%	71.0%	79.3%	77.7%	*67.4%*
Hispanic/Latino	15.2%	6.38%	**8.3%**	7.5%	8.1%	4.2%	*3.8%*
Black/African American	12.9%	13.92%*	9.4%	11.8%	*9.0%*	12.5%	**26.9%**
Asian	4.5%	4.5%	3.1%	**9.7%**	3.6%	4.2%	*1.9%*

Highest percentage by network for each race/ethnicity is in bold, lowest is in italic.
*This number is somewhat misleading in that the average is significantly affected by the prominent percentage of African American actors featured in The CW programming (26.9%). The average number of black actors featured in all networks excluding The CW is only 10.67%

nificance. After all, when a TV character talks about or consumes a branded product in a TV show, that character's race/ethnicity may play a part in how much his/her behavior will influence different members of the consumer viewing audience. There is a distinct possibility that consumers of a different race/ethnicity than the TV character may not be influenced as much as viewers whose race/ethnicity do match that of the TV character.

Targeting Multicultural Markets

When a marketer determines that a product, message, or campaign warrants a targeted approach, at least at the local level, there is an abundance of print and broadcast media choices both in English and in just about every major foreign language necessary. As might be expected, these vary by region and tend to reflect the demographics of the given region. The larger and more established the minority target market, the more likely it is that national or at least regional advertising mediums will be available for marketers wishing to launch broader campaigns.

Cultural differences become increasingly important when a marketer decides to follow a targeted approach. For this, it is essential to have a thorough understanding of the different racial/ethnic groups one wants to target; in fact, the impressive growth of minority-owned research, marketing, and advertising firms suggests it may be necessary to have an insider's perspective.

Two very simple rules which marketers have traditionally broken when they begin to target a new minority group are:

1. Speak and understand the language of your target group; and,
2. Make sure your intended target market can relate to the faces they see in your advertisement.

Excusez-Moi?

Backwards translation is a common tactic used in bilingual research that can be quite useful to ensure that a translated selling message gets across the intended meaning. When translating from English to Spanish, for example, one bilingual individual will translate the original English script to Spanish then a different bilingual individual will translate the Spanish translation back to English. The more similar the original script is to the English translation, the more accurate and proper the Spanish translation. Still, the best advice for any marketer wishing to communicate in a language other than English is to translate the *idea* behind the selling message rather than the actual words in the message. Very few language combinations can rely on literal verbatim translations. Messages that rely on colloquialisms, humor, or a play on words are notoriously difficult to translate successfully.

Hispanics are the largest but by no means the only cultural group that may require a marketer to deliver his selling message in a language other than English. However, because there are so many different nationalities which comprise the group we refer to as Hispanics/Latinos, it is sometimes challenging to find a word or phrase which has the exact same meaning across the many different versions of Spanish with which these distinct groups may be familiar. Depending on the demographics of the target area or the medium itself (there are many Hispanic newspapers throughout the U.S.

specifically targeted to Mexicans, Salvadorians, Cubans, etc.), it may be worthwhile to deliver several Spanish language versions of the same selling message. A similar argument could be made for broadcast advertising, which may require not only a slightly different version of the Spanish language script, but possibly a slightly different pronunciation as well to reflect the most common accent and speech characteristics of the targeted group.

Another way in which a marketer can have a language gaffe in its advertising is through the inappropriate use of slang when targeting certain minority groups. In a 2005 McDonald's TV ad campaign for their double cheeseburger targeted at African American consumers, a tagline referring to the sandwich states "I'd hit it." McDonald's marketers thought they were expressing the affirmation "I would eat that" in a very hip fashion, not realizing the expression they chose was more commonly used to convey a desire to have sex with the object to which the expression was directed!

There are many humorous examples of advertising translation gone wrong from the international marketing arena. U.S. marketers who decide they should translate their selling message when targeting U.S. minority groups should go the extra mile to prevent blunders like these:

- When Pepsi entered the Chinese market, the translation of their slogan "Pepsi Brings You Back to Life" became: "Pepsi Brings Your Ancestors Back from the Grave."
- When the Dairy Association tried to extend its popular campaign "Got Milk?" to Mexico, their ill-conceived translation actually came across as: "Are you lactating?"
- In Italy, a campaign for "Schweppes Tonic Water" translated the name into a less appealing "Schweppes Toilet Water".
- When Kentucky Fried Chicken entered the Chinese market, they discovered that their slogan "finger lickin' good" was inadvertently interpreted as "eat your fingers off."
- The U.S. slogan for Salem cigarettes, "Salem—Feeling Free," was translated for the Japanese market and read: "When smoking Salem, you feel so refreshed that your mind seems to be free and empty."
- When Parker Pens marketed a ballpoint pen in Mexico they attempted to translate the tag line: "It won't leak in your pocket and embarrass you." Unfortunately, the Spanish translation actually read: "It won't leak in your pocket and make you pregnant."
- When Clairol introduced their "Mist Stick" curling iron in Germany, it was brought to their attention that that "mist" is German slang for manure.
- When now-defunct Braniff Air Lines translated a tag line meant to popularize its new seating upholstery, "Fly in Leather," in Spain, it actually read as "Fly Naked."
- The Coors Brewing Spanish translation of its slogan, "Turn It Loose," came across as "Suffer From Diarrhea."

The Man in the Mirror?

Research has shown that when targeting an ethnic consumer group, marketers will benefit if the models or spokespersons featured in the advertisements look like the intended target market consumers. Unlike the tactic of using racially ambiguous models described earlier, when marketers go through the expense of producing distinct advertising for each of the different markets they wish to target, they usually will hire models or spokespersons with which the intended consumer is expected to identify. As simple as this seems, it requires a thorough knowledge of the specific demographics of the different regions where the advertising is planned to appear. The term *Hispanic* or *Latino* refers to a wide variety of nationalities, not all of which look exactly the same. This was made clear in the late 1990s, when Coca Cola was advertising heavily in several Hispanic newspapers throughout the U.S. At that time, an overwhelming majority of Hispanics in the Southwest were of Mexican descent; however, these print ads were being created by agencies in Miami and/or New York where the majority of Hispanics were of Cuban or Puerto Rican descent, respectively. As a result of this, most newspaper ads published in the Southwest at that time featured a group of presumed friends in various settings enjoying a Coca-Cola; however, the faces in these ads bore very little resemblance to the people Coca-Cola was attempting to target in that region; Hispanics of Mexican descent.

Is it the Market or the Individual that is Multicultural?

Although the automotive advertising examples given earlier serve as fairly good examples of advertisers looking beyond the obvious in order to connect better with multicultural markets, few marketers are embracing a radically new way of looking at multicultural markets the way that some academic researchers are starting to do.

Whereas a multicultural market is described as a market where members of several different cultures or subcultures coexist, a multicultural consumer is an individual who embraces and indentifies with more than one culture, usually depending on what the context calls for. The cultural frame switching literature in social psychology has considered how symbols and language can cue either of two distinct cultural identities in bicultural individuals. Cultural frame switching can be described as a specific type of priming, which changes a person's ability to identify, produce, or classify an item as a result of a previous encounter with that or a related item. By activating certain associations in memory, an individual is more likely to think about those associated concepts, ideas, or beliefs and/or to behave in a way that is consistent with those ideas and beliefs when asked to process information.

One of the earliest studies of cultural frame switching conducted by Ying-Yi Hong and her colleagues in 2000 found that different cultural icons (Great Wall of China vs. American Flag) primed either collectivist or individualistic responses in Chinese-American biculturals. It was hypothesized and confirmed that because China is considered a collectivist society where interdependence and group harmony are highly valued, a Chinese cultural prime would elicit responses in keeping with collectivism; and because America is recognized as an individualistic society where independence and self-sufficiency are valued, an American cultural prime would elicit responses in keeping with individualism. Other studies have shown that language can also prime distinct cultural mindsets in bilingual biculturals. Further evidence that bicultural individuals may in effect embrace two distinct identities comes from a recent study of Mexican-American bicultural-bilinguals living in the U.S. conducted by Nairán Ramírez-Esparza and her colleagues in 2006. Their study found that language is capable of cuing either Mexican or American personality characteristics. Subjects who responded to Spanish language personality scales displayed more "Mexican" personality characteristics (as identified in monolingual Mexicans in Mexico) whereas subjects who responded to the same scales written in English displayed more "American" personality characteristics (as identified in monolingual Anglos living in the U.S.).

Language is only one aspect of an individual's culture, but it is a defining aspect for bicultural bilinguals. Recent studies suggest that in some cases it is possible that each of a bilingual's two languages can facilitate different types of thoughts and emotions. A 2008 marketing study conducted by Jaime Noriega and Edward Blair found that bilingual Hispanics reacted more positively to a Spanish language print advertisement for a restaurant when the ad mentioned dinner rather than lunch. The explanation for this result was that because subjects were more likely to associate dinner with family, friends, and the home; and because Spanish rather than English is more likely to be used with these individuals and in this setting, the Spanish language ad was able to access these types of associations in their subjects' minds more easily than the English version of the advertisement. More recently, a number of studies have shown that both English and Spanish can result in different responses from bilingual Hispanics depending on the context of the advertisement. For a Hispanic bilingual who consumes media in both languages it is also quite possible that an advertisement for a printer, for example, may be more effective and/or efficient when delivered in English. After all, one would assume that English is the language more likely to be spoken at work and whatever associations exist within that mental framework have little to do with family or the home. Indeed, a very recent study of Hispanic bilinguals conducted by Ryall Carroll and David Luna and soon to be published in the *Journal of Advertising* has found that selling messages related to work seem to be more effective when delivered in English.

This research stream suggests that from a marketing standpoint, it may be possible to use the language of the selling message as a prime to engage either of a bicultural bilingual's cultural identities in order to differentially access distinct associations in consumers' minds, something that may ultimately aid in persuasion. And because priming is a general phenomenon, it may also be possible to use other aspects of an advertisement besides language to communicate at a deeper and more meaningful level with one's target market.

In other words, this emerging field of study considers multicultural markets not as distinct groups of homogeneous individuals who are somehow different than their general market counterparts, but rather as groups of individuals who at times will reflect and thereby be motivated by either of the two cultures with which they identify: their American culture or their racial/ethnic/national minority culture. Much of this research is still in its infancy, though, so at this time, most marketers still rely on overly simplistic, often arbitrary, and sometimes biased guidelines to determine which language and symbols to use when targeting racial and/or ethnic minority consumer markets.

Update

Since the previous version of this article was written, there have been no significant new insights on cross-cultural communications coming from scholarly academic sources. However, in spite of this, a number of advertisers have been experimenting with new and interesting ways of communicating with these individuals, primarily as part of their general market advertising.

Hispanic Surnames

Within the past couple of years U.S. audiences have been exposed to numerous commercials where the protagonists are identified by their Hispanic family name either via a voice-over or by way of an inconspicuous small label at the base of the TV screen. These commercials are generally presented completely in English and as expected, the appearance of the people depicted in these commercials is probably best described as "ethnically ambiguous" more so than "definitively Hispanic." The family members featured do not necessarily have any speaking roles but instead are shown interacting with one another in typical "slice of life" scenarios consuming the advertised product. The assumption is that Hispanic viewers will notice the Hispanic surname and feel the advertiser is somehow acknowledging their ancestry and perhaps even paying homage to their well-recognized strong sense of family. In following this approach, advertisers also implicitly assume that the average non-Hispanic viewer will either not notice the Hispanic surname or will not care; that is, will not feel excluded by the message.

A less common approach is to have the protagonist identified as Hispanic (again, by mentioning their surname) and at least one actor will utter a Spanish language word or phrase within an English language presentation. This is a bolder approach because even if the average American TV viewer has gotten used to seeing models whose ethnicity is very hard to determine, they may still perceive the non-English word or phrase as foreign, something that could diminish the relevance of the selling message and ultimately its ability to influence. This also assumes non-ethnic viewers either do not notice or mind the protagonists having a recognizable Hispanic surname.

Non-English Advertisements in Mainstream English-language Media

So far at least, this bold approach is only being implemented by Jimmy Johns, the national sandwich chain that prides itself on lightning quick deliveries. These commercials stand out because they are placed in mainstream English language media but broadcast entirely in their respective foreign languages (Spanish, Japanese, and Hungarian), the only English phrase spoken during the entire commercial is the brand "Jimmy Johns" followed by a tag line at the end that is spoken entirely in English. It should be noted however that the average English viewer will completely understand *all* of these commercials. They work simply because they are funny. The comedic scenarios do not require fluency in any of the three foreign languages. This is really key because this means the commercials are likely to work equally well for ethnic viewers who understand the dialogue and for English monolinguals who will still understand these scenarios where a difficult situation is remedied by Jimmy John's ridiculously speedy delivery. With the exception of the Hungarian version which features an alluring young woman taking a bath and later "accidentally" dropping her towel in front of the Jimmy Johns delivery man—a move some commentators have labeled as needlessly sexist, there has been no other negative backlash as a result of this campaign.

This represents a unique and bold approach no other advertiser has ever attempted, certainly not in a national campaign of this scope. These commercials really stand out because of the immediate contrast effect that is created when one is watching English-language television that is momentarily interrupted by a foreign language commercial. There is an immediate recognition by those who understand the foreign language but English monolinguals also cannot help but pay attention as they try to understand why they suddenly cannot comprehend the words coming out of their TV set. However, because these commercials are clearly and visually driven by humor, the average English speaker can immediately understand the scenarios, the problem presented, and the suggested solution—placing an order for Jimmy Johns which arrives in cartoon-like fashion: as soon as the protagonists puts down the phone after ordering.

The Multiracial Consumer

In the 2010 US Census more than nine million people self-identified as multiracial. In order to reflect and acknowledge this demographic shift through advertising, marketers can follow one of two approaches: They can feature more actors and models that appear to be biracial, and/or they can feature more couples of mixed race. The first approach is quite different from the previously mentioned "racially ambiguous" tactic advertisers have been using for years now—using ethnically ambiguous actors and models in their advertising. Although it is a safe bet that a man or woman whose racial or ethnic identity is hard to discern is probably as a result of having mixed heritage, the intent there is not to acknowledge their biracial identity but rather to have viewers of many different backgrounds identify with these protagonist. If an advertiser wants to make it obvious they are in fact attempting to 'connect' with biracial consumers, it must be clear this is the intended identity of the characters they feature in their advertising.

The second way advertisers can acknowledge the growing number of mixed race couples is quite literally to simply feature more of them in their advertising. This is something one can see more of every day. Wherever a number of people are featured together or in a series of vignettes, there is no doubt one is more likely to see seemingly romantically involved couples of mixed race interacting with one another in commercials nowadays.

It is rather interesting that the most talked-about and controversial example of how an advertiser can acknowledge the growing presence of mixed-race couples was by using both approaches together: Featuring a seemingly biracial actor and then confirming that identity by also showing his or her parents. This is the premise of the original Cheerios commercial that set off a firestorm of controversy after a number of unhappy intolerant consumers made their discomfort known through their hateful comments in the commercial's YouTube page. The ad featured a biracial little girl asking her white Anglo mother about the health benefits of Cheerios—we then see her black African-American father waking up from a nap covered in Cheerios cereal. Although ultimately there was an outpouring of support for the company, the majority of it was primarily a reactionary response to the controversy, not to the ad itself. As advertisers continue to reflect and promote the changing face of the American consumer, they must also consider this may not be a reality all consumers will want to embrace or be reminded of.

JAIME NORIEGA, Ph.D., is an assistant professor of marketing in the College of Commerce, DePaul University. Professor Noriega earned his B.S., M.B.A. and Ph.D. degrees from the University of Houston.

READING
15

Contact and Call Centers

MITCHELL A. LIEBER

Lieber & Associates

What Is Customer Contact?

Customer contact is one-to-one individualized communications with a company representative via telephone, web chat or email. When contact is solely by telephone and centralized, the operation is called a call center. Many call centers also respond to emails and web chats and are increasingly called *customer contact centers*. This is usually shortened to simply *contact center*. The term *contact center* is used here to refer to both types of operations. Table R15.1 illustrates the types of customer contact performed in contact centers.

Customer contact has a variety of business purposes spanning a continuum from service to sales. Service purposes include responding to customers with technical support or customer service issues. Sales activities fall into three main areas: leads, ap-

TABLE R15.1. TYPES OF 1:1 CUSTOMER CONTACT

Type of Contact	Description
Inbound telephone calls	Via toll-free or local telephone number
Inbound fax	Via toll free or local telephone number (while largely replaced by more modern media, fax is still used in some businesses)
Inbound emails	Via an email address or web form
Inbound web chats	From a company web site
Inbound SMS	Prospect or customer's cell phone text message
Social media contact	From Facebook, Twitter and other social media
Outbound calls	Dialed manually, by a computer or predictive dialer
Account service	Inbound and outbound calls to service and sell accounts, such as stockbroker clients or business-to-business sales reps with specific account assignments. This may also include personal, 1:1 contact via fax, email, web chat, SMS and/or social media.

* Opt-in mass email and legally designed opt-in SMS messaging campaigns are typically handled outside of the contact center, similar to direct mail, and so are not listed above.

TABLE R15.2. BUSINESS USES OF CUSTOMER CONTACT TYPES

Type of Contact	Typical Uses
Inbound telephone calls	Sales, orders, new account activation, appointment setting, leads, customer service, help desk
Inbound fax	Orders, customer service
Inbound emails	Sales, orders, leads, customer service, help desk
Inbound web chats	Sales, leads, customer service, help desk
Inbound SMS	Sales, leads, customer service, help desk
Social media contact	Leads, customer service, help desk
Outbound calls	Sales, appointments, lead generation, customer service, market research, customer profiling/database update, customer satisfaction surveys
Account service	Sales, appointment setting, lead generation, customer service, help desk, market research, customer profiling/database update, customer satisfaction surveys

pointments and sales. So contact may be for lead generation or lead qualification, or to set appointments for a sales person. Types of sales calls are: sales cultivation, multistep sales, consultative sales, up-selling and cross-selling. In between service and sales is basic order taking. Table R15.2 illustrates the business uses of each different customer contact type or channel.

Where Customer Contact Fits in and How It Affects Results

The video and interactive elements of your new campaign draw people in. The copy sings the right song beautifully. The graphics are stunning. The data strategy captures information that will drive sales. The campaign is done! Not quite. The contact center program must be developed.

Companies that give the contact center little attention often sabotage their program's results for this area can make or break a program. Here's why. Whether prospects contact your business to order or with questions, via chat or email or phone, one thing is certain for many companies. The most personal and intimate communications a prospect or customer will have with your brand will beat the contact center. It is where the *brand promise* that underlies your advertising comes to life or is proved false and deceptive. Which will it be? The attention you give this area determines the answer.

Will your brand be everything the caller expects? Will reps be accessible, knowledgeable, confident and customer focused? Or will they be difficult to reach, poorly informed, unsure or indifferent?

Whether 10%, 20% or 50% of your prospects or customers contact you in this personal medium, you want to win them over rather than write them off or drive them away. Similarly, if you place outbound calls to prospects you are doing so to win them over.

A Different Type of Channel

There are a number of questions to ask when developing a contact center program. Can the selected organization handle the volume of calls, chats, social media contact and emails, in or out? Will the reps be ready to respond to customers and prospects and to do so properly? If the answer is an immediate and unqualified "yes," as it almost always initially is, there's a followup question. Who is taking responsibility if this turns out to be inaccurate and sales are lost? Ask that question, and "yes" may become "maybe." Dig further, and this may become "maybe, but..." or "we didn't know that..."or "that will cost $ more." When conducting contact center programs, the devil is nearly always in the details.

Why? Effectiveness in the telephone channel may be trickier than in any other channel because it is controlled differently.

The contact center is the *only* channel in which individual human beings dynamically interpret and deliver the creative for *each individual impression*. This contrast is illustrated in Table R15.3.

There is an upside to this complexity. If a program is carefully designed, it is possible to tailor communications to each prospect or customer, engendering positive feelings about the company's responsiveness. There is a down side as well. A one-size-fits-all customers approach sticks out like a sore thumb in this most personal of channels, as do sophisticated approaches that fail because they are overly ambitious and implemented poorly or inconsistently. Which occurs is determined by a series of strategic and creative decisions. This is an overview of these decisions, so that you can make choices to help improve program results.

While poor design and structure can cause substandard programs, so can the quality of call center management, organization and staff. Even well-designed programs at quality call centers fail when they are not a good fit. For example, if a company selects a call center organization that is accustomed to following scripts verba-

TABLE R15.3. MESSAGE DUPLICATION AND DISTRIBUTION IN MEDIA CHANNELS

Channel	Control of Message Delivery	Duplication and Distribution
Web	Agency, copywriter, web designer	Reproduced by computers
Email	Agency, copywriter an designer	Reproduced by computers
Broadcast /web TV and Radio	Producer, director and scriptwriter	Recording is played
Print Ads	Copywriter and graphic designer	Printing
Direct Mail	Copywriter and graphic designer	Printing
Telephone	Script or call guide writer	Telephone reps
Web chat / email response	Template copywriter	Contact center reps
Social media	Posts by copywriter	Response by contact center reps (or others)

tim, asking them to take a conversational approach following a bullet point outline (called a *call guide*) may not work. It may be too different from standard operating procedure for management, supervisors and reps.

Design the Call Center Program First

There are key elements that make up each contact center program. To design the program begin at the end with results. What is the purpose of the program and how will you measure its success?

Purpose of the call or contact. Is the purpose customer service, order-taking, lead generation, lead qualification or sales? Do you want to sell consultatively, up-sell or cross-sell? These all affect metrics, and metrics are essential because contact center programs require constant measurement to stay on course.

Inbound tech support and customer service call metrics. The two most important customer service metrics are *customer satisfaction* and *time to final resolution* per issue. Customer satisfaction is measured by asking a question such as, "Have I fully addressed the reasons for your call today or is there something else I can do?" Time to final resolution is the duration of time from the first contact about an issue until it is resolved for the customer. Resolution could occur by the end of a five-minute phone call or during a call back to the customer one hour or 36 hours later.

A metric related to time to final resolution is *first-call resolution*, which is resolution of an issue with no additional calls. Research by the Technical Assistance Research Project (TARP) has demonstrated that it is highly correlated with customer satisfaction. Some companies prefer the net promoter score (NPS) developed by Bain & Company. This is the percentage of customers who respond favorably to the question, "How likely are you to recommend our company/product/service to your friends and colleagues?" These singular measures of customer satisfaction on individual calls are helpful but top level. They will identify if the trend is up or down but won't identify why! So it is also important to delve deeperwith a more detailed annual customer satisfaction survey. Or a detailed survey may be conducted of a percentage of callers over a period of time.

Inbound lead metrics. For inbound leads, the metrics are the percentage and number *of qualified leads* based on clear and established lead qualification criteria. These are typically (1) the inquirer's role in decision making (for B2B whether the caller recommends, specifies or approves the purchase; for consumer programs whether the caller decides, decides with spouse or family member, etc.), (2) purchase quantity, and (3) purchase time frame. Business-to-business marketers also add(4) whether the purchase is budgeted.

Inbound sales. For inbound sales the top metrics are the *percentage of calls that are sales, average sales amount in dollars per call* and *average sales amount in dollars per hour per rep.* Up-sell and cross-sell close rates and sales volume may also be important.

TABLE R15.4. SERVICE LEVEL VS. TRI-LEVEL

	Service Level	Service Level Example	Tri-Level	Tri-Level Example A	Tri-Level Example B	Tri-Level Example C
80% of calls answered within...	...N seconds	80% in 30 seconds	N seconds	80% in 30 seconds	80% in 120 seconds	80% in 0 seconds
99% of calls answered within...			X seconds	99% in 75 second	99% in 240 seconds	99% in 10 seconds
100% of calls answered within...*aka longest wait*			Y seconds	100% in 150 seconds	100% in 360 seconds	100% in 30 seconds

Speed-of-answer metrics for all inbound call types. A contact center must answer a call before anything else can occur, so two speed-of-answer metrics are commonly used. The first is the percentage of calls that *abandoned* (hang up) before being answered, and how long they waited before abandoning. The second is the percentage of time that *service level* is met. Service level is a goal that is expressed as % of calls answered within seconds. An example is 80% of calls answered within 30 seconds, or simply 80% in 30. A more sophisticated metric is *tri-level* which sets speed-of-answer goals for 80%, 99% and 100% of calls. It measures the service delivered to all prospects and customers rather than just 80%. Service level and tri-level are compared in Table R15.4.

Actual numbers vary widely with the type of call center so three tri-level examples are provided. The principle is to have tiered goals and measure 100% of calls.

Sourcing inbound calls and contacts. The most expensive part of inbound telephone programs that generate leads, orders or sales is making the telephone ring. The cost per call of the advertising is much larger than the cost of handling the call. Sales volume in dollars per $100 or $1,000 of media spend, per source, is the true measure of advertising results. Tracking the media source of each call is essential to produce reports that inform advertising purchase decisions.

For campaigns that include TV or radio, each station in a region of the country is usually assigned a different phone number to automatically determine the source in combination with the geographic location of the caller. If the campaign is exclusively print and mail, some marketers add an operator number or extension number tied to individual sources. Unlike TV and radio responders, these callers will still have the media in front of them during the call and can read the number to the telephone rep. For mailed catalogs, a source code is imprinted on the same page as the address to identify the mailing list and any variations in offer and creative being tested. On the web, operator and extension numbers will often work though unique phone numbers are ideal. All of these methods are superior to asking the media source and relying on caller recall.

Sometimes calls generate leads that are followed up by a field sales organization. For these programs it is wise to assign a unique identifier number to each lead to track closed sales back to the database record containing the media source. This enables you to attribute the sales revenue to a specific TV station, mailing list or web ad. Similarly, inbound emails generated via web forms should include *tracking URLs* from the original web landing page. Web chats can indicate the web page from which they originate.

Metrics for email and web chat. Email service level goals typically range from answering 100% of all emails within three hours to a 24 hour turn-around. Web chat service level goals are similar to those of inbound calls and can be more stringent in some operations. While customer chats generate an immediate automatic response, most customers won't wait another several minutes for a live rep to get to them. Emails and web chats are measured with the key customer service metrics also employed for inbound calls, *customer satisfaction* and *time to final resolution*.

Metrics for social media. Social media service level goals (response times) should, ideally, be tight. Social media is situated between one-way mass media (TV, mail, etc.) and one-to-one personal media (phone, email, web chat) because it is one-to-one communication *with an audience* consisting of a like-minded community.

In particular, a negative comment on social media must be addressed quickly and satisfactorily or it can stain the brand. Negative comments unaddressed on social media for hours or days can fester and amplify. Wise companies visibly and quickly take negative comments off-line for immediate resolution, publically indicating that it intends to resolve it. They quickly post that it is resolved when this occurs or gently ask the customer to do so. Customer service metrics, such as *customer satisfaction* and *time to final resolution*, should also be applied to social media customer service.

It is common to see company social media responses to complaints that say: (1) We're sorry you weren't happy, (2) we always (or usually) do a good job and (3) we hope you'll try us again so we can show you that we do a good job. These make the company appear arrogant and cheap. Why? They are all about the company and not about the customer. These responses do nothing to make the situation right and achieve resolution satisfactory to the customer. The social media audience is dissuaded from patronizing these businesses.

Metrics for outbound calls. Outbound calls are most often placed to generate leads, appointments or sales. In outbound calling a presentation to a decision maker is called a *contact*. Making a contact is a pre-requisite to generating a lead, setting an appointment or making a sale. One can't achieve the desired result with a busy signal, no answer, a request to call back to reach the decision maker or a disconnected number. Contacts figure prominently into outbound metrics. Results among contacts are measured in two ways: as percentages and per hour.

One key metric is the *conversion ratio*, which is the percentage of contacts that purchase (or become leads or appointments for those types of programs). This might be 3%, 12% or 20%, depending on the list and program.

Per hour metrics are based on the results produced by one telephone rep on the telephone for one hour. *Sales-per-hour (SPH)* is the key metric (or appointments-per-hour or leads-per-hour). *Contacts-per-hour (CPH)*, *callback- per-hour* and *bad-numbers-per-hour* (disconnected, etc.) are important intermediate metrics. List penetration is also tracked. It is the percentage of the list that has been used up and won't be called again.

Pay-for-Performance for sales calls. Outbound calling is charged to clients by the *phone hour*, which is one rep at their desk calling for one hour. Some large consumer outbound programs negotiate a fee *per closed sale*, which is called *pay-for-performance*. For example, a large cable operator might contract with an outsourcer to cross-sell cable subscribers a *triple play* package that also includes Internet and phone service on a *pay-for-performance* basis. Rather than pay $26 per phone hour, the cable operator might agree to pay $30 per closed sale. A pay-for-performance rate is typically negotiated after a test, which is often paid for on a phone hour basis.

A pay-for-performance rate is always higher than a phone hour rate to allow for variations in results among lists and vendor risk. The huge client benefit is that it eliminates client management of return-on-investment per phone hour. This key financial result is predetermined. However the client must still monitor conversion ratio (which will affect total revenue per 1,000 names), list penetration and call quality. Pay for performance is usually only available if one has a very large ongoing program with lists that produce relatively consistent results.

Training and Scripting

Training. Training is instrumental to success in contact center programs and should address the product or service and its market, as well as the call guide and frequently asked questions. Role playing and simulated calls are also training components. It's smart to have a product specialist from the company visit the call center (whether in-house or outsourced) to train reps on the product. Reps bond with company representatives and identify with the company as a result such sessions. This improves how they represent your brand. It is important to hand out imprinted items your company has, such as t-shirts and mugs, at trainings. These help customer contact reps feel that they are an integral part of the company's team.

Plans must be made for trainings for new telephone reps that join mid-program, and for update and refresher trainings by call center staff or via webinar.

Table R15.5 is a typical training curriculum. Module titles, content and sequence may vary from company to company. It is beneficial to give periodic quizzes as training progresses to make sure trainees are mastering the content. In some contact centers, trainees are required to pass a final exam in order to pass training.

Scripting, call guides and templates. In some regulated businesses, it may be necessary to use a verbatim script for all or certain parts of consumer calls. This may be true in business sectors such as health care, insurance and banking. Also, some clients

TABLE R15.5. TYPICAL TRAINING CURRICULUM

1. The Company	8. Using the Computer System and Database
2. The Market	9. Using the Telephone System
3. Company's Service or Product Lines	10. Role Playing Calls / Contacts
4. The Call Center / Sales / Service Organization	11. Handling Difficult or Exceptional Situations
5. Related Ads, Mailings and E-Mailings	12. Shadowing an Experienced Rep or Supervisor
6. Types of Customer Contacts and Goals	13. Simulated Calls / Contacts
7. Call Guides and Objection-Responses or FAQs	14. Initial Calls or Contacts While Being Shadowed

prefer verbatim scripts. Business-to-business calls typically use *call guides*, which are bullet point outlines that guide the conversation. If reps have proper training and empowerment, call guides result in more conversational and effective calls on consumer calls as well.

Answers to frequently asked questions must always be part of the call guide or script package. For web chats and emails, commonly used replies should be available as templates to be pasted into messages to facilitate speedy and accurate communications. Outbound sales calls always include objection-responses. These are predetermined answers to objections to buying that prospects may raise(however some U.S. states prohibit the use of objection responses).

Other Program Design Components

A successful contact center program is composed of a number of components in addition to purpose, metrics, scripting and training. Here are the most important ones for the majority of programs. Table R15.6 is a checklist that will help you plan a call center program.

Days and hours of operation. Decisions about hours of operation can affect results. Are you open for inbound contacts 24x7x365? Or is it 8:00 a.m. to 6:00 p.m. eastern time Monday-Friday? If so, are the hours displayed with the inbound phone number? Will outbound calling to existing customers be concentrated during evenings and weekends, with a small number of daytime calls? Will the call center's hours be convenient, or at least adequate, for customers in other time zones? Is it worthwhile for an in-house call center in the central time zone to open an hour earlier to accommodate the east coast, and to stay open one or two hours later to accommodate those in the west? Will customers in Alaska and Hawaii accept mainland hours or is there a business reason to remain open later for them?

In-house or outsourced. Will your contact center program be in-house, outsourced or in-house with outsourced overflow? If outsourced, who will oversee and manage the outsourcer? Will they be able to remotely monitor calls? Who will work with the

TABLE R15.6. PROGRAM SET-UP CHECKLIST

Issue	Question	This Program
Purpose	Customer service, lead-qualification, appointment setting, sales, etc.	
Testing	Proven results from testing the offer and lists (outbound calls) or proven/projected response for inbound contacts.	
Integrations	How must the program operationally integrate with other departments, outside sales, web site, advertising, etc.?	
Where	In-house, outsourced or both?	
Seasonalities	How might call volume and staffing needs fluctuate?	
Lead time	Lead time required for testing, hiring, training, system, telephone set-up, etc.	
Goals	How many retained customers, satisfied customers, leads, appointments, sales, etc. is a realistic goal?	
How much	What is the cost overall and per retained customer, lead or sale?	
QA	Who will monitor calls, emails, web chats, etc. and how frequently? This applies both internally (supervisors) and externally (client).	
HR	What are the goals and the timetable for recruiting and hiring? Who is responsible?	
Training	Who is developing and presenting program specific training to reps and supervisors, in how many groups and what is the timing for this? If the calls are outsourced will the client visit to help train on site?	
Scripting	Who is developing and approving scripts or call guides and objection-responses or FAQs?	
Metrics	What metrics and reports measure the program, rep teams and individual reps?	
Inbound Contact Timing	What will trigger calls, emails, web chats and social media and when? How will this affect staffing needs by time of day, week and month?	
Outbound List	For outbound calling, what lists will be used or tested?	
Contests/ incentives	Will there be contests or incentives for reps that reward the desired behaviors and results?	
Supervision	What will be the ratio of direct supervisors to reps and what percentage of their time do supervisors spend to monitor and coach reps? 100%, 80%, 50% or some other percentage?	
Software	What software will reps use to retrieve and enter information for calls, emails, web chats, social media? What configuration or set-up is necessary?	
Telephone	What telephone system configuration is needed?	

☐ top level decisions   ▨ operational decisions which affect program design vendor to develop call guides and training? What arrangements have been made to answer questions for the call center as they arise? Whether in-house or outsourced, is the call center currently staffed to handle the call types and call volumes? If not, what is the plan for adding sufficient staff?

If there are inbound calls or chats, has anyone projected the call and chat arrival pattern and associated volumes? The most extreme arrival pattern is for direct response TV spots, which generate a *spike* pattern. Nearly all calls ring in within 8 minutes of when TV spots air. There are virtually no calls between ads. How will the contact center staff for this? Will there be sufficient trained staff (often at a main and overflow call centers) to handle the spikes when multiple ads air simultaneously?

Similar issues, though less extreme, can also arise with print, mail, email and web advertising campaigns. For example, is all of the direct mail being sent the same day? If so it may all arrive over a two- or three-day period, generating a concentrated influx of calls. The busiest days of some campaigns may have two, three or more times the customer calls and chats as the average day. The busiest hour of the day may be two or three times as busy as the average hour. In such cases, staffing for average days and hours will result in abandoned calls (due to long wait times) and lost customers.

Management. Who is going to oversee and manage the contact center program at the top level? Also, who will be at the top of the chain of command of the telephone reps delivering your company's message one-to-one? Finally, who is going to make sure your company's goals and objectives are being met initially and on an ongoing basis? Will this be someone in corporate marketing, at the ad agency or a call center consultant?

In addition to monitoring reports and results, will the program manager seed lists used for outbound calls (under an unrecognizable name, to receive and evaluate calls)? Will they, a subordinate or a consultant receive these seeded calls? Who will monitor inbound customer contact? Will they, a subordinate or consultant place test calls, chats and emails?

Database and calling lists. Nearly all contact center programs involve databases. Inbound lead programs populate a marketing database with leads. Order-taking programs typically use an enterprise software system to place customer orders, check inventory and provide delivery dates. Customer service and technical support operations use database systems to track issue type, time to resolution and customer information. Each is a very different category of software but all revolve around databases. All require that decisions be made about the information to capture, the reports required and the frequency of reports.

In outbound campaigns, calling lists are generated based on specific criteria. A business-to-business cataloguer's win-back program for lapsed customers may use RFM (recency, frequency, money). It may target customers who are 5-12 months lapsed (recency), ordered more than three times a year (frequency) and spent more than $400 per order on average (money). For large lists, sophisticated multivariate predictive modeling may be used to target those most likely to purchase. For small lists, a simple approach may be taken such as calling every customer from the preceding 12 months who has not ordered within the last 90 days. Calling lists rarely exist in paper form. These are usually electronic lists of prospect or customer records that are selected to receive a call initiated via a computer system.

System programming. Most contact center programs are set-up in computer systems that provide database fields, on-line scripts for reps (in some systems) and reports. It is wise to develop your requirements for each and to put them in writing. Determine in advance if the contact center will provide all of your company's *must haves* and many of its *would like to haves*. Also determine the cost and time frame for doing so.

Outbound calling to consumers. Most outbound consumer calling is to existing customers, recently lapsed customers and to inquirers from the past 30-90 days. Such calls require a well- designed, consumer-focused offer to be effective and to deliver a good return-on-investment. Results often are improved by integrating direct mail and/or e-mail. Cold calling consumers is ill advised and usually unprofitable.

Outbound calling business-to-business. Business-to-business calling is heavily focused on the same relationship-based calling criteria as consumer calls. Also, prospecting calls that are carefully targeted can be effective for niche business-to-business markets, particularly in combination with e-mail and/or direct mail. Such programs are most effective when there are a limited number of sources for the product or service you are selling, and it is essential to the prospect's business. For example, after-market forklift and clamp truck parts for large fleet owners and repair shops meet both of these requirements. A non-niche market that meets neither requirement is photocopier and laser printer paper for offices.

Monitoring calls and communications. Contact centers produce interactions with prospects and customers. The interactions can be counted and the results measured. However the quality of the calls can only be evaluated by listening to them, and for emails and web chats, by reviewing the messages. This must be done internally by call center supervisors and managers. Clients utilizing an outsourcer must also implement their own monitoring program. This oversight is essential to success. Most outsourced contact centers can accommodate real time call monitoring from remote locations and may provide recordings of calls. Similarly they can send emails and web chats for review and evaluation.

It is crucial that monitoring employ a set of objective criteria for scoring communications. *Is friendly* is subjective while *uses customer's name* is objective. Well before a monitoring program begins, the monitoring criteria must be introduced to reps as performance goals and accompanied by training. This helps assure successful calls. It is only fair to measure reps on performance criteria that are clear and on which they have been trained.

Most call centers record calls which are available for later review. However, the best way to help reps improve is to review a challenging call with them immediately afterwards, with or without a recording, and to ask the rep what they would do differently next time. When the experience of the call is fresh, it is a *teachable moment* with an opportunity for the rep to learn how to change what they do on future calls. The experience of the call is long forgotten an hour, a day or a week later and a discussion then is much less effective.

Inbound call IVRs and voice recognition: Some inbound call centers use an IVR (interactive voice response) system to accept touch tone data entered by a caller. Others use a voice recognition system to collect caller information on an automated basis. These forms of automation may be used without live reps but are usually employed to route calls to the proper group of reps, such as sales or service. Most callers don't feel that they are receiving service until they reach a live person. So when designing IVR and voice recognition systems, less is more. It is best to route callers to a live person in as few steps and as quickly as possible.

Social media contact management. If selected call center agents handle social media communications, establish clear rules about (a) what to write when, (b) what not to write and (c) what needs approval from higher up. The company must have a process with service levels (turnaround time deadlines) for approvals from higher ups if responses are to be timely. Next day is usually too late in the social media world.

Selecting an Outsourcer

Contact center programs are handled by outsourcers when there are insufficient resources to conduct them properly in-house. Top-level criteria for selecting an outsourcer include (a)overall competence, (2) a match with your program's written requirements and (c) experience handling similar types of programs. All three are essential.

Overall competence is the sum of the competence of management, supervision, phone reps and of the operations systems and processes. All are instrumental in implementing your program.

It is necessary to create a set of written requirements for your contact center program so that there is a clear set of needs against which to score potential vendors. This also forces your organization to distinguish *nice to have* capabilities and characteristics from *must haves*. Glitzy bells and whistles never substitute for fundamental functionality that may be missing in another area.

The amount of specialization among contact centers may appear remarkable. The reason for so much specialization is that the goal, process, rep style and skills required vary significantly by program type. For inbound programs, handling inquiries to capture basic contact information is different than delivering technical support. Taking credit card orders differs from both. Unlike telephone calls, handling email or web chats requires the ability to write clearly, well and judiciously.

Whether outbound or inbound, it is usually wise to focus your search on contact centers that work in your vertical business area such as insurance, infomercials or health care. Table 15.7 is a checklist that will aid in comparing multiple vendors.

Business-to-business vs. consumer. Business-to-business programs are quite different than consumer programs, particularly in outbound calling. Consumer outbound calling experience is rarely sufficient to conduct business-to-business outbound calling programs and vise versa.

TABLE R15.7. OUTSOURCER SELECTION CHECKLIST

Issue	Question	Vendor A	Vendor B
Similar Work	Does the company do similar work? This means inbound vs. outbound, consumer vs. business-to-business, contact purpose and vertical business area.		
Rep Quality	Listen to calls on a site visit. If you require inbound services mystery shop their clients. How do they do?		
Supervisors & Account Staff	They translate your wishes into rep behavior. Are they knowledgeable? Are you comfortable with them?		
Training	How is the new hire, refresher and program-specific training? Is it sufficient in duration, depth and quality?		
Quality Control	How frequent is monitoring and coaching? Can you easily remotely monitor calls or contacts?		
Staff Turnover	How frequent is rep turnover? How will your program be affected by having new reps this frequently?		
Reports	Ask for and review standard reports. Do they meet your needs? For inbound, require wait time and abandoned call reports. For outbound, require reports on the "no" responses, bad numbers, unreachables and list penetration. Ask the cost and time frame for your custom reports. How often are reports sent?		
Value Added	Will the vendor alert you when your program could be improved or could this wait until you discover it?		
Culture	Is the call center always a pressure cooker or is it usually a pleasant place to work? Happy reps are more likely to treat your customers well.		
Responsiveness	Is the vendor responsive to you? Are their lead times for set-up reasonable and turnaround time for changes acceptable? Are they in the contract? Will they have adequate staff for your program?		
Primary Contact and Escalation	Are you comfortable with the individual who will be your contact, typically an account executive? How far up can you escalate if necessary?		
Fair Contract	Can their contract be modified to protect your interests by adding inbound service level guarantees and more? Is there a way to cancel before renewal?		
Technology	Does the call center have appropriate phone, computer and software technology? What is the disaster recovery plan for outages and weather?		
References	Ask for three references with programs similar to yours and contact them. References that are not enthusiastic are a red flag.		
Cost	Cost is always a factor. Also consider total value. It may be a bargain to pay $3.25 instead of $2.75 for an inbound call. When? If you receive 5% more $200 orders, better customer interactions or more responsiveness at the for $3.25/call vendor. Ask for set-up, training and other non-call fees.		

Geography is a red herring. Many companies use geography to determine which outsourcers to consider. This is almost always short-sighted and limiting. Marketers usually visit outsourced contact centers once or twice a year or four times a year at most. Select the contact center on qualifications first and only consider geography if all other things are equal. Avoiding a poor match between a program and outsourcer is worth an occasional airplane flight or drive. Why? The disastrous results that come from a poor match cost a good deal more in both money and management time than occasional travel.

One vs. discrete inbound and outbound call centers. Another common dilemma is whether to use separate contact centers for inbound and outbound communications or a single vendor for both. If the volume is significant you will want a company that specializes in the area. Some vendors have inbound and outbound divisions and may have the required specializations in both. Others focus primarily on one mode and handle small volumes in the other, and so may only be a match for one. Still other contact centers focus solely on either inbound or outbound communications.

A primarily outbound call center may be able to handle three or four inbound calls a day but will likely be ill-equipped to handle 300 inbound calls a day along with a few emails and web chats, and so will cause your company to deliver poor service and lose customers. An outbound shop will lack the specialized technology, metrics, organization, staff, training and supervision to handle a significant volume of inbound calls. The reverse is true for an inbound shop attempting to handle significant scale outbound campaigns.

Special Program Design Concerns

Contact center programs must exist in harmony with the related business environment. This includes elements that range from the company's branding to a country or state's regulations. Here are a few of the environmental issues affecting contact center programs.

Branding: Company branding can be incorporated into the call. However, incorporating a slogan or catch phrase usually doesn't work. Here's an example. "This is Theresa Smith calling for GE. We bring good things to life. The reason for my call today . . ."

Why doesn't this work? A phone call is a one-to-one personal communications. When was the last time you used a slogan or catch phrase to communicate with someone in a conversation? Slogans are used for crowds via one-way media such as TV, the web and public speeches. Incorporating a slogan into a conversation is out of place and de-personalizes it.

How can branding be incorporated in an appropriate way? The best way is to incorporate the underlying branding principles and to deliver on the brand promise. In other words, behave in a way that brings good things to the caller's life. For example a GE rep might be instructed to say, "If you ever have a problem with this product just call us at 1-nnn-nnn-nnnn or contact us via our web site. We'll solve it for you. This service is a part of our product."

Staff turnover: This is a pivotal concern and varies widely. If most of the reps who initially learn and do well on your program are transferred or leave six weeks or even six months later, then what? How well will the new reps be trained and how well will they do? Don't assume that the initial staff will be there or working on your program for a period of time.Ask about and plan for turnover or assignment to other projects and the additional training this will require.

Toll free numbers: Cross-country calls today cost pennies per minute or are part of a flat rate plan and cost nothing extra. However toll-free numbers continue to be a standard for most inbound calling programs. If the toll-free number is a vanity number, one that spells out a word or phrase, it is helpful to also display the numeric digits in smaller type below. Why? Vanity numbers are easier to remember but more difficult to dial. Also the alphabet does not correlate with numbers on some smartphones, particularly certain Blackberries. They have separate letter and number keys and this makes a vanity number impossible to dial.In catalogs, it is often wise to display the hours and days the call center is open along with the phone number.

Communications style differences within the U.S.: Cultural issues often arise when conducting call center programs. Understand how your market engages. For example, rapport building and relationships are more important in many immigrant Hispanic cultures than they are in Anglo cultures in the U.S. Similar differences arise in socio-economic groups. In business-to-business calling,professions and industries may also have their own cultures. Engineers may request detailed information and care little about the duration of a call, email or web chat session if that goal is being met. However, stockbrokers are very concerned about time and will want to complete their calls quickly. To brokers, time is money.

International issues: Our world continues to shrink due to instant international communications. However, we still retain distinctly national ways of doing things. Call guides, scripts and template email and chat language often need to be restructured to conform to local cultures.

International *free call* numbers are specific to each country. So although it may be using a single Pan-European or other multi-country call center, you will need toll-free numbers for each country. Laws and regulations are different abroad than in the United States. You may find that the use of credit information will be less restricted but the use of personal information will be more tightly regulated in some countries. The specifics of similar sounding laws will also differ. Canada's do-not-call law is not identical to the U.S. law. To successfully operate call center programs in other countries it is prudent to have one or more partners who can advise on these local issues.

Generational differences: People of different ages communicate differently. Most Americans born after 1980 will try a web site and web chat before calling, while those born before WWII prefer to speak with live telephone reps. Baby boomers are a transitional generation. Some boomers prefer web chat while others prefer to place a phone call. In fact, a large percentage of baby boomers will be unable to carry on a web chat. Select multiple communications channels that allow easy access for all relevant market segments.

Click-to-call on the web: Modern commerce today is very web focused and has moved the contact center to the web. This has produced three versions of *click-to-call* at a web site. The oldest enables a visitor to a web page to enter their telephone number, click and receive a call from a contact center agent qualified to handle their request. The customer continues browsing the web site until a telephone rep calls to assist. The customer avoids waiting on hold and navigating a menu of options. The second version of click-to-call is employed by PC and tablet users with Skype, Google Voice or another IP phone service. These customers click on a phone number on the web to connect the call over the Internet, bypassing the phone network. The third version of click-to-call is via smartphones, which are increasingly the device of choice for web browsing. Callers click on a phone number on a web site to place the call via their cell phone.

Offshore contact centers: Some companies chose to use contact centers in the Caribbean, Philippines, Central America, South America, India and other countries to reduce labor costs. Other corporations have global footprints and so operate call centers on several or all populated continents, and may overflow calls to one another. For example, Spanish language inbound calls handled in Spain may overflow during times of peak volume to call centers in Central America or South America because the language is the same (though dialects and accents will vary).

When a sales relationship is not at stake, offshore call centers can do well. However, when a sales relationship is on the line, offshore labor cost savings can be more than offset by increased talk time, a larger number of callbacks and even loss of customers. The reasons are that offshore agents are usually not empowered to do more than read a script and cultural differences also may get in the way. Plan thoughtfully if you are considering offshore for customer service, technical support or sales calls. Here is a formula for calculating financial benefit or loss.

+ Cost Savings
− Cost of Increased Talk Time and Increased Callbacks
− Increased Training, Monitoring, Coaching and Q.A. Costs
− Any Decrease in Sales
− Any Decrease in Lifetime Value of a Customer*
──
= Total savings or loss of using an offshore call center for a particular program

* Lifetime value of a customer (LTV) is the average revenue per year per customer x the average tenure in years of a customer

Use Table R15.8 to help calculate the economic benefit or loss of an offshore call center, based on the formula.

Home Agents: The use of home agents has grown in recent years. Home agents enable a company to hire qualified staff, reduce expenses for physical space and reduce its carbon footprint. They make it possible to employ staff who may not be able to commute easily to a call center. Some companies have agents come to a physical call center one or two days a week and work from home the majority of the time. Other call centers employ agents who work entirely from home.

Home agent teams require extra organizational infrastructure in order to commu-

TABLE R15.8. DOMESTIC VS. OFFSHORE
CALL CENTER ECONOMIC IMPACT

	Domestic	Offshore	Offshore Difference	Offshore Difference Expected
Call costs			+/-	Usually a savings
Cost of increased talk time and/or repeat calls to resolve a customer issue			+/-	Usually an increased cost
Training costs			+/-	Could be + or –
U.S. and overseas Q.A., monitoring, coaching costs			+/-	Usually an increased cost
Change in sales			+/-	Usually a revenue loss
Change in customer LTV*			+/-	Usually a revenue loss
Total			+/-	Could be + or -

nicate company practices successfully to reps and create a contact center culture.These include frequent on-line chats, webinars and teleconferences.Though essential to success, these are easier said than done. Technical difficulties logging onto interviews, orientations and webinar trainings can decrease new hires, breed employee discontent and otherwise sabotage home agent programs.

A number of large outsourcing firms have switched from on-premise to home agents, while others have switched from home agents back to on-premise agents. Some in-house call centers have also switched back and forth. This seems to indicate that home agents can be successful with proper organizational and technological implementation. However, home agents can easily become problematic if required organizational and technical components are not in place or are not functioning well.

Speech Analytics: Speech analytics systems are being used by some large contact centers to identify issues not caught by monitoring or to substitute automation for some monitoring. The most common type of speech analytics was originally developed for the intelligence community. It *listens* to phone calls by transforming speech-to-text and then performs word spotting to find particular trigger words or phrases such as *mad, upset, refund orsupervisor* to identify calls with issues. A highly sophisticated form of speech analytics identifies the tone of voice of customers, in real time, to select those who are upset and alert a supervisor so they may monitor it and intervene if necessary.

Technology in Contact Centers

Contact centers use a wide variety of technology. What's the most common? Headsets, which facilitate receiving or placing call after call with time efficiency. Headsets are where the technology in many contact centers begins. Here are other more important technological tools.

Inbound telephone system: Sometimes called an ACD (automatic call distributor), these systems play announcements to callers, route calls to the appropriate reps and report on calls and rep activity, including rep talk time, call duration, call wait time and percentage of abandoned calls (hang ups while waiting). Some ACDs route web callbacks, chats and emails to agents along with telephone calls.

IVR/speech recognition system: IVR (interactive voice response) systems have prompts such as, "Touch 1 for sales . . ."Increasingly IVRs have speech recognition systems attached so that menus are easier to navigate or eliminated. IVR is often included with inbound phone systems. Speech recognition is frequently an option.

Workforce management system: Workforce management systems are used to project future inbound call volume, the number of reps required at any time to handle projected calls and to schedule reps. In call centers of more than 50 inbound agents, these often costly systems pay for themselves in labor savings. They also result in faster service to callers.

Outbound dialer phone system: There are three types of outbound dialing performed in call centers: preview, power and predictive. With preview dialing,the rep brings up a record, reviews it and clicks to dial. Power dialers automatically pace reps. Once a call is completed, it automatically brings up the next record, waits for a predetermined number of seconds and dials the call for the rep. Predictive dialers are designed to further optimize rep productivity by employing an algorithm to dynamically predict call length as well as the number of no answers, busy signals, disconnected numbers and answering machines. Based on these predictions,dialers dial a certain number of calls for each rep who is currently available for a call and for each rep that it predicts will become available momentarily. When a predictive dialer is used, outbound telephone reps may be on calls as many as 45–50 minutes each hour.

Predictive dialers are specialized outbound phone systems. Power dialing is frequently performed using a predictive dialer set to operate as a power dialer. Preview dialing is usually conducted using contact management or CRM software but may also be implemented on a predictive dialer set for preview dialing.

Email management system: A call center can handle five, 25 or perhaps 50 emails a day using a consumer email tool such as Outlook or Gmail. As volumes get larger and exceed 50–100/day, a more sophisticated tool is needed. Email management systems spot key words in incoming email subject lines and messages to (a) route emails to particular reps and (b) automatically select template responses for reps to modify and send. They include other features that ease management of large numbers of inbound emails.

Web chat software: Web chat software enables web chats between web site visitors and contact center agents. The software also keeps a record of chats and generates reports. It is often provided on a SaaS (software as a service) basis hosted by the software company.

Help desk software: Help desk software is used in customer service and technical support (also called help desk) contact centers to manage time to resolution of issues or complaints. The software enables reps to assign each issue/complaint a ticket or case number, enter a description, categorize the issue and assign it to a group or individual. These systems deliver alerts to agents and supervisors when too much time has elapsed without resolution and produce reports about issues reported and time to resolution. Most automatically generate tickets or cases from customer emails and from a customer web portal. They also have a searchable knowledgebase, populated by your company, that enable reps to locate solutions to issues and which can be part of a customer web portal for self service.

Scripting systems: Exactly what should reps say on calls? Predictive dialers usually include scripting systems while other types of contact center programs may require separate systems devoted entirely to scripting. Sophisticated scripting systems typically read and write to fields in existing Customer Relationship Management (CRM) software, such as Salesforce.com. CRM software is nearly always an inefficient tool in a call center because it requires too many keystrokes to perform each individual function. At scales of 20–50 reps, scripting software usually increases productivity so much that it makes economic sense. It can also improve service and sales.

Cloud vs. premise-based systems: Just as office software has cloud-based iterations, so does call center software and technology. Call center phone systems are now available in the cloud. Software for customer service, sales and other functions are also available on a hosted SaaS (software as a service) basis.

Advantages of cloud-based systems are more rapid installations, the ability to add telephone reps with little notice and the ability to reduce telephone reps monthly or annually to receive a reduction in costs. Home agents are as easily implemented as traditional premise-based agents. There is less in-house technical support required, though an IT staffer must still administer the system. So cloud systems are particularly good for start-ups, fast-growing operations and those with frequently changing home agents. The premise-based system's large initial cost goes away with cloud systems' pay-as-you-go approach.

The ability to implement a call center phone system in 2–4 weeks for roughly $150/agent/month (an average cost) plus the cost of installation/implementation and long distance calls can be attractive. On the desktop software side, the ability to implement a help desk software system in a few days to a few weeks for $25-$70/month/rep is attractive as well.

Many telephone and software systems easily integrate with one another using *web services* technology. This means that functions such as *screen pops* (using a caller's telephone number to automatically locate and open their customer record for the telephone rep), can be implemented inexpensively and quickly.

There can be disadvantages to cloud systems. Reliability and resolution of problems is entirely in the vendor's hands and not your staff's. As a result, clients are married to the vendor's approach and standard time frames. Customers are also beholden to the vendor for implementation, which may take several iterations to be perfected, especially if an implementation is either large or complex. While cloud systems have security measures in place and it appears that hackers have not yet targeted cloud systems, security must always be considered. After 2-4 years the total cost of ownership of a cloud system may be much higher than if the company had purchased premise based equipment, particularly for call center phone systems.

The cloud vs. premise based decision is typically made by comparing needs for speed and flexibility vs. needs to minimize long-term costs and to have direct control over the technology.

Implementing cloud-based systems: Caveat emptor! A cloud system is outsourced, but does not outsource the call center's functional design. The vendor's professional services staff are expert in their technology and you are expert in your business. The canyon between the two is a good system design based on your business requirements. This provides the vendor with something concrete to implement. You will need a team, and perhaps a consultant, to translate your business requirements into call center requirements, so the vendor can translate that into how the system should function. For inbound phone systems this includes one vs. several 800 numbers, IVR menus and announcements, alternate language options, organization of skills groups, overflow routing plans, reports required and usually more than one hundred related details.

In my experience, cloud vendor professional services staff do not analyze your business to provide an effective system design. Leaving this entirely in their hands is akin to hiring a carpenter but no architect to build a new house. The carpenter will make suggestions that initially appear to be good and smart. After living in the house you discover that its design was simplistic, cookie-cutter and is missing a lot of what you need. The same dissatisfaction occurs when cloud telephone system vendors design call centers. Firms try to put patches on these designs but ultimately must start from scratch to fix it, which means paying for set-up twice.

Vendors of traditional premise-based systems are also ill-equipped to design your call center. However, buyers of premise-based systems usually have more staff resources, including staff that work in this area, and so are less likely to expect that design is unnecessary or included.

Legal and Regulatory Compliance

Contact centers are a regulated way of doing business and some uses are more regulated than others. Responding to incoming customer service (non-sales) e-mails and web chats may be governed by the fewest regulations. Inbound customer service (non-sales) is minimally regulated. Outbound consumer sales calls are heavily regulated, although fewer rules govern calling one's customers and recent inquirers. Most business-to-business outbound sales calls are minimally regulated. Unsolicited fax and unsolicited pre-recorded outbound calls *for sales purposes* are illegal in the U.S.

In the U.S. the Federal Communications Commission (FCC) and Federal Trade Commission (FTC) are the primary federal regulators and there are also state laws. Here is a top level summary of some of the major rules. Regulators never consider ignorance as a valid reason for violation of the law and some companies have attracted penalties in the millions of dollars from the FTC. The legal fees and staff time required to respond to regulator inquiries that may lead to a fine can quickly reach hundreds of thousands of dollars.

All countries, including Canada, have their own unique regulations. While some rules in other countries are similar to U.S. law, few are exactly the same. For purposes of simplicity, this overview focuses solely on U.S. regulations.

Any call center compliance program must be based on a more detailed, program-specific and up-to-date review of regulations than is possible here. In many call centers, this is the job of the compliance officer. The compliance officer integrates legally compliant processes and compliance training into the operation. The information provided here is an introduction to regulatory compliance in contact centers.

These are some of the most important regulations in place at the time this was written. This will provide a basic understanding of which strategies, tactics and *good ideas* are legal and which can earn a company fines of up to $16,000 per incident (call) and, in rare cases, possible jail time.

Monitoring and recording inbound and outbound calls: In most states, call monitoring and recording requires *one-party* consent, which can be the phone rep. A written consent form is recommended. As many as twelve states require *all-party* consent. This is a reason you have heard the announcement,"This call may be monitored or recorded." This consent requirement applies to calls originating *or* terminating in all-party states, be they inbound or outbound calls.

Pay-by-phone regulations: U.S. law requires specific processes for paying over the phone, particularly by phone check or by repetitive credit card charges, which is sometimes called auto-pay. Many of these transactions must include a disclosure statement and customer agreement to the transaction, all of which is recorded to comply with the law.

Privacy and data breaches: Contact centers must employ practices to protect prospect and customer information from data breaches. This includes protecting credit card information through processes that are PCI (payment card industry) compliant. However it can also include other personal information, such as telephone numbers. In the event of a breach, the company must promptly notify those who may be affected.

Outbound consumer sales call do-not-call lists: Outbound consumer sales calls are heavily regulated. Every company that places outbound consumer sales calls is required to maintain a company-specific do-not-call list, and to scrub calling lists against it before placing calls. This company specific list is the repository of the telephone numbers of those who have directly asked your company not to call, either on a previous call or via a similar personal communications. During the scrubbing process those on calling lists, and also those on the company-specific do-not-call list, are *scrubbed* (removed) from the calling list.

Consumer calling lists must also be scrubbed against the National Do-Not-Call (DNC) Registry. There are specific exceptions to National DNC Registry scrubbing for existing customers and recent inquirers. Inquiries must have occurred within the preceding 90 days under U.S. federal law. This is made more complex by a handful of state laws that specify a period that is shorter or even zero days. A few states totally prohibit outbound consumer sales calls.

Companies that only call existing customers, recently lapsed customers and prospects who have inquired within the past 90 days are not required by federal law to scrub against the national Do-Not-Call Registry.

Each client company that is required to scrub must pay for its own annual subscription fee to the registry, even if it subcontracts the actual scrubbing to its outsourced contact center or another vendor. The first five area codes are free. As this is being written each additional area code is $59 per year up to a maximum of $16,228 per year for all U.S. area codes. These fees increase slightly each October.

There were more than 220 million phone numbers registered with the national registry as of late 2013, including some cell phones and fax numbers. This averages one phone number each for 72% of the United States' population. Clearly, much of the American public has opted out of receiving cold sales calls.

Computer calls to cell phones illegal without written permission: Federal law prohibits calls to cell phones if a computer dials the number unless the marketer has the cell phone owner's specific written permission to call their cell number, and has obtained it in a way that complies with federal regulations. Marketers subscribe to a service that supplies current cell phone numbers so that these may be scrubbed from calling lists. A SMS message is considered a call to a cell phone.

Sales disclosure and caller ID requirements: The FTC's Telemarketing Sales Rule requires specific types of disclosures during sales calls. Federal law also sets requirements for the transmission of caller I.D. and how calls to the caller I.D. phone number must be handled. Some states also have their own sales disclosure and caller I.D. rules.

State no rebuttal laws: A number of states prohibit the use of objection-responses, sometimes called rebuttals, and at least one requires informing the person being called that it is a sales call and then asking for permission to continue.

Calling hours and days: Federal rules restrict outbound sales calling to specific hours, making early morning and late night calls illegal. Some state laws are more restrictive and vary state to state. A handful of states have statutes that prohibit outbound sales calls on specific holidays such as Christmas. Louisiana determines its no-calling-holidays year-to-year.

Robocalls: Robocalls are automated outbound calls with recorded messages. These are illegal under federal and many state laws if they are placed for sales purposes. Customer service robocalls are permitted under federal law, such as a robocall to notify you that the car you dropped off for bodywork is ready. Congress exempted politicians from most of the federal telemarketing laws including those prohibiting robocalls, citing freedom of speech.

Business-to-business outbound sales calls: With the exception of *non-durable office or cleaning supplies*, business-to-business sales calls are not included in the FTC's Telemarketing Sales Rule and are not required by law to scrub against the do-not-call registry or to make specific sales disclosures. State laws may vary in this regard.

Charity exemption: Charities are exempt from many, but not all, of the federal tele-marketing laws. For example, charities need not scrub against the national Do-Not-Call Registry and so, like politicians, can telephone people on the registry.

Fax: Unsolicited faxes selling products are illegal under federal and many state laws. Faxes are also required to have certain header information by federal law.

Email: Outbound mass emails must comply with federal CAN-SPAM regulation. Among other things CAN-SPAM regulates who can be on the email list and requires that the email include a business street address and an unsubscribe option.

SMS: SMS messages for marketing purposes clearly require written permission under federal law as of 2013. See *computer calls to cell phones*, above.

Responsibility for non-compliance: Prudent companies require their outsourced contact center to take responsibility for regulatory compliance and specify this in writing as part the contract. Some have the contact center indemnify the client company for the results of non-compliance due to contact center company negligence. The contract may also specify activities that the client must carry out as its partner in compliance.

When a violation occurs, the government pursues all parties involvedand has a history of levying the largest penalties against the culpable party with the deepest pockets. It holds corporations responsible for non-compliance by its subcontractors and independent agents, particularly if a corporation does not take the specific pro-active steps to assure compliance by its agents and their employees outlined in past regulatory actions. Most prominently, in 2005 the U.S. Federal Trade Commission (FTC) fined DirecTV $5.3 million for the actions of independent sales agents that sold its satellite TV service. In 2009, DirecTV paid a second penalty of $2.31 million for another set of Do-Not-Call and related violations by its telemarketing firm's sales reps. The telemarketing firm, a much smaller company, was required to pay a penalty of $115,000 in this 2009 action.

If your company is making outbound consumer sales calls, it is essential to make pro-active efforts to regularly, routinely and diligently confirm that you and your contact center are complying with all applicable federal and state regulations. This should include an audit to determine that all parties are properly implementing compliance policies and practices in keeping with applicable regulations. This is a prudent measure for all contact center programs, including those operated in-house.

Finally, be sure the contact center has a process for keeping all relevant staff informed of changes in federal and state regulations.

Contact Center Strategies and Tactics at Work

There are a large number of nuts and bolts in contact center programs. Program managers who strategically select each nut and bolt so that it is well suited to their program usually experience successful results. Here are a few examples of creative approaches to program design that are well suited to specific programs.

Consumer marketer Zappos puts the right people in its inbound call center: The online shoe retailer Zappos has done an exemplary job of creating a service-oriented culture. They begin early and weed out reps who are not fully engaged in Zappos' culture of making customers happy. How? At the conclusion of training Zappos offers trainees $1,000 for doing one thing. That one thing is leaving the company. Think about who must leave and who stays.

JetBlue inbound call center takes off: When JetBlue was a start-up, it wanted to deliver good service by phone. It decided to use 100% U.S. based home agents so that it could recruit better quality reps than might do the same work at a centralized call center and to distinguish itself from airlines with overseas call centers.

American Medical Association uses segmentation and conditional close to boost outbound sales: The American Medical Association (AMA) sold a directory of all physicians with their specialties and professional backgrounds to state medical societies, medical libraries, university libraries and others. A direct mail piece was followed by a telephone call. The outbound business-to-business phone campaign produced 400% more sales than in the past due to two key modifications.

First a section early in the script was tailored to each market segment so that state medical societies, university libraries and others each received a message tailored to them. Second, it was discovered that many buyers required approval from a committee or board to purchase, but usually didn't remember to put the purchase on the meeting agenda. So a *conditional close* was added to the script. Phone reps told such buyers they would be sent an invoice that states the sale is subject to board or committee approval. If approval was received the organization would pay the invoice and receive the directory. If voted down they could disregard the invoice. The invoice assured that the purchase was on the meeting agenda, and it was usually approved.

Lands' End segments inbound staff to handle calls and web chats: Phone calls and web chats require an immediate response while emails require a response within a matter of hours. Contact center reps who can handle both calls and web chats have additional skills and so command higher wages. The incremental cost of hiring only reps who can handle all forms of customer contact is an expensive proposition for a large contact center.

Lands' End was an early adopter of web chat. To deliver speedy service at a reasonable cost it employed a large rep group that only handled phone calls. It also employed a smaller team that could handle phone calls, e-mails and web chats and so was paid higher wages. The second group put emails aside for a short time to handle peaks in web chat or phone call traffic. This enabled Lands' End to deliver speedy service in all media at a reasonable cost. How speedy? Lands' End handled 86–90% of calls within 20 seconds (about 4 rings), according to Angela Rundle, Supervisor for Internet Sales at the cataloguer.

Contact Center Program Success

So how does one decide what's appropriate and what won't cut it in the contact center? Experience helps a great deal. The best is experience designing, implementing *and measuring* contact center programs. The proof of the effectiveness of strategic and creative choices is usually in the numbers.

Secondarily, rely on your personal experience as a business-to-business prospect or customer, and as a consumer. What engages you in contact center programs? What turns you off? Instead of thinking about them as an abstract mass, put yourself in each of your prospects' or customers' shoes. Would that offer appeal to you? Would you like speaking with that telephone rep? Would you answer the question if it was worded that way? What would make you interested in discussing the product or service? Simply thinking about your program through the filter of the golden rule, *do unto others as you would like done unto you*, will help make your contact center program more customer-focused, successful and profitable.

Notes

First North American book rights to Susan K. Jones for publication in *The IMC Handbook: Readings & Cases in Integrated Marketing Communications*, 3rd ed., Racom Communications.

MITCHELL LIEBER is president of the international call center consulting firm, Lieber & Associates, and a frequent speaker and author on customer contact. Lieber & Associates assists companies with call and contact center assessments, strategy, customer experience, management studies, metrics, technology and training. A call center specialist and direct marketing generalist, Mitchell Lieber is past chair of the Board of Governors of the DMA International ECHO Awards. He may be reached at m_lieber@lieberandassociates.com or 1-773-325-0608.

READING
16

Social Media Marketing: Building, Nurturing and Sustaining Relationships

DePaul University

NEIL GRANITZ
California State University, Fullerton

Social media is the second generation of web-based tools (also called Web 2.0), and includes social networking sites (e.g. Myspace, Facebook), social sharing sites (e.g., YouTube, Snapchat, Pinterest), wikis, and blogs. The social use of the Internet has seen explosive growth recently. A Nielsen study found that over 66% of the worldwide Internet population could be reached through social networks—more than through e-mail, which many view as antiquated. According to the Pew Research Center, adoption and use of social media sites is especially high among teens and young adults (a coveted audience by advertisers). Eighty-one percent of online teens use social networking sites, and 42% of online adults use multiple social media sites. A recent study indicates that users spend more time on social media than they do on e-mail. Not surprisingly, college students actually exhibit physical symptoms of withdrawal if they are isolated from social media devices and social media sites.

The use of social media presents significant opportunities for marketers to connect with customers and build relationships in ways they never have before. Whether you are promoting your company, your personal business, your next career move, or a local event, it is critical to understand the value of social media marketing to enhance your business or career. This article will provide you with a better understanding of the new social media landscape, and will present strategies for businesses and individuals to use social media sites to build awareness, increase visibility and engage in conversations with potential and existing customers.

Web 1.0: The Beginning

The advent of the World Wide Web in the early 1990s, and the subsequent rapid increase in the adoption and use of the Web, was fueled in part by innovations from some (now) well-known companies. America Online (AOL) helped to migrate people onto the Web, while Yahoo! and Google made content on the Web easily searchable and accessible. The Internet quickly became an integral part of consumers' everyday lives, especially as a significant and influential source of information for consumers about a variety of topics. At the same time, many companies recognized the potential of the Web to provide consumers with an almost unlimited amount of information at an extremely low cost, and the number of corporate homepages exploded. In addition to providing information, many organizations also began to use their web sites as a vehicle for consumers to purchase products in addition to (or instead of) their bricks and mortar stores. Companies rushed to develop other business models to take advantage of this emergent technology. Some of the new business models that were tested in the early dot-com days included connect-time revenue splits (AOL, USA Today), online auctions (eBay), reverse auctions (FreeMarkets), affiliate/pay-for-performance (Amazon, Barnes & Noble), micro-charging (iTunes), and infomediary models (Travelocity, Kelly Blue Book). Thus began the dot-com bubble.

Unfortunately, many of these early business models were not successful. Even though many companies struggled to integrate this new technology into their marketing strategy, thought leaders predicted that after the dot-com shakeout it would not be a matter of whether or not a company used the Internet, but rather how they used it. Currently, companies' use of web sites to provide information and facilitate purchase of products is ubiquitous. Other business models such as auctions and micro-charging have also been quite successful (e.g., Priceline, eBay, iTunes).

Consumer and organizational use of the Internet continues to evolve. The current focus is on collaboration and sharing of content versus passive viewing of content. This new generation of the Web has been coined Web 2.0.

Web 2.0: The Social Use of the Web

Tim O'Reilly, an early pioneer of Web 2.0, defines it as follows:

> Web 2.0 is the network as platform, spanning all connected devices; Web 2.0 applications are those that make the most of the intrinsic advantages of that platform; delivering software as a continually-updated service that gets better the more people use it, consuming and remixing data from multiple sources, including individual users, while providing their own data and services in a form that allows remixing by others, creating network effects though an architecture of participation and going beyond the page metaphor of Web 1.0 to deliver rich user experiences (O'Reilly, 2005).

Web 2.0 developed through the convergence of several existing technologies (see Table R16.1). The concerted use of this technology (and the related tools) has created new "Principles of Social Media Marketing" (see Table R16.2). Simply stated, Web 2.0 revolves around the social use of the Web to create and share information. Collaboration in this creation of new content can take place through many social platforms, including email, chat rooms, message boards, blogs, micro-blogs, podcasts, social networking sites, video/photo sharing sites, wikis, social bookmarking,

TABLE R16.1. SOCIAL MEDIA TECHNOLOGY TOOLS[1]

Social Networking Software	**Examples**
This software allows users to connect, create, post, and network with other users.	Facebook, MySpace, Twitter, Snapchat, Pinterest
Collaboration Tools	**Examples**
A wiki is a site that allows users to add and amend content and is used primarily for collaborative authoring; these tools often allow individuals to rate a posted comment or document.	Wikipedia, Wikia
Self-Expression Tools	**Examples**
These tools include blogs, vlogs and podcasts. Blog stands for web log and is a personal diary that is available for the public to read and follow. Several blog search engines allow users to find blogs in the blogosphere (community of all blogs). A vlog is simply the video equivalent of a blog. A podcast is a series of audio or videodigital media files which are distributed over the Internet to portable media players and computers; new content is downloaded automatically using RSS (Real Simple Syndication).	Blogs: Blogger, WordPress Blog search engines: Technorati, IceRocket Vlogs: FreeVlog, Rocketboom Podcasts: Ask a Ninja, iTunes
Productivity Software	**Examples**
These are free web-based software tools that offer a toolbox of capabilities similar to desktop software such as Microsoft Office.	Google Docs
Content Tracking Tools	**Examples**
A permalink is a URL for a resource that never changes and is always available. Thanks to the permalink, users can keep track of, filter and search a growing amount of social media content.	Digg, Delicious
Remix and Mashup Tools	**Examples**
A remix is the reworking of an original work. A mashup involves the combination of two or more works that may be very different from one another. An application programming interface (API) is often used to accomplish this. Thus, two different websites are integrated to create a unique third website.	Yahoo Pipes Mashup Search Engine: ProgrammableWeb

[1]Taken from Granitz and Koernig, *Journal of Marketing Education* (2011)

TABLE R16.2. PRINCIPLES OF SOCIAL MEDIA MARKETING[2]

Social Media is participative; users create value. The traditional view of the web has been one-sided with publishers pushing out content to users; however, low cost tools (access to software, Internet, bandwith and open source code) allow mass collaboration.	Example The California Open-Source Textbook Project offers a new model for creating textbooks by leveraging currently available free content, the expertise of faculty and innovative copyright tools such as Creative Commons.
Social media facilitates the free creation and sharing of information. Organizations offer services (in the form of free software) that attract users to their sites and gives them tools to create their environment. These services allow for a high degree of scalability by allowing individuals to share the information that they have created with an almost unlimited number of people.	Example Google delivers free services over the web, such as Google Sites, allowing users to create and edit web pages. Google Sites allows control over who can access and change this content.
Crowdsourcing/Bottom up structure. By users sharing knowledge with the public, the knowledge process is accelerated. Tapscott and Williams (2006) call this "peering": when people self-organize to create knowledge, share experiences or design goods and services.	Example In a bid to find mining locations, Goldcorp opened up their databases to scientists, geologists and engineers in the general population.
Success is based on the ability to harness collective intelligence. O'Reilly (2005) refers to the web as a giant global brain.	Example Social media success stories like YouTube, Facebook and MySpace are from organizations that were able to harness collective intelligence.
Social media is about remix and mashup and creation. End users are rapidly gaining access to content that was once considered proprietary and are exercising the power of creation and distribution.	Example The Chicago Police Department employs a web application called "Clearmap" to mash crime data from their online database with Google Maps.

[2]Taken from Granitz and Koernig, *Journal of Marketing Education* (2011)

mashups, news aggregation, and RSS feeds. Harnessing the collective intelligence of the masses through these platforms accelerates and enhances the learning process and the creation of knowledge.

Similar to the dot-com frenzy, many companies are frantically embracing social media without a full understanding of how/when/why to use it. One thing is for certain—to remain relevant, companies need to embrace social media. The question is: Which social media tools are appropriate, and how can/should companies use them?

How Is Social Media Different?

Before we get into a discussion of the strategic uses of social media sites, a quick discussion of traditional marketing strategy is in order. The marketing "old guard" revolved around the "Four P's": product, price, place (distribution), and promotion. Specifically, promotion includes four main activities: sales promotions, advertising, personal selling, and public relations—all of which an organization can control. However, while an organization has complete control over their public relations strategy, they are at the mercy of independent news sources to spread their message. Possible outcomes of an organization's public relations strategy may be positive publicity, negative publicity, or the very real possibility of no publicity.

When positive publicity results from the public relations effort, the organization benefits in two main ways: (1) consumers tend to trust the message compared to a paid advertisement, and (2) the cost for this publicity is negligible, thus resulting in essentially free advertising for the organization. Thus, the primary goal of a public relations campaign is to build positive word-of mouth (WOM) through trusted independent sources. For example, in the pre-social media days, restaurant-goers might read a review about a new restaurant in the "Food" section of the *Los Angeles Times* online. The restaurant hopes that the review reports favorably on their food, service and ambience, but they cannot control what is written.

The organization embracing social media marketing is faced with challenges similar to their public relations efforts—both are *strategies* over which the company has complete control, but they do not have control over the *outcome* of said efforts. An organization can expect outcomes similar to a PR campaign as a result of their social media marketing efforts: positive "buzz," negative buzz, or no buzz. In a social media campaign, the buzz is no longer created by independent news sources; rather consumers shape the message and share it among their friends. As a consumer whom do you trust more? Companies or people that you regularly interact with? You probably answered the latter! Traditionally, people have shared positive brand experiences with about three people, but share negative experiences with up to ten people. Thus, in the pre-social media era, a positive or negative buzz would build slowly over time. However, today social media gives consumers the ability to disseminate information instantaneously—to potentially be viewed by millions of people. As such, in an accelerated timeframe, consumer chatter on social media sites like Yelp can have a significant impact on the success or failure of your organization. This increases the efficiency of markets where high quality products are revered and quickly made successful, and low quality products are besmirched and briskly disregarded.

Social media platforms developed organically as a means by which people could build and maintain personal relationships, and the "Holy Grail" for social media marketers is to tap into these friendship networks to create relationships with consumers and harness their power to spread positive buzz about the brand. The critical issue for organizations is how they can and should tap into this vast potential. Unfortunately, many companies are jumping into the deep end without an understanding of what they want the social media efforts to achieve. In the next section, we offer guidance to help organizations better understand the strategic uses of social media sites.

Social Media Marketing: A Strategic Philosophy

Before launching into the specific marketing strategy elements, we would like to lay out a general philosophy that companies can use when approaching the use of social media. First, consumers view social media sites as places where they can meet and connect with others; that is also how companies should see it. It is your chance to mix with consumers and put a face on your business. For example, *A Thousand Words* is a blog written by people who work at Kodak Alaris. The byline reads, "We love what we do, and we want to share our stories about imaging and its power to influence our world. We invite you to join our conversation with stories of your own." In this case it is the face of the actual Kodak Alaris employees.

Second, social media marketing is about creating contexts for interaction and engaging a community. It is the next logical step in relationship marketing where companies can create lasting relationships with their constituents. With its Refresh Project, Pepsi built an online community through offline community. They awarded money to people, businesses, and non-profits that had ideas to positively impact their community. Ideas were submitted by constituents and then voted on by the community. The Refresh Project blog also included stories of people who have enacted their refresh projects.

Third, the purpose of social media marketing should be to listen and respond. Companies should draw consumers to their social media sites and listen. If needed, they should respond. Burt's Bees, best known for their beeswax lip balm, had 1,764,467 likes on its Facebook page at this writing. If one peruses the page, there are positive fans who are loving the products or mentioning negative issues they have with the products; Burt's Bees is responding when necessary. For example, a fan comment of , "I love the toothpaste" gets no response; but the comment, "I am a Burt's Bees advocate, but . . . in the past week, my 15-month old and my friend's baby of the same age had a horrible allergic reaction to the Baby Bees Buttermilk Lotion," gets the response, "We are very sorry to hear of the reaction that your child had with our Baby Bee Buttermilk Lotion," as well as contact info so that the customer can follow-up.

Fourth, social media should not constitute your entire marketing plan; it plays one part of your integrated marketing plan where all the pieces work together to create a positive ROI. Corporations should not use social media for the hard-sell; that is the job of your web site and brick and mortar store. Consumers use social media sites to connect with friends and family. This is your chance to be friends with your consumers; friends don't ask friends to buy anything. However, through repeated positive interactions, trust and long-term relationships can develop, which subsequently can lead to sustained sales.

Strategic Marketing Uses of Social Media Sites

In this section, examples of successful and unsuccessful social media marketing strategies are presented. These are organized around the marketing strategies where the use of social media is most advantageous. The outcome of these strategies is reported when it is available; however in many cases the company has not reported the degree of success (or failure) of their social media marketing efforts.

Market Research

It is imperative that every company—no matter how large or small—at least dip their toe in the social media waters. An excellent entry point for the novice involves monitoring what consumers are saying online about their brand. For an organization completely unfamiliar with social media, this might require the company's new social media "expert" to first research the use of social media sites by consumers of their product. This will provide the organization with an introduction to some of the specific sites that are currently popular. Additionally, they can search online resources such as Marketing Land (formerly Sphinn), Wikipedia, or Technorati. A history of these searches can be maintained by bookmarking these articles using social media sites such as Delicious, StumbleUpon and Digg.

After building competence with these social media sites, the focus should shift to "listening" to customers' (actual, former, and potential) online conversations about your brand. General search engines like Google or Bing are effective at casting a wide net to find these conversations. For a large multinational brand, it might be easy to find conversations about your products; in this case, the difficult task will likely be sifting through all of the clutter to find relevant comments. For example, a search for Starbucks (the coffee brand) might result in a huge number of "hits" that may or may not be related to your search. Instead, you might find results related to news about Starbucks, general corporate information, or even hits related to the character Starbuck from the television series "Battlestar Galactica!"[3]. The objective of these searches is to determine where your customers and friends are talking online. Depending on the industry, your customers and friends might be congregating in particular social media sites. For example, wine- related blogs such as *Vinography*, *The Wine Blog*, and *Dr. Vono's Wine Blog*, would be good starting points for a wine producer (or seller) to gauge reaction to their products. A perusal of these sites might also provide clues about other social media sites that are popular with this audience.

Once a comprehensive search has been conducted (and digested), it is important that the ongoing conversations be monitored. Tools like Google Alerts and Really Simple Syndication (RSS) feeds are useful in this regard. Google Alerts is a free service offered by Google that monitors the web for new content. The user enters search terms and when new content is created on blogs, new sites, etc., matching the search

---

[3]More on the importance of search terms can be found in the Social Media Marketing Measurement presented later in this chapter.

terms, an update is sent via email with the updates. The user can control the frequency of these updates: "once a day," "once a week," or "as it happens." RSS feeds give the user a more targeted approach to receive updates about new content, typically from sites that are updated often such as news sites and blogs. By clicking on the RSS icon on a website, the user subscribes to the site and receives automated updates from it.

Listening to consumers' conversations will result in the following benefits. First, the process of searching social media sites will help build knowledge of and comfort with these sites. Second, listening to what your customers are saying is an easy and timely way to collect market research about consumer attitudes, consumer demographics, complaints about your products, new product ideas and uses, and attitudes toward competitors' products. Third, it provides you with an opportunity to participate in the conversation. After finding conversations about your brand on social media sites (e.g., blog posts, videos on YouTube, Tweets on Twitter, etc.), you can comment on the appropriate blog or interact with customers through the social media site. For example, in New York, Pretzel Crisps launched the billboard ad campaign, "You can never be too thin." The ad was seen by many as encouraging anorexia and was posted on the women's blog site, Jezebel, followed by condemning comments and tweets. The next day, Pretzel Crisps sent out an e-mail to bloggers thanking them for their feedback, explaining that they thought the word thin was a good way to describe their product and assuring readers that the ads would be removed.

Ignoring these conversations is dangerous. One of the characteristics of social media is rapid dissemination of information, and if a negative (or positive) buzz is building, it will build fast. In fact, ignoring social media conversations can lead to a public relations nightmare. For example, two Domino's Pizza employees posted a video on YouTube purportedly showing one of the employees putting a piece of cheese up his nose (among other, more disgusting, things) and then onto a sandwich being prepared for delivery. Domino's was not actively listening to online conversations about their brand, and was unaware of this video until advised by a blogger of its existence. Even after being alerted to the video, Domino's did not immediately respond in an attempt to reduce the damage of the video. In the meantime, bloggers discovered the exact location of the store by using other businesses shown through the window to triangulate the location. By the time Domino's reacted to this public relations nightmare, the number of views of the video had surpassed one million in just a few days, damaging the company's reputation and sales. Despite countless examples such as this, a whopping 28% of companies still do not actively monitor social media chatter about their brand.

Blogging & Targeting Influencers

A we**blog**, or "blog," is a web site that which includes written thoughts (about anything and everything) that may include pictures, sounds, and videos. Many early blogs functioned as a type of online diary. For example, Stephanie Klein achieved early fame as a blogger (her blog is called Greek Tragedy) due to her provocative blog about her personal and professional life (think Sex and the City). She abandoned her career as an art director for an ad agency in New York to become a full-time blogger/writer after *The New York Times* ran a story about her in the "Sunday Styles" section. Since then, she has continued to blog, and has also parlayed her success as a blogger into two book deals—both memoirs.

Over time, the blogging community has exploded. This growth is due in part to Blogger.com and WordPress.com, the two most commonly used blogging platforms. Both allow any users to set up blog platforms for free. Blogger has undisclosed millions of users while WordPress boasts over two million active blogs. As a result, blogs evolved beyond people's personal musings and became more focused on particular areas of interest. Some of the more popular blogging subjects include (but are certainly not limited to) politics, music, travel, fashion, and food/drink. As blogging increased in popularity, companies realized the potential for independent bloggers to reach—and influence—large numbers of people. In 2008, Procter & Gamble identified "mommy bloggers" as an important and persuasive group of influencers for their product lines (especially their Baby Care and Family Care business segments). To tap into the potential of these influencers, P&G invited fifteen mommy bloggers to visit the P&G headquarters in Cincinnati, Ohio, for an all-expense paid trip including airfare, hotel accommodations, tours of the P&G facilities, and group discussions with other mommy bloggers and P&G executives about moms, babies, and P&G products. According to P&G, "We've made it clear that we are not pitching products per se, but exploring areas of common interest, such as baby development and how to help moms in this topsy-turvy time in their lives." Of course, P&G hoped that these influential bloggers would blog about their experiences with the company and itstheir products in a positive way—and they did.

A company can also create its own blog. For example, Best Western sponsors a blog, On the Go with Amy, where the author travels the country writing about her experiences. Unlike the above example where an independent blogger promotes the brand (and thus is seen as a credible source), the company-sponsored blog may be seen as a type of advertisement; therefore, it is especially critical that the blog creates value for the consumer. It should deliver fresh and relevant content for your audience that is worth sharing. . . . Otherwise, what is the reason for people to come together and form a community around your brand? For example, on the Best Western blog, Amy visits large cities and small towns in America, reviewing major tourist attraction and off-beat places to visit. A company-sponsored blog is ideal for products with steep learning curves (e.g., high-tech products, baby-related products, or financial services), when there is a lifestyle associated with brand (e.g., autos, alcohol, or travel) or to promote a social mission(e.g., environmental, homelessness, aid to Third World countries).

A major theme of any social media marketing strategy should be openness, honesty, and transparency. The company that fails to heed this advice may suffer a backlash from consumers. For example, Wal-Mart's ad agency (Edelman Worldwide) created and paid for a "flog" (fake blog), "Wal-Marting Across America," documenting the adventures of a couple on a cross-country road trip. Along their journey, the couple parked their RV in Wal-Mart parking lots overnight to sleep. They also frequently posted on their blog about Wal-Mart employees that they purportedly spoke with who all voiced their love of working for the company. However, the "couple" were actually professional journalists who were backed and funded by Edelman. This lack of transparency was in violation of the Word of Mouth Marketing Association's Code of

Ethics, which Edelman helped to create. Chronicled in a major story in *Business Week*, this added to consumers' pre-existing negative perceptions of Wal-Mart, most likely hurting their sales.

Promotions

Currently, one of the most popular uses of social media by companies is for sales promotions. The goal of sales promotions is to increase short-term sales and to get new customers to try the brand—and hopefully become brand loyal. Because of its shortness and immediacy, Twitter, a micro-blogging site, is an ideal tool to use for this. A California pizza chain, Z'Pizza, places ads in local "traditional" media stating that if you followed them on Twitter, you would already know about today's deal. Besides promoting existing specials, there should be online specials to keep consumers following your Twitter account. For example, Jetblue has over 1.79 million followers and tweets its online and off-line deals. Naked Pizza, a New Orleans pizza chain hoping to go national, started to track Twitter inspired sales. In a test, an exclusive Twitter offer brought in 15% of a day's business.

Social networking sites, like Facebook, also provide significant opportunities to increase short-term sales and to foster brand loyalty among current and potential consumers. Sprinkles Cupcakes is an extremely effective example of the successful use of Facebook to promote the brand and to increase consumer engagement with their brand. To rapidly increase their number of Facebook "likes," Sprinkles ran a "BFF Contest." The goal of this contest was to increase the number of likes that Sprinkles had on Facebook to 100,000 (from a little over 30,000). From the start of the promotion until the 100,000[th] like (or the contest deadline), anyone who "liked" Sprinkles on Facebook was entered in the contest. The grand prize was a trip for two to Beverly Hills; the location of the first Sprinkles bakery. This promotion helped Sprinkles to quickly meet (and exceed) their goal of 100,000 likes. (They now have more than 461,000 likes.) To keep consumers engaged with the brand, on Facebook and Twitter, Sprinkles posts a secret phrase that customers can "whisper" at a Sprinkles store to receive a free cupcake.

Einstein Bros. Bagels also used a Facebook promotion to increase engagement with their customers and to obtain new customers. If a consumer "liked" Einstein Bros. Bagels, they could download one in-store coupon for a free bagel and "schmear" of cream cheese. The promotion was a huge success in terms of getting new likes (from 4,700 at the beginning of the promotion to over 336,000 in three days).

Healthy Choice has attempted to exponentially increase the number of people who "like" their brand on Facebook by increasing the value of a coupon as the number of new people joining the page increases during the duration of the promotion. In a little over 24 hours, the number of Healthy Choice fans tripled (to about 53,000 fans); the coupon also grew from 75 cents off to $1.25 off of the next purchase. As the number of likes continued to grow, the coupon morphed into a buy-one-get-one-free offer.

Social media sharing sites, like YouTube, are especially good at increasing engagement among consumers by facilitating the creation of content involving the brand. Procter & Gamble promoted their Crest Whitening Expressions brand through a "catch-phrase" contest. To replace their "Bam!" tagline (made famous by Emeril Lagasse, a celebrity endorser of the brand), Crest asked YouTube users to create and post a video describing their experience with the brand in ten words or less for the Wintergreen Ice flavor. In a similar vein, Klondike sponsored a "What Would You Do?" contest to reinvigorate the brand with a new audience using their classic tagline. In this contest, consumers created and posted videos on YouTube describing the lengths that they would go for a Klondike bar. Not only do these contests increase engagement with the brand (the Klondike winner actually went to the Arctic to film part of his video), but they also have the potential to be viewed and shared by a large number of other people (e.g., going viral) if the video is funny, cute, or otherwise compelling. Interestingly, a popular losing entry (submitted by YouTube user "BriTANicK") still generated significant buzz and has been viewed more thanover 1.2 million times.

Ideally, multiple social media platforms should be used in the sales promotion. For example, Coca-Cola conducted a nationwide search for three people to serve as ambassadors for the company. Coke fans were involved from the outset by voting on the nine finalists. The three winners traveled to every country in which Coca-Cola products are sold (206) over the course of 365 days. The three contest winners used a variety of social networking sites (including but not limited to Facebook, YouTube, Twitter, and Flickr) to document their journey with a focus on finding "what makes people happy" in the various countries they visited.

Customer Service

Customer service is another extremely popular use of social media sites. In fact, many social media sites are emerging as new (and more efficient) replacements for e-mail and phone centers. American Airlines asked customers with complaints to e-mail them. There was a 13% increase in e-mail complaints but a 74% increase in downstream traffic to MySpace. Many social media sites are ideally suited to serve as quick and inexpensive substitutes for the often maligned customer service call centers. For example, Frank Eliason, the (now former) Director of Digital Care for Comcast, was instrumental in spearheading the use of social media sites to assist customers experiencing problems with their Comcast service. Through the Twitter account @ComcastCares, Frank searched for customers Tweeting about problems and asked "Can I help?" He typically was able to address their problem either on the Twitter site or, for more complex problems, he asked the customer to "DM" (direct message; Twitter's version of email) him with their contact information.

JetBlue has similarly also embraced Twitter to help assist customers with problems they encounter with the airline, such as flight delays and misplaced baggage. Additionally, they promote new flight routes and special promotions, provide information about airports (e.g. availability of power outlets and access to WiFi), and monitor (and respond to) conversations about JetBlue occurring in real time on Twitter. Many organizations have discovered that an added advantage of solving problems via a Tweet is that customers with similar issues also can see the solution to the problem. Also, when you publicly solve a problem, you are publicizing good customer service to your constituents.

New Product Development

In a 2006 *Wired* magazine article, Jeff Howe coined the term *"crowd-sourcing"* to describe the use of customers, potential customers, and other stakeholders as your labor pool to produce your product or service. By its very nature, crowd-sourcing is often perceived to be risky for many companies because the more the product/service is crowd-sourced, the less control the company has over the message and the brand image. However, it is also a very powerful tool to generate new product ideas—and to engage customers with your brand.

Crowd-sourcing can be directly or indirectly used to develop new products. Indirectly, using social media to just listen to customers, for customer service or for product promotions may spur the idea for a new product. For example, Ben &Jerry's started an online "Free Cone Day" to complement their offline Free Cone Day. Facebook users could give their friends a "virtual cone" that would appear on their Facebook wall. This promotion helped bring consumers to their Facebook page, where numerous discussions took place regarding favorite flavors, the availability of flavors, and ideas for new flavors.

Other companies have found that changing a package or logo without asking for consumers' opinions first may result in a backlash. For example, Tropicana replaced the long-time symbol of an orange with a straw in it on their packaging with a glass of orange juice. Using social media, customers complained. On Facebook, one customer wrote, "My nine year old freaked out when he saw the new branding. Yikes! We couldn't force ourselves to buy it." Tropicana promptly reverted to their original packaging. Similarly, when the Gap changed its logo from the familiar blue background with white lettering to a white background with black letters and a little blue box there was an incredible amount of outcry against the new logo on Facebook and Twitter. One week later, the company announced (on Facebook) that it would be reverting back to its original logo. Company spokespersons also stated that they should have used social media to involve their consumers in the creation of the new logo. In both cases, consumers rapidly complained that the originals were far superior, and the companies took this information to heart and reverted back to the original designs. Their rapid response likely prevented a long, drawn out battle, which would serve neither company well.

Directly, you can directly ask customers for ideas for new products. Starbucks offers a site, MyStarbucksIdeas, where users can post ideas their own ideas and vote on the ideas of others. At the time of this writing, the idea of Starbucks offering a birthday brew has received 79,400 votes. Modcloth, a small online clothing retailer, lets consumers "be the buyer." Samples of women's dresses are put on the company website for 14 days, and during this time consumers can vote for the dress by clicking on a "pick it!" or "skip it!" button. They can also post comments about what they like and don't like about the dress. This provides the company with extremely valuable customer input, which helps them decide which dresses to produce. When a decision is made to manufacture a dress, consumers who voted "pick it!" are sent an email letting them know about their "win," which reminds them about the brand and encourages purchase of the dress.

Sales

For most companies, directly increasing sales should not be a primary goal of the social media marketing strategy. Social media marketing is about putting a face on a business; it's giving consumers someone to trust. It's really about friends connecting with, creating with, and collaborating with each other. People like to talk about brands and identify with them and their fellow users on their Facebook page; however, they might not respond well on sales-oriented company intrusions. Imagine if every time you invited a friend over to dinner he or she tried to sell you something. Would you continue the "friendship" or stop inviting him for dinner?

However, social media marketing can be effective in generating sales under the right circumstances. For example, Dell offers consumers refurbished computers at low prices via their @DellOutlook Twitter account. According to Dell, the @DellOutlook Twitter account has been very financially lucrative for Dell. Additionally, by including links to their products in their Tweets, Dell is also able to track the effectiveness of each Twitter promotion. An added advantage of drawing customers to the Dell website via Twitter is that some customers decide to buy a new computer after visiting the Dell Outlet site.

Social Media Marketing Measurement

Although many companies have embraced social media, a large number of companies have struggled to determine whether or not their social media marketing efforts have been successful. According to eMarketer, 47 percent of companies worldwide are not able to measure the effectiveness of their social media marketing efforts. (Thirty-five percent reported a similar or greater return or value than from other marketing activities.) Of course, measuring the impact of a social media campaign may be more (or less) difficult depending on the strategic objectives of the social media marketing efforts. For example, measuring the effectiveness of using Twitter by Dell Outlet to increase sales is relatively easy compared to measuring Jet Blue's use of Twitter to improve customer service and provide customers with information.

In a majority of cases it is difficult to measure the impact of social media marketing, especially if it is used to increase engagement among consumers with the brand. How do you know if your social media strategy is helping to increase engagement with your brands? If consumers are more engaged with your brands, they likely will be talking more about the brand online. In fact, this should be a primary goal of any social media campaign. Thus, measuring the success of a specific social media marketing strategy can be done by comparing the online "chatter" before and after the firm's social media marketing efforts. This is actually quite similar to measuring the impact of an ad campaign on increasing brand awareness. For example, the organization measures brand awareness (and or sales) before and after the ad campaign to determine if there are any differences.

The critical issue is how to measure the buzz before and after the social media marketing event. Unlike advertising, there is no consensus on exactly how to do this. An extremely simple method of measuring the impact of your social media marketing strategy is to use a general search engine like Google or Bing to compare the number of conversations about your brand before and after your social media campaign. Of course, selecting the "right" search terms may prove to be extremely difficult. For example, Do you use the brand name? The corporate name? Brand slogans? All of the above?! Even if the "right" search terms are used, for a large multi-national brand measurement still might prove difficult due to the amount of clutter online. However, for a relatively unknown brand (with little to no online conversation prior to the social media campaign), measuring the impact of the social media campaign should be significantly easier.

The quest for an easy, accurate, and customary way to measure the impact of a social media strategy has led to the development of public (for sale) and proprietary measurement systems. IBM developed data mining and text analytics software (sold under the SPSS Modeler brand) to help companies monitor and analyze what consumers are saying about their company, brands, products (and those of the competition) on blogs, Twitter, and other searchable social media sites. This software uses a sentiment-analysis algorithm to gauge consumer emotions in these conversations; this is a relatively new technology that has yet to fully be developed.

Ad agencies, public relations firms, and other related industries have also rushed to develop tools to measure the outcome of a social media campaign. It is crucial for these organizations to gather this data so that they can demonstrate the impact of their services. For example, the Zócalo Group (a word of mouth and social media marketing agency and a division of Omnicom Group, Inc.), in collaboration with DePaul University marketing faculty, developed the Digital Footprint Index (DFI), which measures the outcome of a social media strategy along three dimensions: *height*, *width*, and *depth*. The *height* deals with the degree to which your brand is being talked about online, and tries to determine the overall volume of all brand mentions across online channels. This is determined by examining the number of blog posts, forum threads, tweets, videos, photos, social networking groups, etc. The *width* involves the degree that your brand conversation is being engaged with and shared by consumers. Different than height, the width is the sum of the engagement metrics for each channel analyzed in the height. Examples include the number of comments, thread replies, video views, photo views, Diggs, Twitter followers, bookmarks, etc. The *depth* tackles the issue of whether or not people are talking about your brand in the way you want them to; this includes the presence of a brand's keywords and messages in social media conversations, as well as the tone of the conversation. Are a brand's messages adopted and used by consumers? Are the conversations positive or negative?

At present, the height and width are fairly easy to measure using automated programs (assuming there is consensus on the specific sites to include in the search, which is no easy task), but the valence of the message is difficult to measure using people, and almost impossible to measure using automated programs. For example, let's assume that Starbucks conducts an aggressive social media campaign promoting a line of ten new products. In their attempt to measure the impact of this campaign, there may be three blog posts which all mention Starbucks (the coffee). The first blog post is very effusive about Starbucks, and even includes slogans from their new social media campaign, but the post is vague as to reasons for this love (or even the products the poster likes). The second blog post is a critical evaluation of the new product releases in the style of *Consumer Reports*. Unfortunately, there is no consensus about the quality of the ten new drinks—some receive favorable reviews, but others do not. The third post is a very negative one about the use of social media to promote these new products. Currently, the only way to evaluate and compare the tone and content of these blog posts involves a subjective classification of the three messages.

In summary, when undertaking any social media marketing strategy, it is important that the company designate some measures of the outcome. As the field develops, more accurate, standardized, lower-cost measurement solutions will become available.

Paid Social Media

While social media web sites offer many "free" ways for organizations to market themselves, the stakeholders of these web sites must make money and offer several "paying" marketing tools that businesses can use to promote their product or service. As the specific properties are often changing their offerings, the discussion will focus on the general major marketing abilities that social media properties offer. To find the various options for each social media web site, one usually just scrolls to the bottom of the site and looks for a "business solutions" or "advertising" link.

Banner ads. Banner ads are akin to traditional advertising where the business pays to have their ad appear on a particular page (regardless of the click-throughs). These ads are appropriate when you have to get the word out fast and hit a large general target. On the YouTube homepage, one could find an ad for Liberty Mutual insurance as a sponsor of the 2014 Winter Olympics prior to and during the Olympics.

Targeted advertising. Some social media sites allow advertisers to target ads based upon demographic and personal information submitted to the site by the user. Targeted ads can be very effective in reaching a well-defined but narrow segment. For example, in composing their Facebook profile, a user may have listed that they are a female, aged 20 and like running. As a result, Nike may pay Facebook to place an ad for a female running shoe on this user's site. Furthermore if the user likes the ad, they may click a Like button on the ad and everyone in their network will see the ad and that the user liked it. On LinkedIn, similar targeting can be conducted; Fidelity targets education professionals with special 403k plans.

Content targeting. Some social media sites offer organizations the opportunity to advertise on site pages that match the content of the product or service that the organization is promoting; this is often called content targeting. This type of advertising goes beyond matching search keywords with advertisements; instead it matches the keywords of the search to the contents of Internet Web pages, resulting in more useful and relevant search results. For example, on YouTube, a search for "hot dog" will pull up a promoted video by Heinz entitled, "57 Things You Can Eat with Heinz Ketchup."

Promotional search ads. Social media sites, like Twitter and Digg, allow organizations to have their results show up with the organic results searched by the user. Promotional ads work when you have short fast messages to relay. For example, a search on Digg for the latest news will also bring up the headline "Del Taco does Breakfast", with the byline, sponsored by Del Taco. Or under #nowplaying, a popular twitter topic, Virgin America asks passengers in the air to tweet what they are watching.

Paid participation. In this case, the organization can pay the social media site for greater prominence. These ads are useful when corporations do not yet have enough representation on social media sites to automatically appear high in the results. For example, Yelp advertisers can have their advertisement appear above Yelp search results. Businesses that pay Yelp can also prevent the ads of competitive businesses appearing on their page.

Sponsored social media. Even though they don't even know them, many people feel close to celebrities because they can follow their tweets and Facebook fan pages. While this is not a direct service offered by the social media websites, there are middlemen who represent celebrities and these celebrities can endorse your product on social media sites. Similar to all sponsorships, these ads work best when there is symmetry between the image of the celebrity and the sponsor. For example, Kim Kardashian reportedly has earned $10,000 a tweet while promoting brands like Carl's Jr. and T-Mobile Blackberry.

The Future of Social Media Marketing

The social media marketing landscape is constantly evolving (e.g., the irrelevance of once dominant MySpace and Second Life; the relatively new dominance of Twitter, and popular emerging sites such as Snapchat and Pinterest). It is also difficult to predict what the next hot site will be. Indeed, today's "magic bullet" might be irrelevant tomorrow. At the time of this writing, picture/video based networks (Snapchat, Pinterest, Instagram) seem to be all the rage. Time will tell if these relatively new platforms have staying power. Whatever the next-big-thing is for social media marketing, one thing is for certain:—social media platforms are not silver bullets that will be the salvation of every company using them. However, social media can be an important and extremely effective tool in the marketing mix of any company that chooses to use it.

STEPHEN K. KOERNIG is an Associate Professor at DePaul University in Chicago. Steve has won numerous awards for teaching and research and is currently teaching *Social Media Marketing, Strategic Marketing Tools, Consumer Behavior*, and *Services Marketing*. Dr. Koernig's academic research focuses on social media marketing, e-commerce, and marketing education. His research has been published in leading academic journals including *Journal of Advertising, Psychology & Marketing, Journal of Marketing Education*, and *Sport Marketing Quarterly*. Steve is an American Marketing Association Doctoral Fellow, and is a member of the American Marketing Association and the Academy of Marketing Science. He received his M.B.A. from DePaul University and has a Ph.D. in marketing from the University of Illinois at Chicago.

NEIL GRANITZ is a Professor of Marketing at California State University, Fullerton. In 1999, he obtained his Ph.D. from Arizona State University. Neil teaches Market Research, Strategic Internet Marketing, and Customer Information Strategy. His research interests include e-commerce, ethics, and marketing education. Dr. Granitz has published articles in several journals including the *Journal of Advertising*, the *Journal of Business Ethics*, and the *Journal of Marketing Education*. While at Cal State Fullerton, he has won the award for *CBE Outstanding Faculty Member*, as well as for *Teaching Innovation*. Prior to pursuing his Ph.D., he was the Domestic and International Director of Market Research for Imasco (Canada's third largest company). Dr. Granitz continues to consult for several companies. In his spare time he reads lots of comic books.

Mobile Marketing and the Mobile Decade to Come

How the Mobile Decade Will Change Marketing, Media and Commerce

MICKEY ALAM KHAN
Editor-in-Chief, www.mobilemarketer.com

———————

The nation stands today at a pivotal point where mobile will soon infuse every marketing, media and retail decision just as the Internet did in the last ten years. The Mobile Decade is upon us. Marketers have only to look around this country and see the one thing that consumers today cannot be parted from: their mobile phones. And that device, as the decade wears on, will become the interface between consumer and society.

Are all stakeholders in this economy geared for the major changes down the road? Those who are prepared are already in some version of Mobile 2.0 with their marketing plans. Those who aren't need some more validation before committing time, people and budget to adding mobile to the mix.

Of this all can be certain: mobile will democratize every institution just as the Internet did. It will enhance the value of marketing, content and commerce for some and cut the margins in others. In other words, mobile will level the playing field, empowering consumers even more with information that shifts the balance of power even further away from the marketer. How will this likely play out for marketers as regards brands, agencies, media and retailers?

Brands in the Know

More consumers will rely on their mobile media to tap into news, information, shopping and entertainment. Brands that seek to maintain their edge in this decade will have to roll out 360-degree marketing plans that include mobile advertising on key sites. In addition, they will have to debut mobile-friendly sites and mobile applications to enable an easy, user-friendly two-way communication with their target audience.

Brands will also need a strong Short Message Service (SMS) program to reach out to consumers who choose that medium along with email as their two primary choices for direct marketing. SMS will complement email in loyalty marketing efforts and, equally important, drive traffic to offline channels including retail stores.

Brands cannot afford to be locked out of a mobile relationship with customers and prospects. The alternative is to wish upon themselves the same fate that befell those brands that were stubborn to the attractions—and necessity—of an effective Internet presence in the early- to mid-2000s. Ad agencies, for their part, cannot shelter under lack of education, complexity or inadequacy of metrics any much longer.

Shop Talk

The year 2007 saw the launch of the first Web-friendly Apple iPhone. Several upgraded versions and hundreds of thousands of applications later, the market is now crowded with smartphones from Samsung, HTC, Nokia, Motorola and the fading BlackBerry.

Consumer acceptance of smartphones with their own operating systems from Apple's iPhone to Google's Android has been spectacular. More than two-third of mobile phones in the U.S. are smartphones with Web and application capabilities, and nothing short of computers in their tasking strengths. To top that, Apple's App Store and Google's Google Play store combined boast more than 1 million applications.

Advertising agencies cannot afford anymore to ignore this reality—that mobile is rapidly becoming a critical-mass marketing medium, albeit with margins that are nowhere near print or television. Indeed, agencies will have to restructure themselves financially—lean, mean and with the same sheen.

On the creative front, it's time copywriters were taught how to pen copy in 160 characters or six-word headlines on tiny screens. How to be creative and yet get to the point—that's the dilemma copy folks and art directors will have to face. As for the account management teams at agencies? Better get used to pitching mobile to the clients and writing briefs that understand what mobile is all about: relationship marketing.

Mobile will not come at the expense of TV or radio or other older media. But advertisers will soon discover that mobile media are as efficient, if not more, in attracting and retaining customers.

Medium Is the Message

Media may have the least time before Mobile 2.0 hits in earnest. If the wired Web has cannibalized print media and not returned ad revenues anywhere near old media's, then mobile will simply compound that mess. The media world is about to come to a fork in the road: Either stick to an advertising-supported, free-access model or erect subscription walls to charge consumers for reading on mobile sites and applications.

The history of paid media isn't good. Beyond a few newspapers and magazines that can charge because their content is highly unique, most publications cannot afford to lose traffic over walls that may drive readers elsewhere.

Charging for mobile content will only work if content on the wired Web is also gated. Yes, consumers are conditioned to paying for content (such as some apps) on mobile. However, for most consumers, news is not the same thing as content. News has become a commodity. Readers will only pay if the news is viewed as a brand. And that, in this 24-hour news cycle, is highly improbable.

Which leaves the other possibility as the one to bet the house on: advertising-supported media. Publishers will have to work double-duty to ensure that advertisers are offered media plans that include all formats—print, online, broadcast and mobile.

That said, it is a shame to visit sites of noted publishers and see wasted advertising opportunities. Get a big brand to taste mobile. Give a free month-long trial to new advertisers. Let them experience the power of mobile. And work with them to tailor appropriate messages that resonate with an on-the-go mindset. Simply repurposing online ads for mobile won't cut the mustard.

Make the Buy

As for retailers, mobile's benefit is obvious: driving traffic to stores or call centers. Mobile commerce will change the face of retail as we know it.

Now all of these developments hinge on a few factors. First, that wireless carriers will continue to support new Web-friendly smartphones with affordable data plans and upgrade networks to handle increased bandwidth demands. Next, that consumers are sufficiently convinced of the wider benefits and security of relating with brands through mobile. Finally, that marketers stretch to acknowledge mobile's strengths.

Either way, welcome to the Mobile Decade. Make it memorable for getting things right at the outset. Consumers want to talk; so listen.

Commonsense Dos and Don'ts of Mobile Marketing

From the noise generated by the myriad mobile conferences, blogs and publications, most brands, advertising agencies and publishers just want to know a couple of things: What's working and what's not working in mobile marketing. Here's a stab at that.

First, it's important to dispel the myth that marketers don't get mobile. They do—ask Colgate-Palmolive, Unilever, Gap, Adidas, M&M/Mars, NBC, Kodak, Heineken, ESPN, McDonald's, American Airlines, Sherwin-Williams, Microsoft, AOL, MGM Grand, Johnson & Johnson, Dairy Queen, Jaguar, Skyy Vodka, Ford Motor, The Weather Channel, Discover Card, Procter & Gamble's Gillette, Brita, Jim Beam and Chase.

These aforementioned brands have run mobile campaigns, sites and applications or launched mobile commerce operations. Some of these efforts have morphed into longer-term programs that integrate mobile into overall multichannel outreach initiatives within these Fortune 500 and Fortune 1000 brands.

No doubt mobile will have to work harder to get a larger chunk of marketing budgets. But marketers surely are getting the message that mobile is where they need to be. Consumers—their customers—wouldn't expect any less, not with their newer phone models and better data plans.

Know Your Audience

This leads to the first observation about what's working in mobile marketing: *Understanding the audience and targeting* with appropriate mobile banner and video ads, sites, applications or SMS campaigns—all opted-in, not once but twice by the consumer.

This rule is not exclusive to mobile. A targeted mailer sent to a household has proven to generate sales online, in-store or via telephone. Online banners or emails that sync with the site audience's interests inevitably generate click-throughs and responses to calls to action.

So mobile's not any different. A relevant movie trailer banner ad on an entertainment mobile site will serve both the advertiser and consumer well. Requesting that existing customers opt-in to the marketer's mobile alert programs will also work to great advantage. Ask casino giants such as Harrah's and MGM Grand.

Not surprisingly, it is critical to research the targeted audience's mobile habits. What is it that they consume on the mobile phone and the tablet? How much time do they spend on mobile? What is it that they would like to initiate elsewhere but complete on mobile or vice versa?

Visiting a well-thought out mobile site is such a pleasure. Consider *The New York Times'* mobile site at mobile.nytimes.com. It is hard to admit this, but the mobile site beats the wired Web site simply because the scroll-down interface is easy to navigate and the articles easy to read.

The only casualty about the mobile *New York Times* experience is the advertising. While the banner ad units are quite visible, the *Times* needs to work harder on convincing some of its current online advertisers to add mobile to their mix.

It seems almost strange to see a mobile site without ads—not ones that interrupt the experience, but ones that enhance the overall reading experience by offering a window into commercial applications.

At the risk of sounding audacious, perhaps the *Times* should offer sampling opportunities to key advertisers such as Tiffany, Macy's, Cartier and local auto dealers. And if these advertisers don't have a mobile presence, then the *Times* should work with mobile firms to mobilize their client base. Imagine the brownie points scored if mobile gains significant leads and sales for these firms.

Knowing the audience also includes knowledge of their propensity or willingness to receive permission-based communications on their phones. Mobile may not be for everyone, just like the wired Internet isn't.

But it seems quite obvious that marketers offering value through the mobile site, application, banner ad, coupon or text message will find a welcome reception. Training the customer base to expect quality in mobile marketing communications is a corollary to knowing what makes the marketer's target customer tick.

While many industry observers are waiting for a flash of light to let them know mobile is the new tableau for marketing, those already with toes in the water know where the fish are.

Mobile Works for Database and Loyalty Marketing—Absolutely

One of the most astute uses of mobile—besides employing mobile advertising for branding—is the channel's ability to expand a marketer's loyalty program. And the humble foot soldier of loyalty marketing is SMS text messaging. Yes, text messaging is to mobile what email is to the Internet—the choice tool for communicating one-on-one with the customer.

Marketing need not get too complicated if the goal is to convince the targeted consumer to consume the advertiser's product or service over the competitor's. SMS is the easiest way to communicate that message. It takes some legwork to get fully SMS-enabled. The tools required are a common short code, keywords, approval of mobile campaign from wireless carriers and another channel to get the consumer to text in to opt into a program.

Marketers and retailers can use stores, direct mail, television, radio, print, online and billboards to get the consumer to opt-in—not once, but twice—to receiving coupons or alerts from the company.

Once the consumer is signed up, moderate the communications to anywhere from two messages to four messages a month, maximum. And be upfront with the opted-in consumer about the frequency of messages, company privacy policy and option to opt out at any time. Remember, it's a land grab right now. At some point, the consumer will not agree to sign up for any more mobile loyalty programs or alerts. So it is best to start work on incorporating mobile into the company's overall loyalty program.

Legs to Other Channels

Here's another point to remember: mobile's place in the multichannel context. Mobile is not an island unto itself and contrary to what its most ardent fans would like to believe, the channel's best use is in giving legs to other channels.

Mobile has the potential to drive traffic to retail stores, as has been amply proved with campaigns from restaurant chains and food retailers such as Papa John's, McDonald's, Burger King, Starbucks, Subway and countless others with a physical footprint.

The "American Idol" show on television is proof that text messaging can elect winners simply by action of keyword and short code. Shows such as "American Idol" and "Deal or No Deal" were said to have generated as much revenues for the programmers from texting as they did from advertising. Maybe it's exaggerating it a bit, but the point is that mobile brings interactivity to TV.

Now here's something that agencies don't want to hear about: actual tracking of brand commercials. Image a keyword and short code on spots—not just at the end of the 30-second spot, but in every frame—that invites the consumer to text in. No, it need not turn into a direct response TV ad, but the texts could give the advertiser an idea of the consumer's engagement with the brand's TV advertising.

Ditto with radio. And it's proved to have worked. Oil change giant Jiffy Lube has gone on the record to acknowledge SMS marketing's role in driving traffic to its locations. In most cases, the SMS call to action was run first on radio spots targeted to drivers in certain areas.

What about direct mail and inserts? How about placing targeted keywords and short code on mail and inserts sent to consumers' homes and offices? Ask them to respond via text for prompt fulfillment of the desired call to action. The examples can go on and on. Keep an open mind and a sharp eye on the consumer's needs and market trends.

What Not to Do in Any Circumstances?

It's mostly a bunch of commonsense. Don't abuse the privilege. When mobile consumers opt into receiving communications from brands, they are giving access to their most personal medium.

Err on the side of caution when sending text messages—twice a month, instead of four, for example—or make sure that the banner ad doesn't disrupt the viewing experience on mobile.

It's been said before, and bears repeating here: familiarity breeds contempt. Don't inundate the consumer with messages. Space them out and make sure each message is targeted.

Sensitivity is the watchword here. And privacy. In fact, privacy threatens to snowball into one of the biggest issues threatening online and mobile advertising. Privacy advocacy groups and consumer watchdogs are chomping at the bit to restrain marketers from crossing a fine line. They are doing their best to convince the Federal Trade Commission of the need to regulate behavioral and location-based advertising online and on mobile. The growing popularity of beacons to identify opted-in consumers in stores with relevant offers may give rise to another raft of worries down the road, but the potential for targeted marketing is tremendous.

The privacy groups' worries, while legitimate, will affect marketing based on data and knowledge of consumer actions, even on an aggregate basis. So give no excuse to these groups or to the FTC or to the various attorneys general nationwide who want to make their name on marketing's back.

Finally, be realistic. Mobile's not a cure for what ails other channels. While it's not even realistic to call it a channel—it's a phone, TV, radio, MP3 player, video player, gaming instrument, camera, computer, email tool, SMS enabler and pathway to the Internet—mobile still works best when matched with other channels.

Mobile thankfully does not enjoy the same degree of hype as the Internet did in the late 1990s. Yes, every agency, conference organizer or publisher has tacked on mobile as the new accessory to their offerings, but the venture-capital money inflow has been measured and realistic. The only exception is Facebook's newfound penchant to throw billions at mobile applications, with the jury still in doubt over the efficacy of those moves.

Those in the field know that mobile victories come hard-fought. It is their job now to communicate that mobile has its advantages and its limitations.

One of the truths is that mobile will not replace other channels, but complement them in a manner that no other medium has.

But mobile requires time to show results, and consumers need time to work out their relationship with the mobile device—is it a phone, book, entertainment channel, business tool, news source, video, camera, advertising vehicle or shop? All nine, as time and smart mobile marketing campaigns and programs will prove.

MICKEY ALAM KHAN is editor-in-chief of *Mobile Marketer, Mobile Commerce Daily* and *Luxury Daily,* all based in New York. He was previously editor in chief of *eMarketer* and *DM News,* and also served as correspondent for *Advertising Age.* Reach him at mickey@napean.com.

DRTV and Integrated Marketing

TIMOTHY HAWTHORNE
Founder, Chairman and Executive Creative Director
Hawthorne Direct

Direct response television goes hand-in-hand with many other adver-tising strategies, and should be considered a vital aspect of any com-pany's overall marketing effort.

In a world where consumers are bombarded by thousands of marketing messages daily, it's no longer enough to utilize a single selling channel and expect it to per-form up to snuff. The question is, how does a marketer approach consumers from multiple angles in a time/cost-efficient and effective manner? Simple. By using inte-grated marketing, or the delivery of a consistent message across multiple channels like retail, television, radio, web, mobile, email, catalog, print and direct mail, among others.

In this chapter I'll help you understand how the direct response TV (DRTV) chan-nel impacts integrated campaigns, and walk you through the roots of this often-mis-understood—yet frequently used—marketing medium. I'll show you how the indus-try has evolved, and compare and contrast it with general advertising. Finally, I'll give you the lowdown on DRTV's collaborative qualities, and help you maximize your own integrated ad campaign by tapping into DRTV's unique qualities.

Laying the Groundwork

It may have its roots in Ginsu knives and Pocket Fishermen, but over the last 20 years DRTV marketing has proven itself as a cost-effective, accountable, measurable and powerful way to entice customers to place orders over the phone and via the Internet, or even drive them into retail stores to see and touch the products firsthand.

DRTV is broadly defined as any TV commercial that includes a response mecha-nism (800 number, URL, SMS code or "push your remote's order button") to gener-ate an immediate response to purchase a product or request more information.

225

DRTV commercials can be of any length: 15, 30, 60 second "spots" (short form) or 30 minute "infomercials" (long form). They've been around since the dawn of TV and today are a much bigger business than just oft-seen Snuggies, Ab Rockets and Magic Bullets, now accounting for over $100 billion in annual product sales.

Here are just some of the ways that advertisers, both entrepreneurs and big brands, are using DRTV today:

- Drive prospects to the web.
- Drive retail sales.
- Bypass retail; sell products direct to consumers.
- Introduce new products.
- Educate about complex product benefits.
- Generate leads at low cost.
- Extend product lines of existing brands.
- Increase product and brand awareness.
- Differentiate products from competitors.
- Support all other marketing channels.

When making the case for DRTV, cost is a key driver. For the cost of 30 seconds of media in prime time network TV (8–11 PM), advertisers can fund dozens of DRTV airings across a broad range of stations. Additionally, the direct response metrics of a long or short form DRTV commercial can be accurately tested with as little as $25,000 in media expenditures. Even if a brand's TV budget has been slashed (as so many have in today's economic environment), for example, it will still be feasible to beef up the campaign with a DRTV-driven marketing effort that produces a measurable return on investment.

None of these facts are news to the ears of seasoned DRTV marketers who already know about the medium's power. Commercial television was launched in the late 1940s and early 1950s by a handful of broadcasters who desperately sought programming to fill their airtime. In those days, a typical television station ran only a few hours of network shows in the morning and then again in the evening.

Around the same time, in Chicago, Philadelphia, and Atlantic City, ad men such as Al Eicoff, and entrepreneurs such as the Popeil and Arnold families recognized the profit potential in this new television medium. They were post-World War II sales, marketing and advertising experts who had already made their names by pitching products on radio, through the mail, in newspapers, or live and in-person at state fairs or on Atlantic City's boardwalk (the latter of which was a favorite haunt decades later for one of DRTV's great pitchmen, the late Billy Mays).

Together, these sales innovators created the first long form TV commercials (what would later be called infomercials). Their television commercials ran anywhere from five to 30 minutes or more and featured evangelistic, often outrageous, product presentations. The same fast-paced sales techniques, honed before thousands of fairgoers and seaside vacationers, provided a new breed of television entertainment that, as it happened, also sold products in the millions.

At the time, there were no toll-free 800 telephone numbers and no credit cards. A "call to action" was intended to persuade viewers to send a check or scurry on down to Walgreens. Families in cities across America huddled around their new Philco TVs, entranced by the exciting demonstration of the latest, one-of-a-kind, "must-have" gadget. It was a time of freedom of expression, prosperity and growth in a new commercial industry—which inevitably would come under regulatory scrutiny that mandated change.

The Golden Age

As the "Golden Age" of television took hold in the mid-1950s, major advertisers began to compete for 60-second time slots that sponsored entertainment programming. Infomercial pioneers were dismayed to find that less and less long form infomercial time was available, and what was still available cost a lot more than in the "good old days."

When the quiz-show scandals of the late 1950s struck, all eyes turned to the rapidly growing television medium, its crass commercialism and apparent ability to corrupt American youth. Television programming and its sponsors had greatly disappointed the American public, whose trusting eyes and ears had once watched and listened and earnestly believed in what appeared on their black-and-white living room Zeniths.

In an effort to stem the tide of public dissent and help salvage commercial television, in 1962 the Federal Communications Commission (FCC) slapped new regulations on the industry. From then on, broadcast television stations were permitted to sell a maximum of 12 to 14 minutes of commercial time per hour, thus ending the initial era of the long form infomercial.

A determined bunch of long form advertisers such as Eicoff and Wunderman adapted to the new FCC regulations by running two-minute direct response spots. Positioned as "key outlet" commercials, they tagged the end of their brief product demonstrations with the names of three to six major retailers that carried the showcased product, thus forcing you to buy the product at retail only.

Meanwhile, in 1968, AT&T introduced the next revolution in direct response television (DRTV)–the WATTS line, or toll-free 800 number. Suddenly, a commercial could run nationwide with a centralized inbound phone reception center taking orders from across the country, an innovation that gave new life to DRTV.

No Smoking

The ban on television cigarette advertising in 1970 created an enormous gap in broadcasters' ad revenues. Television media time became plentiful and inexpensive as broadcast stations hustled to fill the commercial airtime that was once dominated by cigarette advertisers. Short form direct response television commercials filled the gap nicely. Products such as records, books, tools, kitchen gadgets, pest control, and arts and crafts proliferated. Companies like K-Tel and Ronco dominated the DRTV market place. Any mass-market consumer item that could be demonstrated, provide immediate solutions, and sell for $9.95 or less, was a prime candidate for short form DRTV ad campaigns.

But it would still be another two decades before DRTV would gain acceptance in mainstream advertising circles. (In fact, DRTV commercials remained a breed apart from major brand television advertising for most of the first 50 years of TV.) Direct response spots were notorious for being low-budget productions that featured hard-sell, rapid-fire pitches and wildly exaggerated demonstrations and claims made by gregarious hosts relentlessly driving home the sale. As a result, the credibility of DRTV ads left much to be desired among consumers, and deservedly so. Unfulfilled or late orders happened too often, and many of the products that were delivered were of such poor quality that purchasers were left disgruntled and disenchanted with the whole business.

In the early 1970s, Reader's Digest dared to apply classic general television advertising concepts to short form DRTV ads in support of its direct-mail subscription campaign. One of the first direct response integrated marketing campaigns, it was executed with style and substance. Thanks to Reader's Digest, DRTV spot advertising regained some face and, in the process, succeeded in waking up Madison Avenue advertising executives to this "new" mode of advertising that actually provided measurable response and still maintained their Fortune 500 clients' image-enhancing style of traditional high-quality spot ads.

Record and audiotape clubs, book continuity programs, magazines and insurance pioneered the upscale DRTV commercials of the 1970s. Time-Life, Columbia House, Publishers' Clearinghouse, Liberty Mutual Insurance, Rolling Stone, Newsweek, Time and Playboy covered the airwaves. What's more, they weren't restricted to late-night fringe time, lowbrow hours, but appeared throughout the day and occasionally even in prime time.

Earning Respect

Creatively, except for their toll-free number DR ordering component, many of the short form DRTV ads were virtually indistinguishable from general advertising, often shot on 35mm film (providing superior production values), and employing experienced union models and actors in compelling fictional story settings. DRTV was slowly earning a bit more respect from the advertising "establishment" on Madison Avenue.

Meanwhile, from the early 1960s to the early 1980s, all was quiet on the long form front. Only the evangelists for God and nonprofit organizations (WorldVision), not products, could taking advantage of the "Power of the Half Hour"™ on Sunday mornings. Savvy ad agencies spent millions in media time for these causes, which generated donations that well exceeded their media investments. Though officially designated as religious or not-for-profit programming, there's no doubt the evangelists borrowed techniques for closing their "sales" from the best boardwalk pitchmen of the 1950s.

The rebirth of long form advertising was due in part to the advent of upstart, advertiser-supported national cable networks such as The Cable Health Network (now Lifetime), USA Network, and Satellite Program Network (now defunct). In the late 1970s and early 1980s, these fledgling networks were wired into only a small percentage of TV households in the United States and were thus ignored by most major advertisers. Like the pioneering broadcast TV stations 60 years ago, they hungered for ad revenues.

Because they weren't subject to FCC rules regulating broadcast commercial time, these cable networks welcomed the cash-up-front advertising revenues from half-hour commercials in the early 1980s. In 1983, The Sharper Image catalog pioneered the multi-product infomercial on cable, a good three years before the Home Shopping Network launched the same format nationally, 24 hours per day, to great success.

Meanwhile, a few risk-taking broadcast TV stations, still under commercial time regulations, began to air infomercials disguised as TV talk shows and "documentaries" for such products as hair restoration formulas and real estate investment seminars. Most of those infomercial campaigns bear no resemblance to today's programs. They typically ran in a limited number of markets at any one time or had brief runs on cable. It wasn't until the summer of 1984 that infomercials were officially born.

Credit Reagan-era deregulation with helping to spur on that official introduction. In June 1984, the FCC officially removed any TV commercial time constraints. The decision to allow TV stations to self-regulate was well founded, the thinking being that if a station began selling more than 12 to 14 minutes of advertising per hour, viewers simply wouldn't watch the station, which would lower the station's viewership/ratings and their commercial rates. It would not be in the financial interests of broadcasters to increase the amount of commercial time sold.

What wasn't expected from this ruling was how entrepreneurs would use their limited long form experience on cable to conceive a new billion-dollar industry. Annual sales from the long form advertising format have skyrocketed. Infomercials generated approximately $10 million in sales in 1984. Today it's a $30 billion dollar industry.

Introducing the Infomercial

The modern infomercial era really began in the fall of 1984, when Herbalife generated millions of dollars in revenues through its weekly, Sunday-evening motivational pep rallies on USA Network. Since then, the short and long form DRTV industry has grown by leaps and bounds, thrived during several economic downturns and even gained mass acceptance by brand advertisers who have come to love the medium's accountability and direct-to-consumer approach.

Because of the tremendous infomercial industry growth and positive effects of self-regulation instituted by the industry's trade group (Electronic Retailing Association— www. retailing.org), major institutions and Fortune 500 and 1000 corporations are taking advantage of this successful, proven marketing channel. Many well-known retailers, financial institutions, publishers, insurance companies and manufacturers have used infomercials to showcase their products, including (but not limited to):

- ✓ 3M
- ✓ American Airlines
- ✓ Apple
- ✓ AT&T
- ✓ Bank of America
- ✓ Black & Decker
- ✓ Blue Cross Blue Shield
- ✓ Clorox
- ✓ Coca-Cola
- ✓ Estee Lauder
- ✓ Fidelity Investments
- ✓ Fisher Price

✓ Ford
✓ General Motors
✓ McDonald's
✓ Microsoft
✓ P&G
✓ Nissan
✓ Pepsi
✓ Phillips
✓ Sony
✓ Target
✓ Toyota
✓ Wal-Mart
✓ Weight Watchers

The list goes on. In fact, companies of all shapes and sizes are using DRTV to get the word out about their products and services. That's because the medium helps companies tell their story in a format that is not only measurable and accountable, but can perform far better than traditional 15- or 30-second branding spots in recall, intent to purchase, enhanced brand awareness. Using "brandmercials" (a moniker we came up with here at Hawthorne Direct), firms like 3M, Black & Decker, Hoover, PETA, and 1-800 Flowers, among many others, are tapping the power of long form and short form DRTV to tell their story right in the consumer's living room and alongside their other multiple marketing channels. With DRTV, results can be closely tracked, and the selling itself takes place either online, or by phone, at a time that's convenient for the consumer. Who can argue with these benefits? No one.

When brand advertisers jumped into the DRTV pool, something else happened. Their first brandmercials pioneered a wave of upscale production values that worked hard to keep the brand tone intact for Fortune 500 firms. In the late-1990s, Apple Computer was an immediate beneficiary, ringing up $92 million in retail sales on a $3 million DRTV investment. Nissan followed with the most successful DR campaign in company history, and paved the way for others to follow in its footsteps.

When these types of Fortune 500 companies integrate DRTV into the advertising mix, they use a format that lends itself to consumer education on the brand itself, and also on the individual products that the label represents. By telling their stories through these longer-format commercials, these marketers can break through the "blur of image" created by most traditional 15/30 second spots, and delve deeper into the true value that the brand delivers to the consumer.

And, proving many skeptics wrong, DRTV has also demonstrated it can do more than just support brands; it can create them too. Guthy-Renker's ProActiv skin care product started with a million dollar DRTV investment (vs. tens of millions for major brand companies) and is a billion dollar brand today. Other DRTV generated brands include: OrangeGlo, OxiClean, George Foreman Grills, Magic Bullet, Total Gym, Victoria Jackson Cosmetics, Bare Minerals, Little Giant Ladder, Shark Vacuums, Murad Skin Care, Magic Jack, Tempur-Pedic, Rosetta Stone, Zumba, P90X, Select Comfort, Max Clarity, Swivel Sweeper, Provo Craft, Bowflex, Oreck Vacuums, Taebo,

Time Life Music, NutriSystem, Space Bags, Nordic Track, Video Professor, Principal Secret, Youthology and Vonage.

Breaking It Down

Again, what most distinguishes DRTV from brand TV advertising is the presence of an *offer to buy*, or learn more about the product, "now." DRTV commercial "product offers" can be broken down into three types, each of which airs regularly and is used by a wide range of marketers. Here's a breakdown of each type:

- One-Step: As in "it only takes one step to buy this product; use your credit card and call the operator or go online now." The classic one-step DRTV offer dominated the industry for its first 50 years, and remains a DRTV staple today. In many viewers' eyes, the "order now and use your credit card" offer defines the medium. It's usually used to sell such products as exercise equipment, kitchen appliances, cosmetics and diet programs priced less than $99.95. The traditional one-step infomercial sells unique products—often not available at retail stores—directly to television viewers. Because of today's high cost of media airtime, the success rate for testing a one-step offer has fallen from one-out-of-two to one-out-of-twenty. These days, infomercials that employ one-step offers are considered high-risk ventures—that is, if the show itself is the only profit-making element. One-step infomercial marketers have adapted to the increased media costs by attracting customers with the one-step offer while making most of their profits on their Internet orders, retail sales (where most infomercial products will eventually end up) and the "back end." Back-end programs may include continuity programs, outbound telemarketing, direct mail, home shopping appearances, catalogs, and more. In fact, roughly 80 percent of Jordan Whitney's (an industry research company—www.jwgreensheet.com) Top Ten Infomercials each month still feature one-step offers. Obviously, high media costs have not deterred one-step marketers.
- Two-Step: As in "call or go online now for more information." Reacting to the squeeze on one-step offers, advertisers have begun turning toward two-step offers, or "lead generators." Major financial service companies such as Progressive and Geico use the two-step approach to successfully generate leads from infomercial viewers. If your product is priced over $99.95 and your one-step infomercial doesn't work, consider changing your offer to generate a lead. You can't get a more qualified lead than someone who has already watched 2 to 30 minutes of your sales presentation. Jordan Whitney defines approximately 20 percent of its top-ranked infomercials each month as "lead generating," and this percentage continues to grow throughout the industry as a whole.
- Driving Online and Retail: The online and retail-driving DRTV commercials are an interesting hybrid of direct response and image awareness marketing. Ninety-nine percent of a DRTV commercial's viewers will not buy immediately in response to seeing the ad (the average infomercial response rate is between 0.2 percent and 0.4 percent). But these millions of non-purchasing infomercial watchers are primed to purchase the product at retail or online, their preferred buying channels, or are influenced to buy later via print, catalog and direct mail

messaging. Corporations such as 3M, P&G, and Black & Decker, which traditionally marketed strictly through retail, have used infomercials with great success to drive retail sales.

Whether they're looking to sell direct, drive consumers to retail and the web, or build their consumer databases, brand advertisers see DRTV as a viable addition to their arsenals. They're using it to educate their consumers in a meaningful, measurable way, while also reaping the rewards of authenticity that traditional TV branding spots simply can't match.

Unique Attributes

In our new, consumer-driven, fragmented media universe, consumers want more relevant information at more touchpoints. They're no longer prompted to try a new product or check out a new service based on a single contact, and have come to expect a more integrated approach that includes print, TV, radio, web, mobile and other advertising techniques.

The economic downturns of the early 2000s and then in 2008–09, further complicated matters, what with consumers doing more comparison shopping and being more frugal. These consumers track down the best deals, clip or download coupons and wait for discounted offers. They tune out messages that are not relevant to the problems in their lives right now.

They also pay more attention to DRTV, which routinely demonstrates product benefits as solutions to everyday problems. With longer selling messages and prominent value based offers, direct response always speaks the language anxious consumers want to hear. Free premiums and discounts are popular any time; in a troubled economy, they're compelling.

Also persuasive are DRTV's longer-format commercials that "tell" along with the "sell." By taking the time to educate consumers on the benefits and features of a particular product or service, DRTV:

✓ Explains multiple product benefits, thus heightening value
✓ Offers in-depth product demonstrations, thus engaging viewers
✓ Introduces real people and expert testimonials, which builds credibility
✓ Repeats key selling messages, which enhances persuasion
✓ Takes customers through a complete sales story, thus deepening understanding
✓ Differentiates from competitors, which boosts preference
✓ Allows for consideration of the purchase decision, which creates purchase justification

Despite these obvious benefits, the road to widespread DRTV advertiser and consumer acceptance has been fraught with obstacles. Since they began, long form television marketers have had to face down accusations of being "boardwalk pitchmen" of dubious reputation, adjust to regulation, deregulation, and re-regulation by federal agencies, and regain the confidence of a disenchanted TV-viewing audience. Through it all, infomercial advertisers have adapted and thrived and will continue to do so in spite of ongoing challenges, such as those that exist today.

In 1985, for example, an advertiser could purchase cable airtime for as little as $50 per half hour (due to minuscule cable viewership at that time), making it easy to realize a success ratio of $5 in revenue for every media dollar spent. A 10-to-1 ratio was not untypical with a hot show. Media time on the same cable channels currently is going for as much as $30,000 per half hour. The industry wide cost of media time has ballooned an average of 500 percent. These prices reflect phenomenal increases in the number of cable subscribers.

In addition, average production budgets have surged from $30,000 per infomercial in 1985 to anywhere from $200,000 to $800,000 per half-hour show today. Both increases reflect a heated-up competitive marketplace. In 1984, there were five infomercials total on the air; today, five to 10 new programs appear every week.

The Quiet Revolution

While DRTV marketers were battling it out with traditional image/awareness advertisers for TV airtime and respect in the 1990s, a quiet revolution toward brand advertisers and retail-driving infomercials started up and has prevailed ever since. Here's a look at how this revolution evolved and grew:

- In 1990, Time-Life Music successfully entered infomercial marketing as the first Fortune 500 Company via their agency, Hawthorne Direct, and Fitness Quest simultaneously launched new products through infomercials and at retail.
- In 1991, infomercial media costs continued to inflate at a frantic pace because of increased competition for limited available time slots ("avails"), while front-end profits and success ratios decreased, and reliance on back-end sales increased. Saturn broadcast the first image-only infomercial (no toll-free number mechanism). Braun, via Hawthorne Direct, produced an infomercial for their Handblender specifically to drive retail sales.
- In 1992, Ross Perot debuted an infomercial designed to educate the nation regarding the details of his United States presidential campaign. Retailers acknowledged the immense impact infomercials have for "as seen on TV" product categories. Juicers sold through infomercials flew off retail shelves. Major advertisers began seriously considering infomercial campaigns: Braun, Redken, GTE and Volvo debuted successful infomercials. Corporate infomercials demonstrated their ability to drive sales at retail while paying for part or all of their TV media airtime with direct response television sales.

DRTV's success has proven that millions of viewers will watch from 2 to 30 minutes of well-produced commercial advertising. At Hawthorne Direct, our internal research shows that consumers are hungry for product information and are growing increasingly skeptical of standard 15–30 second brand advertising.

From my own experience in the industry, I'd say that most brand companies have already embraced the idea that measurable advertising is the way to go, especially in this economy. By 2011, DRTV had evolved to the point where a hybrid DRTV/TRP (Targeted Rating Points—a standard brand media buying methodology) media campaign made sense to many corporate marketing folks, because they could now quantify their TV ad spending both by number of viewers and actual response by those viewers.

Yet $50 billion is still spent every year on general brand TV advertising, with little or no response mechanism. Old habits die hard, and it's no secret that brands and their agencies hate to "ask for the order." Still, DRTV continues to gain traction among those brands, and is particularly attractive to those that are seeking an affordable, accountable advertising mechanism that works well with myriad other mediums.

Why DRTV is so Hard to Ignore

So, what is it about DRTV that makes advertisers swoon and their traditional agencies cringe in fear? In one word, it's the accountability. While the medium comes with many other benefits, one of DRTV's biggest attributes is its ability to accurately and method-ically track exactly where customers are coming from, what they buy (and what they turn down) and how often they come back for more. With this information in hand, advertisers can make quick decisions regarding the best allocation of their marketing dollars—something that traditional TV advertising simply can't match.

DRTV also allows companies to talk directly to their consumers, collect informa-tion from them and educate them in a luxurious amount of time. Using short form and/or long form DRTV commercials combined with other forms of advertising, marketers can not only get their points across, but they can also pound those points home for the TV viewer and web surfer.

Finally, it's hard to ignore DRTV's cost advantages. Spot DR media is regularly purchased as remnant time at 10 to 50 percent off rate card. In the recession-driven soft advertising market of 2008–10, long form DRTV media rates were down between 10 and 20 percent on average, to levels not seen since the turn of the millennium, as TV stations and cable networks responded to deteriorating ad revenues by exchang-ing entertainment programming for paid 30-minute commercial slots. Even today, with people continuing to entertain themselves more at home, TV viewing house-holds and viewing hours are on the rise, always a good sign for DRTV.

Short Form Vs. Long Form

There are two basic DRTV formats: long form, or the 28.5-minute infomercial for-mat, and short form, which comprises any DRTV commercial that is two minutes or less in length (with the most popular being 60, 90 or 120 seconds long). Many long form infomercial products won't succeed in short form because the product requires more than two minutes to fully explain the product features and benefits. Or if your product sale requires creating an emotional bond (via an "improve your relation-ships" self-help course, for example), short form will not cut it.

Think about the classic short form products you've seen over the years and how the products' benefits are quickly understood: classic rock music CDs, the Clint Eastwood movie collection, Ginsu knives, miracle polishers/cleansers, unique tools, Thigh Master, and so on. Most short form products are priced at or below $49.95, and some may even run with a co-existing infomercial campaign.

Short form DRTV spots are placed on TV stations and cable networks by purchas-ing "remnant" time, i.e., media time not already pre-purchased by a brand advertiser. It's "leftover" media time, available at a deep discount, and consequently the time slots rarely can be pinpointed beforehand except in broad dayparts (Morning, Daytime, Late Night). Often, depending on the DRTV short form competition and the strength of the brand advertising market, you will not achieve 100% of your requested time, but rather "clear" only a percentage, from 10% to 90%. Infomercial time slots, on the other hand, are set and secure for at least each upcoming quarter and clear 95 percent of the time.

In general, marketers should use short form when:

- They are selling a less complex product and story.
- Their product has a lower price point ($9.95–$49.95) or coupon offer.
- They need more targeted media placement.
- Their goal is to drive retail, Internet, print, direct mail, radio and/or mobile sales.

Long form is more often used when:

- The company has a more complex product and story.
- The price point exceeds $49.95.
- There is a need for significant differentiation.

There are other factors to consider when deciding which format to use, and when to use both in concert with one another, such as:

Product Type:
Short Form: Simpler, more impulse items; benefits and features need to be easily understood in 100 seconds.
Long Form: Good for more complex products that require more "consideration."

Product Features and Benefits:
Short Form: Only enough time to focus on five or six major product benefits.
Long Form: Plenty of time to go deep into multiple product features and benefits.

Testimonials:
Short Form: Not much time for "real people" testimonials (good actors are more concise); if strong real people testimonials are available, use very brief sound bites.
Long Form: Enough time for real people testimonials who can tell their product story in depth; more potential for evoking emotion and poignancy.

Call to Action (CTA):
Short Form: Traditionally about 20 seconds to state the offer (800 number could be inserted for virtually the entire spot).
Long Form: Traditionally between 2-1/2 and 3-1/2 minute long CTA's; inserted two to three times in the long form program for a total CTA time of almost 10 minutes (long form CTAs are often cut down and repurposed for 1- and 2-minute short form spots).

Price Point:
Short Form: Lower priced product ($9.95–$49.95), trial offers or lead generators
Long Form: Higher priced product ($49.95–$2,995), blind offers and lead generators.

Drive Retail:

Both short form and long form can drive retail, but since short form can play at any time of the day or night it has significantly more reach (number of unique viewers) than long form and works perfectly as a follow-up strategy to a successful long form commercial for driving retail, Internet and other integrated marketing channels.

Strategic Goal:

Within the short form arena there are two distinctly different show types: the one-step offer, and the two-step lead generation approach. Rising media costs over the past 15 years have made it difficult—if not impossible—to get short form DRTV one-step offers to be profitable on immediate sales. But one-step offer short form products are now often run at a loss for months simply to drive the product's retail sales.

Response to DRTV commercials has varied much over the past 25 years, but through it all one constant remains: the success or failure of this type of advertising comes down to the product and the offer. In fact, the product determines which other channels best support short form or long form. For example, an intellectual property DRTV product can hit a home run with radio, whereas a skin product would not. Print supports live seminar DRTV well, but not much else. Online supports it all.

In other words, direct response campaigns are best supported with multi-platform campaigns (TV, radio, Internet, print, mobile). In addition, it has also been shown that long form drives results for short form, which drives online sales. The most successful campaigns know how to harness the power of all media to achieve winning ROI.

Here are a few DRTV "home runs" that have embraced the integrated approach to come out winners:

TABLE R18.1

Product	Total Sales*	Time on the Air
Popeil Showtime Rotisserie	$1.4 Billion+	7 years
George Foreman Grill	$500 Million+	5 years
Jet Stream Oven	$300 Million+	4 years
Magic Bullet Blender	$400 Million+	7 years
Rotozip Tool	$300 Million+	5 years
Swivel Sweeper	$100 Million+	3 years
Juiceman Juicers	$300 Million+	15 years
Miracle Mop	$150 Million+	3 years
Little Giant Ladder	$200 Million+	4 years
Tae Bo Fitness	$600 Million+	2 years
Total Gym	$1 Billion+	14 years
Richard Simmons Deal-A-Meal	$600 Million+	8 years
ProActiv Solution	$2 Billion+	15 years
Carleton Sheets	$1 Billion+	18 years
BowFlex Fitness	$1 Billion+	14 years
Tony Robbins Personal Power	$1 Billion+	15 years

*Figures are anecdotal estimates as of 2010

You probably recognize some or all of these product names, and that's because the companies behind them used (and/or, continue to use) a multi-pronged advertising approach that incorporates DRTV, plus other integrated channels. Not all of them were around for the evolution of Web 2.0 technology, but you can bet they would have <u>all</u> used social networking, online video and mobile advertising to further entrench their messages in their customers' brains.

Powerful Supplements

DRTV effectively supplements a company's existing advertising media mix. Working in concert with your other advertising avenues, DRTV can bolster consumer awareness of your product and provide more information and product benefits than is often possible in other media. By running infomercials on national cable and broadcast television, a product's story and benefits can be shared with millions of additional prospects. Direct sales are made in direct proportion to the number of television viewers. The cost per lead (CPL) or cost per order (CPO) can usually match or beat other direct marketing channels such as direct mail or print ads.

As you plan your infomercial campaign, there are a number of springboards built in to further bolster the success of your product. Back-end direct marketing works off of your infomercial, often resulting in profits that are two to five times those of upfront sales. Continuity programs, upsells, cross sells, list management and more extend profits well beyond your initial expectations. Back-end driven conversions may initially account for 30 to 50 percent of many direct marketers' sales.

Before creating a short form or long form commercial, companies and their DRTV ad agencies should review their customer profile, market research and historical sales results to determine demographic targeting and refine campaign objectives. To structure a productive media test, you'll want to ask yourself a few important questions first. One of the most important queries is: Which of the following do you want your show to achieve? Here are a few of the answers you'll probably come up with:

✓ Make a direct sale (one-step offer).
✓ Generate a lead (two-step offer).
✓ Strengthen customer relationship: increase brand loyalty, develop one-on-one customer database.
✓ Influence purchase behavior: enhance product value, move excess inventory, create sales bump with seasonal or event promotion.
✓ Reach new prospects: encourage product trial and retention.
✓ Launch new product: rapid and inexpensive test marketing.
✓ Demonstrate additional product uses: deepen product understanding and education.
✓ Build brand awareness; clarify differentiation, enhance image.
✓ Sustain and build brand equity: communicate corporate good works, solve a PR problem.
✓ Reposition brand: revive a mature product.
✓ Seasonal retail sales promotion.
✓ Drive retail and Internet sales.
✓ A mix of the above.

The infomercial can handle any of the above, based on its half-hour of product story telling time. Short form DRTV is a bit more limiting, but can still help marketers achieve most of these goals much more efficiently than traditional TV advertising.

Dollars and Sense

Infomercial media buying is highly specialized and much different from brand awareness spot buying or even short form DRTV spot buying. Image spot campaigns usually have established media budgets. Infomercial media campaigns rarely have budgets (other than the initial $20,000 to $50,000 media test). As long as the media buys create profits, infomercial buyers will spend as much as they can.

Brand awareness spot campaigns buy media to obtain a pre-set amount of gross rating points (GRP's = total viewer impressions) and TRP's (targeted rating points = # of rating points among your targeted audience). Traditional infomercial buyers care very little about how many viewers watch. They concentrate on how many pick up the phone, or go to a web site, and order. Image spot buyers purchase airtime to cover six, eight or 13 week "flights," and then take the commercial off the air. Infomercial campaigns can run continuously 52 weeks a year for one, three, five years or more. Spot buyers have difficulty reserving specific 30-second spot periods within any half hour. Infomercial buyers can secure 13-, 26- or 52-week contracts for specific half hours and essentially "own" the time.

Image spot media is planned months ahead, then purchased in 13 week flights all at once, and then left alone to run its course. Infomercial media changes dramatically from week to week based on results, and requires daily cancellation, re-buying, and renegotiation. Image spot campaigns largely have no accountability measurements for success. Infomercial campaigns can measure success or failure within hours of the media run. Image spot campaigns have no need for a historical media database. Infomercial media buyers rely on databases of thousands of previous telecasts and their revenue results to determine future strategy.

Well-Defined Roles

In a DRTV campaign, short form and long form work in tandem with one another. Put simply, short form rounds out and complements the infomercial campaign. Very often, companies will cut 60-, 90- or 120-second commercials out of their infomercial and run a simultaneous short form campaign. Normally, the short form spots are not as profitable as the infomercial, but by reminding viewers of the product (they may have seen previously in the infomercial) in short bursts throughout the day, they can create a synergy with the infomercial to boost profitability.

One other drawback to short form DRTV is that buyers are required to purchase groups of spots (2 to 50) on a weekly basis and measure success primarily on each station's overall results, not individual spot runs. Infomercial buyers can purchase one half hour, or many, on the same station and measure success for each and every individual half hour.

While DRTV airtime rates are clearly lower than the prices for image spots, there are still a few important points for marketers to consider when integrating direct response TV into their IMC campaigns.

Take media efficiency ratio (MER = total direct sales / media cost), for example.

The universal benchmark used by DRTV marketers to determine if a product is paying out and has a potential future in selling direct to consumers, a "positive" MER always depends on the campaign's breakeven (BE) goal. Some products with high Cost of Goods (COG) may require a high BE MER, say a 2 or 2.5 ($250 product sales to every $100 of media spent). Other products that are looking to drive retail or Internet sales may thrive with a MER as low as .3 or .5 ($50 of direct sales to every $100 of media spent).

But what happens when a product doesn't achieve these minimum MERs? If you're at 75 percent of your goal, you should definitely "tweak" the commercial creative and/or offer. This means looking at making changes in your voiceover talent, music, graphic look, product shots, testimonials and re-editing the show elements to add clarity and improve pacing. Even deeper changes might require you to rewrite the show's opening segment and CTA to make it harder-hitting and the offer more enticing.

If, on the other hand, you're at 50 percent of minimum MER goal or less, you'll need a significant show makeover, which might include: repositioning the product, script rewrite, new product name, on-camera talent, testimonials, set and/or setting. Tests that come in at less than 25 percent of minimum MER goal might benefit from a commercial makeover, but from what I've seen, the chances of success will be very low.

As you've just read, DRTV is a completely different animal than traditional television advertising. It comes with its own set of quirks, but can also offer significant benefits that 15- and 30-second image spots cannot. To most effectively integrate the medium into your marketing mix requires a group of talented, knowledgeable individuals who not only know your product, brand and its idiosyncrasies, but who have their fingers on the pulse of this unique advertising channel.

Collaborative Qualities

DRTV in and of itself is a powerful, highly versatile platform. Pair it with other, equally effective marketing channels, and that strength and versatility increases exponentially. Just as with general TV advertising, ongoing DRTV campaigns lift sales in other channels and can be seamlessly incorporated into a fully integrated marketing plan. With its ability to do the heavy lifting while simultaneously delivering efficiency and effectiveness metrics, DRTV can be utilized in a variety of tactical ways.

The most common tactical use of DRTV by major brands is to create a DRTV commercial that powerfully drives retail store sales, while partially offsetting the cost of media with direct sale revenues, producing MER's of .1 to .3 or more. DRTV campaigns have also launched many CRM initiatives within companies new to one-on-one marketing and previously unaware of the value of a large, dynamic customer database.

Companies often repurpose the DRTV footage for point-of-sale displays and to add "sticky" video assets to their web sites. In fact, DRTV has measurably been proven to outperform general TV advertising in terms of delivering vast amounts of valuable information and lifting overall ROI of advertising budgets. Here's a quick look at how DRTV boosts other sales channels:

✓ 75% of all consumers will not buy products direct over TV but 95% of all TV viewers will watch DRTV commercials.

✓ 47 percent of all consumers bought a DRTV product at retail or online after viewing a DRTV commercial.

✓ Infomercial driven retail sales: 2–5 times the number of direct sales.

✓ Web searches can be boosted by as much as 1,230% and paid click through rates by 58%.

✓ Product storytelling, demonstrations and testimonials benefit all marketing efforts by dramatizing product benefits and consumer preference.

Direct response works particularly well with the new round of advertising options that have taken hold over the last few years. With more companies using social networking, the web, mobile advertising and online video to communicate directly with consumers, it just makes sense that DRTV would serve as the perfect adjunct for these forward-thinking marketing campaigns. Instead of simply slapping a 30-second image spot on the TV airwaves and hoping that customers will respond favorably, companies of all sizes—and from all industries—are taking a more proactive advertising approach using DRTV's greater length and economic media costs.

Online video is a particularly compelling option that works extremely well with DRTV. In fact, we've found that online video helps to create consumer trust and ultimately results in more transactions. And research shows that over 60 percent of DRTV viewers go online to learn more about a product or service before ordering. The boom in online video is happening because "videoactive" web sites (using video intensively on formerly text heavy web pages) educate consumers, entertain them and give consumers an opportunity to opt-in to additional information presented in a highly entertaining video format.

With the use of mobile also on the rise, companies are also seeking out ways to effectively integrate mobile with more traditional channels. This is especially critical for firms looking to hit younger demographic groups, from pre-teen to late-20s, who heavily rely on their mobile phones. Gen X (30–45) and Gen Y (20-somethings) are also good responders to mobile offers, making the case for such campaigns that much more compelling. More and more, the CTAs in DRTV commercials are including SMS codes as a response mechanism alternative to 800 #'s and URLs.

On the Horizon

Developments in and around the DRTV industry reveal an exciting future replete with not only individual successes, but also integrated campaigns that are leveraged across various platforms. Seemingly innocuous announcements (such as Dish's late-2010 revelation that subscribers would soon be able to watch TV content on their iPads, iPhones and iPod Touch devices) actually have substantial impact on the way advertisers and their agencies think, and on the methods they're using to reach current, past and future customers.

Put video-on-demand, interactive program guides and DVRs into the "game changers" category, and toss the Internet and its myriad functionalities into the mix. The end result is a multi-channel advertising world that experts like Backchannel

Media's Michael Kokernak boldly make predictions about. Kokernak envisions a "TV Everywhere" portal that not only gives consumers more choices, but that also provides the following benefits:

✓ Integration with web and devices. Leveraging Internet-enabled technologies such as GPS, video cameras, heart monitors, car diagnostic kits, bathroom scales, etc., will allow the user to combine data beyond mobile phones into a video device.

✓ Customization via advertising and content feeds. Tailoring the user experience will require at least two interdependent feeds, notes Kokernak, kind of like how AdWords assembles advertising results based on a consumer's search request. The television industry, when leveraging multiple devices and a return path clickstream, can create a superior experience to the Internet search.

✓ Path to addressable media. Interlaced bound and unbound content will enable the user to monitor and interact with personally identifiable, and unidentifiable, data sources from a variety of devices wrapped around the core video experience.

✓ A personal level of devices—those that can monitor everything from heart rate to the performance of automobiles—will become commonplace and are a part of the natural evolution of Web 2.0. As consumers multitask, they will seek out privacy-protected devices that can be integrated with "television."

Expect these and other predictions to materialize over coming months and years, as the economy rises from the ashes of the recession and makes its way into "rebound" territory. In periods when we experience lower response rates, it makes sense to maximize the revenue of every call, click and order you get. The industry focus is going to be on hot back-end solutions, such as innovative cross-selling, couponing, retail-driving incentives and new, outside the box approaches to maximize DR revenue.

At Hawthorne Direct, we stay on the cutting edge of the advertising industry, while at the same time employing tried-and-true DRTV methods that deliver consistent results. We use highly innovative upsell techniques and back-end programs, for example, to add significant revenue to the initial DRTV and online sales, and to improve our clients' overall ROI.

As marketers roll out more SMS text codes on their commercials' tag pages to enable growing mobile phone response, and utilize other innovative, integrated advertising methods, we'll be right by their sides. By integrating these and other channel innovations with well-thought-out DRTV campaigns, marketers will be able to gain an edge and approach consumers in the fastest, most efficient and profitable manner possible.

Author of more than 200 published articles, TIM HAWTHORNE is Founder, Chairman and Executive Creative Director of Hawthorne Direct, a full-service DRTV and New Media ad agency founded in 1986. Since then Hawthorne has produced or managed over 800 Direct Response TV campaigns for clients such as 3M, Black & Decker, Braun, Discover Card, Time-Life, Nissan, Lawn Boy, Nikon, Oreck, Bose and Feed the Children. Hawthorne is a co-founder of the Electronic Retailing Association, has delivered over 100 speeches worldwide and is the author of the definitive DRTV book *The Complete Guide to Infomercial Marketing*. A cum laude graduate of Harvard, Hawthorne was honored with the prestigious "Lifetime Achievement Award" by the Electronic Retailing Association (ERA) in 2006.

CASE
1

Allstate Insurance: Building Relationships through Email Campaigns

BLODWEN TARTER
Golden Gate University

MARY CARAVELLA
University of Connecticut

DEBRA ZAHAY
Northern Illinois University

Roberta Borst, Marketing Communications Director for Allstate Insurance, was thinking about the future of the recently launched relationship marketing campaign. Aspen Marketing Services, Allstate's ad agency, had done a terrific job of coming up with an email campaign that would help retain existing customers and open doors for cross-selling new insurance products to them. However, a relationship marketing campaign was new to Allstate. Historically, the company had spent about 30% of its corporate marketing dollars on direct marketing, most of it direct mail. (National general market television accounted for the largest portion of the total corporate marketing expenditures.) These direct mail call-to-action campaigns were intended to generate sales leads primarily for Allstate agents. Of course, Allstate had a web site and previously Allstate had experimented with different kinds of email messages to customers. Individual agents had tried different approaches while the corporate marketing group had also initiated a variety of email campaigns. The results had been sufficiently promising that Allstate corporate marketing wanted to pursue a coordinated email marketing strategy to support the field agents. The email-based relationship marketing campaign was a new venture, both in scope and purpose.

The initial results of the campaign were quite good and the corporate marketing team judged it successful by a number of measures. Now, how could Roberta best sell the agents on the value of continuing this campaign and get their support for enhancing it? What was needed to ensure its continued success? The campaign was just ending its first year and it was time to consider what the next steps should be.

Insurance Industry Overview

The insurance industry exists to protect its customers ("insureds" or "policyholders") from the consequences of risk. The insurer charges a premium for insurance coverage against specified risks, such as an automobile accident or a flood or fire in one's home. In the event that something happens for which the policyholder is covered, the insurance company pays, according to the terms of its contract. By extensive modeling of historical data, insurance companies seek to price coverage in such a way that the insurance company has sufficient reserves to pay out for any damages and still make money. Insurance may be the only product that people buy that they hope they will never use!

In the United States, the $140.1 billion insurance industry[1] is highly fragmented and extremely competitive. Insurance agents and brokers sell a host of insurance products but property and casualty and life insurance account for the bulk of the premiums. In a recent year, 53.4% of premiums were attributable to non-life insurance policies and 46.6% of premiums came from life insurance.[2] Personal property and casualty insurance covers automobiles and personal residences, so-called car insurance and homeowners' policies. Life insurance pays benefits upon the death of the insured.

Insurance companies compete for customers based on coverage (do they offer the kind of insurance needed?), price (are premiums competitive?), service (when a claim is made, how prompt and efficient is the company to process the claim?), and reliability and stability (is the company sufficiently well-managed that it will be able to pay out when claims are made?). Reputation is everything.

A highly regulated industry, insurance companies are subject to state laws and are scrutinized on an ongoing basis by state insurance commissioners. Every state has its own rules and regulations. Agents and brokers must be licensed in every state in which they do business and marketing materials must comply with the varying rules imposed by each state. This regulatory environment makes creating national campaigns more complex for insurance companies than for unregulated businesses.

In the insurance industry, a great deal of effort is spent on first acquiring a customer. If nothing goes awry, the company hopes that customers will simply renew their insurance policies year after year. A satisfied insurance customer is often subject to inertia—once he or she becomes a customer of a specific insurance company, it seems like too much work to move. The customer is also a prime target for cross-selling different products, further tying the customer to the company. Discounts on homeowner policies may be available to those policyholders who also have car insurance with a given company, encouraging customers to buy multiple insurance products from the same company. These bundles of products are lucrative for the insurance company and are the basis for a more in-depth relationship between the

---

[1] *Insurance in the United States: Industry Profile*, Reference Code 0072-2087, Datamonitor, November 2008, p. 3. Accessed via Business Source Complete online database, accession number 35416629. Value as measured by 2007 premiums.

[2] *Insurance in the United States: Industry Profile*, Reference Code 0072-2087, Datamonitor, November 2008, p. 12.

customer and the insurance company. However, as the insurance business becomes increasingly competitive, active customer retention efforts become a higher priority.

Company Background

Allstate is the second-largest US personal lines property and casualty insurer, behind State Farm. The company, originally owned by Sears, was started in 1931, during the Great Depression, as a way for Sears to diversify by selling insurance through its stores. Allstate became a public company in 1993. At that time, Sears divested about 20% of its shares in the company, followed by complete divestiture in 1995. Allstate has continued to grow in size and scope, broadening its product offerings over the years.

The company sells property and casualty and life insurance products in Canada and the US. Allstate Protection, which focuses on the property and casualty lines of insurance, accounts for about 90% of total premiums of Allstate. The Allstate Protection business is somewhat concentrated, with about 40% of its premiums from sales in California, Florida, New York, and Texas. Although customers can purchase some products online, Allstate maintains a network of 12,800 exclusive agencies which sell its Allstate-branded insurance products.[3] Allstate's image is of a reliable, well-established company and the longstanding slogan "You're in good hands with Allstate®" has resonated among generations of Americans. Yet, customers can still be lured away from Allstate by lower rates from discount companies because insurance rates are rising.

Like most insurers, Allstate had taken steps to protect itself from losses due to catastrophic events such as hurricanes, tornadoes, and floods. However, catastrophic losses for Allstate were greater in the first quarter of the current years than all of the previous year. Allstate was also feeling the pain of the weakening US economy. Fewer auto sales meant fewer new auto insurance policies. Rising mortgage defaults and fewer home purchases adversely affected the number of homeowner policies. Investment income, another source of financial strength for insurance companies, was reduced in the face of the turbulent financial markets. Retaining current customers at profitable rates and increasing the number of policies per customer could only help Allstate's bottom line.

Early in the current year, Allstate was grappling with the same issues facing many insurers because of the rise of the Internet. The term "disintermediation" means leaving the middleman out of the picture; the Internet allows people looking for insurance to buy insurance directly over the Internet. Even though most consumers don't actually purchase insurance online, they have the opportunity to instantly compare prices and seek the best deal. Readily available information about prices and coverage could weaken the ties that bind an insurance customer to the insurance company. In response, Allstate developed some new, more competitive products.

These product line extensions were ways Allstate was building its customer acquisition efforts. However, Allstate also wanted to retain current customers buying regular product lines and to keep the new customers initially attracted by lower rates.

---

[3] *The Allstate Corporation,* Hoover's Company Records—In-depth Records, June 5, 2009, accessed via Lexis/Nexis Academic database 11 June 2009.

Historically, many agents had not spent a lot of time between renewals nurturing customers. Allstate corporate recognized that helping agents stay in touch with customers could strengthen ties to Allstate and reduce customer attrition. If customers felt that Allstate cared about them and acted in their best interests they might be less likely to leave for lower rates. So while Roberta wanted to create marketing campaigns that strengthened customers' connections with the Allstate brand, she also wanted the campaigns to help agents stay in touch—reinforcing the key role the agents played in delivering the "You're in Good Hands" brand promise.

The Email Relationship Campaign

Thus, Allstate decided to develop a relationship-building email marketing campaign in order to maximize the lifetime value of current customers, offset attrition and ease the cross-selling process. The company wanted the series of emails not just to "push product" but to create a real dialogue with customers, building an emotional tie that lasted beyond the initial decision to buy or the subsequent decision to renew. Of course, by educating customers to help them avoid problems that caused losses, the company also stood to benefit. Fewer losses meant that Allstate paid less to settle claims and enhanced the company's profitability.

In the words of Allstate's ad agency that developed the program, the initial plan was to "communicate to customers on a monthly basis, provide valuable information without selling, and start to build a relationship beyond insurance." By cultivating the trust of the customer, the ensuing loyalty to Allstate would influence customers to renew their policies. Encouraging policyholders to call their agent with questions would begin a conversation between the policyholder and the agent and help customers become more secure about their Allstate relationship and more invested in it.

How did the Allstate email campaign achieve these objectives?

The company concentrated on three aspects: engaging emails from a recognized sender that encouraged action; using a simple, focused, microsite online that reinforced the message of each email and encouraged educational and fun customer interaction, and by creating an ongoing conversation between the policyholder and Allstate. That dialogue started with emails and the Allstate web site but encouraged personal and direct involvement with the Allstate agent.

A series of monthly emails was sent directly from the agent, a familiar name. Email deliverability was a high priority and Allstate's careful compliance with the CAN-SPAM requirements was expected to avoid messages being caught in spam filters. Once a spam filter blocks an email message there is a high likelihood it would never reach the customer. Responsys, Allstate's email deployment vendor, measured deliverability rates as high as 99% against a benchmark of 85%, suggesting that the Allstate campaign was quite effective in this arena.

The creative execution similarly focused on deliverability and legibility. Designed to be scanned quickly, the HTML text appeared on solid color backgrounds without images that are often blocked by Internet service providers. Carefully crafted messages meant that the email preview pane displayed the key information in full. Allstate knew that it had only seconds to grab the attention of its policyholders to encourage them to read the complete message and then act as requested.

Intriguing subject lines "hooked" customers and drove them to the online microsite to further engage with the company. Subject lines such as "Insurance Facts and Fallacies," "Lower Your Insurance Premiums," "Safe Driving" and "Home Preparedness" led visitors to interactive games, quizzes and surveys designed to entice customer interaction. There, visitors could browse more information on the specific topic as well as read other tips, facts, checklists and vital information. The microsite included valuable downloads like a teen driving contract, a home inventory checklist and car games for road trips. There was also a feedback center where customers could rate each page's content on a 1–5 scale.

Like the emails, the microsite had been designed to be easily scanned and simple to navigate, as well as visually consistent with the emails. From Allstate's perspective, the new microsite page templates made updating fast and easy, so fresh content could be added quickly each month. As customers became accustomed to finding new information on the web site they were more likely to visit again and again, prompted by new emails. Relevant partner offers, such as a discount on a home security system from ADT, made the microsite even more attractive to policyholders. Allstate hoped that the email messages had some pass-along value and that recipients would forward the emails to others who might be interested in the content.

With objectives to build customer trust and loyalty, drive awareness and build good will rather than sell policies, Allstate measured the results of the relationship email campaign primarily by click-through rates (CTR) and participation in the web site-based activities. The results had been impressive with a 165% increase in the email click-through rate from two years ago to one year ago, and a recent average unique click-through rate that was 125% over the email marketing industry average.

As specific examples, the company achieved a 72% email open rate and 13.3% CTR with its ECHO award-winning January "Insurance Quiz." The "Lower Your Insurance Premiums" email produced an email click-through rate four times the financial industry average. July's "Summer Driving" email sweepstakes to win a Rand McNally Road Atlas resulted in entries from 42% of unique visitors to the site. Customers also helped choose where Allstate would give its end-of-year charitable donations—65% of the visitors "voted" online in December of the previous year. For examples of the emails and microsite see Appendix 1.

These results were impressive but left Allstate with the question of where to go next. Click-through rates, although high, had not immediately translated into renewals or incremental policy sales—an overwhelming priority for individual agents. Increases in brand equity had not been measured. Agents were generally supportive of the effort. In fact, some customers had called their agents to initiate conversations about existing policies and about new ones. In addition to measurable results, the anecdotal feedback was generally positive. Of course, it didn't hurt that the campaign was funded by corporate marketing, rather than being covered by the regional or individual field agent's budgets.

After the initial launch, it was decided that the emails should be customized for specific areas of the country. Once it was recognized that messages should be geographically targeted, many messages varied by customer location. For instance, an email that suggested ways to prepare for weather disasters could be tailored for tornadoes, floods, or hail, depending upon where the customer lived. This targeting further improved the effectiveness of the messaging, reinforced the corporate/field partnership, and better served the customers receiving the emails.

However, a few agents had been skeptical about the campaign in spite of the fact that the email messages were sent with their names in the "From" line. The agents were more accustomed to direct marketing that specifically called for a renewal or a new sale (e.g., when cross-selling a different insurance product to an existing customer). Other agents simply didn't fully understand how email marketing was supposed to work. So there was still work to be done to deepen appreciation of the value of email marketing in general and about this campaign in particular.

A number of agents asked for suggestions on how to best capitalize on the corporate email marketing efforts to support their own sales efforts. Allstate agents were demographically diverse. Many were unfamiliar with social networking tools and digital marketing. The marketing team helped interested agents integrate their efforts with the overall relationship campaign

Most agents appreciated the corporate efforts to strengthen customer ties to Allstate and to help them build their business. These agents recognized that customer loyalty might make current policyholders more inclined to buy another type of insurance from Allstate and looked forward to the cross-sell opportunities the campaign should open up. But what would the next steps in this effort look like? Should Allstate now include explicit cross-selling messages in the relationship-building campaign or not? The individual agents and the corporate marketing staff were divided among themselves on this question. There was no clear consensus.

So far, the relationship email marketing campaign stood apart in Allstate's corporate and individual agent marketing efforts. There had been an explosion in social media since the campaign began and many consumers reported using Internet search engines rather than calling agents to make decisions on insurance purchases. How could Allstate expand this good start to focus on relationship-building across all sales channels?

Roberta had several ideas for building on this already successful email campaign.

1. **Allstate could continue soft relationship-building email campaigns in order to retain customers.** Creating new and relevant messages that helped build trust in Allstate without explicit selling would be consistent with the campaign just completed. If Roberta went down this path, she would also need to look at how to extend these messages across additional online media.

2. **Allstate could add specific cross-selling messages into the campaign.** Roberta knew that she could analyze the existing customer base to identify who already owned what kind of insurance and what combinations of insurance were most common. For example, were home owners more likely to own automobile insurance and boat insurance? Then Roberta would need to identify to which customers she should offer what additional lines of insurance. Last but not least, once the target was identified, in what ways could she customize the messages to be most effective? How could Allstate transition the messaging from relationship-building, a softer message, to cross-selling, a harder sell? Furthermore, how could Roberta structure a cross-selling campaign in order to measure its effectiveness?

3. **Allstate could develop email campaigns that generated new leads for agents.** People who indicated interest in Allstate insurance but who had not yet purchased a policy needed to be encouraged to apply and then, once approved, to actually buy the insurance. The field agents might welcome this type of assistance, but this was a significant shift away from the original relationship building intent of the email marketing campaign. Where did customer acquisition and lead conversion fit with the email relationship-building campaign?

Of course, there were many ideas floating around. Roberta mentally reviewed her options and reminded herself that she needed to sort through the alternatives and prioritize them. She knew that the company would require full financial justification of the next phase of the campaign. With the recent serious losses, largely due to tornadoes, hurricanes, and hail storms, all marketing expenditures would be scrutinized and evaluated for an adequate return on investment (ROI). Consequently, Roberta might have to collect more data and enhance its analysis to demonstrate the next campaign's value. As she considered how much needed to be done, Roberta directed the agency to provide recommendations for all aspects of the campaign's next phase, from creative to data analysis.

Appendix 1

Samples from the Campaign

EXHIBIT C1.1:
INSURANCE QUIZ, JANUARY

Results

- *Open Rate*   *72%*
- *Click-through Rate*   *13.3%*
- *ECHO Award winner*

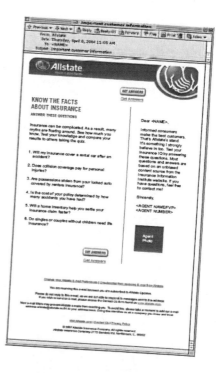

EXHIBIT C1.2: HOW TO LOWER YOUR INSURANCE PREMIUMS, JUNE

Results

- *Delivered*   327,730
- *Bounced*   17,505
- *Open Rate*   64.38%
- *Unique Open Rate*   39.08%
- *Click-through Rate*
  (high)   22%
- *Unsubscribe*   0.1% (336)

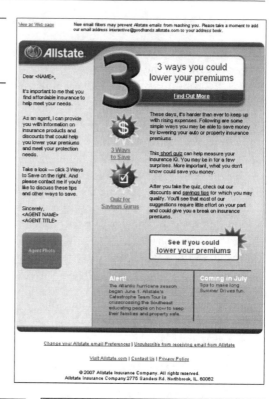

EXHIBIT C1.3: SUMMER DRIVING SWEEPSTAKES JULY

Results

- *Obtained sweepstakes entries from* **42% of unique visitors** *to the site*

EXHIBIT C1.4: ADT PARTNERSHIP OFFER ON MICROSITE

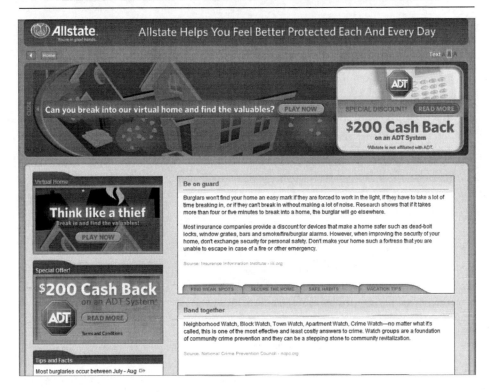

• *Number of leads exceeded ADT's expectations*

Appendix 2

Email Marketing Summary

Advantages: Creates true one to one channel, trackable, measurable, excellent for maintaining and growing a customer relationship using personalized messages

Disadvantages: Difficult to control, driven by end user, limited, not mass, audience

Advantages versus Direct Mail: Faster (3 days vs. 3 weeks), cheaper ($.25 versus a dollar or more), higher response (5% vs. 0.5%).

Response rates (CTR): Vary from 5–10% depending on type of email, audience (list), etc.

Email Uses: Forrester research study of companies doing ecommerce revealed how these firms use email:

- 66% Promotions and discounts
- 48% Newsletters
- 34% New products
- 28% Marketing & advertising
- 24% Alerts and reminders
- 8% Market research

Key email marketing process metrics:

- Bounce rate—undeliverable addresses
- Unsubscribe rate—percent of people who unsubscribe in response to an email
- Open rate—percent of delivered mail that readers open
- Click-through rate—number of links clicked or actions taken divided by the number of opened emails
- Example:
  —100 emails sent
    □ 5 are undeliverable so bounce rate is 5%
    □ 5 people unsubscribe so the unsubscribe rate is 5%
  —40 are opened so open rate is 44% (40/90)
  —10 users actually click through on the requested action so the click-through rate is 25% (10/40)

Elements of CAN-SPAM Act compliance:

- Valid "from" email address, valid reply
- Street address
- Unsubscribe provision
- Label as 'advertising' if the email is unsolicited

How to improve deliverability*

- Use a commercial Email Service Provider with a good reputation with email companies

---

*thanks to Exact Target (www.exacttarget.com) for some of these tips

- Comply with the CAN-SPAM Act (see above)
- Get and confirm permission
- Set content and frequency expectations with customer
- Have a compelling subject line
- Send more relevant content; avoid overly promotional content
- Have an "Address Book" strategy
- Use proper list hygiene
  —Use procedures to remove duplicate addresses from your list
  —Use procedures to screen out addresses on your "do not email" list
  —Check email bounces and correct
- Monitor blacklist reports

Brief Email Marketing Glossary

- **Bounce Rate:** Number of emails undeliverable divided by the number sent
  —**Hard Bounce Rate:** Number of emails undeliverable because of a bad email address divided by the number sent
  —**Soft Bounce Rate:** Number of emails undeliverable for reasons other than a bad email address divided by the number sent
- **Clickstream:** Database created by web site to track user activity on the site
- **Click-Through Rate (CTR):** Number of email offers acted on by clicking a link through to a web page divided by number opened. In online advertising or search marketing, the click-through rate is often instead calculated as the number of users that click on an online ad divided by the total number of exposures. When comparing across media, it is important to understand the calculation being used.
- **Click-to-Purchase Rate:** Number of purchases generated by email campaign divided by number of emails opened
- **Cookies:** Electronic tag on user's computer to enable the web site to recognize that user on their return
- **Dynamic Content:** Changing the email content per user, including personalizing name and other customer information as well as the email content delivered
- **HTML Email:** Emails formatted using the same hypertext markup language used to create web pages. Open rates can only be calculated for HTML emails; rates for text emails and emails opened on many mobile phones cannot be tracked
- **Open Rate:** Number of email offers opened divided by number delivered
  —**Unique Open Rate:** Number of actual people opening offers, divided by number delivered. Accounts for people who look at the email more than once.
- **Permission Email:** Solicitations sent with the receiver's prior permission obtained in some manner; recommended email marketing method
- **Spam:** Lots of unwanted, unsolicited email, gets its name from the famous Monty Python skit in which spam is mentioned so many times that the word becomes annoying! http://www.detritus.org/spam/ And enjoy the song!

CASE
2

American Cancer Society Chicago Chapter May Walk and Roll Event Marketing Campaign

J. STEVEN KELLY

DePaul University

FRANK K. BRYANT

Cal Poly Pomona

RAYECAROL CAVENDER

Virginia Tech

KATE STEVENSON

DePaul University

REGINE VANHEEMS

Université of Paris I—Sorbonne

The National American Cancer Society

This national organization (www.cancer.org) is well known as the premier association that fights cancer. Through its efforts, the National American Cancer Society (NACS) has been able to channel $3.4 billion into funding for cancer research. The NACS can claim that its efforts have supported every major breakthrough in cancer research. Indeed, the NACS has supported 42 Nobel laureates. The organization's leaders and supporters are proud of the fact that 11 million cancer survivors are "living proof" of the American Cancer Society's progress.

That said, NACS research disclosed that although the American Cancer Society was the most highly recognized health charity brand, many citizens had little understanding about the scope of the organization's programs. Therefore, in a recent year, NACS launched a brand revitalization effort. This campaign positioned the American Cancer Society as "The Official Sponsor of Birthdays." The marketing communications asked the public to imagine a world with more birthdays, and highlighted all of the ways the organization saves lives. These included: helping people stay well through taking steps to prevent cancer or detect it early; helping people get well by guiding them through every step of the cancer experience; finding cures through funding and conducting groundbreaking research; and fighting back by encouraging lawmakers to do their part to defeat cancer and rallying communities to join the fight.

One of their main campaigns for NACS is the American Cancer Society "Relay For Life", its signature fundraising activity. It takes place across the country each year, with many of the local and regional events occurring in the spring. The American Cancer Society's community presence is often best felt through Relay For Life, the largest global grassroots movement and cancer fundraiser that involves more than 3.5 million participants. Relay for Life celebrates people who have battled cancer, remembers loved ones lost, and fights back to end a disease that has taken too much away from too many people. The money raised through Relay has helped the American Cancer Society to play a role in nearly every major cancer breakthrough in recent history.

The new "The Official Sponsor of Birthdays" brand effort included a major national advertising launch during April. It included television programs (e.g., "Good Morning America," the "Today Show," "20/20," "60 Minutes," "The View," "CSI," "Amazing Race," "Dancing with the Stars," as well as shows on cable channels); and print publications, including *Better Homes & Gardens, O-The Oprah Magazine, Health, Family Circle, Cooking Light, Woman's Day, Ladies' Home Journal, Prevention* and *Essence.*

The American Cancer Society/Chicago Region

With this background in mind, this case now shifts its focus to one of the major chapters of the American Cancer Society, located in the Chicago region. As the Chicago case opens in fall of the current year, the Vice President of Communications for the Chicago American Cancer Society is fully aware of the national campaigns and programs. That said, his personal responsibility is for the success of the local programs. Like any strategic business unit, the Chicago chapter has financial goals it must meet. Therefore, it is responsible for the marketing of this chapter's own fundraising events as well as assisting with the national programs. Through its 15 community-based regional offices and presence at 50 healthcare partners, the American Cancer Society/Chicago (ACSC) sponsors more than 200 local events—many of them Relay for Life events—each year to raise money. Donors fund $45 million in annual contributions from nearly 400,000 Illinois individuals and companies. To make this happen, ACSC works with nearly 100,000 volunteers.

At this time, the Vice President wants to take a close look at the events referred to as the Walk and Roll fundraisers. These are separate from the other chapter and national ACS office events. In fact, the national events could be said to be competitive to the local events. The local chapter holds five Walk and Roll events in the Chicago area, most in May and one in August (see Table C2.1). Five are in the suburbs, one in the city of Peoria, but the big event is in Chicago the weekend after Mother's Day, usually the second weekend in May. The Vice President wants to focus on this event as a major part of ACSC's fundraising effort. To view the Walk and Roll web site, enter "Walk and Roll" into a search engine.

The results of the previous Spring's events were not up to standard and are out-lined here:

TABLE C2.1

Walk & Roll Event	Date	Money Raised Previous Spring
W&R-Elgin	Sat, May 7	$73,628
W&R-Chicago	Sun, May 15	$523,578
W&R-North Shore	Sun, May 15	$42,587
W&R- West Cook (cancelled—participants urged to join W&R Chicago)	Sun, May 15	$9,830
W&R- Lake County	Sun, May 15	$64,795
W&R- Richland County	Sat, May 21	$6,131
W&R-Peoria	Sat, Aug 14	$1,445

This low level of fundraising results was cause for alarm because it fell well below ACSC's goals and previous year's accomplishments. The Vice President felt that his communications team needed to be assembled to review what could be done to turn this situation around.

In fact, in the previous year, more than 6,000 people had gathered for this annual tradition, raising more than $1.1 million to fight cancer. There were 450 teams of participants, 200 in-line skaters, 500 bikers, and 3500 walkers to total 4,200 actual participants. The rest were volunteers who helped participants and manned the route and booths.

The Chicago Walk and Roll event was the ACSC's longest-standing fundraising event in Illinois. It had begun nearly 40 years previous as the Chicago Bike-a-thon and had grown to include walkers, cyclists, and in-line skaters.

The area had a history of supporting ACSC fundraising events. The very first event was the Bike-a-Thon in 1972, operated along the Chicago Lakefront. Later, walking and in-line skating were added to the event. A second event, in 1974, was started in Skokie, a suburb north of Chicago. It had always been much smaller, with perhaps 600 participants and 60 teams. Much more recently, other events were added. Two years ago, one was held in the northwest suburbs, Elgin, with about 400 participants and 40 teams. Then, four other events were established in the previous year, one far north in Lake County with 450 participants, one West in Brookfield Woods with 300 participants, and two outside Chicago in Peoria and Richland County. All of these were operated in May, except the one in Peoria which was in August.

The plan for this coming Spring/Summer was to hold the following Walk and Roll events:

Elgin, Saturday, May 8
Chicago, Sunday May 15
North Shore, Sunday May 15
Lake County, Sunday May 15
Peoria, Saturday, August 14
Richland County, IL, Saturday, May 22

Background on the Fundraising Environment

The ACSC team reminded each other about the charitable donations environment they had been facing. In the U.S., charitable donations fell 3.6% during the first year of the recent recession. That amounted to $303.75 billion given in the previous year, compared to $315 billion in the year prior to that. This was the largest drop in donations since the 1970s, when the country was going through the oil crisis. High unemployment and foreclosures were prevalent during this time, and may have been a contributing factor to this loss. Forty percent of all charitable gifts are given in the last quarter of the year (October through December). One-third of all donations go to religious groups, which are the biggest recipients of donations. The bulk of all donations come from individuals in the form of small gifts. Giving to human services, health, international affairs and environment and animal-related groups all saw increases in the previous year, while donations to education, arts, culture and humanities organizations fell overall.

Statistics found at www.factfinder.census.gov provided some insights into the current Chicago population:

TABLE C2.2

	Estimate
Total Population	2,725,206
Male	1,333,779
Female	1,391,427
Men and Women's Population	
25 to 34 years	453,165
35 to 44 years	415,807
45 to 54 years	356,586
18 years and over	2,065,028
Male	997,859
Female	1,067,169

Also, income figures helped complete the picture of the greater Chicago community and potential participants in the ACSC events.

TABLE C2.3

Income Less than $25,000	610,454
Income of $25,000 to $34,999	269,893
Income of $35,000 to $49,999	389,145
Income of $50,000 to $74,999	559,553
Income of $75,000 to $99,999	409,265
Income of $100,000 to $149,999	438,021
Income of $150,000 to $199,999	172,813
Income of $200,000 or more	181,475
Median household income (dollars)	$60,057
Mean household income (dollars)	$82,320

The participants in the previous Walk and Roll events fell into the following categories. The vast majority of walkers were female, between 30 and 50 years old. Corporate teams brought in young professionals. The average income of participants was consistent with the national average household income. There was some minority engagement through family and friends teams. For the Chicago Walk and Roll, 48% had 606—zip codes (meaning Chicago city residents), with 50% coming in from the suburbs and 2% from out of state.

Competitive Environment

One cause of the poor donation turnout could be addressed by the level of fundraiser run/walk competition that had arisen in the past few years. The citizens of the area had a wealth of opportunities to participate in such events and raise funds for causes. These are just a few of the events scheduled to take place during the general time period that the ACSC sponsors its events:

- Heart Walk—American Heart Assn., September
- JDRF Walk—Juvenile Diabetes, September
- Walk America—March of Dimes, April
- Mother's Day Walk/Run—Breast Cancer Network of Strength, May
- Memory Walk—Alzheimer's Association, August
- Out of the Dark—National Suicide, May
- Light the Night—Leukemia/Lymphoma, September
- NKFI Gift of Life Walk and Family Health Fair—National Kidney Foundation, June
- Bastille Day: 5K Run/Walk—Mercy Home for Boys, July
- Run for Gus, 5K—Young Associate Board, July
- Fight For Air Run/Walk—American Lung Association, September
- AIDS Run & Walk Chicago—AIDS Foundation of Chicago, October
- Susan G. Komen Walk/Race for the Cure—several races and walks in the summer

A point worth noting is that most of these were not events where winning was a goal. Other events in the area, around the same time, did offer athletic competition. The ACSC team recognized that the amount of preparation required for athletically competitive events did change the perspective of the participant.

The public did seem to want to seek information and involvement in events such as those presented by ACSC. As an example of the popularity of these types of events, a review of key words used for Google search in September showed that the following phrases elicited these numbers:

Cancer walk	246,000
Cure cancer	201,000
Breast cancer walk	165,000
Donate charity	60,500

Current Marketing Program for the Chicago Chapter

The team took a look at the situation they faced in terms of their past communications efforts. Essentially, the ACSC had been adhering to its mission, which it delivered in the message "We save lives by helping people stay well, get well, by finding cures and by fighting back." They had concentrated on these messages because the harsh realities were that on any given day, 170 people in Illinois learned they had cancer, and 70 died from cancer.

Recently, ACSC felt the need to examine the impact of its messaging on the public. The organization undertook brand awareness research to see how they compared to other organizations. In a study done on Illinois residents, for unaided awareness, when thinking about charities that address health problems, the American Cancer Society has the highest overall brand awareness among Illinois residents. This was in comparison to such venerable organizations as American Heart Association, Susan G. Komen Breast Cancer Foundation, American Lung Association, and others. Further, those touched by cancer were more likely to mention American Cancer Society.

When asked what organizations they trusted most for cancer information, the American Cancer Society was rated as "most trusted," even above the respondents' personal physician.

In addition to their messaging toward individuals, the Walk and Roll events offered opportunities for corporations to participate and get involved in the fight against cancer. The NACS gave the IMPACT award to corporations that helped raise awareness and funds to fight cancer. Being involved at this level allowed these corporations to demonstrate sponsorship of the local events, like Walk and Roll. This, of course, showed their customers and employees that they were committed to making an impact on finding a cure for the disease. By sponsoring the events, the companies got brand recognition through Walk and Roll promotional materials, web sites, and thousands of participants wearing apparel with their logos. Also, where appropriate, the companies could give away products at the events, be part of the community, and demonstrate involvement. Finally, it allowed the companies to rally their employees around a worthwhile cause in a family-friendly environment.

The Walk and Roll programs had, in the past, had the following campaign elements:

- Web site—Event information, information on how to raise funds and to donate, stories and testimonials

- Print collateral—Distributed to local storefronts; mailings to past participants
- Past corporate sponsors received materials to mail to their employees
- Kick-off event—Targeted to past teams, top fundraisers and any new prospects secured by committee and staff
- Volunteers—Leveraging personal circles, hanging posters in their communities
- CTA (bus service in Chicago) and Street Pole Banners distributed 30 days out from event
- The local NBC affiliate, Channel 5, was a media sponsor and offered Public Service Announcements 30 days out from event

This was done in the past, but it was obvious that this was not enough to compete with the programs they were facing.

What Did the New Marketing Program Look Like?

The ACSC team recognized in order for the next campaign to meet the target objectives ($2 million in donations, 12,000 participants), it would need to be an integrated, multichannel marketing communications campaign. ACSC would need to grow more volunteers, more participants (walkers and rollers), increase donations, increase corporate teams and sponsorships, gain market share in the Chicagoland walk market (there were a considerable number of events in the summer) and examine what market segments might be included that were not already present.

In order to market the Walk and Roll event, the budget was set at $60,000. ACSC was ready to consider digital and social media options to raise the Walk and Roll event above other charity messages as "the way" to fight back against cancer in Chicagoland.

Noticeably absent from past marketing was any email campaign. The local chapter, despite the years of involvement in these events, had only 5,000 email addresses of past participants. There was a philosophical reason for this: it was felt that people did not make donations via email. For example, potential participants found out about the web site through print materials, mailers and the like. That point of view might be challenged.

A major consideration that those looking into this program should consider is whether the current Walk and Roll name was still relevant. Also, did this or another name align better with the ACSC brand?

Another question was how does ACSC learn how to "digitize" its marketing communications? It was thought advisable to review what some of the local Chicagoland events calendars might offer in terms of creative program ideas. ACSC was not opposed to joining forces with other media and marketing vehicles. Here are a few:

- http://www.chicagoevents.com/
- http://www.mychicagoathlete.com/
- http://www.cancer.org/docroot/home/index.asp
- http://www.yelp.com/chicago
- http://www.meetup.com/find/us/il/chicago/

- http://www.cararuns.org/
- http://www.americanheart.org/

A competitive analysis would help ACS understand its position with regard to all of these events. There was a need to evaluate top walks/runs/bike events in Chicago (both athletically competitive and non-competitive). They also needed to evaluate sponsorship benefits to the corporations and consider creating the team programs.

Of course, any multichannel marketing communications program needs to establish a set of metrics to set benchmarks and to track success. What might be done to measure success of the web site? Should a separate micro-site be used (and for what purpose)? What measurements needed to be set up to track success? Should social media be used, and how? A timeline needed to be set up to show what will be done from now, Fall, to the events and beyond. Methods needed to be examined for capturing participant information to help with future programs.

There were other organizations in the Chicago area that might play a part in the program. Corporations have already been mentioned but perhaps the program to reach out to them could be revitalized. In addition, the Chicago Public Schools have over 150 high schools with over 110,000 students. The College and Career Preparation Department of the Chicago Public Schools has requirements for students to complete a minimum of 40 hours of service between 9th and 12th grade; sophomores must complete a minimum of 20 hours of service in order to be promoted to junior status; and students must spend time preparing for and reflecting on the Service Learning experience. Is this something that Walk and Roll could be a part of? Inviting, but it could be more administrative work than the team had time for.

After a great deal of discussion and nail-biting over the past results, the team suggested that they get some outside points of view about marketing the Walk and Roll event. They suggested posing the marketing communications problem to some graduate students at a major local university.

CASE
3

Amtrak: A Communications Planning Challenge[1]

MARIAN AZZARO

Roosevelt University

T his case presents the details of a positioning and communications strategy problem for a very complex consumer service business: Amtrak. The key question facing Amtrak management and its advisors involved identifying the best communications positioning strategy and determining the best way to choose that strategy in order to build the brand and the business.

Background: Business Description

Amtrak is the nation's passenger railroad. Created by an act of Congress in 1971, Amtrak today is still subsidized by the government and almost wholly owned by the U.S. Department of Transportation. Amtrak is a for-profit company, challenged to achieve commercial success while continuing to meet its public service mission. By law, Amtrak is required to provide a national network of passenger rail service. However, many of the mandated routes are not financially viable. As a result, Amtrak stands before Congress every year requesting budget subsidies.

Amtrak today operates a reasonably efficient version of the national route network mandated by Congress. On weekdays Amtrak runs more than 250 trains daily covering more than 22,000 miles of track. In total it provides rail service to more than 500 cities and towns in 46 states nationwide. In general, Amtrak's service is made up of long-distance routes connecting densely populated short-distance service corridors throughout the U.S. Long-distance trains generally operate daily, offering several choices of passenger service class, including first-class sleeping car service, custom class service, and economy service. Corridor services typically run shorter distances with multiple daily frequencies. The premier corridor service offered by Amtrak today is the new Acela high-speed service on the Northeast rail corridor running geographically from Washington, D.C., north to Boston. Acela is the model for development of rail service in other U.S. federally-designated travel corridors.

---

[1]Much of the material for this case is edited from information available on the Amtrak web site, www.amtrak.com. Other specific sources are indicated in the text or the notes that follow.

EXHIBIT C3.1: AMTRAK RIDERSHIP AND REVENUE GROWTH

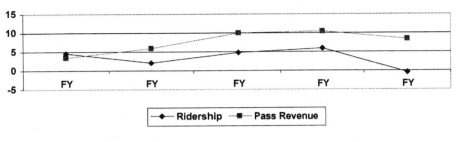

Past 5 Years Percent Change in Ridership and Passenger Revenue

Source: Figures provided by Amtrak

State of the Business

For the past five years Amtrak has successfully grown its passenger business, building revenue by an average of 7.6% per year and building ridership by an average of 3.3% per year (see Exhibit C3.1). For the next five years, Amtrak projects continued growth in passenger revenue at about 4% per year with modest growth in passenger ridership. Much of Amtrak's success can be attributed to its focus on four core strategies:

1. Building public and private partnerships
2. Developing established and new corridor services
3. Revitalizing the Amtrak Brand
4. Delivering improved service quality

Building Public and Private Partnerships

Amtrak began efforts in 1999 to identify commercial and investment partners for strategic business alliances. Today it continues efforts to develop promotional, service development, and investment partnerships. Amtrak envisions such partnerships to be critical to the commercial success of long-distance train service and fundamental to repositioning Amtrak's brand identity.

Developing Established and New Corridor Services

Even as Amtrak launched the Acela high-speed rail service in the Northeast, it was working with other states and business partners to expand improved rail services to other corridors across the country. Amtrak's plan is to leverage expertise and knowledge gained in the Northeast to fast-adapt expansion to the promising corridors of the future:

- The California Corridors, Los Angeles to San Diego and the San Joaquin Valley
- The Midwest Corridor, connecting Ohio, Michigan, Illinois, Wisconsin, Nebraska and Minnesota through Chicago
- The Pacific Northwest Corridor connecting Vancouver, Seattle, and Portland
- The Southeast Corridor between Washington, D.C., and Charlotte, North Carolina

EXHIBIT C3.2: AMTRAK LOGO DEVELOPMENT

Original Logo	New Logos

- The Gulf Coast Corridor between Atlanta and New Orleans
- The Empire Corridor in the state of New York
- The Keystone Corridor in Pennsylvania

Revitalizing the Amtrak Brand and Delivering Improved Service Quality

Amtrak recognizes that its brand encompasses the total experience of train travel, from purchasing the ticket to entering the station to the meals and amenities available during the trip. Proprietary Amtrak research yielded results leading to redefined services, amenities, and offerings; defined service standards to apply throughout the network system; and trained employees delivering the new standards.

In 1999 Amtrak introduced a new brand identity along with its service standards guarantee and the all-new Acela high-speed services to demonstrate its commitment to change (see Exhibit C3.2). The new Amtrak taps into today's consumer values and successfully reflects Amtrak's changing corporate strategies and services.

Cost Management

Most recently, Amtrak has added a fifth core strategy, that of cost management. This strategy is key to Amtrak's chances for success and applies across all of the organization. From train operations to station services to marketing management, all Amtrak employees must seek out and adapt to cost management opportunities. In marketing management, for example, such opportunities will range from buying efficiencies to budget cuts. The Amtrak National Communications plan must reflect this reality.

Traveling Consumers

Amtrak's passengers can be broadly defined as "train interested" travelers. This is a broad sub-group representing about 45% of the total traveling population in the U.S. according to the Yankelovich 2001 *Leisure Monitor*[2]. "Train interested" travelers may or may not have taken a train trip recently, but they have all expressed an interest in doing so within the next two years.

In more specific terms, according to proprietary Amtrak research[3], there are five

[2] Yankelovich Partners, Inc., 2001, *The Yankelovich 2001 Leisure MONITOR*, p. 114.
[3] Amtrak 1998 Market Based Network Study.

EXHIBIT C3.3: AMTRAK CHALLENGES BY NATIONAL TRAVEL MARKET SEGMENT

Consumer Segment	Amtrak Challenges	% U.S. Travelers
Business Travelers	Travel time	22%
Young Family Travelers	Travel time, cost, nearby stations	11%
Footloose/Fancy Free	Travel time, station locations, and flexibility	10%
Older Family Vacationers	Cost and convenient station locations	9%
Senior Experientials	Travel time, convenient stations, and comfort	8%

Source: Amtrak Market Based Network Study

market segments of particular interest to Amtrak. Each segment, defined according to life-style and travel purpose, holds some challenge for Amtrak (see Exhibit C3.3). This segmentation scheme works well in that it captures key differences in travel motivation. The needs of consumers differ significantly when traveling for business versus leisure purposes. Needs also differ when traveling alone as adults or traveling with younger or older children. As would be expected, these differences are significant in many ways.

Despite their obvious differences, most of these segments have one important consideration in common: travel time. Travel time can be both good and bad for consumers. They consider it part of the travel experience, and that can be time well spent or time wasted depending on the experience. Travel time for Amtrak can also be good or bad. A trip on Amtrak is all about time because train travel generally takes longer than air travel. Opportunistically, though, time spent traveling on Amtrak can be part of an enriching travel experience, and this is part of the appeal among train-interested traveling consumers.

Demographically, across all of Amtrak, consumers are older and better educated than the U.S. travel market in general (see Exhibit C3.4), but this is somewhat misleading. Amtrak believes that it is not appropriate to consider all products and services as a whole. Instead, the travel experience and the consumer's expectations differ significantly for long-distance leisure versus short-distance regional travel.

Marketing Communications

The marketing budget for Amtrak is planned each year in the late spring/early summer. Budgets are finalized when the business plan is confirmed each year in October. Amtrak marketing expenditures are allocated annually throughout its system supporting the many products and services of Amtrak.

Seasonality for Amtrak is similar to that of the travel industry in general. Summer is the big travel season. Other than the summer season, peaks occur during key holiday seasons such as Thanksgiving through New Year's and spring break. As with the rest of the industry, Amtrak generally experiences high demand during these peak periods and doesn't typically need to advertise or promote to build ridership. Instead, Amtrak plans system-wide fall and spring promotions designed to build ridership in the "shoulder" periods between peak and off-peak times. The fall program each year

EXHIBIT C3.4: AMTRAK NATIONAL TRAVEL MARKET DEMOGRAPHIC PROFILES

	U.S. Market %	Amtrak %	Index
Gender			
Male	50	48	96
Female	50	52	104
Trip Purpose			
Business	33	26	79
Non-business	57	65	114
Both	10	9	90
Age			
18–34	40	29	72
35–54	47	47	100
55–64	10	20	200
65+	2	4	200
Average Age	40 yrs	44 yrs	
Education			
Less Than HS	3	3	100
HS Graduate	24	20	83
Some College	27	24	89
College Graduate	30	33	110
Graduate School	16	20	125
HH Income			
Less than $45K	41	43	105
$45K–$75K	34	33	97
$75K+	25	24	96
Average Income	$59K	$57K	

Source: Amtrak Brand Tracking and Equity Study

is usually some variation of the Amtrak *Explore America* zonal fares. This fall program is usually targeted more to an older adult audience. The spring program is also generally some kind of special fares promotion targeted more to younger adults and traveling families. In recent years, Amtrak has worked to develop and leverage some highly visible partnerships behind its fare promotions (for example, Major League Baseball in the spring).

Product and Service Highlights

In recent years, the two biggest positive news factors for Amtrak have been the introduction of Acela high-speed rail in the Northeast and its system-wide service training and the service guarantee called "The Amtrak Promise."

Acela High-Speed Rail

Inaugurated in November 2000, Acela was heralded by Amtrak as the fastest train in its history. But Acela is not just about speed. Acela is high-service rail with its superior ride quality, world-class service and amenities, and enhanced speed all backed by a customer satisfaction guarantee. Acela is the pride of Amtrak and its model for service standards on all Amtrak trains.

The Amtrak Promise

At the same time, Amtrak began the monumental task of defining and implementing consistent service standards system-wide across the broad range of products and services offered. This effort started with a core team of managers and employees who defined the set of standards and determined the plan for implementation. The first step in implementation was the "Service Success" training program for all employees and managers. The next step was a service rewards and incentives program designed to keep employees on the service track. Finally, Amtrak offered its customer satisfaction guarantee, "The Amtrak Promise," on all trains, at all times.

Other Amtrak Products and Services

Beyond these more recent developments, it is worth noting that Amtrak offers a full range of products and services for traveling consumers.

Amtrak offers coach class, custom class and first-class service on long-distance leisure trains throughout the country. (It is important to note that first-class long-distance travel on Amtrak includes on-board sleeping accommodations and dining car privileges.) Some of the more outstanding and historic Amtrak routes are:

- The Silver Service operating daily along the East Coast between New York, Washington, D.C., and all points in Florida
- The Auto Train carrying passengers and their cars direct, non-stop, and overnight between Washington, D.C. and Orlando, Florida
- The Coast Starlight operating daily along the West Coast with service between Los Angeles and Seattle
- The Sunset Limited, the nation's only coast-to-coast passenger train, operating between Florida and California
- Several spectacular routes running daily out of Chicago: The California Zephyr, The City of New Orleans, The Capitol Limited, The Empire Builder, and The Southwest Chief

Service schedules for many of these long-distance routes afford travelers a one-of-a-kind travel experience unique to train travel: the first-class, overnight excursion. There are several examples throughout the Amtrak route network where first-class passengers can board a train in the late afternoon or evening in one city, enjoy a fine dinner in the dining car, retire to a private sleeping compartment, and wake the next morning arriving fresh and rested in a new city. Examples include Chicago to Denver on The California Zephyr, Washington, D.C., to Chicago on The Capitol Limited, and Chicago to New Orleans on The City of New Orleans.

For consumers who prefer one-stop vacation shopping, Amtrak offers Amtrak Vacations and Amtrak Air Rail. With one phone call to Amtrak Vacations, consumers can book pre-packaged complete vacations or assemble their own vacation plans including the train, car rentals, hotel accommodations, and tour options of interest. Amtrak Air Rail is a one-of-a-kind partnership between Amtrak and United Airlines allowing consumers to travel one-way by train and one-way by plane virtually anywhere in the U.S.

Overall, much is new and exciting about the new Amtrak. Amtrak is actively engaged in redefining and re-establishing its brand equity and succeeding in its efforts. But the network is expansive; Amtrak has 25,000 employees working in more than 500 cities and towns across 46 states. And, Amtrak's business objectives are seemingly at odds, its public service mission often draining profits from commercial successes. This is the continuing challenge of Amtrak's National Communications efforts.

Questions

1. Which Amtrak product or product group represents the greatest potential for building Amtrak's business? State facts to support your recommendation.
2. Which target audience segment represents the greatest growth potential for Amtrak (consider those mentioned in the case and others not mentioned as well)? State the facts that support your recommendation.
3. Thinking about your audience and product focus recommended in 1 and 2 above, what benefit and support would you recommend for Amtrak's marketing communications focus? Explain how your recommended benefit and support fits with the product and the audience segment. Be specific.

C A S E
4

Busch Gardens®: Planning for a Wild Direct & Interactive Marketing Ride

LISA D. SPILLER

Christopher Newport University

M emorial Day weekend was fast approaching and Dan Dipiazzo, Vice-President of Marketing at Busch Gardens and Water Country USA® in Williamsburg, Virginia, was looking forward to the more *quiet* days of summer. Quiet days of summer? How can that be possible? Isn't Dan responsible for the marketing activities of a highly seasonal theme park? Indeed, Busch Gardens is a successful seasonal business and summer is the peak season for the park—that is, if the marketing strategies put in place for the season are effective. However, for Dan and his marketing team, summertime is primarily a time for planning next year's marketing strategies. Sure, they keep an eye on the current marketing activities, and tweak the special event promotions and media mix as needed, but for the most part, the bulk of the advertisements are produced, media buys are complete, and the summer campaigns are underway. So, for the Busch Gardens marketing group, summer is a relatively laid back time.

Today was not going to be a quiet one though. It was now 9:15 a.m. and Dan was in high gear as he was busy with the last-minute details for his marketing retreat, which was set to begin at 10:00 a.m. sharp. The Memorial Day market planning retreat, which is held annually, each Tuesday after Memorial Day, always begins with a team-bonding experience, such as a wild ride on one of the many thrilling roller coasters featured in the park. This year, Apollo's Chariot® (Exhibit C4.1) is the roller coaster of choice.

As the 10:00 hour arrives, Dan assembles the planning team, which includes his three marketing directors and three managers selected to serve on this year's team. "Let's go get our creative juices flowing with a ride on Apollo's

Exhibit C4.1.
Apollo's Chariot

269

Chariot," he says, and the group takes off toward the giant roller coast. There's nothing like a gripping roller coaster ride to bring out the kid in everyone!

The opportunity to experience the park in action is one of the reasons Dan (Exhibit C4.2) made the move to Williamsburg from his company's corporate office in 2007. A native of the St. Louis Area, he started his career as a reporter and editor for his hometown daily newspaper before making the switch to public relations. He spent 10 years at Fleishman-Hillard International Communications, becoming a senior vice president and partner in the firms's consumer marketing practice. After a decade of agency life he decided to focus on one client and became a public relations consultant for Busch Entertainment Corp.—the theme park company that later became SeaWorld Parks & Entertainment™. Eventually he was hired by the company to become vice president of consumer marketing, and later vice president of marketing strategy and planning. While being at headquarters allowed him to work with all of the company's parks across the country, he was eager to get closer to the "front lines" of the business and see

Exhibit C4.2. Dan Dipiazzo, Vice President of Marketing, Busch Gardens/ Water Country USA

marketing in action. When the opportunity arose to lead the marketing team at Busch Gardens and Water Country USA in Williamsburg, he jumped at the chance.

The roller coaster ride was just what the planning team needed before spending the warm and sunny day inside at the retreat. "Awesome ride!" shouts Cindy, the park's brand director. "Let's ride it again!" "Maybe later," replies Dan. "For now, let's head back to the conference room as we've got a lot of planning to do if we're going to make next year a marketing success story" says Dan. Everyone agrees as they head back to the Busch Gardens office complex.

Busch Gardens Williamsburg

SeaWorld Parks & Entertainment is a leading theme park and entertainment company delivering personal, interactive and educational experiences that blend imagination with nature. Over its more than 50 year history, the Company has built a diversified portfolio of 11 destination and regional theme parks that are grouped in key markets across the United States. (See Exhibit C4.3.) The parks hosted more than 24 million guests in 2012. One of the company's major bases of operation is Williamsburg, Virginia, where its Busch Gardens and Water Country USA parks are top attractions for family vacationers.

Busch Gardens Williamsburg opened in 1975 and is a European-themed park with world-class roller coasters, natural beauty, and shared family fun. Voted the world's most beautiful theme park for 22 consecutive years, Busch Gardens (Exhibit C4.4) offers culinary delights from around the world, unique shopping, live stage shows, and exciting thrill rides.

The park also offers a variety of seasonal events throughout the year. These events include

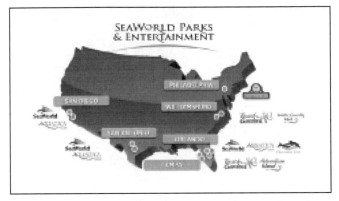

Exhibit C4.3. Sea World Parks & Entertainment Locations

Exhibit C4.4. Busch Gardens Williamsburg

- **Busch Gardens® Food & Wine Festival.** This all-new event features sample-sized portions of superb foods, wines and other refreshments not usually found at Busch Gardens. (See Exhibit C4.5.) Guests can stroll through France to enjoy coq au vin with rosemary roasted fingerling potatoes, linger in Spain for venera con jamón with saffron rice and romesco sauce, and then stop in Germany for pork schnitzel and fine-crafted brews. This festival is held on weekends from late May through June.

- **Glory at the Gardens.** A concert series that offers a sensational lineup of chart-topping contemporary Christian and Gospel artists. Glory at the Gardens combines the best Christian-inspired performances with the park's family-friendly atmosphere for a perfect mix of music and adventure. Concerts typically are held on select dates from May through September.

Exhibit C4.5. Busch Gardens Food & Wine Festival

- **Busch Gardens Live.** Top talent from pop, country and classic rock take the stage for the Busch Gardens Live concert series. Well-known bands and hot up-and-coming artists are featured throughout the spring and summer.
- **IllumiNights.** A summer nightly extravaganza featuring live performances, music and special effects culminating in a park-wide fireworks spectacular. IllumiNights is offered during the summer months of July through mid-August.
- **Howl-O-Scream®.** Dare to venture to the dark side of the gardens for the annual fear fest. Hair-raising scares, sinister shows and gruesome creatures that stalk around the park are the center of attraction in Busch Gardens' celebration of the macabre. Guests go mad with thrills and excitement in anticipation of the horror of Howl-O-Scream. The haunts begin mid-September and continue every Friday, Saturday and Sunday through the end of October.
- **Christmas Town™.** This one-of-a-kind event combines the magic and merriment of the season with stunning Broadway-style shows, unique gift ideas and millions of twinkling lights. Guests may sip on Busch Gardens' signature peppermint fudge hot chocolate while strolling through Christmas Town's Holiday Hills™ a nostalgic vision of mid-20th-century Christmas traditions complete with tin toys and miles of garland. Kids can share their holiday wishes at Santa's workshop and see the park's 50-foot tall, light-animated Christmas tree for a memorable Christmas Town experience. Christmas Town opens in late November and continues on select days through December 21. (Exhibit C4.6)

Exhibit C4.6. Busch Gardens' Christmas Town

- **Water Country USA** is Virginia's largest waterplay park, offering fun for the entire family with a retro surf theme and new resort-style amenities. It is owned by SeaWorld Parks & Entertainment, as is its fellow Williamsburg park, Busch Gardens. Situated on 121 acres, Water Country USA features more than 10 state-of-the-art water rides. (See Exhibit C4.7.)

Exhibit C4.7. Water Country USA Logo

As leading regional theme parks, Busch Gardens and Water Country USA appeal to both tourists, who stay overnight in the destination, and residents, who visit the parks as a day trip. The majority of these guests are families, but the parks also cater to groups and niche audiences, such as military and youth groups. Although visitors come from across the United States and many other countries, the largest concentration of guests come from the region stretching from New York through North Carolina, encompassing major cities including New York, Philadelphia, Baltimore, Washington D.C., Richmond, Norfolk and Raleigh-Durham.

The Amusement Park Industry

The Amusement Park industry includes theme parks, kiddie parks, amusement piers, centers, and parks, and other establishments (excluding fairs, circuses, and carnivals) that operate in part or whole such attractions as mechanical rides, amusement devices, refreshment stands, and picnic grounds (Pearce). There are more than 400 amusement parks and attractions in the United States (Travel & Tourism Handbook).

According to the International Association of Amusement Parks and Attractions, more than 300 million people visit U.S. amusement parks annually, with an economic impact of $57 billion. Exhibit C4.8 presents the top 20 amusement and theme parks based on park attendance in a recent year. According to these statistics, Disney World Resort in Orlando maintained its worldwide dominance with more than 48.5 million visits (TEA/AECOM).

The United States amusement park industry grew by 2.9% in terms of attendance in a recent year (Pearce). According to market analyst IBISWorld, over the five years previous years, industry revenue was expected to increase at an average annual rate of 1.8% to total $13.0 billion, with revenue forecast to grow 2.9% in the previous year alone (IBISWorld). Overall, growth in the amusement and theme park industry was substantial in the most recent year, with Disney California Adventure leading in attendance growth with an increase of 22.6% from the previous year (TEA/AECOM).

According to *The Great American Amusement Parks*, the earliest amusement parks were the European pleasure gardens of the seventeenth and eighteenth centuries. Technological advances, contributed by the United States during the Industrial Revolution, led to the mechanical rides found in today's modern amusement parks (Pearce). Jones's Wood in New York City, established in the early nineteenth century,

	EXHIBIT C4.8: Top 20 Amusement/Theme Parks in a recent year		
Rank	Amusement / Theme Park	Location	Park Attendance 2012
1.	MAGIC KINGDOM at Walt Disney World	Lake Buena Vista, FL	17,536,000
2.	DISNEYLAND	Anaheim, CA	15,963,000
3.	EPCOT at Walt Disney World	Lake Buena Vista, FL	11,063,000
4.	DISNEY'S ANIMAL KINGDOM at Walt Disney World	Lake Buena Vista, FL	9,998,000
5.	DISNEY'S HOLLYWOOD STUDIOS at Walt Disney World	Lake Buena Vista, FL	9,912,000
6.	UNIVERSAL'S ISLANDS OF ADVENTURE at Universal	Orlando, FL	7,981,000
7.	DISNEY'S CALIFORNIAN ADVENTURE	Anaheim, CA	7,775,000
8.	UNIVERSAL STUDIOS FLORIDA at Universal	Orlando, FL	6,195,000
9.	UNIVERSAL STUDIOS HOLLYWOOD	Universal City, CA	5,912,000
10.	SEAWORLD FLORIDA	Orlando, FL	5,358,000
11.	SEAWORLD CALIFORNIA	San Diego, CA	4,444,000
12.	BUSCH GARDENS TAMPA BAY	Tampa, FL	4,348,000
13.	CANADA'S WONDERLAND	Maple, ON, Canada	3,655,000
14	KNOTT'S BERRY FARM	Buena Park, CA	3,508,000
15.	CEDAR POINT	Sandusky, OH	3,221,000
16.	KINGS ISLAND	Kings Island, OH	3,206,000
17.	HERSHEY PARK	Hershey, PA	3,140,000
18.	BUSCH GARDENS EUROPE	Williamsburg, VA	2,854,000
19.	SIX FLAGS MAGIC MOUNTAIN	Valencia, CA	2,808,000
20.	SEAWORLD SAN ANTONIO	San Antonio, TX	2,678,000
Total Attendance			131,500,000

featuring billiards, bowling, and donkey rides, was likely the first major amusement park.

Years later, the legendary resort, Coney Island, began to expand by introducing mechanized rides in 1884 (Pearce). From their inception, roller coasters proved the most popular attractions, as well as the largest and most expensive to build. In 1893, the first Ferris wheel made its appearance at the 1893 Chicago World's Fair Columbian Exposition (Pearce).

Disney was the initial creator of wholesome family amusement with its innovative theme parks, which first opened in 1955. Busch Gardens Tampa Bay soon followed, opening in 1959, primarily as a brewery tour, but also featuring wonderful Bird

Gardens. Hundreds of exotic birds filled the Bird Gardens and the birds roamed free inside a large cage, where the guests were free to pet them (Busch Gardens). Six Flags Over Texas soon followed in 1961, and expanded thereafter (Pearce). Today, America's favorite theme parks include Walt Disney World, Universal Studios/Islands of Adventure, and Busch Gardens, Williamsburg, Virginia (NAPHA, 2008).

While amusement parks and theme parks are terms that are often used collectively and even interchangeably, there are a few important differences between them. Theme parks are primarily differentiated from amusement parks by their areas or "lands" that focus on telling a story.

The environments of theme parks include architecture, landscaping, stores, rides, and food to support specific themes (Geissler and Rucks). Research has revealed that food products are becoming an increasingly important part of the overall theme park experience, ranging from quick snacks and beverages to award-winning, full-service themed dining (Geissler and Rucks). Market survey findings reveal that although people of all ages enjoy going to U.S. amusement parks, the largest percentage of park visitors are ages 18-55 years old (Travel & Tourism Handbook).

Competition

Busch Gardens has several direct competitors, and many indirect ones. Let's briefly examine each primary competitor.

Primary Competitors

Kings Dominion in Doswell, Virginia. Kings Dominion is Virginia's other major theme park, located near Richmond. It offers a number of roller coasters and rides, along with children's play areas, shows and a water park included with the main park. Kings Dominion competes with Busch Gardens for resident day-trippers from the Richmond and Norfolk markets, as well as visitors from Washington, D.C. and Baltimore.

Hersheypark in Hershey, Pennsylvania. Hersheypark, located in the town famous for chocolate, goes head-to-head with Busch Gardens for overnight visitors from the major mid-Atlantic markets including New York, Philadelphia and Washington, D.C. Hersheypark features rides, entertainment, a water park and a zoo, plus on-site lodging and other vacation amenities.

Six Flags parks in Maryland and New Jersey. These parks provide closer-to-home theme park options for potential Busch Gardens' visitors who reside in those areas. The parks are heavy based on thrill rides but offer water attractions, kid's activities and seasonal events.

Ocean Breeze in Virginia Beach, Virginia, is a stand-alone water park that competes with Water Country USA for visits from residents of the Norfolk/Virginia Beach market, as well as attracting beach tourists.

Indirect or secondary competition includes any form of entertainment that could be selected instead of visiting Busch Gardens. For local residents, this includes movie theaters, concerts, theater, plays, sporting events, festivals, putt-putt golf, and many more. For out-of-town guests, this includes planning a vacation or day trip to a different location or planning a vacation to Williamsburg, Virginia, but not including a visit to Busch Gardens in their itinerary.

Customers

The target audience for Busch Gardens is families with children. Families who reside outside of the Williamsburg geographical region are considered potential destination tourist guests of the park. These families visit Busch Gardens while on vacations. Families who reside in the local regional area are considered potential pass members, who would hopefully return to the park for day trips or outings on a regular basis. Busch Gardens offers 1-Park and 2-Park Passes, along with a premier Platinum Pass. Pass member benefits include:

- Complimentary general parking and discounted preferred parking
- Discounted single-day admission for friends and family
- Discounted Christmas Town admission
- A 50% discount on single-day admission to SeaWorld Parks & Entertainment locations
- A 10% discount at select Busch Gardens and/or Water Country USA shops and restaurants
- Savings on stroller, wheelchair and motorized cart rentals and the Pet Kennel
- An EZpay option, which is a monthly payment plan.

In addition to all of the benefits listed above for pass members, Platinum Pass members enjoy unlimited visits for two years on regular operating days from the date of the pass purchase to:

- Busch Gardens (Williamsburg, Tampa)
- Water Country USA (Williamsburg)
- Sea World® (Orlando, San Diego, San Antonio)
- Adventure Island® (Tampa)
- Aquatica Sea World's Waterpark™ (Orlando, San Diego, San Antonio)
- Sesame Place® (Langhorne, PA)

Marketing and Advertising Activities of Busch Gardens

To reach potential visitors, the marketing team uses a comprehensive mix of paid media, direct marketing, public relations, promotions and interactive communications. The media mix and level of activity are adjusted according to the potential of each geographic market and consumer segment. Television and radio advertising are used in most major visitor-source markets. Digital media, including online display advertising, pre-roll video, rich media and paid search, are key parts of the mix, which are targeted according to geography or behavior.

Each year the marketing department produces hundreds of unique printed pieces, including advertisements, direct mail and collateral materials. As shown in Exhibit C4.9, print advertisements are designed for newspapers and magazines and most have a specific all to action—a ticket offer, promotional discount or limited-time event.

Exhibit C4.9. Print
Advertisement

Some advertisements are targeted to specific audiences, such as parents of young children or military families. Others, as shown in Exhibit C4.10, are designed to drive business through ticket- sales partners, which include travel agents, credit unions and hotels.

A significant part of Busch Gardens' direct-mail activity is aimed at its pass members, who purchase a pass good for unlimited admission for one or two years. To acquire new pass members, the park often uses self-mailers highlighting upcoming events and new attractions. To encourage existing members to renew their passes, the park communicates through a combination of e-mail, four-color postcards and a statement-type letter offering a discount for continued loyalty.

In addition, all members receive newsletters, postcards, and annual Fun Tracker calendars, featured in Exhibit C4.11, to encourage park visitation. Historically the theme park mailed out a small flyer to entice these guests to renew their park pass. However, since this group was already familiar with the park, Busch Gardens decided to illustrate the value of the membership pass more demonstratively by showcasing by month all the events, concerts and new offerings at Busch Gardens with an annual Fun Tracker calendar. The inside cover messaging of the calendar was, "We welcome you back," and stressed all the fun that could be had all spring and summer at Busch Gardens. Pass members consistently cite these printed pieces as a primary source for their knowing about events and new features at the parks.

Direct mail also is effectively used by the park's marketers to reach likely tourists. These mailers are targeted both geographically and demographically and typically include a strong call to action for a vacation package or multi-day ticket for both Busch

Exhibit C4.10. Examples of Advertisements Targeting
Ticket-Sales Partners

Exhibit C4.11. Fun Tracker Calendar

Gardens and Water Country USA. A recent direct mailing included a free, ready-to-use ticket to both parks as a powerful incentive to plan a getaway.

Printed collateral ranges from small information cards to large posters. Almost all pieces include a direct call to action, inviting prospects to visit the Busch Gardens' website. Exhibit C4.12 shows a website landing page targeting vacation planners, who were likely enticed by direct response ads or direct mailers.

Many print advertisements are customized for sales outlets, geographic markets or customer segments. The pieces provide an important layer in extending the park's messages where potential visitors work, play and seek vacation ideas.

In marketing to tourists, Busch Gardens relies heavily on mass media and promotions. Mailing lists consist of past customers and prospects from rented lists. The park also reaches prospective tourists through mass media (television, radio, online, newspaper), promotions, local sponsorships and in-market events. A number of tourists travel from Canada to visit the park, therefore, Busch Gardens sometimes creates advertisements translated into French language to appeal to those French-speaking Canadians.

Busch Gardens sometimes honors various groups or professions, such as Enlisted Member of the U.S. Military, Emergency Service Employees, and Healthcare Professionals. As shown in Exhibit C4.13, these groups may receive special admission opportunities on specified days during the season.

Exhibit C4.12. Targeted Vacations Website Landing Page

Exhibit C4.13. Busch Gardens Targeted Offers Honoring Select Groups

Marketing Challenges of Busch Gardens

Dan Dipiazzo leads a team of professionals responsible for all aspects of marketing and sales to support Busch Gardens and Water Country USA. His team coordinates advertising, consumer promotions, digital marketing, pass membership, direct marketing, sales, special events, public relations and community outreach. Busch Gardens' success relies on appealing to both local residents—many of whom visit the park multiple times with an annual pass—and tourists, primarily from the Northeast and Mid-Atlantic regions.

Now that everyone is settled in the conference room with mugs of coffee and pastries in front of them, Dan is ready to get down to business. For the coming year, Dan knows that he needs to include more direct and interactive marketing strategies in his marketing mix in order to effectively tackle the upcoming marketing challenges of Busch Gardens.

Dan begins the Marketing Planning Retreat. "Good morning, again, and I'm glad you are all here," says Dan in a truly collegial and welcoming tone. Dan continues, "I look forward to spending the next six hours with you planning our marketing activities for next year. Let me begin our retreat with an update on our new logo and brand essence."

Dan explains, "As you all know, we've recently conducted extensive research on our brand and worked with our advertising agency to help us to create our new brand image. In addition, we commissioned Mom Central Consulting to conduct a survey to better understand the needs and desires of mothers, the primary decision maker for vacations and family activity planning. Our new logo and brand essence were created on the basis of the research study findings. So, before I show you our new logo, let me overview the key findings of this important research study.

Based on the feedback of nearly 900 moms who participated in the survey, the research revealed:

- 85 percent of moms worry that their children don't experience enough natural, unstructured outdoor playtime;
- kids today spend only two hours during the week participating in natural, unstructured activities such as playing tag, riding bikes and exploring nature, and these activity levels increase only slightly on the weekends;
- both moms and kids see technology as a deterrent to kids playing outside, with 68 percent of moms claiming that their kids spend too much time plugged in;
- 44 percent of kids prefer texting to kickball;
- more than 67 percent of moms feel that family fun often takes a backseat to day-to-day obligations;
- 70 percent of moms rely on vacations as a time for kids to unplug and get away from technology;
- 95 percent of moms wish they could have more fun together as a family;
- 93 percent of kids wish they could have more fun together as a family;
- 93 percent of moms aspire to do more natural, unstructured outdoor activities as a family;
- 58 percent of moms rely on vacation as a way to get kids outside; and

- 69 percent of families say what they love most about a theme park experience is family time togetherness (Busch Gardens, 2013b).

Therefore, planning a family get-away enables families to set aside pressures and obligations and re-connect as a family (Busch Gardens, 2013b). These research findings offer critical information that we need to address in both our new brand image and our strategic marketing directions. Moreover, these research findings underscore the important message that our marketing communications must deliver," Dan asserts.

Exhibit C4.14. Old Logo

"And now it's my pleasure to unveil our new brand look and slogan," as Dan clicks the mouse and the slide projects the old logo (Exhibit C4.14) and then with another click, the new logo and tagline appear as featured in Exhibit C4.15.

"Notice how our new logo features a legible, but somewhat unstructured and free-flowing script in natural shades of green," asserts Dan. "And we have added a new icon—our 'coaster tree,' a symbol that evokes both a roller coaster track and a tree, just like Busch Gardens represents the perfect intersection of thrills and nature." (See Exhibit C4.16.)

Exhibit C4.15. New Logo and Tagline

"Part of our marketing challenge for next year is to effectively integrate our new brand identity to convey the natural fun we offer at Busch Gardens," Dan proclaims with delight. "Beyond the convergence of our new brand image with all of our mass marketing efforts, we need to address four specific marketing challenges," Dan announces.

"As you all know, most of our mass media efforts support our broader brand mes-

Exhibit C4.16. Exotic Birds at Busch Gardens

sage to our main audience, but these four marketing challenges will be an opportunity to use direct and interactive marketing in innovative ways to identify and appeal to specific niches of customers with targeted offers. Are you ready? Here goes: The four unique marketing opportunities that we are challenged to specifically address for next year are: (1) marketing our Preschool Pass to parents and grandparents of preschool children; (2) promoting our Christmas Town™ event to acquire holiday visitors; (3) generating greater awareness and new customers for our new Food & Wine Festival; and finally, (4) identifying and connecting with more groups, versus final consumers, in order to encourage them to plan their group functions at Busch Gardens," Dan concludes.

"Does anyone have any questions before I begin with a more detailed presentation of each marketing opportunity?" Dan asks his marketing associates. "OK, since there are no questions, let me begin." As Dan clicks to the next slide, an image of one of the KIDsiderate rides designed for preschool children appears on the slide (see Exhibit C4.17) and Dan's planning meeting is off and running. Over the next hour or so, Dan presents detailed information about each of the features of Busch Gardens that are the focus of this year's market planning.

**Exhibit C4.17.
KIDsiderate Ride**

Preschool Pass—Families with young children are an important guest segment for Busch Gardens and Water Country USA. While the parks are well-known for big thrills like roller coasters and water slides, they also have a wide variety of activities and attractions for smaller children. The parks feature these elements and special services under their KIDsiderate initiative. Busch Gardens has two distinct children's play areas—Sesame Street® Forest of Fun™ and Land of the Dragons®—plus smaller rides, animal encounters and shows throughout the park. Busch Gardens wants to make sure families with youngsters experience these attractions, so it offers a Preschool Pass, good for free unlimited admission to both Busch Gardens and Water Country USA for children age 5 and younger. (Exhibit C4.18.)

"We need to expand the marketing efforts of our Preschool Pass offer by promoting it to more families with young children and to grandparents," states Dan.

Christmas Town—In 2009 Busch Gardens launched its new holiday event, Christmas Town: A Busch Gardens Celebration, at a time when the park traditionally was closed. The park now opens on an annual basis for this special holiday event in late-November through the end of December. Christmas Town features special holiday shows, dining, shopping, Santa's Workshop and other attractions set amid more than 6 million lights. (See Exhibit C4.19.)

Dan vividly recalls one of the earlier social media promotions the marketing team used to promote Christmas Town. In anticipation of the second year of Christmas Town, the theme park's marketing team leaned on its Twitter account to generate some buzz. At the time of the promotion, Busch Gardens had been positioning its Twitter account (@BuschGardensVA) as the best place online for park guests to find

Exhibit C4.18. Busch Gardens KIDsiderate
Advertisement

Exhibit C4.19. Busch Gardens Christmas Town Mailer

exclusive offers, last-minute deals, giveaways and promotional information. So in October, 2010 the marketing department decided to sell Christmas Town tickets through Twitter for $5—only a fraction of the normal $21.99 price of admission. With one tweet, the offer was live:

> *"Hurry! Limited Time Offer. Buy a Christmas Town ticket for $5. Normally $21.99 Promo Code: BGVACT http:// ow.ly/2Ws90"*

There was not any public relations or other promotional support behind the offer. Still, news of the deal spread quickly from the 4,400 followers and was accelerated by a posting on a local newspaper's blog dedicated to savvy shopping. Soon after, other news organizations picked up on the promotion, including another local newspaper and television station. In six hours, more than 18,000 tickets were sold! Additionally, the theme park had proof there was strong demand for the event, the promotion generated significant publicity, and the Twitter account's profile had been boosted.

The park also has successfully used Living Social and its own email base to promote limited- time, limited-quantity deals for Christmas Town. Dan challenges the team to consider how such direct and interactive channels can be used to distribute offers to reach new visitors without eroding margins from repeat guests.

In addition to appealing to local families seeking holiday entertainment, Busch Gardens works with other organizations in the Williamsburg area to expand the destination's tourist base and raise awareness in nearby markets. Part of this effort includes elevating Williamsburg as a Christmas getaway destination, with Christmas Town as an anchor along with seasonal events at Colonial Williamsburg, shopping at Premium Outlets and other holiday activities. Dan concludes, "We need to proactively market Christmas Town as the center of a memorable holiday destination."

Busch Gardens Food & Wine Festival—The Food & Wine Festival is a natural outgrowth of the park's European theme, and reputation for authentic food and beverages. The event is included with regular park admission, although guests pay as they go for food and drinks. (See Exhibit C4.20.)

The Festival features more than a dozen culinary kiosks serving authentic food tastings paired with unique alcoholic beverages not normally found at Busch Gardens. The event includes live music, interactive shows, chef demonstrations and wine tasting, all set against the naturally beautiful environment of Busch Gardens. Food booths offer smaller-size portions of food and beverages to enable guests to enjoy several different tastes. A special cashless wristband is available so guests can link to their credit cards and conveniently pay for their purchases as they visit all of the culinary locations.

"In marketing this new attraction, we need to reach activity planners as they are thinking about early summer activities or weekend getaways, probably within 2 to 4 weeks before the event begins. Our goal is to encourage food and wine enthusiasts, who may not be our typical guests to visit Busch Gardens in June to experience the Food and Wine Festival," Dan explains.

Exhibit C4.20. Food & Wine Festival Promotional Materials

Group Sales—The success of Busch Gardens relies on the visitation of both local residents and tourists. In addition to individuals, groups are an important part of the guest mix. Past groups that have visited Busch Gardens include corporate employee outings, school field trips, family reunions, church groups, music festivals, cheer-and-dance competitions, and youth groups. (See Exhibit C4.21). Some of these groups visit the park annually and others will alternate years with other destinations.

Discounted admission pricing is available to groups of 15 or more people, with additional price breaks for larger groups. The marketing priority is to attract groups that include both admission tickets and meals, either in the form of a catered picnic

Exhibit C4.21. Youth Group at Busch Gardens

Exhibit C4.22. Group Event Announcement

at the park or meal certificates, which allow group members to dine at their convenience at restaurants throughout the park.

Pricing is most flexible during times of lower demand, typically the spring and some fall dates. Special rates also are extended as an "early bird" offer to groups who schedule their group outings early with substantial lead time. Exhibit C4.22 shows an announcement for a spring group event being held for the students at The College of William and Mary.

In marketing to groups, Busch Gardens relies heavily on mailers, in addition to contact from sales managers and visits to the group Web site. (See Exhibit C4.23.) Mailing lists consist of past customers and prospects from

Exhibit C4.23. Busch Gardens Group Package Advertisements

rented lists. "Identifying new groups will be one of our top marketing priorities for next year," Dan challenges the planning team.

"Whew!" Dan utters as he concludes his presentation of the four marketing opportunities.

Dan has been presenting for nearly an hour now. "So, what do you think? Are you as excited as I am to begin our market planning?" Dan asks the group. As he concludes his overview, he challenges his marketing team: "Unlike decades ago, today's marketing world is replete with figures and statistics that can be gathered and analyzed on a regular basis — and that has only increased in recent years given the rise of digital and social media marketing activities. My request to each of you is this: Please keep in mind that we need to gather the pertinent data to support each of the recommendations that we make in our market planning."

Dan continues, "We also know that our consumers are now savvier than ever. They take in multiple sources of information and seek deals through a variety of channels. They are looking for relevant information presented in an individualized manner. In short, they want to feel like we understand their needs and have a solution that's just right for them and for their families. Also, bear in mind that our new brand campaign was created in response to the recent survey research which revealed that a majority of mothers believe that 'Natural Fun Deficiency' has become a significant challenge, and that an increasing gap exists between how parents spent their childhood and what kids today do with their free time," (Hartman, 2013). Dan adds, "Our theme park offers a natural solution for families to get outside and enjoy time together. So, let's be sure we incorporate our new brand image into each and every marketing strategy we propose for next year."

Dan concludes, "I noticed that most of you have been taking detailed notes. So, let's take a 15- minute refreshment break and then come back to the conference room ready to tackle these marketing challenges, shall we?"

Case Challenges

"Our market planning challenge is to agree on the strategic directions we should take. This includes determining the offer, media, list and creative strategies to be included in next year's overall marketing initiatives. In our previous marketing efforts to tourists, we have relied heavily on mass media advertising. However, next year, I believe we should use more targeted direct and interactive marketing campaigns." Dan states. He continues, "Let's focus on the following key issues and see if we can agree on the strategic decisions for each."

Decision 1: Marketing the Preschool Pass to parents and grandparents of preschool children. Dan realizes that this will require greater targeting and selectivity in reaching these prospective guests. He thinks direct mail and email may be the most productive media options to be explored, but he is open to the suggestions of the marketing team. He would likely need to rent lists to identify and reach these prospective guests. He also wonders if there are any niche publications that may effectively reach this select audience, and hopes his team explores that media option as well. The offer is the Preschool Pass, with its free park admission for children ages 5 and younger, however, how might this offer be effectively positioned to prospective park guests? Are there any other promotional offers that could be combined with the Preschool Pass to make it even more enticing to the target market customers?

Decision 2: Promoting Christmas Town to acquire holiday visitors. Marketing Christmas Town will enable Dan the unique opportunity to work with business partners in the area to jointly promote the greater Williamsburg area as a Christmas getaway destination. Christmas Town would be featured as an anchor along with seasonal events at Colonial Williamsburg, shopping at Premium Outlets and other holiday activities. Dan believes this exciting marketing opportunity offers great promise for Busch Gardens to promote Christmas Town to out-of-town guests. Thus far, most of Busch Garden's marketing efforts for this event have been concentrated on local area residents. What customers and/or customer groups should be targeted? What media mix should be used to promote this unique holiday getaway? What offers will be most attractive to prospective visitors? How will the partner marketing efforts take shape? Dan has so many questions for his marketing team to address.

Decision 3: Generating greater awareness and new customers for the new Food & Wine Festival. The new Busch Gardens Food & Wine Festival kicks off the important summer season for the park. Since this is a new event for the park, the marketing activities will be critical in generating both awareness and visitors. In addition to marketing the event to existing guests of the park, this event may lend itself to be effectively marketed to older and more sophisticated customers and groups. Anyone who enjoys food and wine tasting experiences, even if they don't enjoy thrilling roller coaster rides, are prospective customers for this event. Dan realizes that similar to marketing the Preschool pass, he would likely need to rent lists to identify and reach prospective guests for the Food and Wine Festival. He also believes that there may be some appropriate publications that may effectively reach this select audience. Once again, he and his team needs to determine the most effective offer, media and creative strategies that should be used to market this unique event.

Decision 4: Prospecting for new group sales customers. Dan is interested in identifying and testing some potential business consumer lists that he might rent in his attempt to generate business leads and secure group sales for marketing Busch Garden's group packages. He is interested in testing several lists for possible use in rolling-out his lead generation program to market group packages. Dan would like to identify and explore at least five potential lists to determine which are most productive. Based on the response rate results of the list test, Dan plans to rollout 20,000 direct mail packages to the groups on the most productive lists.

The challenge to the marketing team is to determine which of the lists contain prospects that have the greatest potential in becoming group customers at Busch Gardens? Which five (5) lists should be recommended to Dan for inclusion in his list rental test?

Exhibit C4.24. Busch Gardens Roller Coaster Skyline

Conclusion

It's now late in the afternoon and the market planning retreat is coming to a close. Dan summarizes the four unique marketing opportunities that the planning team addressed for next year, including: (1) marketing the Preschool Pass to parents and grandparents of preschool children; (2) promoting Christmas Town™ to acquire holiday visitors; (3) generating greater awareness and new customers for the new Food & Wine Festival; and (4) connecting with more groups to encourage them to hold their group functions at Busch Gardens. As usual, his marketing team didn't let him down.

Their recommendations were both rich with creativity and based on solid critical analysis. Most importantly, all of their recommendations strategically utilized direct and interactive marketing methods to effectively capitalize on each unique marketing opportunity.

"Well team, it's time to bring our market planning retreat to a close," says Dan. "Today has been a great day and we have accomplished a lot. Let's spend the rest of the week putting together the action plans for each of the strategic decisions we have agreed upon for our marketing campaigns for next year. I applaud your efforts, and now, I'll reward them. Would anyone like to join me in the park? Let's go enjoy a few more roller coaster rides, and then I'll treat you all to dinner at your favorite restaurant in the park." "Now you're talking," replies Cindy in an excited voice. "Let's go!" she shouts to her fellow team members as the team takes off for the park with its gleaming roller coasters jetting to the fluorescent sky. (See Exhibit C4.24.)

Case Questions

1. Given its Pass Member program, Busch Gardens has a sizeable customer database that may be analyzed and used to communicate on a regular basis with its pass members and to promote its many special events and offers. How might you recommend utilizing the Busch Gardens' customer database to address the four specific challenges presented in this case?

2. Each of the challenges presented to the marketing team in this case is focused on attracting new guests to the park. However, there is another critically important marketing challenge to be addressed—increasing guest spending levels when they visit the park. What promotional recommendations would you make to increase this important revenue stream for Busch Gardens?

3. How might Dan and his marketing team utilize digital and social media in addressing each of the case marketing challenges? Dan has made a mental note about the success they had using Twitter to promote Christmas Town a few years ago, so he's interested in exploring more digital and social media methods for possible inclusion in next year's marketing campaigns. How would you advise him?

4. Part of Dan and his team's marketing challenge for next year is to effectively integrate the park's new brand identity to convey the *natural fun* offered at Busch Gardens. Given the market research findings presented in the case, there seems to be great market opportunity for Busch Gardens to present itself as a solution to the problem. How might Busch Gardens capitalize on the expressed desires of both moms and kids? What specific marketing strategies and activities would you recommend to Dan if you were a member of his marketing team?

References

Busch Gardens, (2013a) The History Of Busch Gardens Tampa, http://bgwfans.com/2009/the-history-of-busch-gardens-tampa/ (Retrieved June 7, 2013).

Busch Gardens, (2013b). "Natural Fun Takes a Backseat to Tech Time for Kids & Families: Busch Gardens(R) Survey Reveals Outdoor Fun Decline. New York: PR Newswire Association LLC, May 7, 2013

Geissler, Gary L. and Rucks, Conway T., (2011). "The critical influence of customer food perceptions on overall theme park evaluations." *Journal of Management and Marketing Research*, Vol. 8 (September), pp. 1-15.

International Association of Amusement Parks and Attractions (IAAPA), 2012. Amusement Park and Attractions Industry Statistics. http://www.iaapa.org/resources/by- park-type/amusement-parks-and-attractions/industry-statisticswww.iaapa.org (Retrieved June 4, 2013).

IBISWorld, (2013) Amusement Parks in the US: Market Research Report, January, http://www.ibisworld.com/industry/default.aspx?indid=1646 (Retrieved June 4, 2013).

National Amusement Park Historical Association (NAPHA), (2008). *NAPHA'S 2008 survey results*. Mt. Prospect, IL: NAPHA.

Pearce, Lynn M. (ed.), (2013). "Amusement Parks." *Encyclopedia of American Industries.* Detroit: Gale. *Business Insights: Essentials.* Web. (Retrieved June 4, 2013.)

Staff, (2013). "Amusement and Theme Parks." *Business Insights: Essentials.* http://0-bi.galegroup.com.read.cnu.edu/essentials/industry/713110?u=viva_cnu, (Retrieved June 4, 2013).

The Travel & Tourism Market Research Handbook, (2013), Theme Parks/Market Assessment, 84.1, Richard K. Miller & Associates, pp. 504–509.

Themed Entertainment Association and the Economics Practice at AECOM, TEA/AECOM (2013). "Themed Index: Global Attractions Attendance Report." Rubin, Judith (ed.)

Some of the data provided for this case has been disguised and is not useful for research purposes. The author would like to thank Mr. Dan Dipiazzo for his assistance with this case.

CASE
5

Domino's Pizza:
Growing Sales With Technology

MATTHEW H. SAUBER

Eastern Michigan University

DAVID W. MAROLD

Eastern Michigan University

ALICIA ANDERSON

Eastern Michigan University

S ince 2007, Domino's customers have been able to visit its web site and browse the menu to build their own pizza and add sides such as Buffalo Chicken Wings or Chocolate Lava Crunch Cakes. Customers can watch the simulated image of the pizza they are ordering. The image changes as they select a different pie size, choose a sauce and add pepperoni, black olives and other toppings. They can also watch the price when the order changes and ingredients get added or removed and when they apply a coupon.

Domino's web site also allows customers to track orders with updates. Once the order is placed, a "pizza tracker" communicates with customers in real time and through a bar graph when their order is being processed, baked, checked and sent out for delivery. Over twenty-five percent of all Domino's orders are placed online through the company web site, which is great for impulse purchases according to Dennis Maloney, Domino's VP of Multi-Media Marketing. The CEO, Patrick Doyle, explains that when customers order pizza online " . . . it enhances the ticket, as we can remind them [via pop-up windows] that we sell drinks, chicken wings and chocolate cake too," (Change at Domino's, 2010; Domino's Pizza Investor Presentation, 2010).

Domino's online presence extends well beyond its own web site. The company understands the critical importance of reaching out to its target market using social media. To stay in touch with its customers, Domino's uses major social media such as Facebook, MySpace, Twitter, and YouTube. Through its corporate account, for example, Domino's monitors Twitter feeds around the clock to hear from followers about its brand, products, and services. The company methodically uses social media to review, respond, and react to what fans and followers post. A company representative, for example, responds with instructions on how to ask for a refund if a customer is dissatisfied with the product. Domino's also uses Facebook to make special offers, news, and reminders to place an order. "Digital media affords you the opportunity to go much more in-depth and be much more transparent with your message," says Russell Weiner, Chief Marketing Officer. "We want people to know that we have nothing to hide and that we have a better pizza." (Change at Domino's, 2010).

Company Background

In 2010 Domino's Pizza celebrated its golden anniversary by opening its 9000th store globally. The company has come a long way since its humble beginning. In 1960, brothers Tom and Jim Monaghan borrowed $500 to purchase DomiNicks, a local pizzeria in Ypsilanti, Michigan (Boyer (2007). Eight months later, Jim Monaghan traded his share of the restaurant for a Volkswagen Beetle. In 1965, Tom renamed the business "Domino's Pizza, Inc." (Our Heritage, 2008).

The restaurant had minimum seating, making delivery essential for success. Initially, Tom Monaghan hired laid off factory workers as drivers, compensating them based on commission. With an efficiency focus, the menu was reduced from subs and small pizzas to only offering "regular pizza". The business concept took off, leading to expansion through franchising and the first franchise store opened in 1967 (Domino's Pizza, Inc., 2008).

Expansion

The company continued with its expansion, overcoming challenges including a fire destroying company headquarters in 1968 and a legal battle headed by Domino's Sugar over trademark infringement (Amstar Corporation, 1980). Originally, Monaghan added dots to the logo for each new franchise opened. With the aggressive expansion rate the idea became impractical. There were 200 franchises in operation by 1978. Domino's opened its 1,000 stores five years later. In 1983, Domino's opened its first international store in Winnipeg, Canada (Exhibit C5.1). This paved the way for a global expansion of 1,000 pizzerias overseas—in Europe, Australia, South America, Africa, and Asia—by 1995. In 1997, Domino's opened its 1,500th overseas location (Domino's Pizza Investor Presentation, 2010).

After 38 years of ownership, Tom Monaghan announced his retirement and sold Domino's Pizza to Bain Capital, Inc. in 1998 (Domino's Founder to Retire . . . , 1998). A year later, the company named David A. Brandon Chairman and Chief Executive Officer (Domino's Pizza, Inc., 2008). The company went public in 2004.

Domino's marked the opening of its 8,000th and 9,000th franchise stores in 2006 and 2010 respectively (Domino's Open 9,000th Store, 2010). The company has franchised stores in all 50 U.S. states and 62 foreign countries (Domino's Pizza Investor Presentation, 2010).

As of January 3, 2010, the company reported 8,999 stores in operation worldwide, of which 4,072 were international and 4,927 were domestic stores. Of the domestic stores 466 were company owned and 4,461 were franchise stores (Exhibit C5.2).

Domino's same store sales grew 1.4% domestically and 3.9% internationally in the 2009 4th quarter. The growth rate was smaller (.5%) for domestic stores and more robust (4.3%) for international stores for 2009 as a whole (Exhibit C5.3).

EXHIBIT C5.1: DOMINO'S MILESTONES

1960	Tom Monaghan and his brother, James, purchased "DomiNick's," a pizza store in Ypsilanti, Mich. Monaghan borrowed $500 to buy the store.
1965	Tom Monaghan, renamed the business "Domino's Pizza, Inc."
1967	The first Domino's Pizza franchise store opened in Ypsilanti, Michigan
1968	First Domino's store outside of Michigan opened in Burlington, Vermont
1978	The 200th Domino's store opened.
1983	Domino's first international store opened in Winnipeg, Canada. The 1,000th Domino's store opened. The first Domino's store opened on the Australian continent, in Queensland, Australia.
1985	The first Domino's store opened in the United Kingdom, in Luten, England. The first Domino's store opened on the continent of Asia, in Minato, Japan.
1988	The first Domino's store opened on the South American continent, in Bogota, Columbia.
1989	Domino's opened its 5,000th store.
1990	Domino's Pizza signed its 1,000th franchise agreement.
1995	Domino's Pizza International opened its 1,000th store. First store opens on African continent, in Cairo, Egypt.
1996	Domino's launched its first web site (www.dominos.com).
1997	Domino's Pizza opened its 1,500th store outside the United States
1998	Domino's launched HeatWave®, a hot bag using patented technology that keeps pizza oven-hot to the customer's door. Domino's Pizza opened its 6,000th store in San Francisco, California. Tom Monaghan announced retirement and sold 93% of the company to Bain Capital, Inc.
1999	David A. Brandon was named Chairman and Chief Executive Officer of Domino's Pizza.
2000	Domino's Pizza International opened its 2,000th store outside the United States.
2003	Domino's became the "Official Pizza of NASCAR." Domino's was named Chain of the Year by Pizza Today. Domino's introduced it Pulse Point of Sale, a touch screen ordering, system.
2005	Domino's Pizza Australia opened its 400th store in Aspley, Brisbane. Domino's Pizza United Kingdom opened its 400th store in Wadsley Bridge, Sheffield.
2006	Domino's opened its 8,000th store by simultaneous opening the 5,000th U.S. store in Huntley, Illinois and the 3,000th international store in Panama City, Panama.
2007	Domino's rolled out online and mobile ordering in the United States.
2009	Domino's ranked No. 1 in customer satisfaction per the annual American Customer Satisfaction Index (ACSI). Domino's introduced Pizza Tracker.
2010	Domino's changed its pizza recipe "from the crust up". J. Patrick Doyle became Domino's Chief Executive Officer Domino's opened its 9000th store in New Delhi India Domino's ranked No. 1 in Keys Brand taste test

EXHIBIT C5.2: DOMINO'S PIZZA STORES WORDWIDE
AS OF JANUARY OF THE CURRENT YEAR

	Domestic Company-Owned Stores	Domestic Franchise Stores	Total Domestic Stores	International Stores	Total
Store counts:					
Store count at September 6,					
Previous Year	481	4,456	4,937	3,949	8,886
Openings	–	49	49	140	189
Closings	(14)	(45)	(59)	(17)	(76)
Transfers	(1)	1	–	–	–
Store count at January 3,					
Current Year	466	4,461	4,927	4,072	8,999
Fourth quarter					
Previous Year net growth	(15)	5	(10)	123	113
Net Growth Previous					
Fiscal Year	(23)	(97)	(120)	346	226

Source: Domino's Pizza, Inc., www.dominos.com

Although Domino's does not provide quarterly or annual sales forecasts, the management believes that the following year-over-year growth rates are achievable over the long term:

Domestic same-store sales:	1%–3%
International same-store sales:	3%–5%
Net units store growth	200–300
Global retail sales growth	4%–6%

International Growth

Domino's received 40 percent of sales from the company's international division in 2009. The proportion was expected to grow and surpass the domestic sales in the next three to five years according to the company (Domino's Pizza Investor Presentation, 2010). The company reports many years of same-store sales growth in its international operations. The key growth areas are the top ten markets (Exhibit C5.4) where Domino's has used master franchises—well-financed local businesses with the rights to own, operate many stores and franchise branches as chains. Domino's Pizza Enterprises, for example, owns and operates stores in Australia, New Zealand, France, Belgium, and the Netherlands. The master franchises for the UK and Ireland are publicly traded as Domino's Pizza UK & IRL (Litterick , 2010).

EXHIBIT C5.3: DOMINO'S DOMESTIC AND GLOBAL SALES (PREVIOUS FISCAL YEAR)

	Fourth Quarter	Fiscal Year
Same store sales growth: (versus prior year period)		
Domestic Company-owned stores	+0.9%	(0.9)%
Domestic franchise stores	+1.5%	+0.6%
Domestic stores	+1.4%	+0.5%
International stores	+3.9%	+4.3%
Global retail sales growth: (versus prior year period)		
Domestic stores	+7.4%	+1.3%
International stores +28.1% +3.3%		
Total	+16.4%	+2.2%
Total (on a 52-week basis)	+7.8%	(0.3)%
Global retail sales growth: (versus prior year period, excluding foreign currency impact)		
Domestic stores	+7.4%	+1.3%
International stores	+21.6%	+14.4%
Total	+13.5%	+7.1%
Total (on a 52-week basis)	+4.9%	+4.6%

Source: Domino's Pizza, Inc., www.dominos.com

EXHIBIT C5.4: DOMINO'S TOP 10 INTERNATIONAL MARKETS

- Mexico*
- United Kingdom*
- Australia*
- South Korea
- Canada
- India*
- Japan
- France
- Taiwan
- Turkey

*These indicate publicly traded companies in their home countries

Source: 2010 Chain of the Year, *Pizza Today,* June 2010, www.pizzatoday.com

EXHIBIT C5.5: U.S. MARKET SHARE

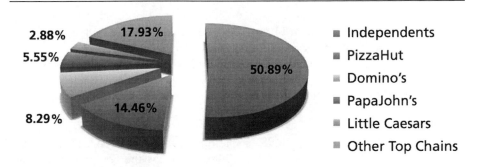

- 2.88%
- 5.55%
- 8.29%
- 14.46%
- 17.93%
- 50.89%

- ■ Independents
- ■ PizzaHut
- ▒ Domino's
- ■ PapaJohn's
- ▒ Little Caesars
- ▒ Other Top Chains

Source: Pizza Power: Report 2009, *PMQ Pizza Magazine*, September 2009.

Industry Overview

Categorically, Domino's Pizza belongs to the Quick-Service-Restaurant (QSR) industry. The QSR industry consists of restaurants with fast food service and limited menus of moderately priced and cooked to order items. The U.S. QSR pizza category is highly competitive, large, and fragmented. With sales of $33.5 billion in the twelve months ended November 2009, the U.S. QSR pizza category is the second largest category within the $230.1 billion U.S. QSR sector. The pizza category is primarily composed of delivery, dine-in, and carryout (Domino's Annual Report, 2010). Approximately *three billion* pizzas are sold in the U.S. each year (Bloomenfield and Associates, 2010). On average, each man, woman, and child in America eats 46 slices, (23 pounds), of pizza per year (Package Fact, 2010).

About 59 percent of pizza outlets in the United States are independently owned. They control 51 percent of the industry sales (Exhibit C5.5). A recent survey reports that 54% of consumers prefer independent stores to chains (2010 Chain of the Year, 2010). The Big Four—Pizza Hut (14.46%), Domino's (8.29%), Papa John's (5.55%), and Little Caesars (2.88%)—as a collective unit, have kept steady sales and market share during the recession.

Pizza Hut

Pizza Hut is a division of Yum! Brands, Inc., the world's largest restaurant company in terms of system restaurants with more than 37,000 restaurants in over 110 countries and territories and more than 1 million associates. Yum! is ranked No. 239 on the Fortune 500 List, with nearly $11 billion in revenue in 2009 (Yum! Brand Annual Report, 2009).

Pizza Hut, based in Dallas, Texas, is America's first national pizza chain, established in 1958. It is the world's largest pizza chain with more than 7,500 restaurants in the United States and over 5,600 restaurants in 97 countries and territories around the world. Pizza Hut became the first national chain to offer pizza delivery on the Internet in 1994. It offered online ordering in all its U.S. locations in 2007 and mobile ordering, through text messaging and web-enabled cell phones, in 2008. Specializing in Pan Pizza, Thin 'N Crispy® Pizza, Hand-Tossed Style Pizza and Stuffed Crust Pizza, Pizza Hut was celebrated as America's Favorite Pizza in 2007.

Faced with 9% decline in same-store sales in 2009, Pizza Hut responded by cutting its pizza prices and rolling out a "$10 any way you want it" promotion that resulted in a dramatic improvement in sales. The company's long term strategy is to transform the brand from "pizza' to "pizza, pasta and wings." They are focusing on improving the speed of their service and have added a new mobile application ahead of their major competitors (2009 Yum! . . . , 2009).

Papa John's

Since opening its first pizzerias in 1985, Papa John's has grown to be the third largest U.S. pizza chain. Headquartered in Louisville, Kentucky, the company had 3,469 restaurants in operations, as of December 2009, of which 614 were corporate owned and 2,167 were franchised restaurants operating in all 50 states and 688 restaurants in 29 countries (Papa John's Annual Report, 2009). Papa John's international development pipeline projects the opening of 1200 new restaurants in the next eight years. Their sales were down 2.3% in the 12 months ended March 31, 2010 (Standard & Poor's Stock Report, 2010).

Papa John's long-term business goal is to build the strongest brand loyalty of all pizza restaurants. The company's key strategies are based on a menu of high-quality pizza along with side items, efficient operating and distribution systems, team member training and development, national and local marketing, developing and maintaining a strong franchise system, and international operations (Papa John's Annual Report, 2009).

Papa John's "traditional" domestic restaurants are delivery and carryout operations that serve defined trade areas. As such, Papa John's is the closest competitor to Domino's.

Papa John's advertising slogan and brand promise is, "Better Ingredients. Better Pizza." Domestic Papa John's restaurants offer a menu of high-quality pizza along with side items, including breadsticks, cheese sticks, chicken strips and wings, dessert items and canned or bottled beverages. Papa John's traditional crust pizza is prepared using fresh dough (never frozen). Papa John's pizzas are made from a proprietary blend of wheat flour, cheese made from 100% real mozzarella, fresh-packed pizza sauce made from vine-ripened tomatoes (not from concentrate) and a proprietary mix of savory spices, and a choice of high-quality meat (100% beef, pork and chicken with no fillers) and vegetable toppings.

In 2001, Papa John's became the first national pizza company to offer online ordering and was the first pizza company to surpass $1 billion in online sales and now has recently surpassed $2 billion in sales (Domino's Annual Report, 2010). In addition to placing orders online at papajohns.com, customers can place order via text messaging and mobile web capabilities of cell phones.

Domino's

Based in Ann Arbor, Michigan, Domino's Pizza is the number one pizza delivery chain in the United States. The company pioneered the pizza delivery business and has built the brand into one of the most widely recognized consumer brands in the world. The Domino's Pizza® brand was named a Megabrand by Advertising Age magazine in 2009. Domino's was also ranked number one in customer satisfaction in a survey of consumers of the U.S. largest limited service restaurants, according to the annual American Customer Satisfaction Index (ACSI).

Domino's operated a network of over 9000 franchised and company-owned stores in all 50 states and 62 international markets. The company had global retail sales of over $5.6 billion in 2009, comprised of $3.1 billion domestic sales and over $2.5 billion international sales (Horovitz, 2010).

Domino's business model emphasizes on-time delivery of quality pizza. The model entails: (1) delivery-oriented store design with low capital requirements, (2) a concentrated menu of pizza and complementary side items, (3) a network of committed owner-operator franchisees and (4) a vertically integrated supply-chain system. Revenues are largely driven from sales through company-owned stores and at franchise levels, comprised of royalty payments and supply-chain revenues.

Domino's operates primarily within the U.S. pizza delivery market. Its $10.3 billion of sales accounted for approximately 31% of total U.S. QSR pizza delivery sales in the twelve months ended November 2009. Domino's and its top two competitors account for approximately 45% of the U.S. pizza delivery market—based on reported consumer spending—with the remaining 55% market share attributable to regional chains and individual establishments (Horovitz, 2010).

Domino's also competes in the carryout market, which together with pizza delivery comprise the largest components of the U.S. QSR pizza industry. The U.S. carryout pizza market had $13.8 billion of sales in the twelve months ended November 2009. Although Domino's primary focus is on pizza delivery, it is also favorably positioned to compete in the carryout segment given its strong brand identity, convenient store locations, and affordable menu offerings (Domino's Annual Report, 2010).

Domestically, Domino's competes against regional and local pizzerias as well as the national chains of Pizza Hut ® and Papa John's. These companies generally compete on the basis of product quality, location, image, service and price. They also compete on a broader scale with quick service and other international, national, regional and local restaurants. In addition, the overall food service industry and the QSR sector in particular are intensely competitive with respect to product quality, price, service, convenience and concept. The industry is often affected by changes in consumer tastes, economic conditions, demographic trends and consumer disposable income (Horovitz, 2010).

According to Dennis Maloney, Domino's Vice President of Multi-Media Marketing, "the recessionary economic climate has contributed to less delivery and more carryout and home cooked and frozen food, substituting for some QSR purchases." (Phone Interview with Dennis Maloney, 2011).

Competitive Analysis Summary

Pizza Hut is the number one pizza chain in the world. It competes in delivery, carryout and sit-down segments of QSR. The recession of 2009 took its toll on Pizza Hut as its sit-down restaurants were hit harder than other segments. Pizza Hut responded by cutting its pizza prices and rolling out a "$10 any way you want it" promotion. It is transitioning itself to be known for pizza, pasta and wings. It also sees itself as a leader in technology and was the first to introduce an application for iPhone.

Papa John's has grown to be the third largest U.S. pizza chain in the 25 years since it was established. It competes in the delivery and carryout segments and as such it is the closest competitor to Domino's. Papa John's advertising slogan and brand promise is: "Better Ingredients. Better Pizza." It is generally agreed that it lives up to its quality promise. In 2001, Papa John's also focused on technology and it became the first national pizza chain to offer online ordering and was the first pizza company to surpass $1 billion in online sales and recently surpassed $2 billion in sales. In addition to placing orders online at papajohns.com, customers can place their order via text messaging and mobile web devices.

Domino's is No. 1 in delivery and No. 2 in the overall pizza chain sales after Pizza Hut. Domino's is striving to be No.1 in technology and to improve the perception of the taste of its pizza and the value it provides to consumers. Domino's Pulse system is arguably the best system in the industry and a demonstration of its leadership in Point of Purchase Database Marketing. The launch of the new pizza recipe and a new menu with 80% changed items between 2008 and 2010 have contributed to sales increases and changing perceptions. Evidence of the industry recognition of the change at Domino's is that in June, 2010, Domino's was named "2010 Chain of the Year" by *Pizza Today*.

Customer Profile

Although pizza is a favorite meal for all Americans, young and old, and more than 95% of population eats pizza, there are variations in consumption based on age, household size, and income. Mintel surveys reports that 21% of people in the 18-24 age category purchase pizza more than three times a month, compared to only 7% of those aged over 65 (Pizza Power Report, 2009).

Among households with children, 20% purchase pizza more than 3 times a month, compared to 12% of those households with no children. Research also indicates that households with annual income of $100,000 and beyond are more likely to prefer pizza from independent, local pizzerias, while households with children are more likely to visit a pizza chain (Corporate Porfile, 2010).

Buying Behavior

U.S. consumer pizza-buying behavior was negatively impacted in 2009 because of the difficult economic environment. As such, consumers reduced their discretionary spending during 2009 in response to increased unemployment and adverse economic conditions. As a result, the QSR Pizza industry sales were approximately 1.0% lower in 2009 compared to 2008. Cost-conscious consumers are opting for less-expensive pizza choices at QSRs and the low-end of the market appears to be saturated. Thus, pizza chains aiming for higher growth are targeting consumers from high-income households (Corporate Profile, 2010)

Other buying trends indicate that consumers are shifting dining-out occasions toward breakfast and lunch and away from dinner in recent years. Consumers are also being attracted to alternative dinner meals from non-pizza QSR chains, including the ones focusing on fresh sandwiches. Many casual diners began using other restaurants that emphasize carryout and curbside meals.

Value consciousness is perhaps the biggest trend among QSR customers. Consumers look for value meals at nearly every QSR outlets, big chains, and small independents. A recent survey by the National Restaurant Association (NRA) reported that 75% of consumers would patronize full-service restaurants more often if they offered discounts for frequent dining or for dining on slow days of the week. The NRA survey also reported that 44% of consumers are more likely to make a restaurant choice based on the restaurant's energy and water conservation practices. Some QSR chains are showing leadership in green initiatives by conserving energy and reducing water use (Corporate Profile, 2010).

Focus on healthy food, for adults and children, is a trend that will stay here. Seventy-six percent of those who were surveyed by the NRA reported that they are trying to eat healthier meals in restaurants compared to two years ago. Forty-five percent said they would frequent quick-serve restaurants more often if the restaurant offered an expanded menu of healthy items for children. Large chains have answered the call by adding salads, flatbreads, whole-wheat crusts, salad-topped pizza, locally grown produce, and organic items to their menus in order to appeal to health conscious consumers (Corporate Profile, 2010).

In its report, "A look into the Future of Eating," the NPD Group has forecasted that healthy foods, especially the ones labeled "organic," will be among the fastest growing consumption trends in the next decade. On the other hand, Mintel's research reports that 84% of surveyed consumers consider pizza as indulgence and they do not care if it is healthy or not (Corporate Profile, 2010).

Domino's SWOT Analysis

Strengths

- *Cost-efficient store model* is characterized by a delivery and carry-out oriented store design, low capital requirements, and a focused menu of quality, affordable pizza, and other complementary items. At the store level, the simplicity and efficiency of operations provide advantages over competitors who, in many cases, also focus on dine-in.
- *Strong brand awareness.* The Domino's Pizza® brand is one of the most widely recognized consumer brands in the world. Consumers associate the brand with the timely delivery of affordable pizza and other complementary items.
- *Domino's PULSE™ point-of-sale system.* Domino's PULSE™, the proprietary point-of-sale system, is installed in every company-owned store in the United States and substantially in all of the domestic franchise stores. Features of Domino's PULSE™ point-of-sale system include:
  —Ability to implement centralized promotional activities throughout the marketing mix, including couponing and flyers as well as communicating back to the consumers in the manner they communicated;
  —Touch screen ordering, which improves accuracy and facilitates more efficient order taking;

—A delivery driver routing system, which improves delivery efficiency;

—Improved administrative and reporting capabilities, which enable store managers to better focus on store operations and customer satisfaction;

—Enhanced online ordering capability, including Pizza Tracker, which was introduced in 2007 and Pizza Builder, which was introduced in 2008;

- *Successful new pizza recipe* with subsequent successful taste tasting and higher sales results

Weaknesses

- Perception by many that Domino's pizza ranks near the bottom on taste;
- Because Domino's business model is heavily dependent upon deliveries, there are areas of the country that it is difficult for the company to expand to and serve;
- Extended menu that may reduce effectiveness of delivery and great service that Domino's is renowned for.

Opportunities

- Great prospects for international expansion in densely populated parts of the world;
- Opportunity to differentiate the brand in terms of health, nutrition, and environmental sustainability;
- Opportunity for growth domestically upon economic recovery in the United States;
- Opportunity for expansion by acquiring local and independent pizza stores

Threats

- Lingering economic doldrums hamper profitability and growth;
- Stronger competition from pizza chains, independents, and take-and-bake options as well as OSR categories other than pizza;
- Healthy eating trend and organic food consumption

Domino's Growth Strategy

Growth is Domino's top business mandate domestically and internationally. The company uses two primary strategies, menu and technology, to grow domestically.

Menu-based Growth Strategy

Domino's has expanded its menu significantly since 2008. To attract the lunch crowd, it added the Oven-Baked Sandwiches line in 2008 in direct competition with Subway. The company also rolled out several BreadBowl Pasta varieties in response to the pasta line from Pizza Hut.

Domino's also expanded its pizza line by launching the American Legends—a line of six specialty pizza varieties featuring 40 percent more cheese than its regular pizza, cheesy crust, and premium toppings—in 2009. The addition of the American Legends was to strike a balance in Domino's pizza offerings to premium oriented customers according to the CEO, Patrick Doyle.

In January 2010, Domino's launched a new pizza recipe to change its reputation from what was one of the bottom of the barrel. It even ran a "self-flogging" advertising campaign that showed that customers commented on Domino's Pizza crust tasting like cardboard and its sauce like ketchup. The new recipe has been credited for Domino's sales rebound in 2010 (Horovitz, 2010).

Starting from scratch, Domino's changed "part of core," beginning with crust up. In the new crust it added butter, garlic, and parsley. The new cheese was shredded instead of diced mozzarella, with a hint of provolone. And the new sauce was made sweeter, with a red pepper kick.

Domino's communicated the arrival of the new pizza to its customers on every box it delivered:

"DOMINO'S NEW PIZZA. 50 YEARS IN THE MAKING

Our hand-tossed pizza is new. It's not a slightly-altered version of the old pizza. It's not the same old product in a fancy wrapper. It's completely new pizza from the crust up. And we're pretty doggone proud of it. Because while it doesn't take long for you to get one, it's taken us 50 years to create a pizza of this perfectitude. Fifty years worth of listening to feedback, tasting cheeses, crafting sauces and trying every possible combination of combinations we could think of. So what's new about it? For starters, everything: our cheese made with 100% real mozzarella and flavored with just a hint of provolone. Our sauce with a dose of spicy red pepper to put a spring in your step. And our garlic-seasoned crust with a rich, buttery taste. Now you may be wondering, is it really different? Will it be as good as they say? Is 'perfectitude' actually a word? Well, there's only one way to find out. Take a bite. Then if someone asks if we actually abandoned our old recipe and completely revamped our pizza, you can tell 'em . . . Oh yes we did."

In a national taste test, sponsored by Domino's and appearing on their web site, three out of five people preferred the taste of Domino's pepperoni pizza, sausage pizza, and extra cheese pizza over Papa John's and Pizza Hut's. Domino's used social media to announce the new arrival by means of its "Pizza Turnaround" documentary on YouTube, showing how they listened to customers who complained about the "old" recipe and how they developed the "new" recipe.

The company's 2010 first–quarter financial results indicate that the new recipe is a hit with the customer. Domino's domestic same-store sales grew a staggering 14.3 percent in the first quarter, while international same-store comparables were up 4.2 percent (2010 Chain of the Year, 2010).

Technology-Based Growth Strategy

Domino's has developed a reputation for innovation in business processes. It pioneered the corrugated cardboard boxes and 3-D car-top signs that are synonymous with the pizza industry. The company strengthened their efficiency with the time saving invention of the Spoodle, a combination of a spoon and ladle. To ensure that customers received the best pizza, the Domino's HeatWave Hot Bag was introduced. This technology utilizes electro-magnetic energy and 3M Thinsulate Insulation to deliver pizza hot and without excess moisture (Corporate Profile, 2010). To improve their daily operations, the Domino's Pulse point of sale system was introduced in 2003

EXHIBIT C5.6: DOMINO'S DIGITAL PIONEERING

1996	Launched its first web site, www.dominos.com
1998	First ordering through interactive television
1999	Direct ordering through Quickorder.com
2004	Launched its dedicated web site for digital marketing
2006	Received Revolution Award as the Best Online Retailer
2007	Launched mobile commerce by introducing SMS pizza ordering service

(Domino's Pizza . . . , 2003). The touch-screen ordering system significantly improved the accuracy and efficiency of order taking.

Early Adoption of Online Technology

Dominos Pizza has led the restaurant industry as an early adapter of online technology to reach customers. It utilized Internet marketing as early as 1996 by launching its web site www.dominos.com (Making Pizza since 1960 . . . , 2010). The first ordering method deviating from the standard call-and-place norm began two years later through a television set (Exhibit C5.6). In 1998, Domino's launched this new ordering method with Open, the "world's first interactive TV platform" in the United Kingdom (Strategic Play . . . , 2005). In the following year, Domino's began a partnership with Quickorder.com, allowing customers to place a delivery or pick-up order directly through the Internet. The user's order was automatically routed to the closest store's point-of-sale system, with a confirmation email sent to the customer (Connor, 2000).

Domino's hired AKQA, an innovative agency with a focus on digital marketing, to create a functional web site to stimulate online ordering in 2004 (Agency of the Year . . . , 2004). The agency's successful feat won Domino's Pizza recognition in the digital marketing world by 2006, with a nomination for a Revolution Award as the Best Online Retailer (Revolution Award . . . , 2006). In July 2007, Domino's began their exploration of the mobile commerce by introducing a SMS pizza ordering service (Domino's Pizza . . . , 2007). To place an order, the customer was required to set up an account online with a keyword attached to their favorite orders and the delivery address. An option for credit card or cash upon delivery allowed the consumer payment flexibility. To place the order for delivery through their mobile phone, the customers sent their chosen word in a text message to 61212 (Domino's Pizza UK, 2007).

Improvements followed the establishment of e-commerce and m-commerce sales channels. Mobile ordering advanced to an application accessible with web-enabled phones at the end of 2007. The expanded sales channel allowed customers more spontaneity in ordering, choosing their desired pizza and side items from the mobile screen. The option of entering an online ordering ID and Password was available to accelerate repeat ordering transactions (Ross, 2007).

In 2007, Domino's reconfigured its online ordering application to include the Pizza Tracker. This monitoring system allowed the customer to view the progressive action of the pizza creation process in real time, from order placement to leaving the store for delivery. Traditional ordering advanced as well with the Pizza Tracker technology. This system was made available to customers who used smart phones to order. Once the order was placed, the customer could monitor it through the Pizza Tracker icon on the Domino's web site (Domino's Launches . . . , 2008).

The "Build Your Own Pizza" feature began to enhance the Internet user's experience in 2008, allowing the customer to create a progressive photo of their pizza with chosen toppings. The ordering system enhancement was combined with other features to assist the store operations. The improved point of sale system provided the restaurant with delivery route maps and optimal scheduling assistance (Jargon, 2009).

In 2008, Domino's entered another television-based sales outlet, TiVo. After viewing a Domino's Pizza commercial, TiVo users can click on the "I want it" to place an order for pick-up or delivery. They can use the Pizza Tracker to watch the progress of their pizza on their TV screen (Liddle, 2008).

Domino's aggressive mobile commerce expansion occurred in 2009. The company entered into a partnership with Air2Web to provide an opt-in mobile coupon service, tailored to the customer's ordering history (Butcher, 2009). In August 2009, a new version of the mobile web site was released, specially designed for iPhone, Android, and Palm Pre users. This mobile site mirrored the web platform by providing the Pizza Tracker with menu visualization, order graphics, and ability to browse and apply available coupons that the customer used (Domino's Pizza Launches . . . , 2009).

New Media Strategy

Although television accounts for more than 90% of Domino's media spending, the company is increasingly utilizing new media, such as online advertising, email, mobile, search, and social networking, to connect with its younger customers. Domino's recently tripled its online advertising spending to promote its new menu and delivery service across a broad range of sites such as Amazon, Ask, Facebook, MySpace, Yahoo, College Humor, and Yellow Pages as well as sites from local newspapers.

Email marketing at Domino's ranges from a variety of special deals, promotional offers, and coupons to new menu item introduction and menu suggestion for special occasions (e.g., lunch, family gathering, gift) to just a simple reminder to order from Domino's. Established customers typically receive weekly email with promotional deals and suggestions.

Domino's search marketing was catching up with its archrival, Pizza Hut. It demonstrated a strong showing in organic search—a testimony to the company's effective advertising and strong web site experience—as opposed to paid search where Pizza Hut made a bigger commitment.

Mobile is one of the fastest growing elements of new media that all the three pizza chains are paying attention to. Although, mobile marketing at Domino's is a small proportion compared to online marketing via the Internet, the company reports that it is growing at an average rate of 20% per month. The growth rate dovetails mobile commerce, the fast growing area of retail purchases in the United States. Shoppers were expected to order $2.2 billion worth of merchandise using cell phones in 2010, $1 billion more than 2009 and five times more than 2008, according to ABI Research Inc., a New York technology research firm. To respond to the rapid growth in mobile shopping, 30% of retailers have installed mobile-commerce web sites (Mattioli, 2010).

Domino's has taken a different approach toward its mobile media. Instead of developing smart phone application to provide access to mobile ordering, Domino's has decided to streamline its web site for mobile access. The advantage of the site is that it requires few clicks for mobile ordering and no downloading or registration for access. By visiting http://www.dominos.com, customers can create an order by tapping "Express Ordering" or "Create Your Own Pizza," examining the menu, special offers and coupons, and using the Pizza Tracker upon placing an order.

Domino's social media strategy is a broad ranging program that encompasses Facebook, Twitter, and YouTube. Domino's engagement in social media was hastened in April 2009 when a prank video, posted on YouTube, showed two employees were abusing and mishandling the food they were preparing in a franchise kitchen. The video quickly spread all over the Internet and received more than a million views in less than 24 hours on YouTube. Domino's President properly responded and discredited the prank in another video posted on YouTube. The company also set up a Twitter account, shortly after the incident, and started answering the questions addressed to Domino's.

Domino's continued using social media to announce the arrival of its new-recipe pizza by its "Pizza Turnaround" documentary on YouTube. They also showed the success of their taste test by beating Papa John's and Pizza Hut on a "Celebrate" page. And they had a "Stop Puffery" campaign, also on Twitter, which made fun of Papa John's (Domino's Pizza Rewards ..., 2010).

Domino's integrated its social media campaign on Facebook by encouraging consumers to try its new-recipe pizza. An interactive contest, "Taste Bud Bounty Hunters", rewarded Facebook users with free food for getting their friends to try the new pizza recipe. On the web site, pizzaholdouts.com, photos were displayed of the top bounty hunter contestants and those pizza holdouts with "wanted taste buds".

Challenges Ahead

As a $5.6 billion company with 170,000 employees and over 9000 stores in 62 countries, Domino's Pizza Inc. is readying to celebrate its 50th anniversary. Basking in the company's success, the management is realistically thoughtful about the list of challenges ahead. On the top of that list are the state of the economy and the maturity of the U.S. pizza market. The question before the management is whether the same-store growth performance is domestically sustainable and achievable in the near future. Per company reports, the U.S. sales rose slightly, from $3 billion to $3.1 billion in 2009. It is expected that quick-service restaurants fare slightly better than full-service restaurants in the coming year, according to the National Restaurant Association. Because of the lingering slowdown in the economy, however, the average amount spent per order won't increase appreciably as consumers continue to hold tight to their wallets.

The international growth is one area that management is hopeful about. Currently over 40% of the company revenues are from the international operation. The proportion is expected to pass 50% in the next three to five years.

The success of Domino's new recipe has created momentum for the brand whose maintenance is subject to proper marketing strategy and execution. Since 2008, Domino's significantly expanded its menu to include multi-variety Oven-Baked Sandwiches, BreadBowl Pasta, and the American Legends line of specialty pizza. While the additions contribute to higher sales and growth at store level, they may complicate order processing, preparation, and delivery as well. Whether the expanded menu would slow down Domino's fast delivery and great service when the economic recovery begins and business picks up remains to be seen.

Case Discussion Questions

1. Discuss Domino's point-of-sale (POS) ordering system. What are the advantages of the new system, for Domino's, its franchisees, and its customers?

2. Analyze the pizza home delivery market. What are the market size and growth? Who are the major competitors? What are Domino's competitive advantages and disadvantages? Evaluate Domino's growth potential in the pizza home delivery market.

3. With the advent of online and mobile ordering, the rivalry among Domino's, Pizza Hut, and Papa John's has been heightened in the past three years. Each company claims that its online/mobile ordering system is as easy to use as blinking. You can engage in online shopping and purchasing by browsing the menu, ordering a pizza, and tracking your pizza in real time from order to delivery on their web site. You can also search for deals, valuable information on nutrition, health, and environment. So, what else can you do on these web sites? Check it for yourself by visiting Domino's, www.dominos.com, Pizza Hut, www.pizzahut.com, and Papa John's, www.papajohns.com. Browse the menu, go over menu items, and decide on a meal from different types of pizzas, side items, and drinks. Check out the listing of various toppings that are offered. Examine the nutritional value of the menu items. After choosing your meal, try to place an order by clicking on the order tab. How many steps you have to go through before completing your order? What information do you have to have to decide on delivery versus carryout? After you place your order, can you track it online from submission to delivery? What other communication / information do you receive after the completion of the delivery? Evaluate your experience with each web site you visited. Which site is easier to use? Which site is user-friendlier? Is ordering pizza online better or worse than ordering pizza over the phone? Why?

4. Domino's recently announced the launch of a new version of its mobile ordering web site, http://mobile.dominos.com. The enhanced version is optimized to access Google's Android operating system, used by iPhone, Palm Pre

and others. Discuss the enhancements of the new ordering site and its marketing implications.

5. What types of data does Domino's collect when it transacts with customers online? Identify at least *five* different ways that Domino's can use customer data to increase sales and market share.

6. Discuss Domino's recent marketing activities using social media. Compare Domino's social-media strategies vis-à-vis those of Pizza Hut and Papa John's. Address Domino's advantages and shortcomings in using social media. How do you think Domino's can leverage social media to better connect with its customers and advance its brand?

References

2009 Yum! Brands Annual Customer Mania Report, 2009.

2010 Chain of the Year, Pizza Today, June 2010, www.pizzatoday.com.

"Agency of the Year: Digital Agency of the Year—Best of the Rest". Dow Jones. 15, December 2004.

"AMSTAR CORPORATION, Plaintiff-Appellee, v. DOMINO'S PIZZA, INC. and Atlanta Pizza, Inc., Pizza Enterprises, Inc. and Pizza Services, Inc., Hanna Creative Enterprises, Inc., Defendants-Appellants.". United States Court of Appeals for the Fifth Circuit. 2 May 1980. http://altlaw.org/v1/cases/525090.

Blumenfeld and Associates, 2010.

Boyer, Peter J. (19 February 2007). "The Deliverer". The New Yorker. http://www.newyorker.com/reporting/2007/02/19/070219fa_fact_boyer.

Butcher, Dan. "Domino's Pizza Exec: Mobile Commerce Growing at Astounding Rate". The Mobile Marketer. 4, September 2009. http://www.mobilemarketer.com/cms/news/commerce/4102.print.

"Change at Domino's." nyse magaine.com, 2010. http://www.nysemagazine.com/dominos.

Connor, Deni. "QuickOrder Brings Domino's Pizza to You in 30 minutes or Less". Network World. 6, March 2000.

"Corporate Profile". Domino's Investor Relations, 2010. http://phx.corporate-ir.net/phoenix.zhtml?c=135383&p=irol-homeprofile.

Domino's 2010 Annual Report, 2010.

"Domino's Founder to Retire, Sell Stake". Los Angeles Time. 26 September 1998. http://articles.latimes.com/1998/sep/26/business/fi-26500.

"Domino's Launches Revolutionary Customer Tool: Pizza Tracker™; Industry-Leading Technology Allows Customers to Follow Progress of their Order Online—Even if they Order by Phone". PR Newswire (U.S.) 30, January 2008.

"Domino's opens 9000th store". Nation's Restaurant News. 11, March 2010. http://www.nrn.com/breakingNews.aspx?id=380448&menu_id=1368

"Domino's Pizza & Breakaway Roll Out of New Pulse POS System". Pizza Marketplace. 5, February 2003. http://www.pizzamarketplace.com/article.php?id=2277.

"Domino's Pizza Enables Ordering by SMS". New Media Age. 26, July 2007.

"Domino's Pizza, Inc." Datamonitor Company Profiles. Datamonitor. 12 November 2008. http://www.datamonitor.com/store/Product/dominos_pizza_inc?productid=1744376E-79E5-49F9-9298-F128768A73E5.

Domino's Pizza, Inc. (2008). "David A. Brandon Biography". Press release. http://phx.corporate-ir.net/phoenix.zhtml?c=135383&p=irol-govBio&ID=115901.

Domino's Pizza Invester Presentation, January 2010. http://phx.corporate-ir.net/External.File?item=UGFyZW50SUQ9MjY5Mjh8Q2hpbGRRJRD0tMXxUeXBlPTM=&t=1

"Domino's Launches Revolutionary Customer Tool: Pizza Tracker™; Industry-Leading Technology Allows Customers to Follow Progress of their Order Online—Even if they Order by Phone". PR Newswire (U.S.) 30, January 2008.

Domino's Pizza Rewards the 'Taste Bud Bounty Hunters'. Restaurant News.Com. 11, May 2010. http://www.restaurantnews.com/dominos-pizza-rewards-the-taste-bud-bounty-hunters/

Domino's Pizza UK (2007). "Domino's Pizza Launches UK's First Ever Text Message Pizza Order Service". Press Release.

http://www.dominos.uk.com/media_centre/pdf/Text%20Ordering.pdf.

Horovitz, Bruce (May 5, 2010) "New pizza recipe did wonders for Domino's sales". USA Today. http://www.usatoday.com/money/industries/food/2010-05-05-dominos05_ST_N.htm Retrieved 2010-06-18

Jargon, Julie. " Business Technology: Domino's IT Staff Delivers Slick Site, Ordering System—-Pizza Chain Rolls Out Point-of-Sale System in U.S. Stores to Woo Customers, Streamline Online Orders". Wall Street Journal. 24, November 2009.

Liddle, A. "Domino's Pioneers 'Couch Commerce,' Expands its Ordering Options with New TiVo Partnership." Nation's Restaurant News. 1, December 2008.

Litterick, David (February 23, 2008). "Colin Halpern sells £4 m slice of Domino's Pizza". The Daily Telegraph. http://www.telegraph.co.uk/money/main.jhtml?xml=/money/2008/02/23/cndomino123.xml.

"Making Pizza Since 1960. . . . ". Domino's Pizza Inc.. http://www.dominosbiz.com/Biz-Public-EN/Site+Content/Secondary/About+Dominos/History/.

Mattioli, Dana (June 11, 2010). "Retailers Answer Call of Smartphones". The Wall Street Journal. http://online.wsj.com/article/SB10001424052748704749904575292

"Our Heritage". Domino's Pizza, Inc.. 2008. http://www.dominos.com/Public-EN/Site%2BContent/Secondary/Inside%2BDominos/Our%2BHeritage/.

Packaged Facts, New York, 2010.

Papa John's 2009 Annual Report, 2009.

Phone interview with Dennis Maloney, Domino's Multi-Media Marketing Vice President, 2011.

"Pizza Power Report, 2009". PMQ Pizza Magazine, September 2009, www.pmq.com

"Revolution Awards 2006: Is Your Work in the Running?". Revolution. 28, February 2006.

Ross, J. "Domino's, Papa John's Look to Build Clientele Via Text Message Ordering". Nation's Restaurant News. 10, December 2007.

Standard & Poor's May 15, 2010 stock report, 2010.

"Strategic Play—Domino's Pizza: Speedy Delivery". New Media Age. 14, April 2005.

Yum! Brands 2009 Annual Report, 2009.

CASE
6

ECB.com: Customer Profiling and Segmentation[1]

DEBRA ZAHAY-BLATZ
Aurora University

BLODWEN TARTER
Golden Gate University

Jin Yang thoughtfully sipped her afternoon coffee, as she listened to her colleague, José Gonzalez, summarize the meeting they had both attended earlier that day. The ECB.com vice president of marketing, Dana Achebe, had invited all the members of the marketing data analytics team to discuss the company's segmentation scheme and how to improve it. Revenue growth had slowed recently and Dana thought that reviewing the customer database and, possibly, revising the target market focus might alleviate the slow growth problem. She suspected that too many customers were one-time buyers and that customer retention was a problem. It was expensive to acquire new customers and she wanted to increase the number and value of purchases made by existing customers.

Jin and José, both newly hired junior data analysts and recent graduates from the same university, had volunteered to review the current situation and recommend a better approach to segmentation and targeting. This was a challenging assignment but one that they were eager to undertake.

ECB.com (formerly Entertainment Coupon Book) sold coupons directly to consumers who use the coupons to obtain discounts for many different types of entertainment. For example, ECB.com would sell a $25 certificate for a specific restaurant for only $10, a savings to the buyer of $15. A $50 seat to a concert might be offered for $25. ECB.com's partners, the providers of the entertainment, used these coupons to introduce new audiences to their services and relied on ECB.com to market the coupons to ECB.com's customers.

---

[1] The case was prepared as a basis for class discussion and is not an illustration of effective or ineffective management. The company and events are fictional. All trademarks are the property of their respective owners. The data in this case may be used for teaching purposes only and not for the creation of other published case material. Only the authors of this case have permission to use the data for this purpose.

Cost-conscious individuals visited the company's website to see what entertainment offers were available. They could sign up for email notices to learn about all of the offers available or choose only the specific categories in which they were interested. Over time, ECB.com expanded its offering to include coupons for restaurants, movies, live theater, concerts, theme parks, rafting, even attendance at blockbuster (and not-so-blockbuster) museum exhibitions. In fact, "entertainment" had become broadly defined at ECB.com, so that the website offered some form of discounted entertainment for almost everyone. However, coupons for dining out in restaurants were the most popular.

In the morning meeting, Dana had provided a brief overview of ECB.com's history of targeting prospective customers. When the company started, the founders used their own judgment to forecast who would be most likely to buy these coupons. Initially, the founders targeted their marketing messages based on their intuition, some primary research about the business concept, and some secondary research about the scope of the entertainment business. They developed specific offers and directed their marketing communications efforts accordingly. As consumers became more aware of ECB.com, and the valuable deals it offered, more people visited the website and purchased coupons. Six years later, ECB.com had sold millions of coupons to thousands of consumers.

José began the recap. "Let's see what we know. Several years ago, ECB.com developed its first formal customer profiles to identify the characteristics of its customers. Then, it developed a segmentation scheme, based on the data accumulated from the inception of the business. The goal was to divide the market into groups of potential customers, or market segments, which would then allow ECB.com to target the most desirable segments. Each segment contained a cluster of people who were alike (or homogenous) in one or more important ways. Each group or cluster differed from the other groups. The segments (or groups) we have been using for a while are classified as *new, engaged, lapsed or inactive*. I wonder if that still makes sense."

Jin interjected, "Yes, our current segmentation is based mostly on R/F/M (recency, frequency, and monetary value). Well, actually, if I remember correctly, it is mostly based on recency and frequency. We know how often people buy, when they buy, and the value of each purchase. That's observable data and collecting it online is so easy! Whenever someone orders, we capture exactly that information. Then we just add it to the customer database. Of course, we do have some demographic data too. That may be useful. But maybe all we have to do to complete this assignment is simply to update the analysis based on more recent data and see what we learn. We think our assumptions about our customers may be wrong, that things have changed. Isn't it just as likely that they haven't changed?"

José considered Jin's comments silently, remembering the direct marketing goal of beating the control. A long-standing practice among successful direct marketers, "beat the control" meant testing your best-performing direct mail package or email or direct response ad (the control) against different executions to try to improve the results of the direct marketing effort. José realized that the control here was the existing segmentation scheme. He also realized that it was usually difficult to beat the control. Maybe this assignment would be harder than he had thought!

Jin interrupted José's thoughts again, adding "On the other hand, we could update the analysis, using ECB.com's data, and add more data from an outside service. Remember when we took that direct and database marketing class? We learned about commercial services that had information about lifestyles, financial behavior, technology usage, and other data that ECB.com can't possibly capture. We could figure out which of those characteristics we think are relevant, take a meaningful sample of the total customer database and have this additional data appended it to the sample. I'm sure we could gain better insight into our customers. And, we would have more data to use in our own segmentation analysis."

Jin and José continued to brainstorm the assignment and how best to tackle it. They reasoned that the ideal customer would contribute the most to generating revenue when he or she would buy frequently, buy higher value certificates, and buy multiple certificates each time. Over the remainder of the afternoon and with further discussion the next morning they concluded that they should first review what the average ECB.com customer looked like. They would first focus on recency, frequency, and monetary value but they wanted to create as complete a profile as possible so they agreed they would look at most of the other types of customer data available too. Just for fun, they each wrote down their best guesses of the characteristics of the average ECB.com buyer. The person who came closest to the actual average order value, the average number of certificates, and the average number of orders would be treated to coffee by the loser—for an entire week.

Once Jin and José had developed the profile of the average customer, they were confident they could develop a clustering method to identify meaningful market segments that was superior to the current approach. They decided they would begin this phase by analyzing the R/F/M of the existing segments (engaged, inactive, lapsed, and new). Once they understood what these segments looked like, the team would try to create meaningful new categories that were similar within the category but different enough to be a truly distinct group.

To begin, José started reviewing the data dictionary (see Appendix) to see exactly what ECB.com data was readily available. He also wanted to decide what data categories were equivalent to the recency, frequency, and monetary value concepts with which he was familiar. Jin took responsibility for researching external suppliers of information that could be used to augment ECB.com's internal data.

Jin and José had already decided that they would base their analysis on 60,000 customer records, randomly selected from the customer database. The subset was large enough to meet statistical sampling requirements but small enough that the data could be manipulated relatively easily for analysis. Once they had refined the segmentation scheme, they could apply it to the entire database.

Then, they realized that they would need to use a single product category, rather than a mixture of products. After a brief discussion, they agreed that using the category for which they had the most data and which contributed the most to ECB.com's revenue made the most sense. This turned out to be dining out, the restaurant category. Once they had a better approach for restaurant coupon buyers, they could look at the other product categories. Tempering their initial enthusiasm to do everything all at once meant a more methodical approach to the analysis, starting with basic customer profiling.

At that point, Jin and José stopped to review some of the mechanics of doing this analysis. They were both experts in using MS Excel®, the standard spreadsheet software. They had used IBM's SPSS® software in their statistics classes and had heard that SAS® could be used for cluster analysis as well. Undoubtedly, there were other software programs that could be helpful. What software did ECB.com have available?

Just then, Dana Achebe stopped by to see how they were doing. When Jin and José explained their plan of approach, Dana smiled. She was interested to see the latest profile of the average ECB.com restaurant category customer and what would be discovered in the review of the existing segmentation scheme. Most importantly, she was looking forward to hear what new clusters the two data analysts came up with. If they could identify a better segmentation scheme, ECB.com could revise its targeting and marketing communications. Perhaps this was the starting point to reverse the decline in revenue growth.

While Dana liked the idea of appending additional data to enhance the ECB.com customer database, she asked that they research the various options available and recommend a data enhancement scheme. She could then decide whether or not she wanted ECB.com to invest in the additional information. The company had already invested in some outside data and by using ZIP codes was able to get information on the customer's DMA, some imputation of income and income rank and customer location (i.e., large metro area vs. suburbs). What other data would help in segmentation? Would an outside firm's segmentation scheme be helpful?

Dana closed by letting the team know that not all of the customer records were complete. To facilitate the registration process, some data was optional and some data was just not in the file. The data on acquisition channel was particularly incomplete. Since some data was missing, Jin and José would need to decide how to handle that.

Appendix

ECB Data Dictionary

DATA DICTIONARY	
Variable Name	**Description**
Unique ID	Unique Identifier for Customer
Transaction/Segment Data	
# Days Since Last Order	# of days since last order (recency) in the last 3 years
# of Orders	# of Orders in the last 3 years
# of Certificates	# of Certificates in the last 3 years
Revenue	Revenue in the last 3 years
Tenure (in days)	# of days since first order with ECB
Lifecycle Tenure Recovery	New = First order with ECB in the last 3 months
	Engaged = Last order was within the last 6 months (and not new)
	Lapsed = Last order was 6–12 months ago
	Inactive = Last order was over 12 months ago
Average Order Value	Revenue / # of Orders in the last 3 years
New Customer Flag	1 = First order with ECB occurred in the last 3 months
	0 = First order with ECB occurred in over 3 months ago
Active Flag	1 = Last order was within the last 12 months
	0 = Last order was over 12 months ago
Subscribed to Email Flag	1 = Customers email address is subscribed to our email program
	0 = Customers email address has unsubscribed from our email program
Marketable thru Email Flag	1 = Customer email address is email marketable (we don't have affiliate partnerships that limit us from emailing to this customer)
	0 = Customer email address is unmarketable, we have affiliate partnerships that limit us from emailing this customer
# of Orders w/a Promotion	# of orders the customer has placed during a promotion percent off
# of Orders w/a 70 Off Promotion	# of orders the customer has placed during a 70 Off promotion
# of Orders with a 80 Off Promotion	# of orders the customer has placed during a 80 Off promotion

# of Orders with a 90 Off Promotion	# of orders the customer has placed during a 90 Off promotion
Acquisition Channel	Channel customer placed first order with ECB, Affiliate, Paid Search, Uncategorized, Null
# of Certificates Validated	# of Certificates the customer has brought to a restaurant and validated (used)
DEMOGRAPHIC DATA	
Customer DMA	Customers DMA Area
Head of Household Age	Actual age, 25 to 84
Marital Status	Single, Married, Missing
Home Ownership	Owner, Renter, Missing
Kids	Yes, No
Age of Kids	Age Mix, Infant/Toddler, Pre teen and teenage, Teenagers
Income Affluence	1 to 5, 1 is highest
Income Rank	1 to 71, 1 is highest
Customer Location Type	Large Metros; Not Top 10
	Large Metros; Suburban, city del.
	Larger Metro Areas; Not Top 10
	Larger Metros; Suburban, city del.
	Largest Metro Areas
	Largest Metro Areas
	Metro Suburban
	Metro Suburban, city delivery
	Metro Suburban, non-city delivery
	Metro Suburban, non-city delivery
	Mixed; But Not Top 10 Metros
	Rural
	Rural; Suburban, non-city delivery
	Mixed; But Not Top 10 Metros
	Rural
	Rural; Suburban, non-city delivery
Ethnicity	African-American, Hispanic, Mixed, White

CASE
7

GreenolaStyle:
Brand on a Mission

DRAI HASSERT

Loyola University Chicago

STACY NEIER

Loyola University Chicago

Our mission: By empowering and partnering with women in marginalized communities, GREENOLA seeks to create a greater awareness and sense of community by standing in solidarity with women around the world. We believe that all women have power to create, nurture, and transform. Each GREENOLA product is hand-made expression of this philosophy, allowing women worldwide to connect to create a better world. Change your look, change a life . . .[1]

. . . and change perspectives about the origins of ethical style. The glitz and glamour of the romanticized fashion industry conjured couture images parading on runways in Paris and Milan. Chicago and Bolivia were certainly never on the radar as the next locations for emerging style. Through the aforementioned mission, Jen Moran, social entrepreneur and founder of GreenolaStyle, changed the landscape of how consumers look not only at fashion but also at sustainable style accomplished through fair trade.

A Day in the Life of a Social Entrepreneur

Jen spent a highly productive day out of the office and in the field visiting with her retail partners. Although Greenola products were found in more than 180 retail stores nationwide, Greenheart Shop, Chicago's premier eco-fair trade nonprofit store in the trendy Wicker Park neighborhood,[2] provided Jen with a barometer of sales and a site to observe customers interact with fair trade products. She observed firsthand how consumers touched the products and read tags for labeling information. She saw con-

---

[1] http://www.greenolastyle.com
[2] http://www.greenheartshop.org/

sumers' reactions to new silhouette fits or to brightened color palettes. In particular, she wanted to talk with Greenheart owners about inventory turn, SKU replenishment, and customer feedback about Greenola's Spring/Summer Sedgewick Line. Chicago's summer street and art fairs substantially increased foot traffic to Greenheart, so Jen needed to plan support and shipment for orders.

Once Greenheart's peak business hours passed, Jen hopped on the Blue Line El train and headed north to her office for planning time. She slipped her train pass away and noticed an email alert on her iPhone: She was not one to resist an email with the subject line of "Sale to a TEE." New markdowns were taken in the Anthropologie store on Chicago Avenue, so a bit of comparison shopping would help her to reduce Greenola's price line for seasonal merchandise. She needed to clear online inventory from the previous season as new SKUs were expected to arrive within the week. Additionally, her upcoming market trip was deserving of some new tees to pack for her meetings with artisans, so she glided, in red canvas TOMS, to transfer from the Blue to Red train lines and indulged in the treasure hunt adventure that always lured Jen into Anthropologie.

Finally back to her office in the Andersonville Galleria, Jen logged her observations from the Greenheart and Anthropologie visits. Although Greenola was yet to invest in a complex CRM system or database, Jen believed that keeping an Excel record of qualitative observations added value to quantitative orders and sales confirmed by the retailer network. Ninety percent of sales derived from current Greenola retailers, so as a wholesaler, Jen wanted a detailed archive to determine how to expand Greenola's brand through her boutique space in the Andersonville Galleria and via e-commerce orders placed directly through www.greenolastyle.com. Balancing the retail and wholesale contributions was an ongoing objective as Greenola gained market share within the competitive apparel and accessories sector.

The day's top priority now shifted to a meeting with Teresa Kuvilla, Greenola's Associate Creative Director. Jen and Teresa were leaving for an annual trip to Bolivia in less than a week, and the itinerary was in constant flux. As they developed a day-by-day agenda, mapping out various co-op and community partners with whom they would visit, Jen's excitement built as she reflected back on the three-year history of Greenola's impact in Bolivia. Jen's expertise and drive for the work to be accomplished was palpable as Jen described to Teresa expectations and opportunities to consider when in the field with Greenola's designers, the women of Bolivia. This would be quite the trip that stood to influence next steps for Greenola's brand strategy.

Greenola's Development into an Integrated Business Model

Fair Trade Defined

Greenola developed with the vision to be a vastly differentiated fashion brand that tied itself to fair trade and sustainable business practices. The initial position that Greenola took was a green and fair trade clothing retailer. Consumers wanted "an ever-changing array of cheap clothes" but "rarely thought about sustainability or quality. In order to consume clothes more ethically, consumers needed to change the way they thought about them."[3] Jen anticipated this point of differentiation would set apart her company on the basis that ethically made and fairly traded clothing was appealing to a wide segment of consumers, both as end users and to give as gifts. Fair trade and sustainability practices were used in the marketing plan to promote these attributes and express a cause-related marketing appeal.

The fair trade movement was an initiative created to enhance the quality of life in underdeveloped countries using a market-based approach to create sustainable production. The original version of fair trade emerged in the 1940s as a philanthropic mission for churches in developed countries. These churches would sell handicrafts from emerging countries and then turn back the profits directly to the craftspeople.[4] Over time the fair trade movement transformed into a global enterprise, where there are currently more than 3,000 grassroots organizations and more than 50 countries involved in the fair trade transaction.[5] The agreed-upon definition of fair trade is "a trading partnership, based on dialogue, transparency and respect, that seeks greater equity in international trade. It contributes to sustainable development by offering better trading conditions to, and securing the rights of, marginalized producers and workers - especially in the South. Fair trade organizations (backed by consumers) are engaged actively in supporting producers, awareness raising, and in campaigning for changes in the rules and practice of conventional international trade."[6]

Fair trade became increasingly relevant to clothing manufacturing due to heightened consumer awareness from media attention on sweatshops and child laborers in developing countries. Greenola was truly a revolution in the fashion industry as typical practices within the industry obscured the origins of the clothes and the factories, farms, and companies responsible for producing the clothing are not represented.[7] Greenola challenged the dominant paradigm through transparent marketing strategies and tactics in the production and distribution of its garments. Greenola's primary goal was to give decision power back to fashion enthusiasts by infusing products with a story of unique travel and community empowerment.

Greenola's business model was a holistic approach that defied traditional economic models that corporations typically replicated to enter markets. Neoclassical economic theory states the purpose of the corporation is to maximize shareholder profits; in order to achieve this, different ways to cut costs in other aspects of the operation were entertained. This model was a powerful tool to generate profits but failed to address what happened when a company no longer used a supplier; production costs were driven up from oversaturation of competitor companies in the market

---

[3] Ethical style: don't donate clothes, repurpose them. Retrieved http://www.good.is/post/ethical-style-don-t-donate-clothes-repurpose-them/

[4] Glazer, S. (2007). Fair Trade Labeling. *CQ Researcher* 17 (May 18): 433-456.

[5] Oxfam International. "Make Trade Fair, Fair Trade: A Definition." Retrieved http://www.maketradefair.com/en/index.php?file=21052002111743.htm&cat=4&subcat=1&select=5

[6] Fair trade label reaches retail market. Retrieved http://www.chicagofairtrade.org/more-about-joomla/clothing/119-fair-trade-label-reaches-retail-market-.html

[7] Retrieved http://www.toms.com/one-for-one

and increasing demands for improved quality of life. The simple answer was to move the company's operations into another emerging country and take advantage of those resources. This approach no longer made sense in a world where massive cultural and technological innovations rapidly changed the way consumers interacted and connected. Global issues were more prevalent and deeply felt through global interconnection enabled through the use of technology like Twitter, Facebook and other social media outlets. Shifts in the political environment, like the Occupy movement and the Tea Party, highlighted economic issues and increased awareness between income discrepancies. Greenola was on trend with these issues and acted on a global scale. Jen's vision addressed global poverty through the idea that consumers will contribute solutions if they receive tangible rewards for what they give. Understanding the outcome of traditional business practices, where companies leave countries upon depletion of low cost production opportunities, guided Jen's own business practices, and influenced her development of a symbiotic, relationship-centered, cyclical, sustainable business.

Greenola's model

Greenola created relationships with producers through in-country fair trade networks, which enabled Jen to work directly with fifty-five women artisans and entrepreneurs in Bolivia. (Greenola's original artisan network included only twelve artisans.) As shown in Appendix A, Jen created a new fashion line for each selling season and traveled to Bolivia to source fabric types, cuts, and colors to fabricate the line. Upon creation, the goods were exported to the United States and sold through three distribution channels: online, retail, and wholesale distribution. Appendix A shows the process represented by Greenola. Consumers in the US then purchased the fashion product, but once they committed to the purchase, information was shared about craftsmen behind the product (Appendix C). Also in Appendix A, the profits Greenola received were used to pay fair wages to producers. This empowered the producers because they were enabled to support their families, give back to their communities, fuel creative expression, and have access to quality healthcare in an economic environment that otherwise would not support their marginalized stature. Jen only traveled to Bolivia one to two times per year, so José Choque became Jen's key contact for cooperative and artisan management located in Cochabamba, Bolivia. José nurtured artisan relationships on the ground in Bolivia with consistency, and partnering with Greenola was in high demand among new co-ops. Artisans knew when Jen visited, and they requested meetings to share product designs. This reaction ran counter to Jen's fond memories of her first trip to Bolivia when she was never asked for hand-outs or charity. Now requests for support were coming from within a much different context.

Jen measured Greenola's success through a triple bottom line approach that took into account: financial success, impact on the community, and impact on the planet. Greenola's social impact objectives were to create jobs, source materials locally, encourage entrepreneurship through artisan training and business education, and to work with artisans' creation of products for local markets (in addition to sales in the US). Greenola also aimed to provide access to quality healthcare to empower marginalized women artisans; breaking the cycle of poverty was to be achieved by Greenola's sustainable business cycle. Consequently, Greenola also donated 10% of its profits to Solidarity Bridge, which provided medical care to Bolivians living in poverty. These relationships were crucial to the development of the Greenola brand as they supported the continued progress of economic indicators in the producers' environment. Although seemingly a small piece of its organizational structure, Greenola had a direct impact on 1,643 patients through its affiliation with Solidarity Bridge. In Greenola's three years of operations, it provided over $55,000 in income for artisans and imported 6,000 goods from Bolivia. An additional $25,000 was anticipated for the upcoming fiscal year.

Perception of Fair Trade

Although Greenola's practices were progressive and capable of redefining how consumers purchase clothing, fair trade was still a long way from mainstream acceptance. During the first two years of business, Jen realized that the green, fair trade concepts fundamental to the marketing plan deterred potential customers within Greenola's target market. Through preliminary attempts to collect primary research through survey data and focus groups, descriptors like *green* and *fair trade* stigmatized how consumers viewed products. Instead of illustrating *ethical*, these traits brought up images of *hippie* or *bohemian*. Rather than attracting a wide array of women within the intended target audience of 20-39, these core competencies narrowed the market to a much smaller segment. Jen wanted to move away from the perception that brought to mind a company like Ten Thousand Villages. Ten Thousand Villages retailed fair trade goods ranging from handicraft gifts to home décor. As a nonprofit, Ten Thousand Villages did not accurately represent the type of business Jen envisioned. As Greenola evolved into its third year of business, Jen decided to instigate a new direction to widen the focus of fair trade as a market position of Greenola as a brand.

The Face of the Greenola Brand

As a social entrepreneur, Jen's ownership of Greenola and the story about how Greenola came to exist motivated Greenola's mission as well as Jen's reputation as the face of the company. Greenola was conceptualized nearly a decade before entering the market when Jen began to attend The Ohio State University to study Fine Arts. Her time at OSU was fast extinct though when Jen did not find an authentic purpose in either her studies or time as a student athlete. She knew she wanted a different trajectory, so she stepped away from OSU and took time to discover the broader calling to which she would ultimately contribute. She began to work at Starbucks part-time and soon progressed to lead her own Starbucks store location. Her team won sales competitions and recognition as a district coffee leader. She expanded her awareness of fair trade principles and the responsible supply chains Starbucks both led and communicated to a global community of stakeholders. The seed—or the coffee bean— was planted: she was thirsty for more fair trade.

Working for a company like Starbucks allowed Jen to pursue her interest in travel. A flexible schedule permitted extended trips to Thailand, Slovakia, and Peru. During these trips, she observed how cultures treated women as second-class citizens; she noticed the juxtaposition of lacking economic opportunities with an abundance of cheap products flooding markets from manufacturing giants like China. This trend was amplified during Jen's first visit to South America. This continent made the deepest cultural impact on Jen, so as quickly as possible, she learned about opportunities to support and nurture South American citizens in need of medical care and education, among all the luxuries Jen herself was awarded as a middle-class American. Through networking, Jen met a non-profit group, Solidarity Bridge, which worked exclusively in Bolivia, South America's poorest nation. Seventy percent of Bolivians lived in extreme poverty and worked for an average hourly wage of $0.22. She immediately traveled to Bolivia to enrich herself with knowledge of the Bolivian women and their inherent struggles.

The influential combination of Starbucks' fair trade commitment, firsthand experience in Bolivia, and training as a fine artist pushed Jen's curiosity its limit: to fully realize the vision of a company committed to doing good business, she needed to return to school. Upon enrollment in DePaul University, she declared an entrepreneurship major. As completion of her degree neared, she was awarded Student Entrepreneur of the Year. She also won the school's business plan competition: the prize money from this accolade afforded Jen the initial investment to begin Greenola as a for-profit, social business organization.

Greenola's Competitive Niche

Jen's vision of Greenola united with sustainable business practices, yet as Greenola approached its fourth fiscal year, priority was given to establishing Greenola's brand equity in a saturated fashion sector. Once brand positioning was achieved, a focused, cohesive marketing mix took priority.

First, current product positioning did not reflect the prevailing fast fashion zeitgeist. Although the sustainable, triple bottom line model was profitable, social and cultural trends shifted faster than Jen could position Greenola. When Greenola was introduced, Jen set out to engage a community of consumers and artisans through primary emphasis on fair trade; maintaining the style of the products was secondary to the social good of Greenola. With so few brands classified as fair trade, Greenola filled a unique niche. However, competitive research indicated TOMS as a dominant brand in the global marketplace. Although TOMS did not uphold fair trade principles, it competed on a sustainable, integrated business model of "One-for-One" cause marketing: consumers bought one pair of shoes, and TOMS gave one pair of shoes to a child who would otherwise have none. According to TOMS, "as of September 2010, TOMS gave over one million pairs of new shoes to children in need around the world."[8] As a TOMS consumer herself, Jen recognized TOMS captured a seemingly large share of market, yet TOMS competed on *cause*. Greenola competed on *fair trade*, so TOMS was not a direct competitor.

Anthropologie fostered brand equity Jen admired as a consumer but did not seek to compete with directly. Anthropologie's consumers were described as "young thinkers who are interested in trend and fashion but don't want to look victim."[9]

---

[8] Labarre, P. (2002). Sophisticated sell. Retrieved http://www.fastcompany.com/magazine/65/sophisticated.html

[9] www.matatraders.com

Anthropologie consumers were 30 to 45 years old, college or post-graduate education, married with kids or in a committed relationship, professional or ex-professional, and earned annual household income of $150,000 to $200,000. Anthropologie offered a "sense of adventure and originality, and the promise of self-discovery.[10] Consumers depended upon feeling a sense of travel when entering stores, and Anthropologie's marketing mix expressed buying "fresh" products that were not necessarily trendy but "new" and "right."[11] Anthropologie did not advertise: the community of shoppers was largely responsible for its stronghold in the market. However, a lacking triple bottom line was incomparable with Greenola's vision to emphasize fair trade. Anthropologie competed on offering consumers a diverse range of sophisticated styles, yet Greenola represented a consistent commitment to sustainability as its core competency.

Although indirect competitors, multinational companies like TOMS and Anthropologie were evidence of broader consumer trends for social responsibility and unique product mixes. Locally, Chicago was becoming home to more direct competition for Greenola. Mata Traders was founded in 2003. Maureen Dunn, Mata Trader founder, returned from several trips to India which inspired a business of imported fashion products directly from "producer groups that paid their workers good wages and practiced the principles of fair trade."[12] Mata is dedicated to "work with organizations that educate, employ, and empower women,"[13] and in the truest sense of community, Mata shares its headquarters and boutique space in Andersonville Galleria with Greenola. Mata focused on India, and Greenola focused on Bolivia. As a social venture, Greenola needed to consider how to capture share of market from leaders like TOMS and Anthopologie while remaining competitive with social entrepreneurs, like Mata, in its hometown backyard.

Competitive Positioning to Branding

Brand Equity

These uncontrollable competitive forces provided Jen an arsenal of attributes to build Greenola's brand equity and control a specific marketplace niche illustrated in Appendix B's strategy canvas. Realizing the mention of *green* confused consumers with connotations of *bohemian* or *hippie, fair trade* stigmatized a faith-based community with strong political undertones. A stronger, edgier appeal was possible without eliminating fair trade principles, and descriptions like *renegade, rebellious, modern,* and *sexy* were more congruent with what fashion consumers demanded from fashion brands' reputations. Greenola's business model was introduced with the tag line, "Fair Trade, Sustainable Style," yet the decision was made to eliminate mention of fair trade from collateral including the company logo, website, and business cards. The tag line was updated to "Style like you mean it." The revised motto made subtle reference to

---

[10] http://www.nyigf.com/TheShow.aspx
[11] http://www.stylemaxonline.com/
[12] http://www.magiconline.com/
[13] http://www.vertcouture.com/

Greenola's mission and underscored consumption with a meaning without directly spelling out fair trade. The new message removed fair trade from the logo but did not obstruct the way the company intended to conduct business. This value was needed to advance awareness of the brand's mission.

Brand Personality

Greenola's product designs also needed to match connotations sparked by attempts to ground brand equity. Some products were inherently constructed with ethnic aesthetics due to Bolivian artisans' backgrounds, so co-ops were coached to capture the sophistication the targeted psychographic would welcome into closets saturated by more recognizable brands. Annual trips to Bolivia demanded Jen's clear communication about trends and design specifications for each season's collections. Recent collections were inspired by the graphic shapes typical in Andy Warhol pieces: Jen named the portfolio of pieces the Sedgewick Line to conjure the spirit of Edie Sedgewick's 1970s stardom. Other recent influences included warrior women, aquatics and mermaids, and serene mythological goddess. Materials, including fabrics, trims, and findings (see Appendix C), were 100% indigenous to Bolivia, so Jen relied on Pantone color forecasts to ensure color matches were on trend. Repositioning Greenola's designs to better align with its emerging brand personality heavily influenced promotional mix decisions.

The Promotional Mix

Traditional Promotion Tactics

Conventional promotional tactics characterized Greenola's early promotional mix. There was no advertising budget, and word of mouth was heavily relied upon. Jen worked to align Greenola with Chicago Fair Trade (CFT) through a business organization membership. CFT prided itself on a diversity of members across four key categories: business members, NGOs, and faith organizations and educational institutions/student groups. Greenola leveraged its CFT membership to gain credibility and access association resources and networking opportunities. CFT introduced Greenola to a variety of Chicago-owned fair trade businesses. Product sectors represented ranged from nondurables like coffee and chocolate to durable handicrafts. Business members with expertise in artisan textiles was fast-growing: apparel retailers in particular began to populate the CFT member list. Therefore, Greenola aligned its vision with the retailing community which best knew the ultimate consumer of fair trade apparel.

Trade association membership opened the possibility to use trade shows as sales channels through which to gain increased presence amongst retailers. The New York International Gift Fair (NYIGF) was held twice yearly and served as host to more than 2,800 companies specializing in "the home, lifestyle, and gift spectrum."[14] Jen attended the January event, and although she instigated relationships with new retailers, the fashion aesthetic Greenola offered as a wholesaler was not a suitable fit for NYIGF. Jen also discovered trade shows in Chicago but considered Merchandise Mart mainstays

---

[14] www.mashable.com

like StyleMax ineffective. StyleMax brought 4000 women's apparel and accessories lines to the Midwest, yet show organizers competed on cost savings to appeal to wholesalers who avoided New York prices for trade show attendance. Greenola's fair trade assortment did not fit the profile of seasoned StyleMax attendees.

On the brink of casting trade shows off as irrelevant to promotion, Jen decided to try Magic in Las Vegas. The third time was a charm where Greenola and trade shows were concerned. Magic's offerings were consistently in line with Greenola's direction as a contemporary fair trade company with modern design. Magic was held in Las Vegas each August to support retail buying seasons for the forthcoming calendar year: August was timed after high fashion trends had been presented during fashion weeks in New York, London, Paris, and Milan. Magic had a competitive edge untapped by NYIGF and StyleMax. Fair trade and eco-friendly exhibitors were dominant among the vendor list of attendees, and Magic communicated with its attendees using interactive, social media including Tumblr and Vimeo, two sites with similar objectives to Twitter and YouTube, but with more avant garde, innovative approaches to content sharing. Magic's marketing initiatives matched Greenola's emerging equity and personality, so Jen found a trade show staple in Magic.

However, back in Chicago, the promotional landscape was becoming less supportive of entrepreneurial fashion brands. CFT did not have the innovative draw Greenola needed to acquire a fashion-thirsty target segment. Retailing connections fostered through CFT membership were invaluable, but introductions to a fashion-forward segment were worthy of exploration. The City of Chicago's Office of Cultural Affairs and Tourism office sponsored an annual fashion week event each October called Fashion Focus. Chicago area designers produced runway shows, and trade associations, including Fashion Group International and Apparel Industry Board Inc., hosted industry seminars. Jen investigated the contribution Greenola might make to Fashion Focus through its supporting website, www.chicagofashionresource.com, but with steep fees and no guarantee of a fair trade-savvy audience, Fashion Focus was immaterial.

Via the Fashion Focus website, Vert Couture was discovered, and Jen thought Greenola hit its promotional jackpot. Vert Couture produced an annual fashion show in Chicago's Millennium Park. The show depended on talented designers formally trained to construct high-end garments and accessories, but unlike the Fashion Focus shows, Vert Couture was an eco-friendly fashion show. An impressive website included an "Eco-Fashion 101" page to define traits like "fair trade," "ethical trade," and "artisans." The website perfectly matched Greenola as a fair trade, social enterprise. However, impressive turned to intimidating when the designers' web page was viewed. Descriptions like "sought after" and "award-winning" were attached to designers' biographies. Bolivian artisans were Greenola's designers, so participation in a couture show didn't honor the organic community from which the garments derived. Vert Couture was evidence that Chicago's fashion community was ready for fair trade style, but Greenola's brand equity and personality were not quite red-carpet ready.

Online and Social Media Promotion

Trade associations, trade shows, and fashion events were standard communication tactics to promote Greenola, but now that Greenola was ready to "Style like you mean it," the brand also needed to interact like it meant it. Early adherence to offline tactics stimulated an urgency to penetrate into digital and social media.

Concurrently, as conventional tactics were executed, Greenola also developed profiles via social media channels including Facebook, YouTube, and Twitter. Accounts were created to demonstrate online presence, but marketing plan objectives did not match the content to be shared via each channel. Facebook (Appendix D) was positioned as a supplement to the e-commerce site. Consumers who viewed the e-commerce site were directed to Facebook, and Facebook fans were directed to www.greenolastyle.com. YouTube was integrated with both Facebook and www.greenolastyle.com. Clips focused on Greenola's fair trade vision and daily business operations but showed very little content about the artisans designing the products and how to style the products in consumers' existing wardrobes. The clips were viewed more like a reel of press releases instead of highlighting the exclusive artisan connections. The relationship between Greenola's website, Facebook, and YouTube presence was more of an afterthought instead of an ecosystem of interactivity through which to engage consumer eyes.

Greenola also had initial presence on Twitter (Appendix D), yet the profile page was rarely updated. Twitter demanded a dependable schedule of tweets and a branded point-of-view to inspire followers, so the original profile fell dormant. However, due to the modernized brand personality, Twitter was fast becoming Jen's go-to social media channel to communicate. Jen took over the Twitter account to establish her personal identity as the face of Greenola and ensure tweets were on message with the brand. With Jen as the source of tweets, the effect of messaging allowed a richer picture of the Greenola customer profile. Jen infused the Twitter stream with tweets about social entrepreneurs in Chicago, new Greenola product introductions, and personal content about herself, including family pictures of her eighteen month old son. Twitter became a unique channel to more aggressively message this personality and gain followers through Jen's social entrepreneurial leadership. Greenola's site and Facebook were promotional mix pillars, yet Jen was eager to take on more social media channels to enhance equity and show personality.

This enthusiasm led Jen directly to Pinterest, a channel considered the darling of the fashion industry's social media mavens. Pictured in Appendix D, Pinterest differentiated itself from Facebook and Twitter as a social bookmarking site, allowing users to create inspiration boards and pin online images fitting of the boards' themes. Synergy was palpable between Pinterest and Greenola from the very start of Pinterest's uptick in the social media landscape. Greenola boards were themed after new collections (like "The Sedgewick Line Inspiration"), but also imaged Greenola's social vision. Boards were created to depict "Ethical Fashion," "We Love Bolivia," and "Recycled Goodness." Jen's individual personality was shared with consumers through a board themed "Jen's Favorite Things." If Jen sustained her relatively early adoption of Pinterest, she saw considerable opportunity to consistently communicate Greenola's differentiated traits and core offerings.

The interactive visual environment stimulated by Pinterest supported the development of online lookbooks (Appendix E). Acting as a digital catalog, key items from each season's collection were styled, indexed, and described. For the most recent Segdewick Line, photographs illustrated ideas about how to wear the designs expected to be most popular. The models in the lookbook were Greenola customers who responded to open casting calls Jen posted to Twitter. The lookbook also served to introduce Greenola consumers to the Bolivian artisans. Interspersed with the Chicago model-consumer images were portraits of the women who designed the products and benefitted directly from sales. Because the lookbooks were primarily intended for use when a seasonal collection launched, the artisan pictures were also connected back to the e-commerce site for a long-term showcase of both who made the product and who wore the product.

The Decision Problem

As Jen readied Teresa for the Bolivian trip ahead, she realized Greenola was at a critical crossroads where fair trade and fashion may not mix. The triple bottom line business model was integrated and maintained for the Bolivian artisans and their communities. Modification of initial positioning and brand personality guided gains in the promotional mix. Progress was unrelenting, yet so were the choices of priorities to address if Greenola wanted to take on powerhouse fashion brand equity. If Jen continued to nurture relationships through CFT association, she stood to enhance her presence as a wholesaler in the fair trade sector. A similar outcome was likely with continued travel to trade shows like Magic. Taking an aggressive interactive presence online helped Greenola to expand from stereotypical connotations of fair trade. Greenola would humanize into its own brand personality through social media and lookbooks, while also humanizing the artisans who created the products. Conventional promotion tactics underscored Greenola as a wholesaler; digital online presence progressed Greenola as a direct-to-consumer retailer. Although each identity offered equity to both Greenola and Bolivian communities, a cohesive strategy needed to be developed. Should Greenola be a wholesaler of fair trade products that happen to be garments and apparel? Should Greenola push to be a retailer of fashion apparel which happens to be fair trade? What opportunities might Jen further address should she decide to claim both identities? How can Jen be an agile fashion brand and maintain her role as the face of Greenola? Her mind was spinning, but she knew how her time on the 10 hour plane ride to Bolivia would be spent.

Appendix A _____

Greenola's Integrated Business Model

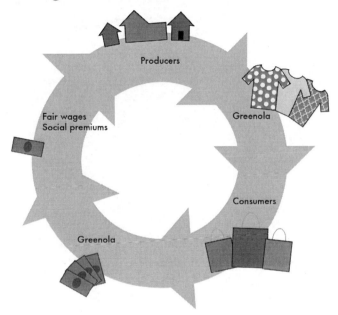

Appendix B

Strategy Canvas

Note: Factors of competition are plotted on the X-axis, and the Y-axis represents high and low quantity of each factor. The gaps between the plotted lines represent the factor on which Greenola might compete.

Appendix C

our materials

Baby Alpaca Fiber

Alpaca Fiber, also known as 'The Fiber of the Gods,' has been used to clothe royalty for over 2000 years. Alpacas are indigenous to South America, and have been farmed in countries such as Brazil, Peru, and Chile for centuries. The high-quality fleece produced by these gentle animals is rapidly becoming more and more popular across the world for some of the following reasons:

* Alpaca fiber is a lighter, softer (it does not contain lanolin) and warmer alternative to wool. It retains its thermal properties even when wet!

* Alpaca fiber is hypoallergenic (and therefore perfect for sensitive skin).

* Baby alpaca produces the highest quality alpaca fleece.

* Alpacas have a very low carbon emission, and they have a low impact on the environment they feed on. They produce a naturally organic fiber that can be knit without any added materials.

* Alpacas are said to "pay for themselves," meaning that the revenue from their fleece (which is shorn once a year) pays for their cost, allowing alpaca farmers to maintain their way of life throughout the year.

Recycled Aguayo Cloth

This colorful, handwoven Bolivian textile is traditionally used for a variety of day-to-day purposes. It is durable enough to hold groceries and carry children, and warm enough to sleep in. We use recycled scraps of Aguayo cloth to create bags, jewelery, and other unique accessories.

Açaí Seed

Although açaí berries are well-known for their incredible health benefits, their seeds are inedible. Once they are dried and polished, these seeds make beautiful beads that are either dyed with natural plant dyes or used in their natural cream color.

Tagua Nut

Tagua, also known as ivory palm, is native to countries such as Ecuador, Peru and Bolivia. After they fall to the ground, tagua nuts are harvested from the forest floor. Tagua is an ethical alternative to elephant ivory, which it closely resembles. Using tagua in jewelery helps to stop elephant poaching by creating a safe, sustainable alternative.

Appendix D

Facebook

Twitter

Pinterest

Appendix E

Lookbook: Sedgewick Line

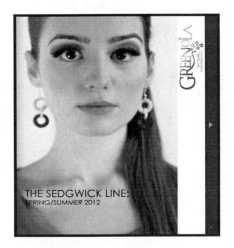

CASE
8

Häagen-Dazs®
Loves Honey Bees

BLODWEN TARTER

Golden Gate University

JACK SAUNDERS

Golden Gate University

I t was mid-summer when Katty Pien, director of the Häagen-Dazs ice cream brand in the United States, sat down to prepare for an important meeting. In a few weeks, the Häagen-Dazs team and its advertising and public relations agencies would start planning the marketing campaign for the next calendar year.

But first, Ms. Pien wanted to review the current Häagen-Dazs Loves Honey Bees (HD_HB) campaign and, quite frankly, to enjoy its run-away success. She thought back to the launch on the previous February. That was the day the company released a press announcement earmarking $250,000 in research grants to scientists studying honey bee Colony Collapse Disorder (CCD) and sustainable pollination at Pennsylvania State University and the University of California at Davis. It was the first of many moves to raise awareness of a serious environmental problem and to link the Häagen-Dazs brand with its solution.

About one-quarter of the country's winged farm workers, the common honey bee, had died the previous winter from an as-yet poorly understood malady. But this much was known: it was taking down whole hives, virtually overnight. Häagen-Dazs had a direct stake in this crisis. More than forty percent of the super-premium ice cream maker's line depends on ingredients that honey bees pollinate. But this was not just a potential strategic supply chain crisis for Häagen-Dazs. Preliminary research determined that the problem was even more far-reaching. Fully one-third of the U.S. food supply was at peril.

Häagen-Dazs had the opportunity to do something that might save the company while helping out the food chain in general. If successful, Häagen-Dazs would emerge not only with its supply chain security restored, but also with a new and timely brand association in "the green space" of sustainability and environmentally conscious business practices.

Of course, the underlying goal was to increase sales of Häagen-Dazs ice cream in an intensely competitive marketplace, but the fundamental opportunity could hold even greater consequence for future profitability. Here was the chance to marry the brand's heretofore understated reputation for all-natural ingredients with the emerging and high-profile ethic of environmental sustainability. Such a brand identity could have extraordinary value as a strategic differentiator if the consumer segment favoring all-natural ingredients also valued companies demonstrably committed to sustainable agricultural practices.

Ben & Jerry's®, a respected competitor in the super-premium ice cream category, had for years claimed a praiseworthy pro-environment corporate attitude. But the Vermont-born firm had been sold to European conglomerate Unilever, and the new parent had done little in years to capitalize on the founders' environmental beliefs. So Häagen-Dazs, even without first-mover advantage, was in a good position to trump Ben & Jerry's with an environmental intervention that was eminently concrete and practical. Häagen-Dazs would set out to bring what could honestly be construed as "health care" to the littlest farm workers in an hour of crisis.

In spite of initial skepticism within the company, HD_HB was succeeding on all fronts when Ms. Pien began to assess progress in July and to consider the brand's moves for the coming year. Sales of Häagen-Dazs ice cream were up in a category that, historically, showed no/low growth. The media and the consumers loved the support that Häagen-Dazs was providing to bee scientists. A few months in the marketplace had given the marketers the information they needed. Nearly 850 separate stories in print, TV, radio, and online described some aspect of the campaign—in its first week. Clearly, news professionals rated the initiative as something consumers would surely want to know about. Just one hundred days into the campaign, the story had racked up almost 188 million media impressions, using standard reach and effectiveness calculations.

The company had received numerous letters, emails, and phone calls from groups and individuals proposing alliances. Some were artists and entertainers, thinking about performances themed to the honey bee plight. Environmental grassroots groups and sustainability enthusiasts signed on with support. Even supermarket retailers were expressing interest in partnering on the campaign.

So planning for the coming year would begin with the sweet hint of success in the air. But first, Ms. Pien reviewed the familiar terrain of the past year. Where were they now and how did they get there?

Ice Cream Industry Background

Häagen-Dazs may love honey bees, but everyone loves ice cream. At least, according to Mintel, more than 90 percent of United States households do. The love of ice cream crosses demographic categories: people of all ages, ethnic groups, and both genders eat ice cream regularly. On average, ice-cream eating households consume a little less than three quarts (or six pints) per month. Ice cream consumption on a per capita basis is reported to have been steady from in the mid-2000s. Given the high penetration among possible consumers and the amount consumed per person, the ice cream market is described as stable, growing primarily as the population grows.[1]

---

[1] *Mintel Ice Cream and Frozen Novelties- US- June 2007* "Household Usage" section. Accessed online.

Not only does everyone love ice cream, ice cream is big business. IBISWorld estimated that, in the United States, the ice cream and frozen dessert category would exceed $9 billion in sales for at-home consumption in a recent year and require more than 7 billion pounds of milk for its manufacture, about 8 percent of the total U.S. production of milk.[2] Including away-from-home consumption in ice cream shops, restaurants and other retail sales outlets brought the total to more than $21 billion.[3]

However, consumption is seasonal. Ice cream is the quintessential warm weather treat, with sales markedly lower in the cold months of the year. In spite of efforts to counter this trend by introducing seasonal flavors, such as peppermint and eggnog, the pattern of consumption remains consistent. Because of this seasonality, promotional efforts for the category are heaviest in the spring and summer.

With the growing problem of childhood obesity and increased concern about nutrition and eating healthy, food manufacturers of traditional ice cream have another reason to worry. Hence, the industry is developing healthier versions of ice cream—light/low fat ice cream, sherbet, no sugar added ice cream, fruit sorbet, fat free ice cream and non-dairy ice cream—as well as offering frozen yogurt and soy-based confections. In recent years, the industry also has jumped on the organic foods bandwagon. *Dairy Foods* reported the introduction of 31 new organic ice cream products in a recent year, increasing to 49 in the next year.[4] This health concern contrasts with the seemingly contradictory trend towards indulgent consumption: "I'm worth it so I will eat super-premium ice cream." The majority (79 percent) of ice-cream eaters still report eating regular, premium or superpremium ice cream rather than the healthier alternatives.[5] Super-premium ice cream, generally defined as 18–22 percent butterfat,[6] is the ultimate in the indulgent category, and Häagen-Dazs occupies a prime position in that category.

Within the super-premium category, Häagen-Dazs competes head-on with Ben & Jerry's. According to Information Resources, Inc., Häagen-Dazs has a 6.6 percent market share of the total ice cream market while Ben & Jerry's has a 5.9 percent share.[7] Other super-premium brands are local or regional with substantially smaller market presence.

Consumers tend to have one or two favorite brands but will eat another brand in a pinch. Given this brand loyalty and the stagnant growth of overall ice cream consumption, any increase in market share is most likely to come from convincing ice cream eaters to switch brands. To entice consumers to choose their brand, ice cream

---

[2] *IBISWorld Industry Report, Ice Cream Production in the US: 31152*, 13 February 2008, p. 13.

[3] http://www.idfa.org/facts/icmonth/page2.cfm accessed 20 May 2008.

[4] "New Products and Marketing, Dairy Market Trends: Ice Cream's Bright Spots: Wellness, FroYo, Novelties and Private Label," *Dairy Foods*, March 2008, p. 44.

[5] *Mintel Ice Cream and Frozen Novelties- US- June 2007*, "Household usage" section.

[6] David Landau, spokesperson for the International Ice Cream Association, quoted in "Adult Appeal," Julie Cook, *Dairy Field*, October 2002. Accessed online http://findarticles.com/p/articles/mi_qa3846/is_200210/ai_n9103025

[7] Information Resources, Inc., based on 52-week sales for period ending 4 November 2007 as cited in "Private Label Drives Ice Cream," *Dairy Foods*. January 2008. Vol. 109, Issue 1, p. 70, 72.

manufacturers typically rely upon a limited set of methods. New products, whether new flavors or new formulations, are common. Price promotions and coupons are also popular. National advertising is rarely used, in part because local and regional brands have relatively small marketing budgets, and in part because national advertising is inefficient for those companies. Public relations efforts tend to focus on new product introductions and flavor sampling, or to be opportunistic. For instance, if there is a major fire, the first-responder firefighters are likely to be served donated ice cream. The margins on ice cream are thin, often less than 10 percent, so creative and cost-effective promotions are required.[8] Ice cream manufacturers must not only convince consumers to switch brands but they must also persuade their retail channels to allocate space—at the expense of other brands. Frozen food case space is very expensive in supermarkets, and manufacturers typically pay meaningful slotting fees for this category.[9]

The ice cream company and the retailer need to be very confident that they can sell more of brand X to justify the additional slotting fees and the cost of adding a new product to an already crowded freezer case. It is more difficult and expensive to expand shelf space for frozen foods than for other food categories. In most cases, physical expansion is not a realistic option, so other products must be displaced.

While more than 60 percent of the nation's ice cream is sold in supermarkets, convenience stores are growing in importance, especially for the smaller-sized packages. Ice cream parlors also are important outlets for reaching consumers, but they tend to be single brand outlets, whether national brands such as Häagen-Dazs or Baskin-Robbins® or local brands.[10]

Häagen-Dazs Background: Positioning and Target Consumers

For Häagen-Dazs, arguably the first super-premium ice cream and one of the best-known brands, distinctiveness is key. Founded in 1961 by New York dairyman Reuben Mattus, Häagen-Dazs has always distinguished itself by its exceptional craftsmanship, high quality standards and all-natural ingredients. Dreyer's Grand Ice Cream, the company that manufactures Häagen-Dazs in the United States, also sells the premium Dreyer's and Edy's® ice cream, The Skinny Cow® low fat ice cream, Nestlé® Drumstick® line of novelties, Dreyer's Fruit Bars—even Frosty Paws® ice cream for dogs. Häagen-Dazs stands alone atop this pyramid of tasty delights.

Häagen-Dazs adheres to a simple rule: absolutely nothing that is not found in the

---

[8] Mark Scott, "Ice Cream Wars: Nestle vs. Unilever," *Business Week Online*, 27 August 2007, p. 12.

[9] According to an FTC study, slotting fees for ice cream range from $2,680 to $12,682 per UPC per store, averaging $10,625 per UPC per store among the admittedly small sample of retail grocers. See Table 5, page 39, *Slotting Allowances in the Retail Grocery Industry: Selected Studies in Five Product Categories*, an FTC Staff Study, November 2003 accessed at http://www.ftc.gov/os/2003/11/slottingallowancerpt031114.pdf 9 June 2008.

[10] *IBISWorld Industry Report, Ice Cream Production in the US: 31152*, 13 February 2008, p. 9–10.

well-stocked household pantry may be used in the making of its ice cream. For example, artificial flavorings and preservatives are out under this rule as are fructose and gums. These are not "unnatural" ingredients but they are rarely found in the typical home cupboard.

Other ingredients, called "inclusions" in the trade, are selected only after exacting searches. Reuben Mattus took six years to find a suitable strawberry for Häagen-Dazs ice cream. Two particular strains, Hood and Totem strawberries, grown in Oregon, are prized for their deep red color and exceptional sweetness. They cost more, but Häagen-Dazs knows that the quality makes these strawberries worth it.

The Häagen-Dazs target consumer is best defined by attitude, rather than by demographic characteristics. The ice cream enthusiast is an ardent fan and consistent consumer of ice cream, seeking out and trying new flavors regularly. This aficionado has high standards and is willing to pay more for the best-tasting ice cream. Other target consumers are those who may not eat ice cream regularly or as frequently, but when they do, they want the very best and they are willing to spend more money for it. At $4.39 a pint, Häagen-Dazs is priced about three times higher than the average regular ice cream, which costs approximately $5.00 for a three-pint (1.5 quart) carton. Häagen-Dazs' convenient pint package allows retailers to put more flavors into the available space while consumers can think of their Häagen-Dazs purchase as an affordable, but special, treat.

More than seventy flavors make up the complete line of Häagen-Dazs branded ice cream. Consistent with the overall industry trend, vanilla flavors are the best-sellers. Recently, Häagen-Dazs had introduced the Reserve Series, its most upscale offering for ice cream aficionados, featuring exotic, gourmet flavors. Beginning with six unusual flavors, including Lehua Honey and Sweet Cream, it later added Fleur de Sel Caramel.[11]

The Idea for the Upcoming Year

Each summer, Häagen-Dazs invites proposals for the following year's marketing campaign. At the current year's "pitch" meeting for the brand's upcoming year plan, the brand management team considered a number of ideas presented by the advertising agency Goodby, Silverstein, and Partners, and the public relations firm Ketchum Public Relations. As usual, the quest was for a theme that underscored the quality message, something that would make the brand, and the company behind the brand, attractive to the upscale customer, a food and fashion enthusiast, not overly concerned about price but highly keen to enjoy the very best.

Some annual campaigns have taken a "democratic" turn, inviting consumers to propose new flavors in a contest format. A couple of years earlier, Häagen-Dazs and the Food Network created a Scoop! Ice Cream Flavor Contest. The finalists were flown to the Häagen-Dazs test kitchens where batches of their flavors were created. The grand prize winner saw her creation—Sticky Toffee Pudding—join the line of Häagen-Dazs flavors. A subsequent flavor contest, in partnership with *Gourmet* mag-

---

[11] "Häagen-Dazs Reserve: For Ice Cream Connoisseurs Only," *Frozen Food Age*, January 2008, Vol. 56 Issue 6, p.10.

azine, resulted in the Caramelized Pear and Toasted Pecan flavor, also added to the Häagen-Dazs line.

For the upcoming year, a Goodby representative floated a new idea. What about "something linked to the environment?" Specifically, what about the honey bee crisis? Honey bees suggested nature, environmental balance, health and happiness. This seemed to work with the all-natural ingredients fetish. The only trouble was: What could Häagen-Dazs do? Häagen-Dazs had no particular expertise in apiary science. Nor did anyone, even the scientists, really know what the honey bee crisis was.

It was simply known by then that the U.S. honey bee population had declined by 25 percent over the past winter, and that agricultural interests (some of them, anyway) were on the verge of panic. Almonds, for example, a $1.9 billion crop and the country's most important horticultural export, depend entirely on honey bees for pollinating the almond trees.[12] And these hard-working insects were suddenly disappearing. In the worst case, almond growers faced potential ruin. Goodby had no concrete idea how Häagen-Dazs might frame the issue to advantage, only a notion that this could underscore the brand's distinctive all-natural, quality positioning. Dori Bailey, director of consumer communications for all of the brands Dreyer's manufactures, had been casting about for ways to enter "the green space." She was at the time inventorying corporate steps on energy conservation, recycling, green facilities upgrades, etc. But so was every public relations office in the country. This was a different idea, dovetailing perfectly with the Häagen-Dazs all-natural positioning. It was a true fit as honey bees were crucial to the growth of the nuts, berries, and fruits on which Häagen-Dazs depended.

The Honey Bee Crisis

There were risks. For example, what if CCD were found to be caused by pesticides? Häagen-Dazs is not an organic brand. The cost of an entirely organic dairy product would force an increase of already premium prices at retail. The brand could not insist that its suppliers eschew pesticides, only that the "inclusions" pass standard USDA testing for health and safety. Could Häagen-Dazs take on the entire agricultural industry?

Ketchum PR suggested Häagen-Dazs form an advisory panel of bee experts, naming it the Häagen-Dazs Bee Board. Meeting with these leaders in apiary science, the team gained some comfort. Pesticides had been around for hundreds of years. There had been isolated cases of bee die-offs as more potent chemicals came into the fields, but after adjustments, the honey bees, until very recently, had done fine with the commonly prescribed doses.

But now, something had changed. Bees were deserting their hives—simply disappearing and presumably dying. Dubbed Colony Collapse Disorder, the cause was unknown. Malnutrition? Mites? Physical stress? Toxic chemicals? Disease? Some lethal combination of threats that separately didn't pose a problem?

According to the USDA more than 90 crops depend upon bees for pollination in-

---

[12] "Record almond crop forecast," *Sacramento Bee*, 8 May 2008, p. D1. Accessed online at http://www.sacbee.com/agriculture/story/921571.html.

[13] *USDA Colony Collapse Disorder Action Plan*, 20 June 2007, accessed at http://www.ars. usda.gov/is/br/ccd/ccd_actionplan.pdf 9 June 2008.

cluding apples, almonds, blueberries, cherries, and pears. That meant one-third of the United States food supply was at risk, worth $15 billion.[13] Bee-pollinated fruits and nuts are essential ingredients in more than 40 percent of Häagen-Dazs flavors, meaning the brand faced a unique strategic supply chain challenge. Typically, a business that foresees supply trouble will search for substitute materials or alternative suppliers, perhaps suppliers unaffected by a regional problem. For Häagen-Dazs, there would be no substitute ingredients. And CCD was not an isolated problem—it was appearing across the continental United States, and in parts of Canada and Europe.

But the problem also offered a unique opportunity to tie Häagen-Dazs to a cause and a legitimate focus on the environment. It required no stretch of the imagination, only some straight-forward explanation, to show how important this issue was to the future of Häagen-Dazs and how logical it was for the brand to promote awareness of CCD. No "greenwashing" here!

The Plan and Implementation

From the vague idea of "something to do with the environment", the honey bee campaign began to take shape. The Bee Board helped Häagen-Dazs understand the science of bees and the mysteries of the CCD problem. From there, the creative ideas flew fast and furious. Eventually, the team settled on a blend of traditional and non-traditional media with emphasis on community involvement. Part of the goal was to enlist everyone to help the honey bees. Häagen-Dazs wanted to raise awareness of the problem and suggest meaningful actions for people to take—while associating Häagen-Dazs with the all-natural ingredients that honey bees help create.

This integrated marketing campaign used virtually all types of marketing communications. Häagen-Dazs launched with the announcement of its $250,000 contribution to the two leading bee science centers in the country. UC Davis used a portion of the donation to fund a fellowship for a bee scientist specifically researching honey bee biology and health. A 30-second television commercial showed the tragically failed courtship of a bee and a flower set to an original operatic score. First aired on national TV, it continued to reach numerous viewers when posted on the YouTube web site.

National Geographic carried an advertorial depicting the potential impact of honey bee declines on crops across the country. Co-sponsored by the National Geographic Society, a map of the United States showed the 35 states in which key food crops were known to be at risk. An ad printed on special flower seed-impregnated recycled linen paper was inserted into selected issues of *Newsweek* delivered to subscribers. Tear out the ad, plant the paper and watch the bee-friendly garden grow! To encourage even more people to plant bee-friendly gardens, which serve as critical food sources for honey bees and other native bees, Häagen-Dazs organized a one million seed giveaway to community groups, garden clubs, parent-teacher associations and schools. If all the seeds were planted, bee habitat would increase substantially.

To use the product itself to carry the honey bee message, a cute HD_HB logo was added to the package of each ice cream flavor identified as bee-dependent. Häagen-Dazs promised to contribute a portion of the profits from the sale of cartons of bee-dependent ice cream to bee research. Buying ice cream, often considered a selfish activity, now served the greater good. While Häagen-Dazs didn't hold a flavor contest for the year the bee campaign was introduced, neither did it abandon the new flavor idea. The schedule called for introducing the new flavor Vanilla Honey Bee simultaneously with the program launch in February. Community tasting events featuring local beekeepers highlighted the new flavor and the work Häagen-Dazs was doing on behalf of the bees.

Häagen-Dazs devoted much of its resources to building the www. helpthehoneybees.com web site. Virtually every Häagen-Dazs message would include the URL of the web site where visitors could read about the CCD problem, the progress in finding a solution, and discover more ways to help. Links to the bee research institutes at UC Davis and Penn State made it easier for people to donate money directly to the research efforts. You could create your own honey bee avatar to email to friends, along with a more serious message about the honey bee crisis.

The team wanted every person in the company to be involved and committed to the cause. Engaging Dreyer's employees started with mailing a packet of seeds and a letter inviting employees to "educate your neighbors, schools, and community groups about the severe situation the honey bees and our food supply are facing," to plant a garden of bee-friendly plants, and to encourage other cause-related non-profit events with a donation of Häagen-Dazs ice cream. Dori Bailey even verified that the plants surrounding Dreyer's corporate headquarters and the production facilities that manufactured Häagen-Dazs were bee-friendly. Furthermore, the Häagen-Dazs team was delighted that Nestlé, the global food company that owns Dreyer's, supported the campaign's premise.

Convincing the sales force that HD_HB would help them sell more ice cream proved to be a more challenging task. After all, Häagen-Dazs was venturing into environmental territory that had been Ben & Jerry's domain for many years. The sales people were, at best, skeptical about the honey bee angle, an issue that few people had even heard of at the time this campaign was being formulated.

Feedback on the HD_HB Campaign— "A Genuine and Authentic Cause"

The Häagen-Dazs internal team was pleased to report that overall sales were up. Based on retailer response, the sales force had high hopes that this growth would continue. Anecdotal evidence suggested that long-sought inroads were being made among certain retailers. A Whole Foods store manager read about the HD_HB campaign in *National Geographic* and created a freezer case wrap featuring Häagen-Dazs and the "Help the Honey Bees" message. Whole Foods was a perfect fit with the Häagen-Dazs brand and this grassroots support was promising.

Consumer response was even more exciting. The Häagen-Dazs team could not keep track of the number of times and places in which the campaign was mentioned online. A Google search in early June showed over 26,000 results for "haagen dazs honey bees" while the same search on Yahoo yielded 50,000 results.[14] Independently-

---

[14] Search conducted by the first author 9 June 2008 at www.google.com and www.yahoo.com.

created videos, reiterating the need to help the honey bees, were posted on YouTube in response to the Help the Honey Bees commercial. A Dane started a Facebook group to "helpthehoneybees" and linked to the official web site. A few commentators questioned the importance of the issue or the motives of the company for highlighting the plight of the honey bees but the vast majority were positive, even enthusiastic, about Häagen-Dazs' actions. Sure, Häagen-Dazs would benefit from the exposure but this issue was serious and solving the CCD problem would benefit everyone.

The beekeeping and scientific community wholeheartedly supported the program. Without exception, they were grateful for the exposure of the problem and did not begrudge Häagen-Dazs any benefit the brand derived from the campaign. Links from the www.helpthehoneybees.com web site led to more than 100 gifts directed to the research teams at Penn State and UC Davis. A Brooklyn, NY beekeeper requested 100,000 seeds to distribute at his local farmer's market, then wrote his own press release promoting the seed giveaway and a flyer explaining the campaign. As these groups experienced the positive impact of the Häagen-Dazs name recognition, they considered more and different actions for the cause partnership.

Equally empowering, employees at all levels of Dreyer's embraced the cause. A Dreyer's employee worked with his children's elementary school in San Leandro, CA to develop a curriculum that included class presentations and a "Honey Bee Day" for planting seeds (accompanied, of course, by donated Häagen-Dazs ice cream). More than 500 students, staff, and teachers participated.

An incidental, but nonetheless gratifying outcome for the Häagen-Dazs team, was the favorable acknowledgement of the campaign by fellow marketing and public relations professionals. The San Francisco American Marketing Association chapter awarded its annual Excellence in Marketing Award for large companies to Dreyer's for the Häagen-Dazs Loves Honey Bees campaign. Advertising pundits reviewed the TV commercials, dedicated web site, and unique print ads in the trade press—and gave the team kudos for the concept, the execution, and the company's commitment to a "genuine and authentic cause."[15]

The Next Steps: The Remainder of Year One and Decisions for Year Two

New ideas were cropping up daily and new partners, both formal and informal, were taking up the issue. With all of this hoopla and increasing momentum, what should Dreyer's do? Now and in the year to come? What would the agencies suggest? What ideas did the company team have? There were so many possibilities for the Häagen-Dazs brand. How would they choose among them?

For the remainder of Year One, should Dreyer's modify the Häagen-Dazs campaign or let it run as planned? The scheduled TV and print advertising had been completed, but the team wondered if more appearances of the operatic TV commercial would be useful. Should they focus on leveraging the now-attentive interest of retailers? How could they capitalize on the sales force's newly developed enthusiasm—

---

[15] Barbara Lippert, "Häagen-Dazs Tries Beekeeping," Adweek, 5 May 2008, Volume 49, Issue 15, p. 30.

and how could they sustain that enthusiasm? What should they do about the continuing overtures from performing artists, documentary producers, and authors?

Of greater import, the team had to decide what they should do for Year Two. Should Häagen-Dazs continue to ride the wave of the heightened focus on sustainability and environmental consciousness? The campaign had momentum now. But what if people grew tired of the theme and enthusiasm waned? If the researchers could not quickly identify the cause of CCD would people grow skeptical that it could be solved and lose interest?

If the Year Two campaign continued with the HD_HB theme, should the company pull back from paid media and concentrate even more on word-of-mouth? Advertising can be expensive but the company controls the message—what is said, when, where, and by whom. Word-of-mouth and viral marketing can spread like wildfire and cost little in terms of cash outlay. However, the consumer takes control of the message, rather than the company. The reach and frequency, as well as the content and context, of the message are unpredictable. How should the Häagen-Dazs team allocate their marketing communications mix?

A new Häagen-Dazs flavor had been introduced annually for several years—and might now constitute a tradition. Is another new bee-related flavor needed? Could one be developed that would be appropriately connected to the honey bee theme?

The company knew that it wanted more people and companies to join with it to raise awareness and to stimulate constructive action towards unraveling the mystery of CCD and sustainable pollination. Häagen-Dazs had no monopoly on the issue which had truly far-reaching implications. How could they inspire even greater grassroots involvement to fund CCD research and to create more nectar-laden gardens to help honey bees survive and thrive? What about starting a non-profit through which donations could be collected and directed to further honey bee research? Could they continue to give away Häagen-Dazs branded seeds to local groups or would people tire of that approach? Perhaps a number of high-quality seed, plant or even garden supply catalog companies would be receptive to linking their name to the Häagen-Dazs brand. Might they join forces with one or more of the many farming cooperatives with crops at risk? How could Dreyer's retain the acknowledged authenticity of the HD_HB campaign and still further the Häagen-Dazs brand?

Katty Pien wondered what alternatives she and her colleagues would focus on and, ultimately, what theme and specific campaign elements they would they recommend to senior management for Häagen-Dazs in Year Two.

Appendix 1

Most Popular Ice Cream Flavors by Percentage

Ice Cream Flavor Percentage

Vanilla 26.0
Chocolate 12.9
Neapolitan 4.8
Strawberry 4.3
Cookie N' Cream 4.0
Chocolate Chip 3.8
Butter-Pecan 3.2
Chocolate Mint 3.2
Vanilla and Chocolate 1.9
Rocky Road 1.6

Source: International Dairy Foods Association. *IBISWorld Industry Report, Ice Cream Production in the US: 31152,* 13 February 2008, p. 9

Appendix 2

The HD_HB Campaign

The Campaign Logo

Häagen-Dazs loves Honey Bees

The Package Logo

Source: helpthehoneybees.com

Appendix 3

Related Web Sites

www.haagen-dazs.com
www.helpthehoneybees.com
www.dreyersinc.com
www.benjerrys.com

C A S E
9

Hi-Ho Silver: Using Metrics to Drive Integrated Marketing Communication Decisions

LISA D. SPILLER

Christopher Newport University

———————

S iobhan Werhan arrived early to work this particular Monday. It was a warm and sunny September morning and the home office of Hi-Ho Silver was already buzzing. She wanted to organize both her thoughts and her reports, as her new marketing intern was due to arrive at 9:00 a.m. Siobhan looked around her office and stole a glance at her wall clock as she began to think about the various marketing projects in which to involve her student intern. As the Marketing Director for Hi-Ho Silver, she was in charge of the multitude of marketing and advertising activities for the company. Siobhan was contemplating which of the various marketing projects would be most beneficial as a learning experience for her new protégé, Kate Stafford. Siobhan smiled as she remembered the first time she met Kate months ago at the nearby university. Kate was one of the students enrolled in the upper-level marketing course in which Siobhan was a guest speaker last semester.

Siobhan vividly recalled the eager and, yet, somewhat surprised looks on the faces of Kate and her fellow marketing students who were in the class. The students really seemed to enjoy learning about the various Hi-Ho Silver marketing programs and advertising campaigns that Siobhan and her boss, Leslie Sink, shared with the class. However, Siobhan remembered seeing how many of the students quickly became "wide-eyed" when she began detailing all of the numbers involved in evaluating each marketing program and measuring the level of effectiveness of each ad campaign. Indeed, the figures seemed a bit mind-boggling for most of the students at the time. But not for Kate. Kate was intrigued and yearned to learn more. As soon as class ended, Kate approached Leslie and Siobhan and expressed her interest and desire to become a marketing intern for Hi-Ho Silver. That's how their relationship began and

———————

Some of the data provided for this case has been disguised and is not useful for research purposes. The author would like to thank Siobhan Werhan and Leslie Sink for both their inspiration and assistance with this case project.

Exhibit C9.1: Siobhan Werhan, Marketing Director, Hi-Ho Silver

now with the new school year underway, Kate was about to get her wish to work closely with Siobhan in marketing Hi-Ho Silver.

Passionate about fashion, design, and creativity, upon graduating from Longwood University with a degree in Communication Studies, Siobhan headed to the big cities. She first worked at Urban Outfitters in Boston, Massachusetts, and then at a small art gallery in New York City. After a few years of big-city living, Siobhan returned home to the Virginia Peninsula because she wanted to work for a small company in an entrepreneurial environment. She began her career with Hi-Ho Silver about five years ago. She started working as a Show Sales Manager and travelled with the jewelry, representing Hi-Ho Silver at retail vendor exhibitions, until the company's owners realized that their small company was large enough to support an in-house marketing team. They moved Siobhan into their Marketing Department and she quickly became the leader.

An important part of Siobhan's job is to constantly gather and analyze the figures associated with and produced by the various marketing activities and use those figures to make solid business decisions. While quantitative analysis is critical to the success of any business, it is especially important for a small entrepreneurial company such as Hi-Ho Silver.

Hi-Ho Silver

Hi-Ho Silver began as a traveling store, selling products wholesale to various vendors. In 2002, Leslie and Chris Sink had the opportunity to open a small retail store operation in Newport News, Virginia, and seized the moment.

The Sinks quickly developed a "growth" business model and began opening retail stores across the Hampton Roads, Virginia, area. Today, after more than 10 years in

Exhibit C9.2: Chris and Leslie Sink, Owners of Hi-Ho Silver

Exhibit C9.3: Hi-Ho Silver
Retail Store

Exhibit C9.4: Nationally Branded Lines of Merchandise Featured at Hi-Ho Silver

business, the Sinks are experiencing overwhelming success at four different retail locations in Williamsburg, Virginia Beach, Norfolk, and their flagship store in Newport News. Each retail store is led by a manager who reports back to the home office. All administrative duties, including marketing, purchasing and accounting, are handled by the executive team lead by Chris and Leslie Sink.

Hi-Ho Silver has grown to become one of the area's largest sterling silver retailers. "It's not fine jewelry; it's not fake jewelry—it's fun jewelry," says Chris Sink. Hi-Ho Silver sells handmade sterling silver and gemstones at affordable prices, offering its customers a product that falls somewhere between the fine and not-so-fine jewelry stores. The company carries a line of silver rings, necklaces, and bracelets that can be engraved by any member of the Hi-Ho Silver staff. Its product lines include both sterling silver items and pewter-wear pieces.

Hi-Ho Silver sells sterling silver pieces sourced from Taxco, Mexico; India; Indonesia; and other international locations. Many items are handcrafted. The sterling silver items range from basic necklaces and bracelets to original pendants. In addition, the company is host to three nationally branded lines, Chamilia, Kameleon, and Honora.

Chamilia is a collection of very fashion-forward handmade beads that may be purchased individually to create a special bracelet or jewelry piece. The line includes a wide variety of sterling silver beads, Murano glass beads, Swarovski crystal beads, and 14k gold beads that can provide an immediate sense of "personalized style" to anyone's jewelry collection.

Kameleon is a flexible line of jewelry that has interchangeable "pops" that can be placed in any of its carriers. Kameleon's base jewelry designs include pendants, necklaces, rings, earrings, bracelets and other accessories. What makes it an interchangeable line are the inserts called JewelPops, which are available in an assortment of designs and literally pop in and out of the base jewelry to match any person's mood and wardrobe.

Honora is a branded line of freshwater pearls. For more than 60 years, Honora has been in the business of value and quality in the jewelry industry. The company is the largest importer of freshwater pearls in the United States and astonishing cultured pearls to create the very best jewelry.

Hi-Ho Silver began carrying the Chamilia beads in 2006 in response to consumer interest. Since that time, the category has exploded in sales. Leslie Sink declares, "Chamilia constitutes a strong percentage of our sales, simply because it gets customers to come back again. It's viral. Not only do customers return for self-purchases, but they also buy gifts for others and get friends and family to come in and buy gifts for them. Lots of new customers have come to us by way of the Chamilia line."

Customers

Hi-Ho Silver customers are primarily middle-aged females who are financially secure. The following data will provide a glimpse of the profile of typical Hi-Ho Silver customers:

- 97% are female.
- 82% are 36 years old and above, with 57% being 46 years old and above.
- 73% have an average household income of $51,000 and above.
- 40% read women's or cooking magazines, such as *InStyle, Lucky, O, Cooking Light,* and *Food & Wine.*
- 41% listen to Alternative and Contemporary music stations in the Hampton Roads area (*101.3 2WD, 93.7 Bob FM, 92.9 The Wave*).
- 73% describe their jewelry style to be Classic and Traditional.
- 58% are on Facebook.

Siobhan regularly conducts customer surveys to gather pertinent data in order to better serve Hi-Ho Silver customers. The survey findings also are used to determine new or continued marketing strategies. For example, information about radio station preferences is compiled to better understand which radio station Hi-Ho Silver customers are listening to, and, thus, which radio stations should be considered for radio advertising allocations. Research also has uncovered the fact that Hi-Ho Silver customers both budget for and actually spend considerably more money when purchasing for gifts for themselves and gifts for family members ($50) as opposed to the amount spent ($30) for nonfamily gifts. Finally, research shows that Hi-Ho Silver customers rank "Quality of Product" and "Price/affordability" as the two most important factors when purchasing jewelry. Siobhan uses customer research whenever possible to help create store promotions and determine the most effective advertising strategies. This attention to customers is paramount to Hi-Ho Silver's business success, and it is what differentiates the company from its competitors.

Both Chris and Leslie Sink recognize that the success of their business depends wholly upon their ability to go above and beyond customer expectations. In fact, the customer is so much in the forefront that, as Leslie says, "We think about them morning, noon and night. At the end of every conversation, every financial, marketing and sales meeting, the question we always ask is: How will this impact our customers?" Leslie also declares, "That regardless of Hi-Ho Silver's phenomenal growth, we want to remain personable, and will bend over backwards to meet the customer."

Customer service functions as the underlying value that guides everything the Sinks do in their business. They strive to find new, fresh, exciting and affordable products for their customer, while maintaining their singular focus on making the customer happy. More important, this belief of "taking care of the customer" doesn't stop with the Sinks. This attitude permeates the culture of the entire Hi-Ho Silver community. Employees are empowered to do whatever it takes to meet and exceed this high customer service standard. This level of customer service is what gives Hi-Ho Silver its competitive edge in the jewelry industry.

The Jewelry Industry

There are many market options available to the consumer for purchasing jewelry and gemstones at retail. The 16 stratified retail markets range from Ultra fine Guild or Provenance-type retail jewelers, well-established good public image retail jewelers, and large retail chain-type jewelers; to the jewelry Artisan/jewelry designer retailers, competitive, independently owned retail jewelry stores, and department stores with leased jewelry departments; to discount stores with jewelry departments, antique dealers, auction houses and online retail jewelers; to cruise ship sellers, kiosk jewelry sellers and pawn shops.[1] Indeed, the retail jewelry market is highly competitive, offering consumers many options to fit their needs, wants, and budgets.

National Jeweler magazine reports that the majority of jewelry-only retailers (79%) are small, independent, family-run businesses that are highly competitive in their local markets; while the remaining (21%) are "majors"—including national and regional chains and online retailers.[2] There are about 28,000 specialty stores selling jewelry in the United States, resulting in annual revenue of approximately $30 billion. This industry is highly fragmented with the top 50 jewelry chains accounting for less than half of the total revenue, 25% of sales revenues and the majority of profits are generated in the fourth quarter, with 25% of annual jewelry sales transactions occurring in December.[3]

The jewelry store industry has lost some of its sparkle in recent years. IBISWorld es-

---

[1] Retail Jewelry Market Analysis, Association of Independent Jewelry Valuers, January 19, 2011. <http://www.seoprofiler.com/analyze/independent-jewellery-valuers.org>, Retrieved June 5, 2012.

[2] Jewelry StoresIndustry Overview, Profile America, 2008, <http://www.immediate.com/images/Jewelry%20Stores.pdf>, Retrieved June 5, 2012.

[3] First Industry Research Report, 2010, <http://www.fastbusinessplans.com/sample-business-plans/jewelry-store-kiosk-business-plan.html?start=3>, Retrieved June 5, 2012.

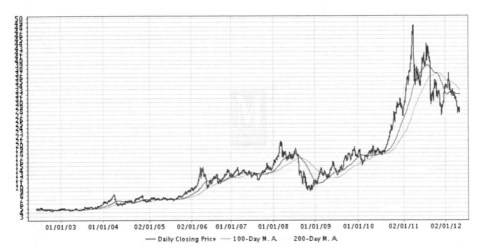

Exhibit C9.5: 10-Year Historical Daily Closing Prices of Silver
(Source: Monex Precious Metals)

timates that revenue has declined at an average annual rate of 1.3% to $29.7 billion during a recent five-year period of.[4] Overall, jewelry stores sales revenue declined 7.5% in 2008 and experienced its biggest drop ever in 2009, following a 25.5% decline in consumer confidence in 2008. However, since 2010, sales revenue has increased slightly each year.[5]

The industry is not projected to return to a steady growth mode because many consumers are still not comfortable spending their incomes on discretionary luxury items during tough economic times. However, as consumers regain confidence and purchasing power over the next few years, industry growth should accelerate.[6] It is expected that some jewelry stores will take the lead, while others will follow. Which jewelry stores will lead may be determined in part by the product lines and items the jewelry store sells.

Included in the definition of a "jewelry store" is the criteria that these retailers sell new jewelry, new sterling and plated silverware and new timepieces.[7] Is there a difference between sterling silver and plated silver? And, does it really matter? Absolutely. Pure silver is relatively soft, very malleable and easily damaged, so it's combined with other metals to produce a more durable alloy. *Sterling silver* is 92.5% silver and 7.5% copper. *Silver plate* is a thin layer of silver bonded through an electrical process, applied to a base metal.

---

[4] Jewelry Stores in the US: Market Research Report, IBISWorld, <http://www.ibisworld.com/industry/default.aspx?indid=1075>, Retrieved June 5, 2012.

[5] Ibid.

[6] Jewelry Stores in the US. Quarterly Earnings Report. By Retail Analyst Nikoleta Panteva. May 2011, <http:// www.ibisworld.com/mediacenter/pdf.aspx?file=Jewelry...Report...>, Retrieved June 5, 2012.

[7] Jewelry Stores in the US: Market Research Report, IBISWorld, May, 2012, <http://www.ibisworld.com/industry/default.aspx?indid=1075>, Retrieved June 5, 2012.

Those jewelry stores specializing in fine sterling silver jewelry have had to endure skyrocketing silver costs while trying to maintain competitive and attractive prices to satisfy conservatively spending consumers. As shown in Exhibit C9.5, according to Monex Precious Metals, the price of silver has increased dramatically over the past decade, rising from approximately $5.00 per ounce in 2003 to more than $28.00 per ounce in 2012, with prices spiking to nearly $48.00 per ounce in a recent year.[8]

Competition

Hi-Ho Silver has several direct competitors, which are small, privately owned stores comparable to Hi-Ho Silver. These retailers carry similar items, including some of the same branded lines of jewelry. Let's briefly examine each primary competitor.

1. *The Mole Hole.* Hi-Ho Silver's largest competitor is The Mole Hole, an upscale boutique carrying a variety of jewelry, clothing, gift and home furnishings and luxury products at affordable prices. Similar to Hi-Ho Silver, The Mole Hole has four locations around the Hampton Roads area, three of which are in the exact same shopping centers as the Hi-Ho Silver retail stores. Although The Mole Hole offers home and décor items in addition to jewelry, the company carries Kameleon, a branded line also featured in Hi-Ho Silver stores, as well as Pandora, which is a direct competitor to the branded line Chamilia carried by Hi-Ho Silver. The close proximity of The Mole Hole to Hi-Ho Silver makes it a formidable competitor.

2. *Simply Selma's* and *The Silver Box..* These two retailers are small boutiques located in the Hampton Roads area that carry similar products and branded lines to those of Hi-Ho Silver. These retailers feature sterling silver jewelry, tableware items, and fashion jewelry. However, each of these companies operates a single retail store, and these are not physically located in the same shopping areas as Hi-Ho Silver stores.

   Hi-Ho Silver also has a few indirect competitors. These competitors offer alternatives to purchasing jewelry items from Hi-Ho Silver retail stores. Let's now overview each secondary competitor.

3. *Silpada Designs.* Silpada is a company that features a wide variety of high-quality sterling silver jewelry. The company doesn't have a physical retail store but sells its hip and classic jewelry via a network of Silpada Designs Representatives who showcase and take orders for Silpada jewelry at informal parties and events hosted by people throughout the community. The hosts are offered free jewelry and sizeable discounts for agreeing to host a party and invite their friends to shop. You can also order directly from the Silpada Designs website.

4. *Pandora and Chamilia.* These branded lines are in direct competition with one another as the Pandora and Chamilia charms are interchangeable and fit onto each other's bracelets. These companies may also be considered indirect com-

---

[8] Monex Precious Metals, <http://www.monex.com/prods/silver_chart.html>, Retrieved June 4, 2012.

petitors to Hi-Ho Silver because customers can order their jewelry items directly from their online websites.

5. **Mass Retailers.** Mass chain retail stores such as T.J. Maxx and Stein Mart may offer similar sterling silver jewelry, including Pandora-style beads and charms, at extremely competitive prices. Although these mass retailers offer great value, their jewelry supply and selection is limited.

Hi-Ho Silver's Marketing Challenges

As with most small entrepreneurial businesses, the biggest marketing challenge for Hi-Ho Silver is to spend its limited marketing budget in the most efficient and effective manner possible. That is precisely what Siobhan is about to discuss with Kate, who has just arrived for her first day of work as a marketing intern. Siobhan wants Kate to comprehend how each marketing decision is made based on careful examination of the respective quantitative data available. This decision process begins with understanding the marketing and advertising budget limits within which they are to market. Exhibit C9.6 reports Hi-Ho Silver's mass media advertising expenditures.

EXHIBIT 6: MASS MEDIA BUDGET

Mass Media Expenses:

Newspaper	$ 6,000
Radio	5,000
Television	12,000
Total	$23,000

Exhibit C9.7 reports the company budgets for marketing activity expenditures on an annual basis.

EXHIBIT C9.7: MARKETING BUDGET

Marketing Expenses:

E-blasts	$ 4,000
Trunk Shows	3,000
In-store Events	2,000
B-Day coupons	2,000
Thank you cards	1,000
Total	$ 12,000

Having a limited budget encourages precise measurement of each and every advertisement and promotional activity in order to determine if the respective return on advertising investment (ROAI) deems the advertisement or activity is profitable and worthy of repeating or not. Siobhan shows Kate two data tables and provides the following example: "Let's say we spend all of the budgeted expenditures for mass media and marketing and we project to achieve $1 million in sales. That means that we will obtain a ROAI of 3.5 percent. How did we calculate that? Based on the data contained in these tables, $35,000 is the total budgeted promotional expenses ($23,000 + $12,000) divided by $1,000,000 (which is our projected sales for the period).

"Mathematically, that generates a 3.5 percent return on our promotional investment." (See Exhibit C9.8.)

EXHIBIT C9.8: RETURN ON ADVERTISING INVESTMENT CALCULATION

$$\frac{\$35,000}{\$1,000,000} = 3.5\%$$

In addition, the ability to make comparisons between the Return on Advertising Investment (ROAI) of one ad versus another is important to be able to make smarter future marketing investments. Siobhan goes on to explain to Kate that *getting the biggest bang for your marketing buck* is of paramount importance for a small entrepreneurial business. "*Shark marketing on a minnow's budget* is the goal here," explains Siobhan. Now that Kate understands the gravity of the budget, Siobhan continues explaining to Kate how to measure and assess each marketing program and activity.

Cooperative Advertising Allowances (Co-ops)

"Each one of the nationally branded product lines that Hi-Ho Silver carries offers a cooperative advertising agreement where each brand will share in the cost of our advertising whenever we feature one of the respective brands in our ads," explains Siobhan. "Really?" Kate exclaims. "That's one sure way to stretch an advertising budget." "Yes, but the challenge is that each advertising co-op is different and you must know how to calculate the way to maximize the value of each co-op," answers Siobhan. Exhibit C9.9 provides the stipulations associated with each co-op.

A challenge often faced by Hi-Ho Silver is determining which branded line should be featured in which advertisements so that the maximum amount of co-op dollars

---

EXHIBIT C9.9: COOPERATIVE ADVERTISING AGREEMENTS

Chamilia—Credit will be applied up to 50% of the cost of each media purchase. Cannot exceed $40,000 annually.

Honora—Will pay up to 100% of media and advertising costs. Cannot exceed 5% of yearly purchases.

Kameleon—Will pay up to 50% of pre-approved advertising costs. Cannot exceed 2.5% of yearly purchases.

can be used to defray the cost of the advertisement. For example, if Hi-Ho Silver's yearly purchases of Honora jewelry in 2012 are $300,000, then the co-op cap for Honora is $15,000 for the year. If Hi-Ho Silver wants to run a television campaign and feature Honora, the cost of the television commercials is about $20,000. Therefore, since that cost exceeds the cap for Honora, Hi-Ho Silver might select another line to be featured, or else pay the additional $5,000 for the television spots. The number crunching conducted beforehand is tied to the fact that some caps are based on a percentage-of-sales figure, while others are a fixed amount. Siobhan constantly manipulates the numbers within each co-op criteria to determine smarter marketing decisions.

Hi-Ho Silver's Marketing and Advertising Activities

Hi-Ho Silver employs a wide variety of marketing and advertising strategies that include both offline and online tactics. Offline marketing strategies include in-store events and signage, special offers and sales promotions, direct mail, telephone marketing, print advertising and public relations. Online marketing strategies include a robust website, e-mail blasts, blog posts, online ads and social media.

Many of the company's promotional strategies are database-driven by its customer loyalty program, the .925 Club. The name, ".925" represents .925 silver which is an indicator that the jewelry at Hi-Ho Silver is the highest quality sterling silver possible. This is why most Hi-Ho Silver items are stamped '.925', to certify the 92.5 % silver content.

Hi-Ho Silver's .925 Club

The .925 Club is another one of Siobhan's responsibilities and is one that she takes very seriously. "The customer database is only usable as a marketing medium if it contains valuable customer data that has been updated and maintained over time," Siobhan says, as she explains the .925 Club to Kate. "Customer data must be collected, segmented, analyzed and then used to target select customers or groups of customers with promotions that match customer interests and desires. We collect customer data when customers sign-up for our .925 Club. We then create a customer record by keying that data into our database. The data we collect includes customer name, contact information (to include both telephone number and email address) date of birth, spouse name (if applicable) and customer interest to include the specific brand or type of jewelry the customer desires." (Please see Exhibit C9.10 for an example of a customer record.)

Siobhan continues, "Based on an analysis of the customer data, such as the date of our customer's last transaction (recency); how often they shop in one of our retail stores (frequency), and how much they spend (monetary), we can determine our most valuable customers based on a Recency-Frequency-Monetary (RFM) assessment. The RFM analysis enables us to assign each customer a 'Loyalty Number' that is recorded in each customer record. Determining the value of our customers helps us to spend our marketing budget most effectively by communicating more often with our more valuable customers who generate greater profitability for our company."

Customer ☒

Customer: 000000000   Customer Since: 02/23/2004   Loyalty No:

First: Hi Ho   M: Last: Silver

Day Phone: 757-591-8912   Ext: DOB: 09/03/2004

Email Address: Company Name:

Address: 705 Middle Ground Blvd

City: Newport News   St: VA   Zip: 23606   Country: USA

Alt Search:

Primary Associate: ☑ Mailing List

Spouse Name:

Spouse Last Name:

Interest

[Addresses] [More] [Misc] [Sales History] [Q and A]   [Apply] [Ok] [Cancel]

Exhibit C9.10: .925 Club Customer Record

Hi-Ho Silver also segments its .925 Club customer database in order to enable its marketing communications to target different customers. The ways Hi-Ho Silver segments its customers include the following:

1. Top sales customers in the last 120 days
2. Top Honora customers
3. New customers in the last month
4. Customers who spend more than $100 within a year
5. Customers who spend more than $200 on necklaces within a year

Hi-Ho Silver uses the database to send targeted, tailored and timed communica-

Exhibit C9.11: Hi-Ho Silver $10 Birthday Cards

Exhibit C9.12: Chamilia Trunk Show Postcard and Sidewalk Sale Postcard.

tions to its customers. For example, on a monthly basis the company sends $10 birthday cards to customers who have spent $100 within the last year. As shown in Exhibit C9.11, these birthday cards can be redeemed at any of its four retail store locations.

Hi-Ho Silver also uses its database to promote specific products and events via email blasts and postcards that are mailed to those customers for whom the company does not have an email address. Two examples include: Chamilia Trunk Show post-

Exhibit C9.13: Membership Benefits of .925 Club

Exhibit C9.14: Miss You Postcard

cards that were sent to just Chamilia customers because of their history in purchasing Chamilia brand items; and a Sidewalk Sale postcard that was mailed only to Newport News retail store customers only as the sale was location-specific. (See Exhibit C9.12.)

As shown in Exhibit C9.13, in order to keep .925 Club members active and encourage repeat purchases Hi-Ho Silver strives to enhance or "upgrade" the benefits members receive.

Club members now receive their 6th pair of earrings free, along with free engraving of purchased items.

"We believe communicating new benefits to our .925 Club members is important to strengthen our relationship and give them 'more reasons to shop often' thus increasing the frequency with which they shop, which in turn will generate greater profitability," explains Siobhan. Kate asks,

"How often do you upgrade the .925 Club benefits?" Siobhan replies, "As often as we can, and if you have any new ideas of what more we might offer our .925 Club members to provide greater value to them, I'd love to hear them!"

Siobhan continues with her explanation, "We also analyze our customer data in order to discern which customers have not shopped in our stores in the past year. We then use that information to mail 'Miss You' postcards to these inactive customers to encourage them to shop with us."

"We track the response that we get on our 'Miss You' mailings to determine whether the 'Miss You' campaign is productive or not. Here again, crunching and analyzing the numbers associated with this campaign provides great insight," Siobhan noted. (See Exhibit C9.14.) "For example, we recently mailed 'Miss You' postcards containing a special 20% discount offer to 536 inactive customers. In response to that mailing 29 coupons were redeemed and generated $2,208.18 in sales, for a net profit of $304.91. More important than the profit earned was the fact that 29 of those 536 inactive customers are now active again," Siobhan boasts.

"So the 'Miss You' campaign is effective in saving lost customers," remarks Kate. "Yes, but just think, the average order for those 29 customers was $76.14 (based on the $2,208.18 sales generated) and if each customer spends an additional $76.14 in the coming year at one of our Hi-Ho Silver retail stores, that will generate even greater profitability," replies Siobhan. She continues, "If each of those 'saved' cus-

**EXHIBIT C9.15: MISS YOU POSTCARD CAMPAIGN
RECENT YEAR RESULTS**

Month	Postcards Mailed	Postcards Redeemed	Sales Generated	Mark Down Dollars	Cost to mail postcards	Gross Profit
Jan	491	21	$1,050	$ (210)	$294.60	$ 545
Feb	486	49	3,725	(758)	291.6	2,675
Mar	495	25	1,402	(256)	346.5	800
Apr	479	58	3,463	(692)	335.3	2,436
May	498	87	5,201	(1,063)	298.8	3,839
June	490	22	1,320	(248)	294	778
July	499	25	1,250	(250)	299.4	701
Aug	468	23	1,379	(275)	289.2	815
Sept	482	18	1,009	(201)	289.2	519
Oct	477	32	2,100	(420)	286.2	1,394
Nov	495	79	4,356	(897)	297	3,162
Dec	462	102	6,129	(1,226)	277.2	4,626

tomers spends only one-half of that amount, the incremental sales generated would still be more than $1,000."

Kate is impressed. "Wow, using a customer database to maintain and strengthen relationships with customers is certainly an important marketing activity," she concludes. "Yes, and the uses of a customer database are limited only by your imagination and your ability to crunch the numbers," asserts Siobhan. "We are constantly trying to analyze the numbers to determine how to convert more inactive customers back to active status again."

"We also track and compare our monthly response rates on our 'Miss You' mailers," explains Siobhan. "Interestingly, the response rates vary considerably by month and we haven't precisely figured out why that is the case. This is an area that requires additional analysis—that's for sure," concludes Siobhan.

"Look Kate," Siobhan says as she holds up a spreadsheet. "Here's a table that contains the data from our recent 'Miss You' Postcard Campaign. Do you see the monthly fluctuations? We need to better understand the impact that timing has on this promotional campaign. For example, if we analyze several years of our Miss You campaign data and determine that year-after-year the response rates and sales generated on the postcards are higher during given months, perhaps we should reexamine our distribution strategy and distribute the cards during specific months, or, perhaps on a quarterly basis instead of monthly. Just think, we might send five months' worth of postcards out in May and mail seven months' worth in December; if we think it would provide a larger return on our campaign investment. I'd like to have you help me streamline the entire 'Miss You' campaign," declares Siobhan. (See Exhibit C9.15.)

"One more thing to consider is that we might want to test various timing options associated with our 'Miss You' campaign," asserts Siobhan. "You see Kate, testing ad-

Exhibit C9.16: Ad Note

vertising and promotional campaigns before rollout to all of our customers is another way we use math and metrics to determine strategy. Direct mail campaigns are perfect for testing since we can select random samples and establish control groups and test groups. Of course, we are not limited to direct mail tests, because we can test almost any promotional campaign and media format. Just more food for thought."

Print Advertising Campaigns

Siobhan opened a large file marked "Most Recent Print Ads" and addressed Kate. "Kate, at Hi-Ho Silver, we need to track, measure and analyze the impact and profitability of each and every advertising campaign. Because Hi-Ho Silver is a small business, we have to spend our advertising dollars wisely. Let's examine a few of this past year's ad campaigns and I think you'll understand precisely the importance of measuring the return on advertising investment (ROAI) associated with each ad campaign."

Ad Note. Siobhan explains, "In this campaign we wanted to advertise to new and existing customers in the local area. We wanted our ad to reach a broad audience across the entire Virginia Peninsula in order to promote two of our retail stores. We decided to use an *ad note* with the local newspaper." An ad note is a small sticker that is placed on the front page of the newspaper and that can be peeled off without damaging the newspaper.

Ad notes offer a powerful front-page top position that truly catches the reader's attention. (See Exhibit C9.16.) "Each ad note was a coupon to receive a 30% discount on an entire purchase at either the Williamsburg or Newport News Hi-Ho Silver stores," clarifies Siobhan.

Geographically Targeted Ads. As Siobhan picked up a couple of print ads and showed them to Kate, she continued, "We often place ads in specific publications to

Exhibit C9.17: Geographically-targeted Advertisements

target customers in a select geographic areas for one of our retail store locations. These two ads are similar in layout and design, however they have a different offer, objective and geographic target market. The first ad was designed specifically for *Beacon* Readers who reside in Virginia Beach and read that particular publication, while the second ad was placed in the Williamsburg edition of the local newspaper and promotes our New Town store in Williamsburg. Both of these ads were measured and analyzed to determine their effectiveness." (See Exhibit C9.17)

"Kate, notice how the two discount offers vary," Siobhan challenged. "Think about the various reasons why we might offer a larger discount in one geographic area versus another. Think also about the impact that the discount offer has on our profitability. Once again, this is where we need to grind some numbers in order to determine the response rate needed on each offer in order to break even on each geographically-targeted advertisement. Of course, we would have to take into account the larger discount in our profit analysis."

"Finally, we can conduct a ZIP Code market penetration analysis for each geographically targeted advertisement by training our store sales associates to collected each customer's ZIP Code area whenever a coupon ad is redeemed at one of our stores," declared Siobhan. "By calculating the market penetration by ZIP Code area, we can determine which areas are more likely to respond to our offers, enabling us to more effectively and efficiently target these customers with future advertisements. In

EXHIBIT C9.18: GEOGRAPHICALLY-TARGETED ADVERTISEMENT ANALYSIS

ZIP Code Area	Pieces Mailed	Responses	Market Penetration % [Response/Mailed]
23451	5,793	60	1.04
23452	2,735	33	1.21
23454	6,731	136	2.02
23456	4,341	119	2.74
23461	7,212	240	3.32
23462	3,308	92	2.78

Exhibit C9.19: Banner Advertisement

addition, market penetration analysis allows us to be selective and mail to only those geographic areas that contain prospective customers who are likely to be receptive." As Siobhan shows Kate a report containing a table detailing market penetration data for a direct mail campaign for the Virginia Beach store, she asserts, "You can see that some ZIP Code areas are clearly more receptive to our offers than others." (See Exhibit C9.18.)

Unlike decades ago, today's marketing world is chock full of figures and statistics that must be analyzed on a regular basis. In carrying out the marketing activities at Hi-Ho Silver, Siobhan finds herself constantly analyzing data—and that has only increased in recent years given the rise of digital and social media marketing activities.

Digital and Social Media

Siobhan picked up another file labeled "Most Recent Online Ads" and began browsing through its contents as she noted, "Much of our promotional focus is online these days. As you can imagine, this has changed from a decade ago when Hi-Ho Silver first opened its retail stores."

Banner Ads. "We create many banner ads such as this one" Siobhan states as she holds up a printed example of an ad banner for Kate to examine. "This banner ad promotes the Chamilia branded line. Notice that this banner ad is time sensitive and encourages immediate action with the words 'Click Here' emphasized in bright red." (See Exhibit C9.19.)

"If you are about to ask whether we track and measure our banner ads, don't bother, because you already know the answer is *yes,*" Siobhan declares to Kate. "But, think for a minute how the measurement of an online ad is different from that of a print advertisement. One thing that I am doing on a regular basis is comparing our banner ad metrics, such as click-through rate, with industry averages and national averages. The rate, in and of itself, is somewhat meaningless without having some basis for comparison. For example, we might compare click-through rates, open rates, conversion rates, or the amount of time spent on one banner ad with results of another. Comparison data usually offers good insight for strategic marketing decision making," concludes Siobhan.

E-Mail Blasts. "We also send out many e-mail blasts to select customer segments," Siobhan notes as she holds up two colorfully printed e-mails to show Kate. "These e-mails are promoting two of our nationally branded lines. The first promotes the Chamilia brand, and it was sent to all of our Chamilia customers. This email offered select Hi-Ho Silver customers an opportunity to have an 'Exclusive Sneak Preview' and be the first to own the new Swarovski Collection created by Chamilia." She continues, "This second e-mail blast example features a creative Kameleon compact that

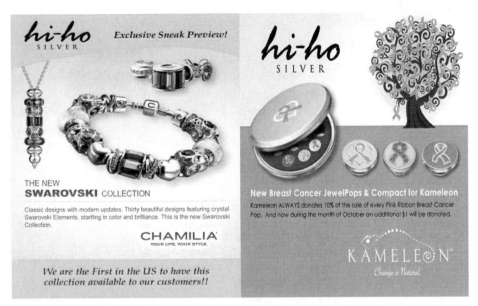

Exhibit C9.20: E-Mail Blasts

also promotes breast cancer awareness. We sent this e-mail to all of our Kameleon customers." (See Exhibit C9.20.)

"Here are the campaign statistics for the Kameleon e-mail blast," states Siobhan as she holds up another report. "We sent out 9,479 emails, 2,060 were opened, which represents a 18.4% open rate; 76 recipients clicked through the email, which represents a .7% click-through rate; and 13 people unsubscribed. As with every e-mail blast, we have to analyze the statistics and determine whether the e-mail met its established objectives."

"In addition to creating banner ads and sending out e-mail blasts, we have to monitor our website and social media conversations constantly and be prepared to respond to customer requests and questions in a timely fashion," noted Siobhan. "Kate, follow me over to my computer so I can better explain to you our digital and social media marketing strategies." With a few quick clicks of her mouse, Siobhan is ready to begin her online show and tell presentation and turns to face Kate who is now looking over her shoulder.

Social Media. "We use social media to promote our four retail stores and our .925 Club," professes Siobhan. "We want people to join our Hi-Ho Silver social network and loyalty program so that we can better serve our current customers and expand our customer base." Siobhan turns and faces Kate and nods, "Here's our 'Welcome Landing Page.' Notice how we encourage visitors to enter their e-mail address and join our Hi-Ho Silver community. We offer landing page contests two or three times per year." (See Exhibit C9.21.)

Next, Siobhan shows Kate the Hi-Ho Silver Facebook page. "We started our

Facebook page in October, 2009 and within three months we had 500 fans," claims Siobhan. "Today, we have more than 6,000 fans. We offer our fans monthly giveaways and new posts on a daily basis." (See Exhibit C9.22.)

"We track and analyze each product that we feature in our daily posts to determine if the post may have had an impact on its sales," reports Siobhan. "For example, we record the quantity sold of each product in the week prior the post, as well as the week following the post. Sales figures vary according to the featured product, but again, it's the comparison analysis of the 'before and after' that is important." (See Exhibit C9.22.)

Siobhan explains, "Some of our online posts include giveaway posts and 'sneak peek' posts. The 'sneak peek' posts are designed to arouse curiosity among our social

Exhibit C9.21: Welcome Landing Page

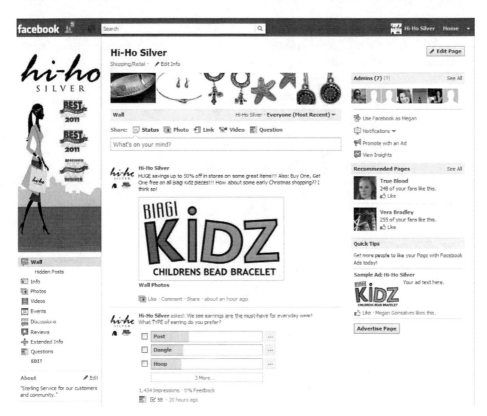

Exhibit C9.22: Facebook Page

network community and offers our customers a chance to see the new product lines and items that will be coming to our retail stores ahead of their appearance. For example, Siobhan says as she holds up a printout of a web page, "Here's a post that provides a sneak peek of a new line of products that our buyers recently picked out in Atlanta. We posted this in January and yet the products were not available for sale in our stores until May." (See Exhibit C9.23.)

Kate shakes her head and marvels, "There are so many different marketing activities, how do you manage to keep up with all of them?" Siobhan replies, "This is only a fraction of what my job of marketing Hi-Ho Silver entails. I haven't shared all of the different in-store promotions and publicity activities for which I am responsible. But, let me mention just one more important program, and then we'll stop there for this morning and move onto tackling some of the marketing challenges with which I'm counting on your assistance." As Siobhan picks up another folder from her desk, she turns to Kate and says, "The final program I'd like to share with you is our charitable donations, which is a form of public relations, and is how our company remains socially responsible in its business operations."

Hi-Ho Silver

A new line our buyers picked out in Atlanta!!! Coming this spring, just in time to celebrate our 10 year anniversary!!

734 People Reached · 11 People Talking About This

Like · Comment · Share · January 19 at 10:55am

Exhibit C9.23: Sneak Peek Posts

Charitable Donations

Siobhan explains, "The Sinks wholeheartedly believe in giving back to the community in which they live and work, therefore, they have challenged each of their four retail stores to donate $500 in products each month to support community charitable events. This requires each retail store manager to maintain good records of the charity, cause or organization to which it donates and I am tasked with overseeing the entire charitable giving program." Siobhan continues, "I often write press releases to support our involvement with a charity and that is good public relations for our company. For example, here's a recent press release that I wrote (as Siobhan selects a page from the folder) announcing that Hi-Ho Silver donated 696 pounds of food to local area food banks." Siobhan reads from the press release, "The donation is a result from a promotion the weekend of November 4th that asked its customers to donate non-perishable food items to any Hi-Ho Silver location in order to receive a 25% discount."

"Okay Kate, so you are likely wondering how I might track and measure the impact that these charitable donations have to the success of our business, right?" challenges Siobhan. "Let me state just a few facts on that subject. First, how many different people do you think see and hear the Hi-Ho Silver brand whenever we make a donation of a necklace and matching bracelet set to a local school? If 200 people attend that school's auction, then there are 200 people hearing about how Hi-Ho Silver supports its local community. Let's say that 5% of those people attending the auction come into one of our retail stores that following week and make a small purchase of a $20 item. That's $200 in sales right there and that doesn't take into account all of the goodwill that is generated by the good deed of the donation itself."

Kate is again shaking her head. "Unbelievable! I think it's outstanding that the Sinks are so dedicated to giving back to the community in such a big way. It is simply amazing given that Hi-Ho Silver is just a small retail jewelry store operation." "Yes, I agree," replies Siobhan. "In fact that's one of the reasons I truly love working at Hi-Ho Silver."

"Now, let's tackle those marketing challenges I have on my plate at the moment and let's see what new successes you can help bring about in marketing Hi-Ho Silver," Siobhan says to Kate. "Shall we?"

Case Challenges

Decision 1: Determine Effective Uses and Allocations of Cooperative Advertising Agreements

Siobhan is always trying to determine which nationally branded products should be featured in which types of media. Part of that determination flows from researching the different kinds of media expenditures each branded co-op will cover, but part of it lies in the maximum usage of the allocated co-op budgets. For example, some companies will not cover online media such as Web ads or e-blasts. Other lines, such as Chamilia, will also run specials and provide co-op dollars for an event. So, Hi-Ho Silver has had to quickly plan, organize, and schedule a Chamilia Promotion or Special Event just to be able to utilize the allotted co-op dollars. If you were Siobhan's marketing intern, what suggestions might you provide to help her be more proactive and efficient in the use of co-op advertising dollars?

Decision 2: Improve the Hi-Ho Silver Customer Loyalty Program

Siobhan is always striving to improve Hi-Ho Silver's .925 Club. While the database marketing strategies she has undertaken thus far with .925 Club members have been very successful, might there be more that she should be doing? For example, she wonders if there might be additional ways to segment the customer database in addition to the five she has shared with Kate. If so, what other segmentation strategies should she employ? What additional customer data might Hi-Ho Silver collect in order to better serve its customers? What additional incentives or benefits might Hi-Ho Silver offer to its .925 Club members?

Decision 3: Revise the Miss-You Campaign on the Basis of Response-Rate Analysis and Recommend a Campaign Test Strategy

Calculate the response rates for each month of the Miss You campaign. What months have the highest and lowest response rates? Based on your assessment of monthly response rates, what might you conclude about the timing of the mailers? What recommendations would you make for revising the Miss You campaign? How might you implement a test strategy to determine the optimal timing for distribution of the Miss You postcards?

Decision 4: Prospect For New Customers on the Basis of Market Penetration Analysis

Based on the market penetration data provided in the case, think about the various reasons why Hi-Ho Silver would offer a larger discount in one geographic area versus another. Think also about the impact that the discount offer has on the company's profitability. Based on the market penetration data, which ZIP Code area would you recommend targeting to prospect for new Hi-Ho Silver customers? Why?

Decision 5: Enhance and Expand the Social Media Marketing on the Basis of a Cost/Benefit Analysis of Current Digital and Social Media Strategies

Social media continues to grow at a rapid pace. Hi-Ho Silver is currently active with Facebook, but has not pursued any other social networks. Recently, Siobhan has been wondering if Twitter, LinkedIn and Pinterest might be worth exploring and joining. She knows that any of these social networks can easily be linked to the current Hi-Ho Silver Website. Should she begin using any of these social networks or is Facebook enough? What's the cost/benefit analysis to joining a new social network? She realizes that if Hi-Ho Silver joins any new social networks, each network must be constantly monitored, managed and updated. If she decides to go ahead and have Hi-Ho Silver join one more social network, which one should it be and why? Also, how should she get started and what offers should Hi-Ho Silver make to get people to connect and engage with Hi-Ho Silver?

Conclusion

As Kate's first day as a marketing intern at Hi-Ho Silver ends, she converses with Siobhan as they walk to their cars in the parking lot outside of the Hi-Ho Silver office complex. "Well Siobhan, I sure learned a great deal today. Thank you." Siobhan replies, "Oh yeah, and what was the highlight of what you learned?" "Well, I now understand that marketing in today's world is all about the numbers." Siobhan responds, "Well, marketing isn't *all* about the numbers, Kate. I agree that number-crunching is critical to determine effective marketing strategies. However, don't forget that it takes solid critical thinking skills to know *what* aspects of a marketing campaign to evaluate; *which* numbers to include in an assessment, *when* and *how* to analyze the data, and *what* action should be taken on the basis of the data analysis. But, I'm glad you like to crunch the numbers, Kate, because you will definitely have an opportunity to do so in almost any marketing career path you ultimately choose. You did a great job today." "Gee thanks," Kate replies with a smile. "I'll see you in the morning Siobhan, and thanks again for all of the hands-on marketing lessons!"

Case Questions

1 What new offers would you extend to strengthen customer relationships and encourage repeat sales for *regular* Hi-Ho Silver customers?
2. What might you offer to entice *prospective* customers to visit a Hi-Ho Silver store and purchase some fun jewelry?
3. What might be some appropriate non-profit organizations with which Hi-Ho Silver should affiliate? Why?

CASE
10

Kiln Creek Golf Club & Resort: On Par for An Integrated Marketing Communications Campaign to Acquire New Members

LISA D. SPILLER
Christopher Newport University

CAROL SCOVOTTI
University of Wisconsin-Whitewater

J amie Connors arrived early at the golf course to play a quick nine holes before work. It was a pristine April morning—warm and sunny. The well-manicured greens sparkled as the rising sun reflected off the morning dew. He was confident that an early round would help him clear his head before tackling the mounting marketing issues affecting Kiln Creek Golf Club & Resort (hereafter referred to as KCGC&R or 'the Club'). The annual meeting with the board of directors and the Club's membership was fast approaching.

As usual, Jamie played very well. Then again, great rounds were *par for the course* for the head golf pro of the facility. He birdied the ninth hole and headed back to his office in the clubhouse. Along the way, he saw the first group of the day preparing to tee off on the first hole. He recognized two of the foursome as members who play a few times a week. "Looking good, Jamie," one of the members cheerfully exclaimed as he pointed to the lush fairway that lay before him. Jamie smiled and agreed with great pride. After all, this course was his baby. As he thanked the golfers and wished them luck, he thought of the irony of the marketing challenges he faced. The Club had a challenging, picturesque 18-hole golf course with driving range, practice putting green, chipping green, tennis courts, swimming pool, clubhouse, gourmet restaurant,

Some of the data provided by the company has been disguised and is not useful for research purposes. The authors would like to thank Jamie Conners for his help in this project.

day spa and inn nestled within a planned community with nearly 3,000 private homes, townhomes, condominiums and apartments. Running a facility of this quality was a golf pro's dream. Despite the quality of the facilities and its convenient location for almost 15,000 nearby residents, club memberships were down. Even with its "open to the public" policy, fewer non-members were playing individual rounds of golf. Jamie was confident that if he could persuade golfers to try the course, the experience would cause them to come back again. The problem was drawing them into the facility.

A Rochester, New York native, Jamie has considered golf both his passion and profession for his entire life. In college, he discovered he had a talent for teaching and coaching. Now a 22-year member of the PGA, Jamie's career had progressed from golf coach for a Florida-based university, to teaching pro at a country club in New York, and instructor at both ESPN Golf and Golf Digest Schools.

The opportunity at KCGC&R was his first in the leadership role. When he arrived three years ago, Jamie saw the entire resort as a diamond in the rough. Everything needed work, but he was confident that with the proper vision and management, the Club could become a thriving facility within the community. He established three priorities that the board of directors accepted. First, the entire golf program from the course itself to the clubhouse, pro shop, and cart garage, needed work. Second, all the other services and facilities needed to be upgraded and/or integrated to enhance the value of membership. Third was marketing. Jamie believed that he had to have a strong product before marketing it.

It took two years, but the first and second priorities were well on their way to being addressed. As the members on the first tee observed, the course was in great shape. The same went for the tennis courts, restaurants, pool, and day spa. What was missing were people. Despite the growing popularity of golf in the area and around the country, memberships and use of KCGC&R facilities continued to wane. Something had to be done to get this facility back on track. It was time to address Jamie's third priority—marketing. The board had been patient, but he was concerned that patience was wearing thin.

Kiln Creek Golf Club & Resort

The Kiln Creek Golf Club & Resort was established in 1991 to provide residents throughout the Hampton Roads, VA area with a recreational club with state-of-the-art amenities. The facility contained a professionally rated 18-hole golf course, pool, fitness center, tennis courts, and a day spa. The club also had a restaurant and lounge for dining and socializing with friends and neighbors as well as rooms for hosting catered events.

The Club was located in the middle of the Virginia Peninsula in Newport News, Virginia, just 30 minutes from the beach and 20 minutes from historic Williamsburg. The Newport News/ Williamsburg International Airport was just minutes away by car, making the facility an easy-to-reach destination.

In addition to all its recreational facilities, KCGC&R included a beautifully remodeled Inn and tastefully decorated restaurant, banquet and meeting rooms. It offered

"Stay-and-Play" get-away packages and hosted numerous weddings and other special parties, events and gatherings.

Since its inception, KCGC&R had hosted more than 5,000 functions. Its banquet and event facilities boasted a Grand Foyer and breathtaking views from the ballroom. Whether a meal with a couple of friends or a party for 350 people, the Club strived to provide patrons with a stress-free, memorable experience.

The facility included:

- 18 Hole, Par 72 Championship Golf Course
- Full Service Golf Pro Shop
- PGA Professional Staff
- Meeting and Banquet Facilities
- Manchester Grill—a casual dining restaurant serving breakfast, lunch and dinner
- 14-Room Hotel overlooking the Golf Course
- Outdoor Swimming Pool
- Outdoor Tennis Facility
- Day Spa
- Fitness Center

KCGC&R initiation and monthly membership fees differed according to the membership category. Membership packages varied based on the number of people joining, facilities that could be used, and where the member resided. The Club offered specific membership packages for individuals and families, residents and non-residents of the Kiln Creek community, as well as specially priced packages for other membership categories. Exhibit C10.1 details the various categories along with their associated rates and fees.

Additional services and amenities for Club members, guests and non-members included golf carts, driving range balls, locker rental and club storage. Exhibit C10.2 lists these services and amenities along with their respective fees.

EXHIBIT C10.1: KCGC&R MEMBERSHIP CATEGORIES AND RATES

Membership Category	Initiation Fee	Monthly Dues	Food & Non-Alcoholic Beverage Minimum
Full Family Golf	$2000	$262	$30
Single Golf	$2000	$223	$30
Senior Golf Family	$2000	$223	$30
Active Military Family	$1000	$223	$30
Weekday Membership Single	$900	$168	$30
Swim/Tennis/Social	$500	$95	$30
Non-Resident Membership	$500	$65	-None-
Junior Sports	$100	$70	-None-
Corporate Membership	$5000	$620	$120

EXHIBIT C10.2: ADDITIONAL KCGC&R SERVICES

18 Holes Guest Play	Monday-Thursday	Friday	Saturday-Sunday
Guest of Member	$37	$40	$48
Non-Member Public	$45	$52	$59
Cart Fees	18 holes—$17.00	9 holes—$9.00	
Driving Range Balls	Member—Free	Non-Member—$7.00	
USGA Handicap Service		$30 annually per member	
Club Cleaning & Storage		$100 annually per member	
Locker Rental		$100 annually per member	
Locker Rental and Club Storage Combined		$150 annually per member	

The products and services offered by the KCGC&R Pro Shop were consistent with other pro shops in the area and included a wide variety of clubs, accessories and clothing. The professionally trained staff at the Pro Shop offered many services to assist golfers in improving their games. In addition to private lessons, golf clinics, and junior golf camps, golf professionals offered club-fitting services. The typical $60 fee was waived with the purchase of a set of golf clubs. The Club also offered several unique packages for members that organized group golf events. Exhibit C10.3 details three available packages.

Although the Club had a variety of recreational facilities, it was first and foremost a golf resort. According to *Golf Digest,* the resort's 6,972 yard, par 72, 18-hole course was rated as one of the five best courses in Virginia. *Tee Time Magazine* recognized the course as one offering the best par 4 holes in the Mid-Atlantic region. The club had hosted the Executive Women's Golf Association two years previous, and held both amateur and professional golf tournaments on a regular basis.

The Golf Industry

Golf is referred to as the "unofficial" sport of the business world (Golf, 2005) and, up until the most recent recession, had been a thriving industry. Recent U.S. Census indicated that there were approximately 12,000 public, semi-private, and private courses across the country with combined annual revenue of about $21 billion. About 25 percent of these courses were owned by non-profit entities such as municipalities, while the vast majority were for-profit facilities. Greens fees represented the largest single source of revenue for private and semi-private courses (about 33 percent), with cart fees, golf lessons, handicapping fees, initiation fees, and pro shop product sales accounting for the remaining 67 percent (First Research, 2010). Greens fees accounted for more than 60 percent of public course revenue.

While facilities and amenities varied significantly within the industry, there were three general categories of golf courses. 'Private' referred to facilities for the exclusive use of members, and typically offered extensive ancillary facilities. 'Semi-private' offered facilities used by members as well as the general public. KCGC&R was considered a semi-private facility. Depending on the available facilities of the club, members

EXHIBIT C10.3: KCGC&R OUTING PACKAGES

Caddy Package:
- Available weekdays anytime
- 18 holes of golf with cart
- Custom-made golf cart signs with player names
- On-course contests
- Unlimited use of practice facility one hour prior to start of event
- Cash only Beverage Service on course
- Post tournament scoring by professional staff
- Par Buffet

Amateur Package:
- Available weekdays anytime, weekends after 1 p.m.
- 18 holes of golf with cart
- Custom-made golf cart signs with player names
- Professionally staffed bag drop
- On-course contests
- Unlimited use of practice facility one hour prior to start of event
- Cash or Master Bill Beverage Service on course
- Post tournament scoring by professional staff
- Create your own menu

Pro Package:
- Available any day at any time
- 18 holes of golf with cart
- Custom-made golf cart signs with player names
- Professionally staffed bag drop
- On-course contests
- Unlimited use of practice facility one hour prior to start of event
- Cash or Master Bill Beverage Service on course
- $4.00 per player in merchandise gift certificates
- "Beat the Pro" Contest (winner receives one complimentary weekend stay at the Club)
- Unique menu customized by the resort's Executive Chef

had access to amenities based on membership type, while the public typically paid a higher fee and could only play golf. 'Public' courses were open to anyone and generally focused strictly on golf. Over the past 50 years, the number of private clubs had decreased substantially, down from 62 percent of all courses in the 1950s to only 27 percent in 2005 (Fore, 2008).

According to the National Golf Foundation (2010) the number of rounds played in the previous three years decreased 0.1 percent, 1.8 percent, and 0.6 percent respectively. This decrease was attributed to both the economic recession and the decrease in the number of "core golfers" who played eight or more rounds per year. Ten years previous, core golfers were estimated at 17.7 million. Four years previous, that figure decreased to

EXHIBIT C10.4: TOP U.S. MARKETS FOR GOLF

Rank	Designated Market Area (DMA)	% of Households that Play Golf	Index (Base = 100)
1	Green Bay—Appleton, WI	25.5	151
2	Grand Rapids-Kalamazoo—Battle Creek, MI	24.0	142
3	Minneapolis—St. Paul, MN	23.7	140
4	Sioux City, IA	23.7	140
5	Palm Springs, CA	23.4	138
6	Ft. Myers—Naples, FL	23.3	138
7	Lansing, MI	23.2	137
8	Traverse City—Cadillac, MI	23.2	137
9	Mankato, MN	22.9	136
10	Wausau—Rhinelander, WI	22.8	135
127	Norfolk, Portsmouth, Newport News, VA	15.2	90
210	Greenwood—Greenville, MS	7.5	44

15 million. The main reasons why people left the sport included the amount of time it took to complete a round, rising costs, and pursuit of other interests.

The decrease in the number of core golfers and rounds played caused 39 of the nearly 4,400 private golf clubs and 800 of the 7,600 semi-private and public courses across the U.S. to shut down between over the previous two years. Another 389 were forced to open their doors to the public (Brinkley, 2010). Median gross golf fee revenue was nearly flat at −0.2 percent nationally in September of the previous year, compared to the year before that. To slow this decrease, some courses had reduced the minimum number of golfers for group rates as well as decreased prices on golf outing/lunch combinations (Schmidt, 2009).

Golfer Demographics & The Newport News Area

There were an estimated 19 million-plus U.S. households where one or more members played golf (SRDS, 2008). As seen in Exhibit C10.4, of the top 10 golf markets, eight were located in the Midwest. The Norfolk, Portsmouth, Newport News (also known as Hampton Roads) designated market area (DMA) ranked 137th out of 210 markets nationwide in golf play.

There are discernable differences between the demographic and lifestyle indicators of the typical U.S. golfer and the residents of Hampton Roads. Exhibit C10.5 compares key demographic data of the golfing population versus all residents of the Hampton Roads DMA while Exhibit C10.6 denotes lifestyle differences.[1]

---

[1] Psychographic data reflects 73 distinct activities measured in the *Lifestyle Market Analyst Report* published annually by Standard Rate and Data Services.

EXHIBIT C10.5: SELECT DEMOGRAPHIC DATA—
U.S. GOLFERS & HAMPTON ROADS DMA

Demographic	U.S. Golfer	Hampton Roads DMA
Median Adult Age	50.4 years	48.3 years
Marital Status		
Single Male	21.9%	21.5%
Single Female	9.4%	23.7%
Married	69.4%	54.8%
Home Ownership		
Owner	79.0%	65.1%
Renter	21.0%	34.9%
Median Income	$70,638	$50,430
Credit Card Usage		
Travel/Entertainment	22.4%	13.6%
Bank Card	86.8%	80.6%
Gas/Department Stores	27.0%	20.3%
No Credit Cards Used	9.3%	16.0%

EXHIBIT C10.6: COMPARISON OF TOP 5 LIFESTYLES—
U.S. GOLFERS & HAMPTON ROADS DMA

Lifestyles	U.S. Golfers %	Index	Rank	Hampton Roads, VA DMA %	Index	Rank
Snow Skiing	16.1	230	1	5.9	84	67
Tennis	13.9	224	2	6.5	105	27
Wines	34.5	184	3	19.1	102	37
Stock/Bonds Investments	34.9	175	4	22.0	111	12
Boating/Sailing	17.1	175	5	12.4	122	2
Real Estate Investments	16.0	172	8	11.1	119	3
NASCAR	18.0	148	22	15.1	123	1
Our Nation's Heritage	9.5	142	26	7.9	118	5
Bible/Devotional Reading	24.8	107	72	27.3	118	4

Local Competition

Southeastern Virginia had a multitude of private, semi-private, and public golf courses. Within a 25-mile radius, there were five private clubs KCGC&R considered its primary competition. James River Country Club was a private, full-service country club situated on the James River in Newport News. It too offered an 18-hole golf course with picturesque river views. It also housed a world-renowned golf museum in its clubhouse. Membership in this club was quite exclusive and the application process included submitting two letters of recommendation or sponsorship from current members.

Kingsmill Resort & Spa was also located along the James River in nearby Williamsburg. It offered three championship golf courses designed by Pete Dye, Arnold Palmer, Tom Clark and two-time U.S. Golf Open champion Curtis Strange. Renowned for great golf, Kingsmill positioned itself as a full-service resort, offering 425 posh guest rooms and suites, a restaurant, and an elaborate spa. It focused its marketing efforts on attracting conferences that included group golfing packages.

Also in Williamsburg were Ford's Colony Country Club and Golden Horseshoe Golf Club. Located on a hill of 3,000 acres of beautiful countryside in Williamsburg, Ford Colony had two golf courses, restaurants and a full-service pro shop. Golden Horseshoe Golf Club offered 45 unique holes of golf. It was one of the top 75 golf resorts around the world, with a rating of 4.5 stars by *Golf Digest*. It also had a full-service pro shop and offered memberships to those who resided within a 75-mile radius. The initiation fee was $5,000 with annual family dues of $4,320 or annual individual dues of $2,895.

Cypress Creek was located in Smithfield, across the James River from Newport News and Williamsburg. It offered an 18-hole golf course also designed by Tom Clark and Curtis Strange. In addition to competition provided by the area country club and resorts, there were a number of public golf courses in the area that offered golfers the opportunity to pay on a daily basis to enjoy either nine or 18 holes of golf. These courses did not require membership.

Previous KCGC&R Marketing Efforts & Challenges

Promoting and building the golf program continued to be the main focus for Jamie and his staff. Ideally, Jamie hoped to attract new members to KCGC&R who would utilize all of the Club's amenities. New member acquisition might be a bit challenging due to the poor economy and all of the local competitors that were vying for golfers. However, Jamie felt strongly that if people came and played the KCGC&R course a few times, they would fall in love with it and join the Club.

Jamie and his assistant, Tyler, had been discussing their marketing strategies. They reviewed the following key facts about KCGC&R:

Reputation and Member Retention

The Club had an excellent reputation among its highly satisfied members. Its annual membership retention rate was approximately 80 percent. In addition to the normal attrition due to the Hampton Roads area military relocations, the sluggish economy had negatively affected its rate of obtaining new members. Most golfers seemed satisfied to use a "pay as you play" approach to golfing—as opposed to joining a golf club or resort and paying both initiation fees and monthly membership dues.

Target Customer

While the KCGC&R customer could conceivably be anyone in the vicinity, the demographic profile of an existing member was a professional between the ages of 30 and 60, with an interest in golf. Interestingly, only three percent of the current members resided in the Kiln Creek community. Despite the high moving rate in the area caused by a significant military population, Jamie thought that the Kiln Creek residential community held an untapped base of prospects.

Unique Selling Point

KCGC&R currently promoted itself as a country club experience. Its positioning statement, *"The country club lifestyle is within your grasp,"* implied that KCGC&R provided members with country club living at a more affordable price. Initiation and dues comparisons with the nearby country and golf clubs suggested that KCG&R was a good value for the money.

Previous Recent Marketing Activities

In the past year, KCGC&R had purchased an advertising schedule on Cox Cable Television that ran for 16 weeks, reaching approximately 12,000 households. The budget for this television campaign that promoted the temporary elimination of the new member initiation fee was $5,000. By its conclusion, the campaign had generated more than 30 inquiries, with 20 new golfers playing the course, and a total of five new KCGC&R memberships.

The club also had a member referral program and had relied on its staff to promote memberships on a person-to-person basis, but these activities had not been overly effective. Otherwise, KCGC&R had not been proactive in promoting the Club to attract new members. Jamie and Tyler needed to address this immediately.

Although the Club had not been proactive in membership marketing, Jamie had tried several promotions to generate awareness and entice people to come and play the course. He placed a small-space advertisement in a neighborhood publication with a circulation of 1,200, targeting Chamber of Commerce members in the surrounding area and emphasizing "Resort Golf without the Resort Fees." The ad offered a special 18-hole golf game rate of $30 for golf during the week and $40 for the weekend (golf cart included) to attract newcomers to try the course. This ad cost $600, garnered a 9 percent response rate, and worked well to generate 108 new golfers to try the course.

Another promotion to generate play was a special game rate offer of $35 for 18 holes (golf cart included), extended to 7,500 members of the Virginia State Golf Association. The cost of this promotion was $900, and it achieved a 2.5 percent response rate, and again was effective in getting new golfers to visit KCGC&R.

A final promotion to generate golfers involved an advertisement offering a golf school with a well-known golf professional at a nominal fee of $20 per two-hour lecture. It was exposed to approximately 18,000 individuals. More than 400 golfers signed up for the school and each was offered a free round of golf at KCGC&R at the conclusion of the lecture. All participants were also invited to sign up for a one and one-half day golf clinic—with 56 golfers accepting and participating. At the conclusion of the golf clinic, these golfers were given a golf card entitling each to return for three free rounds of golf with up to three additional golfers at a special discount rate of $25 each. The cost of this promotion was $7,200, and it achieved a 2.3 percent response rate. Again, it was effective in getting prospective golfers to visit the KCGC&R facility.

With the exception of the television campaign, marketing efforts to date had focused on getting people to try the course. What Jamie discovered through these efforts was that conversion to membership didn't happen naturally. He wondered if conversion had to be its own effort, or if it could be integrated into the campaigns and media he was already using.

KCGC&R Location: The Villages of Kiln Creek

When Jamie first came to KCGC&R, he recognized that its location was both a significant problem and an opportunity. The Club was nestled in an upscale planned community comprising 31 distinct neighborhoods or villages, and 2,918 residences.

The Kiln Creek community was beautifully landscaped, and featured miles of winding bike and jogging paths, social and recreational activities, and an active homeowners association.

With so many residents, strong support of the neighborhood Club could be expected. However to date, less than three percent of the homeowners (70 families) were currently members of the Club. Although KCGC&R was available to the residents, it was not affiliated with the Villages of Kiln Creek and was not automatically included as an amenity for its residents. Interestingly though, the Kiln Creek Neighborhood Homeowners Association promoted KCGC&R as an amenity available to residents, on its web site.

While the Club had an excellent reputation among its highly satisfied members, it had a distant relationship with the homeowners association. Part of this strained relationship was due to strong petitions from the Neighborhood Homeowners Association for the Club to curtail its interests in rezoning and developing a parcel of land previously used for golf, into a residential area. Since 1998, the Homeowners Association bylaws no longer allowed additional villages within Kiln Creek, and this potential new residential development would not be directly affiliated with the currently established Kiln Creek Villages. Therefore, the new residents would not be subject to the Kiln Creek covenants, rules and restrictions nor would they pay annual assessments like the current residents did.

The land rezoning issue was only part of the discourse between the Club Owner and the Homeowners Association Board. Jamie had been informed that the officers of the Homeowners Association Board had made it difficult for the owner to promote the Club for years.

This strained relationship was not good for anyone—the Club or the residents. Prior to the current Club ownership, the previous owners had allowed the golf course to become an eyesore for the neighborhood, which led to a poor golf course reputation. Much had changed in the past decade and the current owner/entrepreneur invested heavily in the KCGC&R and revitalized the golf course. It was now in everyone's interest to move forward and encourage the thousands of Kiln Creek residents to support their local neighborhood club facility.

Where to begin? Jamie thought current Kiln Creek residents who were club members might help the Club establish relationships with other residents. Given the persuasive power of word-of-mouth marketing, he was confident that an innovative referral program would work. How should such a program be structured? How should he reward members for their participation? Also, given the limited number of resident members, even stellar results from such a program wouldn't boost overall membership that much. More would need to be done. He considered various options.

Decision 1—Improve & Build the Relationship with Residents of the Kiln Creek Villages & its Homeowners Association

KCGC&R needed to remediate its relationship with the homeowners association to attract residents to the Club. Jamie knew he must create an attractive offer for the residents of Kiln Creek, but with 31 separate neighborhoods (known as villages) with condominiums, apartments, townhouses and single family homes for diverse demographics, he was not sure of the structure of the offer. Also, should he develop more than one offer? How should the community be segmented? What should be included in the offer(s) for Kiln Creek residents given that they already had a park, tennis courts, clubhouse, and pool facilities as amenities of ownership?

If he decided to go this route, he would also have to determine a promotional strategy including creative approach and media mix. How might sales promotion, perhaps special events, fit into the overall strategy? Jamie's career experiences taught him that whatever strategic direction he and his staff chose, success would depend on consideration of each and every detail.

Decision 2—Acquire More Members beyond Kiln Creek with an IMC Campaign

The Villages of Kiln Creek was an obvious starting point. Where else should Jamie focus his marketing efforts? KCGC&R might benefit from an integrated marketing communications membership drive. Jamie thought he might rent some lists to target specific prospects to get them to come to KCGC&R and play a round of golf. But, what lists should he rent? What demographic profile should he target? As the area's Lifestyle Market Analysis report indicated, golf is not a top draw in Newport News. What should his offer be in this campaign? He also questioned whether a campaign could both attract players and convert members. Marketing efforts to date were good at the former but not the latter.

Another consideration that crossed his mind was targeting businesses to purchase corporate memberships. The facilities were perfect for small business meetings tied into rounds of golf. That would boost the banquet and perhaps the Inn business. Then again, he didn't know if that was trying to accomplish too many things at once.

Summary

So many possible directions! Jamie knew the tasks before him were formidable. The poor economy and the continuing battle with the homeowners association weren't helping matters. The trick was finding the option(s) that best fit his $20,000 a year marketing budget and the know-how of his staff. The board of directors and members meeting was fast approaching. He wanted recommendations he could confidently present that successfully addressed the issues at hand.

Jamie parked his golf cart and headed to his office. Time to grab a quick shower and then get to work. That beautiful course needed more traffic and he was committed to generating it.

Case Questions

1. How should Jamie prioritize his prospecting strategies? Who should be his target market?
2. What media mix should Jamie utilize given his $20,000 marketing budget and the desired prospective customer segments which he was interested in attracting to the Club? How should he allocate this budget between prospect generation and member conversion?
3. What type(s) of special events could Jamie plan at the Club to promote a stronger relationship with the residents of the Kiln Creek villages? How might these be structured to be effective in generating both golfers and new members?
4. How would you suggest obtaining information to help build the KCGC&R prospect database? Should Jamie investigate renting lists of prospective golfers? If so, what segmentation profile should he pursue? What lists and list selects would be potentially effective?

References

Brinkley, Christina, 2010. Admitting Jeans to the Club, *Wall Street Journal*, May 27.

First Research, 2010, Golf Course Industry Profile including Statistics, Trends and Analysis from First Research, February 22, 2010. http://www.first research.com/industry-research/Golf-Courses.html. Retrieved March 22, 2010.

Fore, 2008. View Beyond the Verandah, *Golf Advisory Associates.*

Golf, 2005, http://www.spiritus-temporis.com/golf/social-aspects-of-golf.html, Retrieved March 23, 2010.

Golflink,com, 2009, "How Many People Play Golf in the USA?" http://www.golflink.com/facts_6246_many-people-play-golf-usa.html

IBIS World USA, 2010, Golf Courses & Country Club Industry Research in the U.S. by IBIS World Industry and Company Research Reports and Information, January 13, 2010, http://www.ibisworld.com/industry/default.aspx?indid=1652. Retrieved March 22, 2010.

National Golf Foundation, 2009. National Rounds Played Report, https://ngf.org/cgi/research.asp Retrieved June 1, 2010.

PGA/NGCOA, 2009, *PGA PerformanceTrak News*, October 29, 2009. Retrieved March 23, 2010.

Schmidt, Edward Jr. 2009. Sour Economy No Game-Breaker for Golf, *Meeting News*, 33 (4), March 9, 30.

C A S E
11

McDonald Garden Center

CAROL SCOVOTTI

University of Wisconsin-Whitewater

LISA D. SPILLER

Christopher Newport University

I t was a wintry morning, and Pat Overton, Marketing Director for McDonald Garden Center (MGC), had arrived early to review the coming year's marketing plan. There were several nagging concerns she just couldn't get out of her mind. "So much to do, so little time," she thought to herself. "You'd think that after 37 years in this business, I'd have seen it all. We offer the best products and personalized service. Our prices are competitive with other specialty garden centers. Yet each year, we lose more customers to the big box stores. This job just isn't getting any easier."

She sat back in her chair and surveyed the greenhouse adjacent to her office. Rows of dirt-filled trays were coming to life with tender, green seedlings. It wouldn't be long before those seedlings would start sprouting the fresh buds of spring. With the first flowers came the customers. It was her job to see that those customers kept coming.

Pat couldn't stop thinking about the decisions that had to be made . . . allocating the media mix . . . the future of the rewards program . . . growing the customer base. She decided to take a walk through the network of greenhouses and clear her mind before meeting with her promotions coordinator, Sherry Connell, and the team of associates that assist with marketing activities. Decisions would have to be made soon to be ready for the spring selling season.

The Company

MGC was founded in 1945 as a single retail garden center in Hampton, Virginia. Today it serves the entire Hampton Roads area from its original store as well as two additional retail locations. The Virginia Beach store on Independence Boulevard at Haygood is near a high-income neighborhood on a busy thoroughfare with high visibility. The Chesapeake location is on Portsmouth Boulevard on the west side of the city. Although this area is still somewhat rural, city expansion is moving in that direction. (See Exhibit C11.1 for a map of the area.)

Each retail location operates as a strategic business unit and profit center (also see Exhibit C11.1). Its web site, www.mcdonaldgardencenter.com, serves as an information

EXHIBIT C11.1: ORGANIZATIONAL STRUCTURE OF MCDONALD NURSERIES CORPORATION AND HAMPTON ROADS MAP

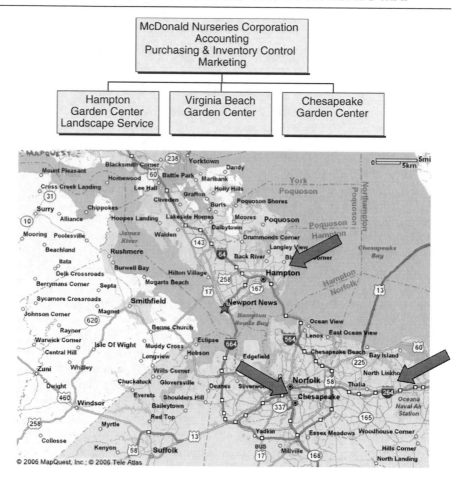

and communication resource for the organization, offering advice, promoting workshops and seminars, and highlighting products. Given the perishability of the plants, there is no option to purchase products online.

The company is owned and operated by Eddie Anderson, a man with a passion for gardening who's dedicated to his customers and staff. Eddie and his crew strive to make MGC the premier garden center in Hampton Roads, offering a wide variety of high quality products and services that enhance the lifestyle of customers for all seasons. MGC focuses on providing customers with the most informative, enjoyable, and successful shopping and gardening experiences possible.

Pat Overton describes herself as being "older than dirt" when it comes to marketing the garden center. Sherry and the staff refer to her as a guru. She's been in the industry since long before many of them were born. Eddie calls Pat and Sherry the dynamic duo and respects their zeal to know who the customers are and what they need. In this industry, strong customer relationships are critical to staying in business.

The MGC Retail Customer

MGC serves both commercial and residential customers. The commercial business serves landscapers and is managed by a separate group from the Hampton location. The typical retail customer is female, 35 to 65 years of age, with a mid-to-upper income. Customers are well educated, married with families, and own their homes. They also tend to be active (busy), civic-minded individuals who enjoy outdoor living and take great pride in their homes and gardens. MGC customers admit they willingly pay more for products because of the added value from the personalized service they receive.

Within the retail side of the business, MGC segments its residential customers by the types of products purchased. These sub-segments include:

- **Collectibles**—Collectors of unique items like Department 56 Villages and Snowbabies.
- **Outdoor Living**—Purchasers of patio furniture, fountains, statues and other outdoor decorations.
- **Indoor Plants**—Purchasers of houseplants and potted items.
- **Color Plants**—Purchasers of annuals and perennials for outdoor gardens, typically do-it-yourselfers.
- **Seed and Mulch**—Typically men who purchase lawn seed, fertilizer, peat moss, mulch, garden rock, etc., for home use.
- **Outdoor Trees and Shrubs**—Purchasers of various sized trees, bushes and shrubs for home use.

Products and Services

The diverse needs of the multiple retail segments MGC serves require an equally diverse line of products and services. In addition to indoor and outdoor plants, MGC also sells gifts and collectibles, seed, mulch and lawn care products, as well as an expansive selection of Christmas products and services. It produces many of the plants it sells to insure their hardiness. Services range from delivery, gift cards and garden advice to landscape design and installation, including tree planting and fountain set-up. Eddie sums up the philosophy of the company in one simple statement; "We know gardening and we share what we know."

Plants are an investment in the garden and home. Purchasing the best quality plants insures this investment. Plant production requires substantial resources—large areas protected from the elements, skilled staff, and lots of water. Despite substantial overhead costs, MGC prices are competitive with other garden centers and specialty stores in the area. However, its prices are usually higher than those of the big box retailers like Lowe's, The Home Depot, and Wal-Mart. Pat laments that maintaining the balance among price, variety, and service becomes more difficult as the big box stores increase their garden products offerings.

EXHIBIT C11.2: RECENT YEAR MARKET SIZE AND SECTOR SALES

All Gardening Product Sales	Four Years Ago	Three Years Ago	Two Years Ago	One Years Ago	Last Year
	$26.5	27.8	29.2	30.6	32.1
—Seeds and plants	8.3	n/a	n/a	n/a	10.1
—Lawnmowers and power tools	7.2	n/a	n/a	n/a	8.7
—Buildings and leisure equipment	5.9	n/a	n/a	n/a	7.4
—Chemicals, lawn care and fertilizer	3.7	n/a	n/a	n/a	4.1
—Hand tools and implements	1.4	n/a	n/a	n/a	1.8

The Gardening Products Industry

In the most recent past year, an estimated 84 million U.S. households participated in some form of do-it-yourself indoor or outdoor lawn and garden activity. This represented about 80 percent of all American households. As seen in Exhibit C11.2, Americans spent $32.1 billion on gardening products that year. The increase in new home sales was presumed to be a major reason for the growth in sales over the past five years.

Garden seeds and plants was the largest sector within the industry. Hand tools and implements such as trowels, shovels and spades, while the lowest in sales revenue, also experienced substantial growth. Much of the sales of garden and leisure equipment were attributed to the purchase of outdoor lawn furniture as homeowners sought to create beautiful outdoor environments to use and enjoy. Garden chemicals and fertilizers showed the slowest growth, in part, because of an overall market trend towards more organic ways to cultivate plants and lawns.

According to Euromonitor International, retail sales of garden products in the U.S. were forecast to grow to $40.8 billion within the next five years. Steady growth was expected over that period, with overall annual sales increasing by approximately five percent a year. The seeds and plants sector was expected to remain the largest, with sales reaching $12.9 billion in the next five years. The buildings and leisure equipment category was expected to reach $9.9 billion, with growth coming from the purchase of luxury garden accents like high-end barbeques, fountains, sculptures, and accessories. Both power and hand tool sales were expected to grow at their current rates. Only chemicals and fertilizer sales were projected to flatten, increasing only about 1.7 percent over the next five years.

Nationally, over half of all garden products were sold between April and June, typically in springtime. However, climatic spring occurs at different times of the year depending on geographic location. The country is divided into eight climate zones, signifying the necessary plant hardiness and the start of the growing season. Exhibit

EXHIBIT C11.3: INDUSTRY SALES BY MONTH & CLIMATE ZONE MAP

Month	Percent of Sales	Month	Percent of Sales
January	0.7	July	6.3
February	0.7	August	5.1
March	4.1	September	6.7
April	14.7	October	6.3
May	29.1	November	4.9
June	12.8	December	7.7

Source: National Gardening Association

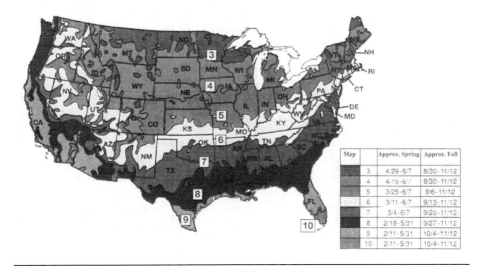

Map	Approx. Spring	Approx. Fall
3	4/29-6/7	8/30-11/12
4	4/15-6/7	8/30-11/12
5	3/25-6/7	9/6-11/12
6	3/11-6/7	9/13-11/12
7	3/4-6/7	9/20-11/12
8	2/18-5/31	9/27-11/12
9	2/11-5/31	10/4-11/12
10	2/11-5/31	10/4-11/12

C11.3 indicates the sale of gardening products on a monthly basis and the various climate zones.

Retail Outlets for Gardening Products

Homeowners shop for gardening products at a variety of retail outlets. Discount stores and home centers topped the list with The Home Depot achieving a 24 percent market share in the previous year. Wal-Mart was second (18 percent) and Lowe's was third (10.5 percent). These three retailers accounted for over half of all residential gardening products sold in the U.S. Price, variety, and location were the primary reasons consumers shopped at these stores.

Garden supply stores accounted for 21 percent of sales that same year, down from 23 percent in the previous year. This category of retail outlet included specialty garden retailers, including the small, independent local or regional chains like MGC.

Customers who enjoy close, personal relationships and advice from more knowledgeable horticulturalists tend to shop at the smaller, locally owned garden centers. However, the composition of this category could possibly change. Rumor had it that The Home Depot planned to open Landscape Supply stores, the first nationwide lawn and garden chain aimed at lawn care and garden professionals. This move was expected to cause more wholesale sales to shift in the gardening supply store category but could make it more difficult for specialty garden retailers to hold market share. With census data indicating that Hampton Roads accounted for 0.5 percent of all households and with the greater propensity of Southerners to use landscapers, the area appeared to be a prime candidate for one of the new Landscape Supply stores.

The Typical Gardener

The breadth of what is classified as gardening is extensive. For some, gardening means having a few potted plants on an apartment balcony. For others, it means various sized plant and vegetable beds. Some of the most extravagant gardens are extensive spaces filled with plants, ponds, and furnishings.

The National Gardening Association estimates that, on average, U.S. households spent $449 on gardening products in the most recent year. This was up slightly from the previous year where the expenditures averaged $440 but down from the year before that, where the typical household spent $466. While practically all American homeowners purchase gardening products, the ones who purchase more than the national average tend to be 45 years of age or older, college graduates with an annual income of at least $50,000. Households in the Midwest and South tend to spend more on gardening activities than those in other parts of the country. The typical buyer is married and lives in a two-person household where both are either employed full-time or retired. Despite industry-wide efforts to involve more children in gardening, those who spend the most on gardening products tend to have no children living at home. Men purchase more lawn seed, fertilizer, power tools and mulch while women purchase more plants, lawn decorations and hand tools.

The Professional Landscaping Business

While the purchase of gardening products has increased over the past several years, so too has residential use of professional landscape and lawn care services. In the previous year, 17.4 million households nationwide spent an average of $556 with service providers in lieu of doing the work themselves. Exhibit C11.4 indicates residential use of these services. The typical residential user of landscaping service is 50 years of age or older, has a college degree, and an annual household income of over $75,000. Research suggests that as homeowners get older and make more income, they are more likely to use professional landscaping companies to handle their lawn and garden maintenance needs.

The residential use of professional landscaping services differs by region of the country. Homeowners living in Southern states tend to rely on landscape professionals more so than elsewhere in the country. An estimated 24 percent of Southern households, including those in Hampton Roads, use outside service providers compared with 16 percent nationwide. This trend is of particular concern to MGC be-

EXHIBIT C11.4: RESIDENTIAL USE OF PROFESSIONAL LANDSCAPING COMPANIES

	Five Years Ago	Four Years Ago	Three Years Ago	Two Years Ago	One Year Ago
Households that Use (in %)	14	15	16	17	16
Households that Use (in Millions)	14.9	16.3	17.8	19.4	17.4
Average Spent per Household ($)	540	543	547	550	556
Total Spent per Year ($ Billions)	9.0	9.7	10.4	10.7	9.8

cause as the income of area residents rises, so too does the likelihood they will hire professional landscapers rather than do the work themselves. How that would impact retail gardening product sales remained to be seen.

Special Events Marketing and Pre-Rewards Program

MGC strives to portray itself as the area's premier, full-service garden specialist, having the most knowledgeable staff that offers sound advice, quality plants, and "no questions asked" guarantees. Pat, Sherry and the marketing staff run several special events each year to highlight seasonal items and activities, as well as drive customers to its retail locations. Some of its big events include:

- **Outdoor Show**—Here customers can discover new products and services presented by local businesses, seeing everything from stir-fry cooking to elegant floral arrangements in a garden setting. This March event features over 80 vendor exhibits, displays, demonstrations, free seminars, activities, and a Kids' Corner.
- **A Butterfly Affair**—This annual event is held each May and includes live-action displays featuring crawling caterpillars and flying butterflies and the plants that attract them. Seminars and "how-to" classes by a butterfly specialist inform attendees of the butterfly life cycle and how to attract them to their yards.
- **Crepe Myrtle Festival**—This is one of MGC's oldest promotional events. "Myrtle Money" is distributed to customers who purchase products between May and July, redeemable at the festival in mid-July. The event features exhibits, booths, and refreshments.
- **Garden Fiesta**—This festival celebrates the spirit and color of the Southwest, complete with Mexican music, sombreros, piñatas and fiesta balloons. The event is held in June and features seminars, "how-to" demonstrations, and activities for children.
- **Designer Days**—Consumers have the opportunity to make their garden visions

EXHIBIT C11.5: MEDIA BUDGET ALLOCATION—
PRE- AND POST- REWARDS CARD LAUNCH

Media Type	Percent of Budget: Pre-Rewards Program Launch	Percent of Budget: Post Rewards Program Launch
Newspaper	65	45
Broadcast (Television and Radio)	20	30
Direct Mail (including Newsletters)	10	22
Other	5	3
Total Budget	100	100

Source: Company

come to life in August with access to landscape designers, "how-to" seminars, and speakers. A "visions" contest awards the creativity of several consumer do-it-yourself garden projects.

- **Grass Roots and the American Red Cross**—This cause-related event is held every Labor Day weekend. The focus is on fall lawn care, with educational programs and putt-putt golf for customers. A portion of weekend's net sales benefits the American Red Cross.
- **Holiday Open House**—This November event features ideas, products, gifts, and time-saving decorating tips for the holiday season.

In addition to these annual events, MGC offers over 50 customer educational seminars throughout the year at each store. It distributes its *Greenleaves* newsletter to approximately 20,000 customers on its mailing list. In years past, most of its marketing budget was spent on promoting the annual events. Getting people to come to an event was thought to drive customer retail traffic to the stores.

As popular as the events were, MGC felt the growing pressures from the big box stores. The Home Depot, Wal-Mart, and Lowe's used low price as a strategic weapon. MGC's marketing budget at that time was 3.5 percent of annual sales. Exhibit C11.5 shows the percent of budget for the media mix before the *Garden Rewards* program was introduced.

The "Garden Rewards" Program

One day about four years previous, as Pat and Sherry strolled through the bodacious gardens of the Hampton store, they realized the company's existing marketing activities wouldn't continue to deliver the results achieved prior to the entry of the mass merchandisers. Pat lamented, "We just can't beat their prices."

Sherry noted, "And the cost of media keeps going up. Cable TV has created so many viewing options for prospective customers, we can't afford to buy time on all those different stations to reach them. Who's to say they're even seeing our commercials?"

Television wasn't the only problematic medium. With more than 33 radio stations in the Hampton Roads area, it was especially difficult to select and expensive to buy enough ad time to reach prospective customers. The power of newspaper advertising was also diminishing as readership rates decreased due to people's busy schedules. As Pat and Sherry reviewed the media mix, they realized that most of their marketing activities were not measurable. They were "mass marketing" to the entire geographic market in hopes of reaching a select group of prospects. The media delivered impressions . . . but no one was sure of the response or the return on the promotional dollars.

Pat and Sherry were sure that the "80/20 Principle" applied to the company's customer base, but they had no way to identify or communicate with that most valued 20 percent. After extensive research, they determined a loyalty program would help the company establish stronger relationships with its best customers. A customer loyalty program would enable them to know the value of each customer and tailor product and service offerings that fit their gardening activities.

While a rewards program appeared to be a sound idea, it wasn't without its challenges. Over the past few decades, several retailers have tried a variety of incentives to build customer loyalty. Results have been mixed. Those able to impact loyalty the most seemed to make their programs the focal point of all promotional efforts. For Pat and Sherry to make their program work, all existing marketing activities would have to be integrated to reflect the importance of the new program. That meant MGC's newsletter, collectibles program, Golden Gardeners program for senior citizens, business partner programs, coupons, and all future advertisements would have to be changed. A "Privacy Policy" would need to be established to let customers know of the company's commitment to protecting information about them. Despite the implementation complexities, Pat and Sherry decided to establish such a program.

"Garden Rewards" had launched nearly four years ago. Membership was free to anyone willing to sign up. Benefits included members-only price discounts, participation in special events, and various program partnership opportunities. Pat and Sherry thought the cornerstone incentive would be the annual rewards attained by accumulating points. Exhibit C11.6 shows the *Garden Rewards* card, list of benefits, and reward point awards.

Just prior to launch, all MGC employees were trained to get everybody "on board" with the program, and change their mass media mentality to a one-on-one marketing mindset. The overall goals of the initiative were to identify current customers and their needs to serve them better. All customers were encouraged to become cardholders. Initial benchmarks were purposely set high—30 percent of all transactions would be recorded in the customer database through card use within the first two weeks of the program launch, and 60 percent of all transactions within the following six weeks.

Within six weeks of the launch, 15,375 customers signed up and used their card at least once. Over 42 percent had used their cards two or more times. The data also revealed findings Pat never expected. For example, the maximum number of times a single card was used in the first six weeks was 26! About seven percent of the cardholders had spent over $1,000 with their Garden Rewards card in the first six weeks of launching the program.

Within six months of the launch, 32,000 Garden Rewards cards had been issued. Over 28,000 cards had been used once and 15,173 cards were used two or more times. One card had been used a whopping 67 times! Was this an anomaly? Not really. During that six-month time frame, a water-gardening customer used her card 55

EXHIBIT C11.6: GARDEN REWARDS CARD
AND PROMOTIONAL MATERIALS

active membership **benefits**

- **Special member discounts on selected plants and garden products**
  ~ Special garden rewards prices on plants and products just for card members.

- **Special member discounts on McDonald Garden Center brand items**
  ~ Extra savings on Lawn Food, Green Leaf Plant Food & more.

- **Special savings on new or exclusive introductions**
  ~ When new plants arrive, members will get early choices and extra savings.

- **Golden Gardeners Day**
  ~ Every Tuesday, members over 60 automatically receive 10% off reg price

- **Greenleaves newsletter subscription for active members**
  ~ The best gardening news for Hampton Roads, mailed to your home — with valuable coupons!

- **FREE local delivery on purchases over $500**

- **FREE registration to seminars and workshops**
  ~ Sign up in advance without a registration fee.

- **FREE pH soil testing**
  ~ Bring a soil sample and we will test the acidity so you know your planting needs.

- **Special Member Days**
  ~ Special preferred member appreciation days with exclusive opportunities.

- **Lost Key program**
  ~ Your key tag assures keys can be dropped in any mail box, return postage guaranteed.

- **Advance notice of selected special events & programs**
  ~ Notification of special customer previews & programs.

- **No annual membership fee**
  ~ Good year after year.
  ~ Not a credit card.

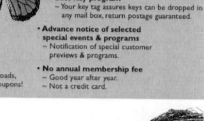

garden reward points

Earn garden reward points on all purchases throughout the year.

Reward Points & Annual Awards

500 to 999 points = $10 gift card

1000 to 1999 points = $25 gift card

2000 to 2999 points = $75 gift card

3000 points and up = $150 gift card

~ Earn one point for every $1 purchase of goods.

~ Use of each card or tag contributes to your total purchases and earns you extra garden reward points throughout the year.

~ Reward points are accrued within each calendar year.

~ Check your point progress on our website: www.mcdonaldgardencenter.com

- Points will be awarded annually; point rewards are awarded by mail before the end of the first quarter.
- All information involving use of this card will be kept confidential and used exclusively to provide you with our special values.
- We reserve the right to change or discontinue the program, card or benefits at any time.
- Returned items will show as adjusted (deducted) points. Points are non-transferrable.

EXHIBIT C11.7: AVERAGE TRANSACTION AMOUNTS— GARDEN REWARDS MEMBERS VS. UNIDENTIFIED CUSTOMERS

Retail Location	Average Transaction: Without Garden Rewards Card	Average Transaction: With Garden Rewards Card
Hampton	$35.15	$44.12
Chesapeake	$33.34	$42.52
Virginia Beach	$38.98	$48.40

Source: Company

times. In addition, overall transaction amounts were found to be higher among card-holders compared to the unidentified customers. (See Exhibit C11.7.)

The Garden Rewards program enabled MGC to divert much of its marketing budget to more targeted media, and in doing so, increase overall profitability. Although the number of retail transactions was down in the first year of the loyalty program as compared to the previous year, average revenue per transaction was up between $9 and $10. While the company continues to allocate 3.5 percent of sales to its marketing budget, the net effect has been a two percent increase in gross margin for the year.

The new focus on the loyalty program caused Pat and Sherry to also allocate more of the budget for broadcast media. Television spots would now focus on the benefits of membership in the loyalty program and invite prospects to visit one of the stores to sign up. The last column in Exhibit C11.5 indicates today's budget allocation figures by media.

Decision #1: Keeping the Offer Fresh

In the time since the launch of Garden Rewards program, over 96,000 customers had obtained and used the card. However, the number of active customers remained at about the same level it did six months after the launch of the program. The challenge Pat and Sherry faced was continuing to identify new ways to keep the Garden Rewards program fresh and persuade more customers to use it. The persistent question at every brainstorming session was "What more can we offer these people? What will entice the different customer segments to shop more frequently and spend more at our stores?"

Popular benefits previously introduced included:

- Two-for-one admission tickets for many of the area's educational and historical museums, including The Chrysler Museum, Endview Plantation, Lee Hall Mansion, Mariner's Museum, Norfolk Botanical Gardens and Virginia Air & Space Center.
- Free local delivery of MGC purchases over $500.
- Bonus points on random days or for the purchase of specific products.
- Advanced notices via email for special events and promotions.

- Free pH soil testing service.
- Lost key program. (MGC supplies its *Garden Rewards* members with a coded key chain. Lost keys could be dropped into any mailbox by the finder, with MGC paying the postage for returning the keys to the owner.)

Sherry assembled ideas for five different postcard mailings planned for the coming year or two and presented them to Pat. The projected costs as well as sample pieces are found in Exhibit C11.8.

Decision #2—Cleaning and Expanding the Customer Base

MGC's database currently held 96,000 records with approximately 12,000 new customers signing up each year. However, only 32,000 were considered active, earning at least 50 reward points in a given year. The longer the company maintained the database, the greater the challenge of keeping customer records current. Knowing that 20 percent of Americans move each year, Pat feared the database had records of people who no longer lived at the addresses on file. With a high percentage of military personnel living in the area, many who had moved might no longer be in the state.

Both Pat and Sherry agreed the records in the database had to be checked for currency and cleaned. The question was how? Once the outdated records were removed, how many "actives" would remain? They also struggled with determining the "right" definition of "active." Fearing the worst, they knew that in addition to efforts to retain existing customers, they would have to do something to attract new ones.

After much research and work with a list broker, they identified several list rental possibilities. But which ones would maximize response for a new customer offer? Exhibit C11.9 provides details regarding several lists Pat and Sherry are considering. Each list also had options for additional segmentation selections to pinpoint who they thought would be the most likely customers. Lists could be further segmented by ZIP code (for an additional $5 per thousand), gender ($6 per thousand extra), state ($8 per thousand extra), income ($10 per thousand extra), education ($7 per thousand extra) and/or marital status ($8 per thousand extra).

In addition to list selection, they also needed to determine an attractive offer. Sherry created two postcard offers to increase membership in the Garden Rewards program, one for free garden gloves, the other for a free geranium plant. (See Exhibit C11.10.) Each offer was determined by looking at product inventory, availability, quantity, cost, season, and broad market appeal. Before making a final decision on the offer, Pat proposed a 500-piece test mailing of both to measure response rates. Each mail piece would cost $0.93 to produce at such limited quantities and $0.39 to mail First Class. Garden glove fulfillment costs were estimated at $4.00 while the geranium plant fulfillment cost was $5.00.

Summary of the Decisions

Pat returned to her office refreshed. Walking through the gardens always helped her clear her head. She sat down, opened her notebook, and made a list of the questions to cover with Sherry and the marketing staff during the upcoming meeting.

EXHIBIT C11.8: SAMPLES OF POSSIBLE UPCOMING POSTCARD MAILINGS WITH ASSOCIATED COSTS

Offer	Potential Segment	Quantity Mailed	Cost per Piece		
			Printing	*Postage*	*Redemption*
Cone-Crazy	Top 600 GR Members	600	$0.50	$0.37	$2.50
Garden		350	$0.50	$0.37	$2.50
Center of the Year	Top 350 GR Members				
Halloween		500	$0.50	$0.37	$5.00
Happy	Top 500 GR Members	413	$0.84	$0.39	$2.50
Birthday	GR customers who spent > $500 in the previous year				
Roses	Top 2000 GR Members	2,000	$0.50	$0.37	$6.25

EXHIBIT C11.9: LIST RENTAL OPTIONS

List	Description	Base Price	Minimum Quantity
American Gardener Magazine	Members of the American Horticultural Society. Avid and master gardeners, professional horticulturalists.	$100/M	5,000
American Private Golf Club Members	Serious golfers who play at private country clubs. Compiled from membership lists and prize recipients at golf events.	$95/M	5,000
Backyard Garden Design	Passionate, creative home gardeners. Subscribe to multiple home and garden publications.	$85/M	5,000
Gardening Enthusiasts	Consumers with a love for gardening and a green thumb to prove it. From seeds to soil, these gardening buffs are open to offers that will help them enhance their gardens.	$70/M	5,000
Hobby Enthusiast Network	Hobbyists with interests ranging from gambling to gardening.	$70/M	5,000
Hispanic Hearth & Home	Individuals who want to improve, decorate, and landscape their property.	$85/M	5,000
Martha Stewart Living Gardening Enhanced	Affluent, paid subscribers who have expressed an interest in gardening. Upscale, well-educated women who love to garden and have the discretionary income to purchase garden products and services.	$105/M	7,500
New Homeowners	Compiled from public sources including county deed records. Updated monthly.	$64/M	5,000

Source: NextMark, Inc.

- What should we do to keep the *Garden Rewards* program fresh and enticing to get members to continue shopping at our stores?
- What level of response can we expect when targeting such small segments of customers like Sherry recommends? What will it cost us to generate that response?
- Of the five postcards Sherry recommended, are there one or two offers that look the most promising? Given the costs and quantities, what response rates are needed for the mailing to breakeven?

EXHIBIT C11.10: SAMPLES OF POTENTIAL POSTCARDS FOR CUSTOMER ACQUISITION PROGRAM

Source: Company

Some of the data provided by the company has been disguised and is not useful for research purposes. The authors would like to thank Pat Overton and Sherry Connell of McDonald Garden Center for their help in this project.

- How should we go about cleaning the database and how many active records are likely to remain once the old ones are deleted?
- How should the *Garden Rewards* program database be segmented? Should we be treating customer segments differently?
- Which of the lists identified look most promising for generating new *Garden Rewards* program members?
- Have we extinguished all the possibilities with what we have in house? How might we prospect for new customers using our current customer database?
- If we do use one or more of these outside lists, should we add additional selects?
- Can we estimate which of the two offers Sherry created for new customer acquisition has the best chance of success? What are the response rates needed to breakeven with each of these options?
- Numbers aside, what do we expect the qualitative impact to be if we go with either of these offers?
- Given the highly competitive environment, are our growth aspirations realistic?

As Pat reviewed her list of questions, she realized the decisions she and her staff were about to make would impact the company for years to come. Just then, Sherry poked her head into the office. "You ready for us?" Sherry asked. Pat replied, "Sure. Let's do it."

Bibliography

Enright, Michael and Heath McDonald, (1997). "The Melbourne Garden Nursery Industry: A Qualitative Review of Marketing and New Product Development Orientation in a Retail Environment," *Journal of Product and Brand Management*, 6 (3), 175–188.

Florkowski, W. and G. Landry, (2000). "An Economic Profile of the Professional Turfgrass and Landscape Industry in Georgia," *The Georgia Agricultural Experiment Stations: University of Georgia,* December.

"Garden Market Forecast: Retail Consumer Behavior," (2003). Unity Marketing, Stevens, PA. www.retailindustry.about.com.

"Garden Market Research," (2006). *National Gardening Association.* www.gardenresearch.com.

"Gardening Products in the USA—October 2005, (2005). Euromonitor International.

Jerardo, Alberto, (2005). "Floriculture and Nursery Crops Outlook," *Electronic Outlook Report from the Economic Research Service,* United States Department of Agriculture, September. www.ers.usda.gov.

Mosquera, Gabrielle, (2003). "Gardeners," *Target Magazine,* May, 26 (5), 65–66.

NextMark List Research Systems. (2006). NextMark, Inc., Hanover NH., www. nextmark.com.

"Population by State," (2006) United States Census Bureau. www.census.gov.

CASE
12

NueMedia, LLC: Redefining Business Media for Customer-Centric Marketing

CAROL SCOVOTTI

University of Wisconsin-Whitewater

O n July 1, Scott Ross sat in his office reviewing the first-half financials of NueMedia, LLC. As president, CEO, and majority stockholder, he was encouraged to see that both revenue and receivables for the Web-based business increased in the second quarter. However, the 18-month-old venture had yet to generate enough cash flow to sustain itself. Another injection of capital would soon be needed to cover upcoming bills.

Starting a new business always has its risks, but starting one amidst an economic recession when banks are on the verge of collapse is especially challenging. Despite federal stimulus money that was supposed to ease the credit market and encourage small business loans, the banks weren't lending. Attempts to obtain support from the Small Business Administration and venture capitalists proved futile as well. NueMedia was a gamble, but Scott was confident its time had come. Unable to procure outside funding, he ultimately decided to finance the business himself by using family savings. "How much longer do I keep this up?" Scott asked himself as he cued up yet another electronic transfer from his personal savings to the business checking account. The reserves he had set aside were running low, and, although optimistic, he still wasn't convinced it was enough to reach the point where the venture would become self-supporting.

Still, after 30 years in business-to-business marketing, he realized that cash flow wasn't the real problem. NueMedia seemed well poised to succeed amidst the sea change transforming the trade publishing industry. However, few people were buying. He wondered how industrial marketers, driven by bottom-line results, could resist having their products and promotional messages available to prospects 24 hours a day, every day, for an entire year for less than the cost of a single half-page ad in a

Note: Some of the data provided by the company has been disguised and is not useful for research purposes. The author would like to thank Ross Scovotti for his help in this project.

monthly trade magazine. "How do I get people to change the way they buy media and evaluate its effectiveness? Businesses will always seek product and process information . . . but only when it is important to their business. A printed magazine that comes out once a month or even once a week isn't customer-centric media. Print is dead!" As he stared at the accounts receivable page on his monitor, Scott pondered what NueMedia's next moves should be.

Business Information Dissemination and the Trade Publishing Industry

People working within industries need specialized, commerce-related information to stay competitive. Business information dissemination is a sector within the much larger communication industry. Historically, business information was published and circulated via printed publications such as trade magazines and newsletters specific to individual industries or segments within an industry. In commercial woodworking for example, printed publications include *Wood Digest, Wood and Wood Products, Cabinet Maker, Modern Woodworking,* and *FDM.*

Published and distributed at specified times of the year (typically monthly), these magazines generated revenue through the sale of advertising space, circulation list rental and, to a lesser extent, subscription sales.[1] Trade publications were successful because they contained data that participants in the industry needed to do their jobs better. They were reliable sources for best practices, information about new products and services, as well as other environmental trends impacting an industry.

The zenith of the printed trade publications sector occurred throughout the 1990s. Large publishers around the world went on a decade-long spending spree, acquiring smaller, industry-specific magazines to create a more diversified portfolio of publications. They benefited from economies of scale and produced publications faster and cheaper by sharing sales, editorial, circulation, and production resources. Plus, a diversified portfolio was thought to protect a publisher from declines or significant changes in specific industries.[1]

At the same time, large publishers discovered another revenue stream in companion trade shows. Companies like Cygnus, Advanstar, Penton Media, Reed Business Information and Cahners established trade show divisions if they didn't already have them or supplemented existing trade shows with acquisitions of related publications.[2] Exhibit C12.1 lists the top 10 group publishers in 2009, along with total advertising pages, for a three-year period. These 10 firms represented more than 81 percent of total ad pages in trade publications. In the next three years, total advertising pages dropped more than 41 percent for the top 10 group publishers and almost 50 percent for all business-to-business publications.

---

[1]Most trade publications have a controlled circulation where qualified subscribers within the industry receive the publication at no charge.

[2] Hough, Michael R. and Jacqueline Tein. 1999. Optimizing the magazine/trade show relationship. *American Business Media: The Association of Business Media Companies.* October.

EXHIBIT C12.1: TOP 10 GROUP PUBLISHERS BY
ADVERTISING PAGES (2007–2009)

GROUP PUBLISHER (NUMBER OF TITLES 2009)	AD PAGES 2009	AD PAGES 2008	AD PAGES 2007	% CHG. 07–09
1. Penton Media (67)	23,969	34,119	40,697	–41%
2. Reed Business (40)	22,093	35,253	40,420	–45%
3. Advanstar Communications (30)	15,466	19,575	21,764	–29%
4. BNP Media (29)	14,436	20,235	28,676	–50%
5. Questex Media Group (21)	9,330	13,615	13,615	–31%
6. Cygnus Business Media (31)	9,173	13,439	18,053	–49%
7. Pennwell Publishing (22)	8,302	10,938	12,492	–34%
8. Randall-Reilly (13)	7,718	10,416	10,755	–28%
9. Nielsen Business Media (19)	7,632	11,676	20,055	–62%
10. McGraw Hill (18)	7,538	10,336	6,692	13%

Source: Access Intelligence LLC, 2010

By 2001 trade publishers were starting to dabble with Internet offerings. However, there was no sense of urgency because they maintained a revenue stream through their print properties and trade shows. They thought they were protected because of the industry diversification achieved during the prior decade's spending spree. The dot-com bust also caused business publishers to delay investing heavily in the new medium. Instead, they duplicated the static content from their magazines onto their websites, as well as sold banner ads and pop-ups as evolutionary marketing.

What they didn't see coming with the rise of the Internet was the simultaneous decline of the economy. Media expenditures historically drop in recessionary periods as advertisers reduce budgets and seek more accountable ways to spend their marketing dollars. The economic recession that began in 2001 hit trade publishers hard as advertisers sought less expensive ways to promote their products and services.

Similar to firms in the consumer marketplace, business-to-business marketers found the Internet an effective, low-cost alternative to expensive print advertising. However, instead of supplementing print campaigns and trade show participation with Internet advertising, business marketers reallocated more and more of their shrinking budgets to online assets. What publishers thought would be an opportunity to gain a greater share of marketing dollars from their advertisers proved to cannibalize sales within their core assets. Laden with the infrastructure created to produce large portfolios of publications, publishers were caught between who they were and what they had to be. Unwilling or unable to see the changing view of print media within the marketplace, group publishers such as Cygnus Business Media were forced into bankruptcy.

As seen in Exhibit C12.2, revenue from trade publications continues to fall. The latest available figures show that revenue for all but the broadcast and pharmaceutical industry publications were down between 2009 and 2010. Losses projected for 2010/2011 are even greater.

EXHIBIT C12.2: REVENUE CHANGE IN B2B PUBLICATIONS 2009 TO 2010 (BY INDUSTRY)

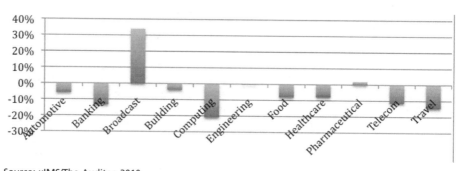

Source: xIMS/The Auditor, 2010

The Launch of NueMedia

NueMedia, the brainchild of two former trade publishers, was formally established in January 2010. Its mission was to unite buyers and sellers within specific industries in a 21st-century business environment to deliver precise information to readers and unparalleled response to suppliers when and where needed.

The idea for NueMedia originated 12 years prior, after Scott had sold a small trade publishing company to a much larger business media firm. By the late 1990s he realized that business use and reliance on technology evolve over time. When first introduced, technology simply replaces manual processes. As a technology develops, business processes are adapted to take advantage of the greater efficiencies created. Eventually businesses and their processes are redefined, requiring industry participants to either change or die. He thought that the impact of the "replace—refine—redefine" evolution on business publishing would be substantial, as he envisioned the industry moving from its company focus with static content on printed pages, distributed in a publisher defined time frame, to a more customer focus with individualized, interactive content stored in a digital environment that would be accessible by end users in their own time frames. He shared these insights with the management of his new parent company and proposed the creation of a virtual community where both current and potential readers and advertisers would belong. However, his proposal fell on deaf ears and Scott eventually left the firm to pursue other interests.

Fast-forward to 2009 and an unexpected phone call from a former industry associate, Sam Jason. A group publisher at a large business media company, Sam's entire team had been recently laid off as part of a cost-cutting effort. His former employer stopped production of three magazines for the commercial woodworking industry. Sam recalled Scott's virtual community idea and proposed they create one to serve woodworkers and finishers. Sam had the industry and editorial contacts; Scott had the marketing strategy and financial management experience. He also had a great track record when it came to finding funds to start new business ventures.

The two worked together for several months before ultimately deciding to the launch the business. In preparation, they contracted with the leading commercial woodworking associations to manage the digital and print communications used to promote annual industry trade shows. This arrangement generated minimal, but immediate revenue and strengthened the venture's credibility among the companies within the industry.

They also purchased the vendor/product database from Sam's former employer as well as the editorial archives and circulation lists of the defunct publications. This provided NueMedia with the cornerstone for its entire business, the database of products and vendors in the commercial woodworking industry, as well as the contact information for both buyers and sellers and a library of useful content. The partners hired a third member of their team, an editor who, like Sam, lost her job in a massive layoff. With the help of their new editor, Scott and Sam established relationships with industry evangelists to write monthly blogs in specific product and process areas.

Next, the partners turned their attention to the platform on which NueMedia content would be delivered. Web sites needed to be created where users could find the product and process information they sought. Neither Scott nor Sam had the necessary expertise so they outsourced web site design and hosting to a nearby company that Scott had done business with in the past. The plan was to launch the first informational/education site, *WoodIQ.com*, by mid April 2010. Subsequent sites for surface finishers, *FinishingIQ.com*, as well as the comprehensive, interactive database of vendors and products in the commercial woodworking industry, *ProductIQ*, would open shortly thereafter. However, programming glitches, unforeseen issues, and miscommunications delayed the launch date six months, inhibiting NueMedia from generating revenue from what was to be a primary source of income.

In the interim, the circulation and advertiser lists acquired in the publication asset purchase enabled the company to generate revenue by selling banner ads in its weekly newsletters, *IQ Alerts*. Focused on hot topics of the day and featuring unique content from industry experts, *IQ Alerts* deliver business information to the industry professional's inbox. Articles that appear in the newsletters link to blog pages on either the *WoodIQ.com* or *FinishingIQ.com* websites, depending on the subject matter. A sample of an e-newsletter is found in Exhibit C12.3.

Buyers, Sellers, and Promotional Offerings

NueMedia differentiates itself from printed publications and companion websites in several ways. Its primary focus is product and vendor information, not industry news and gossip. Woodworking practitioners access the site when they need to buy equipment, components, and accessories to manufacture their products, or when they need to solve an organizational- or process-oriented business problem. Exhibit C12.4 provides the categories of businesses that use NueMedia websites when they need to purchase products or find suitable vendors.

ProductIQ

All commercial woodworkers must buy products to produce their finished goods. The core of NueMedia's portfolio of Internet offerings is *ProductIQ*, a comprehensive

EXHIBIT C12.3. SAMPLE IQ ALERT (NEWSLETTER)

directory of products used by commercial woodworkers and the suppliers who sell them. *ProductIQ* contains information on more than 220 distinct product categories, thousands of vendors, and tens of thousands of actual products. Despite its massive size, the database is fast and easy to search, even for the most specialized need. Every supplier in the industry has administrative access to its company and product listings. Vendors can add new products, modify current product listings, and update company contact information anytime, making *ProductIQ* the most up-to-date buying resource available. The landing page for *ProductIQ* is seen in Exhibit C12.5.

Products search results are prioritized so that Featured Products are at the top of the page, followed by Premium Products, and finally Standard Products. Standard Product listings contain 120-word product descriptions and photo, and are available to any supplier free of charge. Premium sponsorship is available to any vendor who wants to enhance its product listings with a company logo, link to the company website, video demonstration, email response, and branded search. Premium Products are listed above Standard Products within search results. Any number of suppliers may become a premium sponsor. Premium sponsors who want to insure their products are the first listed within applicable search results may purchase a Featured

EXHIBIT C12.4: NAICS CLASSIFICATIONS OF BUSINESSES USING NUEMEDIA

CODE	DESCRIPTION
238330	Flooring Contractors
238350	Finish Carpentry Contractors
321219	Reconstituted Wood Products Manufacturing
321011	Other Wood Product Manufacturing
321912	Cut Stock, Resawing Lumber, and Planing
321918	Other Millwork (including Flooring)
321920	Wood Container and Pallet Manufacturing
321992	Prefabricated Wood Building Manufacturing
321000	All Other Miscellaneous Wood Product Manufacturing
337110	Wood Kitchen Cabinet and Countertop Manufacturing
337121	Upholstered Household Furniture Manufacturing
337112	Non-Upholstered Wood Household Furniture Manufacturing
337129	Wood Television, Radio, and Sewing Machine Cabinet Manufacturing
337211	Wood Office Furniture Manufacturing
337212	Custom Architectural Woodwork and Millwork Manufacturing
337215	Showcase, Partition, Shelving, and Locker Manufacturing

Products listing within a specific product category. Only four Featured Products are available within each of the 220 product categories to guarantee exclusivity and reduce clutter. Both Premium Sponsorships and Featured Products are sold on an annual basis for $2,988 and $600 respectively.

WoodIQ.com & FinishingIQ.com

When woodworking professionals are interested in purchasing a product or need to solve a business problem, they seek advice from knowledgeable authorities. NueMedia affords this guidance free of charge through the content contained in its digital information portals (DIPs). *WoodIQ.com* offers information relevant to commercial woodworking while *FinishingIQ.com* focuses on issues that affect the coating of wood surfaces. Two distinct sites are necessary because fabricating a piece of wood into a product is much different than coating it. While the two processes are needed for the creation of a finished product, having two sites insures that the professional sees information specific to their needs and isn't burdened with clutter.

Within each DIP, blogs written by industry experts are updated monthly and deal with such topics as green/environmental issues, product design, lean manufacturing, tools and technologies, cabinet making, and finishing. Each DIP also features a knowledge base containing an archive of thousands of articles dating back to 2006. The knowledge base is searchable by topic, keyword, company, or any other criteria important to the user. As of the most recent June, users of the two DIPs viewed an average of six pages and spent an average of 48 minutes on the site per visit. There were more than 34,000 members in *WoodIQ.com* and 16,000 members in *FinishingIQ.com*.

EXHIBIT C12.5: PRODUCT IQ HOME PAGE

Membership to the DIPs is free to anyone involved with commercial woodworking. Members sign up online.

Both *WoodIQ.com* and *FinishingIQ.com* contain a buyers guide feature that links to *ProductIQ*. This seamless integration insures that, regardless of the point of entry, prospective buyers find the product and vendor information they seek.

NueMedia generates revenue through the sale of banner ads on the pages of *WoodIQ.com* and *FinishingIQ.com*. Banner ads vary in size, placement, and price. Frequency discounts are offered to those who establish a 3-time, 6-time, or annual schedule within a year. The 2011 rate card for banner advertising on the DIPs is provided in Exhibit C12.6.

EXHIBIT C12.6: 2011 ADVERTISING RATE CARD (MONTHLY)

Ad Type	WoodIQ.com	FinishingIQ.com
Monthly Exposures	10,000	6,000
Leaderboard Banner	$995	$795
Skyscraper	$795	$595
Standard Banner	$595	$445*
Button	$495	$345*

* FinishIQ.com requires a minimum 3x purchase for standard banner and button ads.

FinishingRx

Through the formation of a strategic partnership with the American Wood Finishing Institute (AWFI) NueMedia added *FinishingRx* to its portfolio of offerings in February 2011. An e-help desk and social media site, *FinishingRx* helps professional finishers deal with the constant changes in coatings, technologies, and substrate materials. Finishers post specific challenges they are experiencing with a particular project and obtain real time feedback from finishing experts at AWFI. Help is currently free to any registered member of *FinishingIQ.com*, with feedback guaranteed within 24 hours.

To date, use of this feature has been disappointing. No research has been done to determine why members are not using *FinishingRx* but the partners surmise that they might have overestimated the depth of knowledge of the average member. In doing so, Scott and Sam are concerned that they have stymied the social media aspect of the module. Interestingly, they have discovered that they generate dialogue whenever the editor posts something on a finishing issue on *FinishingIQ's* LinkedIn group.

CountertopIQ.com

In fall 2011, NueMedia plans to add another DIP to its portfolio of offerings, *CountertopIQ.com*. Similar to *FinishingIQ.com*, this DIP will provide relevant information to the subsector in the commercial woodworking industry that deals with marble, granite, manufactured stone, laminates, and wood countertops. The DIP will have unique blogs written by experts in the industry and will also contain a searchable knowledge base. Its buyers guide feature will be similar to its companion sites, with product and company information available through *ProductIQ*. The revenue generation model for *CountertopIQ.com* will be similar to *WoodIQ.com* and *FinishingIQ.com*, however, rates have not yet been established.

The current NueMedia offerings available to the commercial woodworking industry are illustrated in Exhibit C12.7. The business model centers on *ProductIQ*, supported by DIPs for commercial woodworkers (*WoodIQ.com*), professional finishers (*FinishingIQ.com*)and countertop makers and installers (*CountertopIQ.com*).

IQ Alerts

Every month, NueMedia bloggers write original editorial in their specialized areas that is distributed through *IQ Alerts*. One alert is sent every Tuesday with the subject matter rotating on a weekly basis. *WoodIQ.com* and *FinishingIQ.com* members opt-in

EXHIBIT C12.7: NUEMEDIA'S WEB OFFERINGS

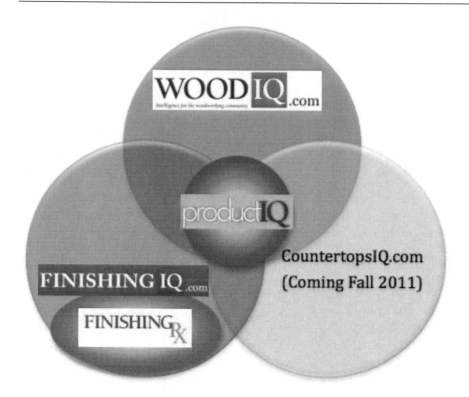

to receive specific titles. This insures that recipients get the content important to their business, minimizing the harm of junk mail. The current portfolio of *IQ Alert* titles include:

- *Green Matters.* News and views on the regulatory environment, woodworkers' best strategies for success in sustainable woodworking and products shaping the marketplace.
- *Woodworking Strategies* (in cooperation with the Architectural Woodwork Institute—AWI). Real-world strategies for improving manufacturing efficiencies via the latest strategies, software, and technologies.
- *Finishing Line* (in cooperation with the Association of Woodworking & Finishings Suppliers—AWFS). A comprehensive look at tools, techniques, and opportunities in wood finishing.
- *Product Showcase.* Highlights new products recently added to the *ProductIQ* website. Products introduced by premium sponsors, as well as featured products are included at no charge. Product with a free listing may be highlighted in the e-newsletter for $695.
- *Cabinet Shop News* (in cooperation with the Cabinet Makers Association— CMA). Content specifically targeted to today's cabinet shop.

The introduction of *IQ Alerts* has revealed a new opportunity for NueMedia to reach even more woodworking professionals. In addition to being sent to members of *WoodIQ.com* and *FinishingIQ.com* involved in a particular sector of the woodworking business, associations also distribute the alerts to its members. Scott explained that aligning with smaller associations generates more qualified users who access the NueMedia sites. More qualified users means greater reach and more value for suppliers.

NueMedia generates revenue through the placement of banner ads in the *IQ Alerts*. Ad prices vary by size and page placement. Leaderboard, skyscrapers, banners and buttons are also available. One-time ad rates range between $895 and $1,495. Frequency discounts are available for 3-time, 6-time, and annual schedules. Cooperative associations receive a small percentage of the ad revenue generated within their specific newsletter.

eBlasts

Qualified lists are as valuable as gold to marketers who want to reach buyers in specific industries with their promotional messages. NueMedia offers an opt-in option to its members to receive information from third parties who sell products that relate to their businesses. NueMedia reviews the content to insure relevance and sends the promotional emails to all or a portion of its members. An eBlast to the master list of *WoodIQ.com* and *FinishingIQ.com* members is $1,995 and $1,445 respectively. Partial runs are available at a rate of $125 per thousand ($995 minimum). Frequency discounts are available.

WoodIQ.com & FinishingIQ.com Platinum Sponsorships

For the advertiser that wants maximum exposure within the woodworking and finishing communities, NueMedia offers a bundled package with eBlasts, leaderboard banner ads on either *WoodIQ.com* or *FinishingIQ.com*, as well as Button ads in newsletters for a rate of $2,695 and $1,995 per month respectively. A three-month minimum is required. This represents a 26 percent savings over buying each individually. To date, no advertiser has purchased a platinum sponsorship.

NueMedia's Marketing Efforts

Nothing sells itself. Even the best products, services, and ideas need marketing if they are to be successful. NueMedia's portfolio of promotional offerings is no exception. While few can deny that the trade publishing industry has its issues, many business marketers are hesitant to stop advertising in industry-specific magazines and redirect their marketing efforts to the customer-centric communication opportunities NueMedia offers. While the number of advertising pages has reduced almost 50 percent over the past three years, business advertisers still rely on print to promote their products. Scott attributes this to fear of what they don't understand. Many don't know how to prepare for a marketing environment where customers are in control of the media and demand customized messages that available when they are interested in receiving it.

Scott admits that NueMedia has struggled with its own promotional efforts. Both he and Sam understand that the challenge they face is more that just getting business media buyers to adopt a new advertising media, it also requires a change in marketing philosophy . . . and that will take time. The lack of a marketing budget doesn't help, but they use the tools at their disposal to persuade business marketers to advertise. Then again, if they had a budget, how should they spend it?

Sam is responsible for sales. He promotes NueMedia's advertising offerings proactively using a combination of eBlasts and telephone-based sales calls. Additionally, all of the NueMedia DIPs and *IQ Alerts* contain house ads that link to a Marketing Services page where interested parties can call or send an email to Sam. When a supplier expresses an interest, Sam demonstrates the sites using *GoToMeeting.com*, an online meeting and collaboration platform. If more specific details and pricing are requested, he creates a proposal and sends it via email or fax. These are the same methods Sam's sales reps used to sell print advertising not too long ago, and both he and Scott wonder if this is the right methodology or if the old model has outlived its usefulness.

Scott considers himself the "back office guy" who handles billing, payments, and interfaces with the website hosting firm. One of his marketing responsibilities is to see that the sites are optimized for top placement in search engine results. To date, he hasn't tried search engine marketing vehicles like Google AdWords because he is concerned that too many unqualified people will respond. "Why would I want to perform a task that creates waste?" he explained. "In business-to-business marketing, it's not about reaching the masses." NueMedia's portfolio of web offerings is relevant to a very targeted niche of business professionals, and he felt that inviting response from woodworking amateurs and hobbyists would cause the sites to lose their value among the professionals and suppliers. Having to deal with amateurs who request help with finishing issues through *FinishingRx*, for example, could be disastrous.

Marketing Decisions

Both Scott and Sam believe their venture can be successful. The concept seems right for the time and a tremendous amount of groundwork has already been completed. Site traffic is up and people are spending more time when they are on the sites. Yet the partners know they have to make some difficult decisions as they determine the direction the firm will take. Their list of questions was extensive.

- Why isn't *FinishingRx* working? Is social media appropriate for the members of the commercial woodworking industry?
- *CountertopIQ.com* is the next scheduled DIP to launch. Where should they focus after that? Should they continue with wood product manufacturing or branch off into other products used in, say, kitchens and baths? When should they consider entering an entirely new industry where the NueMedia model would work and what might that industry be? Where can they find the data needed for a new industry's version of *ProductIQ*? The knowledge base?
- Strategic partnerships and cooperative agreements have provided new sources for reaching woodworking professionals. Should the company try to establish more relationships with the smaller associations? If so, what roles should they play as NueMedia expands?

- To date, no supplier has purchased a platinum sponsorship. Why? Should they continue to offer it?
- What should the sales model be? This is e-media. Does e-media need an e-sales model? If so, what does that mean?
- Is there another pricing alternative to the standard publication rate card? Everybody wants a deal and there are almost 200 product categories that have no featured products. That may be a good place to start. Would they sell these premium positions in *ProductIQ* if they auctioned them off on a quarterly basis? How might the premium sponsors respond to such an offering? How could they protect the "premium-ness" of sponsorship?
- What should they do about search engine marketing? Would advertising within search engines dilute the finite segmentation NueMedia has been able to develop? Would it bring in more qualified users than what the search engine optimization efforts are generating?

The biggest questions on Scott's mind was when the venture would start to make enough money so he could recoup the $150,000 of personal savings he had invested to start the company. Fixed costs were running about $250,000 per year and variable costs totaled 20 percent of sales. Potential doesn't keep the door open and the lights on. Only cash flow does.

References

1. Peltier, Stephanie. 2004. Mergers and acquisitions in the media industries: Were failures really unforeseeable? *Journal of Media Economics, 17* (4), 261–278.

CASE
13

Peninsula Society for the Prevention of Cruelty to Animals (PSPCA)

LISA D. SPILLER

Christopher Newport University

CAROL SCOVOTTI

University of Wisconsin-Whitewater

In 1866, New York resident Henry Bergh decided he could no longer sit idly by and watch a street merchant beat his defenseless horse. On that day, the first Society for the Prevention of Cruelty to Animals (SPCA) was born. Named the ASPCA, or the American Society for the Prevention of Cruelty to Animals, this organization became the first of its kind to exist for the sole purpose of helping make the world a better, safer place for tens of millions of companion pets.

Since that time, hundreds of SPCAs and Humane Societies have been formed across the United States to serve their community's needy and homeless animals. While the primary goal of these organizations is to find new homes for their homeless pets, they also provide humane education to their community's pet owners, provide low-cost medical services to indigent families, and care for sick and injured stray animals. SPCAs also have the difficult responsibility of euthanizing animals that are not adopted. In a recent year, approximately 50 percent of sheltered animals, totaling more than four million animals, were euthanized because people opted to buy pets rather than adopt and because people allowed their pets to breed.

SPCAs generally have small staffs and largely rely on volunteers and private donations to operate. Given that these organizations must raise their own money, they often lack the funds necessary to employ skilled employees or to even engage in the most basic business practices. Modern-day tactics such as direct and interactive marketing are often overlooked or are simply not considered due to a lack of time or money. This was the case for the Peninsula SPCA located in Newport News, Virginia.

Some of the data provided by the company has been disguised and is not useful for research purposes. The authors would like to thank Vicki Rowland for her help in this project.

Peninsula SPCA

Founded in 1967, the Peninsula SPCA (PSPCA) became the only shelter in a four-city region to provide sheltering and adoption services. For over 35 years, the PSPCA provided these services to the best of its ability; however, its adoption rate never exceeded 30 percent. As the nation's best shelters evolved and began attaining adoption rates of 50 percent or more, mounting community demands pressured the PSPCA to reorganize and begin integrating modern-day business practices.

In 2004, a new volunteer Board of Directors was elected to achieve this goal. At that time, there was no marketing plan, no marketing strategy, and no employees were focused on marketing or fundraising. The only marketing activity that the PSPCA engaged in was direct mail, and even this activity was outsourced to a vendor that charged 35 percent for cookie-cutter solicitations. For an organization that relied on donations to exist, this required a prompt overhaul of massive proportions. The first item of business was to form a task force of a few Board members with the sole job of focusing on marketing initiatives. This small group concentrated on creating the PSPCA's first-ever marketing plan and establishing a budget for marketing activities. The next challenge was to create a marketing manager's position and fill that position with someone to handle the marketing duties.

The job went to Vicki Rowland, a 24-year-old college graduate with a love of animals and a keen understanding of direct and interactive marketing. One warm and sunny day in June, Vicki joined the PSPCA as its new Marketing Manager. After all of the introductions and a brief tour, Vicki sat in her office and stared at the current marketing plan. "Where to begin?" She thought to herself. As Exhibit C13.1 shows, the marketing plan had two goals: to increase animal adoptions and to increase funds raised.

EXHIBIT C13.1: PSPCA TWO-YEAR MARKETING PLAN

PSCPA Two-Year Marketing Plan

Goal 1: Increase Adoptions	Estimated cost	Estimated Income
Objective A: Increase Exposure	$12,000	$6,000
Objective B: Increase Media Contact	$600	$—
Objective C: Create Marketing Materials	$1,500	$—
Objective D: Increase Contact with Municipal Partners	$—	$—
Goal 2: Increase Donations		
Objective A: Create Direct Mail Donations	$30,000	$70,000
Objective B: Create Event Donations	$45,000	$157,000
Objective C: Increase Bequests	$—	$—
Objective D: Create Grant Income	$—	$—
Objective E: Create Product Line	$12,000	$17,000
Subtotal	$101,100	$250,000
Labor	$45,000	
Total Cost/Income	$146,100	$250,000

Net Income $103,900

The 'Increase Funds Raised' goal was largely driven by direct marketing principles and will be the focus of the rest of this case. This overall goal was broken down into multiple objectives and numerous supporting strategies, which included creating both a direct mail program and special fundraising events. As Vicki began to get organized, she knew that since the heart of direct and interactive marketing is a customer or client database, her initial efforts should be focused on creating the PSPCA's first real customer database. Vicki quickly organized a team of volunteers to assist her in the tasks associated with database development.

The Database

Vicki investigated several database software solutions and evaluated each on the same criteria: ability to synchronize with the PSPCA's sheltering software, importing/exporting functionality, reporting tools, and price. Ultimately, WiseGuys™, by Database Marketing Solutions, Inc., was selected as it was "user-friendly" and able to be customized to meet PSPCA's needs.

The next task was to import existing donor names and addresses from Excel into the new database. Vicki established source codes and match codes for each unique customer record, which would allow the PSPCA team to analyze which sources provide the most responsive and profitable donors. The next step was to determine appropriate customer segmentation criteria, which would enable messages to be tailored and targeted to each unique segment. Vicki realized she needed additional information in order to create a sound segmentation strategy. She obtained a team of volunteer market researchers from the marketing department of her Alma Mater and began surveying more than 15 of the top SPCAs across the country to learn how they segmented their databases. The results showed that most SPCAs were not segmenting their databases—a result of a lack of time and inability to integrate current marketing practices. Of the few SPCAs that did, the following segments were identified: Donors, Potential Donors, and Volunteers. Exhibit C13.2 provides additional detail about these segments.

The final step in the database development process was to establish ways to generate leads and train volunteers to enter new data. Data entry took much longer than Vicki envisioned, but it was well worth the effort. Vicki created processes to capture new names of people adopting, visiting the PSPCA, and/or participating in a fundraising event. With the database foundation established, it was time to begin executing the marketing plan.

The Marketing Plan
Direct Mail Program

Research revealed that the optimal frequency of direct mail solicitations was four to six times per year. Therefore, the direct mail plan was built around executing four direct mail solicitations per year.

As Exhibit C13.3 reveals, the first solicitation focused on the transformational changes taking place at the PSPCA. It included a callout box that highlighted the work local vets were donating to the PSPCA—a fact that was not known in the com-

EXHIBIT C13.2: DATABASE MARKET SEGMENTATION

A. Donors

1. Cat People—people who specifically love cats.
     Gift History
        a. High—donation $500 plus
        b. Medium—donation $100-$500
        c. Low—donation $items-$100
2. Dog People—people who specifically love dogs.
     Gift History
        a. High—donation $500 plus
        b. Medium—donation $100-$500
        c. Low—donation $items-$100
3. Animal Lovers—people who do not have an animal preference.
     Gift History
        a. High—donation $500 plus
        b. Medium—donation $100-$500
        c. Low—donation $items-$100

B. Potential Donors

1. Cat Adopters—people who have adopted a cat from the SPCA.
        a. Newborns—first six months of adoption
        b. Infants—after six months to one year of adoption
2. Dog Adopters—people who have adopted a dog from the SPCA.
        a. Newborns—first six months of adoption
        b. Infants—after six months to one year of adoption
3. Animal Adopters—people who have other pets from the SPCA.
        a. Newborns—first six months of adoption
        b. Infants—after six months to one year of adoption
4. Participators—participants of raffles, fundraising events, and/or the Petting Zoo.

C. Volunteers

munity and that would inspire confidence in the PSPCA's operations. Another callout box was included that highlighted the story of a rescued dog—the purpose of this callout box was to test how many people would visit the PSPCA's web site to read his rescue story.

This direct mail campaign was distributed to more than 7,000 past donors and cost $2,500. It yielded a 7.1 percent response rate and raised $19,415, which translates into a 677 percent return on investment. This was considered an excellent response that validated the profitability of the direct mail strategy. Vicki was very pleased but wondered, "What more could be done to increase the response rate?"

The results of the subsequent direct mail campaigns can be seen in Exhibit C13.4. Notice the varying response rates on each of the direct mail campaigns.

As Exhibit C13.5 illustrates, direct mail solicitations are not created equal and there are many factors that contribute to their success. The dip in January could have been caused by seasonal fluctuations in donation activity. Or it could have been

EXHIBIT C13.3: INITIAL PSPCA DIRECT MAIL PIECE

This dog was found in the middle of the road, skeletal and missing much of his coat. Read his SPCA rescue story at peninsulaspca.com!

Helping discarded dogs like him...
...is what we do.

Dear SPCA Supporter:

Each day, 10,000 humans are born in the United States. By comparison, 70,000 puppies and kittens are born each day. Since there will never be 70,000 new homes available each day, millions of healthy animals will face early deaths as a form of animal control. Others will be left to fend for themselves against automobiles, inhabitable weather, neglect and cruelty.

At the Peninsula SPCA, we are working very hard to change these statistics on the Virginia Peninsula.

Over the last few years, we have overhauled our management and Board of Directors, replaced outdated financial systems, scrutinized our expenses, improved our relationship with our municipal partners, and examined every aspect of our operations. The transformation continues, and we vow to leave no stone unturned! As a result of this tireless effort, we have proudly established an unshakable foundation for our future.

Now, we need your help!

We are creating an aggressive strategic plan to realize our mission of finding a good home for every adoptable pet. This will be impossible to achieve without your support! The suggested donations below illustrate how your money could be used TODAY to improve the quality of life for our animals. If you will donate to our animals today, we pledge to you that 100% of your contribution (yes, every penny!) will go towards helping the precious animals in our care.

On behalf of all of our animals, I thank you for your generosity and support.

Sincerely,

Doug

G. Douglas Bevelacqua
President, Peninsula SPCA Board of Directors

P.S. We are now on the web! Please visit us at *www.peninsulaspca.com!*

Through the Peninsula Veterinary Association, area vets volunteer their expertise on a rotating basis to treat our injured animals.

❖ PENINSULA SPCA

Your donation will go directly toward improving the lives of the animals in our care. See what your donation could provide:

❏ $15 keeps one homeless animal free of fleas and ticks for one month.

❏ $25 provides antibiotics for one injured animal.

❏ $50 provides complete grooming for one severely neglected pet.

❏ $75 spays or neuters one underprivileged pet.

❏ $100 provides all vaccinations, flea & worm treatments, and a microchip for one homeless pet.

❏   I want to help more!

Name: _____

Address: _____

City, St., Zip

Yes, I want to receive email updates from the SPCA!

email: _____

Visa   Master Card   Discover   (circle one)

Card # _____ Exp. Date:_____

Signature:

EXHIBIT C13.4: DIRECT MAIL CAMPAIGNS
RESPONSE RATE ANALYSIS

Date	Mailing	Number Mailed	Response Rate	Funds Raised	Cost	Net Income	ROI
April Year 1	Helping Discarded Pets is What We Do	7,389	7.10%	$19,415	$2,500	$16,915	677%
Sept. Year 1	Operation: On The Run & Having Fun!	7,390	7.24%	$21,089	$2,500	$18,589	744%
Jan. Year 2	Together, We Changed Lives	8,794	4.97%	$14,759	$3,300	$11,459	347%
June Year 2	PVA/SPCA Clinic Fund	46,000	0.80%	$22,885	$24,000	($1,115)	−5%
	(SPCA Donors)	8,806	2.77%	$13,860	$4,594	$9,266	202%
	(Pet Owner Prospects)	37,194	0.34%	$9,025	$19,406	($10,381)	−53%
Sept. Year 1	Never Again (Disaster Planning)	9,548	4.16%	$16,985	$3,000	$13,985	466%
Dec. Year 2	Holiday Appeal	9,548	6.00%	$27,500	$3,000	$24,500	817%

caused by a more complicated reason such as lack of communication with donors other than solicitations, poor messaging, or a combination of political or market factors. Vicki didn't know for sure. She thought that more time was needed to confirm or rule out the timing or seasonal possibilities. She also thought focus groups or short surveys might shed some light on the significant variation in direct mail results. However, surveys and focus groups take time. In the meantime Vicki had to make decisions about future marketing efforts.

The dip in June is likely to be attributable to an attempt to cultivate new donors. In an effort to expand its donor base, Vicki reached out to the veterinary community to solicit its clients. Since clients of vet clinics own pets, Vicki and her PSPCA team speculated that they would be sympathetic towards the PSPCA's mission and willing to support it financially. Several veterinarians in the area provided Vicki with their customer lists, which the PSPCA mailed, requesting a donation. She knew that prospect solicitations often lose money in the short run; however, the lifetime value of each donor far exceeds the initial gift, so effective prospecting can be a lucrative long-term investment. In this instance, a 0.34 percent response was achieved . . . 112 new donors. Vicki and the team saw this effort as a means of generating awareness and "planting seeds for the future" rather than an unsuccessful direct mail effort.

Overall, the PSPCA direct mail campaigns were highly effective, both in strengthening relationships with its donor base and generating funds for the shelter. However, Vicki and her team were not focused solely on direct mail campaigns to generate both awareness and funds for the PSPCA, they were also busy planning special events.

Special Fundraising Events

Before Vicki was hired, the only fundraising event the PSPCA sponsored was an annual golf tournament. Results had diminished over the years as past participants moved, had lifestyle changes, or just lost interest. Part of Vicki's charge within the new marketing plan was to create and implement profitable fundraising events. The

**EXHIBIT C13.5: GRAPHICAL ILLUSTRATION OF
TOTAL INCOME AND NET INCOME**

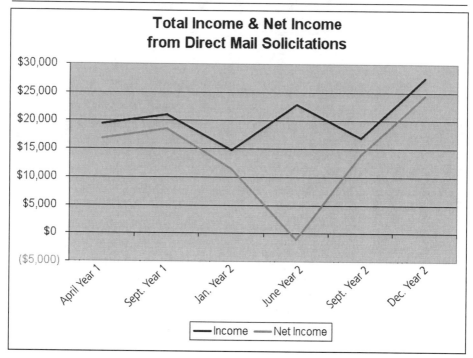

question she faced: What kind of events to run? To determine the most successful fundraising events, Vicki again surveyed top SPCAs across the country. Results indicated the flagship fundraiser of most SPCAs was a pledge walk, with top SPCAs earning between $100,000 and $200,000 each year on that event alone.

The premise of the pledge walk is basic: get individuals to register and raise money from their friends and family. Participants have many ways to raise money: ask in person, mail requests, hold their own mini-fundraisers at work/school/church, etc. Participants can also easily create an interactive, personal fundraising web page that allows participants to email their requests, complete with a picture of their pet. Team formation is encouraged and prizes are awarded for top individual and team fundraisers.

So, how could this simple idea yield hundreds of thousands of dollars? The answer is simple: it's a direct marketing extravaganza. Rather than using a mass request to ask thousands of people for money, a pledge walk provides a fun way for individuals to make requests on behalf of the PSPCA. The beauty of this approach is that each request is a highly targeted, one-on-one plea to the hottest leads of all—friends and family. In addition to requesting donations, registered individuals also ask for their friends and family to register themselves, thus exponentially expanding the PSPCA team's reach.

The PSPCA launched its first dog walk, "Paws for a Cause Dog Walk & Festival," with great anticipation. Following the advice of the Tampa Bay SPCA, the majority of

Vicki and her team's energy was focused on recruiting walkers to fundraise on its behalf. Additionally, Vicki approached many local businesses to sponsor the event and donate via in-kind contributions so that 100 percent of pledges raised from the walkers would benefit the animals. With the help of everyone at the PSPCA and many volunteers, a massive festival was put together to draw non-participants to witness the walk, which included local rescue groups, pet-related vendors, canine games and contests, and canine demonstrations. Exhibit C13.6 presents the direct mail piece promoting this event.

The event was a resounding success and raised more than $77,000. Since only $15,000 was raised in company sponsorships, the remaining $62,000 came from the direct marketing engine comprised of hundreds of motivated individuals making targeted, individualized requests on piping hot leads. Vicki again was extremely pleased with these results and quickly began planning what she would do differently for next year's dog walk and festival.

The Outcome—Year One

As the successes and disappointments of the PSPCA's marketing efforts illustrate, direct marketing is not a success-only journey, and the PSPCA team learned several important lessons along the way. Since it is every marketer's goal to maximize profit on every activity, it is important to recognize the role that measuring and analyzing results play in ensuring that tactics that are effective are repeated and tactics that are not effective are eliminated. It is also vital to recognize the importance of performing solid research to avoid investing in activities that are likely to fail.

At the end of its first year, Vicki and the PSPCA team had raised more than $165,000 from marketing activities and projected raising over $250,000 in the second year. Just as importantly, however, the team's marketing efforts began the critical task of forming thousands of relationships with community members—people that might well become future donors, future volunteers, and hopefully, future families for the homeless animals of the Virginia Peninsula.

The Case Challenges—Year Two and Beyond

Given the successes enjoyed during the first year, Vicki was highly motivated to tackle year two. She revised the PSPCA marketing plan and began to plan more direct mail campaigns and special events. But first, Vicki focused her efforts on a few of the other critical marketing objectives: the development of the PSPCA's new tag line, product line, web site updates and on-line store. Exhibit C13.7 shows the portion of the PSPCA marketing plan pertaining to the "Funds Raised" goal. It also details the related strategies for each of the marketing objectives.

Along with the creation of the new PSPCA tag line, *"Think. Adopt. Love."* Vicki realized she needed to order new PSPCA merchandise to promote the new slogan.

The merchandise included T-shirts, sweatshirts, and hats in a variety of attractive colors. In addition to being displayed in the front reception area at the PSPCA, the merchandise was promoted at all off-site PSPCA events and activities. The staff proudly wore the new apparel with the new tag line to further integrate the brand image and promote animal adoptions. Sales of merchandise were steadily increasing.

Think.Adopt.Love.

Vicki was pleased that the staff and volunteers seemed so in tune with the new PSPCA look and slogan. Of course, Vicki quickly updated the PSPCA web site with its new tag line and began investigating the creation of an online store to further promote the new apparel. With the merchandise displayed and the web site updated, Vicki began to focus on planning the next direct mail campaign and special event.

With the holidays approaching, Vicki's thoughts turned toward a combined appreciation and holiday greeting direct mail campaign. "What a perfect time to thank our donors and volunteers for all they have given us during this past year. Let's host an open house and invite everyone to visit the shelter, enjoy refreshments and a tour of our recent shelter renovations, and view our new PSPCA apparel—which would make great holiday gifts," she exclaimed. The idea was quickly accepted and endorsed by Vicki's Executive Director and the entire PSPCA board. The enthusiasm was contagious and everyone quickly got busy planning for the event. The holiday direct mail piece served as an invitation to the open house, a holiday greeting, and a fundraising effort all in one. Exhibit C13.8 shows this holiday direct mail piece.

The results of the holiday direct mail appeal (previously shown in Exhibit C13.4) were quite impressive. The holiday mailer garnered a six percent response rate, $27,500 in donations, and more than 500 visitors to the shelter for the Open House. Many of the PSPCA friends at the Open House were eager to hear more about the plans for PSPCA's first annual Fur Ball. When Dr. and Mrs. Boxx asked Vicki about the event, Vicki was happy to share details. "The Fur Ball will be a black-tie event which will be held at a local ballroom. Everyone will be able to enjoy an evening filled with cocktails, fine dining, and live music. This event will also feature both silent and live auctions to benefit our animals. But, the real unique feature of this event is that our guests will be welcome to bring their canine and feline companions to the ball and we'll have a dedicated portion of the evening for our guests to show off their furry friends." Everyone thought it sounded divine! Vicki was so enthusiastic that she could hardly wait to get back to preparing for the Fur Ball. Exhibit C13.9 presents the PSPCA Fur Ball invitation.

This inaugural event was a success. Everyone had a wonderful time and established donors brought new donors with them to the event. Vicki was especially glad to see the PSPCA database grow. With three flagship special events held in a one-year span of time, Vicki was both exhausted and totally enthused. A review of the special events shows that the initial dog walk and festival incurred the largest expense, but also generated the most revenue for the PSPCA. See Exhibit C13.10 for a summary of the funds generated via the three special events.

As Vicki began to analyze the outcomes of the direct mail campaigns and special events, she thought, "I know that there is much more we should be doing . . . but what? How can we improve on the foundation we've just established? Act I went well. What do we do for Act II?"

EXHIBIT C13.6: PAWS FOR A CAUSE
DOG WALK & FESTIVAL DIRECT MAIL PIECE

PAWS FOR A CAUSE
DOG WALK & FESTIVAL

Come join us for a fun-packed day to raise money for our animals!

Riverview Park,
Newport News

Sunday, May 20
12:00 - 4:00 pm

EVENTS WILL INCLUDE:

- Demonstrations including the Great American Disc Dog Show
- Police & bomb dog demonstration
- Dog trick workshop
- Tail wagging & dog costume contests
- Avenue of Heroes (local rescue groups)
- Woofstock stage featuring music & entertainment
- Raffle & prizes
- Food & exhibitors

PRE-REGISTER TO BEGIN COLLECTING PLEDGES NOW!

Benefits of pre-registration include:
- Exclusive event t-shirt
- Goody bags
- Prizes for top fundraisers in both individual & team categories
- Pledge packet
- Free personal web page
- Monthly fundraising tips & event updates

PENINSULA SPCA
peninsulaspca.com

Sponsored in part by:

EXHIBIT C13.7: PSPCA MARKETING PLAN—GOAL 2

Marketing Plan Goal 2—Objectives & Strategies

Goal 2: Increase Donations

Objective A: Increase Direct Mail Donations
Strategies:

1. Analyze last two years' direct mail results	$ –	$—
2. Plan/Execute upcoming year direct mail plan	$12,000	$50,000
3. Increase size of database	$18,000	$20,000

Objective B: Increase Event Donations
Strategies:

1. 2nd Annual Paws for a Cause Dog Walk & Festival	$15,000	$80,000
2. 4th Annual All Fore Animals Golf Tournament	$10,000	$25,000
3. 1st Annual Fur Ball	$20,000	$50,000
4. Write playbooks for all events	$—	$—
5. Collect lessons learned for each event	$—	$—
6. Research other shelters for income ideas	$—	$—
7. Fine Arts Shop & Hausers Fundraisers	$—	$2,000

Objective C: Increase Bequests
Strategies:

1. Research how other shelters secure bequests	$—	$—
2. Plan/Execute bequest plan	$—	$—

Objective D: Create Grant Income
Strategies:

1. Create a list of grants the SPCA is eligible for	$—	$—
2. Get grant-writing tips from city contacts	$—	$—
3. Recruit volunteer grant writers	$—	$—
4. Partner with CNU grant writing classes	$—	$—
5. Apply for grants	$—	$—

Objective E: Develop Product Line
Strategies:

1. Research other shelters' product lines	$—	$—
2. Design product line	$10,000	$15,000
3. Establish inventory tracking system	$—	$—
4. Establish display in lobby	$2,000	$—
5. Establish online store	$—	$2,000

Vicki began to make some notes of the marketing challenges she must tackle and the strategic decisions that must be made in order to continue moving the PSPCA on an upward path.

Decision #1—Cleaning and Expanding the Customer/Donor Database

A big concern was maintaining the integrity of the newly created database. People move. Lifestyles and interests change. How and when should the database be updated? Were there other ways to segment customers to make correspondence with

EXHIBIT C13.8: PSPCA HOLIDAY DIRECT MAIL CAMPAIGN

Until he extends the circle of his compassion to all living things, man will not himself find peace.

– Dr. Albert Schweitzer, Nobel Peace Prize 1952

Dear Friend of the SPCA:

Peace. With the holiday season upon us, we hear a lot about peace. We wish it for others, we seek it for ourselves and everything from greeting cards to store displays proclaims its presence. Yet it remains elusive. Maybe Dr. Schweitzer was right.

As a friend of the Peninsula SPCA, you are part of a circle of compassion that has touched thousands of lives during the past year. We hope the support you have given—by making a donation, adopting a dog or cat, or volunteering with us—has provided you with a measure of peace and goodwill.

Together, this is what we have accomplished just this year:

 • Found homes for more than 3,000 animals
 • Reunited over 1,300 lost pets with their families
 • Performed nearly 600 spay/neuter surgeries in our new on-site vet clinic

As the new executive director of the Peninsula SPCA, I am pleased to invite you to visit our "new" shelter, which has undergone extensive renovations in the past several months. The result is a more comfortable environment for the animals in our care and a more welcoming atmosphere for our public.

We welcome you to come to our open house complete with guided tours and refreshments. You also can see our new SPCA apparel for holiday giving!

In the meantime, we are turning to you and counting on your compassion for help, so that we can do even more for the Peninsula's homeless animals in 2008. Your tax-deductible contribution is needed now more than ever before. With your added support, we can realize our vision of saving the lives of all the healthy cats and dogs in our region.

Dr. Schweitzer also wrote that "compassion can only attain its full breadth and depth if it embraces all living creatures and does not limit itself to mankind."

Thank you for helping us embrace our homeless animals.

May peace be with you and your family (both two- and four-legged) during this holiday season.

Gratefully yours,

Ritchie L. Geisel, MBA
Executive Director

Doug Bevelacqua, M.Ed., NCC
Chair

PENINSULA SPCA

Home for the Holidays

Recently, we received a letter from a seven-year-old girl named Lexi Solomon, whose parents had adopted two kittens, Matoaka and Buttons. Concerned about the other homeless animals in our shelter, Lexi made a very thoughtful gift in support of our cats and dogs. Her letter below expresses her compassion and love for our homeless animals.

Read more of our success stories online!

P.S. Remember, mark your calendars now for Saturday, December 15th for our open house celebration!

them even more personalized and relevant? Should there be more information the PSPCA should track in its database? She even wondered about the effectiveness of tracking the age of a customer's pet as many seek a "replacement companion" upon the death of a household animal.

EXHIBIT C13.9: PSPCA HOLIDAY DIRECT MAIL CAMPAIGN

Name: _____ Company: _____ Phone: _____

Address: _____ Email: _____

Fur Ball

Attendees: Qty:
☐ $125 per guest   _____   ☐Sorry, I am unable to attend the event,
☐ $65 per pet   _____   please accept my contribution of: $_____

*Please write the names of those attending (pets and people) on reverse.

Please choose an entrée(s):   Qty:
☐ Roast sirloin of beef au jus with a bordelaise sauce   _____
☐ Pan seared chicken breast with a rosemary veloute sauce   _____
☐ Oven roasted tomato stuffed with barley and grilled vegetables   _____
☐ Herb crusted tilapia with a sun dried tomato cream sauce   _____

Method of Payment: ☐ Cash   ☐ Check

Card #: _____ exp date: _____ Total Payment: $ _____
☐ Visa   ☐ Mastercard   ☐ Discover

For telephone reservations, please call 757.595.1392.
Thank You for supporting the animals!

Decision #2—Establishing Effective Prospecting Strategies

Another major issue that had to be addressed was prospecting for new donors. The immediate fundraising results from the lists provided by local veterinarians were dismal, but Vicki expected prospecting would take time. Vicki knew that her Executive Director was very supportive of investigating future list rental strategies. Vicki recalled a recent conversation: "Vicki, I'm prepared to allocate an additional $5,000 to your marketing budget for next year to support list rental strategies if you believe they will generate long-term donors and a solid return on our investment over time." Vicki's questions were: "Will it be worth it? How long will it take to cultivate new donors? Where could she find appropriate lists? Should she change her fundraising approach to new prospects? What should be the offer and primary message to prospective donors? How should she test the lists to get the most out of her prospecting efforts?

Decision #3—Direct Mail Fundraising Campaign Analysis

Most of the PSPCA direct mail campaigns generated funds beyond the costs incurred in their execution, however, Vicki was troubled by the fact that some were more profitable than others. "Why did some direct mail campaigns generate a larger response rate than others? How can I analyze each campaign to better understand the mindset of our donors? Are our fundraising appeals hitting the right emotional chords? How can I improve each direct mail package? Should I be communicating with our donors more often or less often?" Vicki had lots of questions for which she desired answers.

EXHIBIT C13.10: SPECIAL EVENTS SUMMARY

Event	Paws for A Cause Dog Walk & Festival	Fur Ball	Paws for A Cause Dog Walk & Festival
Date	May 20, Year 2	April 4, Current Year	May 18, Current Year
Number of Participants/Guests	392	169	380
Sponsorship Income	$10,850	$20,250	$6,775
Total Funds Raised	$66,510	$44,894	$49,597
Total Expenses	$15,049	$ 2,979	$ 8,254
Net Income	$62,311	$41,915	$48,118

Decision #4—Special Event Planning

Planning each special event takes time and resources, but the residual effect is worth it. The Dog Walk & Festival and the Fur Ball were excellent events that generated both awareness and funds to support the PSPCA mission and cultivated friends for the shelter. Vicki knew that she would recommend continuing these events on an annual basis. However, she was always searching for other creative ideas for special events. "What other types of events might be effective? Should I be planning more events each year? Should I survey our donors and volunteers for ideas?" These were just a few of the questions Vicki posed to herself.

Decision #5—Animal Adoptions

While the focus of this case and much of Vicki's time has been dedicated to the goal of raising funds to support the PSPCA, she was also mindful of the shelter's mission—to find a loving home for each animal brought to the shelter. Vicki realized that the two goals were not isolated—and in fact, generating community awareness of the shelter, raising funds, cultivating PSPCA friends, and promoting PSPCA special events were certainly having a positive impact on animal adoptions. But, Vicki wanted to do more. She thought to herself. "How can the PSPCA influence or change the mind-sets of residents in the community to think about adopting an animal from our shelter prior to visiting a local pet store? What types of marketing activities can we conduct to attract potential adopters to visit the shelter?" Vicki also wanted to do more to promote the sale of the new PSPCA apparel. She wondered how the new "Think. Adopt. Love." tag line could add value to the promotion of the new merchandise while getting the adoption message out to the greater community. "How can we use the new tag line to increase our animal adoptions?" Vicki thought she might generate more possibilities if she took a stroll through the shelter and visited some of her favorite furry friends.

Vicki returned to her office with a smile on her face. "Animals are the best medicine to cheer a person. What awesome companions they make! The animals in our shelter deserve to become pets of loving families. I have to work harder to help make that happen!" With those thoughts and the images of the faces of those cute puppies and cuddly kittens Vicki had just visited in mind, Vicki was rejuvenated and was ready to begin tackling her strategic decisions with even more passion and determination.

CASE
14

Primetime Developmental Playthings, Inc.

HARLAN SPOTTS
Western New England College
GREG BALEJA
Alma College

I t was 2:00 p.m. on a sunny November afternoon. Laura Thomas and Mary Fischer were sitting in the conference room at the corporate headquarters of Primetime Developmental Playthings (PDP), Inc. As marketing directors, Laura and Mary were working to develop the new marketing plan for the company. It was necessary to devise a strategy to establish a corporate identity for PDP, stimulate consumer demand for PDP products, and maintain retailer loyalty through building consumer store traffic.

Laura and Mary looked around the conference room. Toys from the various PDP product lines filled the walls and corners of the room, which had recently become more crowded with the addition of two new product lines to the current product mix. As they contemplated the future strategy of the firm, Laura and Mary knew they had to get to work. Carson Scott, president of PDP, had asked Laura and Mary to have a draft of their plan on his desk within the next week. Time was an important factor since the company needed to develop a new database structure and put it in operation early next year. The new database was integral for developing new relationship marketing strategies in the future.

Laura and Mary had spent weeks reviewing the various company documents spread before them on the table. The first step required them to clearly define their target market and set marketing objectives. The next step in the process was to develop the marketing strategy they would propose to Carson Scott within the week.

Industry Overview

The United States shipped over 2 billion toys annually and was the largest market for toys in the world. There were over 120,000 individual stockkeeping units (SKUs), with approximately 6,000 new toys introduced every year according to the Toy Manufacturers of America (TMA). Retail sales were estimated currently at $20 billion annually, an increase of 7 percent over the previous year. Manufacturer sales were estimated at approximately two-thirds of retail sales ($13+ billion), up 3 percent over the previous year.

Industry sales were fueled by large annual sales increases in dolls (12.1 percent), ride-ons (10.4 percent), and games and puzzles (7.5 percent). Some categories, however, had not fared so well, with video games (–19.5 percent) and male action toys (–14.1 percent) posting the largest declines (see Exhibit C14.1). Other categories of toys (games, pre-school, infant, and activity toys) exhibited relatively stable sales patterns or intensely hot selling periods due to technological innovations (flying toys, drawing toys, radio-controlled vehicles, toys licensed from popular movies and television shows)—all according to TMA.

As with many industries, toy industry sales suffered from severe seasonality. Almost two-thirds of industry sales occurred between October and December. As one would suspect, the holiday season drove this massive buying trend.

Toy manufacturers attracted consumers through product differentiation. Some toys exhibited fad life cycles, being highly promotional and trendy. In contrast, there were many traditional toys that constituted the backbone of the industry. Given the competitive and volatile nature of the industry, companies started up and went out of business often. Recently, many companies had merged as industry leaders tried to solidify their market positions and competitors worked to achieve differential advantage. Some of the larger past acquisitions included Hasbro's purchase of Tonka in 1991 and Mattel's purchase of Fisher-Price in 1993. In November of 1996, Mattel announced their purchase of Tyco for $175 million. At that time, this acquisition solidified Mattel's number-one position within the industry.

The toy industry could be split into two primary segments, mass and specialty toy markets. While both sectors of the industry produced toys for infants and children, they were drastically different in terms of industry structure, product offerings, and marketing activities.

The Mass Market Sector

This sector was dominant, accounting for approximately 80 percent of industry sales. While there were many toy manufacturers, Mattel and Hasbro dominated in terms of market share and influence. Sales for these two companies have been $3.6 and $2.9 billion, respectively, in a recent year. These larger manufacturers marketed many well-known brands, including Barbie, Tonka, Lego, GI Joe, and Hot Wheels.

Toys produced for this sector were aggressively marketed and distributed through mass merchandising retail chain stores (i.e., Toys 'R Us, Wal-Mart). They also were supported by large expenditures in national television advertising and consumer/ trade promotions (see Exhibit C14.2). Mattel and Hasbro were both among *Advertising Age*'s Top 100 Advertisers, each having spent in excess of $260 million in the U.S. in a recent year. This was a highly competitive industry with dominance of retail shelf space being of prime importance.

According to S&P Industry Surveys, some trends affecting the industry included:

• Increased competition for retail shelf space as mass market toy retailers close stores and cut back on the number of SKUs in inventory

EXHIBIT C14.1: TMA CATEGORY SALES RESULTS

Estimated Manufacturers' Shipments by Product Category
Dollars (First Billing Value[1]) and Units Current Year vs. Previous Year
Volumes have been projected to reflect total industry levels (estimated volumes in millions)

	DOLLARS			UNITS		
Prior	Prior Year	Current Year	% Year Change	Prior Year	Current Year	% Year Change
I. INFANT/PRE-SCHOOL	**$1,345**	**$1,391**	**3.4**	**201**	**207**	**3.0**
Infant Toys*	462	480		73	76	
Pre-School Musical Toys	61	63		10	11	
Pre-School Blocks/Accessories	24	27		4	5	
Pre-School Villages/Scenery Sets*	105	125		9	10	
Pre-School Talking/Sound Toys	64	62		8	8	
Pre-School Learning Toys	50	57		7	8	
Pre-School Tub Toys	14	16		3	4	
Pre-School Role Playing Toys*	170	170		27	25	
Pre-School Push/Pull Toys*	27	25		4	4	
Pre-School Vehicles*	161	180		23	26	
Pre-School Remaining	207	186		33	30	
II. DOLLS	**$1,691**	**$1,896**	**12.1**	**221**	**241**	**9.0**
Large Dolls	331	341		26	27	
Large Doll Accessories	46	49		11	12	
Fashion Dolls/Clothes/Accessories*	693	855		97	113	
Mini Dolls*	220	273		51	55	
Mini Doll Accessories	90	70		9	7	
Soft Dolls	31	30		6	6	
Remaining Dolls/Accessories***	160	170		12	13	
Doll Houses/Furniture*	120	108		9	8	
III. PLUSH	**$921**	**$914**	**−0.8**	**123**	**123**	**0.0**
Musical/Electronic Plush/Accessories	120	125		8	9	
Traditional Plush**	782	767		112	110	
Puppets**	19	22		3	4	
IV. MALE ACTION TOYS	**$926**	**$795**	**−14.1**	**165**	**145**	**−12.1**
Action Figures	687	592		139	122	
Action Figure Accessories*	180	154		21	19	
Male Role Playing	59	49		5	4	
V. VEHICLES	**$1,198**	**$1,213**	**1.3**	**238**	**231**	**−2.9**
Radio Controlled Vehicles*	250	289		10	11	
Remote Controlled Vehicles**	34	38		4	5	
Battery Operated Vehicles	43	36		6	5	
Other Powered Vehicles	24	22		7	7	

[1]First Billing Value: first price paid for an item in the U.S.

(Continued)

EXHIBIT C14.1: TMA CATEGORY SALES RESULTS (Continued)

	DOLLARS			UNITS		
Prior	Current Year	% Year	Prior Change	Current Year	% Year	Change
Boats/Aircraft—Powered	24	24		4	4	
Mini Vehicles	282	261		147	138	
Non-Powered Cars	46	45		9	9	
Non-Powered Aircraft/Boats	34	34		10	10	
Non-Powered Trucks*	156	144		17	16	
Vehicle Accessories	88	95		10	10	
Electric/Battery Car Sets/Accessories	42	44		2	3	
Electric Train Sets/Accessories**	175	181		12	13	
VI. RIDE-ONS	**$722**	**$797**	**10.4**	**31**	**35**	**12.9**
Metal Tricycles	22	21		1	1	
Plastic Tricycles	35	33		2	2	
Other Pedal Ride-Ons	35	34		1	1	
Non-Pedal Ride-Ons	79	91		3	4	
Battery Operated Ride-Ons & Accessories*	172	191		2	2	
Stationary/Rocking/Spring Horses	14	15		1	1	
Riding Sports***	331	370		19	22	
All Other Riding Vehicles	34	42		2	2	
VII. GAMES/PUZZLES	**$1,220**	**$1,312**	**7.5**	**222**	**230**	**3.6**
Card Games*	87	94		34	36	
Dice Games	17	19		5	5	
Word Games	30	30		4	4	
Puzzle Games	18	19		5	5	
Standard Games	35	37		9	10	
Travel Games	35	36		8	9	
Children's Board Games	94	100		13	14	
Pre-School Games	40	66		7	9	
Family Board Games	87	111		8	10	
Adult Board Games	90	97		7	8	
Children's Action Games	182	173		27	25	
Family Action Games*	19	21		2	2	
Strategy Games*	55	56		6	6	
Electronic Handheld/Tabletop Games***	260	271		20	21	
Cardboard Puzzles*	135	144		58	57	
Wood/Plastic/Other Puzzles*	36	38		9	9	
VIII. ACTIVITY TOYS	**$1,821**	**$1,827**	**0.3**	**560**	**573**	**2.3**
Building Sets	366	345		41	39	
Scientific Toys**	55	57		7	8	
Fashion Accessories**	108	95		41	36	
Powered Appliances	21	22		1	1	
Non-Powered Appliances	98	77		5	4	
All Other Household/Food Toys	75	73		19	18	

EXHIBIT C14.1: TMA CATEGORY SALES RESULTS (Continued)

Prior	DOLLARS			UNITS		
	Current Year	% Year	Prior Change	Current Year	% Year	Change
Reusable Compounds*	78	96		25	29	
Mechanical Design	120	122		15	15	
Traditional Kits/Supplies**	196	203		58	60	
Sculpture Kits/Supples	17	17		4	4	
Crayons/Markers/Chalk Etc.**	255	270		182	193	
Crayons/Markers/Chalk Sets & Supplies**	108	116		35	37	
Paint Sets/Supplies**	143	152		83	86	
Sewing, Yarn, String Kits/Supplies	21	22		7	7	
Model Kits/Accessories	123	125		26	26	
All Other Activity Toys**	37	35		11	10	
IX. ALL OTHER TOYS	$3,199	$3,289	2.8	1,049	1,040	−0.9
Water/Pool/Sand Toys**	296	323		67	74	
Audio/Visual Toys	186	191		24	24	
Children's Furniture*	102	109		9	10	
Electronic Learning Aids Hardware	225	263		7	8	
Electronic Learning Aids Software	15	18		2	3	
Sports Activities*	485	507		92	95	
Musical Instruments*	*35	36		2	3	
Pre-School Playground Equipment	127	175		3	4	
Guns/Weapons & Accessories**	187	175		58	51	
Swingsets/Gym Sets & Accessories**	89	96		3	3	
Trading Cards & Accessories**	954	887		561	536	
Mini Figures/Scene Sets*	66	72		15	16	
Miscellaneous Toys***	432	452		206	213	
TOTAL TOY INDUSTRY	$13,043	$13,434	3.0	2,810	2,825	0.5
VIDEO GAMES	$3,148	$2,533	−19.5	67	58	−13.4
TV Video Hardware*	700	638		6	4	
TV Video Software*	1,671	1,302		36	33	
TV Video Accessories*	217	173		9	9	
Portable Video Hardware*	251	213		3	3	
Portable Video Software*	250	169		9	6	
Portable Video Accessories*	59	38		4	3	
TOTAL INDUSTRY WITH VIDEO GAMES	$16,191	$15,967	−1.4	2,877	2,883	0.2

- Number of companies responding = 74
- Figures include imports
- All sales are on a GROSS basis
- Data are compiled through a process which includes a polling of major U.S. toy and game manufacturers, and a comparison of trends with the U.S. Toy Market Index (TMI) and Toy Retail Sales Tracking Service (TRSTS)

*Previous Year Figures Revised
**Limited Sample
***Both Previous Year Figures Revised and Limited Sample

EXHIBIT C14.2: TOY INDUSTRY ADVERTISING EXPENDITURES

	4 Years Ago	3 Years Ago	2 Years Ago	Prior Year	Current Year
Spot TV	$200,268,400	$254,297,400	$267,728,200	$261,132,300	$231,087,800
Network TV	153,035,500	208,497,900	220,508,000	241,601,300	219,015,500
Cable TV Networks	42,840,900	78,503,800	128,620,900	142,513,800	157,133,500
Syndicated TV	93,631,400	102,432,400	117,175,400	190,895,800	194,141,500
Magazines	44,292,100	65,097,700	51,973,700	57,530,400	83,378,700
Newspapers including Sunday Magazines	3,556,000	5,755,600	3,002,900	6,045,800	4,503,500
Outdoor	21,600	62,200	92,100	130,000	83,300
Network Radio	809,400	743,600	18,200	377,600	953,000
National Spot Radio	2,014,900	1,424,900	1,250,900	2,035,500	4,431,600
TOTAL	$540,470,200	$716,815,500	$790,370,300	$902,262,500	$896,670,300

Source: Competitive Media Reporting and Publishers Information Bureau

- Continued industry growth through the marketing of licensed products with tie-ins to televisions shows and movies
- Collectible toys having a major influence on the industry, with Barbie and Matchbox leading the way
- Major manufacturers moving in the direction of multimedia and CD-ROM technology, taking advantage of the increased penetration of personal home computers
- Decreasing resin costs for plastic products over the last year, relieving some of the pressure on profit margins

The Specialty Sector

This sector of the industry was almost the exact opposite of the mass market. It was small, accounting for approximately 20 percent of industry sales according to *Playthings,* and the companies competing in this sector were, for the most part, privately owned. Annual market growth had been steady at 5 percent.

While there were hundreds of companies that manufactured specialty and educational toys, no one company appeared to have the market dominance of a Mattel or Hasbro. It was very likely that a small, privately owned company with a few employees could dominate a product category, but not the overall market. Some of the more well-known names in this sector included Brio, Educational Insights, LearningCurve, Primetime Developmental Playthings, and Playmobile.

Manufacturers in this sector almost exclusively distributed their products through specialty toy retailers. Recently, some of the larger manufacturers, such as Playmobile, had been testing the mass merchandising market. Marketing activities in the specialty arena were reflective of industry size and retail structure. Most companies did not engage in national television advertising or consumer promotions. Trade promotions were limited, with many manufacturers restricting their purchasing requirements to favorable payment terms. Some manufacturers used price-off promotions, but these were usually small (less than 20 percent) and occurred only one time during the year (usually prior to Christmas holidays). From a marketing perspective, this sector of the industry was much less sophisticated than the mass market.

Retail Market Structure

The two primary distribution channels consisted of manufacturer direct to retailer and manufacturer to wholesaler to retailer (TMA). A very small number of companies, such as Discovery Toys, sold direct to consumers. There were over 70,000 retailers across both sectors selling toys and games (TMA). This number included many different types of retailers, from the large mass merchandisers carrying toys as a sideline, to the large, "toys only" merchandisers, to the small, independent toy retailers.

Mass Merchandisers

The mass merchandiser was typified by the "category killer" outlet such as Toys 'R Us, and discount department stores such as Kmart and Wal-Mart. These retailers competed on both selection and price. They carried mainstream toys, both traditional and fad, in inventory and were supported by millions of advertising dollars. Many of the toys carried in these stores were based on popular movie and television programs through tie-in licensing agreements (e.g., *Batman, Star Wars, Star Trek, The Simpsons, Space Jam*). These stores often carried many nationally advertised products and loss leaders to stimulate store traffic. Margins for advertised toys ranged from 15 to 25 percent, while non-advertised toys had margins ranging from 35 to 40 percent (TMA).

Specialty Retailers

The specialty store retailers supported the specialty toy manufacturers. There were approximately 15,000 specialty and educational toy retailers in the United States. The majority of specialty retailers were small, with one to five locations. Recently, a number of chains had begun to expand within the U.S. market, growing rapidly in size. While the total number of retailers had remained constant over the last six years, there did appear to be a high level of turnover with enough new stores opening up to replace the existing stores going out of business.

These retailers actively avoided carrying mass market merchandise because they could not compete in the rough-and-tumble, price-oriented segment of the industry. Instead, they sought to obtain a competitive advantage by providing high-quality developmental and educational toys that made parents feel good about the products they purchased for their children.

While specialty retailers tended to sell higher priced toys, they provided unique product offerings and services to consumers not available from mass merchandisers. Specialty toy retailers were interested in getting to know their customers and determining their need for specific and unique toys. They would even special order specific items for consumers if a particular toy was not in stock. This type of service was in stark contrast to the mass merchandiser, where self-service was standard operating procedure and sales clerks knew relatively little about the products stocked in the store. This resulted in a much more impersonal store experience for the consumer.

Primetime Developmental Playthings: Company Overview

The headquarters for Primetime Developmental Playthings was a renovated loft located in the former warehouse district of Cleveland, Ohio. It was a young, fast-growing company that had increased from 10 to 52 employees in the previous two years. The facilities were rustic, utilizing the open office concept with a corporate culture best described as "West Coast Casual."

PDP was a concept-, rather than an item-, driven company. Its mission could be described as " . . . providing the highest quality toy brands that stimulate children's natural creativity and encourage development backed by a lifetime guarantee." It was a business centered around PDP's relationship with its customers. Thus, all products produced and marketed needed to fit within the overall concept of the company. One of PDP's goals among retailers was to become a leading supplier of toys in the specialty segment of the industry. Among consumers, PDP wanted to have the same name recognition for toys that the "Good Housekeeping Seal of Approval" had for consumer products.

The products that PDP manufactured were sold through specialty toy stores across the country. Independent sales representatives or sales representative organizations sold PDP products to specialty toy store retailers on a commission basis. PDP had no direct control over the sales organizations. All consumer sales went through the retailer; there were no direct sales to consumers.

Founder and president of the company, Carson Scott, had started PDP about three years ago. The company grew out of a struggling retail venture owned by a French company, Best Start Eduplaytion Centers (BSEC). Best Start was a retail specialty toy chain with stores in France, Britain, and Germany, and had opened a chain of U.S. stores based in New Jersey about a decade previous. The chain experienced a number of problems and Scott was brought into the operation to decide whether BSEC should keep, reorganize, or close the retail chain in the United States.

The decision was made to close the U.S. operations of Best Start and Scott jumped from retail to manufacturing with the establishment of Primetime Developmental Playthings, Inc. PDP was started with one product line, Puff N' Chuff Railroad, which was manufactured by a small company in North Carolina. At this time, PDP contracted with a distributor to handle the warehousing and logistics of the Puff N' Chuff product line.

After 18 months of operation, PDP established a customer service department to interface with retailers and customers at the corporate headquarters in Cleveland. In addition to customer service, PDP hired one sales manager to oversee the selling of

PDP products. The distributor maintained the warehousing of products and the independent sales agents were responsible for selling PDP products to retailers.

The distributor's warehouse was located in Bayonne, New Jersey. Another change also took place at this time with the manufacturing of PDP products shifting from North Carolina to Mexico. As with many manufacturers, cost was a consideration in this decision; however, there were also a number of product quality improvements that resulted from the change.

Laura Thomas was the sixth employee hired by PDP. Mary Fischer was the seventh, hired approximately six months after Laura. They had seen rapid expansion in three years' time. PDP's sales went from under $2 million in its first year to over $10 million in its third year of operation (see Exhibit C14.3). The product line grew from one brand to the current eight. Laura Thomas was the marketing director for Puff N' Chuff Railroad, Kinectics Construction Sets, and NuScience Exploration Sets, as well as the new Bake-it Clay Sculpting product line. Mary Fischer, also a marketing director, oversaw the other product lines, including L'Enfant, Primetime Primers, Felt N' Safari and the newly acquired Castlewood line (see Exhibit C14.4 for details). Each product line had an individual marketing assistant.

PDP had been successful and was working to capitalize on the rapid growth of the company to continue the trend. The company had expanded internationally and now had its products distributed in ten countries around the world.

Product Concept

PDP had a philosophy represented by the corporate name, Primetime Developmental Playthings. The product line was designed to provide *developmentally* appropriate toy products to children in their *prime* developing years, from birth to age 15. "Primetime Developmental Playthings' success is not that they just make a good product," said Mary Fischer. "What sets PDP apart from other toy manufacturers is its concept orientation, not a compilation of products with no inter-relationship between the product lines. In PDP, no product stands apart by itself, it is all part of a larger whole. It is a great product design and a great concept for parent-child interaction, the real 'primetime'!"

The product development team at PDP worked with child development experts at a large, public university on the West Coast in the creation of new product lines. These experts reviewed all of the product lines to make sure they were developmentally appropriate. They also created the child development pamphlets included with many of the products to explain to parents exactly what stage their child was in and how the toy could help to enhance certain age-appropriate developmental skills. See Exhibit C14.4 for a complete description of the PDP product line.

While the product line was well developed, Laura and Mary were not satisfied with the level of consumer and retailer understanding of PDP's overarching concept. They knew that any marketing plan must have some product line objectives beyond just sales quotas. In fact, distribution was an area of major importance. While PDP products were distributed in over 3,500 specialty toy stores, not all of the stores carried the complete PDP line. Thus, it would be advantageous to both increase retail penetration and the number of stores carrying all of PDP's products. Within the next two

EXHIBIT C14.3: PRIMETIME DEVELOPMENTAL PLAYTHINGS PERFORMANCE

Figures cited in millions of dollars (000)

	Year 1	Year 2	Year 3	Projected Year 4
Sales Revenues	$1,495.00	$4,562.00	$9,758.00	$12,525.00
Promotional Allowances	14.95	45.62	97.58	125.25
Cost of Goods Sold	807.30	2463.48	4976.58	6262.50
Gross Margin	$672.75	$2052.90	$4683.84	$6012.00
Advertising and Promotion Expense	44.85	136.86	487.90	751.50
Sales Expense	29.90	114.05	195.16	187.87
Administrative Overhead	448.50	1391.41	3122.56	4008.00
Net Profit	**$149.50**	**$410.58**	**$878.22**	**$1064.63**

Numbers are for instructional purposes only and not actual figures.

years, PDP would like a 12.5 percent increase in retail penetration and a doubling of the number of stores carrying the full product line from the current 25 percent.

Retailer Perspective

In discussions about PDP's objectives, Laura related to Mary experiences from her most recent retail store visits. It was clear that there were some difficulties in working with the specialty retailer. While PDP products received good reviews, Laura detected an undercurrent of dissatisfaction with some retailers.

One serious problem PDP faced at both the independent and chain specialty retailers was the merchandising of the various PDP product lines in different areas of the store instead of all together. This merchandising tendency potentially diluted the PDP image and inhibited the cross-sell/upsell strategy. Retailers indicated that they had their own product mix to worry about and did not necessarily see any unique relationship among PDP products. In fact, many specialty toy stores merchandised their product assortments by age group. One specialty toy store in Oregon maintained a web page structured in the same manner as the PDP product line concept.

Retailers were also not satisfied with the sales representatives of PDP always trying to push the bulky displays for PDP products on them. As it was, retailers threw out many of the merchandise displays given to them by manufacturers, instead opting to design their own merchandising plans. This concerned Laura and Mary since the displays were expensive to produce and important for emphasizing the holistic product line concept.

The difficulty with the displays was compounded by the amount of merchandise required to completely fill the unit. The display was designed to have the retailer carry the whole PDP product line. Some retailers wanted to pick and choose products specific for their target markets. The display did not allow for this flexibility. The unit

EXHIBIT C14.4: PRIMETIME DEVELOPMENTAL PLAYTHINGS, INC.

Description of Product Lines

Product	Age	Description
L'Enfant	Birth to 1	This is a complete line of infant toys designed to stimulate the variety of awakening senses experienced by newborns. The first year of life is a powerful year of learning. All products in this line help the infant explore the senses. Included in this line are rattles, teething rings, quilts, mobiles, music boxes, and soft playthings. All products are made in bright and contrasting colors and a variety of shapes.
Primetime Primers	1 to 5	During this time children are beginning to actively explore their environment. They are working through a variety of psychological states as they take command of their bodies. Later during this stage, a lot of emotional and intellectual development takes place. Products in this line include the basic wooden building block sets in a variety of colors, puppet play sets, clay sculpture, wooden pull toys, and a variety of wooden puzzles.
Felt N' Safari	3 to 6	This product line consists of felt playsets with a variety of jungle and zoo motifs to stimulate children's curiosity and learning about animals and rainforests. Playsets are made for both table play and refrigerator play with self-adhesive magnets.
Puff N' Chuff Railroad	4 to 8	This railroad set is very similar to other wooden train sets on the market, such as Brio, Thomas the Tank Engine, and T.C. Timber. Puff N' Chuff includes a variety of characters based on a popular series of children's books. In addition to the wooden train track and trains, buildings and people are available to create complete play towns. The basic set has been immensely popular. Future product introductions will include self-propelled trains using either spring-loaded or AA battery power.
Castlewood	6 to 9	This recently acquired product line allows children to create a medieval castle and town from pre-cut and decorated wooden parts. Consists of a variety of sets that include towers, dungeons, knights, and much more. Each set comes with an informational booklet that provides a variety of interesting facts and details about this fascinating time period.
Bake-it Clay Sculpting	8 to 12	A more advanced art and sculpting kit using a new kitchen oven-firing clay for the budding sculptor in the house hold. Comes with a booklet with step-by-step, illustrated instructions. Also included are finishing paints and glaze for the artistic finishing touches.
Kinectics Construction Sets	8 to 12	This product line contains a number of sets that are a cross between KNEC and LEGOs. The sets provide children in this age range with imaginative play, but at the same time incorporate a number of activities that allow for the learning of basic principles of physics. Includes the use of levers, motion, and sound.
NUScience Exploration Kit	11 to 16	A new and unique product to market, these sets provide children with the basic tools and instruction booklets for conducting science experiments at home. The concept draws upon many household items that can be used to simply and easily demonstrate basic scientific principles. Experiments include biology, chemistry, and physics.

design was also tied into the minimum order requirement for PDP products, which was set at $5,000. This was a large investment for small specialty retailers who might want to only carry the Puff N' Chuff Railroad to round out their wooden train lines, which also included TC Timber and Brio.

In response to the high order size requirements, some small retailers were banding together to purchase PDP products. One retailer placed the order, which was then distributed to the other retailers involved upon arrival. This greatly concerned Laura and Mary, since this activity split up the whole PDP product line across stores. Further, there were some retailers who sold PDP products and never saw a sales representative. This was a lost opportunity to educate retailers on the PDP product line concept.

Marketing Activities

Primetime Developmental Playthings engaged in various activities to market their products, including some trade and consumer promotion, advertising, and direct marketing activities. All promotional activities were directed toward parents—PDP did not target any of its promotions toward children.

Trade Promotion

These activities were fairly limited. PDP on rare occasion would discount the wholesale price of their product to the retailer for special promotions. It was more likely that retailers would receive favorable payment terms that allowed them to pay for the merchandise after it had been sold, a standard industry practice. This was especially beneficial to retailers during the Christmas season.

PDP also provided retailers with cooperative advertising support, usually in the form of displays, flip charts, take-ones, and shelf liners to promote the product line concept at the point of purchase. Laura reiterated that while point-of-purchase materials were made available, retailers did not necessarily merchandise the PDP products as a "system." In fact, it was quite common to walk into a specialty retailer, such as FAO Schwarz, and see PDP products merchandised in different parts of the store. This reinforced Laura's conclusion that not all retailers understood the PDP concept. Any strategy would need to take this issue into consideration.

Retailers were also encouraged to hold PDP "Plaything Playtimes" to enhance store traffic. This was an event held at the retail store providing customers with a chance to actually play with a variety of toys from the PDP product line. PDP supported these events with coloring sheets and other promotional items that children could take home with them. An attempt was made to have a sales or marketing representative from PDP in the retail store to provide additional support. The current staffing levels were making it increasingly difficult for PDP to handle these events.

Consumer Promotions

Consumer promotions were used sparingly. The few promotions used by PDP were restricted to couponing and sweepstake offers to current customers. The problematic issue that Laura and Mary faced was how to implement a promotion to stimulate add-on sales within a product line, and/or cross-selling between product lines without giving away margin on sales that would normally occur anyway. (Since these two promotions were a foundation of PDP's direct marketing strategy, they will be discussed in more detail below.) In discussions with retailers, Laura found they were very hesitant to be involved in price discounting and coupon promotions. These were mainstream tactics for the mass merchandising sector and not part of how specialty stores conducted business. Specialty retailers strongly felt they could not compete on price and therefore were reluctant to reduce profit margins, even if PDP was paying for it.

Direct Marketing Activities

The Primetime Club—The major vehicle for PDP consumer promotions were the direct marketing activities associated with the "*Primetime Club*." *Primetime Club* was a program developed so that PDP could talk with its customers. The club informed members of new PDP products and provided them with helpful developmental tips and information. The ultimate goal of this program was to move customers through the PDP product line as their child grew, and to provide these customers with the ultimate in customer service.

The *Primetime Club* program was initiated by a consumer purchase. Inside each toy package was a warranty card (see Exhibit C14.5). The warranty card collected a variety of data about the consumer, including postal and email addresses, names of children, birthdays, and an inventory of PDP products currently owned. While all products had a lifetime warranty, PDP encouraged the return of the warranty card through the use of a sweepstakes promotion. Unique to the industry, PDP entered all customers who returned warranty cards into a sweepstakes to win free products. This sweepstakes was held six times a year.

Once the warranty card was recorded at PDP, customers then received an invitation to join the *Primetime Club* (see Exhibit C14.6). PDP uses this as an opportunity to collect and verify any information provided in the returned warranty card. Customers were encouraged to join the club by completing the registration card (see Exhibit C14.7). Once the registration card had been recorded at PDP, the customer received a third mailing asking for verification of the information provided. In return the customer received the following benefits: 1) inclusion in the sweepstakes drawing, 2) free gifts for their children, and 3) *Development Dollar$*.

**Development Dollar$**—*Development Dollar$* were personalized coupons for discounts on the purchase of specific PDP products at participating specialty retailers. The information and *Development Dollar$* each parent received depended on the age of the child and the previous buying history of the parent.

Development Dollar$* posed a number of implementation challenges. The logistics of personalization were demanding due to the need for tracking customer purchases. Laura and Mary knew that the challenges created by this program needed to be addressed immediately to avoid any problems that might arise in the future. Also, given the retailers' reluctance to engage in consumer promotions, PDP needed to spend extra time educating and convincing retailers of the benefit of using the *Development Dollar$. Retailers were not quite sure what to do with the coupons and were wary

EXHIBIT C14.5: WARRANTY CARD

L'Enfant
Lifetime Warranty Registration Card

Fill out this warranty card to be automatically entered in a sweepstakes to win $500 worth of L'Enfant toys. Drawings are held six times a year, so be sure to register.

Parent's Last Name	MI	Parent's First Name

Street Address	State	Zip Code

Email Address

Bar Code of Product Purchased

Last Name (1st Child)	MI	First Name	Sex	Mo Day Year

Last Name (2nd Child)	MI	First Name	Sex	Mo Day Year

Please check all of the toys that each child currently owns: _____

	1st Child	2nd Child
L'Enfant		
Castlewood		
Primetime Primer		
Felt N' Safari		
Puff N' Chuff Railroad		
Bake-it Clay Set		
Kinetics Const. Sets.		
NUScience Exploration Kit		

about whether or not they would get their money back from PDP. The *Development Dollar$* program was strictly voluntary on the part of retailers.

The PDP Database—In addition to these challenges, the database used for the direct marketing activities was in need of restructuring. It was definitely in the early stages of development, with most of the information in the database collected from the warranty cards. The database currently had approximately 20,000 to 25,000 names and addresses, with the expectation of increasing to over 60,000 addresses within the next year. Since PDP was a relatively new company, the majority of names in the

---

EXHIBIT C14.6: INVITATION TO JOIN THE PRIMETIME CLUB

(On PDP Letterhead)

Dear Mr. _____:

   I would like to take this opportunity to invite you to join a wonderful organization—PDP's Primetime Club. This organization is devoted to informing parents of new PDP products and providing them with helpful developmental tips and information as their children grow and develop.

   If you become a member of the Primetime Club, you will receive the following benefits:

1. Inclusion in the sweepstakes drawing for a $1,000 Savings Bond,
2. Free gifts for your children, and
3. Free Development Dollar$—Development Dollar$ are personalized coupons for discounts on the purchase of specific PDP products at participating speciality retail stores.

   In order for you to join the Primetime Club, please complete the attached Registration Card. All we ask is that you correct the information that appears on the card. The information contained on the card is based on the information provided on the Warranty Card you recently sent to us. This is a chance for us to verify our records.

   Please drop the completed Registration Card in the mail as soon as possible. Thank you, and I hope that your child is enjoying their new PDP toys.

Sincerely,

Carson Scott

---

database represented customers who purchased, or received as a gift, Puff N' Chuff Railroad products, the first product line.

   PDP would like to more effectively utilize its database to expand its cross-sell/upsell strategy. Managing the size of the database was critical and PDP would like it to grow, but only to the extent that the information can be used. Dave Hudson, advertising and direct marketing director, pointed out that a common problem firms encounter in setting up a database is collecting too much information that will never be used. An additional issue that PDP needed to address was how to integrate the Castlewood database acquired in the recent purchase of Nature's Way Toys, Inc., into the current information system.

   This database operation was critical to PDP's strategy. It was important for them to not only communicate with their customers, but also to figure out how this tool could provide value-added services to specialty retailers. The database generated through the *Primetime Club* could form a powerful bridge between the retailer, the consumer, and PDP. With the impending foray into database marketing, it was extremely important to Carson Scott that PDP be able to calculate the "lifetime value" of a PDP customer, although he was not quite sure how this could be done. Laura, Mary, and Dave all agreed on the importance of being able to calculate the value of a

EXHIBIT C14.7: PRIMETIME CLUB REGISTRATION CARD

Primetime Club Registration & Sweepstakes Entry Card

Complete the information requested and you will receive the following benefits:

1. Inclusion in the sweepstakes drawing for a $1,000 Savings Bond,
2. Free gifts for your children, and
3. Development Dollar$.

Information Currently on File		List any corrections below
Parent's Name	**N. Marcus**	_____
Street Address	**100 N. Macy St.**	_____
City, State, Zip	**Anytown, US 10000–0001**	_____
Email Address	**Marcus@osu.edu**	_____
1st Child's Name	**Katie**	_____
1st Child's Birthday	**08/11/07**	_____
2nd Child's Name	**Matthew**	_____
2nd Child's Birthday	**10/2/09**	_____

___ **All of the information above is correct.**

Would you be so kind as to tell us approximately how many toys you currently own from each of the product lines listed below:

_____ L' Enfant	_____ Castlewood
_____ Primetime Primers	_____ Bake-it Clay Sculpting
_____ Felt N' Safari	_____ Kinectics Construction Sets
_____ Puff N' Chuff Railroad Kits	_____ NUScience Exploration Kits

customer who first purchased a PDP product for a child who was two years old, as compared to the customer who first purchased when the child was ten years old.

The Internet

PDP maintained a presence on the Internet through its own web site, which was promoted to parents in all correspondence. This site contained the complete product line catalog. Aside from allowing parents to examine PDP products, it provided an additional instrument for collecting data from those customers "surfing the Net." Web site visitors were encouraged to correspond with PDP through online discussion groups.

The web site had an additional helpful feature called the "Store Finder." The Store Finder allowed a consumer to find the closest specialty retailer carrying the PDP product of interest. This service made shopping easier for consumers. At the same time, it was a vehicle that helped generate store traffic for the specialty toy retailers that stocked PDP products. Only stores that agreed to accept *Development Dollar$* were included in the Store Finder listing. Still, not every store wanted to be involved with the *Development Dollar$* promotion. This was a perplexing issue for Laura and Mary.

Advertising

This part of the communications program played a minimal role in the marketing activities of PDP. Approximately 3 percent of sales were spent on placing ads in print media promoting PDP and some of its brands to both retailers and consumers. Further, included in the product packaging was a "mini-catalog" that provided consumers with information about complementary products within the product lines they had just purchased. At this point in time catalogs cross-selling other product lines were not included inside the package.

Laura and Mary knew that a major objective was the establishment of PDP's corporate identity. Manufacturers often use media advertising to create an image in the minds of consumers. Was an expanded advertising program the answer?

Consumer Profiles

A wide variety of people purchased toys. The toy industry had been affected by major demographic trends, with Baby Boomers and the "boomlet" having an impact on growth. Toys were purchased by parents for their children or as gifts to other children. The first child would often receive more toys than the second or third children. Many families had two wage earners, resulting in more discretionary income to spend on toys.

Children and teenagers purchased toys for themselves, as well as for gifts to give to other children. It was estimated that children annually spent $1.9 billion of their own money on toys and games (TMA). Grandparents were another major force among consumers buying toys. Spending on toys within this population was large, estimated at approximately 14 percent of retail sales.

The TMA reported that 55 percent of the retail sales reflected a planned purchase on the part of consumers. These consumers were pulled into the retailer after having been exposed to millions of dollars in television advertising to stimulate store visits. Consumer purchases were usually made after comparison shopping, with selections made at the store with the widest variety at the lowest prices (TMA).

There was, however, a difference between those who shopped at the mass market toy retailer as opposed to those shopping at specialty toy retailers. Generally, the primary target market was adults, predominantly women, in their mid 30s, with a relatively high level of education (all had graduated high school with a majority having been to college). Households were small, two to three children usually close together in age (one to three years' separation). Almost all had higher than average incomes, usually from one spouse working full-time. These people had the money to afford higher-priced toys, and higher levels of education made them more concerned about what their children were playing with. These parents wanted their children to grow up to be future presidents, not "vidiots."

The reality was that most customers were small families with one or two children, often more affluent. However, demographic background varied by product line. From the data at hand, Laura and Mary knew that many consumers purchased products in the L'Enfant line as baby gifts. Consumers purchasing Puff N' Chuff Railroad products came from the broader market due to the appeal of a popular children's storybook series. These consumers tended not to shop at specialty toy stores exclusively.

Within the Kinectics product line, children tended to be older, from more upscale families, and had more influence over the purchase of specific items.

Decision Time

The afternoon sun was waning. Laura and Mary sat in the crowded conference room mulling over the myriad issues they needed to address during the development of their marketing plan. The particularly problematic issue was how to increase consumer awareness for the corporate name (PDP), and support their retailer network by increasing store traffic on the limited budget available to them. One of PDP's concerns was that most of its customers were more familiar with the various brand names (Puff N' Chuff Railroad, L'Enfant, etc.) than they were with PDP.

It was apparent that many of PDP's competitors took advantage of the brand equity that was built up over time through the use of mass media advertising. Further, retailers were often more supportive of manufacturers that developed this brand awareness since it translated into increased store traffic and sales. How might PDP develop this level of awareness? Laura and Mary knew that any strategy must strive to achieve the objective of developing corporate identity and/or equity.

At the same time, PDP was not only competing with other specialty toys, but also with mass market toys. Specialty toy stores prided themselves on the extra service and support they gave to their customers in order to differentiate themselves from the mass merchandisers in the industry. With their limited resources, how could PDP help these small, specialty retailers compete? Herein lay the dilemma. PDP wanted to support the retailer, but the specialty toy retailer did not necessarily support PDP to the same degree. It was a basic divergence of objectives. PDP wanted to sell the company and its system, and use its products to generate store traffic. Specialty retailers wanted increased traffic, but were simply interested in selling any product within their store that fits their consumer's needs, which might not necessarily be PDP products. How could PDP profitably maintain consumer loyalty once they get into the store?

CASE
15

The San Francisco Symphony Turns One Hundred: Marketing a Cultural Centennial

BLODWEN TARTER

Golden Gate University

The San Francisco Symphony faced the challenge of a century: to develop a memorable season for the 100th anniversary of the Symphony's founding and then to market it. What should be done to mark this milestone in the history of one of the country's finest orchestras? How could it be used to expand the Symphony's customer base of concert attendees?

Founding of the San Francisco Symphony Orchestra

Just three years after the devastating earthquake and fire of 1906 shook San Francisco to its foundations, leaders of the California city decided to start an "orchestra of the people." This ambitious project was part of an ongoing effort to demonstrate San Francisco's phoenix-like rise from the ashes of disaster. Twenty-one businessmen, committed to the economic and cultural life of San Francisco, formed the Musical Association of San Francisco. In 1909 they began to raise money, hire a conductor and musicians and to find a hall for performances. As a result of their efforts, the then-named San Francisco Orchestra played its first concert on Friday, December 8, 1911. The season ended after 13 performances in both San Francisco and neighboring Oakland.

A Brief History of Many Firsts

Over the ensuing years, the San Francisco Symphony Orchestra has grown into an extraordinary institution of groundbreaking musical culture and popular entertainment. In 1925, the Symphony released its first audio recording. The next year, Standard Oil became the first corporate broadcast sponsor of the performing arts in the United States when it funded the Symphony's debut radio performances. The *Standard Symphony Hour* was the first radio series in the U.S. solely for symphonic music, and it ran for 30 years. The Symphony won its first Grammy award for classical music recordings in 1993, followed by ten more such awards. In 2001, the Symphony formed its own company, SFS Media, to record, produce and distribute its musical performances.

This "artistically adventurous" orchestra has presented over 230 world premieres and commissioned almost 100 new works by a variety of composers.[1] As early as 1979, the San Francisco Symphony began a composer-in-residence program, becoming the model for similar orchestra programs in the United States.

The tradition of long-distance tours began in 1947 when the orchestra covered 9,000 miles across the country performing 56 concerts in 57 days. The tour turned what had been a radio presence into a physical reality for many listeners.[2] The Symphony has since made some 45 national and international concert tours. During most of the year, it is based at Davies Symphony Hall, purpose-built for the San Francisco Symphony and opened in 1980.

Commitment to Music Education

The Symphony's commitment to music education began with its third concert in 1911, which it performed expressly for children.[3] By 1919, the Symphony launched its Young People's series. This eventually became the *Concerts for Kids* program through which nearly 30,000 children each year hear the Symphony with low-priced $5 tickets. The *Adventures in Music* program was established in 1988 to introduce children to music in their school classrooms and to build the Symphony audience of tomorrow. Initially for fourth and fifth-grade students in San Francisco[4], the program has expanded to include first through twelfth graders. Recognizing the power of the Internet, the San Francisco Symphony created www.SFKids.org in 2002, adding online music education. Parents and children can listen to the San Francisco Symphony online and learn even more about music with games and interactive tools.

The focus on music education now reaches beyond children to people of all ages and music backgrounds. *Keeping Score*, a comprehensive program begun in 2006, includes a public television series, an interactive website, a national radio series, documentary and live performance DVDs, and an expanded education program for teachers of students in kindergarten through twelfth grade.

For young, but highly trained, musicians the San Francisco Symphony offers the San Francisco Youth Orchestra. Performing its first concert in January 1982 it was later described as "the finest youth orchestra . . . heard anywhere."[5] Since many Symphony subscribers once played musical instruments, this serves both to educate and foster a lifetime commitment to performance music.

---

[1] *SFS Fact Sheet* http://www.sfsymphony.org/about/default.aspx?id=144

[2] *Music for a City, Music for the World*, Larry Rothe, 2011, p. 100.

[3] Oliver Theil, presentation to the San Francisco Public Relations Roundtable, 25 October 2011.

[4] *Music for a City, Music for the World*, Larry Rothe, 2011, p. 207.

[5] *Music for a City*, p. 193.

Marketing the San Francisco Symphony

Undoubtedly, the San Francisco Symphony has been innovative in its music offerings and education programs. But, it is also creative in its use of marketing and media, building on tried-and-true traditional methods.

The Symphony has three types of adult customers for its regular season.

- *Subscribers* buy one or more series of performances, packages of individual tickets, often based on a theme (for example, music by a single composer such as Mahler), for specific dates and times. Many subscribers purchase these tickets well before the season begins. Subscribers may purchase additional individual tickets at a discount and easily exchange tickets for another performance.
- *Individual ticket buyers* purchase tickets for specific concerts. They may attend the Symphony frequently, but not on the predictable schedule of a season subscriber. They usually don't purchase tickets substantially in advance of the performance.
- *Occasional attendees* are often guests of other customers or attend a performance as a special event.

According to the National Endowment for the Arts, of those who attend classical music performances in the United States, 22.8% are under 35 years of age, 49.5% are 35-59 years old, and 27.7% are 60 years of age or older.[6] The typical symphony subscriber is well-educated, older, and has an above-average income. Younger concert-goers more frequently purchase individual tickets than subscriptions (multiple-performance series).[7] For all age groups, a higher level of education is the best predictor of attendance.[8] About 75% of subscribers once played an instrument or sang with a group and 50% still do so.

People often attend performances with family and friends. For some people, attending the Symphony is a very special event. For others, it is an ongoing part of their social life.

Ticket prices vary by day of the week, by series, and by seat location within the Symphony Hall. A Saturday night loge or premium orchestra seat for a series subscription costs about $140 while a second-tier seat costs about $35. Single ticket prices range from $15 to $150. Subscribers pay less per seat than purchasers of individual tickets, essentially receiving a volume discount. A series ranges from 6 to12 performances and a subscription could be a combination of series. After the season begins, there are occasional time-limited promotional prices for individual tickets to specific programs. Discounts are available for group purchases.

---

[6] *Age and Arts Participation: A Case Against Demographic Destiny*, Mark Stern, National Endowment for the Arts, Research Report #53, February 2011, Table 3, page 38.

[7] *The American Symphony Orchestra: Renewable Audiences Or A Dying Institution?*, Alice Wang, Princeton University Thesis, 2003, http://www.princeton.edu/~artspol/studentpap/undergrad%20thesis3%20Wang.pdf.

[8] *Age and Arts Participation: A Case Against Demographic Destiny*, Mark Stern, National Endowment for the Arts, Research Report #53, February 2011, page 42.

The Symphony advertises in the *San Francisco Chronicle*, the most circulated newspaper in the San Francisco Bay Area. The entertainment section in the Sunday edition regularly features print ads for the Symphony preceding and throughout its season. Each ad includes the Symphony URL and box office telephone number with a call-to-action for ticket purchase.

Radio performances are also a unique form of marketing—they are both product and the promotion of the product. More than 275 radio stations broadcast San Francisco Symphony performances throughout the US and Europe.

Colorful, but not extravagant, direct mail encourages season subscribers to renew each year. Via rented lists, prospective subscribers receive direct mail invitations to purchase one or more series of performances. These rented lists might include subscribers and single ticket buyers from other San Francisco Bay Area musical programs such as Cal Performances or the New Century Chamber Orchestra.

The Symphony has not one, but three, websites. The primary website, www.sfsymphony.org, includes concert schedules and the ability to purchase tickets online. Mentioned earlier, www.SFSKids.org helps children have fun with music where they can listen to performances, learn about different instruments and music, and even compose their own tunes. *Keeping Score*, www.keepingscore.org, a more sophisticated website, features previews of nine one-hour television shows on significant composers and audio recordings, plus lesson plans for teachers to incorporate this material into their own classes.

More than 100,000 people have opted-in to the Symphony email list for both promotional and educational email messages. The list includes many of the more than 1,500 volunteers associated with the Symphony.

The Symphony adopted social media in 2008. More than 56,000 people follow or "like" the Symphony on Facebook, while more than 40,000 people follow it on Twitter. Symphony staff tweet live from concerts or snap photos before and during performances and quickly post them online.

An official Symphony YouTube channel, begun in 2006, includes interviews with musicians, composers and the ever-popular conductor Michael Tilson Thomas (affectionately known as MTT to his fans). Of course, there are video clips of music performed by the Symphony.

All of this is to encourage those who care about the Symphony to seed online word-of-mouth marketing, creating awareness of the Symphony and of specific concerts, leading to sales of subscriptions and individual tickets, CDs, DVDs, and memorabilia.

Planning the Centennial Program Concerts and Events

For its 100th anniversary, the San Francisco Symphony planned an innovative and ambitious 18-week season of performances and programs. An elegant opening gala and a free, public concert in September would kick off the centennial season.

In keeping with the Symphony's heritage of artistic adventure, a month-long new music program was scheduled. Six new pieces were commissioned from different composers[9] and would be first performed as part of the centennial celebration. A week of concerts called *Barbary Coast and Beyond*, would feature music from the 1849 California Gold Rush, generally considered the beginning of modern San Francisco, up to the founding of the San Francisco Symphony in the early 20th century.

The *American Mavericks* program would perform works created by 17 iconoclastic, radical composers in a series of San Francisco concerts. The orchestra would then take the concerts on tour to Chicago, Ann Arbor, and New York City.

Six US orchestras were invited to perform as guests of the Symphony in *The American Orchestra* series. In this unusual program, the orchestras of Los Angeles, Boston, Chicago, Cleveland, New York, and Philadelphia would be heard on stage at Davies Symphony Hall, performing original works commissioned by each respective orchestra.

Other special performances would include the *Sunday Organ Series, Past & Present Music Directors on the Podium*, and concerts for Dia de los Muertos, an important holiday for the Hispanic community, and Chinese New Year.

The Black and White Ball, a fundraising extravaganza since 1956, would take place in early June. Paul Simon and Cyndi Lauper would join the San Francisco Symphony as headliners for the night-long dance party in the streets and buildings throughout San Francisco's Civic Center. Tickets would cost $250 (party only) or $350 (Davies Symphony Hall seats).

A detailed history of the Symphony, the book *Music for a City, Music for the World*, would be published as well. More DVDs and CDs would join the library of San Francisco Symphony musical recordings as the centennial season performances would be captured live for future release. San Francisco's public TV station, KQED, planned a documentary in partnership with the Symphony.

The Marketing Challenge: Expand the Customer Base

The San Francisco Symphony was confident that it had planned a unique centennial season, suitable for this momentous occasion. It also wanted to ensure its long-term viability by using this celebration as a focal point to further expand its customer base.

To help the San Francisco Symphony achieve its goal, you are asked to propose an integrated direct marketing acquisition campaign, using multiple media, to attract 18 to 34 year olds for the centennial season and beyond. Note that this includes two groups: 18 to 21 year olds of traditional college age and 22 to 34 year olds in the early career stage.

The primary objectives of the direct marketing campaign are to:

a. acquire new subscribers who will buy packages of multiple performances (series), preferably before the season begins

b. sell individual tickets to specific performances.

---

[9] Composers John Adams, Mason Bates, Meredith Monk, Morton Subotnick, Sofia Gubaidulina and Thomas Adès

The secondary objective is to sell Symphony merchandise such as CDs, DVDs, and print publications.

Describe the target audience(s) in detail, develop a creative theme for the special centennial season aimed at this target, define the offers and calls to action, detail the media selected and describe how you will measure performance of the campaign. Be sure to justify all of your recommendations.

CASE
16

Star Island:
The Paradox of Management

JAN P. OWENS

Carthage College

Introduction

Star Island is a seaside conference and retreat center, located in the Isles of Shoals off the New Hampshire Coast, in a national historic district. Its nonprofit organization was founded in 1915 based on the ideals of Unitarian Universalism, but the island hosts and welcomes events that represent a variety of beliefs and objectives. Past visitors have included such notables as the artist Childe Hassam and author Nathaniel Hawthorne. Today's family and theme conferences include a range of topics, from spiritual retreats to natural history and ecology, to fine arts workshops and events. A particularly successful event in recent years was a weekend of traditional dancing.

The island has 37 buildings and maintenance facilities and is available only during the warmer weather period of June through mid-September. Its turn-of-the-last century hotel, complete with writing room, sitting room, and dining hall, provides a social center of gatherings. The 1801 Gosport Chapel is a link to its historic past with services lit by candle lanterns. Living quarters are comfortable but basic, reflecting Star Island's commitment to resource conservation. The island is a welcoming venue for a variety of outdoor sports and activities.

Star Island welcomes various combinations of visitors: groups and organizations, family holidays, day-trippers, and singles. They come for specific conferences, events and programs, or simply to spend a day or more in a natural setting by the sea.

The Challenge

For many years, Star Island (hereafter SI) has hosted events and vacation weeks that were organized and administered by outside groups and organizations. These groups would reserve a number of rooms and event spaces on the island, estimating the number of guests. The organizing groups did not post a financial guarantee to Star Island. This meant that the financial stability of SI depended on the skill of others to organize an attractive conference or event and effectively publicize it. When forecasts were met, Star Island covered its expenses. Unfortunately, not all events were equally lucrative. A conference with an esoteric topic might not attract enough participants to break even. Star Island would not only lose money but also suffer the opportunity cost of attracting better planned programs.

Then there was the disaster. In 2007, the fire inspector refused permission for SI to open for the season. Multiple violations of fire and electrical codes resulted in $2 million of repairs and renovations, and more than $1 million is lost bookings, which almost bankrupted Star Island. Victoria Hardy, the new CEO of Star Island, had her work cut out for her. In addition to recovering from the shortened season, she knew that better planning, organizing, and marketing for events had to get into high gear. Active fundraising to support a five-year capital improvement plan was also a priority.

Among other initiatives, Ms. Hardy hired professional staff that included the first-ever "outreach" staff. This was particularly necessary because (a) as an island, few visitors would accidentally come across the location, and (b) SI cannot always rely on word-of-mouth to publicize its conferences and attractions. With her team, Ms. Hardy worked hard to encourage groups to book the island, help put together events that would attract a number of attendees, and help the groups to publicize their events.

The problem remained of groups that booked rooms but fell short of the attendance targets. Financial commitments from groups booking island facilities were placed on a more solid footing but still remained low in the spirit of inclusiveness of the groups and the nonprofit nature of the organization. However, SI would still need to pay its bills and attract and pay a dedicated crew of about 90 employees.

Historical research generated a new means of attracting visitors. It was found that the origins of the America's Cup could be traced to a sailboat named the America that won the Gosport Regatta, held at the Isles of Shoals in 1876. In conjunction with the Piscatuqua Sailing Association, SI has revived the Regatta and now draws hundreds of enthusiasts, some of whom have lunch or brunch in the SI dining rooms or grounds, complete with celebratory jazz music.

SI has also helped to organize and promote broad-interest programs. A Literary Festival features some noteworthy regional authors, and the Star Arts Conference provides a number of workshops, activities, and entertainment that appeal to creative urges. "Theme weeks" have also been popular. The island also hosts nature-oriented programs that take advantage of its seaside environment.

To encourage referrals, SI has developed a plan to offer discounts to regular conference participants who bring a newcomer to the island. It also makes scholarship money available to conference attendees who would like to attend but lack the funds to do so. The growth of "personal retreats" has also been a successful addition to the offerings, with more than 500 bednights in a recent year.

Advertisements in regional media are meant to appeal to a wide range of interests of key target markets. The budget now has a professional who has been hired for outreach in its marketing efforts.

Target Markets

SI needs to attract a mix of groups and individuals to make the season a financial success. The following are identified as some key groups to target:

- **Conference organizers.** This group represents the potential for volume booking, assuming the event proves popular with its membership. These groups have included university groups, topical conferences such as world affairs, and spiritual retreats.
- **Families.** Whether a day outing or a longer stay for a family reunion or to attend a conference, families can be the basis of recurring gatherings. A visit to Star Island can become part of a family's heritage.
- **Special interest groups.** Be it a weekend of folk dancing or a group of friends who want to practice yoga in fresh salt air, SI would like to provide the venue.
- **Individuals.** The quiet and restful atmosphere of SI provides an ideal place for quiet contemplation or other activities for personal enrichment, such as writing or painting. The personal retreat option has already proven successful on a limited basis.

The AdWords Goof and Insight

Students at a small Midwestern college offered to help SI with an assignment using Google's AdWords. AdWords is Google's paid advertisement program, where the results of a Google search results in ads listed in order of the relevance to the search match and the bid for a higher ranking. Misreading the affiliation and programs at Star Island, some of the AdWords used in the test program included "Spiritual Retreat" and "Christian Retreats." The results produced 1,668 and 1,345 impressions respectively, with approximate click-through rates of 1%—not too bad for this medium. "Christian Retreats for Women" earned even higher CTR.

While the objective of these search terms might have been misguided, the results seemed to identify a market segment that might be targeted as potential organizers of retreats on Star Island. Still, "New Hampshire History" earned the highest CTR, although people with such an interest might not have been the most qualified of potential visitors to SI.

Still, the goof got the students thinking: could they identify other trends in the marketplace that could point to good prospects for marketing efforts? Which groups could see SI as a destination for a meeting or event?

Recent Results

Ms. Hardy brought a more systematic level of professional management to SI. This included regular weekly meetings with the management team and closer coordination with the outreach coordinator. Monthly reports to the Board of Directors kept it informed about progress on the strategic plan. Detailed marketing plans were proposed and implemented.

Unfortunately, SI saw a $20,000 operating deficit in a recent year. Still, this was a great improvement over the $150,000 loss in the previous year. Ms. Hardy believed that the weak results were due to (a) no big-name conferences that would attract a high numbers of attendees, and (b) new conferences that falter in a difficult economy. Until the programs at SI were better attended or provided more lucrative financial support, SI would continue to struggle.

The Overall Question

How does Star Island manage the paradox of surviving on conferences and attracting visitors when it does not control much of the content of events of the sponsoring organizations?

Specific Questions for Discussion

1. What does Star Island "sell?" What does it offer?
2. Describe key advertising or direct mail copy that could attract each of the market segments identified in the case.
3. Should Star Island purchase a list for direct mail purposes? How would this list be described, i.e., a list of. . . . How would you cut the list? Locate an appropriate list from the NEXTMARK.com website, and explain your strategy for this direct marketing approach.
4. Besides those listed above, what are some key target segments for Star Island's outreach activities?
5. How should Star Island promote itself to boaters in the coastal area of New Hampshire?
6. How should Star Island bill conference organizers, e.g. minimum guarantees?
7. Are there conferences or events that Star Island might organize that would attract any or all of the target customer groups mentioned in the case? How should it approach these activities?

C A S E
17

TurboTax® Tries Direct Response Television … Again[1]

BLODWEN TARTER
Golden State University

Early in the fall of 2008, David Kirven, director of brand strategy for TurboTax, was reviewing the most recent results of regularly-conducted TurboTax brand research. As the leading tax preparation software in the United States, TurboTax was a mature brand with a large brand advertising budget. Owned by Intuit, the product had been advertised for years using 30-second and 15 second brand commercials on television as well as print and online advertising.

Unfortunately, in late 2008, TurboTax was reaching a point of diminishing returns for brand advertising and wanted a more cost-effective way to drive growth. Among other things, the brand research suggested that the company should better demonstrate how TurboTax worked.

Coming from a background of direct marketing, David Kirven considered the possibility that direct response television (DRTV) might be just the way to achieve a breakthrough in advertising effectiveness for TurboTax. He had long believed that DRTV, with its ability to provide deeper messaging due to its lengthier commercials, could be an effective approach for TurboTax. Unfortunately, past DRTV test results for TurboTax had been disappointing. Yet Intuit had used many other direct marketing channels

---

quite successfully. Frequent testing was part of the corporate culture. Direct mail, email messages to prior customers promoting the new annual versions, online banner ads, and direct response print ads had all been used to generate direct sales of TurboTax products.

David decided it was worth trying direct response TV again, this time with a different approach. He believed there had to be a way that DRTV could work for TurboTax and help achieve the sales goals for the product line. And what about further building brand awareness and brand perception? These were typical goals for general advertising, not for direct marketing. Why not try to do both? If a test was successful, David would then need to decide how to roll out a DRTV campaign for the following tax year.

First, David wanted to review what he knew about DRTV, then to review the company's previous efforts to use DRTV for TurboTax. What had Intuit missed? Had anything changed that could now be used for more effective DRTV?

Direct Response Television Background

According to the Direct Marketing Association, US businesses spent $22.2 billion on DRTV in 2008, driving $151.4 billion in sales.[2]

Historically, short-form direct response television was used to promote unique, low-priced items available only by ordering directly from the manufacturer. Typically priced from $9.95 to $29.95, these products had no retail distribution at launch. Therefore, unique toll-free phone numbers for each network could be used to track the effectiveness of the DRTV marketing program and all sales could be attributed to the DRTV spots. With the advent of the Internet, interested buyers could also place orders online and a unique URL could be used to track sales generated by DRTV. In the more distant past, DRTV response also included mail orders, where the respondent sent payment to a post office box. With no retail distribution, DRTV could be measured as a stand-alone sales and distribution channel.

Successful DRTV products tended to be easy to explain and demonstrate and appealed to broad audiences. Low manufacturing and shipping costs contribute to greater profitability. Short-form DRTV spots are one or two minutes long, usually described as 60-second and 120-second spots, respectively. The longer form of DRTV is known as an infomercial, where the commercial may run up to 30 minutes.

Over time, DRTV has evolved. The most successful DRTV products might subsequently obtain retail distribution, often in the section of a store dedicated to products "As Seen on TV." Now, more manufacturers seek retail distribution at product introduction, rather than waiting to demonstrate demand first via DRTV only. Thus, they combine direct response television and retail presence to maximize sales. Products such as the Snuggie (a fleece blanket with sleeves), One-Touch Can Opener, and ProActiv Solution (an acne treatment) had become financial successes and iconic examples of short-form DRTV, ultimately including retail distribution.

---

[2] DMA 2010 Statistical Factbook, pages 3 and 4, citing DMA, The Power of Direct Marketing, 2009-2010 Edition.

In traditional DRTV, the goal is to generate an order or a lead profitably with a low cost per response (CPR). For orders, this measure is often called cost per order (CPO) and for leads, the measure is often called cost per inquiry (CPI). The medium used most frequently is national cable television, with messages often running late at night, during the day, or on weekend day parts. To be cost-effective, the media is bought with little lead time (often the week before the TV spots run) at heavily discounted rates. Success is measured via response to a unique telephone number and/or a unique URL, often assigned to identify each TV network.

While the goal of DRTV is drive purchases, in comparison, brand advertising's goals are to build brand awareness and increase brand preference. The media objective is audience delivery as measured by gross rating points (GRPs).[3] National network TV and cable TV are frequently used for television commercials delivered on highly-rated programs during high viewership periods. The media is bought well in advance at premium rates. Media cost is calculated on a CPM (cost per thousand viewers) basis. The lower the CPM, the more "efficient" the media buy. Spots are typically 10 seconds, 15 seconds, or 30 seconds long, with an occasional 60-second spot. Traditionally, success has been measured by comparing pre- and post-exposure research results (awareness, preference, purchase intent, etc.) and the inferred impact on sales, rather than by sales directly attributable to watching the specific TV commercials. Segmentation is achieved by identifying programs, channels, and time of day most watched by the target audience and then by placing commercials in those slots.

DRTV has three unique advantages.

1. Huge savings. Media bought on a DRTV pre-emptable basis cost a fraction of what brand advertisers pay for guaranteed slots. A 30-second DRTV spot may cost one-half to one-fifth what a 30-second brand spot would cost. This is primarily due to the lower-cost purchases made at the last minute when there is unsold airtime available.
2. Deeper messaging. For some advertisers, the opportunity to run longer spots (120-second and 60-second) affordably presents a unique opportunity to communicate more features and benefits of their product. The DRTV rule of thumb is "the more you tell, the more you sell."
3. Build a direct relationship with the consumer. A DRTV campaign, with a response mechanism to collect contact information, allows advertisers to build a database of addressable consumers with whom the company can communicate again.

For brand and multichannel marketers, the newest challenge for DRTV is whether or not this medium can support a brand. A "brand response" commercial combines aspects of brand advertising with aspects of direct marketing such as responding to a call-to-action by visiting a website or calling a designated telephone number. Will a

---

[3] Gross rating points measure audience viewing, defined as reach ("the number of people exposed to the vehicles carrying the ad") times frequency ("the number of insertions purchased in a specific communications vehicle within a specified time period"). Lisa Spiller and Martin Baier, *Contemporary Direct & Interactive Marketing*, 2nd ed., page 174.

"brand response" spot be strong enough to drive direct response? Will creative that effectively drives response also have a positive impact on brand image and brand preference? Can a company measure the effect of DRTV across different distribution channels?

As companies demand greater accountability from every part of a business, marketers must justify all forms of marketing communications. Metrics that indicate performance against a pre- established objective are increasingly required. Brand advertisers are beginning to realize DRTV's potential to help them drive sales across multiple distribution channels and are starting to use brand response commercials for this purpose. Fortunately, DRTV can be tested quickly and efficiently. With enough exposure, results for a test can be determined in a few weeks.

In order to develop a new approach to DRTV for TurboTax David Kirven also needed to review the TurboTax product line itself. How could he design an effective DRTV campaign and then test it? Fortunately, he now had a product that was well-suited to offer on DRTV: the TurboTax Online Free Federal Edition, an online-only version for people with simple tax returns.

TurboTax Background

TurboTax was developed by ChipSoft in the mid-1980s and acquired by Intuit in 1993. It rapidly became America's best-selling tax preparation software, selling millions of units annually. Initially, the software ran only on personal computers. With the advent of the Internet and increasingly secure data transmission, Intuit introduced a web-based version of TurboTax. This alternative allowed users to prepare their taxes entirely online and further expanded the product line.

The TurboTax product line has grown over the years with versions that address the least- complicated tax situation to the most complex. For example, the simplest federal tax filing utilizes Form 1040-EZ and a taxpayer must answer relatively few questions. At the other end of the spectrum, a more complex tax situation would involve personal and small-business income taxes or income taxes for corporations and limited partnerships. Therefore, TurboTax developed Basic, Deluxe, Premier, Home & Business, and Business editions for the federal level and the corresponding state software. As an individual's tax situation changes, there are opportunities for TurboTax to sell more sophisticated software versions.

TurboTax also cross-sells state income tax software to buyers of federal editions, as taxpayers must pay both federal income taxes and, in most cases, state income taxes as well. Data entered for the federal return is automatically transferred into the proper place for the state return. Comparative charts on the TurboTax website, as well as on the packages for the physical CDs, help people evaluate the available choices.

TurboTax customers select the appropriate version of software. They then complete their tax filings by a answering a series of software-guided questions. Over time, TurboTax has added features such as online user forums, online tax filing, and access to professional tax preparers for specific questions (sometimes at an additional charge). Buyers are encouraged to register their product in order to receive any needed software updates prior to final filing. From a marketing standpoint, product registrations also capture information about customers that can be used for ongoing communications, building the TurboTax database.

There were more than 16 million TurboTax units of federal tax editions sold in 2006, increasing to a total of 18.7 million federal units provided in 2007.[4] The websites of approximately 1,100 financial institutions, electronic retailers and other merchants and the Yahoo!® Finance Tax Center are channels of distribution[5] where the software can either be downloaded directly to the buyer's computer or an order placed for physical CDs. In addition, consumers can buy the desktop software at physical outlets of retailers such as office supply stores, electronics stores, and mass merchandisers such as Costco. As noted earlier, the user can also sign up for and use TurboTax entirely online, without a download to the desktop.

New editions of TurboTax are created each year, in response to changes in the federal income tax laws of the United States and in the various state tax laws. One cannot use a prior year's version of TurboTax because the income tax forms and rules change annually and changes are often not finalized until late December or early January.

Not surprisingly, the sales of tax preparation software are seasonal. Virtually all purchases of TurboTax take place November-April with the greatest concentration in the 12-week period leading up to April 15, the day on which annual income tax returns are due in the United States. This highly concentrated selling season puts enormous pressure on TurboTax's marketing communications. There is virtually no time in which to make a marketing mistake and correct it.

While TurboTax is the best-selling tax preparation software in the United States, the market is highly competitive. TaxACT by 2nd Story Software and TaxCut by H&R Block are two significant competitors. Each year, there are numerous reviews published comparing tax preparation alternatives to help consumers evaluate their choices.

Not only is there desktop and online software available to prepare income taxes, there are also thousands of professional tax preparers in the United States. A taxpayer can complete his/her own tax return manually, using free forms provided by the Internal Revenue Service (available in print form or downloadable PDFs from the IRS website) and by the state. Using the IRS- provided forms requires the taxpayer to understand the tax code and to perform all the calculations him or herself. In comparison, most tax preparation software suggests the appropriate tax forms based on the taxpayer's situation, calculates required figures, looks up taxes owed based on income levels and checks for errors and inconsistencies within a tax return. TurboTax even guarantees the accuracy of its calculations!

---

[4] http://files.shareholder.com/downloads/INTU/1187583171x0x245400/f8987037-7ede-4406-8cc1- b5e4bef26525/TurboTax_historical_data_for_release.pdf for data on TurboTax sales

[5] Page 7, Intuit 10-K, for fiscal year 2008, report dated 9/12/2008. http://files.shareholder.com/downloads/INTU/1187583171x0xS950134-08-16540/896878/filing.pdf

DRTV and TurboTax

Why had earlier tests of DRTV failed for TurboTax? First, Intuit measured only responses to the unique toll-free phone number and unique URL presented in the DRTV commercial—a standard direct response practice—and these direct sales were too low. The marketing staff suspected that the DRTV tests had driven sales to retail stores and online to URLs other than the unique DRTV URL but they were unable to prove it. Furthermore, the previous tests were national, making it difficult to isolate the impact of direct response television. With no control market, it was virtually impossible to determine if the DRTV ads had driven viewers to retail or other online locations. The specific products offered might not have been attractive enough or the perceived risk of trying TurboTax might have been too great to attract new users to tax software.

David Kirven believed that DRTV could generate incremental sales for TurboTax. A compelling offer, the deeper messaging permitted by longer spots, a strong call to action that would emphasize free online tax preparation, and lower media costs should be effective. He reminded himself that an essential component of good direct marketing practice was continual testing and he wanted to test DRTV again.

David decided to approach the problem as a "brand response" campaign, using brand guidelines in developing the creative and structuring the test so that the impact across different distribution channels could be measured. First, he asked himself, "What offer would compel people to try TurboTax?"

The New DRTV Offer

In the new test, Intuit would offer the TurboTax Online Free Federal Edition, a relatively new product available only online. This service allowed users to prepare their simple federal income taxes online, print and e-file for free.

The overall goal was to convert non-users of tax preparation software to users of TurboTax. The test objectives were to determine whether or not direct response television could generate incremental in-store retail sales and online sales for TurboTax.

The specific objectives of the campaign were to:

1. Drive traffic to the dedicated URL www.getTurboTaxFree.com
2. Monetize customers by up-selling from the Free Federal Edition to a more robust, paid version of TurboTax Federal edition and by cross-selling paid state editions.

The ads would lead the viewer to a dedicated URL where additional information would help the consumer determine if the Free Federal Edition was sufficient for his or her tax situation. For complex tax returns (such as reporting investments), a different version might be needed. To file state tax returns, the respondent would have to purchase the appropriate state edition. Without sufficient up-selling and cross-selling, the campaign would not pay for the cost of production and media, much less contribute to the bottom line. If customers opted for the Free Federal Edition alone the campaign would not be successful—taxpayers had to pay for additional software in order to make the marketing effort profitable.

The Creative Execution

The agency was asked to develop an integrated message that had a look and feel that differed from the regular brand spots. The spots needed to be consistent with Intuit's stated brand attributes: "real, honest, committed, smart, and spirited."[6]

TurboTax first researched three creative concepts, comparing brand perceptions pre- and post- exposure and evaluating "intent to purchase." An animated spot called "Missing Something?" scored well across the board and respondents liked the cute character and fun tone. Featuring a lovable, but flawed, fellow who could not find his tax savings, TurboTax developed 120-second and 60-second commercials. The animated character added visual interest while screenshots showed how TurboTax works specifically and how easy it is to use. TurboTax colors and fonts were used throughout the commercials.

Research findings led to refinements of the concept. To enhance credibility, press reviews and customer testimonials were included in the 120-second spot. Both spots emphasized that TurboTax Free edition was, well, FREE. The call to action was "Go to FreeTurboTax.com. That's FreeTurboTax.com." Unusually, for DRTV, there was no toll-free number to call. Why? The product cost nothing and could be used only online so neither payment nor shipment were required. By going directly to the unique URL a taxpayer could start using TurboTax's Free Federal Edition immediately.

Find the commercial storyboards at the end of this document.
Watch the 60-second commercial at

http://www.youtube.com/
watch?v=qPcaq_govNs

Watch the 120-second commercial at
http://www.youtube.com/
watch?v=c4vL315610Y

The Media

A rigorously designed test was essential in order to obtain meaningful results. TurboTax decided to match seven pairs of medium-sized local markets, utilizing MRI Research on media consumption and Intuit internal data. Each match or pair consisted of two markets with similar characteristics in terms of consumer demographics, market size, retail TurboTax distribution, historical TurboTax sales and registered

---

[6] Intuit Brand Guidelines—Communicating the Brand Personality Version 1.0 04.02.08 at http://torthbandt.com/web/download/Intuit_guide.pdf.

users, PC ownership, Internet usage, and other relevant characteristics. In each paired set, one market would be exposed to the direct response commercials and one market would have no TurboTax television advertising (the control market). With a well-known brand such as TurboTax, the marketing staff anticipated that some viewers would simply go to the main web site, TurboTax.com, rather than the unique URL used in the commercials. Any increase in sales over the control market would be attributable to the use of the new DRTV spots.

The commercials ran for nine weeks during the prime selling period, beginning in February 2009. The initial test was scheduled for three weeks, and then extended through the end of the tax season to eliminate the impact of any seasonality.

All of the media was purchased as "remnant media" at negotiated rates. Remnant TV media, which is simply unsold air time, is subject to pre-empting. The television network can run another spot in place of the DRTV commercial and there is no guarantee of a specific time or program adjacency. Of course, if the advertiser's spot does not run, the advertiser does not pay for the space.[7] To qualify as a DRTV spot, a URL or a toll-free phone number was required.

Air time was purchased in virtually all time slots: early morning, daytime, evening and late news, prime, late fringe and weekend rotations. The media buyer bid on spots based on a specific GRP goal and CPM goal, seeking greater frequency and higher-rated programs, which is standard practice for brand advertising. While this is atypical of DRTV media buying, the media buyers were successful in meeting those objectives. There was also show-specific programming goals achieved, including Good Morning America, Today Show and the news.

The Results

The TurboTax Free Federal Edition commercials ran in the seven local markets designated to receive TV advertising. These seven markets showed a significant lift in online sales overall as compared to the seven matched markets that did not see the DRTV. Retail results were mixed but did not appear to be impacted conclusively by the DRTV. This was, perhaps, not surprising given that TurboTax was promoting a free edition that was only available online.

The direct response television test appeared to be driving incremental, profitable sales. Yet one question remained. If TurboTax had aired a 30-second brand spot instead of the DRTV 120-second and 60-second spots would TurboTax have seen the same lift? In other words, was it the extra airings and exposure or the deeper messaging of the DRTV spots, made possible by the lengthier 60 and 120-second spots that caused the DRTV to work?

To get the answer, a late-season test was conducted in which a 30-second brand spot was tested against the DRTV 120-second and 60-second spots in several additional markets at the same media weight levels. The head-to-head test of the brand and DRTV spots seemed to prove that it was the deeper messaging of the DRTV 120-

---

[7] The "clearance rate" is the percentage of spots ordered that actually run. A media buyer's challenge is to keep costs low enough to have an acceptable profit per sale while running enough spots to generate an acceptable level of sales.

and 60-second spots that was driving incremental sales. Subsequent brand research suggested the DRTV spots had a positive impact on brand image and preference.

Next Steps

David Kirven was pleased with the test results and that he had decided to try DRTV again, in spite of past failures. But, were the results compelling enough to merit expansion or roll-out for the next tax season? Would DRTV be effective only for the Free Federal Edition or could it be expanded to include other TurboTax products? David had time to evaluate the DRTV approach, consider different offers, and different creative before he had to commit his advertising budget to the next concentrated tax time promotional period in 2010. What should he recommend?

The Assignment:
What Should David Kirven Recommend?

- Do you agree with David Kirven's assessment of the success of this DRTV test? Why or why not? What additional information, if any, is needed to assess the "success" of the effort?
- What should TurboTax do with direct response TV for subsequent tax seasons? Should it rollout nationally, expand incrementally, continue to test or cancel DRTV? Why?
- Should DRTV be expanded to include additional TurboTax products and, if so, how? What kind of offer and creative could be utilized? What different approaches for DRTV would be required for TurboTax products that require payment? After all, a free product is a pretty powerful offer!

Appendix 1

The TurboTax Product Line

(income taxes for 2008 filed in 2009)

Standard Retail Prices

Tax Return Preparation Offerings included desktop and online versions of:

- TurboTax Basic, for simple returns, $34.95
- TurboTax Deluxe, for taxpayers who itemize deductions, $59.95
- TurboTax Premier, for taxpayers who own investments or rental property, $89.95
- TurboTax Home and Business, for small business owners, $99.95
- TurboTax state, $39.95
- TurboTax Business desktop software for larger businesses, $109.95
- TurboTax Business state, $49.95
- TurboTax Free Federal Edition online for the simplest returns, no cost

Actual prices charged vary according to specific promotional offers. For example, TurboTax Basic might be provided free via a sponsored promotion with a financial institution or for $19.95 when purchased online and downloaded directly from the TurboTax website.

Retailers often offered TurboTax at promotional prices at various times during tax season. By US law, retailers can charge what they choose for a product.

Product list according to the Intuit 2009 10-K, page 7, downloaded from http://files.shareholder.com/downloads/INTU/1187583171x0xS950123-09-43307/896878/filing.pdf

Product prices based on "Previous year's products" for 2008 tax year products on www.turbotax.com Feb 2011 and http://turbotax.intuit.com/personal-taxes/past-years-products.jsp

| TurboTax | "Missing Something?" | DRTV 120 |

ANNCR (V/O): Ever feel you be . . .

. . . missing something?

Like, oh, say, hundreds of might dollars in tax savings?

Thank goodness...
Free Edition!

. . . there's TurboTax Federal do your simple federal taxes.

The EASY, online way to

And get the maximum refund –

GUARANTEED.

Just answer easy-to-understand questions. TurboTax quickly learns about your unique situation.

And guides you step-by-step.

Then puts the numbers on all the right forms. Does the math.

And helps get you the maximum refund you deserve.

No doubt about it

TurboTax Free Edition is the fast, easy, free way . . .

. . . to get your biggest refund possible.

With TurboTax Free Edition, you also get free online help . . .

. . . and free audit support tools.

Doing your taxes has never been easier

And best of all, with TurboTax Free Edition, you don't pay a penny.

Because it's free to prepare, free to print and free to e-file your federal tax return.

And when you e-file

You can get your refund fast— in as little as eight days!

So why not give it a try?

Millions of others have already used TurboTax products. Just Listen.

| TurboTax | "Missing Something?" | DRTV 120 |

D. Glaser: I thought the Free Edition was fantastic! I wasn't expecting that. So when I saw that it was free... Bonus!

C. Taylor: TurboTax holds your hand and guides you through...every step of the way.

J. Moody: If I had a question, TurboTax beat me to it.

B. Sacchetto: It was really simple!

J. Banuelos: I got a lot of cash. And that's because of TurboTax!

G. Ellmore: I would never go back to a tax store and pay that kind of money again.

ANNCR (V/O): No wonder TurboTax is America's number one brand of tax preparation software!

The Wall Street Journal found TurboTax "Easier to navigate... and understand." In their tests, "TurboTax... came out on top."

USA Today said, "In our annual test drive of tax software, TurboTax was again the winner!"

Isn't it time you used TurboTax? TurboTax is the easy way to do your taxes—and get the biggest refund you deserve!

Visit GetTurboTaxFree.com! Where it's free to prepare, free to print, and free to e-file your federal tax return.

That's GetTurboTaxFree.com. Do it now and get your refund fast—in as little as eight days!

7486 La Jolla Blvd.
La Jolla, CA 92037
Phone: 858.735.7646
Email: Marla@ResponseShop.com

Advertiser: Intuit
Product: TurboTax
Title: "Missing Something?"
Length: :60

ANNCR (V/O): Ever feel you might be...

. . . missing something?

Like, oh, say, hundreds of dollars in tax savings?

Thank goodness...

. . . there's TurboTax Federal Free Edition!

The EASY, online way to do your simple federal taxes.

And get the maximum refund –

GUARANTEED.

Just answer easy-to-understand questions.

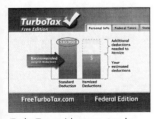

TurboTax guides you step-by-step.

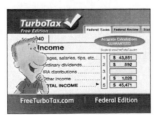

Puts the numbers on all the right forms. Does the math.

And helps get you the maximum refund you deserve.

Plus with Turbo Tax Free Edition, you can get your refund fast.

In as few as eight days when you e-file.

With TurboTax Free Edition, you also get free online help and free audit support tools!

Doing your taxes has never been easier.

And best of all, with TurboTax Free Edition, you don't pay a penny . . .

. . . because it's free to prepare, free to print, and free to e-file your federal tax return.

So why not give it a try?

Go to FreeTurboTax.com. That's FreeTurboTax.com.

The easy way to get your biggest refund possible! Do it now!

CASE
18

VIPER: SmartStart

From Curiosity to Conversion: How VIPER SmartStart Leverages Mobile Technology to Generate New Customers

DAVID W. MAROLD

Eastern Michigan University

LISA D. SPILLER

Christopher Newport University

M ike Simmons sat in his shorts and polo shirt on the patio of his home in Vista, California, enjoying the warm California sunshine while sipping a mug of coffee early one February morning. Although his eyes were taking pleasure in the beautiful view surrounding him, his mind was focused solely on his Smartphone which lay on the table in front of him. While walls of fresh warm air and great beauty enveloped him, he sat there totally immersed in contemplating how to further capitalize on the new mobile app he created for VIPER. Mike's business mind was in high gear.

Mike Simmons, pictured in Exhibit C18.1, is the Executive Vice-President of DEI Holdings, Inc., the parent company of Polk Audio, Directed Electronics, and Definitive Technology. Mike is the creator and driving force behind VIPER SmartStart—the revolutionary new product that allows you to start your car from virtually anywhere with your iPhone. Mike previously served as President of Directed Electronics after joining the company in early 2008. He has led a variety of businesses and has extensive experience in the automotive and

Exhibit C18.1.
Mike Simmons

Some of the data provided by the company has been disguised and is not useful for research purposes. The authors would like to thank Mike Simmons and Ken Gammage for their help with this case.

465

consumer electronics industries. Mike is a Certified Public Accountant. He holds a Bachelor's Degree from the University of Michigan and an MBA from Northwestern's Kellogg School of Management. Mike thrives on tackling business challenges and growing the VIPER SmartStart app is his most recent target.

VIPER SmartStart

VIPER® has been the undisputed heavyweight world champion of car alarms for more than 20 years. Its nearest competitor, Clifford, went bankrupt and out of business more than 10 years ago and its assets were acquired by VIPER. As VIPER's tagline accurately states: NO ONE DARES COME CLOSE.®

But the car-alarm business has plateaued for many years. While still highly profitable for retailers and perceived as necessary by millions of consumers, auto theft has been trending down for some time and the category deteriorated from a "must have" to a commodity that lacks sex appeal.

In the past, VIPER car alarms and remote starters appealed to a very broad cross-section of the population. This was one of the key success drivers for the brand. Young people were overrepresented only because they were more aware of the threat of car theft and content theft and more vulnerable. But, both young and old people bought car alarms—and of course anyone in the cold weather regions is a viable target customer for the purchase of a remote start system in the winter.

However, just as cellular phones were energized by the explosive functionality of the iPhone and other Smartphones, VIPER has been re-energized by a very compelling Smartphone app—along with integrated hardware for the car—called VIPER SmartStart.

Spearheaded by Mike Simmons, VIPER SmartStart debuted on October 12, 2009 with an article in USA TODAY, followed by more than 100 broadcast news stories. VIPER SmartStart instantly captured the imagination of the public, because it was the first app that let users start their cars from virtually anywhere with their Smartphone.

Within hours, Conan O'Brien and Jimmy Fallon mentioned the product in their late-night monologues. It wasn't long before Apple showcased VIPER SmartStart in its iPhone advertising, including a full-page ad in Time and The Wall Street Journal, followed by a 30-second TV commercial. This was wonderful "free advertising" for VIPER that reached nearly half a billion viewers!

The product won the coveted "Best of Innovations" Award at the Consumer Electronics Show in 2010 and has continued to evolve since that time. VIPER has added product features as it expanded platforms beyond iPhone, first to BlackBerry and then to the popular Android Smartphones. The free VIPER SmartStart app has been downloaded by one million Smartphone users as of this writing, and with explosive growth in the mobile market, it's not slowing down anytime soon.

Growth of Mobile Devices

Mike knows that rising Smartphone market penetration is significantly changing the way people use their mobile devices today. He also knows that this mobile wave is what will carry VIPER SmartStart to become a highly profitable product, despite the automobile alarm industry's lackluster sales trend.

In recent years, the number of people who own mobile phones, and Smartphones specifically, has grown significantly. A Warc article states that Google and Ipsos OTX surveyed 5,013 Smartphone owners, and reported that 81 percent regularly surf the net via this route, while 77 percent access search engines, 68 percent leverage apps, and 48 percent stream video.[1] An increasing number of individuals have the Internet at their fingertips constantly. The way that consumers access information is beginning to switch. Savvy marketers recognize the change and are responding in many cutting-edge ways.

The ever-growing array of mobile apps continues to make life easier and more convenient for mobile users—which, in turn, makes new mobiles apps more attractive and in demand. Mobile apps are Internet software programs that run on hand-held devices such as Smartphones. Applications can serve a number of purposes, such as connecting a consumer to a Web site, or providing the software that enables people to perform an action on their device that they otherwise may not have been able to do. "Apps" can come in many different forms, with various programming and functions. Consumers can install apps onto their device in order to tailor them to their preferences. Mobile apps are very empowering to consumers. New mobile apps, such as VIPER SmartStart, are being developed daily to fit consumers' desires for a carefree on-the-go lifestyle.

Automobile Alarm Industry

According to the Federal Bureau of Investigation's (FBI) Uniform Crime Reports, a motor vehicle was stolen in the United States every 40 seconds in a recent year. In that same year, 794,616 motor vehicles were reported stolen. The odds of a vehicle being stolen were one in 270 in the year previous (latest data available based on registrations from the Federal Highway Administration, thefts from the FBI and calculated by the Insurance Information Institute).[2]

Carjackings accounted for only 3.0 percent of all motor vehicle thefts, based on Department of Justice data from 1993 to 2002 (latest available) and occur most frequently in urban areas. In a recent year, the Southern region accounted for the largest share of auto thefts in the United States—37.8 percent, followed by the Western region with 34.2 percent. The Midwest accounted for 18 percent of thefts and the Northeast for 10 percent.[3]

The odds of having an automobile stolen are highest in urban areas. According to the National Insurance Crime Bureau, the top ten U.S. Metropolitan Statistical Areas

---

[1] "Mobile Shaping Purchases: News from Warc.com." *Warc—Ideas and Evidence for Marketing People | Warc.com.* April 28, 2011. Retrieved May May 22, 2011. <http://www.warc.com/LatestNews/News/E-mailNews.news?ID=28212>.

[2] "Auto Theft." *Insurance Information Institute,* June, 2011. Retrieved July 11, 2011. < http://www.iii.org/media/hottopics/insurance/test4/>.

[3] Ibid.

EXHIBIT C18.2: TOP TEN U.S. METROPOLITAN STATISTICAL AREAS WITH THE HIGHEST MOTOR VEHICLE THEFT RATES

Rank	Metropolitan Statistical Area (MSA)*	Vehicles Stolen	Rate**
1	Fresno, CA	7,559	812.40
2	Modesto, CA	3,878	753.81
3	Bakersfield, CA	5,623	669.70
4	Spokane, WA	2,673	586.35
5	Vallejo-Fairfield, CA	2,392	578.69
6	Sacramento-Arden-Arcade-Roseville, CA	11,881	552.83
7	Stockton, CA	3,779	551.43
8	Visalia-Portersville, CA	2,409	544.80
9	San Francisco-Oakland-Fremont, CA	22,617	521.68
10	Yakima, WA	1,266	520.49

Source: *National Insurance Crime Bureau.*
* Metropolitan statistical areas are designated by the federal Office of Management and Budget and usually include areas much larger than the cities for which they are named.
**Ranked by the rate of vehicle thefts reported per 100,000 people based on the concurrent year U.S. Census Population Estimates.

(MSAs) with the highest motor vehicle theft rates are presented in Exhibit C18.2. The state of California ranks the highest with eight of the 10 MSAs earning a spot in the top 10, followed by the state of Washington with two MSAs making the list.

The average stolen vehicle costs the owner $6,600, plus a good deal of hassle. When a vehicle is stolen it requires the vehicle owner deal with the insurance company, rental car agencies, and the emotional trauma of waiting and wondering whether or not his or her vehicle will be returned—returned in decent shape versus being trashed. With an installed automobile alarm system comes security and peace of mind.

The first car alarm is said to have been created by an inventor in Nebraska in the 1920s. The modern car alarm industry grew in the late 1970s. These car alarms consisted of a device that sounded a siren when a person tried to break into a car. The loud, ear piercing sound is familiar to many Americans.

There are different technologies used today to protect against automobile theft:

Active Alarms

An active car alarm works by clicking a transmitter that turns a sensor on or off. When the alarm is triggered, it stops certain functions of the vehicle such as the ignition, fuel circuits or the starter.

Passive Alarms

A passive car alarm activates automatically when the engine is turned off and when the doors are closed. An immobilizer locks the starter and ignition functions when something other than the key is used in the ignition. These systems sometimes lock the doors and engage the emergency lights. The immobilizer sensor can also detect contact on the outside of the car.

In addition, car alarms can be divided into two categories:

- OEM (Original Equipment Manufacturer)—Automobile alarms that are built into the vehicle at the factory.
- Aftermarket—Alarms installed at any time after the car has been built—such as by the new car dealer, an auto accessories store, or the vehicle's owner.

Alarms come with a mix of features. Remote car alarms typically consist of an additional radio receiver that allows the owner to wirelessly control the alarm from a key fob. Remote car alarms typically come equipped with an array of sensors along with immobilizers and motion detectors.

Keyless remote car alarms are typically based on strong cryptography authentication methods:

- Radio receiver
- Immobilizer
- Motion detector
- Wireless USB

Automobile Alarm Competition

Directed's VIPER holds the largest market share in the vehicle security and remote start business. Two key VIPER competitors are Audiovox Corporation (NASDAQ: VOXX) and Compustar (Firstech LLC.) Each of these companies has a competing app product (CarLink and Drone respectively.) However, these "me-to" products are playing catch-up to SmartStart and have received a lukewarm reception at best from dealers and consumers.

Only Audiovox is a public company. The product lines of DEI, Audiovox and Compustar, while they have some product similarities, are not at all "apples and apples" and product comparisons are very hard to come by. With the onset of the great recession in 2008, like many American industries, each of these companies suffered and industry sales as a whole declined.

Perhaps a more formidable competitor is General Motors and the other automakers (see SWOT Analysis below), although this is in part a case of "apples vs. oranges." All passenger cars and trucks sold in America have standard automobile protection equipment—antitheft devices that disable the engine or the drivability of the vehicle whenever someone has tampered with it. These systems typically are silent and do not sound an alarm, but disable the car. Prior to this, car alarms were sold as aftermarket equipment. However, the Original Equipment Manufacturers (OEMs) have eliminated this market by making anti-theft devices that disable the vehicle standard. People who need or desire greater security still turn to the aftermarket suppliers for alarms.

Target Customer Profile

For decades, Directed Electronics regarded its "customers" as the automobile dealers to whom the company sold its alarms as component parts destined to become a part of the automobile itself. Today, the focus is changing from a B2B emphasis to a B2C focus.

Aside from some Do-It-Yourself (DIY) products sold through mass-merchants and distributors, Directed's VIPER brand was created and built in partnership with VIPER dealers—authorized retailers sharing a direct business relationship with Directed. Even though the company advertised VIPER to final consumers, Directed had virtually no ongoing communication with end-users of its products. The company encouraged its consumers to interact with its dealers, and go back to them when they needed service or a replacement remote control. By these activities, Directed encouraged repeat business. Warranty cards returned by these buyers were primarily used for demographic data in aggregate.

VIPER SmartStart has changed all that. Today, Directed's business model is rapidly becoming more consumer-focused. Once the product is installed, the company now has a direct relationship with the end-user, starting with their service plan. Directed Electronics now has both the opportunity and responsibility to deliver world-class customer service to both dealers and final consumers.

With this new consumer focus, Directed has recently established a customer database of VIPER SmartStart customers, segmented by dealer and final consumer designations. For each final consumer, Directed also has captured the type of Smartphone each customer uses—iPhone, BlackBerry or Android—based on the specific type of VIPER SmartStart system purchased. Directed's customer database also contains the e-mail addresses and mobile telephone numbers of each of its final consumers.

A customer profile of Directed's traditional remote start buyers showed they were 50 years old; 58% male with a household income of $60K to $75K. However, because young people are leading the Smartphone revolution, the VIPER SmartStart customer tends to skew younger. The price points are the same, the purchase drivers are still the same (seasonal cold weather for remote start)—but the Smartphone is driving the average age down into the mid-40s.

VIPER SmartStart Market Situation

Building the Brand.

VIPER is a brand with attitude and brawn. Its logo made up of simple bold letters and it often includes the VIPER snake image presented in Exhibit C18.3. Like other

Exhibit C18.3: VIPER Logo Images

great masculine brands of our time, including Harley Davidson and Marlboro, VIPER is confident in its brand voice whether speaking to men or to women. A VIPER is a reptile with intensity. There are grave consequences for those who cross it. The VIPER brand exudes those same qualities. VIPER is the protector. VIPER doesn't take prisoners and it doesn't back down. VIPER says what it means, directly and deliberately. VIPER doesn't apologize for what it is, nor does it try to be something it's not.

These same ideals are at the very heart of VIPER products and the commitment it makes to its customers. Directed has taken VIPER's brand personality and has extended it to its SmartStart product. Mike Simmons is in the process of trying to harness both the VIPER brand personality and the VIPER brand power—as well as the new digital/mobile consumer boom—to effectively market VIPER SmartStart to its target customers. In essence, that's the primary business challenge that Mike is facing.

Let's examine the market situation for VIPER SmartStart with the SWOT Analysis shown in Exhibit C18.4.

VIPER SWOT Analysis
OEM (Automakers) vs. Aftermarket (VIPER)

In summary, VIPER SmartStart not only was first to market with this type of app which has generated solid awareness, but it also holds the number one market position for this readily affordable product and service. The increasing Automaker (OEM) app penetration and the fact that some anti-theft protection is included on all new light vehicles are threats. However, VIPER is the leader in the aftermarket arena (non-OEM) and has opportunities to capitalize there.

Based on the SWOT Analysis, three opportunities to improve sales and penetration logically emerge. They are:

1. Building and enhancing the VIPER SmartStart customer database and developing/ integrating an integrated marketing communication program that enables greater dialog with the actual purchasers of the VIPER SmartStart system.

EXHIBIT C18.4: VIPER SMARTSTART SWOT ANALYSIS

STRENGTHS	WEAKNESSES
• First to market with this type of app • Directed moves faster than the OEMs • Affordable (both product and service) • Universal (not vehicle-specific)	• Requires aftermarket sale and installation • Complexity of aftermarket database integration (which IS vehicle-specific)
OPPORTUNITIES	THREATS
• Enhanced dialog with current users • Huge group of potential customers have downloaded the free app • Increasingly effective renewal communications during cold weather	• Increasing OEM app penetration • Huge OEM advertising budget (though this can also benefit VIPER by raising awareness of the category) • Comes with the car

2. More than one million people have downloaded the free app, but have yet to buy a VIPER SmartStart system. Expanding VIPER's communications to convert these "App Owners" or "hand raisers" to SmartStart purchasers represents a great opportunity.

3. Improving customer communications and strengthening the relationship with current VIPER customers to encourage them to renew their VIPER SmartStart system is needed. The obvious timing for such renewal might be during cold weather months, when customer appreciation for the benefit of a warm vehicle may lead to higher renewal rates. However, this is both seasonal and geographic specific.

Let's explore the product features associated with the VIPER SmartStart system.

VIPER SmartStart Product Features

For VIPER and parent company DEI, the good news is that VIPER SmartStart is not "just" a free app. The full-featured system, made available to paying customers, includes hardware for the automobile that enables drivers to lock/unlock, arm/disarm, and start their car remotely.

This hardware (and installation) is sold at thousands of VIPER retailers across the country, from local aftermarket shops to national retailer Best Buy, and integrates with existing VIPER car alarm and remote start systems.

Results have been impressive. VIPER SmartStart also launched a GPS product allowing users to know exactly where their car is at all times on their Smartphone—along with home control features that allow users to arm and disarm their home alarm from the VIPER app. As shown in Exhibit C18.5, other VIPER app innovations include shared location and roadside assistance features.

Exhibit C18.5. VIPER SmartStart Shared Location and Roadside Assistance Features

The Shared Location feature enables the customer to share his/her location (while in the vehicle) with others via social networking. The Roadside Assistance feature allows the customer to place a roadside assistance request to VIPER Motor Club should the vehicle become disabled. If subscribed to this, the service call is free.

Even though VIPER SmartStart is a new product on a new platform (a Smartphone app), the company is still seeing a wide range of customers for the product because of the broad appeal of Smartphones, which again bodes well for the future. The core price point for a VIPER SmartStart remote start-only system begins at just $299, which is not perceived as a significant barrier to entry.

VIPER Product Line Extensions

For most marketers, line extensions that complement and support sales of the original product are the holy grail. VIPER has also benefited in this way: from VIPER SmartStart, then from the new VIPER SmartStart GPS, new "home control" features in the VIPER app—and now VIPER Window Film, another related product that offers synergies of:

- Seasonality (summer for window tint vs. winter for remote start).
- Customer acceptance (60% of VIPER dealers are already in the tint business).
- Product category (VIPER offers a Security Film that strengthens the glass).
- Technology (VIPER Window Film is non-metallic, so it doesn't interfere with radio frequency (RF) signals, including the cellular signals used by VIPER SmartStart).

Even Directed's car audio brand, *Orion*, is part of the line extension roadmap— because when consumers enhance their ride with expensive aftermarket gear, they'd better invest in a VIPER alarm to protect it!

How did VIPER SmartStart become such an overnight success? What were the stages it undertook to move consumers from awareness to interest to desire to action? Moreover, how did the SmartStart mobile app leap so quickly from arousing consumer curiosity to achieving millions of dollars in sales revenue?

VIPER SmartStart: Leveraging Mobile Technology to Generate New Customers

Let's detail the step-by-step process that enabled VIPER SmartStart to become a success.

- *Step 1:* A free app with attractive features like SmartPark (pinpoints where your car is parked) generates awareness, intrigue and trial. VIPER continues to take advantage of all the publicity surrounding the free app, as well as consumer interest in Smartphone apps in general to manage day-to-day activities. The synergies of the Apple TV commercial, targeted marketing efforts and a boatload of free publicity put the free app in front of millions of prospects

- *Step 2:* Communicating in-app with the one-million plus users who have so far downloaded the free app identifies sales prospects. The company continually enhances the free features of the app, such as SmartPark.

- *Step 3:* Offering information and incentives aids sales conversion, by inviting prospects to join the satisfied users who have the product on their cars and are enjoying the VIPER SmartStart connected lifestyle. By carefully engineering cost out of the product (both hardware and data)—and shifting some up-front costs to service plan revenue, the company reduces sticker shock and entices more users down the purchase funnel.

The long-term strategy for VIPER SmartStart is to continuously improve the value proposition both for free app users and active users—to keep generating interest from new prospects and increasing purchase conversion.

VIPER SmartStart Marketing

VIPER has a history rooted in memorable advertising. From the company's perspective, the number one driver of growth was an award-winning television commercial that ran for more than a decade. In "The Lady, the Thief and the Snake," a classy lady parks her Lexus and arms her car alarm—and we hear the voice of Directed Electronics founder (now Congressman) Darrell Issa say "VIPER Armed." A would-be thief sneaks up on the car, but is frightened away by a VIPER snake inside the vehicle as shown in Exhibit C18.6.

As the terrified thief scurries away, the woman returns to disarm her alarm. Many people still remember this commercial though it hasn't aired in years.

Today VIPER SmartStart advertises in the app itself. These messages are sent to everyone who has downloaded the free app, but have not (yet) become a paying customer. The advertisements featured Exhibit C18.7 are typical VIPER SmartStart ads. Note the confident, cocky and humorous tone of each message. These fit with the brand personality of VIPER.

The company also buys mobile Smartphone advertising from Google's AdMob,

Exhibit C18.6: VIPER Television Advertisement.

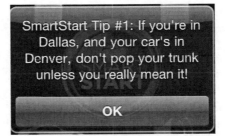

Exhibit C18.7—Examples of VIPER SmartStart Mobile Advertisements

and on The Weather Channel (in select cold-weather markets, using "weather triggered" ads that only launch below a threshold temperature). Not to mention a growing presence on Facebook, Twitter, and YouTube. The company is leveraging new social media opportunities to reach its target demographic and spending less money on traditional advertising.

In other words, the "old media" VIPER systems (formerly advertised in the Yellow Pages, and in car audio magazines that have since gone out of business) have gotten a huge infusion of energy and excitement from "new media" VIPER SmartStart, including social networking integration—because your car needs friends too!

Directed tries to connect with its customers and prospective customers via its Web site. As shown in Exhibit C18.8, some of Directed's mobile advertisements are used to generate traffic directly to the VIPER Web site. As with the previous ads, the tone of each advertising message is slightly humorous and confident. Directed obtains conversions from the mobile messages and many prospective customers decide to purchase a VIPER SmartStart system after receiving the promotional message prompts. Everyone who is not a paying customer receives these mobile marketing messages on a periodic basis.

VIPER Web site visitors are offered an opportunity to register for a free e-newsletter by simply providing their e-mail address. The e-newsletter is distributed to 30,000

Exhibit C18.8—Examples of VIPER SmartStart Mobile Advertisements Generating Web Traffic

users every 60 days (six times per year) with new product updates, system maintenance notes, and miscellaneous VIPER news.

Web visitors are also invited to interact with VIPER via social media. The VIPER Web site invites its guests to "Follow us on Twitter" or "View VIPER SmartStart videos on our YouTube Channel." It also offers its Facebook followers an incentive: "Become a VIPER fan! Every two weeks one lucky person will win a free VIPER SmartStart VSM4000!"

The VIPER Web site engages its visitors with a "share this" button that displays a variety of social networks, such as Blogger, AIM Share, MySpace, StumbleUpon, Digg, Messenger, and many others, with which to communicate and interact on a personal basis. Mike thinks the company can and should do more to connect and engage with VIPER SmartStart customers and prospective customers via social media. In fact, this is an area where he sees real marketing potential.

The Case Challenges

Mike is at a point where he needs to determine how to strategically employ direct and database marketing activities to increase demand for VIPER SmartStart. It is in his tenacious nature to attack a decision problem, stick with it and conquer it. He is deliberating several strategic directions that he might take to capitalize on the VIPER brand image and generate both awareness and new customers for VIPER SmartStart.

Decision Problem 1: Determine how to most effectively allocate VIPER's marketing budget given its new focus on interacting with final consumers.
Mike needs to decide how to best allocate his marketing budget to market VIPER SmartStart. He wants to allocate a large portion of his promotional budget to interact with final consumers, while still spending a portion of his budget on retaining the excellent relationships he has with its dealer network.

How would you advise Mike with respect to allocating his promotional budget? What might Mike do to cross-promote the VIPER SmartStart between the dealers and final consumers to create a synergy in his integrated marketing communication activities? For purposes of this Decision Problem, assume you are dealing with a $1 million promotion budget.

Decision Problem 2: Begin employing database marketing activities given VIPER's new customer database.

VIPER has moved from a distributor marketing system primarily advertising in the Yellow Pages and auto magazines to more modern direct marketing and social media activities thanks to Mike Simmons' direction with the launch of the VIPER SmartStart app. VIPER has begun building a customer database, but with very limited purchase information: name, postal and e-mail address, cell phone, vehicle information (year, make and model), product, services, dealer and usage information.

Assume VIPER's database consists of the last three years of purchasers of all DEI (Directed Products) including VIPER SmartStart and people who have loaded the VIPER SmartStart App on their Smartphone, but have not bought the system (warm prospects). There are about 5,000 likes for VIPER SmartStart on Facebook. Assume Mike Simmons hired you as his new Database Marketing Manager with the task of building a VIPER SmartStart Owner and Prospect Database with a budget of $500,000 to grow owner sales loyalty and prospect sales. Assume some of this $500,000 would go to data enhancement (demographics, lifestyle, etc.) and some to integrated marketing (SEO, emarketing, texting, direct mail, etc.). Staying within the budget, what data would you add to the database and what database marketing programs would you conduct in the next year? Detail quantities, costs and expected rate of response.

Decision Problem 3: Establish a customer referral program for VIPER SmartStart customers.

Mike wants to build a customer referral program for VIPER SmartStart. The referral program will reward customers with a fixed amount of VIPER Services for each referral who purchases the VIPER SmartStart. Mike has allocated a budget of $150,000 to build the program and reward customers in the first year. Subsequent year's rewards of VIPER products are budgeted at $75,000. Consider the amount charged to the program to be 50% of retail. SmartStart Systems start for as little as $299 (MSRP) and yearly service plans begin at $69.99. Develop a detailed plan for a referral program, including type and amount of rewards and media used to promote with budget for each area detailed.

The network of authorized VIPER dealers is a key element in gaining referrals. Be sure to include dealers in your plan to capture referrals. Mike has realized that working with VIPER's authorized dealers is critical to provide after-the-sale customer service and to ensure post-purchase satisfaction of the VIPER SmartStart system. In fact, authorized dealers are so important that Directed has recently created a pop-up window on its Web site (shown in Exhibit C18.9) to remind consumers that if they do not purchase their VIPER System from an authorized dealer, their warranty will be VOID. Thus, there is an important three-way business relationship between Directed and its authorized dealers and consumers that must be taken into account when marketing VIPER SmartStart.

Exhibit C18.9: VIPER Web Site Pop-up Window Message

Decision 4: Prospect for new VIPER SmartStart customers via list rental. Examine current customer market penetration and determine which customer markets have the greatest potential to become VIPER SmartStart customers in the future.

Beyond developing and implementing a customer referral program, Mike has pondered prospecting for new VIPER SmartStart customers via list rental. He realizes that there are many lists of final consumers that may be rented and some may present excellent market potential for VIPER SmartStart. He understands that he must use the appropriate segmenting criteria (geographic, demographic, lifestyle and behavioral) when selecting his lists.

Based on what is known about the automobile alarm industry and current VIPER SmartStart customers, what lists would you recommend that Mike investigate for his prospecting program? What segmentation criteria should he apply to each list? What list selects might he apply when narrowing his selections within a given list?

There are so many different directions Mike may take to prospect for new customers. Where should he begin? Can you help Mike to prioritize the prospects he should target first?

Conclusion . . . The Future

Mike's long-term vision? Key replacement! People want their multi-functional Smartphone with them at all times—but they don't want to carry that heavy bundle of keys. Phase one of the key replacement strategy is already in place: using the Smartphone to unlock and start the car—and using the Smartphone to arm and disarm the home alarm. Is it too much to expect additional hardware to soon be created and made available to enable the Smartphone to take the place of your bundle of keys? Stay tuned for the future as Mike has big plans for VIPER. VIPER may be a long-standing brand, but in Mike's savvy business mind, VIPER SmartStart is just beginning!

Exhibit C18.10: Smartphones
Replace Keys?

Case Discussion Questions

1. Evaluate the car-alarm business in the United Sates. What are the characteristics of the market for car alarms, including the market size and growth? Do you think the car-alarm business has plateaued in recent years? Why? Justify your answer.

2. Given your SWOT analysis in the above, identify key growth strategies that VIPER may pursue in the foreseeable future. Hint: you can look into "security" as a growth theme. Likewise, you may examine "vehicle"—including automobiles—as a direction for growth.

3. VIPER is leveraging social media to reach its target audience and to connect with the online community of visitors and fans. As such, it has a growing presence on Facebook, Twitter, and YouTube. What other social networking sites do you recommend that VIPER use to attract independent visitors and would-be customers such as car buffs and security and technology enthusiasts? Justify your answers.

Zappos: Ensuring a Good Fit

Fortifying Customer Service and the User Experience at Zappos

DEBORAH COWLES

Virginia Commonwealth University

JAN P. OWENS

Carthage College

KRISTEN L. WALKER

California State University Northridge

The Zappos Phenomenon

Since its beginning in 1999, Zappos had become a well-respected and highly successful Internet shopping website. From its early years with Tony Hsieh's $500K investment in Nick Swinmurn's ShoeSite.com startup, a unique approach to serving customers was born. Rather than being just an online display case, the objective was to treat customers well and to make the purchase process as effortless as possible. Beginning with shoes, the site offered deep selection, as well as liberal shipping and return policies. By 2000, the website, renamed Zappos, signaled that it could broaden its product category appeal for future growth. Together with additional investments from Sequoia Capital, co-CEOs Tony and Nick executed this strategy through constant customer attention based on analytics and experimentation, professional and friendly customer service, and innovative technologies to support the enterprise.

Developing a positive and unique company culture was integral to that success: "Zappos.com is more than an electronic shoe store. It is a supportive community that happens to put you in a pair of great-looking shoes" (Pearson 2013). Although Nick left the company in 2006 to develop additional start-ups, Zappos continued to thrive by anticipating and moving with customer preferences not only in the products they wanted, but also in how customers wanted to shop.

During Zappos's early years of growth, the firm relied heavily on affiliate marketing as an easy and affordable way to get its name out. It signed on with an affiliate network, "where online partners, including blogs, shopping sites and comparison sites, drive traffic to Zappos and are paid a commission on the sales completed" (Bell

2009). In the past several years, Zappos has relied more heavily on direct marketing, especially as search engine marketing became more robust. Search engines are a more profitable direct marketing avenue, which allow Zappos to have more control over its message to customers. Zappos has also occasionally used traditional advertising campaigns (e.g., magazines, television), as well as event sponsorship to increase brand awareness.

Amazon.com's purchase of Zappos in 2009 raised initial concerns about its independence. It seemed that Amazon's Endless.com never achieved the success of Zappos, so it took the shortcut to category dominance (Stone 2009). Could Zappos continue to deliver outstanding customer service and nurture excellence and "productive weirdness" in its offices? Could Zappos still keep up with where customers were going in their shopping preferences? After the merger was announced, instead of a standard letter, Amazon CEO Jeff Bezos sent a video to his new Zappos employees, explaining what he had learned from leading Amazon for 15 years and assuring them that he wanted Zappos to maintain its "customer obsession" and unique corporate culture (YouTube 2009). In short, he wanted Zappos to continue to be Zappos. Subsequent financial success and continuous innovation in customer relationships have long since eased the fears of the doubters.

Helping the Customer Make the Right Decision

From the outset, the executives at Zappos understood that buying shoes online was fraught with risks and challenges. Whereas some merchandise categories allowed for a "good enough" fit, customers tend to be very picky about shoe fit and styling. Zappos solved this problem by offering a wide selection of brands for men, women, and children and stocking deep in styles and sizes—also allowing customers to try on shoes at their own convenience and return shoes at no cost to the customer.

Compared to competitors' websites in the early years, the Zappos website offered extensive product information in the listing description and presentation. Each shoe was photographed from at least eight angles. Customers were encouraged to post product reviews and recommendations not only as a form of word-of-mouth communication, but also as an indication of their involvement with the firm and brand. Further, Zappos realized that the varied policies and practices of other online retailers and vendors made order processing, deliveries, and returns problematic. By controlling its own inventory and developing excellent logistics systems located near a UPS hub in Louisville, Kentucky, Zappos discovered that it could deliver a seamless customer experience. With free shipping and returns, and a 365-day return frame, the customer could be assured of finding the right shoes and feeling like a valued customer. At the Zappos website, consumer shopping and decision-making are matched by excellent website navigation tools. From the beginning, the goal was for there to be no "speed bumps" in the entire process.

As customers gained confidence in their relationship with Zappos in buying shoes, requests for additional product categories increased. (Although Tony has in the past dismissed a customer suggestion for AirZappos [an airline run by Zappos] as too great an investment stretch, he has also left the door open: "Who knows what the future holds?") To date, Zappos has added clothing, bags and handbags, homegoods, beauty/cosmetics, and accessories lines. It also developed private label clothing, DH (Deliver Happiness), which helps fund DHW (Delivering Happiness at Work), a consulting firm that provides the Zappos brand of management training for other businesses.

Because Zappos realized that busy consumers might like even more help combing through their vast assortment of products and brands, it launched specialty subsites, such as high-end designer brands at couture.zappos.com, and continues to experiment with microsites launched by a small office of 11 people in the San Francisco-based Zappo Labs. The goal of the 11-person team "is to try out new ideas, work with other tech companies, and develop features that may eventually make it back onto the Zappos home site" (Weir 2013). For example, one platform of curated goods, Glance, seemingly combines products with personalities, tapping more directly into consumer lifestyles. Not all "helpful innovations" were hits, though—the ZN style magazine app lasted only a few seasons.

Zappos knew that the customer had multiple inspirations that motivated shopping before they ever came to Zappos.com. What else could Zappos do to encourage repeat visits from its current customers? What could it do to attract new customers? Forty percent of its sales come from the shoe category (Dishman 2013). What could it do to expand the "share-of-wallet" from its current customers? Who are Zappos's customers, anyway? These were some of the important questions that Zappos User Experience (UX) team members were considering as they faced the challenge of taking Zappos's relationship with its current and prospective customers to the next level. As Jeff Bezos had shared with his new Zappos employees in 2009, "Everyday Is Day 1" (YouTube 2009).

The UX Team

Marilyn Woods was a member of the Zappos UX team, charged with analyzing customer behavior on the website and improving the customer experience. This team included a variety of researchers, product managers, technical experts, and communications associates. By taking good care of customers and anticipating their shopping needs, Zappos believed that sales and repeat customers would follow. Moreover, team members understood the power of the social media, online communities, blogs and other communication venues that consumers use to share their customer experiences. So long as these shopping experiences are positive and unique, then Zappos could expand its customer base as well via referral and recommendation. The UX team's tasks included active observation of customer behavior on the website, customer research, and experimentation, as well as developing a basic understanding of customers.

Marilyn and her fellow team members relied on both quantitative and qualitative approaches to consumer research. Quantitative studies focused on usage patterns, i.e., repeat visits, RFM (recency-frequency-monetary value) measures, trend analyses, and website behavior and activity. The results of these studies often led to improvements to the listings themselves, site design, and basically answering customer questions by providing website information and making sure they could get where they wanted to go. Metrics have always been very important in the success of Zappos, and the digital environment allows for qualitative research reflected in analyzing "voice of the customer" comments, both solicited and unsolicited. For example, the Zappos landing page continues to ask: "HOW DO YOU LIKE OUR WEBSITE? We'd like to get your feedback." The company also has a history of taking unsolicited suggestions very seriously. Customers are encouraged to write product reviews, which are useful both to Zappos and to other customers.

Despite the success of Zappos over the years, Marilyn understood that the company may not be the top-of-mind website for some consumers when shopping for certain items or brands. Although many consumers were aware that Zappos sold shoes, they were not always aware of the other product categories available at Zappos.com. She contemplated: "Is it possible for us to get into consumers' heads when they have a purchase need? Indeed, how can we get inside their heads before they even realize they are shopping? Although the website is doing a great job of offering products and service once customers are there, how can we increase the level of interaction and the relationship intensity—customer engagement—with Zappos?"

Marilyn began by considering how customers searched for products, what search terms they used and how Zappos offered assistance to customers during the user experience. She realized that they searched for products in a variety of ways and used different keywords, but the Zappos UX team manage their keywords well enough to add value to customers' search for products? More importantly, did the UX team add value to the customers' experience with search engine optimization yet manage the costs associated with paid searches based on keywords?

Marilyn also learned more about where consumers were looking for products and/or information about products. She knew all the usual online suspects, including Zappos's parent company, Amazon.com. She also was aware that customers often got product ideas even when they were not actively shopping. They might be reading a Facebook post from a friend. They could be reading an online article about a lifestyle interest when they saw a banner or pop-up advertisement. Current or prospective customers could be on Pinterest, viewing a collection of items from an admired poster, or saving their own scrapbook of impressions. Did they consistently read the tweets from a celebrity they follow? Marilyn knew that newsletters, emails, and other "push" messages were still important sources of consumer information, but she also understood that they were enhanced by connections to the social media. For example, one study found that the average click-through rate was 158% higher for messages that included social sharing buttons, compared to those that did not (O'Malley 2013). The number of users who included social sharing buttons in their emails was increasing rapidly, and included Facebook, Twitter, Pinterest, and even professionally-oriented sites like LinkedIn. Years ago, Zappos had tried to implement its own social network, MyZappos.com, but found that customers preferred to interact with companies and brands via their existing social networks (Dishman 2013).

Facebook

Zappos has a particularly active Facebook brand page with about 1.4 million fans. On average, it posts five new entries a day with items such as new product arrivals, photos, and status updates. Recently, Zappos wanted to get a better idea about which posts were particularly effective in attracting website visitors and sales. One particularly successful campaign included teaming up with Kenshoo Social, a social marketing platform (Lynch 2013). Kenshoo created a Facebook marketing campaign that allowed Zappos to track the posts that were most effective in generating revenue. Within two months, Zappos generated 85,000 visits to its website via Facebook posts. Significantly, 42% of the Zappos posts resulted in sales, and the firm gained much greater insight from important metrics such as revenue per post and revenue per click. In turn, these metrics provided Zappos a deeper understanding of customer behavior beyond Facebook "likes," which may or may not lead to sales. This campaign had an average conversion rate of 1.75% of the Facebook posts, with some reaching 10% conversion rates.

Zappos continued to use many of the innovations from Facebook. It could now place retargeted ads in the news feeds of users, based on each user's browsing activity outside of the social network (Delo 2013). While this targeting tactic began for desktop use only, Zappos knows that mobile targeting capabilities are increasing in the near future. In terms of cost, this format is 82% less expensive than traditional web retargeting.

Pinterest

Marilyn became intrigued with a recent improvement on Pinterest, the image-posting site that reflects the interests of its users in visual form. Shoppers had often complained about how difficult it is to shop from images posted on Pinterest. Unless images had been pinned directly from a retailer's website, hyperlinks and other information that would be useful to shoppers were often rare. Moving beyond the "online scrapbook" capabilities, Pinterest developed "Rich Pins," which are images that can contain much more information directly originating from the pinned image, such as product information and where the item can be purchased. This new capability has attracted a number of major online retailers such as Target and Sephora. While many of Zappos's items have been pinned on users' Pinterest accounts, Rich Pins allows it to attach meta tags that can lead to more specific product and source information, even if the image does not originate at Zappos.

Twitter

For Zappos's Twitter followers, the main interest seemed to be leads to shopping ideas and content marketing, e.g., a popular "what to pack" guide. At other times, the tweets were similar to the enjoyable (sometimes "weird") posts on the Zappos blog composed by staff members. Other tweets included Zappos highlights, musical suggestions, etc. The company was also experimenting with TweetWall, a product that pulls any tweet of a Zappos product instantly over to the Zappos website. Although it wasn't in full use yet, the Zappos Labs office was learning and improving TweetWall to engage consumers. An interesting fact: Although CEO Tony Hsieh has more than 2.8 million followers on Twitter, Zappos.com has just over 17,000. Marilyn was curious: "What does Tony's personal Twitter account offer people that the Zappos account doesn't? And why is the difference in followers so extreme?"

Glance

Although the Zappos home page includes links to a number of other Zappos subsites (e.g., couture, outdoor, rideshop, running, blogs, how-to), as of this writing, there was no link to the Glance website (although customers who knew about Glance could type "glance" into the Zappos search bar and go directly to the microsite). Although Glance is similar to Pinterest, it makes it easier for shoppers who are looking for collections and other fashion ideas. According to Carrie Whitehead, Zappos's product and UX manager, "Compared to the home page of its parent, Glance is spare with just three navigation tabs and a fat photo of the featured collection at the top. The page then picks up where Pinterest leaves off: Two columns of curated collections allow shoppers to click through to pages of product images they can simply 'heart' (think: favorite or like) or click to buy" (Dishman 2013). Hearting items develops a customer profile that allows Glance to refine suggestions in the future and develops style communities within the site. Still, the design and configuration of the site is not left up entirely to curators. Stylists, merchandisers, and buyers at Zappos help to edit the collections. Website analysts have found that viewers are more likely to share their interests if the icons read "Share," "Tweet," and "Pin" rather than Facebook, Twitter, and Pinterest. Marilyn wondered if these terms were like a "call to action" from the perspective of consumers.

Mobile Marketing

Zappos continued to experiment with its messaging strategy, but the mobile website and app were in place. Customers received a 360-degree view of products, as well as push messages when new items were in stock. This development was by no means a second-rate experience for mobile customers; they could browse, search, connect with their social media, view, and buy as if they were on the actual website. The "WOW" was in being able to shop a great website like Zappos whenever and wherever they wanted to do so. The Zappos staff continued to have fun with customers, such as an Easter egg hunt that was available only on the company's mobile apps.

Zappos developed three shopping apps for the iPhone, iPad, and Android. It appeared to Marilyn and the UX team that the mobile sites complement Zappos' Internet channels rather than compete with them. Mobile shopping activity was higher late in the evenings and on weekends, when people don't want to be working at their desks or on laptops (Abrahamovich 2012). It also seemed that consumers found it more acceptable to use an iPhone app for a quick check in social situations, such as Thanksgiving, when the family is watching TV. In these and other social settings, firing up a laptop or an iPad may also seem too much like work.

Branded Mobile Codes

Marilyn and her UX team members were impressed with the growth of mobile marketing, and they believe that it will become an even more critical communication tool in the future. UX sought an easier, more efficient way for customers to connect, and text messages achieve this desired level of efficiency. In the United States and Europe, more than 90% of text subscribers have Internet-ready phones (Ochs 2012). Even better, branded mobile numbers provide easy memory tools for a consumer to connect with a company—in much the same way that customers of Gap need only remember "gap.com" to access its website.

One of the latest developments in mobile communication is the use of branded vanity codes or "StarStar" numbers. Two options are available: (1) common sort codes (CSC), which are five-or-six-digit numbers and (2) StarStar numbers, which begin with ** and can be up to 15 characters long. Instead of sending a text message, consumers can dial these numbers and then automatically receive an instant text message that allows them to access online content. Zappos continued to experiment with push messages that facilitate on-the-go shopping.

What to Do?

Marilyn's head was spinning, but she was excited about the possibilities of this new digital toolkit of options. The real task was how to design the right messages for the right customers, beginning with where they find a desirable product to making it as easy as possible to buy it at Zappos. She knew that an integrated approach was important because customers sometimes used one device and sometimes used multiple devices before the sale was made (Bittar 2013). Some customers feel confident to complete the entire process on a smartphone, while others shop on-the-go, but want to see a bigger picture on a desktop, laptop, or tablet before buying. And Marilyn knew that the tools could be used for so much more than actual shopping and purchase.

References

Abramovich, Giselle, "How Zappos Makes Mobile Unique," *Digiday*, March 20, 2012, www.digitday.com.

Bell, Jennie, "Zappos Milestone: Marketing," May 4, 2009, http://www.wwd.com/footwear-news/markets/zappos-milestone-marketing-2120865?full=true.

Bittar, Christine, "Zappos Takes a Close Look at Consumers' Mcommerce Patterns," Emarketer, February 22, 2013, http://www.emarketer.com/Articles/Print/aspx?R=1009685.

Delo, Cotton, "Facebook Cranks Up Ad Targeting in User News Feeds," *Ad Age Digital*, March 26, 2013.

Dishman, Lydia, "Glance Is Zappos's Gamble on Curated E-Commerce," Fast Company, February 21, 2013, http://www.fastcompany.com/3006108/buyology/glance-zaposs-gamble-crated-e-commerce.

Lynch, Erin, "Zappos Sees 85,000 Site Visits After Facebook Activity," *Multi-Channel Merchant*, February 6, 2013. http://multichannelmerchant.com/news/prnewswire/zappos-sees-85000-site-visits-after-facebook-activity-06022013/.

Michelli, Joseph A., *The Zappos Experience: 5 Principles to Inspire, Engage, and WOW*. New York: McGraw-Hill, 2012.

Ochs, B.L., "Why Apple, Ford, and Zappos Have All Invested in Branded Mobile Codes," WhatsNext, February 2012, WhatsNextBlog.com.

O'Malley, Gavin, "Social Components Boost Email Campaigns," Media Post, March 29, 2013, http://www.mediapost.com/publications/article/196928/social-compoents-boost-email-campaigns.

Pearson, Bryan, "Delivering Loyalty: 10 Lessons From Zappos.com," May 20, 2013, http://www.business2community.com/customer-experience/delivering-loyalty-10-lessons-from-zappos-com-0499293.

Slegg, Jennifer, "Pinterest Introduces Rich Pins for Better Brand Collaboration," *ClickZ.com*, May 22, 2013.

Stone, Brad, "Amazon's Expanding with Deal for Zappos," New York Times, July 23, 2009, http://www.nytimes.com/2009/07/23/technology/companies/23amazon.html?_r=0.

Weir, David, "Local Zappos Labs Experiments to Enhance Online Shopping," May 30, 2013, http://www.7x7.com/tech-gadgets/zappos-labs.

Wilson, Keith, "How to Adjust to the New Customer Journey," *iMediaConnection*, May 1, 2013,http://www.imediaconnection.com/content/34074.asp?imcid=nl.

YouTube, http://www.youtube.com/watch?v=-hxX_Q5CnaA.

Racom Communications Order Form

QUANTITY	TITLE	PRICE	AMOUNT
_____	*The Language of Marketing Technology*, P. Wiland/J. Downs/S. McKee	$39.95	_____
_____	*The Social Current*, **Allie Siarto/Richard T. Cole**	$24.95	_____
_____	*Contemporary Direct & Interactive Marketing, 3rd Ed*, **Lisa Spiller/Martin Baier**	$69.95	_____
_____	*Google This: The New Media Driver's License®* **Richard Cole/Derek Mehraban**	$24.95	_____
_____	*Aligned*, **Maurice Parisien**	$19.95	_____
_____	*How to Jump-Start Your Career*, **Robert L. Hemmings**	$19.95	_____
_____	*This Year a Pogo Stick . . . Next Year a Unicycle*, **Jim Kobs**	$19.95	_____
_____	*Professional Selling*, **Bill Jones**	$59.95	_____
_____	*Follow That Customer*, **Egbert Jan van Bel/Ed Sander/Alan Weber**	$39.95	_____
_____	*Internet Marketing*, **Herschell Gordon Lewis**	$19.95	_____
_____	*Reliability Rules*, **Don Schultz/Reg Price**	$34.95	_____
_____	*The Marketing Performance Measurement Toolkit*, **David M. Raab**	$39.95	_____
_____	*Successful E-Mail Marketing Strategies*, **Arthur M. Hughes/Arthur Sweetser**	$49.95	_____
_____	*Managing Your Business Data*, **Theresa Kushner/Maria Villar**	$32.95	_____
_____	*Media Strategy and Planning Workbook*, **DL Dickinson**	$64.95	_____
_____	*Marketing Metrics in Action*, **Laura Patterson**	$24.95	_____
_____	*The IMC Handbook 3rd Edition*, **J. Stephen Kelly/Susan K. Jones/Richard A. Hagle**	$49.95	_____
_____	*Print Matters*, **Randall Hines/Robert Lauterborn**	$27.95	_____
_____	*The Business of Database Marketing*, **Richard N. Tooker**	$49.95	_____
_____	*Customer Churn, Retention, and Profitability*, **Arthur Middleton Hughes**	$59.95	_____
_____	*Data-Driven Business Models*, **Alan Weber**	$49.95	_____
_____	*Creative Strategy in Direct & Interactive Marketing, 4th Edition*, **Susan K. Jones**	$49.95	_____
_____	*Branding Iron*, **Charlie Hughes and William Jeanes**	$27.95	_____
_____	*Managing Sales Leads*, **James Obermayer**	$39.95	_____
_____	*Creating the Marketing Experience*, **Joe Marconi**	$49.95	_____
_____	*Brand Babble: Sense & Nonsense about Branding*, **Don E. Schultz/Heidi F. Schultz**	$24.95	_____
_____	*The New Marketing Conversation*, **Donna Baier Stein/Alexandra MacAaron**	$34.95	_____
_____	*Trade Show and Event Marketing*, **Ruth Stevens**	$59.95	_____
_____	*Sales & Marketing 365*, **James Obermayer**	$17.95	_____
_____	*Accountable Marketing*, **Peter J. Rosenwald**	$59.95	_____
_____	*Contemporary Database Marketing, Second Edition* **Lisa Spiller/Kurtis Ruf**	$89.95	_____
_____	*Catalog Strategist's Toolkit*, **Katie Muldoon**	$59.95	_____
_____	*Marketing Convergence*, **Susan K. Jones/Ted Spiegel**	$34.95	_____
_____	*High-Performance Interactive Marketing*, **Christopher Ryan**	$39.95	_____
_____	*The White Paper Marketing Handbook*, **Robert W. Bly**	$39.95	_____
_____	*Business-to-Business Marketing Research*, **Martin Block/Tamara Block**	$69.95	_____
_____	*Hot Appeals or Burnt Offerings*, **Herschell Gordon Lewis**	$24.95	_____
_____	*On the Art of Writing Copy, 4th Edition*, **Herschell Gordon Lewis**	$34.95	_____
_____	*Open Me Now*, **Herschell Gordon Lewis**	$21.95	_____
_____	*Marketing Mayhem*, **Herschell Gordon Lewis**	$39.95	_____
_____	*Asinine Advertising*, **Herschell Gordon Lewis**	$22.95	_____

Name/Title_____

Company _____

Street Address _____

City/State/Zip _____

Email _____ Phone _____

Credit Card: ☐ VISA ☐ MasterCard
　　　　　　　 ☐ American Express ☐ Discover

☐ Check or money order enclosed (payable to Racom
　 Communications in US dollars drawn on a US bank)

Number _____ Exp. Date _____

Signature _____

Subtotal	_____
Subtotal from other side	_____
8.65% Tax	_____
Shipping & Handling	_____
$7.00 for first book; $1.00 for each additional book.	
TOTAL	_____

Racom Communications, 150 N. Michigan Ave, Suite 2800, Chicago, IL 60601
312-494-0100, 800-247-6553, www. Racombooks.com